THE
PACIFIC
REGION

CANADA

ALASKA

Barrow

Porcupine

Nome

Yukon

Kuskokwim

Fairbanks

CANADA

Anchorage

Seward

Juneau

Kodiak

Skagit

Lake Chelan

Lake Roosevelt

Spokane

Everett

Seattle

Bellevue

Tacoma

Yakima

Olympia

Yakima

Snake

WASHINGTON

Walla Walla

Columbia

Portland

Pendleton

Salem

Corvallis

Williamette

Deschutes

John Day

IDAHO

Eugene

Bend

Umpqua

OREGON

PACIFIC OCEAN

Rogue

Klamath Lake

Goose Lake

Medford

Eureka

Eel

Redding

Sacramento

Reno

Lake Tahoe

NEVADA

Clear Lake

Santa Rosa

Sacramento

Napa

Stockton

San Francisco

Oakland

Fremont

Modesto

Palo Alto

San Jose

San Joaquin

Salinas

Fresno

Salinas

CALIFORNIA

KAUAI

OAHU

NIIHAU

Kaneohe

MOLOKAI

Honolulu

Wailuku

LANAI

MAUI

KAHOOLAWE

HAWAII

Hilo

HAWAII

Bakersfield

Santa Barbara

Burbank

Los Angeles

San Bernardino

Anaheim

Palm Springs

Long Beach

Santa Ana

Irvine

Indio

Newport Beach

Escondido

Salton Sea

Oceanside

San Diego

ARIZONA

MEXICO

THE
PACIFIC
REGION

The Greenwood Encyclopedia of
American Regional Cultures

Edited by
Jan Goggans with Aaron DiFranco

Foreword by William Ferris, Consulting Editor

Paul S. Piper, Librarian Advisor

GREENWOOD PRESS
Westport, Connecticut • London

Library of Congress Cataloging-in-Publication Data

The Pacific region: the Greenwood encyclopedia of American regional cultures / edited by Jan Goggans with Aaron DiFranco; foreword by William Ferris, consulting editor.

   p. cm.

   Includes bibliographical references and index.

   ISBN 0–313–33266–5 (set : alk. paper)—ISBN 0–313–33043–3 (alk. paper)

   1. Pacific States—Civilization—Encyclopedias. 2. Pacific States—History—Encyclopedias. 3. Pacific States—Social life and customs—Encyclopedias. 4. Popular culture—Pacific States— Encyclopedias. 5. Regionalism—Pacific States—Encyclopedias. 6. Alaska—Civilization—Ency- clopedias. 7. Regionalism—Alaska—Encyclopedias. 8. Hawaii—Civilization—Encyclopedias. 9. Regionalism—Hawaii—Encyclopedias. I. Goggans, Jan. II. DiFranco, Aaron. III. Series.

F851.P1955   2004

979'.003—dc22   2004056061

British Library Cataloguing in Publication Data is available.

Library of Congress Catalog Card Number: 2004056061

ISBN: 0–313–33266–5 (set)

     0–313–32733–5 (The Great Plains Region)
     0–313–32954–0 (The Mid-Atlantic Region)
     0–313–32493–X (The Midwest)
     0–313–32753–X (New England)
     0–313–33043–3 (The Pacific Region)
     0–313–32817–X (The Rocky Mountain Region)
     0–313–32734–3 (The South)
     0–313–32805–6 (The Southwest)

First published in 2004

Greenwood Press, 88 Post Road West, Westport, CT 06881
An imprint of Greenwood Publishing Group, Inc.
www.greenwood.com

Printed in the United States of America

∞™

The paper used in this book complies with the Permanent Paper Standard issued by the National Information Standards Organization (Z39.48–1984).

10 9 8 7 6 5 4 3 2 1

We would like to acknowledge the untiring work of those at the Pacific Regional Humanities Center who offered advice and support to the project: Jack Hicks, Kristen Koster, Ron Saufley, John Van den Heuvel, Georges Van Den Abbeele and Michelle Yeh. To the contributors who worked so hard, under so many unexpected stresses, we offer our thanks for your graciousness. To Anne Thompson and Rob Kirkpatrick, we offer our thanks and admiration for the scale and success of this project. Finally, to the many scholars and writers who sent enthusiastic proposals and inquiries, we also say thank you, and hope that we will work with you one day.

CONTENTS

Contents

FOREWORD

Region inspires and grounds the American experience. Whether we are drawn to them or flee from them, the places in which we live etch themselves into our memory in powerful, enduring ways. For over three centuries Americans have crafted a collective memory of places that constitute our nation's distinctive regions. These regions are embedded in every aspect of American history and culture.

American places have inspired poets and writers from Walt Whitman and Henry David Thoreau to Mark Twain and William Faulkner. These writers grounded their work in the places where they lived. When asked why he never traveled, Thoreau replied, "I have traveled widely in Concord."

William Faulkner remarked that early in his career as a writer he realized that he could devote a lifetime to writing and never fully exhaust his "little postage stamp of native soil."

In each region American writers have framed their work with what Eudora Welty calls "sense of place." Through their writing we encounter the diverse, richly detailed regions of our nation.

In his ballads Woody Guthrie chronicles American places that stretch from "the great Atlantic Ocean to the wide Pacific shore," while Muddy Waters anchors his blues in the Mississippi Delta and his home on Stovall's Plantation.

American corporate worlds like the Bell system neatly organize their divisions by region. And government commissions like the Appalachian Regional Commission, the Mississippi River Commission, and the Delta Development Commission define their mission in terms of geographic places.

When we consider that artists and writers are inspired by place and that government and corporate worlds are similarly grounded in place, it is hardly surprising that we also identify political leaders in terms of their regional culture. We think of John Kennedy as a New Englander, of Ann Richards as a Texan, and of Jimmy Carter as a Georgian.

Because Americans are so deeply immersed in their sense of place, we use region like a compass to provide direction as we negotiate our lives. Through sense of place we find our bearings, our true north. When we meet people for the first time, we ask that familiar American question, "Where are you from?" By identifying others through a region, a city, a community, we frame them with a place and find the bearings with which we can engage them.

Sense of place operates at all levels of our society—from personal to corporate and government worlds. While the power of place has long been understood and integrated in meaningful ways with our institutions, Americans have been slow to seriously study their regions in a focused, thoughtful way. As a young nation, we have been reluctant to confront the places we are "from." As we mature as a nation, Americans are more engaged with the places in which they live and increasingly seek to understand the history and culture of their regions.

The growing importance of regional studies within the academy is an understandable and appropriate response to the need Americans feel to understand the places in which they live. Such study empowers the individual, their community, and their region through a deeper engagement with the American experience. Americans resent that their regions are considered "overfly zones" in America, and through regional studies they ground themselves in their community's history and culture.

The Greenwood Encyclopedia of American Regional Cultures provides an exciting, comprehensive view of our nation's regions. The set devotes volumes to New England, the Mid-Atlantic, the South, the Midwest, the Southwest, the Great Plains, the Rocky Mountains, and the Pacific. Together these volumes offer a refreshing new view of America's regions as they stretch from the Atlantic to the Pacific.

The sheer size of our nation makes it difficult to imagine its diverse worlds as a single country with a shared culture. Our landscapes, our speech patterns, and our foodways all change sharply from region to region. The synergy of different regional worlds bound together within a single nation is what defines the American character. These diverse worlds coexist with the knowledge that America will always be defined by its distinctly different places.

American Regional Cultures explores in exciting ways the history and culture of each American region. Its volumes allow us to savor individual regional traditions and to compare these traditions with those of other regions. Each volume features chapters on architecture, art, ecology and environment, ethnicity, fashion, film and theater, folklore, food, language, literature, music, religion, and sports and recreation. Together these chapters offer a rich portrait of each region. The series is an important teaching resource that will significantly enrich learning at secondary, college, and university levels.

Over the past forty years a growing number of colleges and universities have launched regional studies programs that today offer exciting courses and degrees for both American and international students. During this time the National Endowment for the Humanities (NEH) has funded regional studies initiatives that range from new curricula to the creation of museum exhibits, films, and encyclopedias that focus on American regions. Throughout the nation, universities with regional studies programs recently received NEH support to assist with the programs that they are building.

The National Endowment for the Arts (NEA) has similarly encouraged regional initiatives within the art world. NEA's state arts councils work together within regional organizations to fund arts projects that impact their region.

The growing study of region helps Americans see themselves and the places they come from in insightful ways. As we understand the places that nurture us, we build a stronger foundation for our life. When speaking of how she raised her children, my mother often uses the phrase "Give them their roots, and they will find their wings." Thanks to *American Regional Cultures*, these roots are now far more accessible for all Americans. This impressive set significantly advances our understanding of American regions and the mythic power these places hold for our nation.

William Ferris
University of North Carolina
at Chapel Hill

PREFACE

We are pleased to present *The Greenwood Encyclopedia of American Regional Cultures*, the first book project of any kind, reference or otherwise, to examine cultural regionalism throughout the United States.

The sense of place has an intrinsic role in American consciousness. Across its vast expanses, the United States varies dramatically in its geography and its people. Americans seem especially cognizant of the regions from which they hail. Whether one considers the indigenous American Indian tribes and their relationships to the land, the many waves of immigrants who settled in particular regions of the nation, or the subsequent generations who came to identify themselves as New Englanders or Southerners or Midwesterners, and so forth, the connection of American culture to the sense of regionalism has been a consistent pattern throughout the nation's history.

It can be said that behind every travelogue on television, behind every road novel, behind every cross-country journey, is the desire to grasp the identity of other regions. This project was conceived to fill a surprising gap in publishing on American regionalism and on the many vernacular expressions of culture that one finds throughout the country.

This reference set is designed so that it will be useful to high school and college researchers alike, as well as to the general reader and scholar. Toward this goal, we consulted several members of Greenwood's Library Advisory Board as we determined both the content and the format of this encyclopedia project. Furthermore, we used the *National Standards: United States History* and also the *Curriculum Standards for Social Studies* as guides in choosing a wealth of content that would help researchers gain historical comprehension of how people in, and from, all regions have helped shape American cultures.

American Regional Cultures is divided geographically into eight volumes: *The Great Plains Region*, *The Mid-Atlantic Region*, *The Midwest*, *New England*, *The Pacific Region*, *The Rocky Mountain Region*, *The South*, and *The Southwest*. To ensure that cultural elements from each state would be discussed, we assigned each state to a particular region as follows:

The Great Plains Region: Kansas, Nebraska, North Dakota, Oklahoma, South Dakota
The Mid-Atlantic Region: Delaware, District of Columbia, Maryland, New Jersey, New York, Pennsylvania, West Virginia
The Midwest: Illinois, Indiana, Iowa, Michigan, Minnesota, Missouri, Ohio, Wisconsin
New England: Connecticut, Maine, Massachusetts, New Hampshire, Rhode Island, Vermont
The Pacific Region: Alaska, California, Hawai'i, Oregon, Washington
The Rocky Mountain Region: Colorado, Idaho, Montana, Utah, Wyoming
The South: Alabama, Arkansas, Florida, Georgia, Kentucky, Louisiana, Mississippi, North Carolina, South Carolina, Tennessee, Virginia
The Southwest: Arizona, Nevada, New Mexico, Texas

Each regional volume consists of rigorous, detailed overviews on all elements of culture, with chapters on the following topics: architecture, art, ecology and environment, ethnicity, fashion, film and theater, folklore, food, language, literature, music, religion, and sports and recreation. These chapters examine the many significant elements of those particular aspects of regional culture as they have evolved over time, through the beginning of the twenty-first century. Each chapter seeks not to impose a homogenized identity upon each region but, rather, to develop a synthesis or thematically arranged discussion of the diverse elements of each region. For example, in turning to the chapter on music in *The Pacific Region*, a reader will discover information on Pacific regional music as it has manifested itself in such wide-ranging genres as American Indian tribal performances, Hawaiian stylings, Hispanic and Asian traditions, West Coast jazz, surf rock, folk scenes, San Francisco psychedelia, country rock, the L.A. hard-rock scene, Northwest "grunge" rock, West Coast hip-hop, and Northern California ska-punk. Multiply this by thirteen chapters and again by eight volumes, and you get a sense of the enormous wealth of information covered in this landmark set.

In addition, each chapter concludes with helpful references to further resources, including, in most cases, printed resources, Web sites, films or videos, recordings, festivals or events, organizations, and special collections. Photos, drawings, and maps illustrate each volume. A timeline of major events for the region provides context for understanding the cultural development of the region. A bibliography, primarily of general sources about the region, precedes the index.

We would not have been able to publish such an enormous reference set without the work of our volume editors and the more than one hundred contributors that they recruited for this project. It is their efforts that have made *American Regional Cultures* come to life. We also would like to single out two people for their help: William Ferris, former chairman of the National Endowment for the Humanities and currently Distinguished Professor of History and senior associate director for the Center for the Study of the American South, University of North Carolina at Chapel Hill, who served as consulting editor for and was instrumental in the planning of this set and in the recruitment of its volume editors; and Paul S. Piper,

Reference Librarian at Western Washington University, who in his role as librarian advisor, helped shape both content and format, with a particular focus on helping improve reader interface.

With their help, we present *The Greenwood Encyclopedia of American Regional Cultures*.

Rob Kirkpatrick, Senior Acquisitions Editor
Anne Thompson, Senior Development Editor
Greenwood Publishing Group

INTRODUCTION

In the age of high-speed Internet dial-up, instant text messages, and satellite feeds, time and space do not so much disappear as they become deceptively malleable. Chat rooms peopled with cross-country, even cross-continent, participants convince us that time zones are eminently traversable barriers, that geography can be overcome by a flat screen panel, that people exist in an all-hours/all-access space limited only by the occasional need for human sleep. The world is ideas; perhaps the world is *an* idea—at least that is what devices at our disposal seem to say.

In many ways, college and university departments, along with documentarians and writers, provided pathways down which such ideas could more easily slide, by exploring social and cultural ideologies, by looking deeply at the extent to which humans constructed certain ways of looking at tribes, at places, at behaviors. Challenging outdated notions of "primitive" cultures, for example, anthropologists and sociologists began to understand that the notion of "primitive" was neither hard nor fast, that it was an idea shared by only certain people—usually those with more access to print opportunities—but certainly not an inherently right or even widespread idea. Similarly, our understanding of certain geographies also came into question. Was the South, and the food and politics and language with which we identified it, a place or an idea about a place? What about the Midwest, another place marked not simply by well-known cultural patterns but by stereotypes? And the West—for many scholars and writers, it was immediately clear that the West really never was a place; it was always an idea, a proposed mix of destiny and destination. The belief that the West was simply a cultural construct thus made it that much easier to believe that its geographical boundaries and its demographic differences carried little meaning to a modern American citizen, a belief that contemporary global practices and policies reinforce daily.

The Pacific Region has long been crafted out of a popular mythos, with cowboys and Indians giving way to surfers or loggers or spa-ers. For many, the West appears as one place—a maverick, sometimes arrogant blend of people and places in eastern Oregon, California, and Nevada. For others, that place looks more like the Pacific Northwest, with its flannel shirt obstinacy encompassing western Oregon, Washington, and British Columbia. Southern California presents its own sun-golden mirage. Meanwhile, the noncontiguous states project their own iconic and iconoclastic distinctions: Hawai'i is Hawai'i; Alaska, Alaska. Each of these areas has long had its own popular identity. Even as shifts occurred, in the Pacific Northwest, for example, backwoods logger to bunker builders to World Trade Organization ralliers, stereotypical images remained nearly hermetically sealed, with little room for fluid or fluctuating boundaries. Covering five states and including three island groups, these cultural perceptions impart a complicated mix of identities on the region.

How, then, are we to define regional culture in the Pacific, a place made of theories, fantasies, tall tales, and broken dreams?

Much of the West's culture depends on its stories, whether tall or true. Native peoples carried their culture in their mouths, so to speak, relying on an intricate oral tradition that explained both the geography and the society in which they lived. As the Pacific Coast became an officially "discovered" place, first by Spanish, then Mexican settlers, then by westward-moving U.S. citizens, and finally by eastward-moving Asian cultures, the historical pattern of settlement depended to a large extent on stories passed from those who had witnessed the West to those who wanted to see it for themselves. In John Steinbeck's *The Grapes of Wrath*, the financially troubled Joad family is drawn west by a flyer promising work in the Edenic orange groves of the West. The fact that nearly seventy years after its publication the novel still draws heated debate over the veracity of Steinbeck's plot and serious scholars debate in painstaking detail whether or not such flyers really did exist during the Great Depression attests to how seriously the West takes its fabled stories, how much our concept of culture relies on the tales we tell and others tell about us.

Steinbeck's novel, thought by many to be the quintessential novel of life in California, has gained that reputation largely through its heartbreaking plot: the family pushed west by poverty, goaded on through all sorts of misery and pain by the golden promise of the western state's bounty and abundance, only to find that even in the West people starve, land is unavailable, society has turned mean. As much as the paradisiacal riches it has promised to wave after wave of immigrant and migrant, the West is even more famous for its broken promises, the dreams it engenders in the common man and woman without, seemingly, any intention of fulfillment. The great western expeditions, Lewis and Clark, the Donner Party, the countless gold rushes in California, Washington, Alaska, even the gilded lure of Hollywood—all began with the dream of finding something better, and all ended with the simple fact of the West.

That western dream has long been most often embodied by California, a state whose imaginative construct is sometimes greater than that of all others. While, for example, both Alaska and Washington had gold rushes, it is often the Mother Lode years that American history books cite: The bracing and often brutal tide of migrants and immigrants drawn into Sacramento and San Francisco forms the narrative through which we understand that epoch of our country's history.

Poetically, it is the very fact of California's long-standing popular mythos that highlights how important regional culture is, even in the face of a world both virtual and insistently global. If by the West we, too, often mean stories of the West, California insists that we look beyond the narrative and acknowledge that we also mean a landscape so diverse that eleven different bioregions exist in the state—areas marked by differences in climate and topography so abrupt as to make them seem like other lands. Regionalism asks us to recognize a simple but elegant truth: that culture takes place within place, in response to place. Crafts, language, dance, music, clothing—all respond to physical features of climate, topography, biota. Migratory waterfowl on the Pacific flyway are drawn to marsh basins fed by salmon-heavy mountain rivers visited and revisited in their turn by bear, beaver, or white-tail deer; each and all feed culture, both literally and metaphorically. Land and water connect us, and it is not by coincidence that the region's greatest poet, Gary Snyder, spent forty years on the opus that he eventually titled *Mountains and Rivers without End*. The most aqueous of life forms relies on the long, hot dry landscapes that result from constantly heaving tectonic plates. The desert's geological mirror is the mountain, and both rely on the river's tangent path to the ocean.

While the Sierra Nevadas have had their share of press, the most binding of the region's geological formations is known as Cascadia—the Great Cascade volcanic chain that stretches from Northern California through British Columbia to Alaska. Roughly 300 miles long, the chain's peaks—Mt. Lassen, Mt. Shasta, Mt. St. Helens, Mt. Hood, Crater Lake, and Mt. Rainier—were all formed by the subduction of the Juan de Fuca Plate, now deep in the Pacific Ocean's floor. The actions of the Juan de Fuca Plate, while raising mountains along the coast, also formed the Cascade's mirror range, the Hawaiian Archipelago, in the middle of the ocean. Thus, a single geological shift created a virtual ring of volcanoes, all inspiring various customs for recreation, exploration, and mythology.

Just as the landforms invoke diverse cultural responses, rivers create watersheds in which life systems respond in immediate ways. Like plants clustering in riparian colonies, peoples have long settled by rivers, developing foodways, social rituals, and sports, to name a few, that rely on the river's habitats. Indeed, the entire Pacific Rim is the watershed of the great Pacific Ocean. Along with the region's five major rivers—the Colorado, Los Angeles, San Joaquin–Sacramento, Columbia, and Yukon Rivers—the Pacific Ocean itself acts as a great sixth river, a basin into which all the others flow, and the medium that embraces the Pacific Islands. Yet even while these shared waterways and ranges connect us, tribal movement, immigrant shifts, and migrant patterns all generate new responses to the same place. Consequently, the very geographical ties that bind us will often result in differences among us. The river systems running throughout the region, their natural courses unimpeded by state boundaries, find their waters hotly contested, victims of political manipulations and sources of controversy among farmers, fishermen, ecologists, and developers.

The Pacific Regional Humanities Center's National Endowment for the Humanities (NEH) proposal bluntly and accurately characterized the region as marked by contrasts, conflicts, and compromises. Those qualities are partly the result of the region's vast size. To travel from San Diego, California, to Sitka, Alaska, would take eighty-two hours and fifty-two minutes, a nearly incomprehensible trip of 3,070.46 miles. To hold a teleconference among all the region's members would demand the negotiation of five time zones. At 1:30 P.M. in California, it would be 12:30 P.M. in Alaska, 11:30 A.M. in Hawai'i, 10:30 A.M. in Samoa, and 7:30 P.M. in

American Samoa and Northern Marianas. But it is not simply a matter of size. Diversity permeates the region in all possible forms. California alone houses the lowest point in the Western Hemisphere, Death Valley, and the highest point in the contiguous forty-eight states, Mt. Whitney. Setting out on a typical winter morning, travelers might begin by digging their cars out of the three or four feet of snow that fell around June Lake, face whiteout conditions traveling south on Interstate 395 east of the Sierra mountain range, and stop to fill up the gas tank at Lone Pine, in good seeing distance of Mt. Whitney's 14,495 feet; as long as the car did not overheat, Death Valley's Furnace Creek would offer lunch, only a mile or so from Badwater, at 282 feet below sea level, the lowest point in the Western Hemisphere. The entire trip, discounting stopping time, takes four hours and twenty-five minutes.

Like the land on which they have settled, the region's peoples are marked by extreme, even abrupt, ethnic and cultural differences. This region, first envisioned as the "Pacific Rim" by Mark Twain, is defined geopolitically by a distinct mix of nations, languages, beliefs, and practices. To the south, Mexico, Central America, and South America; to the north, Canada; to the west, the Philippines, Korea, Japan, and China; to the east, an older United States, one that has long harbored conflicted responses to Henry David Thoreau's dictum: head west. To paraphrase the center's proposal, the Pacific West's demographics have been shaped by waves of imported agricultural labor, tides of explorers and pioneers, and literally, boats of refugees. At this moment, the region is experiencing major historic demographic shifts and redefinitions with profound social, economic, and cultural implications for the region itself and the United States in general.

The following chapters face the challenge of defining the undefinable—a culture in a region of many cultures.

In surveying the architecture of the Pacific's microregions, Julie Nicoletta, Merry Ovnick, and Spencer Leineweber demonstrate how, even as design styles have been imported from throughout the world, Pacific habitations and buildings have molded themselves into the environment. For centuries the Northwest Coast's dense forests have provided materials to diverse settlers, used to construct wooden-plank longhouses among coastal tribes as well as San Francisco's Victorian homes. Hawai'i's and California's milder climates permitted more open constructions, from indigenous grass- and brush-thatched dwellings to the cool, Spanish-influenced adobe Mission style. And while twentieth-century influences from Richardson Romanesque to post–World War II suburban tract homes give towns and cities the feel of commonplace Americana, the region also includes daring designs in concrete, steel, and glass. Asian-influenced resort hotels rise out of Hawai'i's shores; the Seattle Center's Space Needle stands against coastal storms; and Los Angeles' urban skyline boasts influences in Internationalism and Futurism, as well as the structured fantasies of Disneyland's Main Street and Frank Gehry's unconventional Disney Concert Hall.

The diverse attempts to build the Pacific environment mirror the variety of artistic lenses brought to the region's landscapes. As Linda Noveroske Rentner and Janet L. Steinbright demonstrate in the chapter on art, the nineteenth century explosion of people in the Pacific coincided with a growing taste for American genre painting. Scenic representation of settler and mining life would blossom into appreciation of the Pacific's tremendous terrains during the nineteenth-century fascination for landscape painting. Early artistic influences came belatedly from Europe and the East Coast, but Pacific artists imbued their work with a dynamicism and vision reflecting the conditions of the region. Such rebelliousness often found its most radical forms in ethnic-political and countercultural art, yet the region's nourishing cultural environment has made it one of the leading edges of the avant-garde. However, as Rentner and Steinbright remind us, time-honored practices still produce exquisite art. Outside of Euro-American legacies stand the works of remarkably skilled Native Alaskan artisans, whose knowledge of the region's natural materials and carefully attended traditions provide a luminous aesthetic that continues to influence regional art.

Indigenous art forms—from Alaskan ivory carving to California basketry to Hawaiian lei arrangements—are but one mode by which the Pacific culture makes use of the region's incredible ecological composition. In the chapter on ecology and environment M. Kathryn Davis outlines the contours of an environment of extremes, one that includes an arctic subcontinent, a 1,600-mile-long volcanic island chain, Death Valley's depths, and North America's highest mountain at over 20,000 feet—the Denali peak of Mt. McKinley. Though sublimely dramatic, these lands are also extremely fertile, providing some of the richest agriculture, forests, fisheries, and even oil reserves in the nation.

Such varied environments have nonetheless offered welcome conditions for a population almost as extreme in its ethnic composition. The Pacific Region is profoundly multicultural, embracing peoples from around the globe. The first human footfalls in the Americas most likely made their way through Alaska into the continent's interior, and First Peoples continue to persist in the region despite onslaughts of immigrants beginning with the California gold rush. Agriculture continues to draw millions of workers into the region, particularly from Mexico and Central America. Yet while Mexican immigrants comprise a vast majority of newcomers, the Pacific Region is still the preferential destination for immigrants of all nationalities. As a vector on the Pacific Rim, the region also has witnessed a remarkable influx of immigrants from throughout Asia. In the chapter on ethnicity, Aaron DiFranco and Kella de Castro Svetich elaborate on the formative influence peoples from Asia have had on the history and social institutions of the region, an influence perpetuated and reshaped by ongoing trans-Pacific diasporas.

The cosmopolitan mix of the Pacific has also made it one of the flashpoints of the fashion industry, thanks in no small part to the glamour of Hollywood. Hollywood's image factory, however, is counterpointed by an established textile and clothing industry that responds to the lifestyle and environment of the region. Susan B. Kaiser and Linda B. Arthur explain how wilderness and outdoor outfitters have responded to people's desires to explore the rugged terrain of the region. The Pacific atmosphere of leisure and ruggedness they describe infuses the region's major fashion trends, from Levi's evolution from mining-camp work pants to hipster style as well as the rise of business-casual dress.

That its influence can be felt from fashion to politics is one of the enduring legacies of Hollywood. From cinematic art to business acumen to technological wizardry, Hollywood's reach is compelling, and having the film industry's heart in the Pacific West profoundly influences the culture's perceptions, its illusions and delusions, of the region. In the chapter on film and theater, Georges Van Den Abbeele, John T. Caldwell, Jan Goggans, and Jeff Purdue's insightful discussion describes not only the regional impact of a national institution but also the influences the region has had in representing scenes from across the globe. Hollywood's titanic presence, however, is not the only model for film in the region. The authors demonstrate not only the growing importance of independent studios, festivals, and art house projects to the Pacific West but also the extent to which film has been used to document and comment on the region's social and political issues.

When cultures begin the task of articulating and defining themselves, folklore, tall tales, and myth are born, as Barre Toelken shows in his chapter on folklore. Drawing on a wealth of regional manifestations or the local imagination, the most famous of which might be Bigfoot, or Yeti, Toelken takes readers through a fascinating maze of Münchausens, domestic arts and crafts, gods and goddesses—all of which create a dynamic story of how generations of Pacific Westerners have made sense of the landscape that has alternately inspired and confused them.

The "dizzying array" to which Kimberly D. Nettles, Melissa Salazar, and Alice McLean first allude in their chapter on food of the Pacific Region describes not simply the "climates, land types, animal and plant products, and peoples" but also the foods, foodways, and food cultures that have grown to be physical, religious, and cultural sustenance for many of the region's peoples. No aspect of culture is more closely tied to the land than food, and the long tug and pull that the West's people have entertained with the land they have alternately conquered and been conquered by is reflected in what the authors aptly name an "amalgam" of cuisines and cultural practices.

Languages of the Pacific Region, as Kevin Donald, Ritsuko Kikusawa, Karen Gaul and Gary Holton show, have been profoundly shaped by the large-scale, and long-term, patterns of migration and immigration. From European and Asian inroads on the original tongues of the Pacific Islanders to the polyglot of South American, African, Asian, and European influences on the mainland, Pacific regional language has been as fluid as the rivers the region supports. In the process of taking in the words and ideas of various visitors and conquerors, native languages have been changed and have, in turn, left their own imprint on the languages that have succeeded them. Various new movements to preserve the native languages of the region are thriving, even as new dialects continue to evolve.

Regionalism and literature have, historically, been linked in a marriage that has been as rich and creative as it has sometimes been contentious. In the Pacific Region, aesthetic responses to the landscape and the many cultures that have shaped lives in response to it have always factored in the physical demands of a geography that has been demanding, even intractable. Western authors have long had to "prove" themselves as they compete not only with those authors embraced by the more entrenched system of eastern publishing houses but also as the rugged writers who can "take on" what it means to be in the West. Jack Hicks, Michael Kowalewski, and Chris J. Sindt explore the fiction, nonfiction, drama, and poetry of the Pacific Region, showing the various movements, both geographic and aesthetic, that have come to form a fertile body of what we now call Western literature.

Often a culture's first form of responding to its surroundings takes the form of music. With a geography, topography, and hydrology diverse enough to spawn a multitude of responses, music has long been one of the region's most important "languages." As the chapter on music by Pauline Tuttle, Valerie Samson, Sydney

Hutchinson, Rob Kirkpatrick, and Jan Goggans demonstrates, the region has a rich musical history, beginning with a long tradition of song and dance by the region's First Nations Peoples. As musical forms traveled from the East and Far East into the Pacific Region, Asian American dance and music, with its unique style and instrumentation, became a crucial component of the region's musical identity. And just as music traveled into the region via eastern migratory patterns, it also came up, with the many South and Central Americans who sought new lives in *El Norte*. The chapter traces the important contributions of Mexican American song and dance to this region. An analysis of contemporary and popular music shows that despite the many homogenizing efforts ethnic groups have suffered, the varied cultures of this region continue to find diverse expression in their music.

As with music, religion in the Pacific has responded to an eclectic fusion of traditions and response to place. Jeremy Bonner, Vivian Deno, and Aaron DiFranco highlight the religious miscellany that has formed in the region, from indigenous rituals to Spanish Catholicism to the rise of independent churches and sects. Despite these influences, the region evinces a strong spiritualism, virtually unmatched elsewhere, that also generally eschews dogma and institutional forms. This tendency and the Pacific mix of peoples have resulted in the rapid growth of charismatic, nondenominational Pentecostal faiths. One of the most pervasive and regionally grounded movements, Pentecostalism has demonstrated a strong appeal among individualistic westerners. Such individualism and intense spiritualism have also permitted the spread of Buddhism throughout the Pacific Region. Originally imported by Asian immigrant communities from China and Japan, Buddhism has attracted a wide body of non-Asian adherents, especially since the end of World War II.

Sports frequently are invented in response to place, and for many of the Pacific Region's most popular and long-lived sports, it is true that the culture of recreation has grown out of regional topography. As Mont Christopher Hubbard, Andrea Ross, and Patrick Moser show in their chapter on sports and recreation, surfing, in particular, is intrinsically related to the survival activities of the region's indigenous peoples. In addition, as new arrivals to the region introduced new cultures, attitudes toward the land played a major role in the development of sports culture, particularly wilderness sports. Yet many of the region's most popular sports are East Coast imports, sports that can be played nearly anywhere at any time.

The temporal march from past to present, as certain cultural aspects reveal it, shows a constant tension between what people do to the lands on which they live, and what those lands do to the people who inhabit them. Never a fully compatible nor a completely hostile relationship, a culture's relation to its place is at the heart of what we understand to be regionalism. As we watch early in the twenty-first century, the pressures of corporate globalism are profound and incessant, and many fear the flattening of human societies into one vast monocultural shopping mall. To be certain, the retro powers of nationalism, fundamentalist religion, and feudal tribalism constitute a complex of fearful responses out of an understandable desire to have a place on earth. There is also a danger that advocates for a renewed sense of the powers of *place*—an appreciation for the many regions that make us one—sometimes exercise a provincial nostalgia, a yearning backward for an Eden that never existed. The culture of the American Pacific is challenged to meld past and future into something wholly new, and there is no better spokesperson for that vision than Pultizer Prize poet Gary Snyder, as he writes in "A View of the Pacific Region":

> Call it the Eastern Pacific, or the western edge of North America; it reaches from the ranges down near Baja up northwest past the Mt. St. Elias and beyond; all of Alaska and the Aleutian arc on out to the Date Line. Into the mid-Pacific, the Hawai'ian islands and the further Pacific islands under U.S. care. West of the Great Basin, the Sierra / Cascade / rim of granite and volcanoes, and the benign Pacific Slope with its westward rivers, forests and grasslands, and summer mountain snowfields.
>
> The salmon is the magical traveler that binds it together, weaving the many threads of streams together with the deeps of the north Pacific. Humpback whales that feed on herring in Sitka Sound will calve in the warmer waters of Hawai'i. The albacore and tuna cruise south through all the island realms.
>
> Hawai'i is a remarkable human mix; and Alaska, too. Alaska still has dozens of Russian Orthodox chapels, a memory of imported reindeer herding experiments from Finland, Aleut fishermen who were interned in Japan during WW II and who speak a little of that language; and in the library a few books left from Russian times when there was Aleut literacy—writing their language in a well-adapted Cyrillic script. Fort Yukon was the farthest westward reach of the Hudson Bay Company. Russian fur traders pushing east came within a few hundred miles in the same era. Texan oilmen work on the giant platforms that go into the Chukchi Sea.
>
> Meanwhile, in San Francisco, anybody can now get the traditional Polynesian-style geometric tattoo designs (which are often seen among young Hawai'ian men—a sign of pride). The whole west coast, with its ethnic and racial crossovers and its tolerance of difference, keeps on inventing a new trans-Pacific regional culture of backpacking, tea ceremony, varietal wines, *animé* movies, computer programming, *zazen*, organic vegetables, gridlock, and Burning Man. We can look ahead to—East-Asian Hispanic? Anglo-Raven Clan-Confucianists? We can only hope that the spirits of Douglas fir, redwood, cedar, liveoak, and especially salmon will guide us past gridlock and smog to a new culture of the far west, and the vast Pacific.

ARCHITECTURE

Julie Nicoletta, Merry Ovnick, and Spencer Leineweber

ARCHITECTURE OF THE PACIFIC NORTHWEST

As part of the American West, the Pacific Northwest has been shaped by the following factors: extraction of natural resources, urbanization, ethnic diversity, and the presence of the federal government. Unlike the rest of the West, however, the region, located far up in the northwest corner of the United States, was isolated for much of its history. In *The Pacific Northwest: An Interpretive History* historian Carlos Schwantes notes that after initial explorations, the Pacific Northwest "remained a colonial hinterland for the next two centuries and thus was economically vulnerable to forces beyond its control."[1] All these elements shaped architecture in the region.

The extraction of natural resources for consumption elsewhere, beginning with the fur trade and shortly thereafter including logging, mining, fishing, ranching, and farming, drew money out of the region, leaving little capital for constructing truly significant architecture on a par with that of San Francisco or cities in the East. This resource-based economy has also made the region vulnerable to boom-and-bust cycles for much of its history. Development was slow until the coming of the railroad.

Just as significantly, Euro-American settlement in the region coincided with the Industrial Revolution; this, too, had an effect on architecture. The mechanization of sawmills, for example, produced standard-sized lumber early on. With the arrival of the railroad in the 1870s, building materials could be shipped easily throughout most of the region, so even in the arid areas east of the Cascade mountains, wood was readily available by the late nineteenth century. Despite a diverse population made up of many ethnic groups, building construction was often speculative and rarely reflected cultural differences or ethnic influences. Builders tended to copy forms and styles from the eastern United States. Not until the mid-twentieth century did the Pacific Northwest exhibit its own creativity in design, when architects began drawing on the region's unique natural landscape of forest, water, mountains, and plains for inspiration.

Rapid urbanization since the late nineteenth century has characterized the development of much of the Pacific Northwest, especially along the West Coast where most of the population has settled, and around Spokane in eastern Washington, Boise, and Anchorage. Transportation hubs, where the railroads met ports and highways concentrated capital and people into urban centers, required a variety of public and private buildings, such as courthouses, schools, train stations, churches, warehouses, and dwellings. Construction, using standardized materials—sawn lumber and prefabricated windows, doors, and trim—allowed rapid construction but not always a diversity of forms.

Finally, the presence of the federal government, first through the establishment of forts to fight Native Americans in the nineteenth century and later, in the twentieth century, through the construction of large military bases, dams and hydroelectric power systems, and sites such as Hanford Nuclear Reservation in Washington, resulted in some of the region's largest public works projects.

Prevalent Elements of Architecture in the Region

Native American Architecture

The most populated area before contact with Euro-Americans was along the coast, where water and soil provided abundant resources. Wooden longhouses were the most common building type in villages located along the coast. Constructed of cedar, which the Northwest Coast Indians believe to have spiritual properties, these structures were supported by a post-and-beam timber frame covered by broad, vertical planks and roofed with three-foot-long cedar shingles. Depending on the location and tribe, the houses could have either gable or shed roofs. Also known as plank houses, these structures served a central function in Northwest Coast Indian life as dwellings and as the site of religious rituals and potlatches. Sometimes the most prominent houses in each village were painted with elaborate designs representing the crests of the chief and his family. Though all longhouses from precontact times have disappeared, many reconstructions exist, for example, at the Makah Cultural and Research Center in Neah Bay, Washington, and the Museum of Anthropology at the University of British Columbia in Vancouver. The form continues to inspire Northwest architecture today. A prominent example of a modern building loosely modeled on a plank house is the Museum of Anthropology (1973–1976) at the University of British Columbia (UBC) in Vancouver. Architect Arthur Erickson (b. 1924) designed a building using an enlarged version of the post-and-beam system made of reinforced concrete with large glass walls to allow for natural light. The effect is reminiscent of a plank house, but the structure functions as a modern exhibit hall for the display of Northwest Coast art and artifacts. Many Native Americans living east of the mountains used round, subterranean pit houses for shelter. By the mid-eighteenth century, however, some groups such as the Yakima, Nez Perce, and Umatilla were erecting rectangular houses with pole frames covered by woven reed mats. None of these survive. In Alaska, in addition to the plank houses of the Haida and Tlingit, the Eskimos along the north and western coasts built semisubterranean houses of sod, driftwood, and

A reconstruction of a Makah longhouse in Neah Bay, Washington. Courtesy of the Makah Cultural and Research Center.

whalebone; in the interior, the nomadic Athapaskan Indians erected moss- or bark-covered structures; and the Aleuts lived in partially subterranean buildings accessed through a hole in the roof. Few of these structures stand today, but as Alison K. Hoagland notes in *Buildings of Alaska*, many Native organizations "are reconstructing traditional dwellings as outdoor museums."[2]

European Settlements

The first permanent settlements built by Euro-Americans were posts established to facilitate trade, mainly in furs, with Native Americans. The Hudson's Bay Company (HBC), the American Fur Company, and other companies competed with each other to trap beaver for their pelts and establish trade relations with the indigenous population. Companies built their forts throughout the Northwest; the most important one was the HBC's Fort Vancouver (1825–1860) on the north bank of the Columbia River near its junction with the Willamette River. This fort served as the headquarters for the HBC's vast Columbia Department that covered much of the American West and British Columbia. Under Chief Factor John McLoughlin (1784–1857), Fort Vancouver became a self-sufficient community with scores of buildings. A village grew outside the fort's stockade, complete with houses, churches, a school, a sawmill, and dairies. Scotsmen, French Canadians, Hawaiians, and Native Americans, including local Chinooks and Iroquois from the East, were among those making up the fort's diverse population. But fort buildings followed a common pattern, typically modest one-story log or timber-frame structures with gable roofs arranged in rows around an open yard. Chief Factor McLoughlin's large, white house with its broad veranda stood out as unusually re-

Photograph shows view of officers' quarters and other buildings at the Hudson's Bay Company's post at Fort Vancouver, on the Columbia River. Courtesy of the Library of Congress.

fined, a reflection of McLoughlin's larger-than-life personality. In the twentieth century, the National Park Service reconstructed the buildings at Fort Vancouver, providing visitors with a good sense of the appearance of these trading posts. In Alaska the Russian-American Company, chartered in 1799, quickly gained control of the fur trade in that northern land, encouraging settlement during the Russians' 126-year occupation. Although the Russian population in Alaska never numbered more than 800, they left a legacy of architecture, primarily Russian Orthodox churches that continue to be built today. Saint Nicholas Russian Orthodox Church (1893–1894) in Juneau survives as the only remaining octagonal-plan Russian Orthodox church in the state. Throughout Alaska, the onion domes of these churches act as significant landmarks and as a reminder of the state's early history.

Northwest Architecture in the Nineteenth and Early Twentieth Centuries

Homesteaders soon followed the trappers, traders, and Protestant missionaries who had already begun settling the region in the first few decades of the nineteenth century. By 1841 the first organized wagon trains had crossed the continent in search of good farming and ranching land. It is not surprising that Euro-Americans tended to settle where the Native Americans had—primarily in the Willamette Valley and around the Puget Sound, given the wealth of resources in those areas. Most pioneers followed the Oregon Trail, which led them along the Columbia River gorge and into the Willamette Valley, where the rich soil allowed for excellent agriculture.

Though some of the trading posts established in earlier years lasted for decades, the farming families who settled the region in the 1840s and 1850s created more permanent communities. What is now Washington State was settled beginning in the late 1840s by families moving north from the Willamette Valley. By the early

The Yesler family's house stands on a hillside overlooking the sawmill owned by Henry Yesler, one of the first industrialists in Seattle, 1859. © PEMCO–Webster & Stevens Collection; Museum of History & Industry, Seattle/Corbis.

1850s small communities had been established along the Puget Sound up to what is now Bellingham. Constructing houses and barns, of course, was the most immediate concern of settlers. Along the coast and in the river valleys, they used timber from abundant forests to erect their dwellings. Although settlers typically built log houses first, local entrepreneurs, such as Henry Yesler (1810–1892) in Seattle in 1852, soon constructed sawmills, enabling inhabitants to erect houses and other buildings that more closely resembled structures in the eastern United States. Such buildings reflected the popular architectural styles of the day, though they were usually more simple in form and decoration than one might find in the East. In the 1850s and 1860s common styles included the Greek Revival, Gothic Revival, and the Italianate. Builders might use pattern books to design and construct buildings that reflected eastern trends, but they frequently made changes to suit individual needs, local climatic conditions, and available materials, creating variations of standard designs. Builders in Oregon, particularly in Lane County, erected covered bridges to protect the wood frames from rapidly deteriorating in the damp climate. Surviving bridges are twentieth-century versions of earlier ones.

The isolation of the region, the small population, and the lack of affluence meant that buildings were conservative in style and materials. Alaska, even more remote from the Lower Forty-eight and sparsely populated, also adopted styles from the more established parts of the United States, but its architecture tended to be plainer still. As the most abundant local material throughout much of the region, wood served the needs of many builders, but structures often lacked the permanence and distinction of stone or brick buildings. In Seattle, for example, the first building of the University of Washington, established in 1861, was the most elaborate edifice for many years to come. Standing two stories tall, the white Classical Revival style building with its Ionic columns and cupola presented an impressive appearance, yet it was constructed entirely out of wood. Russian settlers built a similarly elaborate building in Sitka in 1857; the log customhouse had exterior horizontal planks, wooden corner quoins, and cornices with modillions transforming the building into an Italianate structure common throughout the United States at the time.

Railroads connected the Pacific Northwest to the rest of the country when the transcontinental railroad arrived in Portland and Tacoma in 1883. With the trains came an explosion in population, construction, urbanization, and the number of professional architects. Spokane and Tacoma, which had small settlements before the railroads, sprouted overnight into cities with ambitious goals to dominate their respective regions. Merchants, land speculators, and entrepreneurs eagerly promoted their cities as forward looking and prosperous. Architecture was a way to embody these dreams in physical form. Railroad stations became important as the main point of arrival for visitors and new inhabitants. Tacoma's domed Beaux Arts–style Union Station (1909–1911), designed by Reed & Stem and now a federal courthouse, still anchors the old warehouse district just south of downtown, though today it is accompanied by new museums and a growing campus of the University of Washington. Another way for cities and towns to show their promise was to become a county seat and erect an imposing courthouse such as Willis A. Ritchie's (1864–1931) Romanesque Revival Jefferson County Courthouse (1892) in Port Townsend, Washington, with its soaring tower and thick stone walls, or the similarly styled courthouse (1909) in Baker City, Oregon, built of locally quarried gray volcanic stone.

Commercial buildings exhibiting styles such as the Renaissance Revival or Romanesque Revival style, with arches and carved ornamentation, also contributed to a city's prosperous appearance. Substantial warehouses of brick and stone rose along Tacoma's main thoroughfare, Pacific Avenue, near the railroad depot and docks of Commencement Bay. Spokane, centered on a series of dramatic waterfalls, boomed in the 1880s when five railroads were built through the city. A gold rush during this decade brought additional wealth, seen most prominently along Riverside Avenue with its mix of Beaux Arts– and Classical Revival–style structures. Seattle and Portland erected prosperous commercial districts near their ports and railroad stations. Portland, in particular, embraced cast-iron architecture in the late nineteenth century. Builders quickly adopted this method of construction because of its strength and protection against fire; slender iron columns supporting the structure opened up the walls for more windows. An elaborate interpretation of the Italianate style was employed in many of these buildings. Despite some demolition over the years, downtown Portland has the largest collection of cast-iron buildings on the West Coast. Prime examples include the Centennial Block (1876, 1899) and the Mikado Block (1880, 1886), both in the Yamhill Historic District. In contrast, the frontier nature of Alaska in the late nineteenth century, fueled by gold booms in Juneau in 1880, along the Yukon River in 1893, and then along the Klondike River in 1896, produced mining towns of vernacular log houses and false-fronted commercial buildings during this period.

The influx of new arrivals in the region placed new demands on housing. Hotels located near the railroad stations provided temporary lodgings. Urban devel-

Downtown Portland, 2004. Courtesy of Corbis.

opment and a growing economy produced a greater distinction between the classes. Laborers coming to work in the timber, shipping, or railroad industries lived in boardinghouses intermixed with the warehouses. Wealthy men and women built impressive mansions located not too far from downtown or the waterfront but far enough away to be free of the noise and dirt. Like more modest houses in the region, mansions were usually built of wood but in styles of the period—Queen Anne or Eastlake, for example, which featured towers, turrets, and elaborate jig-sawn trim, in some cases piled on like frosting, to highlight the abundant use of lumber, seen, for example, in the remaining mansions of Spokane's Browne's Addition. As cities grew and the downtowns became crowded with commercial structures, the wealthy moved farther away from the center, leaving their old neighborhoods for new inhabitants. In Seattle, First Hill, Capitol Hill, and Queen Anne Hill became known for their tree-lined streets and stately houses representing the latest in architectural styles. One of the best-known houses from the early twentieth century, the Stimson-Green Mansion (1899–1901), was designed by Spokane-based architects Kirkland K. Cutter (1860–1939) and Karl G. Malmgren (1862–1921). The half-timbered mansion drew its inspiration from the English Arts and Crafts Movement, newly introduced to the Northwest at this time. Cutter designed similar baronial houses for the wealthy in Spokane.

Urbanization was so rapid along this stretch in Seattle (Second Avenue and Marion Street), that tents were used until permanent structures could be built, 1889. Courtesy of the Library of Congress.

Houses

The majority of Northwest inhabitants, however, lived in modest wood-frame houses. By the early twentieth century, real estate developers began building tracts of houses on speculation in the region's largest cities. These were located in previously undeveloped areas further from downtown; streetcars provided transportation for workers. Architectural styles favored at this time throughout the region included various interpretations of the Colonial Revival and Tudor Revival and, to a lesser extent, the Mission Revival. By the 1910s and 1920s the Craftsman bungalow had come into vogue; these buildings with their broad gable roofs and front porches became popular for buyers in a range of income levels. Often designed from architectural pattern books or plan books, bungalows could be simple one-story, two-bedroom dwellings or two-and-one-half-story houses with built-in cabinets and leaded windows. Developers also began constructing apartment buildings designed for inhabitants of varying incomes. Some included one-room or two-room apartments for single people, whereas others had much larger apartments of three bedrooms to accommodate middle-class families. As old streetcar suburbs have been rehabilitated over the past thirty years, many of these buildings have been renewed and offer housing to residents who prefer to live close to the city center, providing an alternative to new developments on the outskirts. Others lived far more modestly; in mining towns and in the forests where logging took place, housing was often of a more temporary nature—canvas tents or railroad cars converted to barracks that could be rolled in on rails. In the eastern part of the region where farming and ranching dominated, barns and houses, usually of wood, sometimes of stone, dotted the countryside surrounded by wheat fields in the Walla

Walla Valley and the Palouse and ranches on the plains of eastern Oregon. These rural vernacular buildings were typically constructed by builder/owners rather than trained architects. Alaskans drew on popular forms, such as the bungalow, but built them as simpler one-story buildings with fewer decorative elements such as wide eaves, leaded glass, and clinker brick.

The Boom in Northwest Cities in the Late Nineteenth Century

The region's booming economy attracted architects in search of work. After fires devastated the downtown areas of Seattle and Spokane in 1889, both cities quickly rebuilt themselves with structures that were more impressive than before. Solid brick and stone structures replaced the wooden ones that had been destroyed by the conflagration. The disaster provided many commissions for architects. By this time, commercial and public buildings were regularly designed by men who had training in architecture. Some of these architects, including Willis A. Ritchie and Edwin W. Houghton (1856–1927), had been educated and trained outside of the region and brought with them a knowledge of architectural advances in the nation. Rather than draw on pattern books, these designers looked to the eastern United States and Europe, adding a new sophistication to the urban landscape. Thus, the new downtowns reflected innovations such as the use of iron, steel, and elevators to erect taller structures in styles such as Richardsonian Romanesque, the Romanesque Revival, and the Chicago School. For the first time, these cities had buildings whose design could begin to rival those of Chicago, Minneapolis, and San Francisco. Seattle's Pioneer Square remains today one of the most intact late-nineteenth-century commercial districts in the region; one notable edifice still standing is the Pioneer Building (1889–1890) by Elmer Fisher (c. 1840–1905), who designed numerous buildings in the city. An arch supporting two attached columns of rusticated stone blocks marks the facade of this unique structure.

The boom-and-bust cycles of the region influenced land development and landscape design, as well as architecture. The Tacoma Land Company, an arm of the Northern Pacific Railroad, commissioned Frederick Law Olmsted (1822–1903), the landscape architect of Central Park in New York, to design a plan for the city of Tacoma in 1873. Olmsted, who favored naturalistic designs for parks and towns, proposed a scheme with parks and long blocks formed by curved roads to follow the steep hills of the new city. Ultimately, economics won out; the company decided it could not afford to spend money on parks or on oddly shaped building lots. It settled on a grid plan because square or rectangular lots were easier to describe and, therefore, easier to sell. The grid, the most common urban plan throughout the Midwest and the West, prevailed in the Northwest, too, despite the region's hilly terrain. As cities matured and parks were seen as a more important component of urban life, however, more open space was required. The Olmsted Brothers firm, founded by Olmsted, was commissioned by the city of Seattle to devise a comprehensive park plan in 1903. Although there was not much undeveloped land left, the firm came up with a cohesive series of parks, some formal, some more wild, that provided open space for the city's residents. Olmsted Brothers also designed a park plan for Spokane in 1906, similar to that in Seattle, with large parks linked by boulevards. Portland was laid out with a spine through its center known as the Park Blocks. These would have run the length of the city, but the central blocks fell into private hands and were developed. Also at this time, the conservation movement had spread to the Northwest. The federal government established two national parks in the region: Mount Rainier (1899) and Crater Lake (1902). Denali National Park (1917), Olympic National Park (1938), North Cascades National Park (1968), and several more parks in Alaska followed. These parks helped define the region's connection with the natural environment by preserving striking natural landscapes near metropolitan areas.

Immigrants' Influences

The booming economy of the late nineteenth and early twentieth centuries attracted new arrivals not only from across the United States but also from around the world, most notably from Scandinavia, China, and Japan. Although these ethnic groups have left a legacy of descendants who remain in the region today, their impact on the built environment is less obvious; more research needs to be done in this area. Time and cultural assimilation have erased many architectural elements that distinguished the buildings of specific cultural groups. In rural areas of Washington, Oregon, and Idaho, Scandinavian immigrants also erected their own buildings, thereby introducing building forms and methods from their homelands, such as log buildings and timber-frame construction, that survived at least for a short time. Even traditional forms could be found in cities, such as the old Finnish Temperance Society in Seattle (built 1902) with its narrow, one-room width, though its exterior resembles American examples of commercial buildings. But industrialization and standardized building materials and components soon crowded out transplanted building practices. In other cases, single events contributed to this trend. In 1885, for example, the Chinese were rounded up in Tacoma and put on trains headed south, destroying the city's Chinatown. Although a similar event occurred in Seattle the following year, some Chinese returned shortly thereafter to create a thriving, though contained, Chinatown at the south edge of downtown. In 1942, President Franklin Roosevelt (1882–1945) issued his executive order sending Japanese and Americans of Japanese descent to internment camps during World War II. This action decimated Japanese neighborhoods overnight; most residents did not return to their homes after the war, leaving many buildings to neglect and demolition. Much of Japantown was promptly demolished by the city of Seattle, clearing the way for the construction of Yesler Terrace, a low-income housing project that accommodated African Americans arriving in the city seeking wartime jobs. Today, small Chinatowns stand in Portland and Seattle; a much larger one exists in Vancouver, British Columbia, galvanized by new immigration in the 1980s and 1990s. Some unique structures survive from the early twentieth century, however. A Japanese American sento, or public bathhouse, remains in the basement of the Panama Hotel (1901) in what was Seattle's Japantown. Nihon Go Gakko (1922, 1926), the Japanese Language School in Tacoma, served as a cultural center for young Japanese Americans. One of only two such buildings on the West Coast (the other is in Seattle) to survive into the twenty-first century, this building suffered demolition by neglect at the hands of the University of Washington, Tacoma, and was torn down in 2004. Recent immigration has had a more visible impact on the built environment. Buddhist temples have been built throughout the region in modern yet traditional styles; see, for example, the Idaho-Oregon Buddhist Temple (1955–1958), Ontario, Oregon, designed by Kichio Allen Arai (1901–1966), or the Thai Buddhavanaram Buddhist Temple (1991–1999) in Auburn, Washington, with its steeply pitched gable roofs held up by wooden boomerang-shaped supports.

Northwest Fairs

By the early twentieth century, architecture in the Pacific Northwest reflected a place that had become urbanized and industrialized, but the region was still isolated from the rest of the country. Having built up the region, business leaders wanted to draw attention from the nation and the world. Encouraged by the success of world's fairs in Chicago (1893) and St. Louis (1904), community leaders in the Northwest launched two fairs—one in Portland in 1905 and one in Seattle in 1907. Both fairs had the goals of furthering the expansion of the American Empire across the Pacific and to boost the two cities' standing as economic and cultural centers on the West Coast. The fairs also demonstrated a growing rivalry between Seattle and Portland as they battled for primacy in the Northwest. Though most buildings were designed in revival styles, the forestry pavilions at each fair captured the spirit of the region by using giant unhewn logs for the buildings' frames, as well as their walls and columns. The erection of skyscrapers was another way to convey the region's economic prowess through height and technological innovation. Portland, Seattle, and Spokane all gained tall buildings of usually ten to twelve stories, their steel skeletons clad by terra cotta tiles, brick, or stone. The Smith Tower (1914) designed by Gaggin & Gaggin rose forty-two stories above Seattle and was the tallest building west of the Mississippi for years.

Northwest Building and Architecture in the Twentieth Century

A growing economy and the region's location on the Pacific Rim brought an influx in public and private spending. World Wars I and II fueled construction of new or enlarged military installations, including Fort Lewis, McChord Air Force Base, and the Puget Sound Naval Shipyard, all in Washington. The wars also spurred private investment in manufacturing, especially related to defense. William Boeing (1881–1956) established the Boeing Airplane Company in 1916 to capitalize on the United States' entry into World War I. The company expanded during both world wars and, after World War II, moved into the production of commercial aircraft. Boeing's strong manufacturing base helped drive the Puget Sound economy. Its significance is embodied in the 747/767/777 plant (1966, 1979–1980, 1990) in Everett, Washington, which is the world's largest building by volume, encompassing 472 million cubic feet. The company's size, however, has made the region vulnerable to the aircraft manufacturer's economic ups and downs. During the Great Depression the construction of large public works projects, such as Grand Coulee Dam (1935–1941) and Bonneville Dam (1937), both on the Columbia River, and smaller projects in national forests and parks, such as Timberline Lodge (1936–1937) designed by the U.S. Forest Service on Mount Hood and Paradise Inn (1917) by Heath & Gove on Mount Rainier, employed thousands of laborers.

Also during this period, the architectural profession in the Northwest matured

Government projects, such as Hanford Nuclear Reservation in Washington, resulted in some of the region's largest public works projects. Courtesy of the National Archives.

considerably. In 1914 both the University of Oregon and the University of Washington established architecture programs, which educated young designers in academic architectural traditions, primarily the Beaux Arts, emphasizing a reliance on historical styles and monumental settings, the standard curriculum in most schools of architecture at the time. The presence of these programs helped solidify a strong local base of architects in cities such as Portland, Eugene, Seattle, and Spokane. In the 1920s, however, elements of the architecture of European modernists, with its rejection of historical detail and ornament, began entering the curriculum. Walter Ross Baumes Willcox (1869–1947) at Oregon and Lionel Pries (1897–1968) at Washington each had a profound impact on a generation of students. A 1928 graduate of the University of Washington, Paul Thiry (1904–1993) is known in Seattle for bringing modern architecture to the Pacific Northwest. Although he had few commissions during the 1930s, the houses he built in Seattle during the decade showed a clear understanding of the European International Style in his use of spare, geometric forms, clean lines, and new building technologies. Other important contributors to the rise of modernism in the Northwest were John Yeon (1910–1994) and Italian-born Pietro Belluschi (1899–1994), both of whom practiced in Portland. Belluschi's Equitable Building (1944–1948) in downtown Portland was the first glass-box skyscraper erected in the United States. A second generation of architects after World War II, most notably Arthur Erickson (b. 1924) in Vancouver, British Columbia, continued in the modernist vein, though in a more expressive manner. Erickson's hallmark in the 1960s and 1970s was the use of post-and-beam construction for domestic and public buildings that allowed for a strong framework and large expanses of glass to open up the buildings to their surroundings, thereby connecting exterior and interior spaces.

Economic Boom Times

The postwar era brought a new economic boom to the region and a surge in population. Workers who had come to the Northwest to labor in factories or on bases remained after the war. The construction of new roads, interstate highways, and tract housing fueled suburbanization, which dramatically transformed the region. Many families left the cities to move to new suburbs of modest houses on the outer edges of cities, becoming dependent on cars for transportation. Freeways had a major impact, frequently dividing neighborhoods and destroying urban fabric. Highways erected along the Willamette River and Puget Sound cut off the downtown areas of Portland and Seattle from their waterfronts. In 1974 Portland tore down its Harbor Drive freeway to create a park and reunite the city with its river, but Seattle has yet to do the same with its elevated highway, the Alaskan Way Viaduct.

Suburbanization and postwar affluence contributed to a flourishing Northwest interpretation of modernism. Influenced by the modern, unadorned International Style and by the low-slung California ranch house, Northwest architects frequently interpreted the style in wood, continuing the tradition of timber construction in the region. In addition, they rediscovered nature and incorporated it into their designs. The use of wood limited the scale of buildings; thus, the style is seen mostly in houses but also in small-scale offices, libraries, and churches that fluidly merge interior and exterior space. Architectural elements such as overhanging eaves, broad expanses of glass windows, and decks take advantage of the Northwest landscape. Frequently these buildings turn away from the street, focusing instead on backyards or inner courtyards. Over the years their facades have become obscured by the vegetation surrounding them. John Yeon and Pietro Belluschi in Portland, Paul Hayden Kirk (b. 1914) and Wendell Lovett (b. 1922) in the Seattle-Bellevue area, Kenneth Brooks (1917–1996) and Royal McClure in Spokane, and Arthur Erickson in Vancouver are among the many architects who created excellent examples of this style; see Yeon's Watzek House (1936–1937) and Belluschi's Burkes House (1944–1948), both in Portland; Kirk's Magnolia Branch Library (1962–1964) in Seattle; McClure's Studio Apartments (1949) in Spokane; and Erickson's Smith House (1965) in West Vancouver.

During the 1960s, 1970s, and 1980s, world's fairs put the Northwest on the international map. The Century 21 Exposition in Seattle in 1962 served as a watershed for urban development in Seattle. Sited just north of downtown, with Paul Thiry as supervising architect and Lawrence Halprin (b. 1916) as landscape architect, the fair presented numerous futuristic structures with attenuated forms and space-age elements, embodied most effectively in the Space Needle designed by Victor Steinbrueck (1911–1985) and the firm of John Graham, Jr. (1908–1999). The site became the Seattle Center after the fair, spurring the creation of many museums and cultural institutions housed there. Twelve years later, Spokane hosted Expo '74. Like Century 21, this fair was built in the center of the city in an industrial area once dominated by railroad structures; today the site is Riverfront Park. The landscape architecture firm of Robert Perron and Associates designed a plan with formal elements closest to the city's business district that gradually gave way to a more natural terrain closer to the falls. The glass-and-steel Washington State Pavilion, designed by Walker, McGough, Foltz & Lyerla, still stands as a civic auditorium and convention center. The last fair in the Pacific Northwest was Expo '86 in Vancouver, British Columbia. Most of the pavilions were arranged along the north shore of False Creek and demolished at the fair's end. False Creek had become an industrial mess, but the fair provided an opportunity to clean up the site and develop it for housing and commercial purposes afterward. Canada Place, the Canadian government's pavilion, was designed as a permanent structure and rises along Burrard Inlet as a convention center. The structure's fabric roof supported by poles in the form of sails provides a striking counterpoint to the boxy glass towers of downtown Vancouver. All three fairs were economically successful, though in every case the majority of visitors came from the Northwest, making the fairs more regional than global in their impact. Located in or near the city center, the expositions helped to redefine urban space, fuel cultural development, and reorient the region to the rest of the world.

Alaska's Architectural Development

For much of its history, Alaska's architectural development has lagged behind that of the Lower Forty-eight. Its isolation and lack of a variety of construction materials have proven challenging. As with the rest of the Pacific Northwest, wood was employed frequently in log buildings or wood-frame houses, but brick had to be imported, since Alaska has no good sources of clay. Concrete became a popular building material beginning in the 1920s and has been used widely in public and commercial structures, including the Alaska Railroad Depot (1942) in Anchorage, an interesting combination of Art Moderne and Beaux Arts Classical styles, and the Art Deco U.S. Post Office and Court House (1932–1933) in Fairbanks, designed by George Ray of Washington, D.C. Alaska has remained dependent on the extraction of natural resources; oil has been its most significant resource since the 1960s when the Atlantic Richfield Oil Company discovered a giant oil field at Prudhoe Bay. This boom has brought great wealth to the state, along with a growing number of residents. Still, Alaska's relatively small population cannot yet support an architectural school; all architects are educated elsewhere, and large commissions tend to go to architects from outside the state, for example, the Alaska Center for the Performing Arts (1985) in Anchorage, designed by Hardy Holzman Pfeiffer Associates with Livingston Slone of Anchorage. This postmodern building was controversial for its design, cost, and lack of accessibility, but its glass, brick, concrete, and stucco exterior has created a cultural focal point for the city. Commissions such as this one have led to more sophisticated buildings being erected in Alaska but have also made much architecture in the state appear less distinctive from other parts of the region and country.

Recent Developments in Northwest Architecture

The past twenty years have seen new developments in the region—the rise of the high-technology and tourism industries. This shift has moved a portion of the economy away from natural resources and manufacturing, helping to further diversify the region as employers have sought highly educated workers. Alaska, in particular, has been dramatically affected by the rise of the cruise industry, which brings hundreds of ships to coastal towns during the summer, temporarily flooding them with visitors. In addition, the population of the Northwest grew dramatically through immigration from the rest of the nation and the world, particularly Asia and South America, increasing urban density but also encouraging suburban sprawl. Portland, which implemented an urban growth boundary in the 1970s, and Vancouver, British Columbia, have dealt with their growth better than most other cities in the region, by encouraging high-density urban development and supporting it with rapid-transit systems. Portland, in particular, has been honored by planners and architects worldwide for serving as a model of what cities should strive to be. Seattle, on the other hand, has not been as successful in controlling sprawl or in building a mass transit system that adequately serves its population. The difference can be seen among these three cities, where Portland and Vancouver have far more lively downtown areas at all hours of the day than does Seattle. As in the past, the western part of the region, near the coast, has experienced most of the growth, whereas the eastern part of the region has had a less robust economy and has had to contend with declining populations in its cities. Rural areas, particularly east of the mountains, are still dependent on logging, mining, agriculture, and ranching, making them more vulnerable to economic cycles. Bend, Oregon, and Sequim, Washington, which have become centers for retirees and outdoor enthusiasts, are exceptions but perhaps the wave of the future.

With an influx of new inhabitants and new ideas, the Pacific Northwest has become much more cosmopolitan. Greater wealth from the high-tech and biotech boom has led to more construction and more commissions of well-known architects. Clusters of skyscrapers now dominate the skylines of the major cities in the region, though most are glass boxes with little character or aesthetic connection to the region. Northwest-based architects such as Wendell Lovett and George Suyama, and firms such as BOORA, NBBJ, and LMN Architects, have garnered major commissions including the homes of high-tech millionaires and billionaires and large-scale projects, such as the Simonyi Villa (Wendell Lovett; begun 1987), Medina, Washington, the new federal courthouse in Seattle (NBBJ; 2004), and Benaroya Hall for the Seattle Symphony (LMN; 1998). Other architectural commissions have gone to internationally known architects as patrons seek to put the region on the global map. The first such commission was the Portland Building (1980–1982), in Portland, designed by Michael Graves (b. 1934). It is one of the best-known representations of the postmodern style, with its allusions to classical style and decorated facades, even though it has been plagued by structural problems. Cultural institutions have sought wider notoriety by hiring famous architects to design unique structures. Examples include the Experience Music Project (2000) by Frank Gehry (b. 1929), a colorful if amorphous blob of reflective panels over a curving steel frame; the Seattle Public Library (2004) by Rem Koolhaas (b. 1944), a high-tech structure in which the interlocking web of the steel skeleton is visible through a glass skin; and the Vancouver Public Library (1995) by Moshe Safdie (b. 1938), a clever take on the Colosseum in Rome but gradually unraveling to create a public space at the entrance of the library itself. These structures have raised the bar for design in the region.

As the economy shifts away from a dependency on the exploitation of natural resources and on the federal government, architects in the Pacific Northwest will need to become increasingly innovative in meeting the needs of its inhabitants.

Continued economic development based on white-collar jobs and growing diversity will fuel the construction, perhaps of architecture that will reflect more global influences over time, while still retaining a connection to the region's natural landscape. As the Northwest becomes more urbanized, planners and architects will also have to become more adept at designing transportation systems and high-density structures that can accommodate multiple uses in ways that will make metropolitan areas inviting places to live and work.

ARCHITECTURE OF NORTHERN CALIFORNIA

Despite the years of pre-European contact inhabitants and their dwellings, no architectural remains from that time exist in Northern California, perhaps because of a reliance on adobe—both the structure of adobe dwellings so prominent in Alta California and the mud/water mix of adobe itself. Even the missions along El Camino Real, the 21 mission chain begun by Franciscan missionaries in 1769, relied on adobe with tile roofs, which would ostensibly protect the walls from rain. With the transfer of California from Spain to Mexico, however, the system was secularized and many of the missions fell into disrepair and deterioration.

Even as late as the Gold Rush, as prospectors flooded the banks of the Sacramento and San Joaquin rivers, structures, entire cities even, were temporary. Still, even with the lack of any wood frame structures, the Gold Rush saw an actual style of architecture evolving: one architect, Thomas Larken of the then trading port, Monterey, introduced strong redwood timber framing of houses but stayed with the structural practice of adobe walls, attaching a two-story veranda to protect and stabilize the walls.

It was not until the emigration of Midwestern families, however, following the wave of prospectors, who came out to the San Francisco and Sacramento regions, that the need for more stable housing drove architects to begin using wood. Eastern architects, realizing the need for immediate housing, traveled west for the opportunity, and in San Francisco, particularly, they designed many sophisticated buildings and began a professional journal—*The California Architect and Building News*. At the same time, a number of self-trained designers and builders were also busy constructing homes and buildings in response to the great demand for them. Generally, these builders and designers relied on popular design handbooks and borrowed liberally from revival styles such as Classical, Gothic, and Italianate. Toward the end of the nineteenth century, Victorian architecture, particularly Queen Anne ornamentation, was popular on houses, as the abundance of redwood finally became clear to builders. With no apparent irony, architects also "introduced" a revival of Spanish-Mexican mission architecture, which had become nationally popular after the World's Columbian Exposition in Chicago.

It was not until the early twentieth century that professional architects began to truly develop a Northern Californian style. First and most famous was Bernard Maybeck, who arrived in San Francisco in the 1890s. He drew on a variety of styles and regional inspirations, and his signature was the use of shingles and stained wood. He was the center of the Craftsman movement in the Bay Area, and served as mentor to Julia Morgan, a distinct architect herself and one of the country's first prominent female architects. Allowed, after much effort, to study at Ecole des Beaux-Arts, Morgan returned to the West Coast in 1904, and throughout her

46-year career, designed nearly 800 buildings, clubs, churches and schools, including the Hearst Castle, a project that lasted for decades.

In general, the open feel of the raw West characterizes Northern California architecture: an emphasis on the outdoors, and particularly a design that used wood for both interior and exterior tended to bring the outdoors, in. Many of Frank Lloyd Wright's ideas influenced a developing regional vernacular that relied on the "ranch house," long, single-story houses with rambling floor plans, large windows, and attached garages that insisted on a casual, informal feel and design.

ARCHITECTURE OF SOUTHERN CALIFORNIA

Sunny Southern California, with its imagery created by boosters, filmmakers, beachgoers, flamboyant politicians, aerospace technocrats, and a diverse population, has a rich and varied architecture through which four themes thread: (1) how structures relate to nature, (2) how imported styles are reinterpreted in California and reexported, (3) innovative work, and (4) the temporal question.

Accommodating Nature

Southern California's much-vaunted climate—Mediterranean on the coast, warmer and drier inland—has encouraged architectural accommodation from the earliest times. By 500 C.E. the Native American peoples in the region's coastal and foothill zones had evolved a settled culture with a dietary staple of acorn mush and a house type known as the *jacal* ("hah-kahl") formed of pliant poles anchored in the ground in a circle and tied at the top to form a dome-like shape. Cross poles tied to it formed a frame that was covered with brush thatch or woven brush mats, leaving a down-wind opening for the entrance. Basically upside-down baskets, jacales were flexible in wind, sufficient protection in the mild weather, and easily replaceable as soot or vermin necessitated. They were temporary dwellings, and they disappeared under the onslaught of European culture.

When the Spanish, disappointed in

Corridor, Santa Barbara Mission, 1820. Courtesy of Merry Ovnick.

17

The California Cure

Consumptives, and persons debilitated by age, over-work, or disease, will find in . . . Southern California a climate remarkably mild and healing. . . . The seeker after health has open to him a . . . choice of pleasant health-resorts . . . and thoroughly comfortable hotels and inns, where even the most delicate invalids may rest with enjoyment. . . . [S]unny rooms, open fires, broad piazzas [verandas] sheltered from the wind by glass enclosures—all these now supplement the natural advantages.[3]

1542 to find no sign of gold or advanced native civilizations, finally decided to settle Alta California as a defensive outpost and mission enterprise in 1769, they were not put off by Southern California's apparent lack of building material. The gnarly oaks that produced abundant acorns for the Indians did not yield good timber. No matter. Spain's similar climate, its centuries of occupation by the Moors, and the colonial experience in Mexico had familiarized Spaniards with packed earth and adobe construction. Clay soil, mixed with water and binders such as straw, could be shaped into building blocks in frame molds, sun-dried, laid up, and mud-mortared into mission and *presidio* (fort) walls by conscripted Indian laborers. Stone, fast-growing cane, fired clay tiles, and lime plaster rounded out the building materials—all locally accessible. The Spanish brought other architectural traditions appropriate for the climate: Covered corridors kept east- and west-facing walls in shade; long experience with water scarcity had led to expertise in aqueducts, dams, hydraulic fountains, and systems for recycling water.

After Mexico's independence from Spain in 1821, liberalized landownership and foreign trade laws facilitated the rise of a culture of ease and imported comforts among the largest landholders, the rancheros who could produce the cattle hides and tallow sought by foreign trading companies. They built adobe houses, often U-shaped around a courtyard or patio, with covered corridors on ground and upper floors protecting heat-banking adobe walls from the elements and extending social space and domestic tasks to the out-of-doors.

Morey House (Victorian). Courtesy of Merry Ovnick.

Long after the United States acquired Alta California in 1848 and the cattle-ranching economy foundered from droughts, floods, debts, labor shortage, and Texas beef, eastern and midwestern Americans flocked to Southern California in response to a barrage of advertising touting near-miraculous cures for various ailments in the balmy air and sunshine of Southern California's winters.

Hotels, sanitariums, and private residences in the 1870s and 1880s featured commodious verandas for basking in this atmosphere. The terraces and sleeping porches of the 1910s, patios of the 1920s, glass walls of the moderns, and the postwar orientation to the backyard continued the regional emphasis on indoor-outdoor living.

Nature is not always benevolent. Earthquakes are one regional hazard. In 1812, an earthquake along the San Andreas Fault, which runs from the Gulf of California to Bodega Bay, north of San Francisco, severely damaged the missions made of unreinforced masonry: adobe blocks, stone, and bricks. A soaring vaulted basilica at San Juan Capistrano was left in ruins. The original bell tower at San Gabriel collapsed, the raw wound still visible today. Nature was stingy when it came to water resources, too.

Contesting Nature

The mission padres had constructed reservoirs, aqueducts, hydraulic fountains, and cisterns, putting recycled water to industrial and crop use. Twentieth-century engineers redesigned Nature on an even grander scale. At the turn of the century, landlocked Los Angeles won federal funding for a man-made port at San Pedro. The city population topped 100,000 in 1900 and more than tripled that number by the time the port was completed in 1913. Every businessman's anticipated profits and every homeowner's equity value were keyed to growth. In spite of the semi-arid climate, lush lawns, exotic plants, and year-round blooms had become synonymous with the Good Life. To ensure both growth and gardens, the city of Los Angeles tapped a water source 233 miles to the east, completing an aqueduct in 1913. Subsequent Southern California importations from the Colorado River to the east (1941) and the Feather River in the north (1973) made possible the suburban sprawl for which the region is so well known.

A beacon celebrating technology's triumph over Nature, the Los Angeles Department of Water and Power (Albert C. Martin and Associates, 1963–1964) flaunted its surfeits of imported water and hydroelectric energy with a glass-cored stack of cantilevered sunshades. With its interior lights on all night, the building becomes a column of light surrounded by fountains and a reflecting pool. The 1970s energy crisis mandated turning off the lights and fountains until solar panels could be installed to continue the effect. Continuing development in the region has led to recent water struggles in Santa Barbara, Ventura County, and San Diego. It is hard to change a culture nourished on a long-advertised subtropical image at odds with a land of little rainfall. And yet a 1978 plan to develop the former site of Hughes Aircraft and an adjoining marsh not far from Los Angeles International Airport aroused environmentalists who mounted a twenty-year battle to save the wetlands. In 2003, in a hard-fought compromise, Playa Vista, a community of dense residential and commercial development for 13,000 people interspersed with parks and a 200-acre ecological preserve, may be the blueprint for future development throughout the region, in keeping with the Southern California Association of Government's conviction that future traffic, air quality, and quality of life in Southern California will require densification interspersed with open space.

The same sequence of accommodation (such as Native American structures and Spanish building materials), innovation (water engineering), and repair or retrenchment parallels the story of architectural style development. Southern California's importance, architecturally, traces, on the one hand, to the process of importing, adapting, then reexporting borrowed traditions and, on the other, to liberated experimental work that has won attention elsewhere for new ideas, not always adaptable to other regions.

Import → Adapt → Export

Verdant landscaping dependent on borrowed and diminishing water supplies provides an appropriate setting for architectural representations of fantasized pasts. In the 1870s, freelance writers and railroad hirelings wrote hyperbole-laden articles about the romantic possibilities of floral bowers, vine-covered verandas, and varied scenery stretching from deserts to mountains to ocean shoreline. Helen Hunt Jackson followed a successful 1883 travelogue—*Bits of Travel at Home*—along this vein with her bestseller novel *Ramona* (1884), which idealized the Spanish past as a time of sincerity, simplicity, faith, and a kind of gentility now lost forever. Tourists poured off the trains intent on visiting the crumbling ruins of the missions and the sites and scenery described in the novel. Popular magazines, novels, and films would continue to burnish this myth of "Old California" into the 1950s.

Flights of Fantasy

Redlands, San Diego, Los Angeles and its neighboring communities, and Santa Barbara all experienced real estate frenzies in the mid-1880s, triggered by a railroad fare war. Vacant lots were auctioned to beguiled tourists, then resold to others as values skyrocketed. By mid-1888, after an unusually bad winter and heavy flooding had dampened tourist appeal, property values adjusted downward, speculators went bankrupt, and new home construction declined. But what had been built displayed particularly unrestrained imagery that set the tone for the region. Exotic borrowed traditions, onion domes, "Moorish" motifs, and Chinese moon gates flourished on wood frame houses from mansion to middle-class scale. Wood was, just then, reasonable and available because the redwood forests of Northern California and the Northwest were being exploited, the lumber shipped down the coast and brought into inland towns by the railroads. At this same time, industrial technology began turning out hot-pressed "carving" and lathe-turned spindlework at affordable prices. But there is a temporary note about wood frame houses, appropriate to a generation that bought property on a tourist whim in a place they had been drawn to because it was different from home. The 1880s boom established a pattern of borrowing attention-getting imagery foreign to settlers' source locations, even in the case of more permanent commercial buildings. The Bradbury Building (George H. Wyman, 1893), an investment office structure in Los Angeles, drew its inspiration from science fiction.

Purloined Pasts

While the old Spanish missions had, with varying degrees of refinement or simplification, followed the course set in Mexico of adaptations of Baroque curved and recurved facades, arcades, and shell niches (except the Santa Barbara mission church, completed in 1820, an adaptation of Vitruvian Classicism), the predominantly Protestant American newcomers to California in the 1890s to the 1910s had no direct claim to the ecclesiastical and historical traditions these building forms represented. The Mission Revival style that became popular in those decades reflected the romanticized myth of the Spanish Past popularized by writers, artists, and publicists. The Riverside Mission Inn (Arthur B. Benton, 1902–1914), along

Smiley Library (Mission Revival). Courtesy of Merry Ovnick.

with countless small flats, commercial buildings, schools, and libraries, sported the Mission *espadaña* facade. Both the Santa Fe and the Southern Pacific Railroads adopted the style for terminals across the Southwest in the early decades of the twentieth century. But when it came to the design for the California-Panama Exposition in 1915, San Diego leaders rejected the Mission Revival mode in favor of more grandiose Spanish references. Bertram Grosvenor Goodhue, of the renowned eastern firm of Cram, Ferguson and Goodhue, was chosen as the lead architect because of the favorable publicity his name and his dramatic conceptualization would bring to the exposition. He favored the elaborately ornamental Churrigueresque facades, Mudejar ceilings, and sophisticated details borrowed from Spanish history and the high culture of colonial Mexico. The aim was to build "a city-in-miniature wherein everything that met the eye and ear of the visitor were meant to recall to mind the glamour and mystery and poetry of the old Spanish Days." Borrowed Spanish grandeur, with no direct link to California history, was fine for a fair, for, as the architects put it, "it must be remembered that Exposition Architecture differs from that of our everyday world in being essentially of the fabric of a dream. . . . It should provide, after the fashion that stage scenery provides—illusion rather than reality."[4] For these same reasons, exercises in Spanish Baroque embellished movie palaces (among them the Million Dollar Theater, Los Angeles, Albert C. Martin, 1918; and the Fox Arlington in Santa Barbara, Edwards, Plunkett and Howell, 1929–1931), city halls (Pasadena, John Bakewell, Jr.), the rotunda and council chamber of Los Angeles City Hall (Austin Whittlesey, 1926–1928), churches (St. Vincent de Paul, Los Angeles, Albert C. Martin, 1925), and well-endowed schools (Gates Laboratory, California Institute of Technology, Pasadena, Bertram G. Goodhue and Elmer Grey, 1917).

Italian traditions inspired Abbot Kinney's 1905 Venice-of-America project, a housing development on Venetian canals with a commercial center modeled after St. Mark's Square (Norman F. Marsh and C. H. Russell). In the 1920s, the Uni-

Goodhue, Balboa Park. Courtesy of Merry Ovnick.

versity of California Los Angeles' new campus at Westwood appeared in more serious Italian garb, this time Tuscan Romanesque, for Royce Hall (Allison and Allison, 1928–1929), Powell Library and the campus plan (George W. Kelham, 1927–1929). Cross-town rival the University of Southern California (Bovard Auditorium, John and Donald Parkinson, 1920–1921) and the nearby Los Angeles County Museum (Hudson and Munsell, 1913) had introduced the same look and material (brick and terra cotta), which they originally termed "Spanish Renaissance."

Designing Domesticity

Domestic architecture proved less academic and more creative. First, the American Arts and Crafts Movement, or Craftsman Movement, roughly 1901 to 1917, was imported, adapted to the region, then exported nationwide.

Three rustic retreats—a mountain cabin for attorney Henry O'Melveny (Sumner P. Hunt, 1897), a Sierra Madre home for railroad counsel Edgar Camp (Charles and Henry Greene, 1904), and a Pasadena residence for ranchero family descendant Arturo Bandini (also by Greene and Greene, 1908)—were published in *The Craftsman*, a monthly magazine published from 1901 to 1916 by eastern furniture manufacturer Gustav Stickley. The magazine was dedicated to the moral reform of the urban and suburban middle class by aesthetic means (and to the promotion of Stickley's furniture). *The Craftsman* called for "plain living and high thinking," a rejection of the Victorian aesthetic of excess and display. Although interior illustrations in *The Craftsman*'s pages depicted inviting retreats of quaint but nonspecific historicism, cozy inglenooks, and an efficient use of space, the exterior renderings were often at odds with the magazine's call for simplicity.

It was not until 1905 that *The Craftsman* presented an exterior that a modern taxonomist would classify as the bungalow or the "Craftsman style." Then, in the 1907 recession, *The Craftsman* terminated its art department. For sixteen issues, the familiar cozy renderings were missing. Instead, photo-illustrated articles by West Coast builders and architects showcased small bungalows and grand winter homes in Southern California, realizations of the Craftsman aesthetic adapted to

Craftsman photo, typical California bungalow. Courtesy of Merry Ovnick.

the benign climate. In October 1908 *The Craftsman* resumed its house articles, artists' renderings, and building plans. The magazine was rededicated "mainly to designs for dwellings of small and moderate cost" and promised to continue articles by outside architects, "especially the bungalows of the West and the Pacific Coast, which come so closely to our own theory of the building art that is most expressive of our national life."[5]

Apparently responding to reader feedback, the national magazine embraced the blend of features that California builders had presented in its pages. The woodsy bungalow we think of as synonymous with the Craftsman aesthetic was thus actually born in California, nurtured by local builders and their clients who had been inspired by the interior renderings in the early issues of *The Craftsman*, adapted to meet Southern California conditions. It featured wood beams and wood wainscoting (featured prominently in the early *Craftsman* illustrations and adopted wholesale in Southern California); expanded fenestration (important to a population drawn to Southern California by climate claims); horizontality (not consistently featured in Craftsman houses before 1909), which California architects exaggerated by widening the overhanging eaves as protection from the sun and by lowering the pitch of the roof, since they had little concern about rain runoff or snow pack; outdoor living spaces (which *The Craftsman* had presented in earlier vacation houses but which Californians could utilize year-round); Greene and Greene's trademark mix of clinker brick and cobblestone chimneys and foundations; and the informal lifestyle (unevenly represented up to this time in *The Craftsman*'s pages). In the 1910s the California bungalow sprang up across the nation, whether suitable to the climate or not.

Silent Film Stages

In the 1920s, historically derivative styles originating in motion picture set design principles were also exported and adopted nationwide. Extensive tracts of every price range proliferated, particularly in Los Angeles during its second great boom, this one peaking in 1923. They exhibited three new features not common in the pre–World War I period: a marked attention to texture and value; crowded style references in miniaturized scale; and fragmentation into a multiplicity of volumes. These features came from motion pictures.

Silent filmmakers, taking advantage of the sunny climate and varied topography, built permanent studios in Hollywood, Edendale, Santa Monica, and Culver City in the 1910s. World War I crippled European film production and concentrated the world's movie production in the Los Angeles area. As audiences demanded increasingly complex story lines, moviemakers, challenged by the limitations of black and white and uncertain if their viewers could read the subtitles, experimented with various means of making sure their audiences could vicariously "get into" the story. Art directors learned to add otherwise-unnecessary objects and exaggerated texture to compensate for the flattening effects of early lighting technology. If this was a film about medieval times, the castle behind the characters had to have identifiers—a moat and drawbridge, maybe crenellations and a turret, all crowded within the frame of the picture behind the character action. To this end, motion picture sets were made in four-fifths scale or less, with multiple volumes, each of them a ministage for some action in the story. The deep relief of the fragmented surfaces, often deeper than reality, helped to overcome the problems of depth and texture posed by silent movies' early film quality, poor lighting, and unfamiliar black-and-white action. Viewers became accustomed to packed references, exaggerated texture and relief, and multiple volumes, and accepted these features as standards of beauty. By 1920, filmmakers had built up a repertoire of stylistic motifs that indicated, however inaccurate historically, certain storied times and places. They had established a set of features that meant Ancient Babylon, Exotic Baghdad, Medieval Castles, Quaint European Villages, Colonial America, the Wild West. The public was educated in architectural references by silent film. And as soon as the twin dampers of war and the 1919 influenza epidemic were past, the streets of Los Angeles blossomed with reflections of that education.

Riche Residence. Courtesy of Merry Ovnick.

Beginning in mid-1919 and peaking in 1923, Los Angeles experienced a phenomenal population and real estate boom period. The population doubled between 1920 and 1925. City building permits shot up from 6,000 in 1918 to 62,000 in 1923, 76 percent of them for single-family residences. Real estate developers carved out large tracts from former bean fields for auto owners not dependent on trolley access. They hired film stars to grace gala openings. The houses that sprang up in response could have come straight from the silver screen.

The favorite of the 1920s decade was the Spanish Colonial or Mediterranean. Enclosed patios, serenade balconies, wrought iron, and polychrome tile accents abounded throughout Southern California and, for similar reasons of fictionalized Spanish roots, climate, and an automobile-driven boom, in Florida.

Santa Barbara remade itself in this image. Leading citizens of this resort town had seen to the preservation of the mission and several adobes dating back to Spanish times. An active Community Arts Association asserted itself in aesthetic issues, enthusiastically supporting the private development of shopping arcades (El Paseo, James Osborne Craig, 1921–1922) and villas for wealthy Santa Barbara and Montecito clients by architects George Washington Smith, Reginald Johnson, Carleton M. Winslow, Sr., Myron Hunt, and others in the composite Spanish Colonial and Italian references it labeled "California Style." After a destructive earthquake in 1925, Santa Barbara created an architectural review board. Within nine months, it processed over 2,000 designs, and the town emerged from the disaster a Spanish Colonial theme dream. The results were so attractive, so evocative of the romantic myth of "Old California," that developers planning upscale communities at Palos Verdes and Rancho Santa Fe instituted style controls to assure total conformity to the same theme there.

Successful architects of the 1920s such as Sylvanus Marston, Roland P. Coate, Gordon B. Kaufmann, Wallace Neff, Pierpont Davis, Paul R. Williams, and Morgan, Walls, & Clements were versatile in a wide range of other period reference styles, as well. In all of these cases, an abundance of motifs packed in close proximity, recessed and projected forms accentuated by light and shadow, and attention to texture, including a heavily troweled plaster surface then referred to as "jazzed stucco," hark back to the aesthetic standards shaped by silent movies. As movies were seen nationwide, these characteristics also show up nationwide, but Southern California's building boom, its model style–consistent developments, and the exchange of designers and patrons between real and reel life made the phenomenon a major characteristic of regional identity.

Fantasyland

In this place where make-believe is taken seriously, Disneyland represents the ultimate merger of fantasy, borrowed pasts, and the built environment. The Anaheim theme park opened in 1955. Walt Disney and a team of animators and movie art directors set out to create theme-consistent vistas through a carefully planned layout, structure heights, and landscaping. Disneyland's versions of a nineteenth-century Main Street, a fairytale castle, a frontier fort, a pirate's lair, a haunted mansion have served, for better or worse, as the visual reference guide for these types of building for the last three generations, not just in Southern California, but around the globe. Tomorrowland's promise of a space-era future was likewise appropriate to Southern California because the region really was the site of innovative design and space-age technology. Disney, himself a media pioneer, employed modernist Kem Weber to build his studio in Burbank in the 1930s.

Braly Block. Courtesy of Merry Ovnick.

Invention → Attention → Emulation

Steel Frame and Terra-Cotta

After the collapse of the 1886–1888 boom with its impulsive speculators, seasoned investors bought up unfinished developments and downtown lots, prepared to pour capital into long-term investments. Sugar scion John D. Spreckels (1853–1926) headed to San Diego and rail baron Henry E. Huntington (1850–1927) to Los Angeles to consolidate and extend streetcar systems throughout their regions in profitable association with suburban real estate developers. Homer Laughlin, a wealthy pottery manufacturer from Ohio, commissioned commercial buildings and, in 1900, a pottery works in Los Angeles that would supply much of the terra-cotta ornamentation to the region's most important buildings over the next two decades. Steel frame construction, the particular pride of Chicago, was introduced to Southern California in 1898 in the six-story Homer Laughlin building (originally leased to a department store, now Grand Central Market; John Parkinson). It was overshadowed by the fourteen-story Braly Block, with its ornate terra-cotta cornice, in 1902 (John Parkinson), as Los Angeles' downtown, now a streetcar hub, grew skyward.

Reinforced Concrete

Reinforced concrete was still an experimental building method in the early 1900s. Thomas Fellows, an English-trained architectural engineer who had studied under William Morris (1834–1896), later at the Franklin Institute in Philadelphia, with experience in steel construction in Pittsburgh, came to Los Angeles around 1900, where he left a trail of pioneering work in reinforced concrete. Architect Charles Whittlesey, renowned for his grand Mission-style lodges in the Southwest for the Santa Fe Railroad, essayed a reinforced concrete Annex to the Homer Laughlin Building while Fellows was on his staff in 1905. Earlier the same year, prominent contractor Carl Leonardt, who had not worked in the new medium before, built a concrete warehouse bearing his name, perhaps with Fellows' help. In 1906, Whittlesey, with Fellows on his payroll, designed the Philharmonic Auditorium Building on West Fifth and completed the Lissner office building on Spring Street, all of them advertised as fireproof structures. After the 1906 San Francisco earthquake and fire, reinforced concrete was an attractive option for residences. The Lanterman house in La Cañada, a grand-scale Craftsman-style bungalow now open for public tours, was built of concrete in 1915 (Arthur Haley).

Experiments in Expression

In San Diego, Irving Gill brought a new look to regional architecture. Arriving in 1893, the young architect fresh from the Chicago office of Adler and Sullivan, where he had worked along with Frank Lloyd Wright (1867–1959), simplified the Mission Revival, the shingled Craftsman, and the Prairie styles to a more Spartan geometry. As early as 1905, he had reduced Baroque Mission arches to pierced openings in flat walls—not an attempt to replicate the past, merely a nod to the region's favorite myth. By 1912, Gill had adopted the newly patented tilt-slab construction method by which reinforced concrete was poured in place in molds incorporating window and door frames, then tilted up and fitted to adjoining walls. Inside, he poured concrete floors and eliminated moldings. Outside, he experimented with tinting his white walls to play off the colors of foundation plants and vines. Gill's reductionism won him clients, not only in the San Diego area, but also in Pasadena, Los Angeles, Long Beach, Santa Monica, and the industrial community of Torrance.

Wright is due a nod for his brooding, pattern-molded concrete block work in Los Angeles in the 1920s. His son Lloyd Wright carried on his father's ideas with more theatrical verve, perhaps because he had previously worked in the film industry and many of his clients and associates were movie people.

Gill's La Jolla Women's Club. Courtesy of Merry Ovnick.

A New Look

If we omit everything useless from the structural point of view we will come to see the great beauty of straight lines, to see the charm that lies in perspective, the force in light and shade, the power in balanced masses, the fascination of color that plays upon a smooth wall left free to report the passing of a cloud or nearness of a flower.[6]

The International School

It was two young Viennese modernists, R. M. Schindler and Richard Neutra, who made Southern California a showcase of the International School. Rudolf Schindler, who had been a student of Otto Wagner and a disciple of Adolf Loos, European progenitors of modernism, was inspired by Wright's 1910 Wasmuth Portfolio to believe that in the United States clients would be more open to creative architecture than in tradition-bound Europe. In Los Angeles, he did find exceptional individuals looking for truly unique houses, often for steep hillside sites. One of Schindler's most important works was the Lovell Beach House in Newport Beach (1925–1926) for holistic health columnist Phillip Lovell. Raised on pilotis (columns or piles used to raise the base of a building above ground level), like the villas of his contemporary, Le Corbusier, the house is composed of projected concrete solids and recessed glass "voids," evoking a precision machine composed of interlocking parts, integrated by scale, and unified by repeated forms and textural contrasts. In 1923, Schindler perfected the concrete "slab-cast wall," in which the wall was laid up vertically one band per day as the forms were repositioned. Much of Schindler's work verged on the expressionistic, and he was soon eclipsed by his compatriot Richard Neutra. A 1929 Los Angeles house for Schindler's former client Lovell made Neutra's fame. The prefabricated steel frame was assembled in forty work hours, with factory-made steel casement windows slipped into their frames and the concrete panels shot in place. The architect and client publicized this vision of replicable housing forms and construction methods that could be adapted to low-cost housing and yield tranquil and efficient dwelling space for the future. For his minimalist interiors, transparent walls erasing the barrier between house and nature, and machine aesthetic, Neutra was recognized as one of the masters of International Modernism, along with Mies van der Rohe, Le Corbusier, and Walter Gropius. His work and that of Schindler and their immediate followers and contemporaries, J. R. Davidson, Harwell Hamilton Harris, Gregory Ain, and Raphael Soriano, found avant-garde clients among science and art professors, progressive educators, and creative figures in the entertainment business. They also found a public forum in *California Arts & Architecture*, edited by John Entenza.

During World War II, when wartime controls restricted building, architects pondered the looming challenge of housing a generation of returning soldiers. Entenza's magazine sponsored a 1943 contest for designs that would meet limited budgets and size constraints, yet satisfy the dreams of this generation. The results were all crisply modern, modular houses of great efficiency, designed to integrate with their garden surroundings. In 1945, *Arts & Architecture* offered a sequel in which clients would actually commission winning designs to be showcased in the magazine. Case Study houses by Charles and Rae Eames, Pierre Koenig, and other modernists won national coverage.

The Futuristic

In addition to these high modern architects, Southern California was the scene of a considerable number of more prosaic Streamline Moderne works in the 1930s, partly because of the continued health of the region's oil and film industries and partly because military orders to the region's airplane and shipping industries, beginning in 1938, lifted the pall of the Depression earlier than in much of the nation. Commercial buildings by major firms such as John C. Austin, Morgan, Walls & Clements, and John and Donald Parkinson and houses and apartments by designers Milton J. Black and William Kesling contributed to a futuristic image of the region. Contributing an absurdist edge to this image, the automobile culture had stimulated corny programmatic structures in the 1920s: a piano store shaped like a piano, ice cream shops like an ice cream cone, and so on. By the postwar period the taste for such eye-catchers had evolved to "googie" (so named for a coffee shop by John Lautner) drive-in eateries, car washes, and auto showrooms with rakishly tilted slab roofs, acute angles, and glass walls, taking modernism to space fiction theatricality for the sake of grabbing the attention of passing motorists.

Postwar Tracts

In spite of their borrowed references to the imagery of television westerners of the postwar period—barn siding, shutters, dove cotes, and hayloft openings above the garage—the extensive tracts of ranch-style houses that filled interior valleys from Santa Barbara to the Mexican border between the late 1940s and the late 1960s also represented the perfection of mass-production efficiencies in construction and marketing. Their orientation to the backyard reflected both the outdoor life and the desire for privacy in cookie-cutter suburbs.

Ephemeral or Permanent?

Native jacales, wood frame Victorians, Schindler's modernist essays, and postwar tract houses were built for the moment. Mission Revival, Tudor, Spanish Colonial, and ranch themes spoke of escapism rather than of commitment. Bungalows and modern experimentation were motivated as much by commercial cost-cutting or attention-getting as by human accommodation, efficiency, or permanence. These contradictions came together in the 1970s when residents began to think about roots and what was happening to landmark buildings in the face of downtown redevelopment and rampant suburban sprawl. San Diego created an Old Town historic district. Angelenos fought a plan to replace an eclectic but beloved 1926 Central Library (Bertram G. Goodhue and Carleton M. Winslow) and succeeded in winning a retrofit and expansion that preserved open space as well (Hardy, Holzman, and Pfeiffer, 1993). Deteriorating Victorians were moved to Heritage Park in San Diego, Heritage Square in Los Angeles, or gentrified and restored by a new generation of owners banded together in neighborhood associations and enticed by tax breaks. Historical societies and preservation organizations proliferated, giving sell-out tours and lobbying to preserve old buildings newly recognized as priceless symbols of continuity with the past and keys to local identity. Los Angeles, which had become a major metropolis in the streetcar era with a downtown stymied by inadequate parking, narrow streets, and un-air-conditioned office buildings, entered a renaissance of loft conversion in the late 1990s, with entrepreneurs retrofitting historic high-rise office buildings for loft living. The discovery that the escapist and experimental buildings built for their fleeting moments had, over time, formed an accretion of images that, all together, gave the region a unique and even lovable identity was an important awakening. Besides fostering preservation and restoration, the new interest in the regional past attracted postmodernist work that acknowledged and apotheosized history. Michael Graves' San Juan Capistrano Library (1983) evokes the Mission heritage but attends to functionality, with natural lighting in the transept reading room, a children's play area in the tower, and a cloister ambulatory through the stacks.

The region's ambivalence about temporality is symbolized by two recent monuments: the Catholic Cathedral of Our Lady of the Angels (José Rafael Moneo, completed in 2002) and Disney Concert Hall (Frank Gehry, completed in 2003). The cathedral, sited on the edge of a freeway gulf for maximum motorist visibility, began with a brouhaha over the attempted demolition of the historic St. Vibiana Cathedral (Ezra F. Kysor and W. J. Mathews, 1871–1876), skirting cultural heritage protections. It was the particular goal of the client, Cardinal Roger Mahoney, that the new cathedral be built to last 300 to 500 years. To that end, 149 base isolators and 47 slider base isolators ward against earthquake damage. To prevent heat cracks from developing in the reinforced concrete walls from the tremendous pressure of scale and thickness (up to four feet, in places), the project imported 40,000 cubic yards of a Danish concrete that could keep cool under those conditions. Thousands of sheer alabaster panels create a translucent ceiling and upper walls. And then, because alabaster will turn opaque if it gets too hot, an outer layer of glass protects the alabaster, with circulating air in between. While the building has no right angles, the bell tower (with bells from the California missions), the orientation of the altar, and the placement of the crypts observe long Catholic traditions. The cathedral's design for permanence takes on a fortress likeness, with impassive walls to the surrounding sidewalks and the freeway. Only when one makes the effort to enter its interior plaza does it come to life.

Cathedral. Courtesy of Merry Ovnick.

The Disney Concert Hall shouts its

Disney Hall. Courtesy of Merry Ovnick.

liveliness and defies all traditions. Challenged steelworkers assembled soaring curls of stainless steel, some matte, some polished, into a restive sculpture that seems ready to blow away on the next wind. Whether the material will weather well, the aesthetics please or pall, the concert hall fill and profit will decide whether the imaginative design will prove to be ephemeral or lasting architecture.

Southern California, set in an enviable and "improved" environment, a place of man-made myths and experimentation, long marked by short-term structures, is finally mature enough to appreciate and preserve its past and its remaining open space but young enough to celebrate a lyrical revolution.

HAWAIIAN ARCHITECTURE

Hawai'i is particularly sensitive to the dominant aspects of both culture and climate; these influences are often experienced in the extreme. While Hawaiians lived in relative isolation from the West for more than 1,500 years, 400,000 workers for the sugar plantations changed the demographics in less than 50 years. For 1,600 years, the land, with plentiful water and sun, had sustained the economy, first with taro, then with sugar cane. Only in the last 10 years has the major crop changed, with 6 million tourist arrivals per year. The architecture has also shifted from being a direct result of cultural needs and climatic response to serving a cosmopolitan international community at the crossroads of the Pacific.

Early Contact

Captain James Cook (1728–1779), when first sighting the island of Atooi (Kauai, Hawai'i) in 1778, noted, "[E]verything we meet with, worthy of observation."[7] Fortunately, his artist John Webber was well qualified to record these observations in detailed pencil sketches. Sixty-one line engravings illustrated in the 1784 edition of *A Voyage to the Pacific Ocean* for the Lords Commissioners of the Admiralty brought the first images of Hawai'i to the world. These images show people adorned with geometric drawings, *kakau*, and decked in flower wreaths, *lei*; small communities of grass houses, *ahupua'a*; and large stone places of worship, *heiau*. The people and language resembled in many aspects similar circumstances that Cook had observed in Tahiti. The people were gracious to Cook, perhaps mistaking him for Lono, as he had arrived just at the time of annual season-end celebrations, *makahiki*.[8] The billowing sails on his ships replicated the ceremonial staffs of Lono, the god of agriculture. When he returned weeks later with a broken mast, the celebrations were over, and Cook was killed.

The communities were roughly triangular in shape, organized interdependently from the mountains, *mauka*, to the sea, *makai*. Directions in Hawai'i still bear these descriptors. The fishing village traded with the farmers of the midlands; the farmers traded for wood from the upland people. Groups of grass buildings with individual functions, *hale pili*, were enclosed by open spaces with low walls. At the ocean's edge these mortarless walls surrounded ponds of cultivated fish, *loko ia*, or in the midlands, irrigated fields, *loi*. The architect, *kuhikuhi pu'uone*, was trained to consider the position of mountains and lowlands, water sources, sun, and wind and rain patterns. All measurements were done in multiples of the hand and arm. These buildings were only used for protection during inclement weather, most activities occurring out-of-doors. The houses were remarkably simple, with design elements specifically supporting the often-changing climate: low door openings to minimize winds; steep roofs to shed heavy rains; strong yet flexible timber posts; and easily replaceable light grass coverings. The house was considered to have a soul, the thatch over the doorway left uncut as the umbilical cord, *piko*, until the proper birth rituals could be celebrated.

The worship places were the most intriguing to Cook, and he describes one clearly:

> It was an oblong space of considerable extent, surrounded by a wall of stone, about four feet high. The space enclosed was loosely paved with smaller stones, and at one end of it stood what I call a pyramid (oracle tower), *lana nu'u* . . . composed of small poles interwoven with twigs and branches. . . . [I]t had originally been covered with a thin, light gray cloth . . . [with] pieces of wood carved into something like human figures.[9]

The building forms changed very quickly after Western contact. Russian Louis Choris (1795–1828), an artist on the circumnavigation voyage of Otto Von Kotzebue (1761–1819), created some of the most important images of Hawai'i and its people that exist. His sketches from 1816 are the last view of everyday life while the old feudal order, or *kapu* system, was still in force. Choris was encouraged to publish his drawings, and he produced and sold by subscription a beautiful volume of color lithographs under the title *Picturesque Voyage around the World* (1822). Choris is best known for his paintings of Kamehameha I (1736–1819), the king who united all the islands, and his queen Ka'ahumanu (1772–1832). If one looks carefully at these images the detail of the architecture also begins to emerge—finely woven mats with colored geometric patterns for furniture, softly draped cloth for interior walls, tightly wrapped timber posts, and plastered masonry walls with wood lintel at openings.

Missionary Period

When Kamehameha died in 1819, his strong control using the *kapu* system also died. Within the year the small nation went into turmoil, and rigid obedience to the powerful leader was broken. The islands were ready for the onslaught of religious fervor and the Western architectural ideas of the Congregationalist missionaries. Sent by the American Board of Commissioners of Foreign Missions from Boston, Massachusetts, the first of many companies sailed into Honolulu harbor in April 1820 on the Thaddeus.

A precut house that would provide suitable living quarters for the missionaries arrived at the end of December on board the brig *Tartar*. This wooden house was typical of New England architecture, with clipped eaves to allow the sun to warm the southern walls, small windows to protect from ice and snow, a narrow central staircase, and many small rooms. It was completely unsuitable for the intense tropical climate or the culture of small buildings with individualized functions. It was more than a year before they received permission from the king to assemble it, where it still stands today as the First Frame House (1821).

Most of Honolulu at this time was concentrated in a village about half a mile from the mission compound. Although not the capital city, which was at Lahaina, Honolulu was the focus for commercial enterprise in the 1830s and had nearly 400 foreigners engaged in business practices with the 10,000 native residents. The village began to have formal roads laid out by 1838, with straightening and sidewalks often requiring the demolition of foreigners' houses.

The most common building material for Western-style houses during this period was adobe. The bricks, 10×20 inches, were dirt and straw pressed into molds and baked in the sun. Spanish settler Don Francisco de Paula y Marin (1774–1837) had brought the technology for adobe to Hawai'i as early as 1811. By 1847 the number of adobe houses, mostly lived in by foreigners, was 345.[10] The only adobe building still standing today is the Adobe School House (1835) on the grounds of the large coral church Kawaiahao (1841). Coral stone cut from the sea was also used despite the difficulty in cutting it from the reef at low tide and dragging the large $36 \times 24 \times 12$ inches blocks inland. The work of mining it resembled cutting up the surface of a pond frozen over and prying out the pieces with levers. By 1831 a lime kiln was opened to speed the construction of Western-style buildings. Chunks of coral were stacked in a hivelike shape over wood with a tall pole sent down to the center of the pile. Water was added to the quicklime to make whitewash and lime for mortar. Most of the houses illustrated in sketches of this period have bright plastered facades glistening in the sun.

The difficulty of obtaining materials for construction has always been present in Hawai'i. While small timbers, *ohia*, were readily available, large timbers often came from shipwrecks. Finish lumber was either the native *koa* or white pine from the state of Maine. The frustration of finding suitable craftsmen was also present, and native builders were often trained by shipwrights. Roofing materials presented the most difficult material, as the missionaries were strongly adverse to the dampness presented by the thatched *pili* roof. *Koa* shingles were used until corrugated iron proved to be the most durable.

Monarchy Period

The knowledge of the evolution of Honolulu in the mid-1850s is best revealed in the remarkable lithographs of 1853 from the sketches of Paul Emmert (1826–1867). In a series of views from the top of the Catholic Church, Emmert provided not only four contextual views of Honolulu but also fifty-four detailed drawings of individual buildings. Although there are a few transitional Western-style buildings with thatched roofs, most are large two-story wood or brick structures. Many of the supplies for building at this time were shipped precut from the Pacific Northwest. In 1850 more than 400 precut homes were built in Honolulu. Emmert's drawings show simple classical-style buildings beginning to adapt to the tropical climate: steep roofs to shed heavy rain, covered porches to shade the walls, and large windows and door openings to allow for the trade winds.

The Hawaiian royalty, *ali'i*, were not to be outdone by the strange ways of foreigners' construction. For the first Western-style royal palace, *'Iolani*, walls were constructed from plastered coral blocks, yet the decorative elements were all in wood: a high-pitched roof, dormers centered in each elevation, surrounding verandas, and a screened observation deck at the roof level. The weight of the steep roof was carried by posts at the outer edge of the porch, *lanai*. The steep roof allowed the warm air to rise, and the overhanging eaves kept out the sun and rain. This same basic form without the decorative embellishments was also used at two native churches built about this same time. Kaumakapili Church (1839) and Waioli Mission Church (1841) both had high-pitched thatched roofs, with surrounding verandas. These verandas were eight to ten feet wide to accommodate the overflowing native worshippers. To allow for the rain-shedding pitch and an appropriately scaled plate height at the edge of the veranda, the slope of the veranda rafter was changed over the wall line. This created a distinctive change in pitch and a softening of the overall form. It is this double-pitch roof that is called a Hawaiian roof today. Another transitional building was at Kaniakapupu (1845), in the upper valley of Nu'uanu. This structure had white plastered rubble rock walls with cut coral corners and a large double-pitched wood shingle roof with surrounding veranda. Both Waioli Mission Church and Kaniakapupu remain today. Not completely convinced of these Western accommodations, in each royal compound there was still a larger thatched house for entertaining and sleeping.

Theodore Heuck (1828–1874), a carpenter, engineer, and architect, arrived from Australia in 1850 and was the first to advertise his architectural services in the *Commercial Advertiser*. He served in the legislature of the Kingdom from 1864 to 1867 and designed the Queens Hospital (1860), Royal Mausoleum (1871), and 'Iolani Barracks (1871). Heuck returned to Germany in 1874 after being knighted in the Order of Kamehameha I and died in his native Hamburg. Another foreign arrival was J. G. Osborne (1830?–1880) of Yorkshire, a brick mason. The first building he constructed was the Kamehameha V Post Office (1870) built entirely of concrete blocks made on site. While the cement was imported from California, the building technology used was quite advanced: The aggregates were finely graded, iron reinforcing bars strengthened concrete spanning openings, and the cracks of hydration were minimized by daily wetting. It is believed to be the oldest extant precast concrete block building in the United States.

The second official government building, Ali'iolani Hale (1874), was designed as a royal palace, but the need for governmental offices changed its use during construction to the legislature and the court. Built in a Renaissance Revival style, the materials were imported brick, large double-hung windows, and white plastered exteriors. Although the second 'Iolani Palace was begun in 1876, a certain exuberance was added by King David Kalakaua (1836–1891) after he returned from his impressionable voyage around the world. Kalakaua greatly enjoyed the circumstances of his royal station, and his Victorian Italianate–style palace would have pleased any king of Europe. Thomas J. Baker (1826–1903), a builder from San Francisco, designed the structure in locally made brick with heavy stucco detailing. Most of the decorative construction materials were imported, including cast-iron Corinthian columns, decorative ironwork, cast plaster cupids, Greek maidens etched into door glass, and extensive millwork of Port Orford cedar. Other Hawaiian royalty built similarly ostentatious Western-style residential buildings, but always with the adjacent thatched house or lathed walled bungalow for sleeping purposes.

Plantation Architecture

The cultivation of sugar literally changed the face of Hawai'i by influencing the cultivation patterns and the demographics of the islands. Sugar cane, which arrived in Hawai'i in the Polynesian voyaging canoes in 500 C.E., eventually became Hawai'i's dominant industry. When American-born William Hooper (1809–1854) hired twenty-five natives to cultivate his 12 acres of cane, the first commercial sugar plantation began in Koloa, Kauai, in 1835. Land leases extended this plantation to 980 acres, and the plantation and mill became Ladd & Company. The demand for sugar caused by the California gold rush and the Civil War changed the scale to a plantation crop. Most of the land fell into the control of foreigners rather than the natives at the Great Mahele of 1848, when the land was divided into crown (government) lands, royal family lands, and land available to the commoners, maka'ainana.

Since sugar is a highly labor-intensive crop, the demand for unskilled labor was met by the importation of more than 450,000 indentured contract laborers representing eight distinct ethnic groups from 1890 to 1940. Their housing and specialty structures developed into a unique vernacular type that is the most distinctive built resource of the rural landscape in Hawai'i today. These buildings are important for the development of an efficient construction system of vertical plank walls and for the modifications made to meet the demands of different ethnic groups. Canec board pressed from the bagasse of sugar cane was used as both a structural and finish material.

The first plantation houses were built by the immigrant workers and often reflected the vernacular traditions of the country of their birth. An early plantation grouping outside of Hilo had pitched thatch roof with the traditional *katsuogi* and *chigi* of the minka farmhouses of Japan. These early houses were very makeshift, and social problems and inadequate sanitation became intensified. Many of the plantation communities that still exist today are a result of the 1919 standardized housing program of the Hawai'i Sugar Planters Association (HSPA). The HSPA was formed in 1895 to support the technical and agricultural requirements of the burgeoning sugar industry. As a result of worker strikes due to poor living conditions, the HSPA developed a standard set of house and sanitation drawings that were sent to all member plantations. Hundreds of these homes can still be found on all islands.

Though separated from their homelands, and fit into standardized housing, the laborers retained a strong sense of national identity by adapting a number of structures to promote cultural traditions. To the Japanese, a hot bath was a daily must that went beyond just being clean. The Japanese *ofuro* ranged in size from one-person wooden tubs to thirty-person concrete boxes. Laundry houses were constructed by four families in the Portuguese camps, and washing and drying became a social event among neighbors. Shinto shrines and Buddhist temples were created from the basic residential form with carved religious decorative elements. A dozen Chinese Tang Society buildings were constructed in 1906 throughout the islands by a crew of mainland Chinese carpenters. Each of these buildings was the same two-story form with a room for meetings on the first floor, a room for ancestor veneration on the second, and wide porches at each level for gathering. Four remain today.

In addition to the housing and ethnic structures, commercial buildings were also built. Most plantations operated a general store, and smaller camp offices were located in the field to take care of the administrative tasks of worker scheduling, paycheck distribution, and record keeping. Later free enterprise developed larger two-story commercial buildings clustered near the mill buildings. These buildings had rooms for traveling salesmen and first-floor stores for the latest in goods from California and Asia.

Territorial Architecture

Hawai'i became a territory of the United States in June 1898 under circumstances designed to protect American interests rather than the native people. The power of the throne was more than undermined when the reciprocity treaty of 1887 gave control of Pearl Harbor to the United States. Many pro-American interests controlled both the economy and the sugar lands. With annexation the American interests were protected, and Hawai'i experienced a building boom. The structures built at this time reflected the typical American idiom of Richardson Romanesque and were built from locally quarried and dressed bluestone. Clinton Briggs Ripley (1849–1910), a California architect, arrived in 1890 specifically to take advantage of this economy. He built both large commercial structures, such as Pauahi Hall at Punahou School, and smaller residences. It was his later partnership with Charles William Dickey (1871–1942) that was to prove particularly influential to the architectural landscape. Dickey was the grandson of the missionary William Alexander (1805–1884) and consequently had many important contacts in Hawai'i. The lava rock structures still standing from that partnership are the Irwin Block (1898), the Bishop Estate Building (1896), and the Model Progress Block (1898). The one with the most courageous Romanesque detailing and openings and form reflective of the Hawaiian climate, the Number One Fire Engine House (1898), has been demolished. Ripley and Dickey's largest commission at this time was the six-story Stangenwald Building (1891) with the first elevator in Honolulu and rich terra-cotta detailing in a style reminiscent of Louis Sullivan. Although Dickey returned to California in 1909, he opened an office in Honolulu in 1919 with a junior partner, Hart Wood (1880–1957). Wood supervised many of the buildings designed by Dickey while in California, and together they worked on the design for the Alexander and Baldwin Building (1929), their largest and most successful commission. The contributions of each of these talented architects can be seen easily in the careful proportions of the multistory facade. The rich terra-cotta ornament and murals executed by Einar Cortsen Peterson (c. 1885–1986), a Swiss-born artist already known for his decorative work in Los Angeles, are particularly notable. Details of oxen and sugar cane, Chinese characters of good fortune, and sailing ships represented the Alexander and Baldwin family fortunes from the sugar industry.

There was soon to be plenty of competition for Hawai'i's architects. One of the most prolific was Oliver Green Traphagen (1854–1932), who arrived from Duluth, Minnesota, in 1897 and constructed many buildings in Italian Renaissance eclecticism, including the Judd Building (1898), the Kakaako Pumping Station (1901), the Mendonca Building (1900), and the first large hotel in Waikiki, the Moana Hotel (1901). Despite its heavy styling, the Moana was the first large commercial structure to acknowledge the climatic needs with low eaves, substantial windows, sheltering balconies, and roof gardens.

Most mainland architects were invited to Honolulu by the influential families of missionary descendants. Bertram Goodhue (1869–1924), a New York–based architect, was invited to plan the campuses of Punahou and Kamehameha Schools. Goodhue's drawings for the future Honolulu show Mediterranean-style buildings with tile roofs and covered loggias. His sketches were not well received by the business community but were noticed by Mrs. Anna Rice Cooke (1853–1934), who desired a public home for her extensive collection of East Asian Art. Goodhue designed the Honolulu Academy of Arts (1927) in a Mediterranean style with simple rough plastered walls, heavy tiled roofs, and intimate courtyards. These courtyard gardens were designed by Catherine Jones Thompson (1887–1985), the first landscape architect in Hawai'i, also known for her sensitive design of the Punchbowl Memorial Cemetery (1949) and the 'Ewa Plantation master plan (1932). Thompson shaped the gardens for Ralph Adams Cram (1863–1942) when he designed the Central Union Church (1924) with little response to the culture or climate in an ecclesiastical form more reminiscent of Sir Christopher Wren. Julia Morgan (1872–1957), known for her sensitive designs for the Young Women's Christian Association (YWCA) in California, also designed the Honolulu YWCA, Laniakea (1927), the Homelani Columbarium (1926) in Hilo, and a residential facility for women, Fernhurst (1928), since demolished. Morgan's YWCA building is a multicourtyard scheme with open loggias; the courtyard gardens and swimming pool were designed by Thompson. Thompson's greatest contribution was her classical approach to garden design utilizing indigenous plants and Asian motifs; the corpus of her work contributed to a specific regional style for Hawai'i based on natural elements.

Another striking image of Hawai'i was brought to the world in the winter of 1941. "Remember Pearl Harbor" and the smoking ruins of the battleship USS *Arizona* began the U.S. intensive involvement in World War II and stopped major construction in Hawai'i for nearly twenty years. It was not to resume with any intensity until Hawai'i became a state in 1959.

Statehood Architecture

The State Capitol Building (1965) designed by John Carl Warnecke (1919–) was inspired by the strong forms of the Hawaiian landscape. The volumes of the curving legislative chambers mimic volcanoes erupting like islands from the sea. The edges of the central open-air courtyard curve upward with blue mosaic tiles. The upper office floors are supported by forty staggering columns with shapes like palm trees. This building has an originality and enthusiasm for the unique landscape conditions not found in any of the other Federalist or Classical Revival state capitol buildings.

The economic growth presented by statehood in 1959 created a consequent surge in construction. Many of these buildings captured the benefits presented by the climate and the now multicultural society. The First United Methodist Church (1961) by Alfred Preis (1911–1993) and the Outrigger Canoe Club (1964) and Pacific Club (1961) by Vladimir Ossipoff (1907–1998) are exemplary examples that blended the line between building and landscape. Both men were foreign immigrants to Hawai'i, Preis from Austria and Ossipoff from Russia by way of Japan. Their work has strong roof lines and deep overhangs and uses dark woods and native stone, in what has been described as a local or *kama'aina* style. Preis' unusual cantilevered USS *Arizona* Memorial (1962) honors the men lost in the attack on Pearl Harbor and receives the largest number of tourists per year (1.5 million) to any site in Hawai'i.

The growth of this tourism industry was greatly increased by the federal spending on airports and transportation systems after statehood. Jet planes arrived from both East and West to take advantage of the climate, the mix of Asian cultures, and the American economy. Large resort hotels grew out of the newly formed lava of the Big Island. The first ones blended Asian elements with broad open spaces, blurring the line between inside and outside. The Mauna Kea Beach Hotel (1965) by Skidmore Owings and Merrill was developed by Laurence Rockefeller (1910–) and houses his spectacular Asian art collection. The later hotels were 350-foot walls sheathed in pink Italian marble and tinted windows with no acknowledgment of the climatic conditions or the multicultural society. Office towers in Honolulu were designed by international firms and are no different than the new buildings found in any other international city.

RESOURCE GUIDE

Printed Sources

Abbott, Carl. *Greater Portland: Urban Life and Landscape in the Pacific Northwest*. Philadelphia: University of Pennsylvania Press, 2001.

Apple, Russell A. *Hawaiian Thatched House: Use–Construction–Adaptation*. San Francisco, CA: National Park Service, Western Service Center, Office of History and Historic Architecture, 1971.

Crowley, Walt. *National Trust Guide Seattle: America's Guide for Architecture and History Travelers*. New York: John Wiley and Sons, 2003.

Dubrow, Gail, with Donna Graves. *Sento at Sixth and Main: Preserving Landmarks of Japanese American Heritage*. Seattle: Seattle Arts Commission, distributed by University of Washington Press, 2002.

Hawkins, William John, III. *The Grand Era of Cast-Iron Architecture in Portland*. Portland, OR: Binford and Mort, 1976.

Hoagland, Alison K. *Buildings of Alaska*. New York: Oxford University Press, 1993.

Jay, Robert. *The Architecture of Charles W. Dickey: Hawaii and California*. Honolulu: University of Hawaii Press, 1992.

Kalman, Harold, Ron Phillips, and Robin Ward. *Exploring Vancouver: The Essential Architectural Guide*. Vancouver: University of British Columbia, 1993.

King, Bart. *An Architectural Guidebook to Portland*. Salt Lake City, UT: Gibbs Smith Publisher, 2001.

Nabokov, Peter, and Robert Easton. *Native American Architecture*. New York: Oxford University Press, 1989.

Ochsner, Jeffrey Karl, ed. *Shaping Seattle Architecture: A Historical Guide to the Architects*. Seattle: University of Washington Press, 1994.

Roth, Leland, ed. *Buildings at the End of the Oregon Trail: Tour Guide*. Produced in conjunction with the 18th Annual Meeting of the Vernacular Architecture Forum, Portland, Oregon, June 11–14, 1997.

Sandler, Rob. *Architecture in Hawaii: A Chronological Survey/Text*. Honolulu: Mutual Publishing Company, 1993.

Schwantes, Carlos Arnaldo. *The Pacific Northwest: An Interpretive History*. Rev. ed. Lincoln: University of Nebraska Press, 1996.

Williams, Richard G. *Style and Vernacular: A Guide to the Architecture of Lane County, Oregon*. Portland: Oregon Historical Society, 2000.

Woodbridge, Sally B., and Roger Montgomery. *A Guide to Architecture in Washington State*. Seattle: University of Washington Press, 1980.

Web Sites

Hawai'i Museums Association
August 16, 2003.
http://www.hawaiimuseums.org/

Northern California Architecture
http://www.cr.nps.gov/nr/travel/santaclara/bayareaarchitecture.html

The Oregon History Project
Oregon Historical Society. August 16, 2003.
http://www.ohs.org/education/oregonhistory/index.cfm?CFID=9930&CFTOKEN=83276116

Has online versions of primary and secondary documents related to Oregon history and architecture.

University of Washington Libraries Digital Collections
University of Washington Libraries. August 16, 2003.
http://content.lib.washington.edu/

Large collection of historic photographs of Washington State and the Pacific Northwest.

Washington HistoryLink.org
History Link. August 16, 2003.
http://www.historylink.org/

The online encyclopedia of Seattle, King County, and Washington State history.

Organizations

Alaska Office of History and Archaeology
550 West 7th Avenue Suite 1310
Anchorage, AK 99501-3565
http://www.dnr.state.ak.us/parks/oha/index.htm

This state office carries out the responsibilities of the State Historic Preservation Office.

Historic Preservation League of Oregon
3534 Southeast Main Street
Portland, OR 97214
http://www.hplo.org/index.htm

Statewide historic preservation advocacy group.

Oregon Historical Society
1200 Southwest Park Avenue
Portland, OR 97205
http://www.ohs.org/

The photographic archives include over 2.5 million images from prestatehood to the present day.

Oregon State Historic Preservation Office
1115 Commercial Street Nebraska, Suite 2
Salem, OR 97301-1012
http://www.shpo.state.or.us/index.php

Society of Architectural Historians
Marion Dean Ross/Pacific Northwest Chapter
http://www.sahmdr.org/

Washington State Historical Society
1911 Pacific Avenue
Tacoma, WA 98402
http://www.wshs.org/

Collections of artifacts and documents related to Washington State history. Large photograph collection of buildings in the state.

Washington State Office of Archeology and Historic Preservation
1063 South Capitol Way, Suite 106
P. O. Box 48343
Olympia, WA 98504-8343
http://www.oahp.wa.gov/

Washington State's primary agency with knowledge and expertise in historic preservation.

Washington Trust for Historic Preservation
1204 Minor Avenue
Seattle, WA 98101
http://www.wa-trust.org/index.htm
Statewide historic preservation advocacy group.

Archives

Bishop Museum Photographic Collection
1525 Bernice Street
Honolulu, HI 96817
808-847-3511; 808-848-4182 (archives)
http://www.bishopmuseum.org/research/cultstud/libarch/archphoto.htm/

Hawai'i State Archives
'Iolani Palace Grounds
Honolulu, HI 96813
808-586-0329
http://www.statehi.us/dags/archives/

Hawaiian Historical Society
560 Kawaiahao Street
Honolulu, HI 96813
808-537-6271
http://www.hawaiianhistory.org/

Hawaiian Mission Children's Society Library
553 South King Street
Honolulu, HI 96813
808-531-0481
http://www.lave.net/~mhm/lib.htm

Historic American Buildings Survey/Historic American Engineering Record, Prints and
Photographs Division
Library of Congress
101 Independence Avenue, SE
Washington, DC 20540
http://memory.loc.gov/ammem/hhhtml/hhhome.html

Kaua'i Historical Society
4396 Rice Street, Suite 101
Lihu'e, HI 96766
808-245-3373
http://www.kauaihistoricalsociety.org/

Kona Historical Society
Highway 11
P. O. Box 398
Captain Cook, HI 96704
808-323-3222
http://www.konahistorical.org/

Maui Historical Society
2375-A Main Street
Wailuku, HI 96793

808-244-3326
http://www.kauaihistoricalsociety.org/

University of Hawaii, Hawaiian Collection
University of Hawaii at Manoa Library
2550 The Mall
Honolulu, HI 96822
808-956-8264
http://libweb.hawaii.edu/uhmlib/

ART

*Linda Noveroske Rentner
and Janet L. Steinbright*

ART IN THE PACIFIC REGION

Museums devoted to the visual arts of California, Oregon, Washington, Alaska, and Hawai'i present visitors with one of the most rich and diverse artistic traditions in the world. The art of the region comprises a most stimulating history, from the earliest petroglyphs,[1] pictographs,[2] and cave paintings up through the most recent, contemporary innovations in the art world today. From the dramatic mountain ranges of the Pacific Northwest to the lush, tropical landscapes of Hawai'i to the glacial grandeur of Alaska, natural inspiration for the landscape artist is and has been abundant. For the portraitist, the conceptual artist, the sculptor, and the craftsperson, the dynamic overlap of cultures has provided ample fodder for development of new and vital modes of expression. For the performing artist, the venues and public willingness to embrace the creative spirit have provided the opportunity for groundbreaking work. The communities of the Pacific Region are a fiercely proud and accepting group that has taken care of its artists. As such, creativity and skill have flourished for many centuries.

Early Native American Art

Before the indigenous peoples of North America ever had first contact with European explorers and settlers, they had already developed their own sophisticated artistic tradition. Because the climate of the Pacific Region was generally temperate, the Native American tribes had ample time to turn their efforts toward activities that not only ensured their survival but enriched their lives. Though very little of this precontact artwork survives today, its history has been preserved in the stories and legends of the Native Americans. While their artwork was for the most part functional in nature—the concept of "art for art's sake" was foreign to them—it was created with careful attention to detail, and always with the underlying con-

Petroglyphs like this one in Pu'uloa, Hawai'i Volcanoes National Park can be found all over Hawai'i. Courtesy of the National Park Service.

cept of communication. Robert Tyler Davis, author of *Native Arts of the Pacific Northwest*, describes it thus:

> The Indians of the Northwest coast of America developed a culture with a tremendously rich artistic expression. The expressions were sometimes powerful and dramatic, sometimes fine and delicate, but always they were alive. The art is one that had something to say, and what the artist made was not only useful in the material sense but functioned also in telling part of the story of a whole culture.[3]

The earliest examples of native art found thus far in the Pacific Region are of petroglyphs and pictographs, an ancient form of carving and painting the living rock. In Southern California, the Kawaiisu tribe (still extant today) boasts some of the most beautiful ancient rock carvings to be found. In the Mojave Desert, many of their stories are incised into the rocks near Steam Wells, a natural spring. These carvings, some of which date as far back as 10,000 B.C.E., have prompted many theories as to the nature and culture of the tribal life since time immemorial. The prevailing interpretation to date is that these petroglyphs and pictographs reflect the belief that water sources from the earth are dwellings of supernatural spirits. They appear to depict stories of shamans', or medicine men's, encounters with the spirit world.

In Hawai'i, similar petroglyphs have been found throughout all of the islands, incised into the smooth lava rock. The Kanaka Maoli, or native Hawaiians, carved their own memories into the landscape from as early as 1,500 to 2,000 years ago. When the first Polynesian settlers came to the island, they had no known written language, so they recorded their stories through oral tradition and by representing images of people and animals in the lava rock. These fascinating carvings, many of which are still visible today, inspired Ansel Adams (1902–1984) to create a photographic essay on the wonders of the islands.

Alongside their proliferation of rock art, the dominant form of artistic expression of the native Hawaiians took the form of building their oceangoing canoes. One thousand years before Christopher Columbus (1451–1506) sailed across the Atlantic, the Kanaka Maoli were developing the sacred art of exploration. The construction of their massive, double-hulled canoes—some of which reached seventy feet in length—was surrounded by solemn ceremony. The Kanaka Maoli would select the tallest and strongest Koa trees from the

On the Hawaiian Islands, artistic endeavors would not change significantly until their first contact with prominent European explorers, namely, Captain James Cook in 1778. Courtesy of the Library of Congress.

forest, hollow them out with stone adzes,[4] and carve the bows and sterns of the vessels with images of their gods to protect the voyagers. All the while, strict protocol was observed; they chanted and danced to ensure that the favor of their gods was present throughout the entire process. The process did not end with the completion of a vessel; rather, the ceremony continued with the actual voyage into the vast, open ocean. Tradition prevailed in these wondrous times; artistic endeavors would not change significantly until their first contact with prominent European explorers, namely, Captain James Cook (1728–1779).

Captain James Cook's ships, the *Resolution* and the *Discovery*, came to the Hawaiian Islands in 1778 during a four-year circumnavigation of the globe. The artists who accompanied him were responsible for executing drawings, paintings, and sketches as a way of visually recording what they encountered there. They recorded the features of the land and sea, the indigenous plant and animal life, and the native peoples who inhabited the island. During their interactions with the native Hawaiians, they traded with them extensively, introducing them to sophisticated carving tools, items such as pencils, paints, and paper, and European theories of artistic representation. Though Cook's stay ended in tragedy (in one of many brutal skirmishes between the natives and the visitors, Cook was killed after his men fired warning shots that killed several Hawaiians, one of which was a chief), the impact of the European explorers on the development of art in Hawaii would be lasting.

Cook also made contact with the Native Americans of the Pacific Northwest Coast in 1778. This European contact, in addition to encounters with the Spaniards in 1774, profoundly influenced the art of the Native Americans. The introduction of steel tools and materials such as beads and blankets fueled their artistic output immensely. Before the introduction of new methods and materials, however, the coastal tribes had developed their own methods that displayed high artistic merit.

Though remaining examples of actual artwork from this precontact period are scarce, the history of these objects and traditions is still very much alive. An amazing phenomenon can be observed among all of the tribes that comprise the Pacific Region: though their individual styles and cultures can be seen in their artwork, there are several unifying themes that run through almost all of the tribes that make their art instantly recognizable as that of the Pacific Region. Similar iconography, artistic processes, and ceremonial functions span many of the tribes that were, paradoxically, kept separated by features of the land.

The most apparent unifying characteristic is that of the importance of ceremony in their lives. They stood on ceremony to ground their people in traditions that worked to protect and promote the prosperity of the tribe. They practiced regular rituals to communicate the history of their people, to cure sickness, and to frighten away evil spirits. The subjects of their legends and stories in particular were of paramount importance; ceremonies were performed as a way of passing on the guardianship of their lineage and customs to future generations. The artwork that accompanied and enriched these practices was functional, the aesthetics in service of underlining the significance of the experience. There was very little artistic specialization among members of the tribes; whole communities worked equally to produce those items essential to their traditional practices. There was no concept of connoisseurship or elitism as there is today. Pieces were not made to enrich the aesthetic quality of a particular person's life but to preserve the heritage of the whole tribe.

Rank within the tribe, though not a signifier of who had the right to accumulate art, was a distinguishing feature of the artistic iconography used during these rituals. Connections with deities and spirits entitled certain families to "possess" not only significant songs or rituals but certain symbols. If the family's lineage included a particular animal, for example, only this family could display the animal on their clothing or other possessions. Both the animal and its surrounding lore were effectively their property. They were considered totems, or spirits of protection, and the Native Americans developed strict protocol for displaying and passing on their totems to future generations. The relationship of man to animal was the cornerstone of their spiritual beliefs. Depictions of animals could be formal and stylized, abstracted, or naturalistic, depending on the artist's vision of those factors that were most important to communicate the presence of the animal in its proper context. All depended on the purpose of the ceremony in which the animal's spirit would make its appearance.

For the ceremonies enacted before contact with European explorers and settlers, costumes, masks, and other objects were made primarily of shredded cedar bark. The men made and wore elaborate mantles around their shoulders, and the women wore cedar bark shirts, hats, and capes. Even though they had only the most basic tools—such as the stone adz—at their disposal, they worked wonders, for they understood the nature of the materials with which they worked. Not only did they create stunning costumes and utensils out of cedar bark, but they fashioned the horns of mountain goats and sheep into spoons, ladles, and bowls that they then decorated with figures depicting stories of the tribe. These costumes and utensils were decorated with relief sculpture, hair, shells, bone, and occasionally abalone shell, which was plentiful among the tribes of California. The tribes of the Pacific Region were masters of living effectively within their environment and the most accomplished artists for enhancing that experience with meaning and imagination. They utilized the materials and tools that they had and created beautiful works of art to accompany their ceremonies, well before the European explorers came in and changed their way of life forever.

The European explorers introduced the Native Americans to many new art techniques and materials. They brought with them such concepts as perspective and such materials as paint, flannel, buttons, and pearls. This had a monumental effect on the style of Native American art. Though the tribes retained the original character and flavor of their art, the introduction of so many new techniques and media caused a major expansion of possibilities for individual expression. The artists still followed the conventions of their culture, but they had freedom within these conventions to create more innovative and varied interpretations of their traditional iconography.

As the European explorers affected the artistic output of the Native Americans, they also affected the clothing and other materials that they used in daily life. Their everyday clothing eventually became somewhat European in style, as did their tools used for hunting, eating, and building. Their ceremonial items, however, were a different story altogether. The formerly cedar bark capes and shirts were replaced by elaborately painted and beaded blankets, and their food dishes and utensils became even more richly decorated. Their ceremonial staffs, pipes, and boxes took on the bright colors and detailed carvings that only commercial paints and tools could function to create. One of the most important iconographic symbols in Native American art, the eye, became a brightly colored illustration of what the Native Americans saw as the most essential component of most works of art: the window to the spirit that lives within everything. Black, red, and blue-green paint (occasionally accompanied by yellow and white) became the primary colors used on ceremonial masks, costumes, and totem poles.

Perhaps the most innovative appropriation of European technique and material into Native American style, though, was evident in the ornate headdresses worn by tribal chiefs. These tall, cylindrical headdresses were usually made of alder wood and decorated with mineral paint, shells, and feathers. They are perhaps among the greatest examples of combining traditional forms with new media.

Even as the Native Americans appropriated these outside influences into their art, the most poignant focal point in this process is that they managed to retain their individuality. In their costumes, masks, dance rattles, blankets, paintings, totem poles, and other functional items required by society, they kept their sense of who they were and where they were from. Though the ever-encroaching settlers eventually displaced them from their homeland, the unique yet all-encompassing art of the Native Americans in the Pacific Re-

Display of Northwest-coast Native American baskets, masks, wooden figures, a ceremonial painted board, and other objects, c. 1901. Courtesy of the Library of Congress.

gion served its original purpose; to keep their traditions and heritage alive. Even today, advocates of Native American tribal history work relentlessly to preserve the rich traditions of their ancestors. It is an excellent testament to the perseverance of a way of life that will always work within its given circumstances to proudly declare itself.

The Age of Exploration

In 1542, Juan Rodríguez Cabrillo (?–1543) and his crew arrived at Point Reyes, California. They were the first known Europeans to artistically represent the Pacific Coast of America in European fashion, pen on paper. Though their maps were wildly inaccurate (they depicted California as an island), these aesthetically pleasing maps would be the first of many works by artist explorers in the Pacific Region. Artists would, for several centuries, continue to record the wonders of this new world in drawings and paintings. It was no matter of pure fancy that prompted such a proliferation of two-dimensional works; it was for posterity that they chose to document, as much as possible, the land and the new ways of life that they discovered.

During the Spanish Period (1769–1822), much of the Pacific Coast of America was claimed as "New Spain." Missions (establishments for educating and Christianizing Native Americans), presidios (military garrisons charged with protecting the missions), and pueblos (communities for the Spaniards to settle in) were established to colonize the land and protect the realm from Russian fur trappers on the Northwest Coast. This period saw the emergence of a wealth of mission art—usually religious wall paintings that decorated the interiors of the Spanish missions. As the missions were established to convert and educate the Native Americans in a European style of life, the mission wall paintings served largely to instruct them in the stories of European Christianity. Many examples of these works are still extant today, the most famous of which is probably the mission of San Juan Capistrano, between Los Angeles and San Diego. Established November 1, 1776, by Fr. Junipero Serra, it is still in use today and is considered the oldest church in California.

In 1822, Mexican revolutionaries broke the Spanish rule over much of the North American West Coast, ushering in the Mexican Period (1822–1847). With this shift in power came changes in artistic styles and subject matter. The major trends included art that focused on the scientific recording of flora and fauna, wealthy gentlemen with the means to travel and produce "fine art" on their journeys, and above all, artists' depictions of man's presence in and ability to dominate the wilderness. Views of America's West Coast began to look more and more like European landscapes, as evidenced by such works as William Smyth's (1800–1877) *The Mission of San Carlos, Upper California* (1827, watercolor). The setting is peaceful and pastoral, executed with clear mastery of European theories of perspective and composition. The view of the ocean and the formerly rugged landscape is tamed and civilized by the dominating presence of the mission building in the painting's middle ground, as well as two figures of "natives" in the foreground. It is an excellent example of the explorers and settlers who arrived by ship and exercised their power over a land that they perceived as wild and uncivilized.

Not all art of this period came from explorers arriving by ship, however. As Eu-

William Smyth's *The Mission of San Carlos*, Upper California. The Art Archive/Navy Historical Service, Vincennes, France/Dagli Orti.

ropeans were arriving from nautical circumnavigations of the globe, so American artist explorers of the land were coming across the expansive plains and vast mountain ranges to record what they regarded as the final frontier. While individual motivations for exploring the West were numerous and diverse, probably the single most significant factor in the American push westward was the discovery of gold in California. Ever since James Wilson Marshall uttered those legendary words "My eye was caught with the glimpse of something shining in the ditch," life on the frontier would be forever changed. The gold rush, which lasted from 1848 to approximately 1864,[5] would inspire not only an entirely new style of genre painting but also the discovery of wilderness vistas that stimulated artists to travel long distances to paint the magnificent landscapes. The lure of gold that brought hundreds of thousands of prospectors to the West would have a lasting impact not only on the economy but also on the development of art that strove to be uniquely American.

Gold Rush Art

Though only a small percentage of the original gold rush genre oil paintings, watercolors, prints, and drawings survive today, they comprise a fantastic visual account of the rapid development of life in the Pacific Region.[6] Nearly every day, new towns sprang up around mining sites, and already established small towns became bustling cities. Depictions of the ever-increasing pace of life, as well as por-

The Pacific Northwest and Alaskan Gold Rushes

It is important to note the several less famous, though equally as significant, Alaskan gold rushes. Between 1849 and 1920, scattered discoveries of gold in Alaska prompted sweeping northward migrations. Just as the artist explorers had discovered stunning natural subject matter in their travels toward California, so they found equally inspiring substance in the landscapes and inhabitants of the Pacific Northwest. The craggy coastline, lush valleys, and temperate climate of Washington and Oregon would motivate many artists and other travelers to settle there and make their homes in the haunting beauty of the Northwest Coast.

traits of prospectors and entrepreneurs, dominated artistic subject matter. Also, the influx of immigrants from all over the world brought cutting-edge artistic styles to these scenes. A widespread taste for American genre painting and a booming economy provided the patronage necessary for thousands of works of gold rush art. All these factors combined set the stage for a great leap in artistic productivity.

Portraits of prospectors and scenes from their daily lives were a very popular subject in gold rush art. Excellent examples of these are E. Hall Martin's (1818–1851) *The Prospector* (1850, oil on canvas), Henry Bacon's (1839–1912) *The Luck of Roaring Camp* (1880, oil on canvas), and Rufus Wright's (1832–1900) *The Card Players* (1882, oil on canvas). Though these scenes were often sentimental and romanticized, they attest to the prospector's lives outside their feverish search for gold. They offer a poignant glimpse into the pioneering spirit and the camaraderie that often characterized gold rush communities.

Another widespread subject of gold rush art was the representation of mining scenes. Works like William McIlvaine's (1813–1867) *Panning Gold* (n.d., watercolor) and W. Taber's (1830–1916) *Steam Gold Dredger Ascending the Sacramento* (1849, ink and gouache on paper) provide detailed views of the actual process of searching out and extracting gold. Through these images, there exists a meticulous record of panning, dredging, digging, and other forms of mining as they were actually practiced.

The third major subject of gold rush art—scenes of the ever-increasingly populated cities—is evident in William Birch McMurtrie's (1816–1872) *View of Telegraph Hill and City, North of Montgomery Street* (1849, watercolor on paper), and R. Godchaux's (1878–?) *Vue de San-Francisco en 1851* (1851, gouache on paper). These scenes offer views of the changing way of life, particularly in California, for which the gold rush was responsible. Not only were prospectors flooding in from all over the world, but entrepreneurs were arriving and capitalizing on the needs of a population that was increasing exponentially.

The gold rush provided more than new subject matter for artists; along with it came developing communities that demanded works of art to enrich their lives. Though the lure of gold was the original impetus that brought so many people to the Pacific Region, it was for the beauty of the land and the promise of a prosperous life that many remained. Those artist explorers who stayed in California, Oregon, and Washington often established studios and created markets, contributing to later developments of art in the Pacific Region. As they explored, sometimes settled, and incorporated new subject matter into their art, the artists of the Pacific Region ushered in one of the most memorable periods in American art.

Albert Bierstadt's *The Domes of the Yosemite*. Courtesy of the Library of Congress.

The American Renaissance and the Golden Age of Landscape Painting

The latter half of the nineteenth century is often regarded as a classic era in American art. In the Pacific Region, art would grow and develop exponentially as artists looked more and more toward the glorification of their homeland and less toward emulating the styles and movements of the European masters. Though artists working in America retained this European influence to varying degrees, such as that of the Munich School in Germany and the Barbizon School in France, the general focus shifted distinctly toward development of a uniquely American style. This style would have a tremendous impact on genre painting, other forms of media, and above all, landscape painting. Though the Civil War (1861–1865) had a profoundly disturbing effect on America, the desire remained for images of America as a pristine paradise. Landscape artists, perhaps moved by the need for Americans to return to the pleasures of pride in their country and the resilient spirit of the pioneer, would answer that call.

A very wise and witty writer, Mark Twain, once had this to say about Albert Bierstadt's (1830–1902) *The Domes of the Yosemite* (1867, oil on canvas):

> One sees these things in all sorts of places throughout California, and under all sorts of circumstances, and gets so familiar with them that he knows them in a moment when he sees them in a picture.
>
> I knew them in Bierstadt's picture, and checked them off one by one, and said "These things are correct—they all look just as they ought to look, and they all belong to California."

> But when I got around to the atmosphere, I was obliged to say "This man has imported this atmosphere; this man has surely imported this atmosphere from some foreign country, because nothing like it was ever seen in California."
>
> I may be mistaken, for all men are liable to err, but I honestly think I am right. The atmospheric effects in that picture are startling, are full of variety, and are charming. It is more the atmosphere of *Kingdom-Come* than of California.[7]

Twain's criticism of Bierstadt's most famous work is obviously meant to be taken as tongue-in-cheek, but it reveals one of the most prevalent themes in the Golden Age of Landscape Painting: improving upon a natural setting that is already beautiful. In the decades of the 1840s through the 1880s, landscape was easily one of the most popular subjects in American art, for it was with a certain nationalistic pride that artists sought to record the great wilderness vistas of the West. Subjects such as Yosemite, Donner Lake, and the Oregon Trail were among the favorites of the great landscape masters. They sought to record the natural beauty of the West before it would forever become domesticated, and this desire prompted them to use their often European-inspired techniques to cast their subjects in the most flattering possible light.

Before the completion of the Transcontinental Railroad in 1869, the trek to the Pacific Coast was an arduous one. The journey claimed the lives of many pioneers, but those who made it were to be rewarded with views of some of the most awe-inspiring terrain in America. Word of these unparalleled landscapes made it back to the East Coast, and as a result, many artists undertook the journey in search of sublime subject matter. Photographers Eadweard Muybridge (1830–1904), Carleton Watkins (1829–1916), and William Henry Jackson (1843–1942) were among them, and their photographic essays on the Rocky Mountains, Yosemite Valley, and the Oregon Trail, among other places, were vital in providing reliable visual accounts of the Pacific Region's unsurpassed beauty. Their photographs would not only inspire many landscape artists to travel west; they would also contribute to the Conservation Movement and the formation of the National Park System.

Probably the most famous of the landscape painters of the American West were Bierstadt and Thomas Moran (1837–1926). They, among many others, elevated the scenery of the Pacific Region to a kind of mythological status. Influenced by the Munich School,[8] the Barbizon School,[9] and the second generation of the Hudson River School,[10] they created lasting images of a pristine wilderness, poignantly underscored by the presence of ever-encroaching settlers. Their works were to become records of a transient beauty, a rugged landscape that Americans sought to dominate even as they lauded its natural allure.

Examples of Bierstadt's masterful representation and manipulation of the Pacific Regional landscape can be seen in his works *The Domes of the Yosemite* (1867, oil on canvas), *In the Mountains* (1867, oil on canvas), *Puget Sound on the Pacific Coast* (1870), and *The Oregon Trail* (1869, oil on canvas). In *The Domes of the Yosemite*, Bierstadt depicts a haunting view of Yosemite's famous Half Dome, which had, in the words of Mark Twain, "the atmosphere of *Kingdom-Come*." This same type of celestial atmosphere permeates most of Bierstadt's landscapes, attesting to the prevailing notion of the Pacific Region; it belonged to America but also to the realm of other-worldliness that would soon become familiar iconography in American landscape painting.

Moran also endowed his landscapes with heavenly atmosphere. Originally from Long Island, Moran traveled to the West to paint Yosemite and other views of the Sierras. The influence of his mentor Joseph M. W. Turner is evident in his works, particularly in *Domes of the Yosemite* (1872, oil on canvas). Moran's palette of earthy colors bathes the mountains in a warm glow, set off strikingly against a dark foreground. Famous for their lustrous atmospheric qualities, many of Moran's works would eventually grace the offices of influential U.S. congressmen and aid in inspiring a growing American population to travel west and settle among the natural wonders.

Other artists such as Frederick Ferdinand Schafer (1839–1927), William Keith (1838–1911), and William Hahn (1829–1887) also made the journey to the Pacific Region to immortalize its vistas in landscape paintings. Their works captured the mountain ranges, rivers, coastal views, and groves of redwood and sequoia trees for which the West Coast was, and still is, famous. Though large numbers of pioneers would soon domesticate the land with their homes and businesses, the works of the American landscape painters provide a lasting and poignant visual account of some of the nation's most treasured land. Today, one can still visit many of these sites. And while the views have changed—sometimes subtly, sometimes dramatically—the spirit of the rugged wilderness remains.

Not only did the West Coast of the continental United States inspire artists to undertake difficult journeys in search of subject matter; the Hawaiian Islands also provided unparalleled natural beauty for their work. Though not yet officially part of the United States, the Hawaiian Islands were an immensely popular destination for naturalists and landscape painters. Then known by many visitors as the "Sandwich Islands" (so named by Captain James Cook in honor of the Earl of Sandwich), artists, pioneers, and missionaries arrived there from all over the world.

Subjects of Hawaiian landscape paintings varied widely, from coastal views to scenes of mission settlements to volcanoes both active and dormant. The art of Hawai'i had evolved from the pencil or pen on paper drawings of the early explorers to sophisticated watercolor and oil paintings by masters. Among these masters were Titian Ramsay Peale (1799–1885), John Prendergast (1815–?), and James Gay Sawkins (1806–1878). All artists who had learned their skills in other countries, they found themselves, in one way or another, transfixed by Hawai'i's unique landscape.

Titian Peale, son of the famous American artist Charles Wilson Peale (1741–1827), traveled to Hawai'i as a naturalist for the U.S. Exploring Expedition in 1840. Peale's works during this expedition included, among others, *West Crater of Kaluea Pele from the Black Ledge* (1841, oil on board), *Volcano of Kaluea Pele as Seen from the Side of Mauna Loa* (1841, oil on board), and *Kilauea by Day* (1842, oil on canvas). Peale's depiction of the Kilauea Crater shows clouds of steam, gas, and smoke issuing from the earth in the middle ground, with a group of Native Hawaiians in the foreground. Lieutenant Charles Wilkes, the commander of Peale's expedition, had this to say about the Kilauea Crater:

> We hurried to the edge of the cavity in order to get a view of its interior. . . .
> When the edge is reached, the extent of the cavity becomes apparent . . . the

vastness thus made sensible, transfixes the mind with astonishment, and every instant, the impression of grandeur and magnitude increases.[11]

Apparently, the phenomena of the Hawaiian landscape mesmerized nearly everyone who witnessed it.

John Prendergast arrived in Honolulu in 1848. Though he left later that year for the promise of California's gold rush, his painting of Honolulu remains today as one of the original records of Diamond Head juxtaposed with the emerging Alakea streets. *Honolulu Looking toward Diamond Head* (1848, watercolor) depicts his view of the city in translucent watercolors. His subtle washes and keen observation distinguish his work as that of a master. Accurate detail coupled with aesthetic qualities display Prendergast's confident and unquestionable skill as a painter.

James Gay Sawkins, an English artist who set up a studio in Honolulu, also painted the views of Oahu with reverence. In *Hilo from the Bay* (1852, oil on canvas) the mountain peaks of Mauna Loa and Mauna Kea are visible in the background of Hilo, a popular resort town for both visitors and residents. The snowy peaks of the two mountains provide a fascinating contrast to the busy, tropical settlement in the middle ground. These types of startling combinations would find their way into many Hawaiian landscapes of this period.

Though the lure of Hawai'i brought travelers from all over the world, not all artists in Hawai'i at this time came from abroad. Native Hawaiians, influenced by the influx of artists particularly from Europe and America, also began to develop advanced techniques in oil and watercolor painting. Joseph Nawahi (1842–1896), for example, was a Native Hawaiian whose artistic output, though relatively small, showed off his extraordinary talent. His work *Hilo from Coconut Island* (1868, oil on canvas) attests to his ability, even though he was an amateur painter, to appropriate the most current techniques into his perception of the island that was always his home.

In the 1880s, painting in Hawai'i took a most exciting turn. Great volcanic activity on Mauna Loa and Kilauea Crater brought more artists to the Hawaiian Islands than ever before. The resulting trend, dubbed "The Volcano School" (also termed the "Little Hawaiian Renaissance"), prompted a vast range of spectacular paintings of the Kilauea Volcano and Diamond Head. Artists such as Charles Ferneaux (c. 1835–1913), Joseph D. Strong (1852–1899), and Jules Tavernier (1844–1889) came from America (Ferneaux and Strong) and France (Tavernier) to see the legendary volcanic eruptions. Though they painted and drew a wide variety of subjects, their volcano paintings are considered to be the most striking and memorable of the era. Increasing numbers of Hawaiian residents were developing a taste for collecting artwork, and the familiar subject of the volcano was an extremely popular one. In particular, the families of the early missionaries had the financial means and the desire to encourage a major increase in artistic activity.

Ferneaux, Strong, and Tavernier all employed relatively similar methods in their works on volcanoes. They undertook often difficult and dangerous climbs to attain the most dramatic vantage points and positioned themselves to make quick, skillful sketches. Because of the noxious gases and heat, it would have been impossible to execute finished pieces *en plein air*,[12] so these were completed later on in their studios. For the most part, their paintings retained an impressive amount of the spontaneity and freshness of their sketches, capturing the flow of lava and the vigor of the actual eruptions. Excellent examples of these successful paintings are Ferneaux's *Night View 1880–80, Eruption from Hilo Bay* (c. 1881, oil on canvas) and Tavernier's *Kilauea by Night* (c. 1887, oil on canvas). The public reception of their prolific bodies of work was overwhelmingly positive, and Tavernier is still regarded by many today as the all-time greatest painter of the volcano.

Sculpture, Printmaking, and Photography

While landscape of everything from Hawaiian volcanoes to pastoral scenes dominated the development of painting in the Pacific Region, other forms of media were also becoming more prominent at this time. Particularly in the last decade of the nineteenth century, sculpture, printmaking, and photography were bursting onto the scene as legitimate art forms. Civic enhancement during the post–Civil War years prompted the rapid spread of new public buildings and spaces, often in the neoclassical style, and sculptors found ample work in beautifying these sites. The growing availability of printmaking machinery and materials allowed artists to explore this medium that had previously been reserved largely for illustration and reproduction. Photographers began to realize the potential for taking their trade beyond accurate recording of images and to push the boundaries of photography into the realm of formal aesthetics.

Sculptors Douglas Tilden (1869–1935), Julia Bracken Wendt (1871–1942), and Arthur Putnam (1873–1930) were three of the premier artists of the West Coast. Their work embraced the popular Beaux Arts style and helped to put American sculpture on the map. As the glorification of America and its history was the prevailing trend, bronze and marble sculpture was often executed in service of memorializing important people and events. Tilden's *Memorial to the California Volunteers* (1906, bronze) still stands today in San Francisco as a prime example of the tremendous skill displayed by the American sculptors in commemorating regional and national history.

Printmakers, though less concerned with monumental commemoration, due to the nature of the media in which they worked, also gained recognition for the leaps and bounds by which they advanced their artwork. Working in woodcut,[13] monotype,[14] and etching,[15] printmakers advanced their craft beyond mere representation of extant imagery and capitalized on formal innovation. Printmaker Clark Hobart (1870–1948) was one such artist. His monotype print *Spirits of the Cypress* (1915) is obviously unconcerned with naturalism; instead, it captures, as its title suggests, the "spirit" of the cypress tree. The cool, winding greens and blues, set off by splashes of warm earth tones, invite the viewer to experience the essence of nature rather than a strict reproduction of it. While this type of expressiveness had belonged previously to the realm of painters, printmakers were now delving into the realm of abstraction and aestheticism.

Photographers at this time were also experimenting with diverging techniques. One of these was the documentary style, in which the photographer would capture moments from significant events, like the monumental sculptors, or everyday scenes, like the American genre painters. Popular subjects in the West were photographic essays on Native Americans, "exotic" cultures, dramatic scenery, and the lives of farmers. Special emphasis was placed on portraying people as individuals, rather than stereotypical images. Carleton Watkins (1829–1916) was one of the greatest of these photographers. His photographs of the Pacific Northwest reveal the haunting natural beauty and individuality of some of the most sublime terrain in the country.

The other emerging trend, known as Camera Pictorialism, was drastically different than the straightforward documentary style. Camera Pictorialists experimented with everything from focus, light, and vantage points to chemical processing and gloss finish to achieve unusual effects. This technique generally reduced regular images to their pure, formal characteristics, obscuring reality to achieve abstracted aesthetics or painterly qualities. Anne Brigman (1869–1950), who was born in Hawai'i and then moved to California, was the premier Pictorialist of her time. In 1949, she published a book of her poems and photographs titled *Songs of a Pagan*, containing photographs of nudes juxtaposed with trees and rocks, provocatively blurring the line between human and nature.

The advances in photography, painting, printmaking, and sculpture in the latter half of the nineteenth century and the early twentieth century were indicative of the dynamic nature of artists in the Pacific Region. Their innovative uses of traditional art forms would continue to expand and redefine the art world throughout the twentieth and twenty-first centuries. Artists, inspired by the vibrant culture of the Pacific Region, would climb to the forefront of the art scene and eventually rival the epicenters of the East Coast, France, Germany, Italy, and England as the latest Western artistic hotbed. With the twentieth century came a veritable explosion of new styles, and the Pacific Region could count itself among the pioneers of the newest and most exciting movements in art history.

The Modern Era

To definitively pin down the exact dates of the modern era is to attempt the impossible. So many movements, artists, and regions overlapped and influenced each other that it is difficult to deduce where and when things started, where they developed, and when they ended, if they ended at all. With regard to the evolution of artistic style, though, the modern era can be considered to have started roughly in 1890 and to have "ended" just before the Americans entered World War II. However, while the timeline of the modern era is problematic, the general qualities are fairly straightforward. Rather than simply trying to imitate reality, modernists focused on departing from tradition and inventing new forms of expression. From Impressionism to Surrealism to Geometric Abstraction, modernists constantly questioned the standard perception of reality and aimed toward uncovering novel inroads into understanding new ways to represent the world around them.

In the Pacific Region, artists simultaneously pioneered their own techniques as they observed and emulated styles from around the world. Two of the most influential events on artists of the modern era were the Armory Show (New York, 1913) and the Panama Pacific International Exposition (San Francisco, 1915). The Armory Show, though it took place on the East Coast, had a tremendous effect on art across the entire United States. The show exhibited over 1,250 paintings, sculptures, and decorative works by artists from both Europe and America, and though it was lambasted by many critics, it would forever change the face of American art.

The modernist's chief aim at the time was to raise awareness of the changing definition of fine art and open up new possibilities for expression, and the Armory Show brought these values to the attention of a surprised, if not scandalized, public.

Impressionism

The Panama Pacific International Exposition of 1915, though not focused only on modernism, brought together over 4,500 works by American artists, in addition to roughly the same number by artists from other countries. All of the most recent artistic movements were represented, including French Impressionism. It is thrilling to imagine what this would have been like for the artists of the Pacific Region, many of whom had never before seen original works by French Impressionists. At the exposition, they came face to face with styles they had only previously glimpsed in magazine pictures. Though modernism had long since been established in Europe, the Pacific Region was generally far behind the latest artistic trends. A few artists, such as George Gardner Symons (1861–1930) and William Wendt (1865–1946), had experimented with Impressionism, but they were clearly in a minority. Not until the Panama Pacific International Exposition would West Coast artists start to make the leap from being several decades behind the latest movements to being right on the cutting edge.

Impressionism quickly caught fire in the Pacific Region. The arid landscapes of Southern California were perfect material for impressionistic splashes of light, while the extraordinary coastal views of Northern California, Washington, and Oregon seemed ideal for broken brushwork and bird's-eye views. In Hawai'i, the bright, tropical landscapes and glowing volcanoes could not have been better suited to the Impressionistic style.

Southern California can claim to be the birthplace of Impressionism on the West Coast. Symons and Wendt, having experimented with their own interpretations of the style for many years, came into their own with the influence of the Panama Pacific International Exposition. Wendt's *Where Nature's God Hath Wrought* (1925, oil on canvas) is a beautiful example of landscape that lent itself exquisitely to Impressionism. This view of the area around Los Angeles depicts the juxtaposition of rocky hills and mountains with a dry, grassy foreground, cast in golden light that evokes a feeling of the peacefulness in the time of day just before the sun begins to set. Signs of human presence in the landscape are only hinted at; Wendt obviously sought to portray an image of land forged by a divine presence.

Another early Impressionist in the Pacific Region was Childe Hassam (1859–1935), who worked extensively

Panama Pacific International Exposition of 1915. Courtesy of the Library of Congress.

in Portland, Oregon. Southeast Oregon's Harney Desert inspired Hassam to create nearly forty paintings of that area alone, which were eagerly snapped up by Portland collectors. One of the most lauded artists of the Panama Pacific International Exposition, Hassam exhibited no less than thirty-eight paintings there, all in a room of their own. Hassam's fascination with the smattering of arid climates in the Pacific Region would keep him traveling and painting up and down the West Coast for many years.

Impressionism in Hawai'i, though not so directly influenced by the Panama Pacific International Exposition, was flourishing as well. In 1917, the Hawaiian Society of Artists was formed when artists recognized the need for a unified group to promote the arts. Soon after came the Honolulu Art Society in 1919, a group that contributed significantly to establishing Hawai'i's first permanent art museum. Through their tireless work and promotion through art exhibits, it became apparent that Hawai'i was beginning to fully embrace modernism.

Among these prominent artists were D. Howard Hitchcock (1861–1943), Lionel Walden (1861–1933), William Twigg-Smith (1883–1950), and Esther Mabel Crawford (1872–1958). The work of these artists, though representative of varying individual styles, demonstrates a distinctly Impressionistic influence. Hitchcock's *Kona Shore* (1934, oil on canvas) is an example of his break with an earlier, more conservative style and a move toward the more modern approach that seemed so well suited to the Hawaiian seascape. Walden's *Luakaha: Evening* (c. 1916, oil on canvas) shows the Impressionistic treatment of the Hawaiian tropics, with glowing amber skies and mountains set against cool foliage in the foreground. Twigg-Smith chose a more urban subject for his work *Hilo Sampans* (1917, oil on canvas) and applied the painterly techniques of the Impressionists to a harbor scene. Esther Mabel Crawford's *Chinese Rice Farm, Hanalei, Kanai* (1929, oil on canvas) is a Cézannesque landscape depicting workers in a rice paddy, though the workers draw little focus. Crawford shows herself a true master of color and brushwork with this painting; the combination of hazy blues, greens, and violets with splashes of bright reds and yellows gives the palpable sensation of a balmy day in the fields.

Postimpressionism

Overlapping the period of Impressionism, the influence of Postimpressionism also found its way to the artists of Hawai'i. Though the movement had long since peaked in Europe, artists such as Juliette May Fraser (1887–1983), Joseph Henry Sharp (1859–1953), Cornelia MacIntyre Foley (1909–   ), and Arman T. Manookian (1904–1931) display distinct echoes of Postimpressionism in their work. From poignant portraits to scenes of marine life, their paintings exhibit the solid formal characteristics that would eventually evolve as a whole into movements like Cubism and Abstraction. For example, Fraser's *Lei Sellers ("Change, Please")* (c. 1941, oil on canvas) is a masterful harmony of strong form and color celebrating the peaceful era in Honolulu before the bombing of Pearl Harbor. Fraser's bold use of the palette knife and a veritable spectrum of primary colors lend this work a stunning vibrancy, and the thick, black, linear outlines around the figures give them visible weight and presence. It would be a short step from this style into the more radical forms of modern art.

Artists on the U.S. West Coast were also shifting from straight Impressionism to Postimpressionism. While Impressionism had largely come from imitation of styles that had evolved elsewhere, Postimpressionism in the Pacific Region had a more organic development. It was pure in the sense that it was not mere appropriation of a European style that had peaked over twenty years earlier, but it grew naturally out of experimentation with Impressionism, pushing the style farther toward subjectivity of the individual artist. Though the results often resembled European work stylistically, this was due to the inherent proclivity of the artist to gravitate toward modes of expression that best suited his or her needs, rather than straight mimesis. On the West Coast, this meant that Postimpressionistic work began to resemble that of the Fauvists[16] in France and the expressive brushwork of Van Gogh, rather than the more formulaic Pointillism.[17]

After the Panama Pacific International Exposition, Impressionism in the Pacific Region quickly progressed into Postimpressionism, and artists began experimenting with innovative uses of light and color. The West Coast's first official group of modern artists, the Society of Six, epitomized the prevailing attitude of the new modernists; they painted purely for the delight of pleasing the eye. There was no underlying intellectual message in their work other than the communication and visual interpretation of the beauty in their surroundings. The artists that made up the Society of Six—Selden Connor Gile (1877–1947), August Gay (1890–1949), Maurice Logan (1886–1977), Louis Siegriest (1899–1989), Bernard von Eichman (1899–1970), and William Henry Clapp (1879–1954)—can accurately be termed Postimpressionists because their styles grew out of reinterpreting and expanding themes that had their roots in Impressionism. Most of their styles were predominantly Fauvist, but Clapp, the last to join the Society, paradoxically remained a Pointillist. His work *Poplars at Hayward* (n.d., oil on canvas) exemplifies his mastery of this difficult and disciplined technique.

Postimpressionism spread rapidly throughout the entire Pacific Region, and even if it lagged behind European Postimpressionism on the timeline, Pacific artists imbued it with an energy and vitality that distinguished it as its own legitimate regional style. Artists used Postimpressionism to express their own visions of widely diverse subject matter, from the seaside art colonies of the coast to the painters of deserts, Native Americans, cowboys, and even urban landscapes. Concerned more with expression of a particular theme or mood than with naturalistic representation, this tendency toward subjectivity would lead artists further down the modernist road toward Abstraction, Cubism, and Surrealism, as well as more nontraditional forms such as assemblage and metal sculpture.

Abstract Art

Abstraction, as a pure concept, can be concisely defined as that which either extracts from an image its most basic formal characteristics or has no beginning or end in natural representation. Translation of this process from concept to actual works of art, however, can take an infinite variety of forms. Some artists use living models, everyday scenery, or still life as subject matter to be manipulated, while others work solely through their own impetus, or what is known as automatism.[18] Styles emerged, ranging from Synchronism to Abstract Expressionism, freeing artists to express themselves in whatever methods suited their aims. The definition of art itself became completely fluid, encompassing whatever style or medium one chose to invent or perpetuate.

Synchronism, developed by California artist Stanton MacDonald Wright (1890–1973), is a form of Abstraction based on color relationships. In *Conception Synchrony* (1915, oil on canvas) Wright demonstrates the underlying concept of Synchronism: reproducing actions of the human body or spatial positioning of a stationary object through the interaction of warm and cool colors. His idea, widely accepted by color theorists, was that color relationships reproduce the sensations of physically projecting or receding in space through formulaic arrangements. Though Synchronism did not catch on as a major movement, it encompasses one of the main themes of Abstraction: Naturalistic representation is not necessary to convey the essence of subject matter.

More mainstream forms of Abstraction tended toward Minimalism, Cubism, Abstract Expressionism, and Surrealism. Minimalists, influenced by European artists Piet Mondrian (1872–1944) and Ad Reinhardt (1913–1967), distilled natural forms down to their most basic formal elements, line and color. While some of these were manifested as geometric compositions in basic primary colors, others followed more organic formats, where the artist would simply record the most basic impressions of curves, lines, colors, and shapes. West Coast artist Edward Corbett (1919–1971) exhibited this looser type of minimalism in his work *Mt. Holyoke #2* (1960, oil on canvas). Here the impression of a mountain is nothing more than subtle gradations of mauves and pinks, the sky behind it suggested in white, with the merest hint of lavender shading.

Cubism, pioneered by Spanish artist Pablo Picasso (1881–1973), had its influence on artists of the Pacific Region, though it never took hold there as a major movement. The style's influence can be seen in the work of Los Angeles artist Knudd Merrild (1894–1954). Merrild essentially broke apart three-dimensional subjects into two-dimensional space, simultaneously representing all angles. He also experimented with manipulating two-dimensional surfaces by physically cutting out parts and raising others beyond the surface of the picture plane. His piece *Volume and Space Organization* (1933, paint, wood, and metal) exhibits these techniques, melding together the practices of both painting and sculpture.

Abstract Expressionism took hold of the art scene in the Pacific Region most visibly during the years following World War II. The idea behind it, looking within oneself rather than to the outside world for inspiration, was a particularly poignant one during these years of rebuilding and reflection. Hassel Smith (b. 1915) was one of the West Coast artists who embraced the Expressionistic style in order to move viewers to experience joy and celebrate life, rather than dwell on the somber mood of a nation that had just been through a harrowing experience. Smith's painting *The Buffalo Dance* (1960, oil on canvas), though completed over a decade after the end of the war, encapsulates this whimsical spirit. Though there is no discernible buffalo as the subject of the work, the title reflects the playfulness of the work itself. Other West Coast artists, such as James Budd Dixon (1900–1967), would eschew even the most cursory references to tangible objects and revel in the play of color and form for its own sake. Dixon's *Red and Green #1* (1948, oil on canvas) is this type of work; no recognizable realistic subject matter can be found in either the work itself or the title. It is merely a pure expression of emotion, played out in bright color and set off by black negative space.

Surrealism

Surrealism, though not a major movement in the Pacific Region, nevertheless became the preferred style of a number of West Coast artists in the 1940s. Surrealists worked within one of two main methods: illusionism, which involved combining realistic representation of subject matter arranged in unrealistic combinations; or automatism, which called for the artist to create straight from the subconscious. Eugene Berman (1899–1972) worked in the illusionistic style that had been made famous in the United States by Salvador Dalí (1904–1989). Berman's *Nike* (1943, oil on canvas) displays the odd juxtaposition of a woman robed in red with an additional figure apparently transporting a rocklike form on its head. Though not meant to convey any particular narrative, this type of image is meant to invoke the logic of dreams or the doorway to the subconscious. The alternative strain of Surrealism, automatism, can be seen in the work of Stanley William Hayter (1901–1988), a Parisian artist who had been driven into exile on the American West Coast during World War II. Hayter worked with a variety of materials, from paint to acid, splashing them onto canvases or etching plates to create lines and color forms and layering compositions to create pieces based on exploration of movement and space.

Nontraditional Art

Though many artists worked in the two-dimensional formats of painting, drawing, and printmaking, this dynamic period of modernism also paved the way for artists working in more nontraditional formats. Metal sculpture and assemblage became very popular among the Pacific Regional artists, prompting everything from miniature to colossal-sized works, small collages to mural-sized assemblages. These three-dimensional works followed the same tenant as the two-dimensional works; it was no longer necessary to ground a work of art in an empirically realistic theme or subject. Exploration of the potential inherent in different media, or the compulsion of the artist to manipulate material for its own sake, was reason enough to create.

Metal sculptures by Ernest Mundt (1905–1933) and Claire Falkenstein (1908–1997) demonstrate the boundless innovation of Pacific Regional artists in this period. Mundt's *Desire* (1945, brass and copper wire) is an example of miniature sculpture that encompasses the ideals of Expressionism. The complex forms of twisting wire extend outward as if prompted by a jolt of electricity, evoking spontaneity even in a work that must have been carefully constructed. Falkenstein's *Structure and Flow #2 (Wave)* (1965, copper tubing and glass) reveals a similar propensity but on a much larger scale. Again, though much time and effort must have been employed in the placement of materials, the overall sense of this sculpture is one of chaos, imagination, and the potential for movement.

In the Pacific Region, sculptors, painters, printmakers, and artists working in other media had by the peak of the modern era caught up with their European counterparts. The onset of mass culture and the immediacy of communication had propelled artists into a completely new area, where innovation took precedence over technical skill. Novel concepts and styles became the ultimate goal, hurling artists into a veritable race toward the next stages of development. For the past several centuries, American artists had either lagged behind or kept an even pace in that race, but by the second half of the twentieth century, they would begin a lasting trend of vying for, and often taking, the lead.

Artists from Minority Cultures

Even before the civil rights movement began sweeping across the nation in the 1950s and 1960s, minority artists were making their voices heard in the Pacific Region. The large Asian American population in Seattle and Hawai'i was stimulating interest in collecting art of the Far East, as well as encouraging absorption of the culture and philosophy that went hand in hand with Asian art. California's Latino artists both worked to preserve their artistic heritage and made grand political statements through works such as large murals. African American artists, inspired by the Harlem Renaissance of the 1920s, made great advancements by ceasing to imitate European styles and deriving techniques and subject matter from African traditions. Native Americans began, once again, to protest the U.S. government and their long history of violating Native Americans' rights. Feminists, gays, and lesbians also found their voices, promoting their ideals and values in art that demanded recognition of their presence and rights in America. While art had always been, to a degree, a reflection of the culture from which it originated, it was now taking a more active role. Rather than merely reflecting ideas, it was fast becoming the perfect medium to instigate political change.

Asian American Artists

Asian Americans, a term that encompasses a broad range of people—those of Indian, Indonesian, Philippino, Vietnamese, Chinese, Japanese, or Korean descent—had contributed to the growth of art in the Pacific Region for many years. After World War II, however, new American immigration laws encouraged a major rise in immigration from the Pacific's Eastern rim. Asian themes and styles, which had evolved over millennia, began to merge with American styles with increasing intensity. Artists such as Masami Teraoka (b. 1936) displayed the conflation of traditional Japanese art with American art in both style and imagery. Teraoka's humorous narrative series *McDonald's Hamburgers Invading Japan* (1975, watercolor) describes the sense of clashing cultures in an accessible format. Hung Liu (b. 1948), who identified both as a feminist and as a Chinese American artist, employed both photography and painting to make her statements on minority issues. In *Judgment of Paris* (1992, oil on canvas, lacquered wood), Liu turned to antique imagery to present the confusing combination of Eastern and Western standards of beauty and femininity. Even today, the melding of cultures is still a major issue in Asian American art.

Hung Liu's *The Maiden*. Courtesy of the Library of Congress.

African American Artists

African Americans had little presence, population-wise, in the Pacific Region before World War II, but in the second half of the twentieth century, the advancement of northern urban industrial centers prompted a large, northward migration of blacks coming from the South in search of steady work. Once in the Pacific Region, they formed strong communities and worked to promote awareness of African American cultural heritage by combining traditional African iconography with contemporary issues. Sculptures, paintings, and especially large wall murals were excellent media for making bold statements; they beautified the neighborhoods, reinforced positive values, and taught younger generations about pride and respect. In the last forty years, tremendous advancements have been made in support of African American art. Samella Lewis (b. 1924), for example, who has spent much of her life in California, was one of the first people to set up galleries and periodicals devoted exclusively to African American art. Largely influenced by her groundbreaking work, art museums, art educational institutions, and cultural societies devoted to the promotion of African American art and culture have sprung up and continue to appear all over the Pacific Region.

63

Native American Artists

Native Americans in the Pacific Region were also finding their voice during the post–World War II years. While many of their artists aim to preserve ancient traditions through works in ceramics, weaving, and leather and bead work, others combine their traditional imagery with modern materials and methods. The irony of this combination is often palpable and intentional, simultaneously bridging contrasting cultures and belief systems while underscoring their fundamental differences. California artist Frank L. Day (1902–1976) of the Konkow Maidu tribe spent over a decade traveling across North America to learn about different tribal traditions and used oil on canvas to express his conceptions of the stories he had gathered. His works, such as *Toto Dance at Bloomer Hill* (1973, oil on canvas), are reminiscent of folk art and aim more toward overall content and symbolism than Western ideas of perspective and realism. His body of work as a whole chronicles the heritage of many Native American tribes, leaving an important visual record of their customs and beliefs. Other Native American artists, such as Frank D. Tuttle, Jr. (b. 1957), turned to abstraction to achieve similar ends. Though nonrepresentational, abstract Native American art is often used as a formal means to depict the symbols and legends so vital to the identity of the Native American tribes.

Latino Artists

Bold statements about cultural issues also rose to the forefront of the West Coast's large Latino population. Latinos—those of Mexican, Central American, or South American descent—had long been treated as second-class citizens in the United

A wall painting on a housing project in Boyle Heights depicts Che Guevera and reads "We are not a minority." © Stephanie Maze/Corbis.

States, and the second half of the twentieth century was time for radical changes. As activist César Chávez formed the United Farm Workers organization in 1962 to protest the treatment of fieldworkers, Latino artists did their part to raise awareness through posters, murals, and political cartoons. These works of art carried their message through scenes of proud workers, passionate written messages painted in eye-catching colors and styles, and attractive images of traditional activities. The thirty-two-foot mural *We are not a minority* (1979, acrylic on stucco), by the Chicanos en Aztlan, proudly declares a powerful message: Gone are the days of tolerating oppression. In a more symbolic format, the same message comes through in Willie Heron's (b. 1951) mural *The Wall That Cracked* (1972, enamel and acrylic on stucco). Not only did Heron execute a masterful scene of Chicanos breaking through the symbolic wall that separated them from their inalienable rights, but he also invited others to take up brushes and to add their own messages to the piece. Today, the mural still graces the side of the bakery on which it was originally painted, and people continue to contribute to its evolution in an ongoing communal message.

Feminist, Gay, and Lesbian Artists

Not only did ethnic minorities in the Pacific Region take up this powerful medium to express their political views, but women, gays, and lesbians also found ways to fight oppression through art. Spurred on by the women's liberation movement, Judy Chicago (b. 1939) and Miriam Shapiro (b. 1923) pioneered The Feminist Art Program in the early 1970s. Chicago and Shapiro developed a whole system of feminist iconography, turning traditional "female" symbols that had been primarily reinforced by male artists into statements of pride in females' unique attributes. Antiquated ideas of women's place in society, limited abilities, and "legitimate" female ambitions became ironic statements about the absurdity of female subjugation. The Feminist Art Program simultaneously honored the achievements of creative females from times past while breaking new ground for women's potential to make giant strides in the art world.

Another group that can be considered a minority—gays and lesbians—also made their presence known in Pacific Regional art. Though homoeroticism in art has been present for millennia, all over the world, it was rarely considered to be legitimate subject matter for American art until the second half of the twentieth century. Even as East Coast artists such as Thomas Eakins (1844–1916) painted homoerotic scenes in the nineteenth century—usually under the guise of physical fitness or leisure activity studies—the homosexual element remained largely unacknowledged. The gay liberation movement had its origins in 1950s Los Angeles and San Francisco, though homosexually oriented art did not become mainstream until the 1970s, even if Beats, hippies, Bohemians, and other countercultural groups had accepted homosexuality as a significant and perfectly acceptable part of life long before mass culture was ready to do the same. Scenes of gay, lesbian, and transgender lifestyles, only some of which contained erotic elements, became the artistic way of raising awareness for the rest of the American public. Fine art, poster art, street art, graphic art, and performance art were and still are utilized as media for art by and about gays and lesbians. San Francisco, home to one of the largest gay and lesbian populations in the world, has been the most prolific city in the Pacific Region, turning out a magnitude of art with gay and lesbian themes.

Just as other minority groups create art to promote their cultures, gays and lesbians, who to this day fight a difficult battle for rights and acceptance, often use art for political or personal statements on pride, self-love, and identity.

While art of minority groups is by no means limited to the Pacific Region, there is a certain element, though difficult to discern, of life on the U.S. West Coast and Hawai'i that seems to draw out the rebellious spirit in its artists. Ethnic minorities, feminists, gays, and lesbians have been extremely active in the Pacific Regional art scene for centuries, even as different cultures expressed resistance to their messages. Art has always been an ideal way to express—allegorically, expressionistically, or sometimes literally—the desire for radical change.

Postmodernism to Contemporary Art

Pinning down the exact dates of the postmodern era in art is just as problematic as creating a specific timeline for modern art. Because postmodernism is still very much a part of the Pacific Regional art scene today, it is difficult to take an art historical perspective on the movement as a whole. Its characteristics are as fluid as the wide variety of cultural advancement that influences it. It is, however, safe to say that the recent output of minority art had a tremendous impact on ushering in the postmodern era. The spirit of pluralism inherent in art coming from a range of individuals and groups is what distinguishes the beginning of the postmodern era; the focus shifted from attainment of universal expression to the acceptance of many different forms of expression. Emphasis on the individual, the unique, the innovative became imperative. Though art critics and historians religiously attempted to streamline art into a unified phase, they eventually accepted the legitimacy of an era that could scarcely be contained under one umbrella term. From the 1970s into present day, art of the Pacific Region has evolved into a confusing yet stimulating array of styles that can be grouped together by, if nothing else, their eclecticism.

As any style, revival, imitation, or satirization of art has been fair game for the past thirty years, it is only possible to provide a brief sampling of those trends that comprise the postmodern era in the Pacific Region. From the need to identify with ancient traditions to the desire to broaden the very definition of art, Pacific Regional artists have turned out work that pleases, amazes, and provokes its viewers. As the pace of life around the world has sped up to a rate that leaves the general public breathless to keep up, so has the artistic output changed and expanded at a dizzying rate. Though it has morphed into an amalgam of mixed messages, it embodies the spirit of the diverse culture that produces it. Artists of Hawai'i, Washington, Oregon, and California, whether they embrace globalization or hold fast to individual tradition, are all part of the exciting drive toward capturing the spirit of multiculturalism.

In Hawai'i, the twentieth century brought tremendous changes to the landscape, economy, and industry of the islands. It would be impossible today, with its towering high-rises and widespread tourism, to characterize Hawai'i as the pristine, untrammeled jewel of the Pacific that it once was. Like the rest of the Pacific Region, these traits can only be observed in national or state parks and reserves. Rather than struggle to domesticate the land, the emphasis has been placed on preservation. No ground remains uncharted; the land and the old ways of life are the responsibilities of those that work for their continuance. Artists have taken up this cause in many forms, from promoting native traditions to reflecting the changes that modern life has brought. The establishment of the State Foundation on Culture and the Arts in 1965 positioned Hawaiian artists to work within a network of excellent support and education in achieving their vital contributions to this growing trend of individuality and reflexivity.

Hawaiian artists such as Satoru Abe (b. 1926), Dorothy Faison (b. 1955), Tadashi Sato (b. 1923), and Doug Young (b. 1951) are just four members of the bustling Hawaiian art community that has been such a force in contemporary art. Abe, who works in both painting and sculpture, produces fascinating works in both mediums. *One Tree* (1985, copper and bronze) displays a juxtaposition of organic shapes with man-made imagery, evoking the struggle between human's need to both dominate and appreciate nature in a montage of pattern and chaos. Faison's work, while both autobiographical and universal, reflects the spirit of postmodernism in its combinations of feminine and geometric imagery—vibrant color with solid, flat forms. In *Ritual Protection* (1993, oil on canvas) Faison communicates a melding of the natural with the abstract, providing an enticing look at the possibility of gendered forms coming together in space. Sato, influenced by Hawaiian artist Isami Doi (1903–1965), uses conceptual art together with formal abstraction to. create works that speak of nature from a personal standpoint.

On the U.S. West Coast, artists work with similar themes in equally varied media. Rick Bartow (b. 1946), Paul Berger (b. 1948), William Morris (b. 1957), and David Simpson (b. 1928) provide a small yet diverse cross section of the plethora of styles and media in which Pacific Regional artists reflect their fluctuating worlds. Bartow fuses traditional Native American imagery with contemporary aesthetics in works such as *Wolf and Deer* (1993, charcoal, pastel, graphite on paper), reflecting his own personal search for identity. A Vietnam veteran, perhaps in search of catharsis, Bartow lays himself bare in his work, freely expressing those conflicting needs and desires that are so familiar to contemporary Americans. Berger represents those artists who are moving beyond even the "traditional norms" of postmodernism and incorporates digitized imagery into contemporary art. Originally a photographer in the filmic sense, Berger now combines computers, digital cameras, and graphics into his artillery, refusing to ignore the place that modern technology occupies in everyday life. His work *World 2AA* (1989, inkjet print) incorporates the latest technology of the time into iconic imagery, layering scanned video stills, photographs, and computerized linear drawing in the medium of pixels on a computer monitor. Morris, a sculptor who works with materials too numerous to list, explores the dichotomy of death and the affirmation of life. His work explores the idea of the remains of things once living, manipulated to encourage a particularly life-affirming point of view. A gifted glass artist, his *Cineary Urns*, some of his finest glass work, was created as a deeply personal response to September 11, 2001. David Simpson (b. 1928) comments on human psychological space in a manner both individual and universal, adopting the popular modernist style of hard-edge geometric abstraction. With this choice, Simpson calls into question the personal attachment to a decades-old style as a feasible means to look into human psychology. In Simpson's *Gradiva's Palace* (1976, acrylic on canvas), the vast blackness of the canvas, punctuated by only a single, narrow strip of umber, viewers may figuratively wander through the space in any manner their minds choose to take them.

Contemporary art is so complex and diverse that the truth is worth repeating:

The Pacific Region has entered a time of uncertainty, as confusing as it is stimulating. It is up to the individual artist to determine the most effective way to communicate whatever force drives him or her to create art. Judgment of merit can no longer be grounded in any presently dominant aesthetic but must be placed in the context of each individual artist's experience. Though this has to some degree always been the case with art, now more than ever the emphasis is on the individual as a conduit of the combined influences, training, and skill level afforded each artist. To be sure, art of differing styles and media will always find acceptance in some way, whether it is merely the personal satisfaction of the creator or worldwide recognition.

A true melting pot of cultures and ethnicities, the Pacific Region produces art that speaks not only to all of its residents but to an entire world full of people who are perhaps learning the value of their own ability to contribute something of themselves. It is within this spirit of multiplicity that the artists of the Pacific Region find their inspiration and, through the needs of public yearning for fresh vision, that they continue to view and interpret a changing world through changing eyes. In possession of a past as stimulating and revolutionary as that of any other area of the world, Pacific Regional art displays a wide range of reactions to this history. Whether its artists express reflection, appreciation, outrage, or desire for change, the causal element is almost always grounded in the dynamic nature of its evolution. This evolution has not only brought the Pacific Regional art scene to the place it occupies today—at the forefront of artistic innovation—but, perhaps more important, it has provided a supportive environment that regards its artists as a vital component of its infrastructure. Art has and will continue to have significant value in the Pacific Region and as such both mirrors and enriches the lives of its diverse communities.

While it is true that certain techniques, processes and functions do bind the many artistic communities and geographies together within the Pacific Region, the vast cultural differences have also created sub-regional and even counter-regional movements. Hawai'i's isolated position, for example, created a separate visual aesthetic, one that is interpreted in specific cultural and even political ways by Native Hawaiians. That aesthetic is influenced by the growing political cry for Hawaiian sovereignty, but we can also see, historically, that Hawaii has been less influenced by European artistic traditions than the mainland. Similarly, Alaska, separated by not simply an ocean but a whole country, inhabits an isolated position, one that Alaskans have in many ways cherished. Like the Hawaiian sovereignty movement, heritage preservation movements in Alaskan culture have become more prominent lately, but they have always existed. Thus, Alaskan Native art provides a key to the culture, one that can be read visually, aesthetically, and accurately.

ALASKA NATIVE ART

Protecting a Precious Heritage

Archeological evidence indicates that Alaska Natives have inhabited parts of Alaska for at least 10,000 years. Anthropologists believe they originated in Asia and migrated to present-day Alaska by walking across the Bering Land Bridge or by traveling in boats. The oral history carries stories of migrations from the south also. However, many Alaska Natives believe they did not come from another place but had origins in Alaska from the very beginning.

All Alaska Native traditions possess oral accounts of a Great Flood and of subsequent migrations of their people to higher, dry land. Some of them went to the interior of Canada; others to southern shores. When the waters subsided in southeast Alaska, the people returned to the coast, traveling down rivers, under and over glaciers, returning to the land rich with resources they knew would sustain them. Clans relate these oral narratives of migration at public gatherings.

Between 1741 and 1784, Alaska and its resources were sought after by both Russian and English explorers. In 1784, the first white settlement was established in Alaska on Kodiak Island by the Russian government. Russians coveted the elegant fur of the sea otter for trade. In 1867, Alaska was purchased by the United States from Czarist Russia, and a new form of government dominated.

The practice of creating Alaska Native art, which is an intimate part of the culture, experienced major cultural disruption with European and American contact. Visitors, who came to exploit Alaska's natural resources, brought new ways of perceiving the world, different types of behavior and religious beliefs that they imposed upon the local populations. This resulted in the forced cessation of traditional Native ceremonies and the creation of the accoutrements that accompanied them. Totems and regalia were burned; potlatches ceased; masked dances were banned. Shamanistic practices were forbidden.

It was not until the early 1970s that both the Western and traditional societies living in Alaska began to realize that a very rich and meaningful tradition was almost totally lost. Native people began looking to this lost heritage in order to find out who they were and where they came from in order to pass this legacy on to their children. Language revitalization programs were formed. Cultural programs were reinitiated. Ceremonial practices like potlatches, winter ceremonies, and bladder festivals were given new life. Art began to flourish again. With the help of the few living Native elders left who knew the history, museum collections that had preserved the artwork, and archeological excavations that returned material items reflecting tradition, Alaska Native culture and art are again flourishing.

Cultural heritage programs and legislation like the Silver Hand Program,[19] which provides authentication of Alaska Native artwork, the Marine Mammal Protection Act,[20] which protects traditional subsistence materials for Alaska Natives' use and the Native American Graves Protection and Repatriation Act (NAGPRA),[21] which returns objects of cultural patrimony and funerary items to Native groups, assist in this effort to preserve and sustain this important heritage.

The Term *Art* in Alaskan Languages

The term *art* does not exist in the indigenous languages of Alaska's Native people. What is recognized and called art today was for Alaska Native people a means of decorating utilitarian items, displaying lineage or empowering physical objects with spirit. The concept of art for art's sake did not take form until European explorers and visitors arrived in the North in the eighteenth century, and the local people realized the ornamentation they had been giving to their clothing, containers, implements, and tools was sought by these visitors. It was as a result of this contact that ivory began to be carved into sculptures for sale rather than used as amulets to ensure luck for the hunter, and masks were made without see-through eyes, no longer meant to be worn but hung on a wall as works of art. Therefore, when the term *art* is used, it is in this context and for lack of a better word to describe the unique visual creations of Alaska's first people.

There are eight major cultural groups living in Alaska today, their distinctions being mainly linguistic: Inupiat, Yup'ik, Athabascan, Alutiiq, Aleut, Tlingit, Haida, and Tsimshian. There are also cultural variations influenced by lineage, history, and physical environments. The eight Alaska Native cultures are diverse. Twenty-one distinct languages were originally spoken, and the groups, to this day, maintain strong ties to their respective regions. Local environments and resources created differences in the food they ate, the types of transportation they utilized, their dwellings, the distances they needed to travel to obtain food, and their ability to establish and maintain permanent dwelling sites.

Despite the cultural and environmental differences, Alaska Native people shared many characteristics. Their economy was based on a subsistence use of the land. They were all hunters and gatherers and did not engage in agriculture. This implied a need to travel long distances from their settlements in order to obtain subsistence resources. This way of life strongly influenced the imagery and meaning depicted in their art. Animals were taken for food and clothing, but no part of the animal was wasted. The use of animal parts for artistic expression was common, influenced by availability and spiritual beliefs. Skins, antlers, whiskers, fur, baleen, feathers, tusks, teeth, intestines, and bones were used in innovative ways. Natural materials taken from the land were also utilized: grass, roots, and bark for baskets; wood for carved implements, boats, masks, and sculpture; stone for tools and carvings; clay, lichens, bark, minerals, and berries for dyes.

As there was no written language among these groups, history and mythology were related through stories told orally. These were also used to educate the young by passing on cultural values and beliefs. Much of the art gives visual image to these stories.

Another similar characteristic was reverence and respect for the land and animals that provided for the people, a symbiotic relationship that was valued above all else. Respect was key; when it was absent, the resources often disappeared, and the people went hungry. This was viewed as a spiritual relationship with all of nature and is quite apparent in the art. Alaska Natives were conscious caretakers of the environment because of this spiritual relationship.

Becoming aware of these cultural and environmental influences promotes an understanding of why the visual expressions have taken the forms they have. The physical and spiritual connection to place, to the land and sea, is a primary influence for Alaska Native art. The work also reflects the material available to the artist. As with most indigenous art, it emerged from a need to relate to the physical environment, to tell a particular story, to relate history or express a connection within the spiritual realm that includes both the animate and inanimate.

Masks were made by all of the Alaska Native cultures. Masks of animals and birds used in ceremony connected the wearer and the observer with the spirit world and made visual the intimate connection between man and animal. The oral history contains stories of this connection when all were one before animals, humans, birds, and fish were sorted out, each to their own kind.

Amulets carved in the form of the animal a hunter was seeking were used to ensure luck and to appease the spirit of the animal so that it might give itself to the hunter and return the following year. Other carvings were used to protect the hunter on his often-dangerous journey. A good example of this are the carvings placed on Yup'ik kayak stanchions, a smiling male (husband) face and a female (wife) frowning face placed symmetrically in the craft, symbolically creating balance and providing protection.[22]

Totem poles in the Southeast embellished with animal and human figures record the history and identity of a clan or group of people. They also illustrate how events that have taken place or stories from the oral history were used as symbols of honor for important people, or served as the final resting place for important tribal members.

Woven and folded containers were originally used for utilitarian purposes, to store and carry goods. Baskets were made by all of the Alaska Native groups but in varying styles and from the materials available to them in their respective regions. They displayed designs woven into the warp or weft using dyed material such as grasses or seal gut. Some had designs applied to the surface, carved onto lids or coiled into rows. After contact with Europeans, baskets became a prized market item, and the designs and purpose changed to suit the strangers' tastes.

Other types of containers included bentwood or carved boxes and bowls, gut and skin bags, fur and leather pouches and cases, and birch bark baby cradles.

Clothing was made from furs, skins, gut, and bark. The designs identified the person, family, or some aspect of the culture. Ceremonial regalia was more highly ornamented than everyday wear.

Today, with a cash-based economy, village life has transformed drastically, but Native people still rely heavily upon the land for materials for their art and the physical and spiritual sustenance it brings.

The Athabascans

The Athabascans are dwellers of the Interior, the boreal forest. They live along rivers, which are used for transportation in summer and winter. Due to the great geographical distances of the Interior and the scarcity of game in many years, the Athabascans often had to travel over hundreds of miles to hunt. Life was spent between three or four seasonal camps. Access to limited resources resulted in forming small groups rather than large villages. They spoke eleven distinct languages.

This mobile lifestyle did not allow time for the creation of objects other than the bare necessities. However, the Athabascans did become known for their skin and fur sewing and elaborate ornamentation on clothing employing porcupine quills and, later, beads.

Porcupine quillwork predates the use of cut glass beads before contact with Europeans. The quills were flattened, sewn down with sinew or woven into a sinew warp to create bands of embroidery on clothing and bags. The quills either were used in their natural color or were dyed with natural dyes extracted from berries, minerals, and bark.

The larger glass pony beads were introduced into Alaska in the eighteenth century by the Russians and were readily adopted. In 1847, Hudson's Bay Company forged its way into the Interior and set up a trading post at Fort Yukon on the Yukon River and supplied the smaller glass seed beads in trade for furs in compe-

Beadwork in Baby Belts or Straps

The most striking examples of beadwork being produced today are the baby belts or straps. Originally designed for carrying a baby on the back, these sought-after pieces have shown up in art collections worldwide. Often containing over 10,000 beads, the straps are roughly five feet long, five to six inches wide, and take six months to a year to create. Baby straps are made for newborns by grandmothers or other women close to the family as a special gift.

tition with the Russians. The women eagerly used them, drawn to the bright colors and textures that could be incorporated into their work. Early examples show a combination of quills and beads; later, only beads were used.

Dentalia, ocean mollusks obtained in trade with groups living in coastal areas, were also worked into the designs. Used on knife sheath straps, necklaces, and clothing, these items became signs of wealth and power; only a privileged few could wear them.

Floral designs have dominated Athabascan beadwork from early in the nineteenth century on and were probably introduced by Europeans.[23] The most-desired backing material for beadwork embroidery is Native-tanned smoked moose hide. When tanned properly, the skin becomes like felt and is easy to sew on. After contact, beadworkers started using felt with a backing of paper or other material for stiffness.

The other craft for which the Athabascans are known is their work with birch bark. Birch bark containers were used to store berries and other food for winter, were employed as cooking pots, and were used for carrying everything from just-gathered food to babies. For storage, grease was put on top of the food and a lid applied.

Two methods were used for cooking. If people were out on the trail and needed to cook food quickly, it was put into the birch bark container with water and placed directly over the fire. The burned container was then disposed of. The other method was to heat rocks and place them in the container that held water and the food. The water became hot and cooked the food.

Baskets were used to pick berries in the field and then transport them home. Baby carriers or cradles made of birch bark are the forerunners of the modern-day plastic carriers. The cradle was slung from ropes so it could be rocked or simply carried with the infant aboard. The Athabascan women today make beautiful baskets and produce colorful beadwork, all highly prized by collectors.

The Tlingit, Haida, and Tsimshian

In southeast Alaska, the Panhandle, the Tlingit reside with their Eyak neighbors to the north, and to the south, the Haida and Tsimshian people. The latter two groups migrated from Canada to settle in Alaska, the Tsimshian to Annette Island near Ketchikan and the Haida, who were originally from the Queen Charlotte Islands, to Prince of Wales Island. Eyak speakers are very few today.

Sarah Malcolm

Sarah Malcolm of Eagle (1905–1992) developed unique forms: a woman's sewing basket with compartments for all her sewing implements and cylindrical baskets, the patterns of which were derived from old metal coffee cans.

The Tlingit, Haida, and Tsimshian people belong to the Northwest Coast culture that calls the coast between Yakutat in Alaska through Canada south to Washington State home. This group shares a highly developed social structure which includes the clan system, communal dwellings, similar artistic expressions, ceremonies and oral history.

Due to an abundance of rich marine resources, the Northwest Coast people of Alaska enjoyed relative stability in their everyday lives, dividing their time between winter settlements and summer fish camps. They developed elaborate artwork employing a style of design called Northwest Coast formline which basically uses only three elements joined by a black undulating line or border called a formline.

Crest Art

Great importance is placed upon clan affiliation and identification within the culture. Most of the art is related to crest designs that represent these clans. Connected with each clan is a story, and out of that story an animal, bird, fish, or an element from the landscape that was selected by the group to represent them. Using the formline style, these crest designs are carved into wood and woven into textiles. They display a well-developed sense of proportion and symmetry. Today, the crest designs are also engraved on silver and gold jewelry.

Carving

Northwest Coast artisans created very sophisticated carvings: masks, frontlets, bowls, spoons, and leaders' staffs. They hewed large monumental totem poles and shorter structural house posts, all of which tell stories, honor important people or events, and identify clans. A distinct type of pole served as a mortuary structure to hold the cremated remains of leaders. The Haida exclusively carve a stone known as argillite. Elaborate bowls and pipes are carved from this rich, dark stone.

Chilkat

Using mountain goat wool and cedar bark, the Tsimshian and Tlingit developed woven ceremonial garments called Chilkat robes, named for the Chilkat Valley, near Haines, home to famous weavers. Men designed and painted a pattern board, and women wove the formline design into a robe. In later years, wool blankets, trade items, were turned into ceremonial robes and covered with formline crest designs in shell buttons, and more recently, beads and felt appliqués.

Raven's Tail

Another woven textile, recently given the name Raven's Tail, was previously referred to as the "northern geometric style."[24] This form probably predated

Seven Chilkat Indian men and boys posed, standing, full length, in native dress. Courtesy of the Library of Congress.

73

the Chilkat, and unlike the Chilkat, these weavings are dominated by geometric designs, not the curvilinear formline shapes. They follow more closely the design elements of the twined baskets

Basketry

Basketry was highly developed on the Northwest Coast. The materials used were spruce root and cedar bark, which were twined and plated. Dyed grasses and other materials were added for contrasting designs, which were geometric bands representing objects in nature. A unique style is the lidded rattle top baskets. Pebbles or shot would be gathered and put into a hollow knob, which, when shaken, would rattle.

Large woven hats were also twined out of spruce roots or cedar bark. Utility hats to be worn in canoes had no designs except a coating of paint as a preservative. If the hat belonged to a high caste person, it might have crest designs painted on it.[25]

The Inupiat

The Inupiat live in the far North along the North Slope and on the West Coast of Alaska, with the demarcation line being the village of Unalakleet. They continue to engage in subsistence activities relying heavily upon whale, seal, walrus, caribou, fish, and birds. The climate of their homeland is extreme—very cold temperatures and, in the far North, many winter months without sun. During the summer, however, the sun returns and at solstice never sets. The land is flat and, for the most part, treeless.

The Inupiat are well known for their ivory and whale bone carving and, more recently, baleen basketry. As a people, they coexist with large herds of walrus from which the ivory is taken along with the meat. This is also true of the baleen, which comes from the mouths of bowhead whales, another marine mammal the indigenous people are allowed to hunt under the Marine Mammal Protection Act.

Eskimo ivory carver, 1912. Courtesy of the Library of Congress.

Ivory

Two types of ivory are used for carving in Alaska, fresh from the walrus and ancient mastodon, mammoth, or walrus ivory dug from the earth. Tusks from male walruses can measure more than three feet and weigh ten pounds. It is a desirable material due to its color; its hardness, which ensures durability; and its workability. The Inupiat fashion a wide variety of small carvings depicting animals and other aspects of their environment. Today they also make jewelry for the market including bracelets, earrings, pendants, and pins. Other market items are the elaborately carved cribbage boards and whole-carved tusks that often depict scenes from Inupiat village life. Carved pipes are also an item created for the market.

Mineralized ivory, incorrectly referred to as "fossil ivory" is ivory that has been buried in the earth and has taken on coloration from minerals.[26] Ranging from beige to dark brown, old ivory pieces include newly created work from raw, dug-up ivory to the prehistoric pieces from the Old Bering Sea, Okvik, Ipuitak, Punuk, and Thule periods. The earliest of these periods, the Old Bering Sea I, is dated from 200 B.C.E. Due to the durability of ivory, artifacts from prehistoric times exist today, providing valuable records for research into early Inupiat culture and its connection with Asia.

Baleen Baskets

Yankee whalers began commercial activity in Alaskan waters in 1848. When commercial whaling was terminated in America, baleen basketry was initiated at the suggestion of an American whaler living in Barrow, Charles Brower, sometime between 1914 and 1918.[27] It is said he asked a local artist to try making a basket out of baleen copying the Athabascan or Eskimo coiled willow root style. The art spread to other Inupiat villages, and today the baskets command a high market price and are sought by collectors. Baleen is a keratinous material found in the mouths of plankton-eating whales, a material that is stiff and takes a lot of manipulating to be manageable.

Furs

The Inupiat are also known for their skin and fur sewing, elaborate parkas, mitts and boots, all created for the cold, harsh environment of the North. Eskimo dolls illustrate in small scale the furs used for the clothing. Some dollmakers such as Eva Heffle of Fairbanks (originally Kotzebue) make dolls engaged in traditional Inupiat activities such as hunting, trapping, berry picking and traveling by dog sled, thus extending the purpose of dolls to contemporary education.[28]

The Yup'ik

The Yup'ik live in western Alaska along the Bering Sea Coast, in the Yukon Kuskokwim Delta and in Bristol Bay. The Siberian Yup'ik live on St. Lawrence Island, closer to the Russian mainland than Alaska. The mainland subarctic terrain is flat, treeless, and punctuated by many drainages. Over half of the land is covered by water. The islands Nelson, Nunivak, and St. Lawrence are situated in the shallow Bering Sea, which thrives with marine fauna. The inland drainages supply large quantities of driftwood that the Yup'ik use for their dwellings, steam baths, boats, masks, bowls, spoons, and a variety of ceremonial accessories.

Basketry

An abundance of wild beach grass (*Elymus mollis*) grows in the low sandy areas of western Alaska. The Yup'ik gather this grass several times in spring and summer, cure it, and weave it into baskets. Yup'ik basketmakers are very innovative in applying ornamentation to these coiled containers. In addition to dyed grasses, they used dyed seal gut, yarns, animal parts, and carvings. The older baskets employ basically geometric designs, but the contemporary work has expanded to include embroidery depicting scenes and animals. As is the case with all of the cultures before European contact, dyes were extracted from natural materials. Today the basketmakers prefer the convenience of commercial dyes, which retain their color longer and do not take the extensive time involved in the collection and processing of natural materials. However, a few Yup'ik artists such as Rita Blumenstein[29] still work with earth dyes and teach the old techniques.

The Yup'ik are also known worldwide for their complex, highly symbolic wooden masks. Made to be used in winter ceremonies, the designs were usually directed by the *angalkuq*, or shaman. Elders say the masks were prayers for certain things, to relate to the spirit and animal world or to depict a voyage of a shaman who could travel to other worlds.[30] Once the mask was used in ceremony, it was thrown away, as its purpose had been fulfilled.

The Yup'ik, like the Alutiiq, Aleut, and Inupiat, were superb sewers of gut or intestine. Mainly using the fine membrane of seals, they created capes, jackets, hats, and bags that were waterproof and often ornamented with beaks, feathers, yarns, and grasses. They used an ingenious method of sewing in blades of grass along the seams for further waterproofing. The grass would swell when wet and seal the seam. They used the same technique on the seams of their skin kayaks. The Yup'ik between the mouth of the Yukon River and the Kuskokwim River also used fish skin to make garments and bags.

The Aleut and Alutiiq

The traditional land of the Aleuts is the Aleutian Islands, a chain that stretches 1,300 miles out into the Bering Sea. Their neighbors, the Alutiiq people, inhabit Kodiak Island, the Alaska Peninsula, the lower Kenai Peninsula, and the Prince William Sound region.

These two groups were maritime people, living on or close to coastal regions. Like the Inupiat, they relied heavily on the marine mammals. They developed highly maneuverable and seaworthy skin-covered kayaks for traveling and hunting on rough, stormy seas. For rain wear in the extremely wet climate, they sewed seal gut parkas with high precision, making them waterproof. They ornamented these garments with natural dyes, feathers, puffin beaks, or carved figurines from ivory, bone, or wood.

Hunting Hats

Bent wood hunting hats are world renowned for their form, ornamentation, and practical application. These hats had wide visors to protect the kayaker from the sun, rain, and glare from the water. They were made in several versions: long and short visor, open and closed crowns, and a helmet form. They were decorated with sea lion whiskers, beads, carved ivory amulets, and painted designs that might relate stories of the hunt or summon an animal helping spirit. It is thought that the effect they sought to achieve was zoomorphic.[31] The hunter in his animal skin (kayak) looked like a magnificent sea mammal as he approached his prey, with feathers and beads on his head moving in the wind.

The Hunting Hat Tradition

Contemporary Alutiiq hunting hat maker Jacob Simeonoff carries on his people's tradition by creating these masterpieces of bent wood ornamented with pigment, ivory, beads and feathers. His sister June Pardue, an Alutiiq tradition bearer, stated at the Qayaqs and Canoes traditional boatbuilding project in Anchorage in 2000 that the beads on the hat clack together in a high wind, warning the hunter to return to shore as a storm is building.[32]

Basketry

The Aleuts in the Chain are best known for their finely woven grass basketry. The women gather wild rye and barley beach grass from sandbars close to the shore, cure it carefully so it turns a soft, consistent color, and twine it into baskets and mats. Historically there were three weaving groups that produced variations in style, technique, and shape in the basket forms: Attu, Atka and Unalaska.[33] The finest weavings are purported to contain as many as 1,300 stitches per square inch.[34] Grass dyed with natural materials, feathers, silk floss, and other yarns were used for creating designs in a technique called "false embroidery." The colored material is wrapped around the weft but does not appear on the inside of the basket. The designs changed from the traditional geometric designs to floral motifs upon contact and conquest by Russia in the eighteenth century.

The Future

Alaska Native art today is growing and changing. Young artists are studying the work of their ancestors and are replicating, interpreting, extracting from, and in some cases, giving it new form and meaning. The art is in dynamic transition. New totem poles are being carved and raised in traditional ceremonies. Some tell the old stories, but some address the contemporary Native experience.

In 1992 a group of women in Sitka wove a Raven's Tail robe that includes designs representing clear-cut logging by local corporations and the impact of a cash economy.[35] Many artists, like Susie Bevins Ericsen/Qimmiqsak,[36] have addressed the devastation of their culture in their artwork and its results—

An example of Aleut baskets. Courtesy of the Library of Congress.

alcoholism, abuse, and suicide. Other carvers, like the late Larry Beck, use unusual materials such as car parts, glass, and plastics for creating three-dimensional forms.[37] Some artists are taking the traditional design forms and expanding upon them, resulting in new, exciting expressions.

Today Alaska Native art is being used to record, preserve, inform, and process experience and to inspire a whole new generation. Just as with the traditional expressions, contemporary work is based on stories, but these stories are new and the images are new; still there exists a need on the part of these artists to connect to tradition, to maintain that spiritual thread to the ancestors. The result of this blending is a dynamic body of artwork that can rival any in the world today.

RESOURCE GUIDE

Printed Sources

Black, Lydia T. *Glory Remembered: Wooden Head Gear of Alaskan Sea Hunters.* Juneau: Friends of the Alaska State Museum, 1991.

Davis, Robert Tyler. *Native Arts of the Pacific Northwest.* Palo Alto, CA: Stanford University Press, 1954.

Duncan, Kate. *Northern Athapaskan Art: A Beadwork Tradition.* Seattle: University of Washington Press, 1988.

Fienup-Riordan, Ann. *The Living Tradition of Yup'ik Masks: Agayuliyararput: Our Way of Making Prayer.* Seattle: University of Washington Press, 1996.

Fishback, Kurt Edward. *Art in Residence: West Coast Artists and Their Space.* Portland, OR: Blue Heron Publishing, 2000.

Fitzhugh, William W., and Aron Cromwell. *Crossroads of the Continents: Cultures of Siberia and Alaska.* Washington, DC: Smithsonian Institution Press, 1988.

Holm, Bill. *Northwest Coast Indian Art: An Analysis of Form.* 1965. Seattle: University of Washington Press, 1975.

Jones, Suzi, ed. *Eskimo Dolls.* 1982. Anchorage: Alaska State Council on the Arts, 1999.

Larsen, Dinah, ed. *Setting It Free. An Exhibition of Modern Alaskan Eskimo Carving.* Fairbanks: University of Alaska Museum, 1982.

Lee, Molly. *Baleen Basketry of the North Alaskan Eskimo.* Barrow: North Slope Planning Department, 1983, Seattle: University of Washington Press, 2000.

Paul, Frances. *Spruce Root Basketry of the Northern Tlingit.* Sitka, AK: Sheldon Jackson Museum, 1981.

Plagens, Peter. *Sunshine Muse: Art on the West Coast, 1945–1970.* Berkeley: University of California Press, 2000.

Samuel, Cheryl. *The Chilkat Dancing Blanket.* Seattle, WA: Pacific Search Press, 1982.

Shapsnikoff, Anfesia, and Raymond C. Hudson. "Aleut Basketry." *Anthropological Papers of the University of Alaska* 16 (1974): 41–69.

Steinbright, Jan, ed. *Alaskameut '86: An Exhibit of Contemporary Alaska Native Masks.* Fairbanks: Institute of Alaska Native Arts, 1986.

Museums, Web Sites, and Places of Interest

Alaska

Alaska State Council on the Arts
411 West 4th Avenue, STE 1E
Anchorage, AK 99501-2343
http://www.educ.state.ak.us/aksca/

Anchorage Museum of History and Art
121 West 7th Avenue
Anchorage, AK 99501
http://www.anchoragemuseum.org/

University of Alaska Museum
P. O. Box 756960
907 Yukon Drive
Fairbanks, AK 99775-6960
http://www.uaf.edu/museum/

California

Berkeley Art Museum/Pacific Film Archive
2621 Durant Avenue
Berkeley, CA 94720
510-642-1437
http://www.bampfa.berkeley.edu/

California African American Art Museum
600 State Par, Exposition Drive
Los Angeles, CA 90037
213-744-7432
http://www.caam.ca.gov/

California Arts Council
1300 I Street, Suite 930
Sacramento, CA 95814
http://www.cac.ca.gov/

Crocker Art Museum
216 O Street
Sacramento, CA 95814
916-264-5423
http://www.crockerartmuseum.org/

Fine Arts Museum of San Francisco
Legion of Honor
34th Avenue & Clement Street
San Francisco, CA 94121
415-863-3330
http://www.thinker.org/

Fresno Art Museum
2233 North First Street
Fresno, CA 93703
559-441-4221
http://www.fresnoartmuseum.org/

Los Angeles County Museum of Art
5905 Wilshire Boulevard
Los Angeles, CA 90036
323-857-6000
http://www.lacma.org/

Museum of Contemporary Art San Diego
MCASD La Jolla
700 Prospect Street
La Jolla, CA 92037-4291
858-454-3541

MCASD Downtown
1001 Kettner Boulevard
San Diego, CA 92101
619-234-1001
http://www.mcasandiego.org/

Museum of Latin American Art
628 Alamitos Avenue
Long Beach, CA 90802
562-437-1689
http://www.molaa.com/

Oakland Museum of California
1000 Oak Street
Oakland, CA 94607
510-238-2200
http://www.museumca.org/

San Jose Museum of Art
110 South Market Street
San Jose, CA 95113
408-271-6840
http://www.sjmusart.org/

Hawai'i

The Arts at Mark's Garage
1159 Nuuanu Avenue
Honolulu, HI 96817
808-521-2903
http://www.artsatmarks.com/

Bailey House Museum / Maui Historical Society
2375-A Main Street
Wailuku, HI 96793
808-244-3326
http://www.mauimuseum.org/

Bernice Pauahi Bishop Museum
1525 Bernice Street
Honolulu, HI 96817
808-847-3511
http://www.bishopmuseum.org/

The Contemporary Museum
2411 Makiki Heights Drive
Honolulu, HI 96822
808-526-1322 ext. 30
http://www.tcmhi.org/

Doris Duke Foundation for Islamic Art (Shangri La)
4055 Papu Circle
Honolulu, HI 96816
808-734-1941
http://www.hawaiimuseums.org/mc/isoahv_shangrila.htm

East–West Center Gallery
1601 East-West Road at the corner of Dole Street
Honolulu, HI 96848
808-944-7111
http://www.eastwestcenter.org/

Hawai'i State Art Museum
No. 1 Capitol District Building
250 South Hotel Street, 2nd Floor
Honolulu, HI 96813
808-586-0900
http://www.state.hi.us/sfca/

Hawai'i State Foundation on Culture and the Arts
250 South Hotel Street, 2nd Floor
Honolulu, HI 96813
http://www.state.hi.us/sfca/

Honolulu Academy of Arts
900 South Beretania Street
Honolulu, HI 96814
808-532-8700
http://www.honoluluacademy.org/

Hui No'eau Visual Arts Center
2841 Baldwin Avenue
Makawao, HI 96768
808-572-6560
http://www.huinoeau.com/

Maui Arts & Cultural Center
1 Cameron Way
Kahului, HI 96732
808-242-2787
http://www.mauiarts.org/

University of Hawai'i Art Gallery
Department of Art, University of Hawai'i at Manoa
Honolulu, HI 96822
808-956-6888
http://www.hawaii.edu/artgallery

Oregon

Coos Art Museum
235 Anderson Avenue
Coos Bay, OR 97420
541-267-3901
http://www.coosart.org/

Favell Art Museum of Western Art & Artifacts
125 West Main Street
Klamath Falls, OR 97601
541-882-9996
http://www.favellmuseum.com/

Hallie Ford Museum of Art
Willamette University
900 State Street
Salem, OR 97301
503-370-6300
http://www.willamette.edu/museum_of_art/

Oregon Arts Commission
775 Summer Street NE, Suite 200
Salem, OR 97301-1284
http://www.oregonartscommission.org/main.php

Portland Art Museum
1219 Southwest Park Avenue
Portland, OR 97205
503-226-2811
http://www.pam.org/

Schneider Museum of Art
1250 Siskyou Boulevard
Ashland, OR 97520
541-552-6245
http://www.sou.edu/sma/

University of Oregon Museum of Art
1233 University of Oregon
Eugene, OR 97403
541-346-3027
http://uoma.uoregon.edu/

Washington

Center on Contemporary Art
410 Dexter Avenue North
Seattle, WA 98109
206-728-1980
http://www.cocaseattle.org/

Frye Art Museum
704 Terry Avenue
Seattle, WA 98104
206-622-9250
http://www.fryeart.org/

Henry Art Gallery
University of Washington
15th Avenue NE & NE 41st Street
Seattle, WA 98195-1410
206-543-2280
http://www.henryart.org/

Maryhill Museum of Art
35 Maryhill Museum Drive
Goldendale, WA 98620
509-773-3733
http://maryhillmuseum.org/

Museum of Northwest Art
121 South First Street
La Conner, WA 98257
360-466-4446
http://www.museumofnwart.org/

Northwest Museum of Art
2316 West First Avenue
Spokane, WA 99204
509-456-3931
http://www.northwestmuseum.org/northwestmuseum/

Seattle Art Museum, Downtown
100 University Street
Seattle, WA 98101-2902
206-654-3100
http://www.seattleartmuseum.org/

Tacoma Art Museum
1701 Pacific Avenue
Tacoma, WA 98402
253-272-4258
http://www.tacomaartmuseum.org/

Washington State Arts Commission
234 8th Avenue SE (corner of 8th & Franklin)
P. O. Box 42675
Olympia, WA 98504-2675
http://www.arts.wa.gov/

Wing Luke Asian Museum
407 7th Avenue South
Seattle, WA 98104
206-623-5124
http://www.wingluke.org/

CANADA

ALASKA

Barrow

Denali
Natil Park   Porcupine
Nome   Alaska Range   Fairbanks
                        Mt. McKinley
              Kuskokwim   Wrangell Mts.
              Anchorage   St. Elias Mts.
                                              Juneau
              Kenai
              Mts.

Mt. Baker
Puget Sound
Basin
Skagit
Olympic   Everett   Lake   Lake
Mt. Olympus   Seattle   Chelan   Roosevelt
Mts.   Glacier   Columbia   Spokane
              Tacoma   Peak   Grand Coulee   Spokane
              Olympia   Mt. Rainier   Dam   Wenatchee
              WASHINGTON   Yakima   Valley
                        Yakima   Snake
                        Valley
                        Mt. Adams
                        Columbia

Portland   Columbia   Columbia
Mt. Hood   River   Plateau   Blue Mountains
Salem   Gorge
Willamette   Columbia River
Valley   Deschutes   John Day   Basin
Eugene   OREGON   IDAHO

PACIFIC
OCEAN

Umpqua   Crater Lake
Rogue   Natil Park   Goose
              Klamath   Lake
              Lake

Mt. Shasta
Klamath
Mts.
              Lassen Pk.
Eel   Sacramento

CALIFORNIA

Clear
Lake   Lake
              Tahoe   NEVADA
Sacramento   SIERRA NEVADA
Napa Valley
Napa   Stockton
San Francisco   Oakland   Modesto   Mono
              Fremont   Lake
Palo Alto   Yosemite   Sequoia
              San Jose   Natil Park   Natil Park   Death Valley
              Salinas   San Joaquin   Fresno
                                        Mt.   Badwater
                                        Whitney
              Salinas   Central   Mojave
                        Valley   Desert
              Bakersfield
Kauai
Mt. Waiialeiale   Santa Barbara   Los Angeles   San Bernardino
Niihau   Burbank
              Oahu   Molokai   Long Beach   Santa Ana   Palm Springs
Honolulu   Maui   Anaheim   Irvine   Imperial   Colorado
              Lanai   Kahului   Newport Beach   Valley   Salton
              Kahoolawe   Oceanside   Sea
HAWAII   San Diego   ARIZONA
              Mauna Kea   Hilo   MEXICO
              Mauna Loa
Hawaii   Kilauea Crater

ECOLOGY AND ENVIRONMENT

M. Kathryn Davis

Diversity is the defining characteristic of the Pacific Region, and this very characteristic is what makes it difficult to discuss it as a coherent place. The physical geography of this region has been a central factor in shaping human society, and people have reshaped the natural environment in both obvious and subtle ways. The most obvious involves transportation systems, settlement location, population, and commerce. Physical geography has impacted human society through climate, soil conditions, and diverse geophysical features such as imposing mountain ranges, active volcanoes, seemingly bottomless lakes, and the Pacific Ocean. Environmentally and ecologically speaking, the region contains a variety of landscapes, from the country's harshest deserts to some of the lushest rainforests in North America. The region is a place of contradiction with the most awe-inspiring wild and scenic places as well as some of the most urbanized and built landscapes. It is this diversity and contradiction that give the Pacific Region its personality and mystique.

LANDFORMS AND CLIMATE

The region's diversity makes it difficult at best, and in many ways impossible, to discuss it as a region in terms of landforms and climate. In this section the discussion will necessarily be guided by analysis of the area within discrete subregions in the greater Pacific Region. These subregions include the Columbia Plateau; California; Pacific Coastal Region; Hawai'i; and Alaska.

The Columbia Plateau

The Columbia Plateau actually has more in common with the intermontane west than with the coastal regions of Oregon and Washington. It lies east of the Cascade

Mountain range in Oregon and Washington and includes hills, plains, ridges, and mountains ranging from a few hundred feet to over 10,000 feet in elevation. The plateau has a semiarid climate, and precipitation varies from ten to twenty inches a year, with little or no summer rain. Much of the area is grassland primarily covered in bunchgrass, which supports a large ranching industry in eastern Washington and Oregon. Ponderosa pine and Douglas fir are the dominant tree species. There is abundant fauna including pronghorn antelope, deer, elk, mountain sheep, and feral horses. Cougar, coyote, bobcat, and foxes are scarce primarily because of state-sponsored extermination campaigns geared toward protecting the cattle industry.

The term *plateau* is not completely accurate in a geophysical sense because of the lack of topographic uniformity. It is primarily covered with basalt lava flows, and its most defining, and for decades mysterious, geological feature is the channeled scablands located in eastern and central Washington. The channeled scablands were created by raging floodwaters released when ice dams holding back Lake Missoula in northwestern Montana repeatedly burst during the last Ice Age. Lake Missoula was a massive Pleistocene lake estimated to contain more than ten times the present flow of all the current world rivers combined. During the last great Ice Age, the Cordilleran Ice Sheet extended far enough south to block the Clark Fork River and create a massive glacial lake. The Ice Sheet was about 3,000 to 4,000 feet thick at Seattle and around 5,000 feet thick at the U.S.-Canadian border. The ice dam is estimated to have been approximately 2,000 feet high, stretching east up to 200 miles, creating an inland sea in the area we know as Montana.

Periodic catastrophic failures of the ice dam released torrents of water, ice, dirt, and rock debris down the Columbia River drainage to the Pacific Ocean. According to U.S. Geological Survey (USGS) estimates, at maximum height and extent, the lake probably contained more than 500 cubic miles of water. When the pressure behind the ice dam built to the point of bursting, it sped toward the Pacific Ocean. The water must have shaken the ground as it thundered, at speeds reaching nearly sixty-five miles per hour, across the basin, gathering soil, trees, and rock on its way. The lake probably drained in less than forty-eight hours. Scientists believe this process was repeated, probably dozens of times, over a period of about 2,500 to 3,000 years, sending torrents of water raging to the Pacific Ocean and carving the gorges seen today in the channeled scablands. The floods moved about 50 cubic miles of earth, piled gravel thirty stories high, and carried 200-ton boulders from the Rocky Mountains to the Willamette Valley. They also created giant ripple or wave marks that in some places are three stories high. When the

The Columbia River Gorge today. Courtesy of Getty Images/ PhotoDisc.

glaciers retreated about 13,000 years ago, they left a landscape scoured and carved by their movement over thousands of years.

The Columbia River Gorge is about 100 miles long and 3,000 to 4,000 feet deep in some places. The northern wall of the Gorge is the southern border of Washington, and the southern wall is the northern border of Oregon. The Columbia River Basin is the fourth largest river basin in the United States and drains about 250,000 square miles in parts of seven states. This includes much of Oregon and Washington as well as all of Idaho. The Columbia River itself is about 1,200 miles long, with its origin at the base of the Canadian Rockies in southeastern British Columbia. There are 250 reservoirs, 150 hydropower projects, and 400 dams on the river and its tributaries. There are 18 dams on the mainstream Columbia and its major tributary, the Snake River. It is the most hydroelectrically developed river system in the world and generates more than twenty-one kilowatts of electricity. Electricity generated on the Columbia River system has stimulated economic growth in the Pacific Northwest since World War II. During World War II it was crucial to the war effort and powered such defense industries as aluminum plants, shipyards, and the development of the plutonium atomic bomb at Hanford. While fish ladders and other methods of aiding salmon migration and spawning have been incorporated into dam design since 1938, the dams are still one of the primary reasons for the catastrophic decline in salmon populations in the twentieth century. Even though fish ladders do help salmon get upstream, the survival rate is often low, and reservoirs cover spawning areas with silt and deep water, so many fish surviving the fish ladders do not find an acceptable spawning ground.

Smaller than the Columbia River Basin but as important in terms of human settlement and economy is the Puget Sound Basin. This basin was carved during the Pleistocene Ice Age by at least one large and probably several small glaciers. The Puget Sound Basin covers about 16,000 square miles, with 80 percent of that land and 20 percent water. The Sound itself is really an estuary where saltwater from the Pacific mixes with freshwater from a multitude of rivers. The average depth is about 450 feet, while the deepest portion, located north of Seattle, is about 930 feet deep. The soil in this area is relatively young and immature, with only a shallow accumulation of organic material except in the southern and western regions and river valleys.

Pacific Coast Region

The North Pacific Coast is a subregion about 2,000 miles long that stretches from Alaska's Cook Inlet to the northern tip of California. Just as the Columbia Plateau has more in common with the intermontane region, northern California has more in common with the coastal regions of Oregon, Washington, and Alaska. Diverse mountain ranges and narrow coastal plains dominate this area. The coastal ranges are relatively low except in northern California, where the Klamaths reach elevations of 9,000 feet and are heavily glaciated. In Oregon and Washington the coast ranges only average about 1,000 feet in elevation. North of the Columbia River transverse river valleys are dominant characteristics, with the primary valleys found along the Columbia, Umpqua, and Rogue Rivers. The Willamette Valley, a broad alluvial plain 15 to 30 miles wide and 125 miles long with very rich soil, is one of the most important agricultural areas of this subregion. The Olympic

In the heart of the Olympic Mountains in Washington. Courtesy of Getty Images/PhotoDisc.

Mountains are much higher than the coast ranges, with the highest, Mount Olympus, reaching 8,000 feet. The Olympics receive abundant heavy snowfall that maintains over sixty glaciers. High peaks of mostly volcanic mountains dominate the inland ranges. The Cascades range from Lassen Peak in northern California to southern British Columbia. The Columbia River Gorge divides the northern and southern portions of the range. Mount Lassen is one of only two active volcanoes to erupt in the twentieth century. Mt. Shasta is the tallest of the range at 14,162 feet. Crater Lake is one of the world's deepest lakes and is actually the caldera of ancient Mt. Mazama. In Oregon, volcanic Mt. Hood stands at 11,225 feet. The northern portion of the Cascades is more granitic than volcanic but does include Mt. St. Helens, the other volcano in the range to erupt in the twentieth century. Mt. Adams, Mt. Rainier, Mt. Baker, and Glacier Peak are the other dominant peaks of the range.

The Cascades experience heavy snowfall, with extensive glaciation and very cool summers. There are about 750 glaciers in the northern Cascades, which is two-thirds of all active glaciers in the contiguous United States. Mt. Rainier alone has over 40 glaciers. Finally, Alaska is dominated by the St. Elias Mountains at the intersection of Alaska, the Yukon Territory, and British Columbia. Alaska boasts the highest coastal mountains in the world. This includes the Kenai and Wrangell Mountains and the Alaska Range.

Climate and vegetation in the North Pacific Coast Region are very distinctive and contribute to its attraction for hikers and campers. The climate is dominated by a temperate marine climate with very low winter temperatures only in lowland regions of south-central Alaska and highlands in Oregon, Washington, and northern California. Precipitation is abundant, and winter cyclonic storms travel east across the open Pacific for 1,000 miles before crashing into the northern reaches of this region. Precipitation is variable, depending on height and location of mountain ranges. For instance, the southwest Olympics average 150 inches per year, but the northeast Olympics, just 75 miles away, average only 16 inches. There is considerable snowfall in the far northern reaches, with an annual average of 80

Mt. Shasta in California. Courtesy of Getty Images/PhotoDisc.

feet in some places. Winters are generally cloudy and damp, and mild temperatures, light winds, coastal fog, and low clouds mark summers. The best description of the region along the northern California, Oregon, and Washington coast in the winter is gray. When it is not raining, it is still gray and dreary. The rugged beauty of the coastline has a mystical quality found in few other places.

California

California is the most ecologically and environmentally diverse region on the North American continent. California is physically so isolated that until completion of the Central Pacific Railroad in 1869 it was one of the most isolated, inhabited places on earth. It took less time and less money and was more comfortable traveling to China or Australia than to Chicago or New York. It was also this physical isolation and the resulting high transportation costs that forced California into industrial and agricultural self-sufficiency. The Sierra Nevada, a 450-mile-long range in the center of Eastern California, was an imposing and usually impenetrable barrier between California and places east. California also claims environmental distinctiveness in its varied geographical landforms. For example, San Francisco is the world's largest landlocked harbor. The lowest and highest points in the lower forty-eight states are found in California. Badwater, in Death Valley, is 282 feet below sea level, while less than 100 miles away, Mt. Whitney is 14,495 feet in elevation. California also claims to be home to the world's oldest and largest trees, including a Bristlecone pine estimated to be around 5,000 years old. Mono Lake, the oldest lake in the United States, at approximately 7,000 years old, is found on the eastern side of the Sierra. Lake Tahoe, the largest alpine lake in the country, straddles the border between California and Nevada. In one, admittedly long, day a person can wake up, have breakfast in the desert, eat lunch and play in the snow at Lake Tahoe, and eat dinner on the beach.

California's primary environmental characteristics are also what initially attract people to the region. This includes a dry summer subtropical climate, abundant sunshine, mild winters, dry summers, and relatively dry winters. California's summer climate is characterized by calm, sunny, rainless days and mild, rainless nights. Inland areas, however, are very hot in the summer. While the climate is commonly referred to as classic Mediterranean, summers are actually more comparable to North Africa and Israel and are hotter and drier than Italy, Spain, or Greece. The winter climate is variable, with a rainy season generated by Pacific cyclonic disturbances. Winter rainfall ranges from 10 inches in San Diego to 20 inches in San Francisco to over 100 inches in far Northern California. Low-growth shrubs and coastal sage dominate vegetation in the coastal zones. The valleys and low mountain areas of Central and Southern California are characterized by chaparral, while the central valley was historically natural grassland. Ponderosa pine, Lodgepole pine, and various firs dominate the mid- and upper-mountain slopes. California is famous for its giant Sequoias, which grow at middle elevations (4,500 feet to 7,500 feet) along the western Sierra Nevada Mountains.

In geologic terms, California is a severely faulted region, with the San Andreas the most famous and recognizable fault. The entire state is an unstable crustal zone, and earthquakes are frequent, unpredictable, and often deadly. The Loma Prieta earthquake of 1989 killed sixty-five people and did $8 billion in damage. In 1994 the Northridge quake killed fifty-seven people and resulted in $7.2 billion in damage. Floods are also serious concerns in California, with nearly all precipitation falling in winter. Urban areas are extensive usually, and inadequate drainage systems contribute to destructive mudslides and floods in inhabited areas. Forest and brush fires occur during the extensive dry season, particularly in late fall, with Santa Ana winds, chaparral, chamise, and other hot-burning vegetation creating perfect conditions for wildfires in Southern California. Destructive floods, mudslides, and wildfires most often occur in areas of the most expensive homes and exclusive communities. California's wealthy citizens prefer homes in areas that are somewhat isolated, have the best views, and are surrounded with "green space." Unfortunately most of the green space is not actually green but dry and fire prone.

Hawai'i

Hawai'i is the smallest region of the United States and is located 2,100 miles to the southwest of California. It is a 1,600-mile string of islands, but the term *Hawaiian Islands* commonly refers to a 400-mile stretch of about twelve islands. The total area is about 6,500 square miles or the approximate area of New Jersey. There are eight major islands: Hawai'i, Maui, Oahu, Kauai, Molokai, Lanai, Ni'ihau, and Kaho'olawe. The islands are actually the tops of a mountain range pushed upward by volcanic activity and modified by erosion. The volcanoes are younger from west to east, and Mauna Loa, at 13,679 feet, is the world's largest active volcano. The two major active volcanoes on Hawai'i (the Big Island) are expanding the size of the island. In fact, when Kilauea erupted in 1960, it added about 500 acres of new land to the island. The volcano is also destructive, and in 1990 an eruption destroyed over 100 homes. Flat land in Hawai'i is scarce, even around the coastal fringes. Sheer cliffs and rugged steep-sided canyons with abrupt elevation changes characterize the islands. There are three controlling factors influencing climate here:

The islands are located on the tropical fringe in the ocean, which means generally mild temperatures and abundant moisture.

Northeast tradewinds blow in the summer, and although weaker, they are still persistent in the winter.

The terrain's height and orientation are the primary determinants of temperature and rainfall variation.

The onshore tradewinds are usually accompanied by some cloud cover, high relative humidity, temperatures that range from mild to warm, and brief but frequent showers. Rainfall, influenced primarily by geographic location and the island's terrain, varies within as well as between islands, with windward islands receiving much more precipitation than leeward. For example, on Kauai, Mt. Wai'ale'ale is supposedly the rainiest place on earth and averages about 476 inches of rainfall annually. Only fifteen miles away, the average annual rainfall is a mere 20 inches. Variations like this are found on all the islands except Kaho'olawe, Lana'i, and Moloka'i, which all have relatively low precipitation. Within the city of Honolulu, one location might have an average annual rainfall of 93 inches, while five miles away the annual average is only 25 inches. Temperatures in the lowlands tend to be mild with little change. For instance, the average January temperature in Honolulu is 72 degrees, while the average July temperature is 78 degrees. Tropical hurricanes occur usually about twice in a decade and normally originate off the

The coastline of Honolulu. Courtesy of Getty Images/PhotoDisc.

west coast of Mexico or Central America. Hurricane ʻIwa in 1982 and Hurricane ʻIniki in 1992 caused considerable damage. The Hawaiian Islands have lush, beautiful vegetation. While there are serious problems with introduced species, Hawaiʻi maintains its sense of a lush tropical paradise in many areas of the state.

Alaska

Alaska is the northernmost state in the Pacific Region, nearly one-third lying in the Arctic Circle. It is approximately 1,480 miles long and 810 miles wide. Most of Alaska is surrounded by water—the Arctic Ocean to the north, the Gulf of Alaska and the Pacific Ocean to the south, and the Bering Sea to the west. To the east and south, Alaska borders Canada. Covering over 650,000 square miles, Alaska is the largest of the fifty U.S. states and more than twice the size of Texas.

Alaska's land elevations run from sea level to 20,320 feet above sea level, the height of Mt. McKinley, which is the state's highest point as well as the highest point in North America. Lakes and rivers dot the state. Alaska's longest river is the Yukon, nearly 1,900 miles long.

With its immense size, Alaska has a number of environmental regions, ranging from ice fields with severe glaciation to rainforests in the southern coastal areas. Alaska, geographically, consists of four main areas, including two mountain range systems, a central plateau, and a coastal plain. The Pacific Mountain System runs from the Aleutian Islands down through south-central Alaska to Northern California. It includes several major mountain ranges, among which is the Alaska Range, home to Mt. McKinley. A second major mountain system is the Rocky Mountain System of Alaska, composed of the Brooks Range and its foothills. In between these two ranges are the Central Uplands and Lowlands, an area making up the largest land area in Alaska. Finally, the Arctic Coastal Plain, which lies north of the Rocky Mountain System, makes up Alaska's tundra region, where the ground is permanently frozen.

Precipitation varies greatly in the state. The central plains and uplands often average less than 10 inches of rain per year, whereas the Cordova-Valdez region, in the Prince William Sound area, may experience 200 inches or more. Anchorage, in the interior basin, averages about 25 inches of rain. Mean annual temperatures range from the low forties in the maritime areas in the south to about ten degrees Fahrenheit north of the Brooks Mountain Range along the Arctic Slope. The central and eastern portions of the continental interior experience the largest contrasts in seasonal temperatures, averaging maximum temperatures in the upper seventies in the summer; winter's lack of sunshine, on the other hand, may drive the temperatures to minus fifty degrees or more, sometimes for weeks at a time.

According to ongoing studies by the Arctic Climate Impact Assessment, a team of experts assessing global warming in the Arctic, temperatures in Alaska have risen four degrees over the last thirty years, indicating global warming. If global warming continues, it will seriously impact Alaska: as ice melts, rising water levels will cause coastal damage; cycles of flooding and drought will be more severe; and climatic perturbations will result in outbreaks of disease in native populations.

BUSINESS, ECONOMY, AND ENVIRONMENT

In the Pacific Region, perhaps even more than in other regions of North America, the environment has affected business development and shaped the economy. In turn, commerce and economic development have affected the environment in significant, and often permanent, ways. At first glance, the most obvious impacts include environmental constraints on transportation systems, settlement location, and development of commerce around natural resources. Climate is both a limiting and expansive factor in the entire region. Snow pack determines how much water is in reservoirs at the end of the wet season, but a quick snowmelt can also result in severe damage from mud slides and floods. In other words, ample precipitation in the region has both positive and negative implications for economic development.

The most prominent commonality in this region's economic development is the reliance on natural resources and tourism. Some places in the region are dependent on a single resource, while others enjoy a diversified economy. Towns have been subject to the availability of resources and changing technologies. The region is characterized by boom-and-bust economies, and at times, entire towns have disappeared after a bust. In the past couple of decades the Pacific Region has begun a transformation to economic development based on a different valuing of the landscape. The landscape itself is increasingly the growth industry in the Northwest. Some of the most significant growth is found in rural areas in skiing, hunting, rafting, retirement communities, and vacation homes. Technology has allowed people to live in one state and work in another. For example, there was a significant movement of people from California to small towns in the Northwest, establishing new residences while maintaining their jobs in California. This transformation of the economic base is best characterized as a transition from extraction to attraction. Farmland becomes suburban communities, and logging roads become mountain bike trails and playgrounds for off-road vehicles. Forested land is cleared to make way for large vacation homes that people will visit only once or twice a year. The ideal of the rustic cabin in the woods has transformed for many into a fully furnished home with all the amenities. Native vegetation is replaced with exotic and other nonnative species. Familiar plant life appears to be a kind of "comfort food" for the soul, allowing people who relocate from urban to rural areas a sense of familiarity and even control over their environment. The environmental impact of this transformation is no less damaging than extractive industries.

Agriculture

The entire region is agriculturally productive and dependent upon irrigation. How dependent varies according to environmental and climatic conditions. There are some historical similarities in the development of agriculture. In the entire Pacific Region agriculture began as a subsistence activity, but production grew with increasing population and as urbanization increased. Technology, primarily for moving water, turned marginal lands into productive agricultural regions in the most arid areas. This technology included dams, diversion canals, and irrigation, as well as mechanization of agriculture. In the region as a whole the federal government has invested significant financial resources in agricultural production.

Agriculture is an important economic sector in the Columbia Plateau region and is heavily dependent on irrigation, although increasingly dryland farming techniques are being employed successfully. The Palouse is the region encompassing eastern and central Washington and northeast and north-central Oregon. It is the most important agricultural region in the intermontane west primarily because of its rich prairie soil. The Palouse, with its abundance of winter wheat, is the highest-yielding wheat-producing location on the continent, as well as an important source of dry peas, lentils, barley, clover, and alfalfa. The Blue Mountains region in northeastern Oregon and southeastern Washington is the nation's leading source of pea production. The Yakima and Wenatchee Valleys lie in the rainshadow of the Cascade Mountains and enjoy a near-perfect climate for agriculture. Two-fifths of the nation's apples come from this area, and other important crops include hay and field corn for cattle, hops, and potatoes. In the 1990s an enormous expansion of vineyards and boutique wineries on both sides of the Columbia began to rival California's Napa Valley. The Willamette Valley is the largest and most developed agricultural region on the Oregon side of the Columbia River. Its crops include wheat, fruits, oats, pasture grasses, grapes, and mint. An important agricultural development is the Columbia Basin Project in eastern Washington. This project is an attempt to increase agricultural production in the area, especially expansion of potato and corn output. This particular area of Washington is semiarid, and its natural vegetation is primarily sagebrush. Irrigation water from the Grand Coulee Dam is used for center-pivot irrigation, which is a much more efficient water delivery system that also requires less human labor. As in other arid sections of the region, irrigation is helping turn marginal lands into productive farmlands. While the short-term gain is impressive, there are important environmental consequences that will be discussed in a later section.

Usually when people think of farming and food production as well as agricultural technology, their minds turn to the Great Plains or the Midwest regions of the United States. However, California is the leading agricultural state in the nation, and the total value of farm products sold is higher in California than any other state. Eight of the nation's ten most productive agricultural counties are in California. The success of California's agricultural production is due to a combination of human and environmental factors. The state has abundant sunshine, fertile soil, and a long growing season. These factors combine with elaborate irrigation systems and cutting-edge farm management techniques to make California the important food production region that it has been for nearly a century. Where water was lacking for agricultural (and urban) development, elaborate aqueduct systems were created for moving water from one region in the state to another.

The most important technological advances in agriculture have been developed in California, including the tractor. California agriculture depends on a mobile, mostly foreign-born labor force. It is highly specialized, depending on mild winters and long growing seasons or rainless, low-humidity summers. Most agricultural techniques and legal institutions in the West were developed in California. These include western water law, control of alkali, deep-well drilling and pumping techniques, large dam building, joint stock irrigation districts, legislation restricting dumping of mining debris into streams and rivers, and technological development. Two percent of U.S. farms and about 10 percent of gross farm receipts are found in California. California grows about 40 percent of the nation's fresh fruits and vegetables. Milk is the state's number-one product in terms of value, and the important milk-producing regions are the San Joaquin Valley and San Bernardino-Riverside. One in every five glasses of milk in the United States comes from California. The second-most valuable product is beef cattle, primarily raised in the San Joaquin Valley. Fully 90 percent of the nation's grapes are grown in California, and the state is also the national leader in nursery products such as trees and plants.

The great Central Valley contributes 75 percent of the state's total farm output. It has some of the richest soil in the nation but barely any water; so it is dependent on California's elaborate system of irrigation projects, including the Central Valley Project and the California Water Project. The Sacramento Valley, the northern one-third of the Central Valley, has more precipitation and so is less dependent on intensive irrigation. The primary crops of the Sacramento Valley include rice, almonds, tomatoes, sugar beets, wheat, hay, cattle, milk, and prunes. The San Joaquin Valley at the southern end of the Central Valley is arid and requires heavy irrigation. Its crops include cattle, milk, grapes, cotton, hay, oranges, and almonds. The Salinas Valley has the richest farmland in the entire nation and is renowned for lettuce, artichokes, broccoli, cauliflower, and Brussels sprouts. The Oxnard Plain lies along the coast between Los Angeles and Santa Barbara. It is declining as an agricultural region because of increasing land values and the aesthetic value of its proximity to the ocean. It is still, however, an important region for a variety of vegetables and citrus. The Imperial Valley in southeastern California is irrigated by water drawn from the Colorado River. It is an important source of field crops such as vegetables, wheat, and alfalfa. Although not as important economically, there are also numerous citrus orchards in the Imperial Valley. Finally, San Diego and the Napa Valley are important regions for high-value crops such as nursery plants and vineyards, both heavily dependent on irrigation.

Alaska is not a major agricultural producer. There is very little arable land in Alaska, and two-thirds of the state's cropland is located in the Matanuska Valley at the head of the Cook Inlet just inland from Anchorage. There are only a few dozen marginal farms because production costs are too high, and crop options are too limited by environmental constraints. There is a short growing season, although the long hours of summer sunlight are good for the production of oats, barley, potatoes, hay, and cool-climate vegetables. There is some livestock raising, and greenhouse farming has been an important adaptation to climatic limitations.

Only one-tenth of the land in Hawai'i is arable. Forty-two percent of the total land area is government controlled. Seventy estates, trusts, and large landowners own another 47 percent. This leaves only about 11 percent available for private ownership. Agricultural land does have productive soil, no frost, abundant rainfall, and abundant groundwater. The first cash crop grown for export was tobacco during the first half of the nineteenth century. Between the 1820s and 1870s ships stopping for provisions provided a small market for agricultural products. During the California gold rush Hawai'i was an important supplier of fruits and vegetables to the mining regions as well as San Francisco. This agricultural boom only lasted for about a decade. By the mid-nineteenth century specialized plantation crops became the foundation of the regional economy. Sugar cane has been the leading crop for more than a century, with pineapple a close second. Both, however, have been in a steady decline for at least a decade. The third most important crop is

Harvesting pineapples in Hawai'i, 1915. Courtesy of the Library of Congress.

macadamia nuts. Other major crops include coffee, livestock, floriculture, and nursery plants. Hawaii is famous for Kona coffee, which is grown on a two-by-twenty-mile strip of slope on the leeward side of the Big Island. It is the smallest growing area for one of the world's most famous coffees. Three-quarters of Hawai'i's agricultural land, mostly on the Big Island, is now engaged in beef cattle ranching. Most of the ranches are large, and animals are raised on pasture grasses rather than hay and grains. Most beef cattle are sold for local consumption, and the hides are exported. Even with so much land devoted to beef production, it supplies only about 30 percent of the local demand. Dairy and poultry are both expanding on the four largest islands. The recent decline in the importance of sugar and pineapple, though, has opened new opportunities for individuals to engage in agriculture. Plantations are being transformed into small- and medium-sized farms on prime agricultural land. Most of these farms are less than ten acres each. The only agricultural products in which Hawai'i is self-sufficient are sugar and milk. Everything else, including beef, is imported.

Industry

Agriculture is not the only, or even the most important, economic sector of the Pacific Region. There are diverse industries that run the gamut from federal government to tourism to high-tech to natural resource industries. Each area of the region is primarily dependent on a different type of industry. Alaska, the nation's largest state in area, has a population of around 623,000. High labor costs, transportation costs, and complex environmental regulations conspire to keep industrial development at bay. Even though Alaska has the lowest taxes in the United States, its geographic isolation and environment keep it relatively undeveloped in terms of industry. There is considerable conflict in Alaska over conservation versus economic growth. The sensitive natural environment is impacted by competing claims of different groups. Important and contentious controversies rage around issues such as Native Alaskan land claims, oil reserves, and natural resource exploitation. While there is significant government employment, the economic base of this area is found in its natural resources.

Oil, gas, seafood, and tourism are Alaska's primary industries. The importance of tourism has been increasing over the past decade, although there was a brief tourist boycott in 1994 in response to the state's "wolf management" program. This program allowed local hunters to shoot 80 percent of the wolves in an area the size of Northern Ireland. The program was canceled in 1995 at least partly in response to negative publicity. It does not appear to have permanently damaged the tourist industry, which is on the rise. Tourism has been the state's major growth industry, increasing 86 percent between 1989 and 1998. This growth has been driven in part by the cruise industry. Over 200 cruise ships travel through the Inside Passage each summer, but the highest growth rates are still in highway and ferry travelers. Ferries are increasingly popular as a mode of transportation for tourists interested in visiting Alaska, and the emphasis of the Alaska Marine Highway System has shifted from carrying cargo to carrying passengers. In fact, ferry travel has become so popular that in order to get a sleeping cabin on a ferry traveling the Alaska Marine Highway, travelers usually need to book their reservation a year in advance. In the summer, ferry decks become campgrounds, with passengers pitching small tents wherever there is an open space on deck.

The seafood industry is increasingly impacted by the farmed fish industry. Farmed salmon is steadily eroding the value of wild-caught salmon. Adding to this problem, British Columbia recently lifted a moratorium on farming Atlantic salmon in its waters. Alaska's groundfish industry, however, remains the world's largest single-species fishery, but the value of that fishery fluctuates with changes in Asian economic health, particularly in Japan. One new area of economic growth is in the service sector, which has traditionally been low producing. As in the rest of the country, Alaska's population is aging, and projected employment increases are heavily tilted toward service industries tied to aging such as health care. The increasing pressure of aging adults on the state's infrastructure and social safety nets could outweigh what positive impact this might have on the economy.

The state government still depends primarily on revenues from the oil and gas industries. The industry spends an estimated $2.1 billion annually in the state. One of the Bush administration's goals was to open the Alaska National Wildlife Refuge to oil exploration and production. So far that proposal has failed to garner enough votes in Congress. However, it will continue to be hotly debated as a solution to our dependence on foreign oil. The oil and gas industry is Alaska's largest non-government industry and generates about 20 percent of the private sector payroll and about 12 percent of private sector jobs. The industry spends nearly $2 billion on goods and services, which is roughly equivalent to the state's general fund expenditures. Wages in the oil and gas industry are nearly three times higher than the statewide average, and this continues to attract people to Alaska. Without realizing that the cost of living is exceedingly high, there are still many who travel

Photograph shows two men operating oil equipment in connection with the Trans-Alaska Pipeline, 1977. Courtesy of the Library of Congress.

to Alaska expecting to strike it rich working on salmon boats or in the oil and gas industry.

In the Pacific Northwest as a whole there are some commonalities in terms of industry. The forest products industry is a major source of income generation. Commercial fishing is also important, and this is one of the world's major fishing regions. Salmon, although declining for decades, is still the dominant species. The catch in the 1990s totaled only about 3 million fish, a small percentage of the 50 million fish caught annually in the nineteenth and early twentieth centuries. Fewer and fewer fish are able to return upriver to spawn and 50 percent of the catch in the 1990s was hatchery bred. Other important species include pollock, herring (mostly roe for the Japanese market), Pacific cod, and sablefish. Halibut is the largest, most valuable bottom fish in the region. A halibut can live up to thirty-five years and reach a weight of 500 pounds. It is on the menu of most upscale restaurants. Shellfish are another important species, although king crab has all but disappeared and has been replaced most notably by snow crab. Crabbing in Alaska is dangerous work, but men and women return to it season after season. Fishing is more than a job; it is a way of life, an identity, and as such impossible for most fishers to give up.

Another important natural resource in this region is water. There is great potential for hydropower generation primarily due to the many dams on the Columbia River. The principal markets at present are the large cities of Washington and Oregon and major aluminum plants scattered throughout the region. Future energy markets in California and other western states are being developed and will provide a tremendous economic boost that will replace income lost in the timber and fishing industries. Oregon and Washington will benefit financially, but the problem of increasing unemployment and pressure on social systems will not be so easily resolved. The energy crisis suffered by California in 2001–2002 proved the need for additional sources of hydropower, and the Pacific Northwest has this in abundance. Deregulation of the energy industry opens new markets, and Oregon and Washington have such an abundance of hydropower generation in place that they can offer perhaps the most competitive prices in the future. California's energy problems have the potential to make Oregon and Washington quite wealthy.

With an eye toward solving conflict over the pace of growth and development, Washington State passed the Growth Management Act in 1990 to guide the state in "smart" growth. This act is credited with netting about 600,000 new jobs in the 1990s. While Boeing downsized in the mid-1990s, the potentially disastrous impact was mitigated by Microsoft's expansion and the growth of the high-tech and biotech industries. In addition, the state attracted national warehousing and distribution facilities to the Seattle–Tacoma area. Industrial construction and growth continued throughout the 1990s, and although Washington is experiencing the same economic downturn as the rest of the country, its impact is not nearly as severe as in other areas such as California.

Oregon has successfully transitioned from an economy based primarily on fishing and timber to one of the most diversified economies in the country. This transition began prior to World War II when cheap hydropower encouraged development of metal and paper industries. In the 1970s a boom in home building generated by low interest rates and baby boomers coming of age and buying homes gave new life to the timber industry. But when interest rates increased dramatically in the 1980s, the housing boom collapsed, and this, combined with changes in federal land management policies in the early 1990s, drastically reduced timber harvests in the Pacific Northwest. Oregon was, however, poised to capture a segment of the high-tech industry, and employment in the high-tech sector grew from 22 percent in 1990 to 28 percent in 1997. Oregon now claims one of the top twenty most diversified economies in the country, with an economic base that includes high-tech, forest products, agriculture and food processing, tourism, metals, and transportation equipment. Rural areas, however, are still dependent on natural resource industries and suffer under economic downturns. Diversifying rural areas will be a challenge for the state over the next decade at least. Most rural areas continue to grow in terms of employment opportunities and population, but wages are significantly lower than in urban areas. The fact that Oregon's industrial base is concentrated on the production of capital goods rather than on consumer goods shelters it somewhat from the country's economic downturn. There were, however, signs of slowed growth and increasing unemployment in 1998.

Hawai'i's economic development is limited due to its isolation and lack of natural resources. There is no significant income available from mineral deposits, and commercial fishing has been only marginally successful. At one time the sandalwood trade was important, but the forests have been depleted and are no longer economically viable. The largest industry in Hawai'i by far is tourism. Summer is the busiest tourist season, with June the peak month and a secondary season in December and January. Although tourists visit all the major islands, the hub of the industry is located on Oahu. In fact, 72 percent of Hawai'i's private sector jobs are located on Oahu, as is 72 percent of the state's population. Fifty percent of the hotels rooms are located in Waikiki. The tourist industry attracts about 6.5 million visitors each year, with an average 125,000 tourists in the islands each day. Two-thirds of the westbound tourist business comes from the mainland United States and most of them from California. Many are repeat tourists who return to the islands again and again. Three-fourths of the eastbound tourists are from Japan. A dramatic increase in tourists from Japan over the past decade or so has stabilized this sector of the economy. Westbound tourists tend to stay longer, while east-bound tourists spend more money on their vacation. The past couple of years have been difficult for Hawai'i's tourist industry, although it appeared to be rebounding in late 2003. The international drop in travel following September 11 caused a short-term setback for Hawai'i's tourist industry. Just as it had nearly recovered, the SARS outbreak was another shock for the industry to absorb. Indications in November 2003 were that the industry had not only recovered from these two setbacks but had actually begun to increase.

The second largest industry in Hawaii is the federal government. Some of the nation's largest military bases are found in this strategic location. Pearl Harbor is the headquarters for the U.S. Pacific Command. One in five persons in Hawai'i's labor force works for the federal government, usually on military establishments. The U.S. Armed Forces spends about $2 billion annually in Hawai'i. Construction is an important sector of the economy, and the federal government provides most of the contracts. While residential construction on Oahu is declining due to lack of developable land, the construction industry is on the upswing, owing to military contracts. The state anticipates billions of dollars in federal contracts for repair and maintenance of military housing units as well as construction of about 15,000 new units. Although Hawai'i relies primarily on only two industries, the economy remains relatively stable, owing to near-perfect conditions for tourism and its strategic military location.

More than any other state in the region, California's economic character has always been boom and bust. A land boom in 1880 began a steady stream of migrants to Southern California. Northern California, particularly the San Francisco Bay area, had experienced phenomenal growth during the gold rush. In 1845 California's population was around 5,000 and less than 10 percent Anglo. In 1850 the population had grown to 100,000, and was 90 percent Anglo. Southern California boosters were eager to catch up to and surpass the economic, political, and population dominance of San Francisco. Los Angeles County's population tripled to nearly 100,000 between 1880 and 1890. Initially the primary industry was agriculture, mainly oranges and grapes. When a railway line reached Los Angeles from San Francisco in 1876, the agriculture industry began to boom. This accelerated in the late nineteenth and early twentieth centuries with the introduction of refrigerated railroad cars, improved canning technology and methods for freezing produce, farm machinery improvements, and sophisticated irrigation systems. But agriculture did not long hold sway in Southern California. Oil was discovered in the late nineteenth century, and in the early twentieth century the movie industry relocated to Southern California. The movie industry was central to economic and population growth as well as urban expansion in the early twentieth century. In addition to the motion picture industry, the garment and furniture industries and aircraft and defense industries were dominant in the years leading up to World War II.

Oil has remained important, and Southern California ranks fourth in the nation in production. Most production is in Southern California's coastal regions, but small fields have also been found in the southern San Joaquin Valley. It is likely that there are other, possibly extensive, oil fields in the state that have not been discovered. Four of ten of the nation's most productive oil fields are located in California. In 1965 Long Beach sold the first major offshore leases to oil companies.

California's offshore reserves are among the largest in North America, and in order to avert controversy, offshore platforms were disguised as islands with palm trees, waterfalls, lights, and so on. But in the 1990s offshore drilling was ended due to successful lobbying by environmental groups concerned about the potential for disaster from an oil leak. This will continue to be an issue of debate in the future. The vast reserves off the California coast and in the Alaskan wilderness will continue to tempt our leadership's will to preserve the environment.

Southern California's nonfarming sector of the state's economy is decidedly postindustrial. The defense industries that had been the mainstay of the economy since World War II declined about 50 percent during the 1980s and early 1990s. The primary economic sectors are now electronics, high-tech research and development, and service industries. The low-tech sectors of the economy, primarily the clothing and furniture industries, are, much like California agriculture, dependent on immigrant labor. Sweatshop conditions are the foundation of the clothing and furniture industries, and many of the workers are undocumented immigrants from across the border. The entertainment industry maintains its dominance in Southern California but in the 1990s became much more prominent in Northern California as high-tech became an integral part of moviemaking. New forms of computer-generated animation have been responsible for a shift in industry power and money to the San Francisco Bay area and its immediate environs. This highlights another interesting pattern in California's geography: there has always been a competition for power and influence between Northern and Southern California characterized by shifts from one region of the state to the other, primarily catalyzed by economic change.

In Northern California, government and high-tech have been the prominent agents of industrial growth. The government is the largest employer in San Francisco, which is second only to Washington, D.C., in numbers of federal employees. The south bay is one of the ten leading industrial centers in the country, with Silicon Valley in the lead. But Silicon Valley, like many California industries, was characterized by a boom-and-bust mentality. The bust occurred in the late 1990s, and many small companies simply disappeared. The major technology industries, such as Apple, IBM, and Sun, are still around and apparently entering another growth phase. It remains to be seen if this new growth will be controllable or if we will see a new version of the gold rush in Silicon Valley and the attendant boom-and-bust economy.

URBAN AREAS

There are only a few large cities in the Pacific Region, most located in California, but urbanization continues at a fairly rapid pace throughout. In 2001, California's population was around 35 million, and according to projections, that number will swell to nearly 40 million by 2010. Most of the population lives in urban regions of the state. Today, California's population growth rate is nearly double that for the entire country. More than one-third of foreign-born residents in the United States live in California. While 10 percent of the U.S. population is foreign born, 25 percent of California's population is foreign born. California has the second highest birthrate in the country and the highest rate of teen pregnancy.

In the 1980s there was a net gain of 800,000 people with 50 percent of them born in the state and 50 percent migrating in from other states and countries.

In the 1990s there was a net loss of people to other states, many relocating to Oregon, Washington, Idaho, and Montana while maintaining their employment in California by telecommuting. Ironically, as people left California looking for better quality of life, clean air and water, and open space, they created conditions similar to those they were trying to escape. For example, Oregon's population grew 1.8 percent between 1990 and 1997, with 70 percent coming from other states. The impact of this growth has been increasingly congested roads, overburdened infrastructure, and concerns about air and water pollution. California's urban areas, however, have struggled with these concerns for decades and partly as a result are distinctive in both form and function. The most accurate characterization of California's urban environment is urban sprawl. California's love affair with the automobile, which began when the first vehicle rolled into the state, remains the catalyst for this pervasive sprawl.

Southern California

Southern California can be characterized as the only megalopolis on the West Coast. Its extent ranges from Palm Springs to Santa Barbara, Lancaster to the Mexican border, and San Diego to Santa Barbara. Southern California's urban regions are mostly located in lowlands and valleys. Los Angeles, with a population of nearly 10 million, is the major center of this megalopolis, which is connected by a highly developed, although increasingly inadequate, freeway system. The city of Los Angeles is a minority city, and although the largest group is Latino (40 percent), there is no clear majority group. The Los Angeles region increasingly resembles East Coast and midwestern cities more than other cities in California or the Pacific Region.

San Diego is California's second largest city, with a population around 1.3 million. Around 49 percent of the population is white, 25 percent Latino, and just under 14 percent Asian. By 2020 projections place San Diego's population at around 1.7 million. This is one of the state's most rapidly growing urban areas. San Diego's economy is primarily dependent on tourism and the military. It is homeport to two aircraft carriers and several other ships from the Pacific Fleet. Its beautiful climate and landscape make it a popular tourist destination. Its location makes it a strategic naval location. While urban sprawl threatens to bring San Diego under the influence of the Los Angeles megalopolis, the city fights to maintain its identity and independence from the greater Los Angeles area.

The San Francisco Urban Area

From the gold rush to World War I, San Francisco was the largest city in the western United States. The population in 1848 was 800 and by 1850 had grown to 35,000. Over the next decade it continued to grow at a phenomenal rate, reaching 50,000 by 1860. Since World War II there has been a significant diffusion of metropolitan focus in the Bay Area with three major areas of development: San Francisco, San Jose, and Oakland. The Bay Area, although connected by transportation routes and commute traffic, is not a megalopolis but rather three discrete regions with none dominant over the others. San Francisco, one of the least industrialized cities in the United States, is most known for its character, beauty, history, and culture. Because of its location on a peninsula, the city can only grow up, not out, so growth is constrained by its environment and geography. As a consequence, it has one of the densest populations in the country and the densest west of Chicago. San Francisco's economy is primarily based on tourism and finance.

According to the 2000 census, San Francisco's population was 776,773. In 2002 the population was estimated at 744,881, a decrease of more than 30,000 in only two years. In contrast to Los Angeles, San Francisco is not yet a minority city but is moving in that direction. According to the 2000 census, about 44 percent of the population was white, while the next largest group, Asian, represented 30 percent of the city's population. The next largest group was Latino, at only 14 percent. Housing is tall, narrow, close together, and very close to the street. There are few yards, although there are many parks and playgrounds. Many of San Francisco's neighborhoods have a very distinctive ethnic character, and at times, traveling from one to another feels almost like moving from one country to another. The language, food, smells, and architecture are reminiscent of another place and often another time in some of the neighborhoods. All of this contributes to the city's very cosmopolitan ambiance.

The East Bay is a sprawling urban complex dominated to a certain extent by Oakland but only because it is the largest city. It is a region of contrasts, with some of the Bay Area's most affluent neighborhoods and most poverty-stricken ghettos. There are several small commercial areas but no major industry outside of the port of Oakland, which is one of the world's largest container ports. Oakland's population first mushroomed after the 1906 earthquake when many people opted to move across the Bay rather than remain in San Francisco. According to the 2000 census, Oakland's population was 399,484, and unlike other cities in the Bay Area, the population increased between 2000 and 2002, with current estimates at 412,777. Projections estimate continued growth for Oakland, topping out at around 476,000 in 2025. While Oakland is a minority city, it is the only large city in California with African Americans holding a slim majority at nearly 36 percent of the population. Thirty-one percent is white, 15 percent Asian, and 22 percent Latino. In 2002 the Forbes Annual Survey of the Best Places in America for Business and Careers ranked Oakland eighth in the country.[1] The same year San Francisco dropped from third to fifty-fourth and San Jose from first to sixty-first. In addition, *Newsweek* ranked Oakland as one of the country's top-ten technology cities in April 2001.[2] While San Francisco and San Jose are experiencing a clear downturn, Oakland in many ways is growing stronger and more influential both politically and economically.

The South Bay is also characterized primarily by urban sprawl and is clearly an industrial region. It has undergone a phenomenal transformation from agriculture and food processing to durable goods manufacture and urban service industries in a very short period of time. There have been increasing concerns about limiting urban sprawl in the South Bay in the face of incredible population growth during the Silicon Valley boom years. Property values skyrocketed, and new, large homes and gated communities appeared seemingly overnight. Green space became increasingly squeezed and native fauna and flora overrun by jogging and bike paths that wound through mountain lion habitat. The South Bay is still struggling to come to terms with the residual effects of the boom and dealing with the ramifications of the bust. The urban center of the South Bay is San Jose, California's third largest city. The population of 894,943 in 2000 was fairly evenly distributed, with 36 percent white, 30 percent Latino, and nearly 27 percent Asian. In 2002 the population was estimated around 925,000, a surprising increase considering the economic impact of the Silicon Valley bubble burst. Even so, many new, luxury housing units sit empty—a testament to the consequences of California's continual pattern of boom-and-bust economies.

Urban development in the Central Valley has been increasing primarily because of lower land values, allowing construction of new, affordable homes and increasing numbers of people willing to commute to jobs in the Bay Area. There are nine primary urban areas in the Valley from Redding to Bakersfield, but the only one even resembling a metropolitan area is Sacramento, the state's capital city. Sacramento has experienced growth in population at an explosive rate in the 1980s and 1990s. Manufacturing companies, particularly in the aerospace industry, have been relocating to the Sacramento area over the past ten years because of lower land prices and lower cost of living for employees. With the exception of San Diego, California's primary cities are minority cities. This is perhaps a precursor of the changing face of the state in the future.

Alaska, Washington, and Oregon Urban Areas

The largest city in Alaska is Anchorage, where 260,283 of the state's 626,932 people live. The population is around 70 percent white, 7.3 percent Native American, 5.8 percent African American, 5.5 percent Asian, and 5.7 percent Latino. The next largest city is Juneau, with a population of only 30,711, and Fairbanks is close behind with 30,244.

Portland and Seattle are the two major cities in the Pacific Northwest and are remarkably similar in size and character. One important similarity is a relatively small downtown area as the hub of a large metropolitan area. The 2000 population of both cities was just over half a million, with Seattle at 563,374 and Portland at 536,240. The greater Seattle metro area population in 2000 was 3,275,847, and the greater Portland metro area was around 1.95 million. The population of both cities is overwhelmingly white. Seattle's population is 70 percent white, 8.4 percent African American, 13 percent Asian, and 5.3 percent Latino, while Portland is 84.3 percent white, 8.7 percent Latino, 4.1 percent Asian, and 2.4 percent African American. Portland, indeed the entire state, is currently in a significant growth phase, with the state's population projected to increase by 27 percent between 2000 and 2010. Portland's population growth rate from 1986 to 2000 was around 2.2 percent, with total population growth from 1990 to 2000 at 21 percent. Both Seattle and Portland are industrial cities with high-tech at the center. The U.S. military is one of the largest employers in the Puget Sound Region, with five military bases. In terms of revenue, Boeing is still Seattle's largest employer, with Microsoft third. Tourism is Seattle's fourth largest industry. In contrast, one of Portland's largest growth industries is biotech, primarily in the health care sector. The number of jobs in the greater Portland metro area increased by 43 percent between 1990 and 2002. Although Portland is a beautiful city, tourism is not a significant sector of the economy, and the city seems to be a stop along the way to somewhere else rather than a destination. In contrast, Seattle is an important tourist area for the region.

Hawai'i's Urban Areas

Hawai'i is realistically a one-city region. Fully 80 percent of the population of the islands live in Honolulu. The city contains most of the economic, political, and military activity. It also has increasing population density, in some places more than 50,000 persons per square mile, and the problems that go along with dense populations. Traffic congestion has been increasing for the past twenty years, with the number of cars tripling since 1970. This is a reflection of the growth of the tourist industry. Most of the cars on the road are rentals driven by tourists. The city suffers from problems caused by unregulated high-rise construction and lack of sewage treatment facilities. Raw sewage is still dumped into the ocean. Most of the population growth comes from people moving in from other states. In the 1980s alone, population increased 23 percent, and 70 percent of the population is not Hawai'i born. Development in urban areas has proceeded at a breakneck pace without concern for human or ecological welfare. Resort hotels, roads, and golf courses are continually being developed. In 1960 there were about 5,000 visitor accommodations; by 1999 that number had risen to 70,000. This rapid urbanization and resort development are dangerous to the island's fragile ecosystem. New zoning and land-use restrictions might help if they are implemented soon enough to make a difference. But the tourist industry is so important that it is unlikely that development will be curbed on any significant scale.

ECOLOGICAL ISSUES

A fact of life in Southern California, smog, is created by the intersection of environmental conditions and human agency. The physical location of Los Angeles in a basin, where wind speed is low and mountains and ocean air act as a lid, keeps the pollution created by massive numbers of automobiles trapped in the basin. Commuting is one of the most important factors in air pollution in the Los Angeles region. The average commuter in this area spends triple the time in the car of any other commuters in the country. While air quality is improving because of stringent regulations introduced in the 1990s, it remains a health problem with potential for continuing ecological degradation. This, however, is only one of the myriad ecological issues in the state. As already mentioned, wildfires—especially when the hot, dry Santa Ana winds blow across the hills toward the ocean—cause significant ecological damage as well as creating situations ripe for other problems. Because wildfires are most common in the late fall, massive precipitation often falls on the heels of disastrous fires. With vegetation burned, there is nothing to hold the hillsides in place, and mudslides further damage an already wounded environment.

California's most serious environmental problems stem from four primary factors: (1) urbanization and rapid population growth; (2) massive water projects and irrigation; (3) industrial waste; and (4) residual effects of the gold rush. Rapid population growth and urbanization put pressure on every aspect of California's environment. As previously stated, California has built massive water delivery systems to supply water to growing urban areas and to agriculture. These projects are responsible for habitat destruction in the Delta and San Francisco Bay. Annually, 60 percent of the natural runoff in the Delta–Bay watershed is diverted into California's aqueduct system. Only a tiny percentage of the state's riparian, tidal wetlands, and fish-spawning habitat remains viable. All salmon species in the state are either listed as endangered or being considered for that designation. California agriculture is dependent on irrigation and uses, inefficiently, most of the water moved through the extensive aqueduct system. Because subsidies result in farmers paying significantly below market value for water, there is little incentive to conserve water or to use more efficient irrigation methods. These subsidies are now going to turn into a profit-generating opportunity for farmers in the Imperial Valley under an agreement designed to reduce California's use of water from the Colorado River. Under the agreement brokered by Interior Secretary Gale Norton in 2003, farmers will continue to pay only a bare fraction of the cost and will be allowed to sell the water to Los Angeles or San Diego at fair market value.

Manufacturing is one of the grossest polluters in the state. The environmental damage caused by industrial waste is not just the product of aging facilities and obsolete technology. While the high-tech industry has figured out how to put massive amounts of data on a single, tiny chip, it has not come up with a method of doing that without releasing toxic chemicals into the environment. Indeed, most of the worst superfund sites in the state are located near high-tech industries. It is ironic that the late-twentieth-century equivalent of the gold rush is leaving the same legacy as the mid-nineteenth-century gold rush. The legacy of the gold rush is not at all shiny and bright. California continues to suffer increasing environmental degradation as a direct result of mining practices from the mid- to late nineteenth century. Habitat degradation primarily due to hydraulic mining moving tons of earth and water is, of course, still impacting the state. However, one of the most dangerous legacies of the gold rush is mercury contamination of most of the state's waterways as well as soil. Hydraulic mining flushed arsenic, mercury, cyanide, and acid into California's soil, groundwater, lakes, and rivers. Many abandoned mines were never cleaned up and continue to leach toxins into the environment. Mercury was used in mining in Northern California, and between 1850 and 1900, about 26 million pounds were used by the industry to extract gold from ore. Later erosion and drainage dispersed mercury further into the environment on a broad scale. Clear Lake currently contains about 100 tons of mercury. The state continually advises against eating fish caught in California's waterways because of mercury contamination.

A limited land mass and increasing population pressures exacerbate many of the ecological problems Hawai'i is faced with. Hawai'i's isolation from continents or other islands of appreciable size resulted in flora and fauna that are both limited in variety and unusual in comparison with other states. While tourism is the primary industry, it also contributes to environmental problems in significant ways. Energy development, wastewater and sewage management, watershed protection, land use change, overcrowded beaches, increasing traffic on narrow roads, and increased pressure on natural resources are only some of the problems generated by the tourist industry. This double-edged sword in which tourism provides most employment and economic gain for the state is also one of the most environmentally damaging. The other major industry, the military, is equally if not more damaging to Hawai'i's natural environment. The military is responsible for Hawai'i's superfund sites and is not just a gross polluter of air, water, and land but contributes to environmental degradation in other ways. Unexploded ordnance has been dumped in several places on the islands. Beaches are isolated from public access and used as target ranges for bombing practice.

Sugar and pineapple plantations are responsible for large areas of arable land contaminated with chemicals. Topsoil is also gone, and soil nutrients have been so depleted that it is doubtful whether much of the land is capable of agricultural production. As former plantation lands have been taken out of production and sold, people building homes there have experienced unusually high rates of asthma, autoimmune diseases, and reproductive problems. Some of the plantations have been subdivided into five- or ten-acre farms and sold to private parties. The purchasers often find that the soil is so depleted that their dreams of establishing a small farm will not come to fruition any time soon.

Hawai'i is a classic island environment exhibiting the typical fragile ecosystem. More than 95 percent of the state's species are endemic to the islands. As with many other island ecosystems, it did not take long after contact for most species to be exterminated, significantly endangered, or displaced by humans and alien species. The only mammals native to Hawai'i are the monk seal and the hoary bat, and both are endangered. Since Captain James Cook (1728–1779) landed for the first time in 1778, more than 4,000 seed-bearing plants have been introduced. There are also more introduced freshwater fish, birds, and reptiles than natives. Introduced species include sheep, goats, pigs, cattle, dogs, and cats, feral as well as domesticated. Exotic introduced species include mongoose and axis deer. Feral animals destroy plants and other animals and are a clear danger to the survival of the limited native species that remain. They can also be dangerous if accidentally confronted in the wild. Feral pigs are perhaps the most well known example of this danger. Unfortunately, feral animals have also provided a foundation for a new tourist attraction, sport hunting. Sport hunters are becoming increasingly vocal opponents of any proposals to exterminate the feral pig population.

The loss of native species is not as well known. According to the Environmental Defense Fund, Hawai'i is the global capital of endangered species.[3] Hawai'i's ecosystems are among the most endangered in the United States. Hawai'i has lost a greater percentage of flora and fauna than any other state. Nearly 300 species are on the Endangered Species List. Hawai'i also has about 410,000 acres of coral reef that is in serious danger due to a variety of pollution sources. More than 70 percent of all U.S. plant extinctions have taken place in Hawai'i, and more than 25 percent of the country's endangered plants and birds are in Hawaii.

The Columbia River Basin is important habitat for five species of anadromous salmon (pink, Chinook, Coho, chum, and sockeye) as well as steelhead, smelt, shad, and lamprey. Salmon stocks have declined dramatically in the twen-

Salmon fishing in the Columbia River in Oregon, 1899. Courtesy of the Library of Congress.

tieth century for a variety of reasons. From the late 1800s to early 1900s, over-fishing put tremendous pressure on the population of salmon along the Pacific Coast. But other factors in the twentieth century, such as habitat destruction from farming, cattle grazing, mining, logging, road construction, and industrial pollution, have further reduced the salmon population, and most species are considered endangered. As mentioned earlier, dams especially impede spawning because they destroy spawning habitat and the salmon's ability to get upstream.

The Puget Sound Basin suffers from severe pollution attributed to several causes but primarily population growth and urbanization, military, and industrial waste. While dumping toxic waste has been severely reduced, the damage will impact the health of water, soil, plants, animals, and humans for a long time. About 90,000 acres of the seafloor are considered moderately to highly contaminated. Urban growth is arguably the biggest threat to the health of the region. Population in the area surrounding the Sound is expected to increase by about 1.3 million by 2025. A large military presence also contributes to contamination of groundwater and soils. Thirty-one sites in the region are polluted enough to be on the Superfund list, and thirteen of them were created by the army and navy. Some of the greatest volumes of wastewater come from overburdened sewage treatment plants run by local governments. Many of these plants are so old and outdated that they cannot handle the pollution created by rapidly growing populations and are actually major sources of heavy metal contamination.

The oil spill in Prince William Sound in 1989 was the largest oil spill in American history as well as the most recognizable. Nearly 11 million gallons of crude oil spilled. While this caused severe ecological damage from which Alaska and the Sound region are still struggling to recover, there are many other ecological problems that plague the state. It was also not an isolated incident. Oil spills occur with alarming regularity in Alaska; although all are damaging, some are devastating. In 1998 the Trans-Alaska pipeline in Prudoe Bay exploded, damaging nearby landscapes. Even so, the current administration in Washington, D.C., and some in Alaska would like to increase Alaska's economic dependence on its oil reserves. Alaska has oil reserves that the administration would like to open for

The Alaska pipeline. Courtesy of Getty Images/PhotoDisc.

drilling. However, the reserves in question are located in the Arctic National Wildlife Refuge, and in March 2003 the U.S. Senate voted down a proposal to open 1.5 million acres of the Refuge to drilling. Alaska also has the largest fairly intact coastal temperate rainforest in the world along a 1,000-mile arc of coastline. Deforestation has been an ongoing problem in Alaska since the early twentieth century. Much of Alaska's timber industry was generated by the pulp market rather than lumber. Most of the pulp was produced for rayon and cellophane rather than paper products. While Japan was a primary export market for lumber, the market has dropped dramatically in the past few years. High production costs in Alaska make the pulp and timber industry unable to compete with Washington and British Columbia. While this creates economic problems for communities reliant on this industry, it is good news for the forests.

The industry that is increasingly responsible for damage to Alaska's ecosystem is the cruise industry. As previously mentioned, this is one of Alaska's growth industries, and it comes with a host of potential and actual problems for the environment. Federal law prohibits ships from dumping waste within three miles of the shoreline. Generally, the company policy of cruise ship lines is to dump beyond twelve miles. However, "accidental" discharges in harbors and ports are becoming increasingly commonplace. These discharges can do substantial damage, considering the amount of waste that is generated on cruise ships. For example, in August 2002, a cruise ship discharged 40,000 gallons of partially treated sewage into Juneau Harbor. In general, an average cruise ship generates about 100 gallons of wastewater per person per day. This includes about 10 gallons of sewage and 3.5 kilograms (7.7 pounds) of solid waste per person per day. While one of the most significant ecological problems, waste discharge is not the only issue. Up to 10,000 visitors a day disembark in towns with infrastructure for around 1,500 to 2,000 permanent residents.

Cruise ships also collide with whales, discharge treated sewage into fragile ecosystems without knowledge of the long-term impact, and carry alien species on their hull and in their ballast. While this is an increasingly important industry for Alaska in economic terms, it is increasingly deleterious in human and ecological terms. There is a great deal of conflict in Alaska between conservation and economic growth. Different stakeholders have different priorities, often at odds with one another. For example, debates over oil, Alaskan Natives land claims, whaling by Native peoples, and tourism all involve groups competing for their "share" of a limited and sensitive environment. Alaska's isolation means that there are relatively few opportunities for economic growth, especially when trying to maintain the environment.

The Pacific Region as a whole has 166 sites on the Superfund National Priorities List (NPL) for cleanup. California has the most, with more than twice the number of sites as Washington. There are 96 NPL sites in California clustered in five regions. Santa Clara

Ecological Effects of Cruises on Alaskan Towns

With cruises along the Alaska coast, towns are often overrun with people, noise, refuse, and waste. Sitka alone gets about 225,000 cruise ship passengers a year. And the summer cruise season in Alaska is very short. The citizens of Sitka voted overwhelmingly against building a wharf that would allow cruise ship passengers to disembark directly into downtown. They hoped that by forcing the ships to transport people by lifeboat they could limit the number of visitors.

County has 23 sites, and 16 of them are located at high-tech companies. Washington has 48 sites, with most clustered around the south Puget Sound area and Spokane. Four of the sites are located on the site of the Hanford nuclear facility. There are 11 sites in Oregon, most along the Columbia River and in the Portland metro area. Alaska's 7 sites are divided between Anchorage (3) and Fairbanks (4), and 4 of the 7 are military sites. Finally, Hawai'i has the fewest, with 4. Three of the 4 are located at Pearl Harbor, and the other is located at the site of the Del Monte plantation on Oahu. In other words, all 4 are located on Oahu.

CONCLUSION

While the Pacific Region has many significant problems in terms of increasing population, urbanization proceeding at a pace the infrastructure cannot keep up with, and environmental degradation, it is also one of the most beautiful regions in the United States. Most of the country's wilderness areas are located in the West. About 10 percent of Washington's total acreage is designated wilderness area. Three percent of Oregon's total acreage, 14 percent of California, 16 percent of Alaska, and 4 percent of Hawai'i's total acreage are designated wilderness. In addition, Oregon has forty-seven wild and scenic rivers, while there are three in Washington, fourteen in California, and twenty-five in Alaska.

The Pacific Region is an integral part of the Pacific Rim economy and the center of the high-tech industry in the West. It is beautiful, wild, urbanized, highly populated, and underpopulated. It is a place of intense urbanization and unspeakably beautiful wild and scenic places. It is the most agriculturally productive region in the United States and has some of the most serious ecological problems affecting the water needed to continue adequate food production. Hollywood and Disneyland attract visitors from all over the country and indeed all over the world. Extreme skiers trek to the peaks of Alaska, and the excitement of river rafting on the wild rivers attracts people from all over the world. The Pacific Region is a place defined by its diversity and contradictory nature. In some ways, it is paradoxical in nature. It is extremely dry and wet, urban and rural, rich and poor, conservative and liberal, and it is all this at once.

RESOURCE GUIDE

Printed Resources

Durbin, Kathie. *Tongass: Pulp Politics and the Fight for the Alaska Rain Forest.* Corvallis: Oregon State University Press, 1999.

Goble, Dale D., and Paul W. Hirt, eds. *Northwest Lands, Northwest Peoples.* Seattle: University of Washington Press, 1999.

Klein, Ross A. *Cruise Ship Blues: The Underside of the Cruise Ship Industry.* Gabriola Island, British Columbia: New Society Publishers, 2002.

Merchant, Carolyn, ed. *Green versus Gold: Sources in California's Environmental History.* Washington, DC: Island Press.

Walker, Richard. "California's Golden Road to Riches: Natural Resources and Regional Capitalism, 1848–1940." *Annals of the Association of American Geographers* 91.1 (2001): 167–199.

Organizations

Earth Share of Washington
1402 3rd Avenue, Suite 817
Seattle, WA 98101
http://www.esw.org/index.php

An alliance of environmental organizations dedicated to proactive environmental programs.

Ecotrust
Jean Vollum Natural Capital Center
721 NW Ninth Avenue, Suite 200
Portland, OR 97209
503-227-6225
http://www.ecotrust.org/index.html

Pacific Northwest action group promoting economic, ecologic, and socially equitable planning for the region.

Natural Resources Defense Council
71 Stevenson Street, #1825
San Francisco, CA 94105
415-777-0220
1314 Second Street
Santa Monica, CA 90401
310-434-2300
http://www.nrdc.org/

The Natural Resources Defense Council is a national, nonprofit organization that brings together scientists, lawyers and environmental specialists to promote environmental policies.

The Sierra Club
85 Second Street, 2nd Floor
San Francisco, CA 94105
415-977-5500
http://www.sierraclub.org/

The oldest environmental organization in the country, founded by conservationist John Muir.

ETHNICITY

Aaron DiFranco and
Kella de Castro Svetich

Even as discussions have begun taking a broad focus on the landscape called "Pacific Rim culture," that culture has long been recognized as being composed of a plurality of ethnic practices and sociopolitical identifications. The Pacific Region's vast, varied landscape—from Alaska's Arctic tundra to the Southern Hemisphere shores of American Samoa to the temperate ranges and river valleys of the country's western coast—is home to a population as amazingly varied in its ethnic composition. The 2000 U.S. Census recorded 45 million people living throughout the region, among them some of the most distinctive populations in the United States.

California is central to understanding the region's demography. The most populous U.S. state since 1964, California was home to over 33 million people—an astounding 12 percent of the national population—in 2000 and still continues to grow. Over 500,000 individuals continue to enter the state every year, and only with recent economic and geopolitical troubles have these numbers started to slow. The region's geography perpetuates historical trends, such as ongoing northward migration from Mexico, and trans-Pacific treks by Chinese, Filipinos, Japanese and other Asians, as well as continued arrivals from Russia and Denmark. Although thousands of Americans still respond to the dictum to "Go West," most of the new arrivals to California are foreign born. Indeed, 25 percent of the state's current residents have immigrated from other countries, making it one of the most cosmopolitan, multicultural mixes anywhere. More immigrants choose to live in California over any other state, promising a continuous flux to the region's ethnic composition. While California's vast immigrant population makes it a major focal point in demographic discussions, indigenous cultures also thrive throughout the region. Over 400 federally recognized tribes, bands, and villages are located in the region. This includes ethnically (and legally) distinct Native Alaskans as well as Native Hawaiians. Hawai'i itself is unique in its population, a crossroads of the Pacific Rim where Asian and European immigrants mix with Polynesian and Micronesian residents.

While the East Coast has historically presented itself for transatlantic diasporas from Europe and Africa, the West Coast has absorbed waves of immigrants from all points along the Pacific Rim as well as migratory pulsing across the interior of the continent. Russian, Spanish, British, and U.S. governments have all supported exploration and colonial settlement of the Pacific: a variety of rich agricultural regions, rangelands, forested reserves, coastal fishing, and mineral wealth have inspired the grand claims of nations as well as the simple claims of people looking to make a life. More recently, the digital economy has inspired transformations of the Pacific's ethnic composition, as the high-tech industry draws people from Calcutta to Cleveland. These claims have not gone without challenge by indigenous peoples of all territories, including the Chamorro of Guam, Aleut throughout the Bering Strait, confederated tribes in the Pacific Northwest, and remnant tribes of California's rancherias. Even while preserving much land-based cultural tradition, native groups have transformed in response to the contemporary American scene: Native Alaskan villagers have become shareholders in trust of their land and resource rights; California tribes renegotiate their existence in the wake of the 1988 Indian Gaming Regulatory Act.

Discussions of culture unfortunately favor those ethnicities of a certain gravity—large enough, dense enough, persistent enough—which initiate and preserve identities in and against broader social currents. Yet it should not be forgotten that the Pacific Coast population offers a multicultural flux of peoples. According to the 2000 U.S. Census, the metropolitan areas affixed to Los Angeles and San Francisco have foreign-born populations of almost 30 percent (approximately 1.5 million people each). Although U.S. nation building—even to the present moment—has operated to permit a European-heritaged "white" social hegemony, groups of all backgrounds have maintained cohesive ethnic ties while building culturally plural foundations throughout the Pacific. While this chapter emphasizes the broader historical movements of ethnic groups, it should be remembered that each of these groups also consists of a plurality of people with differing practices, political struggles, and cultural loyalties.

INDIGENOUS PEOPLES OF THE PACIFIC REGION

Natives of Alaska

The Alaskan subcontinent has long been recognized as the major gateway through which human cultures migrated and eventually came to settle both the North and South American continents. The low sea level of the earth during the last Ice Age exposed as dry land the area between the Asian and American continents that is now the Bering Strait. Called Beringia by anthropologists and geologists, this arctic grassland provided a natural "land bridge" that nomadic peoples crossed pursuing game and other food supplies. This land bridge was exposed from about 50,000 years ago until the Ice Age ended around 10,000 B.C.E., and plausible speculation suggests that migrations into North America may have occurred severally during this time. However, most accounts place the first major wave of human migration from Siberia into Alaska at approximately 15,000 years ago, just as the Ice Age was winding down. Following animal migrations, this first wave traveled along several routes, including a coastal route along the Pacific Ocean, through North, Central, and South America. A second migratory wave out of Siberia between 8000 and 5000 B.C.E. brought peoples speaking Na-Dene languages who came to inhabit northern and western North America. These peoples were followed by Eska-Aleut speakers during the next two millennia, who spread north across North America to Greenland and whose present-day Alaskan descendants include the Aleuts, Aleutiiq, Inupiat, and Yup'ik.

While evidence for a sustained human presence in Alaska has been dated to the end of the Ice Age 15,000 years ago, most ancestors of contemporary Alaskan Natives arrived during the second migration wave 5,000 to 10,000 years ago. A variety of social alignments exists among Alaskan Natives, connecting peoples from differing yet contiguous regions. Kinship, base territory, language ties, regional grouping, and even corporate associations have all been factors shaping identity among the Alaskan peoples, and it should not be forgotten that

Kaw-Claa. Tlinget native woman in full potlatch dancing costume, 1906. Courtesy of the Library of Congress.

Alaska is the largest state of the United States. Generally speaking, at least eleven distinct native cultures have established themselves, although organizations like the Alaska Native Heritage Center emphasize five major "groupings" according to geography and common social and linguistic practices: Aleut and Alutiiq villages are scattered along the southern edge of the state and across the Aleutian Islands; Yup'ik and Cup'ik peoples occupy the coast and immediate inland of southwest Alaska; Inupiat and the associated Saint Lawrence Island Peoples dwell in the far north regions; Athabascan villages spread throughout the state's interior; and Tlingit, Haida, Eyak, and Tsimshian cultures share the southeast panhandle bordering British Columbia. Within these groupings, various village and clan organizations have historically influenced the development of each culture. For example, nine Athabascan ethnic groups are known by their varying dialects, and these language groups can be further divided into local bands. Aleuts sometimes warred among themselves, making raids on rival villages and taking captives, as did other native groups. Tlingit and Haida were known as fierce warriors, with Haida raids extending as far as Puget Sound in Washington.

Traditionally, the Native Alaskan peoples were subsistence hunters and gatherers who grounded their lifestyles in the various migratory species of the region. Across the state, a wide selection of berries, wild greens, and roots were used by native groups, though hunting and fishing provided most of their sustenance. For

Microblades

A significant part of the archaeological record of human migration into Alaska has been the uncovering of microblades, small stone hunting tools presumably used by nomadic hunters following caribou and other locally common mammal herds. Their presence at various sites suggests that early peoples slowly penetrated the state between 11,000 and 6,000 years ago. However, the character of artifacts changes after this point. More distinctive regional styles emerge, implying a developed acculturation and persistent dwelling in the given landscapes. Also, microblades quickly fade in prominence in favor of points for spears, harpoons, lances, and the like. Many researchers read these changes in relation to local and global environmental changes, as boreal forests began succeeding the grasslands throughout the Alaskan interior. The discussion of the shift from microblades reflects a truism regarding the ethnographic study of cultures: that culture evolves in relation to the local environment and its available resources. For example, given the length of Alaska's coastline—33,000 total miles, equal to that of the continental United States—and the abundant ocean and freshwater resources, the development of harpoon and lance blades by the arriving peoples for fishing and sea-hunting seems eminently obvious. Yet it would be a mistake to simply "naturalize" these adaptations, for they are bound not only to the landscape but also to a complex of social traditions and evolving practices that define and determine ethnic identity.

Athabascan villages in Alaska's interior, a network of major rivers provided a rich salmon harvest. This diet was supplemented by caribou, moose, beaver, and other small mammals as well as waterfowl and numerous other migratory birds that nest there in summer. Coastal communities, including the Yup'ik, Alutiiq, Haida, Tlingit, and others of the southeast, also took advantage of the seasonal salmon runs. However, coastal and island cultures also developed distinctly impressive ocean travel and hunting methods. For example, Inupiaq villages in the northernmost regions relied primarily on the spring and summer arrival of large marine mammals such as walrus, bowhead, and beluga whales. Such hunts led to the use of large skin boats, which could hold over a dozen people and extremely heavy cargoes. Aleuts used single-person *baidarka*, or kayaks, to hunt the Steller sea lion—their primary prey—as well as seals, sea otters, and whales. Whales were also hunted from single-hunter kayaks using poison-tipped harpoons. Alutiiqs used similar kayak hunting practices, as did some Yup'ik communities, who also used kayaks to set driftnets. Whitefish, rockfish, herring, shellfish, sea urchins, seaweed, and other marine resources also supplemented native diets.

At the cusp of the contact era, as European and U.S. concerns began pushing farther along the northern Pacific Coast, the native population of the Alaskan region stood at an estimated 80,000 to 100,000. Because of Alaska's remoteness and large size, contact came relatively late and in irregular stages. While the growth of the fur trade brought Europeans and Americans to the state's southern portions in the mid- and late 1700s, direct regular contact with native villages in the central and far north regions did not occur until the middle of the nineteenth century. Russian exploration by Ivan Federov (d. 1733) and Vitus Bering (1681–1741) initiated contact with Aleut peoples in the first half of the 1700s, and the radical growth of the fur trade—particularly in sea otter pelts—during the rest of the century brought the expansion of Russian influence across the Aleutian Island chain to the mainland and down along the state's southern coast. Although Aleuts and Alutiiqs at first welcomed trade with the Russians, who brought glass beads, tobacco, firearms, and other provisions, their villages were soon ravaged by disease and, despite resistance, subjugated by force and conversion. The Russian American Company also financed Orthodox missionaries to administer their colonial holdings. Among some villages, the Aleut in particular, this resulted in the spread of Russian Orthodox practice, intermarriage with Russian settlers, as well as the development of native language writing systems grounded in the Cyrillic alphabet. Native peoples were also exploited for their talents: the unparalleled skill of the Aleuts in the kayak made them formidable hunters, and Russian companies relocated them to areas rich in prey—even as far south as California—and forced them to hunt. When Russians discovered seal breeding grounds on the uninhabited Pribilof Islands in 1786, they established an Aleut outpost there; descendants of these relocated villagers still live on the islands today.

The opening of the north Pacific fur trade drew other foreign interests to these areas as well. When Captain James Cook (1728–1779) reached Cook Inlet in 1778, his reports brought U.S. and British concerns to the region, both of whom hoped to undermine the Russian fur monopoly expanding eastward. American traders provided firearms to the Tlingit and Haida, who then resisted Russian incursions into their territory. In 1802, the Tlingit under Katilan drove the Russians off Sitka Island. Though the Russians retook the island in 1805, they were never able to extend further into Tlingit or Haida lands. British traders also provided weapons and ammunition to native villagers, and when they established Fort Yukon in 1847, they completed an overland trade route that dealt directly—for the first time—with interior Athabascan trappers. Russian companies soon switched their attention to Alaska's western rim, where they also encountered an already established thriving trade in which coastal Inupiat dealt beaver, mink, and other pelts from Athabascan villages to Siberian Chukchi groups across the Bering Strait.

During the mid-1800s, British and American whaling industries also discovered the wealth of Arctic waters, thus beginning regular contact with far north Inupiat and St. Lawrence Island villages. This contact brought with it substantial material trade for these groups as well as the familiar ravages of imported disease. The effects of commercial whaling also devastated local communities as walrus and bowhead whale populations were virtually eradicated: 75 percent of the St. Lawrence Island population died of starvation in 1878–1879 when a devastatingly unsuccessful hunting season was followed by severe winter storms.

When Russia chose to eliminate its Alaskan colonial holdings in 1867, U.S. Secretary of State William Seward (1801–1872) negotiated the purchase of the territory for $7.2 million. Many Native Alaskan groups argued that Russia had little claim to "ownership" of Alaskan lands, particularly the Tlingit and Haida whose territories were being reserved as national forests. The U.S. government nevertheless asserted possession of the entire territory, reinforcing their authority by shelling Tlingit villages from a U.S. naval ship. The early U.S. territorial era saw an expansion of commercial fishing, timber harvesting, whaling, as well as mining after the 1896 discovery of gold in the Yukon. Settlement in Alaska by white Westerners was relatively slow but steady, continually increasing tensions over property rights and American encroachment. Territorial disputes reflected cultural disputes as Alaskans, like other tribes confronted by U.S. assimilationist policies, came under a missionizing educational system that rejected native languages. Sharp drops in Native Alaskan populations through the turn of the twentieth century due to imported smallpox, tuberculosis, and influenza as well as frequent strains to food resources brought the native population to a record low in 1909. Native Alaskans would become a minority in the territory by 1940.

Tlingit and Haida villages had already been pursuing numerous land claims with the U.S. government since 1929, yet these claims became more problematic in 1959, when Alaska became a state and 108 million acres of land—much of it traditional native lands—were reserved for state use. In response, native villages organized in protest. In 1966, the Alaskan Federation of Natives (AFN) formed to help resolve disputes over Native Alaskan rights. However, it was the discovery of oil in Alaska that finally enabled native, state, and business interests to work toward a resolution to the land claims. The Alaska Native Claims Settlement Act (ANCSA) of 1971 distributed cash compensation and landholdings to Alaskan Natives but also completely altered the social and political landscape by distributing these assets among twelve regional and 200 village "corporations." No longer direct inheritors of traditional lands, Native Alaskans became shareholders in their local land assets. ANSCA did not settle all disputes between natives and the state and federal governments—indeed, hunting and fishing rights became more contentious after its passage—but it did enable natives to manage and invest corporate monies for the benefit of local shareholders. Though these corporations have met with mixed success, their existence as both cultural and commercial institutions was reaffirmed in 1988 when ANCSA was amended to help protect corporation resources. Because of the northern territories' remoteness, as well as the relatively late era of contact, Alaska's native cultures have had some success at maintaining traditional lifestyles, but they have also labored firmly to adjust to modern conditions.

Tribes of the Pacific Northwest

The Haida and Tsimshians were also relatively recent arrivals to the Alaskan region, having migrated northward in the 1600s and 1800s, respectively, from areas of what is now British Columbia. Here they found dependable marine and freshwater food resources as well as abundant forests for household materials. Indeed, the temperate forests of these coastal areas have inspired similar lifestyles along the continent's edge—relatively stable settlements of cedar-plank houses; salmon dependence supplemented by various tubers, fruit, small game, and other seafood; strong river canoers; great skill in woodcraft and weaving—and these southeastern Alaskan villages are usually identified as belonging to a larger "Northwest Coast Culture" running through British Columbia to the north edge of California. Where these evergreen forests met the Pacific, tribes like Washington's Skagit, Hoh, Nisqually, and Chinook and Oregon's Tillamook, Siletz, and Coos built lifestyles that—like the salmon they harvested—depended on the freshwater rivers running through the Cascade and Coast Ranges to the ocean. Whaling culture was also common among some northwestern Washington coast tribes. Some whaling groups like the Makahs and Ozetts had migrated south along the Canadian coastline, but Quinaults and Quileutes developed their whaling practices originally off the Pacific Northwest shores.

Different cultures, however, developed in the Washington and Oregon interiors—almost eighty different tribes were present in the Pacific Northwest before contact with nonaboriginals. The Plateau cultures that spread from the Cascade Mountains across the watershed of the Columbia River formed an important trading link between coastal groups and the buffalo hunters of the Great Plains.

In this semiarid plain pressing across northern Idaho to the Rocky Mountains, tribes like the Spokane, Cayuse, Palouse, and Nez Perce came to supplement their river-centered cultures with horse economies. Though many tribes—particularly those of the Puget Sound area—were relatively peaceful, and extensive trade networks developed, tribes often skirmished with each other, sometimes raiding for slaves and goods, other times fighting for control of particular territories, particularly along the Lower Columbia and the valleys of its Willamette and Deschuttes tributaries. Language familiarity often led the way to alliances, as between Cayuse and Nez Perce, and these and other Plains tribes like the Paiute pushed against the older Salishan- and Chinookan-speaking peoples north of the Columbia River.

The arrival of Russian, Spanish, British, and U.S. fur interests at the end of the eighteenth century precipitated the radical transformation of the Pacific Northwest tribes. The American Robert Gray (1755–1806) sailed the Oregon coast in 1788, and the Britain George Vancouver (1757–1798) penetrated into Puget Sound in 1792. Both found tribes skeptical of the newcomers' intentions yet eager to trade for manufactured goods including clothes, cooking implements, knives, firearms, eastern tobacco, flour, and other foodstuffs. Pacific Northwest coastal tribes traded sea otter and seal; inland tribes dealt in beaver and mink. These furs were traded in East Asia for exotic goods that the maritime traders would then bring to Boston and London markets. Although traders occasionally used tribal rivalries to sell items like firearms and to force open lands for trapping, they generally preferred peace among the tribes so that energies could be focused on fur trade activities. Numerous outposts rose and fell during the early decades of the nineteenth century, establishing ties in the heart of tribal territories. These outposts forever altered the subsistence lifestyles of the inhabitants and brought a new commercial economy into Spokane, Colville, Umpqua territories, as well as among tribes clustered around the lower and middle Columbia River.

Tensions were often heightened between Northwest tribes and fur companies, especially when supplies failed to arrive at these outposts as expected. Various disease outbreaks contributed to debates raging among some Indian communities regarding whether trade should be continued. At the same time, a slow trickle of settlers began finding their way into the territory after Meriwether Lewis (1774–1809) and William Clark (1770–1838) led their Corps of Discovery mission down the Columbia to the Pacific in November 1805. Methodist Protestant and Roman Catholic missionaries followed in the 1830s, while increasing traffic along the Oregon Trail in the 1840s brought social and cultural pressures to the traditional inhabitants. Laws like the Homestead Act (1862) and the Donation Law (1850) extended the U.S. government's claims in the region while offering parcels of land to settlers. The increase of European and Yankee settlers as well as changes in game resources from the fur trade agitated local tribes and also increased intertribal tensions as groups were displaced out of their conventional territories. Even the rapid exhaustion of the buffalo was felt in the Pacific Northwest as dwindling herds prompted confrontations between Plains and Plateau tribes.

The pressures on land, food resources, and tribal health ignited a series of conflicts between Pacific Northwest tribes and the U.S. authority. The Cayuse War was the first of the so-called Indian Wars in the region, initiated when a band of Cayuse under Tiloukaikt (d. 1849) attacked the Protestant mission at Waiilatpu and killed Dr. Marcus Whitman (1802–1847), his wife Narcissa (1808–1847), and fourteen others. The attack came in retribution after mission "medicine" failed to stem a measles plague ravaging the Plateau tribes in 1847. The Cayuse often killed shamans who failed to cure patients, and they also blamed the mission for guiding into their lands settlers who carried a disease that killed over 200 members of their tribe. Among the conflicting cultural codes of settlers and diversely allied tribes, this act spurred spreading skirmishes and retaliations. The U.S. territorial authority spent several years attempting to bring the perpetrators to account, and Tiloukaikt and several others were eventually sentenced to hang.

Even while government agents worked through the mid-nineteenth century to forge treaties among the Northwest tribes, eight other wars, some of the last to pit the U.S. military against indigenous sovereign tribes, continued over the next three decades. Involving each distinct culture region of the territory, these wars also carried different instigating impulses. Tensions in the Northeast corner had been building for some time before the discovery of gold in Colville, Washington, and the rush of miners through the state accelerated war with the Yakima in 1855. The effort to secure tribes on newly designated reservations also stirred conflicts like the Bannock-Paiute War of 1878: Displaced onto the Fort Hall Reservation and unable to follow their traditional subsistence practices, hungry Bannocks led a revolt that spread into Oregon and among Umatilla Reservation Indians there. The eventual defeat of the militants resulted in even greater fragmentation as tribes were broken among reservations. Among those especially confounded by reservation confinement were many Paiute, who were force-marched north over 300 miles to share land with their old foe the Yakima at Yakima Reservation. Members of "unrecognized" tribes continued to be held and sent indiscriminately onto reservations through the turn of the century.

As stark as these conflicts could be, they are counterpointed by the statesmanship and guidance of many tribal leaders in the face of overwhelming threats to their people. Notable among them are Chief Seattle, Chief Joseph the Younger, and Sarah Winnemucca. Seattle (1786–1866) had been a great leader among Puget Sound tribes, leading raids against other tribes there as well as against early fur trade settlements. Yet Seattle's skill as a diplomat outshone even his formidable military skills, and he deftly negotiated with missionaries, fur traders, and the U.S. territorial governor. Although debates continue regarding the authenticity of his most famous speech, an elegant 1854 address accepting treaty restrictions for his people, his stature and dignity have garnered him lasting respect, especially among those who live in the city bearing his name. Chief Joseph (also Hin-mah-too-yah-lat-kekt, 1840–1904) was a leader of the Nez Perce. When gold was discovered along reservation lands in 1863, the Nez Perce resisted further containment on a far smaller reservation. Hounded by the army, Chief Joseph and his 700-member band began a rebellious 1,400-mile retreat toward the Canadian border. The band eventually surrendered, yet their courage and boldness won the admiration of many. Joseph's poignant surrender speech drew national attention, and for the rest of his life, he would speak out against government Indian policies. Sarah Winnemucca (also Theocmetony, 1844?–1891), originally a Northern Paiute from Nevada, served as an interpreter at several military outposts before joining the Paiute at the Malheur Reservation in Oregon. When fallout from the 1878 Bannock War forced Paiute prisoners to Washington's Yakima Reservation, Winnemucca marched with them and struggled for their release and the return of their

Malheur lands. Government authorities balked at the release of the captives, however. In defiance, Winnemucca initiated a nationwide lecture tour advocating for the Paiute and published in 1883 *Life among the Paiutes: Their Wrongs and Claims*, one of the first books by a Native American woman.

These engagements between U.S. interests and Pacific Northwest tribes during the later stages of nineteenth-century U.S. nation building bore several distinctive impacts. Tribes were undoubtedly fractured by their relocations to reservations, but they did not undergo the often radical displacements of East Coast tribes. Also, a more continuous, modern tradition of political negotiation grew between the confederated tribes and federal and state governments, particularly over issues of land-use rights. On the other hand, the history of Northwest tribes through the twentieth century generally follows the changes in U.S. government Indian policies in operation across the country. Allotment policies at the end of the nineteenth century seized millions of acres of native lands until the 1934 Reorganization Act returned some autonomy to tribal governments. A reversal of approach in the 1950s encouraged the formal termination of tribes and their landbases. Although many tribes resisted termination policies, other individuals found themselves off reservation among a growing, pantribal

Chief Joseph, half-length portrait, facing front, wearing warbonnet and several necklaces, 1903. Courtesy of the Library of Congress.

Indian population in cities like Seattle, Vancouver, and Portland. Since the 1975 Indian Self-Determination and Education Assistance Act formally reversed the government's termination policy, many tribes have been able to reembrace their cultural heritage. This includes potlatch ceremonies, which had been banned since the turn of the twentieth century, elaborate feasts in which the host gave himself and his possessions to the community. Increasing political organization and intertribal collaborations have also allowed groups like the Affiliated Tribes of the Northwest Indians, originally founded in 1953, to continually advance Native American projects throughout the region. Today these tribes still represent a vital component of the Pacific Northwest, engaged in industry, environmental management, artistic productions, and every other facet of life.

California Indians

California's large, diverse terrain—from the Shasta Mountains to the southern deserts, from the Sierra Nevada across the Great Central Valley to the Sacramento River Delta—enabled over 500 different tribes to establish themselves, and the state is believed to have held the densest concentration of peoples north of Mexico before Western contact. Conservative estimates place this population at 300,000 inhabitants with over 100 languages spoken, including Athabascan, Algonquin, and Uto-Aztecan languages. Over fifty different cultural groups had been established before the coming of Europeans, although these groupings—primarily according to language families—often lump together dozens of independent tribes differing in custom, belief, and territory. Northwest Coast culture spread among tribes like the Yurok and Talowa into the state's redwood forests. Food resources were abundant throughout most of California, with acorn and salmon providing subsistence for tribes in the state's northern and central regions. The Central Valley's expansive landscapes and variety of game prompted numerous stable and unique societies, and some independent villages grew to over 1,000 members. This is also true of the Chumash villages on the south-central coast. In the southland, tribes including the Serrano, Luiseno, and Cahuilla developed practices similar to those in Sonoran desert regions throughout the Southwest. Basketry of various material and styles reached exceptional artistic levels among the state's tribes. Vast trading routes flowed within the state, moving worked obsidian from the northern mountain ranges, pottery from the southern deserts, and even soapstone out of the Catalina Islands.

The first great alteration to Native Californian culture began in 1769 with the founding of a string of Spanish Catholic missions that stretched from San Diego to San Francisco. Authorized by Spain to oversee the colonizing of the region, the missions—with their usual military garrison—introduced domesticated crops and animals and pressed native converts to work the mission lands. Although some Indians embraced mission life and its benefits, many rebelled against confinement within the mission work camps as well as changes in religion, food, and language. Disease was also a recurrent problem within the mission confines, as were sexual assaults on the indentured Indian population. The consistent tensions resulted in several uprisings against the local missions: Mission San Diego was destroyed by the Kumeyaay in 1775 and—after it was rebuilt—by the Quechan in 1781; Chumash Indians raided Santa Barbara and Santa Ynez in 1824, the last of the mission revolts. The secularization of the missions after Mexican independence precipitated their downfall: California Indians fled them in increasing numbers until the system collapsed in 1848. Many of the former mission Indians, however, became peons laboring in servitude on the new ranchos granted by the Mexican Republic. Remoter tribes of the north and montane regions maintained their independence a little longer, but those close to missions and ranchos were frequent targets of raids.

Even while the Spanish and later Mexican authorities confined, conquered, and exploited California tribes—sometimes employing them as manual laborers, sometimes as mercenaries—these authorities generally sought to consolidate the native inhabitants within colonial society. This practice changed dramatically with the arrival of U.S. control of the state and the onslaught of gold seekers after 1848. The destruction wrought on coastal tribes by the mission system was but a precursor to the carnage faced by the rest of the state's tribes in the wake of the California Gold Rush. Forty-niners raced throughout California's interior, initiating a campaign of brutal terror against the Indians with the consent of government authorities, ruining land and food resources in the process. When miners and squatters pushing into tribal lands inevitably encountered resistance, the U.S. military authority and local armed militias raided and massacred the already besieged Indians. In the first decade of statehood, the California legislature provided $1.5 million to help "suppress" Indian hostilities, which in practice simply promoted the further extermination of Native Californians by bounty hunters, "Indian Killers," and hastily formed bands of armed settlers. Despite California's entrance into the Union as a "free state," California Indians were deprived of almost all civil rights, as state law allowed them to be held as indentured servants. By 1860, "vagrant" Indians and Indian children could be legally placed under the keeping of white citizens until males were forty years old and females were thirty-five. These conditions fomented an Indian slave trade, whereby parents were murdered and their children were sold to other settlers. New outbreaks of disease also decimated populations, although, ironically, former Mission Indians were less likely to be infected by the new plagues.

The U.S federal government was quick to recognize the chaos of competing land titles during the heat of the Gold Rush, but in the end they did little to protect tribal claims. Congress dispatched three commissioners to the state in 1851 to negotiate treaties with California tribes. Over the next year, eighteen treaties were signed by more than 100 native groups—a far-from-complete reckoning of all the state's tribes—that should have set aside approximately 8 million acres in reservation land and guaranteed certain provisions and protections. Due to public opposition to reservations (consid-

Ishi

Emblematic of the nineteenth-century history of social devastation is the life story of Ishi (c. 1862–1914), the last member of the Yahi. When Ishi walked down from the Lassen Mountain area of Deer Creek to the town of Oroville in 1911 and turned himself over to the authorities, he was the sole survivor of a once fierce tribe that had cloaked itself from European American trespasses for half a century. He was starving, the rest of his band had disappeared from their territory or been killed, and the last of his tools and provisions had been stolen. Taken in by butchers at the local slaughterhouse, he was later befriended by University of California anthropologist Alfred Kroeber. Ishi accompanied Kroeber to San Francisco, where he lived in the University of California Anthropology Museum and instructed Kroeber and the public in the skills and practices of his California alpine band. He became an instant celebrity, beloved by hundreds of museum visitors and others who sympathized with the culturally orphaned man. With his death in 1914 of tuberculosis, the last original mind of the Yahi gave way to legend. Yet this is a legend with a still-active cultural legacy. In 1961, *Ishi in Two Worlds: A Biography of the Last Wild Indian in North America* was published by Kroeber's wife Theodora—also a close companion of Ishi's—thereby keeping his story alive. Millions of schoolchildren learn the tale of Ishi, and scholars have long discussed Ishi's possible kinship with other tribes. When it was discovered that Ishi's brain had been removed for research following his death and was still in archival storage, public outcry supported the efforts of several tribes seeking its custody. Under the 1990 Native American Grave Repatriation Act, Ishi's brain was turned over to affiliated Redding Rancheria and Pit River tribes—tribes closely related to the Yahi. His brain and cremated remains were reunited at a secret burial site in Ishi's home region around Deer Creek.

ered by the masses as sites of future gold strikes), Congress never ratified the treaties and placed them in secret files for the next half-century. In the meantime, California tribes were nevertheless relocated to reserves on marginal land under corrupt oversight. They were never informed of other recourses to establish land titles and were effectively dispossessed. Nonreservation tribes sought out remote, not-yet-occupied lands or—like the Yahi—went into hiding as state anti-Indian policies continued throughout the end of the nineteenth century. Indian resistance was ongoing but never capable of stopping the flood of gold seekers. The most significant and last major conflict in California, the Modoc War of 1872–1873, began when the government ordered the Modoc tribe of Northern California into Oregon's Klamath Reservation. Goaded from the reservation by their historic enemies, the Klamath, a group of Modoc guided by Keiutpoos, also known as Captain Jack (1838?–1873), twice returned to their homeland near the Lost River and scored several victories over their vastly more numerous military pursuers. After an exhaustive engagement, Keiutpoos surrendered and was hanged with four others; the rest of his band was relocated to Oklahoma.

The native population of California—reduced from 300,000 to 150,000 during the era of Spanish and Mexican control—plummeted to under 20,000 people by the end of the nineteenth century, a 90 percent decline in just fifty years. Growing concern for the remaining California Indians, particularly for destitute, non-reservation Indians, prompted some government intervention, especially once the "lost" treaties of 1851–1852 were rediscovered in 1905. Numerous Indian advocacy groups arose after 1900, such as the Northern California Indian Association, which helped compel the government to develop "rancheria" homesteads for landless Indians in the state's north. Despite ongoing pressures on California Indians to give up their cultural practices—through Indian schools, land allotment policies, and missionizing—California Indians persisted and began pressing their legal claims with some success. By mid-century, however, the U.S. government hoped to end all federal obligations to Native Americans and initiated a so-called Termination policy. The policy called for a divestment of tribal holding, which would then be disbursed among individual tribal members. Promising economic self-sufficiency, the policy ended in complete failure and cultural destruction for many of the twenty-three California reservations and rancherias that underwent termination. Ironically, among those devastated by the policy were the confederated Klamath, Modoc, and Yahooskian Band of Snake Paiute of the Klamath Reservation, who had managed to set aside their enmity and rebuild a strong, economically stable community.

Reaction to termination and anti-Indian discrimination led to vigorous political activism, especially among younger, urban-centered Indians of various backgrounds who had been relocated to the state under other federal programs. In 1964, a small group of Sioux Indians crossed over to Alcatraz Island in the San Francisco Bay and claimed the defunct island prison for themselves according to old treaty provisions that granted surplus federal lands to the Sioux. This group was quickly dispersed, but it led to a second demonstration on November 9, 1969, and a prolonged occupation beginning November 20, 1969. Inspired by the first attempt and frustrated with government Indian policy, a mix of about 100 Indian college students and urban Indians from the Bay Area occupied the island under the guidance of Richard Oakes (1942–1972). The occupiers, who called themselves "Indians of All Tribes," remained on Alcatraz for nineteen months, demanding that the federal government give them the island for an Indian cultural center, university, and museum. During this time, over 5,000 Indians from across the country joined the protest group, some staying for a single day, some for the duration. Numerous factors contributed to the end of the occupation on June 11, 1971—factional rivalries, a fire, lack of fresh water—but the occupation ignited a rebirth in Native American ethnic pride and advocacy. National pantribal organizations such as the American Indian Movement (AIM) followed from the occupation, but just as important were advances in California. Native American Studies programs were initiated at numerous state universities, including a doctoral program at the University of California, Davis. Following the example of the Alcatraz occupation, Native Americans and Chicanos claimed a former army site—also in Davis—as surplus federal territory in 1971. Negotiations led the U.S. government to grant the land's title to D-Q University, the first and still the only institution of higher learning controlled by indigenous peoples located outside a reservation.

The official end of the federal termination policy came with the passage of the 1975 Indian Self-Determination and Education Assistance Act, and since that time several rancherias have reversed their termination. The Self-Determination policy has enabled native tribes in California and throughout the region to reinvest in their cultural heritage and gain political advantage. A significant advance in the economic fortunes of California tribes occurred following the 1988 Indian Gaming and Regulatory Act, which allowed Native American tribes to open casinos and other gaming facilities on their lands. Since the 1990s, gaming has been actively pursued by many California tribes seeking to reverse their economic fortunes and is currently the largest growth industry in the state. How gaming will eventually impact both California Indians and the state as a whole is yet to be seen, but the growth of tribal gaming has reinvigorated many regions throughout the state and given many tribes the means to preserve their cultural heritage for the future.

Indigenous Islanders: Hawai'i and the Pacific Territories

The native peoples of Hawai'i have their roots in the Polynesian culture infusing the islands scattered across the Pacific Ocean. Indeed, Hawai'i forms one corner of the so-called Polynesian Triangle, with New Zealand and Easter Island forming the other two corners of the cultural region. Hawai'i has served—even to the present—as an important stop for trans-Pacific trade, but only with the arrival of Polynesians sometime after 300 C.E. did the island chain establish a more permanent population. Most likely coming from the Marqueses Islands in large, ocean-voyaging canoes, these early inhabitants introduced plants and animals of Asian and Melanesian origin, including chickens, pigs, taro, coconut, banana, and sugar cane. In 500 C.E. the first temple, or *heiau*, was erected on the main island, and this new indigenous population came to occupy the entire archipelago over the next four centuries. However, a second wave of Polynesian migrants—this time from Tahiti—made the ocean crossing to Hawai'i in the thirteenth century. The Tahitians conquered and enslaved the islands' populations and fundamentally changed the culture of the region. A line of high priests was initiated, as well as ruling chiefdoms for each island. The mature Kanaka Maoli culture of Hawai'i involved complex social classes with structured feudal mores, highly developed spiritual ceremonies, sophisticated fisheries, and irrigated agriculture on communal lands.

Western contact with the islands began with a visit by Captain James Cook in 1778. Although he was killed in the islands during his second voyage in 1779, his announcement to the world of the islands' presence transformed the indigenous lifestyle. The islands became a major stopover for merchant ships sailing between Asia and the Americas, introducing forged metal and firearms to the Native Hawaiians—as well as cholera, measles, and venereal diseases. As in other instances, these traders precipitated colonial encroachment into native lands, but not without first effecting political unification. Kamehameha I, an *ali'i* (feudal chieftain) on the main island of Hawai'i, saw the military potential of imported weapons: after

A statue of the great Kamehameha. Courtesy of the Library of Congress.

acquiring firearms as well as a schooner with cannon, Kamehameha began a campaign for control of the islands. First consolidating his power over the Big Island, he extended his reach across the entire chain in 1810 and thereby established the sovereign Kingdom of Hawai'i.

Despite this establishment of a Hawaiian nation, traditional culture became increasingly eroded after contact with foreign traders. The integrated religious-political *kapu* system began fading when Kamehameha's son Liholiho (King Kamehameha II) ascended to the throne in 1819. Missionaries landing the next year quickly converted many of the native inhabitants. The islands' tropical climate and fertile lands also prompted commercial agricultural ventures to form, with foreign investors leasing Kingdom lands. At this time, the general Hawaiian populace did not have landownership rights, but increasing pressure over land use led Kamehameha III to change the provisions of property ownership. His Great Mahele of 1945 reserved some lands for the crown and offered the rest for purchase by *ali'i* and commoners. However, this distribution was often confusing and led to the Native Hawaiians' eventual loss of lands to non-Hawaiians, especially once foreigners were allowed to purchase land after 1850.

Through the middle of the nineteenth century, Hawaiians faced increasing political, cultural, and commercial threats. By 1848, the native population had dwindled to under 90,000 (from a precontact level of over 300,000). Sugar, coffee, pineapple, and other plantations continued growing and solidifying their holdings, particularly in the wake of increasing mainland demands due to the California Gold Rush. Contract workers from China, Japan, Portugal, Puerto Rico, and elsewhere were brought in to meet the growing labor shortage, increasing the fragmentation of Hawaiian culture. With the loss of lands after the Great Mahele, more and more native peoples drifted into growing urban areas.

The Kingdom struggled continuously yet skillfully against various colonial maneuvers by Russia, Britain, and the United States, but the increasing power of foreign business interests led to its downfall. Non-Hawaiian sugar cane interests colluded with the U.S. Consul in Hawai'i and overthrew the government of Queen Lilioukalani in 1893. Annexation of the islands as a U.S. territory followed in 1898, with statehood granted in 1959. During this period Hawaiian culture was essentially driven underground; it struggled to survive while Euro-American commercial interests dominated control of the islands.

Since statehood, Native Hawaiian culture has been undergoing a tremendous renaissance, encouraged in part by the islands' popularity as a tourist destination. Although transformed by the trans-Pacific migrations of the last two centuries, Native Hawaiians have been able to firmly reexert many forms of cultural self-determination and preserve their heritage. These efforts are paralleled by potent political activism: Not only have Native Hawaiian groups sought and won concessions from the United States for the annexation of the Hawaiian lands, but numerous organizations continue to pursue sovereignty claims for the Native Hawaiian population. Sovereignty remains a primary political issue, although varying agendas—from more local control of native resources to secession from the United States—have been put forth by nativist groups.

Hawai'i is not the only U.S. Pacific Region with a Polynesian cultural heritage. Samoans of the American Samoa territory—the only U.S. territory south of the equator—consider their islands to be the fount of Polynesian culture. Traditional culture is still very strong on these islands, and families teach *Fa'a Samoa*, the Samoan life philosophy, to each generation. "Modernization" came to the islands in the 1960s, although the U.S. Navy had been administering the territory since the turn of the twentieth century. The islands have U.S.-style education and government systems, yet Samoans still ground their culture in the harvest of the islands' coconuts, taro, yams, papaya, as well as tuna and shellfish from the ocean surrounds.

While the islanders of American Samoa are U.S. nationals, those of Guam and the Commonwealth of Northern Mariana Islands are U.S. citizens. The indigenous Chamorro and Carolinian peoples of these Micronesian islands have seen much of their original cultures transformed radically by Asian maritime trade routes and earlier Spanish colonization, for example, in the adoption of Catholicism. Like in American Samoa, ocean and tropical crop resources direct most of the culture. However, as in Hawai'i, centuries of international trade have transformed the population: Filipino and Chinese ethnicities have long settled the islands, and Asians in general make up a majority of the population.

Peoples from throughout the Pacific islands have long migrated within the region, and the Pacific states hold the largest number of Pacific Islanders in the country. Hawai'i is home to many different Polynesian (e.g., Samoan and Tongan), Micronesian (e.g., Chamorro, Palauan) and Melanesian (e.g., Fijan) ethnicities, but many of these groups have also made it onto the mainland. Hawaiians first began arriving along the Pacific Coast as crewmen on nineteenth-century trading vessels, several of whom actually settled in the Portland-Vancouver area. Currently, almost as many Pacific Islanders call California home as they do Hawai'i, and significant Samoan and Tongan populations have established themselves in San Francisco and Los Angeles.

CROSSING THE SOUTHERN BORDER

Hispanic, Chicano, and Latino

Formative colonial impact on the Pacific Region began with the exploits of Spain. While Spanish exploration and subsequent trade found its way to almost every point in the Pacific Region, its legacy for California's ethnic landscape is particularly significant. The Spanish claim to and naming of "California" in the sixteenth century eventuated in the eighteenth-century "settlement" of the territory by an extensive mission-presidio-pueblo system. The Spanish empire had long used "the cross and the sword" together in its colonial conquests, founding mission outposts near large native populations with nearby military presidios ready to quell any local unrest. When the government authority in New Spain (Mexico) decided to expand settlement into their colonial holding of Alta California—roughly the territory of the current U.S. state—it organized a "Sacred Expedition" under the command of Captain Gaspar de Portolá and including a cohort of Franciscan missionaries led by Father Junipero Serra. The Expedition proceeded along the California coast and established a series of missions beginning with San Diego de Alcala in 1769 and ending at San Francisco in 1776. The Spanish government also promoted the settlement of regional pueblos, towns that helped supply both missions and presidios with food and skilled artisan services. Over the next sixty years, a chain of twenty-one missions, four presidios, and the pueblos of San Jose and Los Angeles were developed and confirmed a distinct Hispanic presence in the state.

The California missions not only worked to convert native inhabitants to the Catholic faith but also implemented a process of acculturation by which local peoples were habituated to Spanish language, culture, and social and economic practices. The mission system was often coercive, but its influence altered after Mexico gained independence from Spain in 1821. The new government permitted trade with other foreigners in the region, such as the establishment of Russian trade outposts north of San Francisco, a practice forbidden under Spanish rule. Mexico also allowed foreigners to own land if they became citizens of the new government and converted to Catholicism. Such policies encouraged the further diffusion of Spanish Mexican culture, but the character of that culture changed with the dismantling of the mission system. The young Mexican government took civil control of the missions in 1834 and attempted unsuccessfully to convert them into pueblos for the remaining Mission Indians. However, lands throughout the state were also continuously disbursed in large tracts to settlers. Where secular land grants before 1834 numbered only a few dozen, almost 800 land grants were given after that year, eviscerating the missions and leading to the establishment of Californian rancho culture. Vast cattle ranches, employing both Mexican and Indian *vaqueros*, spread throughout the state. Most notorious was the rancho of Mexican General Mariano Vallejo (1802–1890), covering almost 100,000 acres. Vallejo employed displaced natives as mercenaries who raided other tribes for rancho workers, including the 1829 attack that killed 200 Wappos (a city in Northern California still bears Vallejo's name). Most land grants went to well-

Mexican migrant woman harvesting tomatoes. Santa Clara Valley, California, 1938. Courtesy of the Library of Congress.

connected individuals like Vallejo. These individuals largely consisted of incoming Mexicans, but some land grants also went to European and American settlers like the German-born Swiss Johann August Sutter. Although rancho culture was seriously diminished after the gold discovery at Sutter's lumber mill near Sacramento, it nevertheless had a lasting effect on Californian traditions, including the disposition of the state's agricultural and cattle industries.

The new, nonnative population—approximately 15,000—was primarily of Hispanic descent when Mexico ceded Alta California to the United States in 1848, and these Californios could immediately become U.S. citizens under the Treaty of Guadalupe Hidalgo. Although the treaty also protected property claims and cultural practices, the tumult of the Gold Rush continuously impinged on the rancho lifestyle. Even today, descendants of this original Spanish Mexican population press for legal rights under the terms of Guadalupe Hidalgo.

Mexican peoples—including indigenous populations like those from the border regions of Sonora—have continued to migrate north into California and the Pacific Region since that time, variously encouraged by economic opportunities and occasional government-sponsored programs. California's massive agricul-

César Chávez, 1966. Courtesy of the Library of Congress.

tural industry in particular has traditionally depended on seasonal migrant workers from Mexico, especially after the growth of Central Valley farming during the first half of the twentieth century. At this time a Chicano identity began to take root as a wave of Mexican contract laborers came to work California fields in the 1930s and 1940s. Although these laborers eventually came under the formal auspices of a binational "Bracero Program" begun in 1942, they came into frequent conflict with white American migrants displaced into the West by depression era dust bowl conditions. *Chicano* began as a derogatory term during this time, perhaps directed first toward indigenous Nahuatl speakers from Mexico's Morelos region. Whatever its origins, Chicano identity has made space for both Hispanic and non-Hispanic indigenous peoples from Mexico. As the influx of Mexican workers increased, even after World War II, a stable sense of community among this migratory generation developed. During the civil rights era, Chicano identity was embraced by many Mexican American activists, including some aligned with the California-based United Farm Work-

Dolores Huerta, VP of United Farm Workers, during grape pickers' strike, 1968. Arthur Schatz/Time Life Pictures/Getty Images.

ers (UFW) labor movement led by César Chávez and Dolores Huerta. The Chicano identity's political emphasis and ties to migrant farm labor distinguish it among Pacific ethnic subcultures, although its legacy can be unfamiliar to other Mexican- and Hispanic-heritaged peoples in the region.

Mexican American remains a multilayered ethnicity in the Pacific, vitalized by familial and cultural ties maintained by ongoing migration. The Bracero Program and its aftermath brought Mexican immigrants into all parts of the region. In Washington's fertile valleys, for example, Tejanos—workers of Mexican descent from Texas—started arriving to fill labor shortages caused by World War II. Both permanent and temporary residents, including non-Spanish-speaking native peoples, continue to flow into the Pacific Region, feeding the area's need for cheap labor. Furthermore, children of these newcomers promulgate a new generation acculturated to American society. The Mexican influence in regional cuisine, music, and language has until recently been stronger than the communities' political influence, in part because of racial discrimination and in part because of the transitory conditions many Mexican migrant laborers endure to support their families. This situation is changing, though, as Mexican American communities, especially in Southern California, have become increasingly politically active. Mexican American communities are most prominent throughout California, where close to 10 million Mexican Americans live.

Although Mexican American and Mexican ethnicities form the dominant Hispanic influence in the Pacific, other Spanish-inflected immigrant groups from around the world provide the region with a varied texture. Chileans and Peruvians arrived to work mines during the California Gold Rush. Basque immigrants from northern Spain first settled along the eastern slopes of the Sierra Nevada in the late nineteenth century and eventually spread as far north as Spokane and Seattle. Basque settlement was also encouraged in the 1950s, bringing more skilled sheepherders into the Pacific Northwest. In addition, Filipino immigrants carrying the legacy of Spanish colonization in their own homeland have historically had close ties to Mexican communities in the Pacific Region, including in the establishment of Californian farm labor unions.

In the last century, Latin American immigrants from Caribbean, Central American, and South American countries have relocated to the Pacific Region due to various economic and political conditions. Puerto Ricans were drawn early to the West Coast fishing industry, and small, established communities can be found in Los Angeles, San Francisco, and Seattle. A small community also formed in Hawai'i when laborers came to work sugar cane plantations in the early twentieth century. Émigrés from Cuba found their way to coastal cities after that country's political upheavals in the 1960s. Further refugees from Bolivia and Chile in the 1970s settled in Washington and California. During the last four decades, political volatility in Panama, El Salvador, and Ecuador has sent an increasing number of people northward, assisted by various refugee organizations. Multiplying numbers from Latin American locales continue to arrive in the Pacific and form sizable communities, and growing numbers have moved into urban areas—as Guatemalans have in Los Angeles—taking advantage of industrial and food service jobs. Although the vast majority of Latino/a and Hispanic ethnicities remain in California, these populations double almost every decade in Oregon and Washington.

ASIAN AMERICANS IN THE PACIFIC REGION

As early as the eighteenth century, Chinese and Filipino immigrants began to trickle into what would eventually become the United States. In 1789, the Pacific Region hosted its first arrivals from Asia when Chinese shipbuilders landed in Hawai'i en route to British Columbia. The first Chinese sugarmaster arrived at the turn of the century, and by the 1840s, a handful of Chinese sugarmasters had settled in the Hawaiian islands. Steeped in centuries of sugar cultivating tradition, these early immigrants came from China's Guangdong Province to establish some of the first sugar plantations in Hawai'i. Because the decline in Hawai'i's indigenous population effected a need for labor, in 1852, 195 Chinese contract laborers arrived in Hawai'i to work on the sugar plantations. Like the sugarmasters, these Chinese laborers came primarily from the Fujian and Guangdong Provinces in southwestern China, areas whose inhabitants had been adversely impacted by the intrusion of Western powers after the Treaty of Nanjing forced open Chinese ports for trade. Between 1852 and the turn of the century, 50,000 Chinese arrived in Hawai'i to work on the plantations. This influx surged especially as demand for sugar dramatically increased and the 1876 Reciprocity Treaty allowed Hawaiian sugar duty-free entry into the United States. Labor conditions on the plantations were horrific. The workers plodded long hours for very little pay, and they were subject to the exploitation and abuse of the largely European American oligarchy that owned the plantations. Many Chinese workers left when their contracts expired and found gainful employment farming rice or establishing small businesses.

On the mainland, the 1848 discovery of gold in Coloma, California, drew thousands of hopeful Chinese to the Sierra Nevada foothills, where they worked as miners or as merchants of

Chinese workers panning for gold in California, c. 1855. A man in a coolie hat digs as another man kneels and sifts. Hulton Archive/Getty Images.

shops catering to the Chinese community. Their numbers decreased after the Foreign Miner's Tax was imposed in 1853 but began again to enter the Pacific Region when, beginning in 1865, Chinese laborers were actively recruited to work for the Central Pacific Railroad Company, which was responsible for the western stretch of the Transcontinental Railroad. These workers endured dangerous conditions in the Sierra Nevada mountains. Blasting through mountain granite and laboring through the Sierra's treacherous winters, many Chinese railroad workers died in explosions or from exposure. By 1869, when the two lengths of railroad finally met in Promontory Point, Utah, the western span had employed up to 10,000 Chinese at any one time. The Chinese laborers, who had made up 90 percent of the railroad's construction workforce, were not invited to the events celebrating the conclusion of the track's construction.

The completion of the Transcontinental Railroad found many Chinese workers unemployed. Some turned to agricultural labor along the West Coast, while some found work in the canneries, fisheries, railroads, or lumber mills of the Pacific Northwest. Others were enticed by the discovery of gold in Alaska and the Yukon. In the wheat fields of California or in the burgeoning fruit industry along the West Coast, early Chinese Americans worked as field hands; a select few were able to lease land and work as tenant farmers, raising fruit and nut trees, potatoes, onions, or asparagus. Many of these farmers offered the Pacific Region their agricultural expertise, influencing not only crop cultivation but also breeding, such as Ah Bing of Oregon, who bred the Bing cherry. In urban areas like Seattle and San Francisco, thousands

In the heart of Chinatown, San Francisco, California, 1926. Courtesy of the Library of Congress.

of Chinese labored in manufacturing throughout the 1870s and 1880s, particularly in clothing sweatshops. Others found employment in domestic service, and entrepreneurs opened restaurants or laundries. Chinese laundries in particular employed substantial numbers: In 1880, more than 5,000 Chinese were working as laundrymen in California.

To sustain a growing population of Chinese consumers, restaurants, stores, churches, schools, and entertainment venues began springing up in areas such as Seattle, Portland, San Francisco, Los Angeles, and the California Central Valley. These blocks of businesses also marked residential areas, further demarcating certain areas as "Chinatowns." Such ethnic enclaves became centers for the social organizations that helped Chinese Americans to cohere as an ethnic community. In Hawai'i, the first Chinese association was organized in 1854, and in 1868, a Chinese Sunday school was founded. In 1851, the Chinese in San Francisco formed the Sam

Yup and Sze Yup associations and, in 1857, opened a school for children. Later in the nineteenth century, the Chinese Consolidated Benevolent Association (or the Chinese Six Companies) united social organizations with the common goal of challenging anti-Chinese legislation and assisting Chinese immigrants in America. Initially formed in California, the association saw branches appear throughout the Pacific Region states, including Portland, Honolulu, and Seattle.

Despite these gestures toward empowerment through solidarity, laws disenfranchising and excluding early Chinese Americans attenuated the immigration influx of the mid-1800s. In 1858, California barred the entry of Chinese and "Mongolians," and the 1882 Chinese Exclusion Act effected a nationwide ban on Chinese immigration. The 1906 earthquake and its consequent fires, however, destroyed all birth records in San Francisco, thus allowing many Chinese immigrants to claim citizenship, which in turn enabled the entry of thousands of "paper sons" and "paper daughters." Most of the Chinese who arrived under these circumstances entered the United States through San Francisco, and eventually the Angel Island Immigration Station was established in 1910 to process these and other immigrants. At Angel Island, the Chinese were subjected to endless questioning and humiliating physical examinations, and they were often kept incarcerated on the island for several months. These Chinese expressed their fear and desperation through poetry carved into the walls of the station's barracks; these works, some of which can still be seen today, are regarded as some of the earliest examples of Asian American literature. Angel Island Immigration Station closed in 1940 but is currently under restoration as a National Historic Landmark.

Like the early Chinese immigrants to the Pacific Region, Japanese laborers first arrived in Hawai'i. Coming primarily from an area in southwestern Japan, these immigrants left their homeland after increasing industrialization began displacing agricultural workers. Arriving in 1868 and 1869, this initial cohort was badly treated, and Japan forbade emigration until finally allowing a small group of laborers to land in Hawai'i in 1885. Shortly thereafter, the 1894 Irwin Convention negotiated the arrival of 29,000 Japanese contract laborers to work in the sugar plantations. Between 1894 and 1908, 142,000 Japanese came to Hawai'i, and like their Chinese counterparts, they encountered horrific working and living conditions as they planted, tended, harvested, and processed sugar under the oppressive domination of the plantation owners. After the 1900 Organic Act ended contract labor in Hawai'i, 34,000 Japanese left the islands for the U.S. West Coast; this exodus continued until 1907, when Executive Order 589 prohibited Japanese migration from Hawai'i to the mainland.

Japanese immigrants working on the mainland in the late nineteenth century found agricultural employment along the Pacific Coast. Beginning as migrant workers in California, many Japanese followed the seasons' crops, moving up and down the mainland coastal states, farming various fruits and vegetables. In Washington, the Japanese worked on the railroad, as well as in the strawberry fields and oyster farming industry. Some of these early Japanese immigrants to the mainland found the opportunity to lease land as tenant farmers and eventually to purchase land before the implementation of California's Alien Land Laws in 1913. Japanese farmers eventually became so prolific that when the United States entered World War I in 1917, they provided over 90 percent of the country's produce. Japanese immigrants on the mainland also worked as fishermen along the entire sweep of the West Coast, including British Columbia and Alaska. Some worked in the salmon canneries of the Pacific Northwest and Alaska. Others worked as domestic servants, or the more entrepreneurial became, like many Chinese, merchants. The latter established businesses catering to other Japanese immigrants, or they worked as importers, primarily of silk, which in the early twentieth century was the most valuable import from Japan into the United States.

In 1907, the Gentleman's Agreement strictly limited Japanese immigration to the United States. A loophole in this agreement, however, allowed for the entry of Japanese wives, and the consequent wave of "picture brides" fostered a second generation of Japanese Americans. These families settled primarily in California, in urban areas such as San Francisco and Los Angeles, or the farmlands of the Central Valley. The Japanese American population particularly flourished in Hawai'i: By 1923, Japanese constituted 40 percent of the islands' population. As these communities grew, Japanese sections of town emerged in Hawai'i, as well as in the mainland West Coast states. The establishments within a typical *nihonmachi* (Japantown) featured Buddhist and Japanese Christian churches, Japanese-language schools, English classes, immigrant associations, boarding houses, and other businesses. Labor unionization also united Japanese Americans living in the Pacific Region during the early part of the twentieth century. Despite plantation owners' attempts to segregate ethnic groups, the 1900 end of contract labor in Hawai'i signaled the beginnings of workers' unionizing and striking. On the mainland and on the islands, Japanese workers created several labor organizations. In Ventura County, California, Japanese and Mexican workers formed the Japanese-Mexican Labor Association and in 1903 successfully struck for wage increases. In 1919, Japanese workers in Hawai'i formed the Federation of Japanese Labor, ultimately renamed the Hawai'i Laborers' Association. Escalating labor unrest—as well as anti-Japanese hostilities—ultimately effected the passage of the 1924 Immigration Act, which completely barred the entry of Japanese into the United States.

Although a small contingent of Koreans landed on Pacific shores in 1888, the major number did not arrive until 1903–1905, when 7,000 Koreans, like their Chinese and Japanese predecessors, immigrated to work on the Hawaiian plantations. Many subsequently moved to the mainland Pacific Region, where they worked as agricultural laborers and tenant farmers, particularly in California's Sacramento and San Joaquin Valleys and in Washington's Yakima Valley. They harvested peaches, plums, grapes, beans, and tomatoes; Korean Americans who were able to lease land farmed rice, potatoes, or other crops. Among the more successful agricultural enterprises was the Kim Brothers Company of California, which included in its triumphs the creation of the nectarine, a cross between a peach and a plum. Other early Korean Americans established hotels, restaurants, groceries, barbershops, and laundries throughout the Pacific West Coast, and those who did not pursue self-employment found work in mining, on the railroads in Oregon and Washington, or in the Alaskan canneries. In 1910, Korean "picture brides" began to arrive, thus ensuring the perpetuation of a second generation of Korean Americans. These families dispersed throughout the Pacific Region, with the majority of Korean Americans located in California and Hawai'i. Korean immigration to the United States was halted in 1905 by the Japanese government, who had taken Korea as its "protectorate" and therefore established its own diplomatic control regarding emigration.

Despite their small numbers, early Korean immigrants to the Pacific Region were eventually able to establish community networks and businesses that strengthened their ethnic solidarity. Christian churches provided important support organizations, particularly since the presence of Christian missionaries had effected the conversion of many Koreans in their homeland. These churches often served as centers for the homeland independence movement that united many Korean Americans in the common cause of liberation from Japanese colonization. Other social organizations assisted and advocated for the Korean community in the Pacific Region states. The Friendship Society emerged in San Francisco in 1903, and the California Mutual Assistance Society, in 1905; in 1907, the United Korean Society was established in Hawai'i. In 1909, the United Korean Society and the California Mutual Assistance Society united to form the Korean National Association, an organization active in the establishment and support of schools, social and cultural programs, Korean-language education and newspapers, and other resources vital to the welfare of Korean Americans.

With the exclusion of Chinese, Japanese, and Korean immigrants, Hawaiian planters realized the need for alternative labor. The Philippines, a spoil of the Spanish-American War (1898) and the Philippine-American War (1899–1902), would fill this lack. As citizens of a U.S. territory, Filipinos were considered U.S. nationals: they held American passports and could move freely between the Philippines and the United States, but they were not eligible for citizenship, nor were they allowed to purchase land. They were, however, somewhat Westernized through the proliferation of American education and culture throughout the Philippines. Many spoke some English before they arrived in the United States, and after almost 400 years of Spanish colonization, the citizenry of the archipelago was predominantly Catholic. After the 1903 Pensionado Act, a small number of Filipino scholars arrived in the United States, but the first major wave of Filipino immigrants began in 1910, when approximately 4,000 arrived in Hawai'i as plantation workers. They came primarily from the northwestern provinces of the Philippine archipelago, where the land was unsuited to the cultivation of export crops; or they hailed from the Visayan island of Cebu, a sugar-producing region whose people were experienced in the art of cultivating the valuable crop. From 1907 to 1935, close to 56,000 Filipino immigrants arrived in Hawai'i, and by the late 1920s, Filipinos were the largest ethnic group of plantation laborers in Hawai'i.

On the mainland, Filipinos also filled the gap left by Asian exclusion legislation. This group of Filipino immigrants was, as with other Asian groups on the mainland, largely comprised of men who worked as migrant laborers following the seasons' crops up and down the Pacific Coast states. However, unlike their Chinese, Japanese, or Korean counterparts, Filipino immigrants to the U.S. West Coast missed opportunities to purchase or lease land, those possibilities having been extinguished by Alien Land Laws in California, Washington, and Oregon. Relegated to agricultural stoop labor, Filipino migrant workers moved throughout California, Oregon, and Washington's Yakima Valley, planting, tending, and harvesting crops as diverse as cotton, oranges, asparagus, spinach, strawberries, beets, and hops. In the absence of other job opportunities, Filipinos also worked on the Pacific Northwest railroads and all along the West Coast in the service industry, where they filled positions as houseboys, dishwashers, or janitors. Filipinos also moved into Alaska, where they worked in the canneries, met and married Native Alaskan women, and settled in the region. By the 1920s, some opportunities arose for entrepreneurship, with some Filipinos opening businesses such as gambling halls or restaurants in urban areas like Seattle and San Francisco. By 1930, close to 80 percent of the mainland Filipino American population resided in the Pacific Coast states, with the majority living in California.

The plunge of the Great Depression throughout the 1930s posed economic challenges to immigrants and exacerbated existing racial hostilities against Filipinos and other nonwhite groups. The country's economic strife lowered farmworkers' wages, and in a bid to resist pay decreases, Filipino farmworkers began to unionize in Hawai'i and in the mainland Pacific Region. In Salinas and Stockton, California, Filipinos organized to form the Filipino Labor Union, which ultimately led several successful strikes during the 1930s. Like Japanese workers, Filipino agricultural laborers in California united with Mexican workers to form interethnic labor organizations such as the Field Workers Union, established in 1936. In Alaska, the Filipino cannery workers, known as "Alaskeros," actively organized against oppressive working conditions. Filipinos were ultimately scapegoated as a major cause of the country's economic woes and, as such, were the targets of hostility and violence, especially throughout Central California. Anti-Filipino sentiment culminated in the 1934 Tydings-McDuffie Act, which planned for gradual independence of the Philippines over a ten-year period and also limited to a paltry fifty the number of Filipinos allowed to immigrate to the United States annually.

Unlike other Asian immigrant groups, Asian Indians came to the United States not via Hawai'i but primarily by way of Canada and the Pacific Northwest. These were mainly Sikhs from the Punjab province of northwest India who came to North America when British colonization increased taxes and dispossessed many of their lands. After Canada toughened immigration requirements, Asian Indians began arriving directly on the U.S. West Coast, working on the railroads and in the lumberyards of the Pacific Northwest, then moving southward to California when anti-Asian hostilities began brewing in the North. Like other Asians, these immigrants built churches and established social organizations in the Pacific Region. Many of these turn-of-the-century immigrants entered the United States via San Francisco, where in 1905 the first Hindu temple in the Western world was built. The first *gurdwara*, or Sikh temple, in America was completed in 1912 in Stockton, California. Throughout California, Oregon, and Washington, Hindustani organizations united Sikhs, Hindus, and Muslim immigrants in the common cause of Indian freedom from British rule; the Ghadar Party, rooted in the Pacific Region, formed a particularly powerful faction of the Indian independence movement.

Between 1900 and 1923, the number of Asian Indians in the United States had climbed from approximately 2,000 to 7,000, with the majority located in California. Despite antimiscegenation laws and legislation that prohibited the immigration of Asian Indian women, a second generation was perpetuated by Asian Indian men who married Mexican women and settled throughout California. Other Asian Indians worked as tenant farmers or laborers in California's Sacramento, San Joaquin, and Coachella Valleys, where they raised and harvested cotton, cantaloupe, celery, grapes, and lettuce. Asian Indian entry into the United States peaked between 1907 and 1910, but the 1917 Immigration Act ultimately demarcated a "Barred Zone" that excluded Asian Indian immigration altogether.

The bombing of Pearl Harbor on December 7, 1941, dramatically impacted the fates of Asian Americans throughout the Pacific Region. On the mainland West Coast, Japanese Americans suffered the abuse and injustice of internment after Franklin Delano Roosevelt (1882–1945) signed Executive Order 9066 on February 19, 1942. Even prior to the order, authorities had begun arresting thousands of Issei (first-generation Japanese American) men along the mainland Pacific Region despite a series of investigations that concluded that Japanese Americans were not inherently inclined toward treason. The Japanese American populations of California, Oregon, Washington, Arizona, and Alaska (two-thirds of whom were Nisei, or second-generation) were evacuated to camps hastily erected in some of the western states' most desolate regions—Tule Lake and Manzanar, California; Poston, Arizona; Topaz, Utah—ten camps in all housed a total of over 110,000 Japanese American internees. Families were forced to sell their homes, businesses, and belongings, and what property was not purchased at abusively low prices was looted from deserted homes, as the internees were allowed to bring with them only what they could carry. One estimate places total property loss suffered by interned Japanese Americans at $1.3 billion, with a net income loss of $2.7 billion.

While Japanese Americans suffered devastating abuses during and after World War II, other Asian American groups realized possibilities for improvements in their status within the United States. Executive Order 8802 (1941) illegalized racial discrimination in the defense industries, thus allowing Asian Americans (including women) opportunities to move into professional positions outside of ethnic enclaves. In California, Filipinos worked in San Pedro's shipyards, as well as military aircraft plants throughout the state; Chinese Americans labored in the shipyards of coastal California and Seattle. During the war, California's land laws (ultimately determined unconstitutional by the state supreme court in 1952) were revised to allow Filipinos to lease land, and Filipinos often took over property vacated by Japanese Americans headed for internment, particularly farmland in agriculturally rich areas. The war also spurred many Asian Americans—Chinese, Korean, Filipino, Asian Indian, and Japanese—to join in the war effort: In California, 40 percent of the state's Filipino population enlisted in the First Filipino Infantry Regiment, many Koreans joined the California National Guard, and the famed 442nd Regimental Combat Team included many West Coast Japanese Americans.

The cultural face of the Pacific Region also shifted as legislation excluding Asian Americans underwent eventual repeal. The Chinese Exclusion Acts were rescinded in 1943, and shortly thereafter, Chinese, Filipinos, and Asian Indians were granted citizenship rights; in 1952 Japanese and Koreans finally became eligible for citizenship. Although the entry quotas for these groups remained low (averaging somewhere around 100 immigrants per ethnic group), Asian Americans won, with their citizenship rights, the right to purchase land. Also strengthening Asian American communities, the 1945 War Brides Act allowed for the entry of Chinese, Filipino, Japanese, and Korean wives of American servicemen, further engendering a second generation of Asian Americans, many of them mixed-race individuals. These postwar families tended to settle primarily in the Pacific Region: in 1960, more than half of the 1,115,669 individuals who reported Asia as a "country of origin" on the U.S. Census lived in the Pacific Region states, the majority of them in California and Hawai'i.

Twenty years after the end of World War II, the 1965 Immigration Act marked a watershed moment in Asian American immigration history that would profoundly impact the demographics of the U.S. Pacific Region. For the first time in American history, immigration quotas that had favored Western countries now shifted to benefit Asian countries that had been historically excluded from or limited immigration into the United States. The new quotas favored family reunification and entry of professionals, most of whom arrived in the United States along the West Coast's many points of entry. Since the passage of the 1965 act, close to 6 million Asian immigrants have entered the United States; the majority of whom have come from the Philippines and South Korea. The post-1965 cohort of Asian immigrants to the United States has settled predominantly in the Pacific Region states, particularly in Hawai'i and California.

Since 1965, close to 1.5 million Southeast Asian immigrants have arrived in the United States; this group is predominantly composed of refugees fleeing war-torn Vietnam, Cambodia, and Laos. Between the fall of Saigon in 1975 and the 2000 U.S. Census, over 1 million refugees arrived from those devastated areas, and even now they continue to arrive from temporary refugee camps in countries such as Thailand. Although resettlement programs originally dispersed these refugees across the country, many pursued secondary migrations in order to reunite with family, many of whom were in California. As a result, large populations of Southeast Asian Americans (including Vietnamese, Cambodian, Laotian, Hmong, and Mien) reside in the Pacific Region metropolitan areas: Orange County, California, is home to one of the more populous Vietnamese American communities in the United States, and the California Central Valley city of Merced hosts one of the largest Hmong communities in the nation. The Southeast Asian American population stood, at the 2000 census, at 1.8 million; close to 800,000 of those individuals reside in the Pacific Region states.

These Southeast Asian immigrants have created their own opportunities in the U.S. Pacific states, as have other Asian American groups in the region. Within ethnic enclaves, Asian-run businesses thrive, especially in metropolitan areas, but Asian Americans have found entrepreneurial possibilities even outside these enclaves. The first of a successful chain of Cambodian-owned donut shops was opened in La Habra, California, and the manicurist salon has been a fruitful investment for Vietnamese entrepreneurs, particularly in California, where 60 percent of the licensed manicurists are Vietnamese. Korean American–owned grocery stores proliferate the Los Angeles area, and Asian Indian Americans own and operate a range of hotels and motels across the nation. The country's economic shift from manufacturing to high-tech service industries also effected changes for the Pacific Region states. Asian Americans have been particularly visible in the high-tech industries of California's Silicon Valley, as well as in Seattle, as highly skilled technical workers and entrepreneurs establishing their own businesses. Asian Americans have also enjoyed high numbers in professional roles such as engineering and the medical field.

The professionalization of Asian American immigrants and their successive generations has resulted in the increasing visibility of an educated, Asian American middle class that began to emerge just after World War II and has grown increasingly since 1965. In the education arena, the Asian presence had grown so strong that Asian American Studies programs began to appear in colleges and universities throughout the Pacific Region, primarily in response to the 1968 San Francisco State College student strikes, which demanded ethnic studies programs. The number of Asian Americans enrolled in Pacific Region universities and colleges has increased dramatically throughout the end of the twentieth century and into the twenty-first. Close to 20 percent of the University of Washington's student body is Asian American; for the University of Hawai'i this percentage stands closer to 42 percent. In the fall semester of 2000, Asian Americans represented 40 percent of the undergraduates at the University of California, Berkeley. At the secondary level, Lowell High School, a prestigious college preparatory school in San Francisco, became the site of tensions between ethnic groups as the Chinese American student population moved into the majority. Consequently, in 1983, race-based enrollment caps were set at 40 to 45 percent, thus limiting the entry of qualified Chinese American students. These caps were eliminated in 1999, when a court settlement determined that the San Francisco Unified School District's institutions could not select students based on race.

Because of their representation in higher education, as well as their seemingly high household income, Asian Americans have been represented as a "model minority," a misnomer that does not account for the vast majority of Asian Americans who deal with socioeconomic and political disadvantages. Furthermore, although Asian Americans occupy a significant portion of professional positions, they are underrepresented in supervisory roles. In California's Silicon Valley, where Asian American workers hold one-third of the jobs, only 12.5 percent of management are Asian American, testimony to the "glass ceiling" hindering Asian Americans' professional progress within the Pacific Region. Asian American groups are, moreover, not immune from poverty: in 2000, 10.4 percent of Asian Americans were living below the poverty level, while the same status was attributed to 7.7 percent of white non-Hispanic Americans. Southeast Asian refugees are particularly vulnerable to poverty: a staggering 62 percent of Hmong and 42 percent of Cambodian refugees in the Pacific Region live in poverty, and half of the Vietnamese refugees in California remain on public assistance.

Aside from the indication that racial discrimination keeps Asian Americans at an economic and professional status lower than that of white Americans, violent acts of racial hostility persist in the Pacific Region. In 1989, five Southeast Asian American children were gunned down in their schoolyard in Stockton, California, apparently murdered by a white American man resentful of the area's large Southeast Asian population. In 1992, the acquittal of the policemen accused of beating Rodney King erupted into riots throughout the Los Angeles area; Korean business owners were particularly targeted in this multiethnic melee that resulted in damages of $1 billion, the majority of which was sustained by Korean Americans. During the 1990s, interracial conflicts persisted between Asian American and African American students at Skyline High School in Oakland, California, and threatening E-mails targeting Asian American students have repeatedly made their way through the University of California. Legislation in the Pacific Region states has also worked against Asian and other ethnic minorities. In California, Proposition 227 passed in 1998, effectively ending bilingual education in favor of English-only instruction, and in 1996, Proposition 209 prohibited the state from using affirmative action.

Despite these setbacks, Asian American culture has proliferated throughout the Pacific Region, and activism in the arts, the media, and politics has heightened the visibility of the multiple ethnicities that sustain this diverse area of the United States. Cultural centers of all Asian ethnicities thrive in the Pacific states, particularly in California, Hawai'i, and Washington. Bookstores and galleries devoted exclusively to the works of one or more Asian ethnic groups have sprung up throughout the metropolitan areas of the Pacific Region, as well as in suburban areas with high concentrations of Asian Americans. Asian American writers with roots in the Pacific Region are far too numerous to enumerate, but noteworthies include *M. Butterfly* (1988) by playwright David Henry Hwang (1957–), a native of Los Angeles; and Maxine Hong Kingston (1940–), whose Stockton Chinatown childhood is immortalized in *The Woman Warrior* (1976). Pacific Region theater groups—such as the Asian American Repertory Theaters in Stockton and San Diego—focus on productions written, directed, and performed by Asian Americans. While an Asian American presence in Hollywood has been tenuous at best, the formation of Asian American media organizations such as Visual Communications (formed in Los Angeles in 1970) demonstrates Asian Americans' tenacity in the face of marginalization. In the political arena, of the approximately 2,000 Asian Americans acting as elected officials in the United States, three Pacific Region states—Hawai'i, California, and Washington—boast the highest numbers of Asian American political representatives.

As of the 2000 U.S. Census, Asian Americans comprise 4 percent of the nation's population. While this number may seem low on a national basis, over half of all Asian Americans reside in Hawai'i, California, Oregon, Washington, and Alaska, with the highest concentrations in Hawai'i, which is 41 percent Asian American, and California, which is 11 percent Asian American. When these numbers are adjusted to include mixed-race Asian Americans, they jump to 58 percent for Hawai'i and 12.3 percent for California. The numbers of Asian Americans living in the Pacific Region also vary according to ethnicity. While 75.9 percent of Japanese and 70.5 percent of Filipinos live in the Pacific Region states, the majority of Asian Indians make their homes in the Northeast. Across the United States, 97 percent of Asian Americans live in metropolitan areas; in the Pacific Region these include San Francisco, San Jose, Los Angeles, Honolulu, San Diego, and Seattle. A recent trend toward the suburbanization of the population reveals more Asian Americans relocating from the urban metropolis into relatively affluent, middle-class suburbs, such as the Los Angeles suburb of Monterey Park, which is 61.8 percent Asian.

The significant populace of Asian Americans throughout the Pacific Region has profoundly impacted the cultural shape of the region. The metropolitan areas of California, Hawai'i, and Washington all sustain Chinatowns, Little Manilas, Koreatowns, Japantowns, Little Saigons, and other Asian American business and residential neighborhoods. San Francisco's Chinatown encompasses a profusion of shops and businesses that have become a major tourist attraction but still support its estimated 100,000 Chinese American residents, some of whom have been in California for at least five generations. In Daly City, just south of San Francisco, Asian Americans—mostly Filipino—comprise more than half of the population. In this crowded suburb, Filipino grocery stores like Goldilocks, Max's, and Jollibee exemplify establishments that have come from the Philippines to prosper in the San Francisco Bay Area.

Clearly the label "Asian American" cannot begin to encompass the many ethnic and cultural variations that have shaped and continue to shape the landscape of the Pacific Region. Under its "Asian" designation, the 2000 census lists Asian Indian, Bangladeshi, Bhutanese, Burmese, Chinese, Filipino, Hmong, Indo Chinese, Indonesian, Iwo Jiman, Japanese, Laotian, Malaysian, Maldivian, Nepalese, Okinawan, Pakistani, Singaporean, Sri Lankan, Taiwanese, Thai, Vietnamese, and still a number of respondents identify under "Other Asian, not specified." The Pacific Region, with over half of the nation's Asian American population, marks the site of the group's historical development, from their first settlements in Hawai'i and along the West Coast to their dispersal throughout the nation. With roots reaching back to the eighteenth century, Asian Americans in the Pacific Region have made countless contributions to the area's culture, technology, and economy, and as this population continues to grow, so, undoubtedly, will the contributions of this diverse group.

FROM "THE EAST"

Euros, Yankees, Anglos, and "Okies"

While Spain turned away from its other Pacific territorial claims, relinquishing the Oregon territory to the Russians, British, and Americans as it concentrated on its Californian mission system, the migration of various other European ethnicities into the Pacific Region continued. This was primarily precipitated by mercantile trade exploits in the Northwest at the turn of the nineteenth century. Russian influence in Alaska consolidated in 1784 with the founding of a permanent outpost on Kodiak Island, and this influence expanded as a monopoly on trade and exploration was granted to the Russian American Company, directed by Aleksandr Baranov (1746–1819), in 1799. Colonization of the Alaskan territories was stable yet never extensive, and the Russian presence was kept to the southern coast of the state. However, the cultural impact of Russian settlement was helped along by Russian Orthodox missionaries who labored to convert Native Alaskans and educate them in Russian traditions. Orthodox churches, such as St. Michael's Cathedral in Sitka, still serve as the most visible and vital reminders of Russian settlement. In 1804, construction began on the town of New Archangel on Baranof Island, which became the capital of Russia's imperial holdings in the region. Renamed Sitka after the sale of Alaska to the United States, New Archangel became an important international trade center, the first major port in the Pacific. The residents of the town, however, were themselves comprised of various ethnicities. The Russian empire's Grand Duchies provided much of the labor pool for the Russian American Company, and Lithuanians, Finns, Swedes, Baltic Germans, Latvians, Ingrians, and others comprised large segments of the Russian colonial population. Indeed, several of the territories' first governors were of Finnish background.

Similar scenarios existed in other parts of the region. In nineteenth-century Oregon Country, which extended from California to the Alaskan border, agents for the British Hudson's Bay Company, the Canadian North West Company, and the American Fur Company came from a variety of backgrounds. The North West Company, for example, was founded by Scottish immigrants and employed many French Canadians out of Montreal. Members of the American Fur Company were known among the native tribes as "Boston Men": Boston was the port of origin for these traders' ships, and the name reaffirms the Northeast Coast heritage of many of the trappers. Also prominent among these fur outposts were Métis, trappers of mixed French and Indian ancestry, as well as members of northeastern Iroquois tribes. Although most of these trappers came simply as operators of the fur trade with little intention of owning property in the region, a number inevitably established homes and formed the vanguard of further settlement. For example, in 1829 a French Canadian trapper named Etienne Lucier founded one of Oregon's first farm communities in an area still known as French Prairie. More significant for settlement, though, was the expansion of fur company outposts to accommodate the growing trade. In 1824, the Hudson Bay Company revitalized its operations north of the Columbia River by developing agricultural self-sufficiency: In just over a decade of operation, Fort Vancouver became a sprawling trade settlement with over 500 white emigrants working its farm and fur operations.

Only with the opening of the Pacific Northwest via the Oregon Trail was large-scale homesteading by European and European American immigrants able to be initiated. In 1841, the first emigrant party, the Bidwell-Bartleson party led by Thomas Fitzpatrick, left Westport Landing on the Kansas River for California with 100 farmers and their families. Along the way, some of the party changed their minds and headed for Oregon Country. "Oregon Fever" caught on: This group's decision to head northward was repeated by almost two-thirds of immigrants heading west before 1848. Much of the initial movement was made by European Americans—predominantly of English, Dutch, German, and French heritage—long established in eastern and midwestern states like New York, Pennsylvania, and Iowa. These were soon followed by the great immigrant tides pouring out of north and western Europe, including French, Dutch, and British émigrés, as well as especially large contingents of Irish facing famine and Germanic peoples facing political upheaval. The overflowing Germans and Irish also enlisted in the military and formed a sizable part of the troops dispatched to the Pacific Northwest to deal with Indian troubles. Agricultural and logging settlements in the area soon arose, but just as the areas around Vancouver, Seattle, and Portland began to grow into stable towns, the 1848 discovery of gold in California radically shifted the temper and character of Pacific settlement.

Global Migration and the Gold Rush

The U.S. nationalistic spirit of "Manifest Destiny" was driven by ideological and economic desires, and it could only be feasible once political authority of the West Coast states was assured. In 1846, President James K. Polk (1795–1849) negotiated a settlement with Britain over disputed claims to the Oregon Territory, which ceded lands south of the 49th parallel to the United States and established the present-day border between Washington and Canada. Immediately thereafter, fallout from the Mexican-American War allowed the United States to annex California, where a small concentration of European and European American settlers had been already agitating against Mexico's authority. The United States now controlled the major West Coast port areas: San Diego, San Francisco, Astoria, Vancouver on the Columbia River, and Seattle on Puget Sound.

However, Manifest Destiny would not become reality without the tsunami of peoples into the region after the January 1848 discovery of gold at Sutter's Mill on California's American River. Before the discovery of gold, the "Anglo" population of the state (as the non-Hispanic northern European and European American immigrants were called) numbered only a few thousand clustered in the state's northern regions, the most cohesive "ethnicity" of which were Mormon settlers. Almost overnight, however, the California Gold Rush began a migration of global proportions. News spread like wildfire through the state, then diffused first to Hawai'i and then Oregon via maritime trade routes. People from these routes, including Hawaiians, Mexicans, South Americans, and eventually Chinese, had a headstart toward the region. Not until December 1848 was the discovery publicly confirmed by President Polk, prompting "Forty-Niners" from every continent and from every American region (as well as new arrivals to Oregon and Washington) to stampede toward California. Ships from around the world floated empty in the harbors of San Francisco, Monterey, and Los Angeles, abandoned by crews scrambling into the goldfields. In 1849, California's population grew from less than 20,000 to more than 100,000. Statehood followed in 1850. In three years, the population climbed to over 250,000. While this population spike was occurring, the California Indian population was spiralling downward, decreasing by 80 percent in the two decades following gold discovery.

Among the great diversity of ethnicities entering California, European immigrants still comprised a major cohort. British, Irish, German, and French immigrants dominated the new arrivals—as they did throughout the United States at the time. Cornish immigrants from England were especially prevalent, given their experience in mines. Additional enclaves of Scandinavians, Dutch, Italians, Belgians, and other nationalities formed throughout the mining camps. San Francisco became a cosmopolitan mecca for gold seekers as the wealth poured out of the Sierra Nevada into the city. These foreign émigrés joined their European American counterparts in the plains and foothills, where boomtowns sprang up overnight.

The tenor of the state, influenced by the greed and suspicion of gold hunters, changed radically with the flood of European American and European settlers. The indigenous population was decimated. The Hispanic Californio population became dispossessed as gold seekers swarmed over their lands. Chinese and other Asians were almost immediately segregated and subjected to racially discriminatory laws. Many of the new European arrivals, particularly the Germans and the Irish, labored to assimilate to the "Anglo-American" culture spilling into the state from the East. Cornish and Welsh miners, as English speakers, often became mine foremen, and small populations still live in the Sierra Nevada foothills. Although the various European ethnicities were generally more acceptable among the white European American authorities than racially and culturally "foreign" groups, ethnic tensions still persisted for them in the booming scramble for gold. The 1850 "Foreign Miners' Tax," for example, crafted discriminately against Chinese miners, was later applied to Mexican and European communities. A French contingent centered around the town of Sonora began an uprising against the tax that was soon joined by German and Mexican miners. Their successful resistance halted the tax's further application and became known as "The French Revolution."

Even as the big boom of the California Rush began to subside and individual placer mining was replaced by corporate hydraulic mining, gold still drew thousands into the Pacific Region during the latter half of the nineteenth century. Discoveries in the Oregon mountains and eastern Washington in the 1850s and 1860s brought northward many who were tired of the struggles in California. Gold had been found in Alaska as early as 1849, but the 1897 discovery in Canada's Yukon Territory sent 30,000 "stampeders" further north into the Klondike. Not everyone who arrived in the Pacific during these rushes came to stake a claim in the fields, however. Many built businesses supplying the miners with food, clothes, and goods. Such was the example of Levi Strauss (1829–1902): a German Jew born in Bavaria and trained as a tailor, Strauss sought to provide tents and wagon covers to the miners. When this enterprise failed, he designed durable work pants for the miners that were so popular they became an icon of American culture: Levi's blue jeans.

European Waves at the Turn of the Twentieth Century

Germans and "Russian Germans"

European immigration into the Pacific Region following the gold rush era generally follows the historical trends for the entire country. Germans continued to be a major immigrant force, establishing themselves first in agricultural regions from Spokane to the Central Valley. The lumber baron Frederick Weyerhaeuser (1834–1914) controlled almost 1 million acres of forest in the Pacific Northwest, and his Weyerhaeuser Timber Company recruited thousands of European immigrants for its mill operations. Later generations of Germans moved into metro areas, establishing *Turnvereins* (German Gymnastics Societies) and *Turnerbunds* (American organizations emphasizing physical fitness education, offshoots of the *Turnvereins*) as well as German American societies in cities like Seattle and San Francisco. A notable subgroup are the so-called Russian Germans, migrants to the plains of Poland and the Ukraine who founded similar grain harvesting practices in towns like Odessa, Washington, and Lodi, California. The nineteenth-century arrivals also included many German Jews, who, like Strauss, helped promote stable businesses in the aftermath of the gold rushes.

British, Irish, and Canadians

Scottish and English heritages continued to be a major influence in the region through the end of the 1800s. The Irish were employed laying track for various railroad operations, particularly on the Northern Pacific Railroad, and they also worked coal mines under Cornish supervisors. Although ethnically distinct, British immigrants were often readily assimilated into mainstream U.S. culture because of language and cultural affiliations. This effect has been even stronger on the West Coast due to smaller concentrations of Irish, Scotch Irish, and English immigrants and because of the differing racial confrontations with Mexican and Asian immigrants experienced in the nineteenth-century West. Only a few British or Irish districts have persisted into the twenty-first century. However, a lasting British legacy has been felt in the Pacific Region through the influence of Canadian immigrations. Canadians continue to make up one of the largest "foreign-born" populations in Washington today, and they have maintained ongoing social, cultural, and political ties with their homeland across the 49th parallel. Despite their prominence, language and cultural practices similar to mainstream "American" culture have led some to speak of Canadians as an "invisible minority."

Scandinavians

A sizable population of Scandinavians moved into the Pacific Northwest in the late nineteenth century—especially after completion of the Northern Pacific Railroad in the 1880s—and continued settling there well into the twentieth century. Most skipped across the northern United States, leapfrogging through Scandinavian settlements in Wisconsin, Minnesota, and the northern Plains. A significant draw was the similarity of the northern Pacific Region's mountain and river landscapes with their home countries. Rural Norwegians and Swedes formed the majority, but Finns, Danes, and Icelanders also arrived in the Oregon and Washington interiors. This group helped establish logging communities and assisted in exporting lumber to the booming California economy. These groups also built cranberry bogs, promoting another agricultural sector still in operation today. Artisans and laborers of all kinds joined the stream. Danes frequently worked as household servants, while Finns worked maritime industry throughout the Northwest, even into Alaska. In the twentieth century, urban populations began to coalesce in the area. Scandinavian pockets of every variety began to arise in towns from Junction City and Astoria, Oregon, to Tacoma, Bellingham, and Everett, Washington, and Seattle's Ballard District became a tremendous hub of Scandinavian American culture.

Scandinavian groups also moved into California but in more isolated pockets, like the Swedish enclave of Kingsburg, known as "Little Sweden" in the early twentieth century. Finns and Norwegians moved into the northern logging regions of Humboldt and Mendocino Counties. Danes showed a special fondness for the state: California has the most Danish-born residents of any state, especially in the metropolitan regions of Los Angeles and the San Francisco–Oakland Bay Area. The Danish town of Solvang in Santa Barbara County, settled in 1911, is still a tourist attraction visited by thousands.

Italians

Immigration into the Pacific from southern and eastern Europe increased before the turn of the twentieth century, and large numbers continued until the 1930s. The fishing industry along the West Coast initially attracted many Italians to the region, although many ended up working as dockworkers. By the time of their arrival, most of the prime agricultural lands were occupied, and Italians provided manual labor in Washington coal mines, Oregon lumberyards, and California urban factories. Southern Italians also worked rail lines in the Pacific Northwest, especially around Spokane, and construction became a major occupation in the early decades of the century. Many of those who came to California—like the chocolate baron Domingo Ghirardelli (1817–1894)—settled in San Francisco's North Beach District. These newcomers—mostly northern Italians—also brought with them a great love of wine, and many seized on the fledgling wine culture begun in the Spanish missions. They developed family-run wineries in the Sonoma and Napa areas surrounding San Francisco that served as forerunners to the massive vineyards in Northern California today.

Eastern Europeans

Slavic immigrants also made their way into the Pacific Region in the early decades of the twentieth century. Russians, Poles, Croats, and Serbs have all made entrances to the West Coast in the 1800s, with enclaves still persisting in all major coast cities. Indeed, Croats settling the San Pedro area near Los Angeles helped develop the tuna industry, and a large Croatian cohort still thrives in the area. Second-wave Slavic immigrants often continued to exchange Mediterranean and Adriatic shores for the Pacific, particularly around Puget Sound, where Montenegrins, Serbs, and Croats sailed purse seiners after salmon, herring, and other fish for the Washington canneries. Croatian and Slovenian Slavs also worked coal mines around Tacoma. Economic distress and social unrest in the decaying Ottoman and Austro-Hungarian empires prompted small Ukrainian, Bulgarian, and Romanian enclaves to develop in Los Angeles and San Diego.

Greek and Portuguese

Small Greek and Portuguese communities secured themselves on the West Coast at this time as well, drawn like others to expanding fishing opportunities as industrial canneries were built on the Alaskan coast, in Seattle, and at Monterey, California's "Cannery Row." Greek enclaves often grew alongside new Italian and Slavic communities in Seattle, particularly among Serbs and Montenegrins who shared the same Greek Orthodox religion (Poles, Croats, Slovenes, and Slovaks share a Roman Catholic practice with Italians). Coffeehouses arose as social centers in Seattle and Tacoma. Many Greeks also landed in mining towns throughout the West Coast mountain ranges, but others found work in the region's growing textile mills. Portuguese from the Cape Verde Islands and the Azores have spread into Northern California from San Francisco through the Napa Valley to Sacramento and the San Joaquin Valley. In Napa they followed Italians in fostering the state's wine traditions, while dairy farm communities were built alongside the Dutch in the southern valleys. Los Angeles, Seattle, and San Francisco continue to support small but vibrant communities of Greeks and Portuguese.

Dutch

The Dutch communities in Southern California became leaders of the state's dairy trade. Dutch dairy farms concentrated in towns on the outskirts of Los Angeles like Chino, Artesia, Bellflower, and Hynes. A Kleine Nederland (now Paramount) was built in the area in the 1920s that served as a vibrant social center. Although concentrated cultural enclaves have faded in the state, half of all Dutch immigrants since World War II still come to California. Modest communities also grew in Oregon and Washington early in the 1900s, the most notable being around Spokane. Farms and dairies proliferated the city on lands compared to the Dutch countryside, and several Dutch-controlled banks dominated Spokane's business operations. The nearby town of Lynden holds an annual Holland Days Festival.

Russians

The Russian legacy in the Pacific Region made it a welcome destination for many trying to escape the political unrest within the Russian empire from the 1880s until the Bolshevik Revolution, as well as during the Soviet period. West Coast ports provided gateways for many Russians into the United States, with some choosing to stay and revitalize the region's older Russian heritage. Alaska and the Pacific Northwest absorbed most of these immigrants, although large concentrations also formed in San Francisco and Los Angeles. This new wave of Russians often lived alongside the new Slavic communities who shared their language, lifestyle, and Orthodox religion. In Seattle, Russian and Greek communities helped found the St. Spirodon Orthodox Church, which was also attended by communities of Bulgarians, Gypsies, Serbians, Syrians, and Ukrainians (Ruthenians).

Jews

Jewish communities and organizations—both religious and ethnic—have also spread throughout the Pacific Region. Los Angeles currently has the third largest population of people of Jewish heritage (after Israel and New York), and this is partly attributable to the succeeding waves of immigrants around the turn of the twentieth century. Immigrant German Jews had settled communities throughout the region in the late 1800s, and in the early 1900s, Russian Jews escaping the pogroms in their homeland followed them and, finding welcome, established synagogues in urban areas that helped them transition into American life. Another wave of Jewish immigrants arrived in the 1920s, these coming from eastern European areas like Poland and the Balkans. Members of this latter group helped build the fledgling film industry. With roots initially in New York, filmmakers discovered the paradisical weather of Southern California and moved into Hollywood and Los Angeles. Jewish studio founders like Samuel Goldwyn (1882–1974), Adolph Zukor (1873–1976), and Jesse Lasky (1880–1958) helped lead Hollywood into its first golden era and became prominent members of Los Angeles society.

In-migration to the Pacific Region: America Goes West

California has always held its own version of the "American Dream," cast in the heady days of the gold rush and crystalized in the glitzy lights of Hollywood's moving picture show. As elusive and illusionary as those California dreams may be, the state became a major destination for relocating Americans throughout the twentieth century. Numerous significant industries, including agriculture and fishing, have prompted massive movements of both white and black Americans from the Northeast, South, and Midwest, helping make California the most populous state since 1964. Midwest transplants formed a remarkable 80 percent of the Southern California population in the 1920s, with Los Angeles' population doubling to over 1.2 million during the decade. Hollywood, nearby oil fields, and a burgeoning automobile trade helped sustain the metropolitan area, as did the draining of water from once fertile Owens Valley to slake the municipal thirst.

Although the stock market crash of 1929 decimated the West Coast economy, refugees of the Great Depression continued to arrive. The dust bowl conditions of

Oklahoma dust bowl refugees on the road in San Fernando, California, 1935. Courtesy of the Library of Congress.

the 1930s sparked an exodus out of Oklahoma, Texas, Missouri, and Arkansas—as chronicled by John Steinbeck (1902–1968) in *The Grapes of Wrath* (1939)—into the state's agricultural fields. Arriving via historic Route 66, these "Okies" often clashed with Mexican, Filipino, and other Asian migrant field-workers moving through the Central Valley. The film industry struggled through this era, and a scandal-plagued oil industry was caught off guard. Yet these industries proved savvy enough to use the influx of cheap labor to expand urban growth around Los Angeles. Other refugees from the era spilled northward into Oregon and Washington. Ozark influence from Arkansas and Missouri spread into the Pacific Northwest bottomlands, as did southern highland culture from Kentucky, Tennessee, and Virginia.

Westward migration increased during the buildup to American involvement in World War II. The bombing of Pearl Harbor forced the United States to fortify its Pacific borders, and military growth expanded base operations and demanded new industrial output. Shipyards, steel works, and airplane manufacturing plants sprang up throughout California and Washington as the country mobilized, helping to produce massive aircraft carriers for the new Pacific Fleet and planes for the Army Air Corps. U.S. Army and Naval Bases from San Diego to Alaska also demanded a huge labor force to help with daily operations and the crafting, transporting, and loading of supplies. Civilian-run factories like Boeing outside of Seattle also required large workforces to keep up with the demand for airplanes and other equipment. The demographic effect of the war was just as drastic as the economic effect, as millions remained to settle on the Pacific Coast even after 1945.

European American migration to the West Coast persisted throughout the latter half of the twentieth century for a variety of reasons. Military bases located in the region continued to inspire many service members to remain in the Pacific after they left active duty. At the other end of the spectrum, the counterculture movements of the 1950s, 1960s, and 1970s drew segments of the youth population to the West Coast. Beatniks, hippies, and "mainstream" anti–Vietnam War protestors—of various ethnicities though predominantly "white"—ingrained themselves in Pacific communities. More recently, the tech and dot-com booms of the 1980s and 1990s motivated another westward migration into areas around Seattle (where Microsoft is headquartered), Portland, Los Angeles, and the Silicon Valley near San Francisco.

European immigration continues into the Pacific Region, although changes to immigration "quotas" with the passage of the 1965 Immigration and Nationality Act and the hegemony of "white" mainstream American culture have meant fewer enclaves of distinct ethnic nationalities have had the means to form. Nonetheless, more recent arrivals have kept ethnic cultures vital and diverse. Jewish refugees from the Holocaust found help among West Coast Jewish communities, as have refugees from various Soviet satellite states. After the failed 1956 revolt, Hungarians found relief among remnant nineteenth-century communities in the Sierra Nevada. Baltic dissidents from Latvia, Estonia, and Lithuania have been aided by groups like the International Refugee Organization (IRO). The IRO's Seattle offices have helped relocate them and others from Eastern Europe—Poles, Slovaks, Czechs—with the assistance of Slavic groups who arrived earlier in the century. Ongoing conflict in the Balkan countries of the former Yugoslavia has prompted a new wave of Croat, Serb, and Montenegrian immigrants into areas like San Pedro and San Francisco. The end of the Soviet regime has encouraged a number of immigrants from the Eastern Bloc to seek better economic opportunities in Pacific metropolitan areas. This has included another migration of Russians who have revitalized areas of San Francisco, Los Angeles, Seattle, Anchorage, and Portland.

AFRICAN AMERICAN ARRIVALS

Although African American communities have not been as abundant throughout the region as in other areas of the country, Pacific communities have played important roles in the formation of regional and national culture. African sailors were among the first nonnatives to navigate the Pacific coastline on the trade ships of the eighteenth century. Several black or mixed black and Indian heritage families were among the original fourteen that established the pueblo of Los Angeles in 1793. Black pioneers were among the first American settlers, including George Washington Bush (1790?–1863), who in 1844 was one of the first non-British to set roots north of the Columbia River in what is now Washington. African Americans—some slaves, some indentured, some free—also came in large numbers during the California Gold Rush. The free-for-all atmosphere of the mine camps ironically carried an egalitarian streak that generally frowned on black slaveholding, even though California Indians were still regularly forced into servitude on ranches. Black communities in the state remained small, but those successful during the gold rush were able to use their influence to promote abolition and social causes. Consequently, Washington, Oregon, and California were admitted to the pre–Civil War Union as free states. In the Pacific Northwest, African Americans were later recruited as strikebreakers in the 1880s and 1890s, pitting them against Italian and Irish coalminers.

African Americans came to the Pacific Coast in growing numbers during the first decades of the last century, frequently working the expanding rail service as porters and Pullman stewards. Maritime trades also provided job opportunities on ferries, on the docks, and—especially during World War I—in the shipyards. Greater numbers would not begin arriving until the end of the Great Depression, and then their numbers rose dramatically, following the broader national migration trends westward. The promise of factory work drew thousands to the region, and the black population of the West Coast quadrupled as newcomers accompanied military mobilization through the Pacific Region during World War II. African Americans arriving in the West hoped for and sometimes found more freedoms in the steelworks and aircraft factories of the modern, growing metropolitan areas, but they still faced fervid discrimination and were kept to menial and often dangerous tasks even

This African American worker, using a portable electric drill on a YP-38 sub-assembly in a large western aircraft plant, was trained in a very short time to do fast accurate work. Courtesy of the Library of Congress.

among military base operations. When a bomb explosion killed 300 African Americans at the Richmond Naval Station in 1944, outrage ensued over racist segregation, negligent oversight, and unsafe conditions for blacks in the military. African Americans who refused to return to work after the explosion were later court-martialed, enflaming civil rights activists who advocated for desegregation of the armed forces. After the war, many recent African American arrivals remained in the West's burgeoning urban areas—Oakland, Los Angeles, Seattle—building lasting communities and providing labor and leadership for the Pacific Region's industrial growth. From 1930 through 1980, over a million African Americans moved into California alone, with two-thirds of them coming from the South.

Throughout the second half of the twentieth century, African Americans in the region maintained vigorous, socially and politically engaged communities. A decelerating military industry, fiercer job competition, and growing ghettoization and urban sprawl in the post–World War II period strained many black inner-city communities, however, particularly those in Los Angeles. At the same time, such communities were developing a proud political identity fostered by the civil rights movement, and they also began confronting the racist attitudes of mainstream American society. Antidiscrimination strikes and social protests were organized in many West Coast cities, such as the 1963 San Francisco Taxi Strike. However, African American frustration over wretched social conditions finally reached its breaking point in 1965 when the Watts district of Los Angeles erupted in violence. When a white police officer pulled over a black driver in the black community of Watts, a crowd gathered and began taunting the officer. A second officer from the all-white L.A. police force, called as backup, began to strike out at the crowd with his baton. As word of this violence spread through the populace of South Central Los Angeles, it incited a massive rebellion among the area's African American citizens as well as some in the Mexican American community. For six days the Watts Riot raged, resulting in thirty-four deaths, over 800 arrests, several thousand injured, and millions of dollars in property damage from looting, fires, and other attacks on property. The Watts Riot was not only the first major eruption of mass violence during the civil rights era but also the largest race riot the United States has yet seen, attesting to the deep dissatisfaction the African American community felt about the progress of racial reform at the time.

The militant attitude expressed in the Watts Riot held nationwide in other violent clashes and the ensuing "Black Power" movement. On the West Coast, Bobby Seale (b. 1936) and Huey Newton (1942–1989) organized the Black Panther Party in Oakland in 1966. In 1969, a second chapter of the Black Panthers opened in

Seattle, the city that held the highest rates in the United States for racially motivated sniping and firebombing during the late 1960s. South Central Los Angeles remains an electrifying core of African American culture, fostering cultural expressions as diverse as segments of the Black Arts movement of the 1960s and 1970s, as well as seminal rap and hip-hop artists of more recent decades. However, Los Angeles also remains actively charged by its racial history: In 1992, riots again swept through the city after a jury found four white officers of the Los Angeles Police Department not guilty of using excessive force during their arrest of Rodney King, a black truck driver. The four officers' furious beating of King, videotaped by a passerby and replayed nationwide on television newscasts, sparked more rioting in southeast Los Angeles, as well as mass protests in San Francisco, Seattle, Las Vegas, New York City, and Atlanta. Behind the protests in Los Angeles, however, one can also perceive ongoing strains within the multicultural urban society building in the Pacific: the rioters' anger was frequently directed at Korean immigrant–owned convenience stores, highlighting the ongoing pressures between new and established ethnic communities. Nonetheless, African American civic leaders still play important roles in building the multicultural society of the Pacific West and have helped foster a bold, dynamic community on the coast.

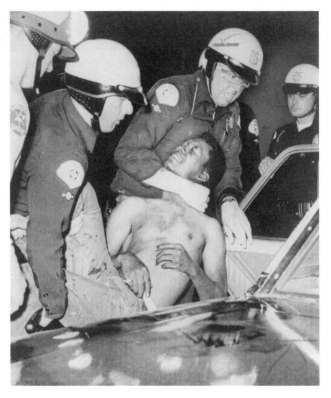

Los Angeles police hustle an African American rioter into their car during the Watts Riots in Los Angeles, 1965. Courtesy of the Library of Congress.

MIGRATIONS FROM THE MIDDLE EAST

Immigration into the Pacific Region by peoples of Middle Eastern heritage prior to World War II did not match the magnitude reached by migratory waves from Asia, Europe, and Central America. Yet important settlements, primarily in California, were established in the region that helped prepare the way for increased influxes from Arab countries in the latter half of the twentieth century.

Significantly, some of the earliest arrivals from that area now referred to as the Middle East were neither Muslim nor Arab. Rather, they were Armenian and Assyrian groups fleeing the persecutions of the Ottoman empire at the end of the nineteenth century. Despite its crumbling authority, the empire actively repressed various minority populations, which included numerous ethnic Christian communities such as the Armenians and Assyrians who had inhabited Persia and the south Caucasus regions for millennia. When Turkish nationalist aspirations at the turn of the century led first to massacres and then to brutal mass relocations, the ensuing diaspora brought thousands of refugees into California. On the eve of World War I, the Central Valley town of Fresno had a teeming Armenian community of thousands working in the agricultural and building trades. More Armenian refugees arrived with the war's aftermath, spreading populations through Pasadena and Los Angeles as well as further up the Central Valley toward Sacramento. Assyrians also moved into the Central Valley, primarily around the Turlock-Modesto area south of Sacramento.

While Armenians and Assyrians formed the largest concentrations of Middle Easterners arriving in the early 1900s, several other smaller groups from the "Greater Syria" area trickled into the West Coast states. These were generally Semitic Christians of various sects but also Muslim and Arab ethnicities, and they included Lebanese and Syrian communities that formed in Los Angeles, as well as Egyptian Copts. Often the local neighborhoods offered support to these new arrivals through established religious communities: Assyrian and other Orthodox ethnicities found backing among Greek and Eastern Orthodox churches around San Francisco and Seattle, and Arab Muslims gravitated toward Asian Indian Islamic centers established in Southern California. The largely Christian disposition of this initial wave did not stir much antagonism among mainstream American society, but many still struggled to assimilate as Pacific culture sought to classify these Middle Easterners indiscriminately as Asians or Muslim Africans.

Armenian and Assyrian immigration to the region continued throughout the latter half of the twentieth century, much of it coming from Iran and Iraq, where these populations had been pressed, after World War I. This includes the large Chaldean contingent that has settled in and around the San Diego metropolitan area as well as a growing Syriac community in Los Angeles. Both of these latter groups are culturally similar to Assyrians but differ in religious practice: Chaldeans tend toward Catholicism, Syriacs follow a Syriac Orthodox practice, while Assyrians are Eastern Orthodox. At the same time, a burgeoning Armenian cultural movement has been supported on the West Coast, with extensive support building in the Seattle-Bellevue areas of Washington and a "Little Armenia" having been designated in East Hollywood by city officials. Following Armenia's independence from Soviet authority in 1991, the Armenian population has experienced a reawakening of cultural pride, holding celebrations and political rallies throughout the region.

Increasing immigration from Arab-speaking countries has given California the largest population of Arab Americans in the United States. Much of this influx was spurred by ongoing conflicts in the Middle East after World War II: the hostility between Israel and its Arab neighbors, particularly the 1967 War; civil war in Lebanon; the Islamic Revolution in Iran and the following Iran-Iraq War; and the 1991 Gulf War. A surge of Iranian immigration began following that country's 1979 revolution; a decade later Iranians—predominantly Muslim but also Jewish and Christian—were in the top ten of immigrant nationalities entering the United States. A sizable majority of these immigrants settled in Southern California, where over a half-million Iranian Americans now live. Almost one-fourth of Arab Americans in the state, however, are of Lebanese heritage, and Lebanon still provides a large percentage of new immigrants. Egyptians and Iraqis also currently comprise a large proportion of Middle Eastern immigrants to the region,

Evolutions: Gay and Lesbian Identity

At the cutting edge of discussions of identity is the new focus on gay and lesbian America, where twenty-first century debates over "gay marriage" and civil rights have brought renewed prominence to sexual identity. Prominent throughout Pacific history has been the formation of "bachelor communities." Pioneers first heading into Pacific wilds were predominantly men, as were the thousands of forty-niners rushing into the gold fields. Other sojourners—Chinese working goldmines and railroads, Scandinavians in Northwest logging communities, Mexicans and Filipinos in the agricultural fields—often arrived without the company of women, sometimes because of the hazards of travel, sometimes due to the expectation of returning home after one's fortune was made, sometimes because of legal restrictions. These bachelor communities, while outwardly conforming to the sexual norms of the day, did provide a cultural atmosphere acquiescent to alternative gender identities. At the turn of the twentieth century, modern sexual identities—among both men and women—had emerged in areas like the San Francisco Bay Area, and with another surge in sex-segregated communities during World War II, the stage was set for a growing political movement. With the creation of the Mattachine Foundation (and later Mattachine Society) and the rise of the San Francisco Beat Movement in the 1950s, Los Angeles and San Francisco became centers for the growing Gay Liberation Movement. Lesbian and gay culture gained growing acceptance during the 1960s counterculture and 1970s activism, particularly after New York's Stonewall Riots in 1969. In 1978, the "Rainbow Flag" was designed by Gilbert Baker for the San Francisco Gay Freedom Day Parade and has since become an international symbol of lesbian and gay identity.

Gay and lesbian culture blossoms throughout every state in the region, but San Francisco remains its symbolic capitol. In 1977 Harvey Milk (1930–1978) was elected to the San Francisco Board of Supervisors, the first openly gay man elected to office in California. The San Francisco Bay Area has had one of the largest gay and lesbian populations in the world, and Milk was a pioneer in bringing the community together. He was assassinated a year after he was elected, and when his murderer received a light sentence, it sparked the U.S.'s second gay riot, the "White Night Riot," on May 21, 1979. Milk's energetic and open advancement of gay and lesbian rights has inspired many, and San Francisco remains at the cutting edge of legal advocacy. In 2004, for example, newly elected mayor Gavin Newsome deemed anti-gay marriage state laws unconstitutional and authorized marriage licenses for gay and lesbian couples. Though the California Supreme Court later halted these marriages, the act prompted a reconsideration of current marriage laws.

as do Palestinians, although the Palestinian diaspora has been difficult to track officially because these immigrants often move through other countries such as Jordan or Lebanon. Palestinians have nonetheless developed strong enclaves in California, particularly in San Francisco and the surrounding metropolitan area during the 1980s, where many owned neighborhood grocery and convenience stores. Newer Somali arrivals from Africa have also begun building ties with Muslim Palestinian groups in San Francisco as well as the shifting Afghan population in the Northwest.

Across America, Arab and Muslim communities like those from Afghanistan have become increasingly prominent in response to the focus placed on them since the events of September 11, 2001. Despite the political tensions these groups currently face, they have also won strong local support from the Pacific population. When reprisals directed toward Arab and Muslim Americans were feared after the World Trade Center and Pentagon attacks, Japanese and other Asian American communities who remembered the trials of internment rallied and spoke out in support of Arab and Muslim populations. Such action can only further a legacy of interethnic contact and support that drives a diverse, dynamic Pacific population.

SUMMARY

The Pacific Region's extreme ethnic diversity makes the area one of the most complex and dynamic cultural landscapes in the nation. Its history of settlement, from the first human migrations from Asia into Alaska to the millions arriving every year in Honolulu, Seattle, Anchorage, Portland, San Francisco, and Los Angeles, endows it with a heritage at once similar yet uniquely distinct from other regions in the United States. A remarkable plurality of native groups has persisted through the devastating impacts wrought by waves of immigrants, and Native Alaskans, Native Hawaiians and American Indian tribes from Puget Sound to the Mohave Desert continue to affirm their cultural and political identities within twenty-first century society. Russian, Spanish, British, and U.S. colonial enterprises have all left their imprints throughout the territories, bestowing lasting legacies that have enabled later migrations—from Mexico, from post-Soviet republics, from the American Midwest—to surge into and reconceive the limits of regional identities. The land has provided a generous bounty for new arrivals over the last two centuries: agriculture, fishing, timber, and oil and mineral mining industries have all attracted immigrants of varied ethnic origins and still form a significant base of the region's economy. The California Gold Rush initiated one of the most massive movements of people in modern history and stood as a precursor for later global migrations through the twentieth century. This includes more recent enclaves of Nigerians, Ethiopians, and Afghanis from Seattle to San Diego. It also cast the Pacific as a seam where East and West merge, as Asian and European immigrants converged on the region and sparked transethnic cultural fusions. Ethnic tensions in the Pacific have been some of the fiercest and most dramatic in the country, but as the twenty-first century proceeds, the region presents itself at the multicultural vanguard, with thriving ethnic communities and cosmopolitan urban centers embodying the ideal of a pluralistic American society.

RESOURCE GUIDE

Printed Sources

Baldassare, Mark. *California in the New Millennium: The Changing Social and Political Landscape*. Public Policy Institute of California. Berkeley: University of California Press, 2000.
Chan, Sucheng. *Asian Americans: An Interpretive History*. New York: Twayne Publishers, 1991.
Dinnerstein, Leonard, Roger L. Nichols, and Davis M. Reimers. *Natives and Strangers: A Multicultural History of Americans*. New York: Oxford University Press, 1996.
Eargle, Dolan H., Jr. *The Earth Is Our Mother: A Guide to the Indians of California, Their Locales and Historic Sites*. San Francisco, CA: Trees Company Press, 1986.

Ethnic Identity in California: A Guide to Organizations and Information Resources. California Information Guide Series. Claremont: California Institute of Public Affairs, 1981.

Halliday, Jan. *Native Peoples of Alaska.* Seattle, WA: Sasquatch Books, 1998.

McKee, Jesse O., ed. *Ethnicity in Contemporary America: A Geographical Appraisal.* 2nd ed. Lanham, MD: Rowman and Littlefield Publishers, 2000.

White, Sid, and S. E. Solberg, eds. *Peoples of Washington: Perspectives on Cultural Diversity.* Pullman: Washington State University Press, 1989.

Videos/Films

Ancestors in the Americas (a three-part series). Prod. Loni Ding. Center for Educational Telecommunications, 1998–2001.

Shades of California. Huell Howser Productions, 2003.

The West (an eight-part series). Dir. Stephen Ives. Public Broadcasting Service, 1996.

Web Sites

Model Minority: A Guide to Asian American Empowerment
June 9, 2004.
http://www.modelminority.com/

A web site devoted to contemporary Asian American issues.

Organizations

Angel Island Immigration Station Foundation
P. O. Box 29237
San Francisco, CA 94129-0237
415-561-2160
http://www.aiisf.org/

California Indian Museum and Cultural Center
5250 Aero Drive
Santa Rosa, CA 95403
707-579-3004
http://www.cimcc.indian.com/

Islamic Center of Southern California
434 S. Vermont Avenue
Los Angeles, CA 90020
213-382-9200
http://www.islamctr.org/

Nordic Heritage Museum
3014 NW 67th Street
Seattle, WA 98117
206-789-5707
http://www.nordicmuseum.com/

Polynesian Cultural Center
55-370 Kamehameha Highway
Laie, HI 96762
800-367-7060
http://www.polynesia.com/

Slavic Cultural Center
60 Onondaga Avenue
San Francisco, CA 94112
510-649-0941
http://www.slavonicweb.org/scc.html

FASHION

Susan B. Kaiser and Linda B. Arthur

A wide array of images comes to mind when thinking about fashion in the context of the Pacific Region; indeed, the concept of fashion itself becomes more elastic. In many ways, fashion calls the idea of a region itself into question. Fashion may not seem stable or "real" enough to represent a regional sense of place, especially in the face of homogenized brands (e.g., Nike, GAP, Levi's) in a global economy. Ambivalence about fashion's ability to represent a sense of place certainly applies to the Pacific Region—itself a complicated and constructed concept. This region promulgates a sense of being alternative, natural, casual, and as creating innovations that fit into people's everyday lives, rather than following conventional concepts of what is "proper." Through casual clothing separates (e.g., jeans, T-shirts, running shoes) that are often linked in some way to "real" goals (e.g., functionality, comfort, performance, freedom), fashion becomes more than *high* fashion in the Pacific Region. In fact, fashion becomes a wide range of options: from the creation of a new kind of runway (the Hollywood red carpet) to business casual attire (i.e., aloha shirts, khaki pants, jeans) to active sportswear and outdoor apparel.

So, how can fashion of the "Pacific Region"—defined as including the states of Alaska, California, Hawai'i, Oregon, and Washington—be captured and represented? A whole host of images surface: from aloha shirts to blue jeans to Alaskan parkas to active sportswear to outdoor "gear" to beachwear to Hollywood glamour, to name just a few. And the more we look into the varied cultural histories within the Pacific Region, the more complicated the array of images become. In addition to the drastic differences in geography and climate (ranging from the warm breezes of the Hawaiian islands to freezing temperatures in Alaska), the cultural diversity within the Pacific Region is remarkable.

Despite the incredible cultural diversity within the Pacific Region, some similar elements of a shared story surface: escape from the rigidity or formality of the Eastern United States or Europe, the colonization of indigenous cultures (i.e., native peoples), and the creation of new (more white) collective identities that continued to erase cultural difference, despite ongoing international trade and immigration, especially in relation to Mexico and Asia. And yet dominant culture finds ways to establish the "authenticity" of certain forms of dress (e.g., the hula skirt, Mexican folkloric skirts, Eskimo parkas) for the tourist industries within the Pacific Region, so as to have a sense of roots with a sense of place and to profit from a sense of roots and regionality.

Frequently, in the Pacific Region, it is a complicated situation of moving back and forth: between moving forward with a sense of discovery towards new and more hopeful possibilities for the future, and stepping back for a reality check—checking in with the natural environment and with the indigenous populations who first settled them, in order to make sense of it all and to understand how and why people dress and change as they do.

INTERCULTURAL NEGOTIATIONS: HOPE AND HEGEMONY

In the present day, business relations with Asia and Mexico (and many other locations in the world) are a central component of the Pacific Region. Intercultural relations with Asia are not new. To understand the complexity of the Pacific Region's interactions with Asia, one needs to look to the shared cultural roots of some Native Alaskan peoples with Asia. Alaskan "Eskimos" (Inuit people) share similar parka clothing styles, fur embroidery, and geometric and floral themes with Asia, suggesting that there was direct contact in the distant past. At the same time, there are important differences: North Pacific cultures have very distinctive geometric embroidery that incorporates reindeer hair and other artifacts linked to reindeer. There is also a strong tradition of making and wearing masks that flourished among native peoples of the Pacific Northwest. It is estimated that Alaskan Athabascan people migrated to the North Pacific and Pacific Northwest a few millennia ago.[1]

Similarly, the history of Hawai'i is deeply integrated—economically and aesthetically—with diverse Asian cultures. Today the majority of Hawaiians descend from Asia, although there have been intercultural marriage and other influences. Multiple Asian influences also help shape the cultures of other states in the Pacific Region—especially California.

Historical, Intercultural Influences on Pacific Dress

This intercultural influence on Pacific dress dates at least to the sixteenth century, when Spanish Mexican explorers Juan Rodríguez Cabrillo (?–1543) and Bartolomé Ferrer (1499–c. 1550) searched for cities of gold and inland waterways within what is now the United States. When they failed to find them, they shifted their focus toward Asia. Since the early 1570s, the Manila Bay (in the Philippine Islands) had served as a strategically located harbor, able to receive silk from China as well as spices from various islands in the south of Asia, items in heavy demand in both "New Spain" (Mexico) and Europe. Accordingly, an active trading system flourished across the Pacific Ocean. What is now known as California became very important in this trans-Pacific trade, because it was the first location to be reached after a long journey across the ocean from Manila en route to Acapulco. In the beginning of the seventeenth century, Sebastían Vizcaíno (1550?–1615) "discovered" what was to become an important port—one that he named Monterey. Below is a quote from his letter to King Felipe III (1578–1621) of Spain from Mexico on May 23, 1603:

> The area is very populated by people whom I considered to be meek, gentle, quiet, and quite amenable to conversion to Catholicism and to becoming subjects of Your Majesty. The Indians have strong bodies and white faces. The women are somewhat smaller and have nice features. Their clothing is made from sealskins. They tan and dress the hides better than it is done in Castile. Seals are found in abundance. . . . They have a large amount of flax and hemp, from which they make fishing lines and nets for catching rabbits and hares. . . . The coast is populated by an endless number of Indians, who said there were large settlements in the interior. . . . They are very knowledgeable about silver and gold and said that these metals can be found in the interior.[2]

It was clear that the "Indians"—so labeled because the original aim of European colonists had been to sail westward in order to seek a shorter trade route to the "East" (in a search for India)—had some knowledge that was valuable in the hopeful search to find new materials (e.g., gold, silver, silk) and to reinforce their dominance. "Hegemony" is a concept that refers to the need to have control and power—to become dominant, with the recognition that this is not just an outcome; rather, it is a *process*. And hegemony, as a process, is not achieved strictly through bloodshed or acts of war. Rather, it is a process that recognizes that some kinds of negotiation need to take place. The peoples who are to be "conquered" or controlled have some knowledge or perspective that needs to be understood. Further, these peoples cannot be controlled (and learned from) strictly through brute force. Instead, there is a need to understand deeply what they want and can gain from a new cultural intervention. In the case of "Indians" or Native Americans, accounts of early settlers or colonists from New and Old Spain (and elsewhere from peoples of European descent) tended to describe the needs and desires of Native Americans for food and clothing (or, at least, materials that would keep them warm and/or make their lives more pleasant in other respects). Some of these early settlers understood that the

Two Nunivak women look out to sea wearing waterproof parkas. Courtesy of the Library of Congress.

159

process of controlling and colonizing other peoples requires knowing something about what they might want and need.

The land known today as California has had human inhabitants for at least 10,000 years. In fact, by the time of European contact, California probably had the densest population of diverse peoples later called "Indians" north of Mexico. However, California remained isolated from Europe and Asia until the early sixteenth century, when Spain sent an expedition to Mexico. The idea was to use the "tried-and-tested" method of sending soldiers and missionaries to develop a colonial order that dominated indigenous populations. Between 1769 and 1846, the population of Native Americans had diminished to one-third of its earlier size, due in part to the introduction of new diseases by the colonizers. The early colonial Mexicans (Californios) became a ranching elite.[3] In the process of displacing Native Americans literally, there was a symbolic erasure of many of their cultural ways, including their native dress customs.

To some extent, hegemony (dominance, control) cannot be achieved if people do not want something, and the western traders coming to the Pacific Region were able to observe at least some signs of something (including clothes) being desired. In the 1770s, in the San Francisco Bay Area, Native American men dressed for a festive occasion as they interacted with Spanish colonizers. In the words of Vicente de Santa María at that time:

Some had adorned their heads with a tuft of red-dyed feathers, and others with a garland of them mixed with black ones. Their chests were covered with a sort of woven jacket made with ash-colored feathers; and the rest of their bodies, though bare, were all worked over with various designs in charcoal and red ochre, presenting a droll sight. . . . We gave them glass beads and other little gifts, which they put in their reed container. . . . They are very fond of trading. All of them hanker for our clothes, our cloaks most of all, and so as to make them warm they show us with sad gestures how they suffer from the cold and even say the words *coreoc cata*, "I am cold." . . . On this day it came off colder than usual, and of the poor unfortunates on board, those who could do so took refuge under my cloak, showing with piteous looks how keenly, being stark naked, they felt the chill. Luck, it seems, offered a sailor's long coat to Supitacse, the oldest and least forward of them all, as soon as he came on board, and he took it at once and kept himself warm in it, huddling in corners. When it was time to leave, he most considerately put the garment back where he had taken possession of it."[4]

Sixty years later, Juan Bandini (who came to Alta [mainland] California in the 1820s with his father, who was a trader) wrote the following in his description of Alta California: "The only thing that makes the foreigners want to trade here is the untanned cattle hides and tallow. It is well known here that nothing else will ever be able to serve as money, for scarcely any money circulates."[5]

A somewhat similar pattern of colonization occurred in Hawai'i, although there are some important differences (e.g., the missionaries were Protestants from New England rather than Catholic missionaries from Spain via Mexico). Between 1778 and 1819 a number of explorers came to the islands; between 1820 and 1900 the missionaries arrived, and between 1900 and 1960 a new kind of commercialized

culture—a tourist industry—fostered a reappropria-
tion and reinvention of some of the symbols of earlier
Hawai'i: most notably the hula girl, who wore a bra
top, a grass skirt, and leis as she moved and swayed.[6]
When the missionaries arrived in Hawai'i, they found
a population used to expressing status differences
through appearance. While the missionaries wanted
to "cover the heathen's nakedness," Hawai'i's queens
desired Western-styled dresses (holoku) to assert their
elevated status. The missionaries wanted New
England–styled homes to be built, and Hawaiian
women wanted calico for dresses. By exchanging their
husbands' labor for calico, Hawaiian women quickly
adopted the holoku as standard Hawaiian dress by the
1850s.

Indeed, a lot of the initial motivation for exploration in the Pacific Region was economic. There was
an incentive for trade, for new materials, and this incentive gradually forced Native Americans into a
different economic system: one that evolved from a
system of a subsistence economy (i.e., take or use only
what you need) to one that involved the trade of goods
and, eventually, a monetary economy. For example,

Little girls perform a traditional hula dance
for tourists. Courtesy of Corbis.

Hawaiians were also forced by Western immigrants to
move toward a currency-based economy. Before Westerners arrived, Hawaiian
people wore garments made of kappa—a soft fabric made from the bark of the
wauke (mulberry) tree, which girls and women stripped, pounded, and dyed. Kappa
was also a form of currency, used to pay taxes. The tradition died out after about
100 years of Western influence (beginning in the late eighteenth century). However, the wide range of colors, natural dyes, and unique patterns used in the production of kappa were transferred onto fabric through wooden stencils until this
became too labor-intensive and faded away. The practice was revived, however, in
the latter part of the twentieth century, when it had the potential to represent indigenous identities but also to appeal to collectors and tourists.[7]

Similar trading patterns can be identified in the case of Athabascan craftswomen
in Alaska. In the late nineteenth century, their traditional porcupine quillwork designs were replaced with beadwork. Colored glass beads had become an item with
economic trade value—a kind of value that had not been assigned to the traditional
quillwork. Colored glass beads were obtained from Russian, American, and Hudson's Bay Company traders and began to circulate as a form of currency among
Athabascans. Athabascan women used beads to trade for skins to make their family's clothing. Also, as men's tunics were decorated with beads, they were preserved
as family wealth.

Koryak seamstresses—also in Alaska—used trade items such as beads to decorate dance coats (knee-length coats with a flared skirt, full sleeves, and with the
wrist area and hood trimmed with fur). Elaborate embroidery patterns embellished
white caribou fur that was arranged in geometric patterns. The additional use of
beads and metal objects that were obtained through trade produced sounds that

increased the value and prestige of the dance coats and also served as protective amulets. The dance coats were worn to welcome whales as hunters caught them along the shore.[8]

The Pendleton Story

Much of this trade sets the stage for the Pendleton story, which directly links the cultural history of Native Americans in the Pacific Region (and beyond) to the commercial realities of a modern economy. This fascinating account can be understood more deeply by analyzing the ways in which Native American cultural and aesthetic preferences became commodified—that is, how what was valued intrinsically for its beauty and tradition became converted into a system of exchange.

The Pendleton family roots in the Pacific Northwest date back to 1863, when Thomas Kay, a young Englishman, arrived in the Oregon Territory. Oregon was known for its ideal conditions for raising sheep and producing wool, as well as its moderate weather and plentiful water. The town of Pendleton, Oregon, was a major railhead serving the Columbia Plateau as a wool-shipping center for sheep growers of the region. Originally, Pendleton made Jacquard Indian trade blankets that were richly colored and patterned. In 1909, the Bishop family established a new and efficient factory that produced vivid blankets inspired by the colors of Native Americans from the Nez Perce nation near Pendleton for the Navajo, Hopi, and Zuni nations. To understand the importance of these blankets' intercultural trade, it is important to look back historically.

Prior to the influx of European settlers, blankets had been used by Native Americans for centuries. These were often made from the hides or pelts of small animals that had been sewn together or woven from wool, feathers, down, bark, and cotton. When the Europeans arrived, it became evident that wool blankets had high trading value. Originally the trading blankets had patterns in plaid and block designs like the traditional Hudson Bay's blankets. However, the Pendleton pattern designers learned about the native mythologies and design preferences of their customers and melded their aesthetic and cultural preferences with new blanket technologies. These blankets were popular not only among Native Americans in the Pacific Northwest; routinely, carloads of blankets traveled to the Southwest for trade with Native Americans there, in exchange for silver jewelry, wool, or other items of value.

To this day, Pendleton continues to produce Native American blanket designs, which have become collectors' items and also cater to the tourist trade. Approximately 50 percent of sales are still to Native American populations. They can be described as a symbol of "authentic" style and one that Pendleton's own contemporary trade discourse characterizes in a way that continues to emphasize the link between Native American cultures and "nature":

NEW FOR 2003: THE GIFT OF LIFE. Native American beliefs are closely tied to the natural world. Universally, rain—and water itself—is considered to be life-giving and life-sustaining. For all tribes, daily activities revolve around rain and water. In the Northwest, rivers and precipitation are abundant.[9]

Pendleton makes the point that although popular style changes, traditions do not change as easily or as readily. So the company has to strike a delicate balance between continuity and change as it continues to produce Native American blankets.

In 1924, Pendleton introduced wool plaid shirts, using some of the colors and aesthetics derived from the Native American blanket designs. The shirt became a very popular item in men's wardrobes, as it was warm, durable, and comfortable. Although in many ways it has become a symbol of the Pacific Northwest, the Beach Boys helped to popularize the image more widely in the 1960s, especially the Umatilla wool shirt. Pendleton describes the shirt as "a 10 oz. weight that can tackle the coldest temperatures or be worn as a casual jacket alternative."[10]

Motives for Intercultural Negotiation

The Pendleton story is instructive because it points to the importance of intercultural negotiations as a major factor in the history of the Pacific Region as a whole. Intercultural—and indeed international—motives helped shape the history of Northern California. Arguably, one of the primary motives for Spain to expand into what is now Northern California in the late 1760s was Russia's entry into this area. Since the explorations of Vitrus Bering in the 1740s, Russian companies had been coming to the area to hunt seals and sea otters; their furs were a valuable part of the developing trade with China. By the end of the eighteenth century, the Russian American Company was the only company that had been authorized by the Russian government to hunt and trade in North America. This company used the knowledge of the native people of the Aleutians and Kodiak Island to develop its sea otter operations. The company established its own base at Fort Ross, north of Bodega Bay. Here, stock such as sheep was raised for its profitable trade value. Their hides were shipped to Alaska, and a lively, illegal trade emerged between the Russians and the northern Spanish settlements around the Francisco presidio, which produced goods that were exchanged for food and the permission to hunt for sea otters. In the 1820s, British and American firms traded with missions in California for the hides and tallows of cattle."[11]

Meanwhile, although some California Native Americans managed to maintain something of their community structures and habits, it became difficult to compete in an economy that was increasingly dominated by large private ranchos. In a society where wealth was based on land, many Native Americans lost their self-sufficiency and worked as wage laborers on the ranchos or in the pueblos.[12]

In the mission of San Luis Rey de Francia, wines were produced and sold to the English or Anglo-Americans for clothing, linen, hats, coffee, tea, and other commodities. The women of the mission produced shirts and other products. However, traditional practices still existed:

On this occasion the clothing is of feathers of various colors, and the body is painted, and the chest is bare, and from the waist to the knees they are covered, the arms without clothing. In the right hand they carry a stick made to take off the sweat. The face is painted. The head is bound with a band of hair woven so as to be able to thrust in the *cheyatom*, our words.[13]

From the 1820s, the Santa Fe Trail had become opened to Missouri, furthering the fur trade between Santa Fe and the Plains Indians east of the Rocky Mountains. Between 1825 and 1840, a number of trading negotiations occurred between the trappers and Indians.[14] Yet in the late 1820s, the only traders in the area of Northern (Alta) California were English, Anglo-American, and Russian and some Mexican ships. The British brought goods and money to exchange for hide and tallow. The Anglo-Americans sailed out of Boston with a number of goods on board, and they left with hide, tallow, and any money they could garner. The Russians came with money in search of grain and meat.[15] By the 1840s, the California rancho had become a central feature of the hide and tallow trade—a trade that dominated the local economy. Routinely, rancho cattle were slaughtered, then put on Anglo-American ships. The hides often ended up in New England to be made into leather for the growing shoe industry; these materials have been described as the resources for the "first American industrial revolution."[16] Yet some of the natural resources of the area, it was becoming evident, were not finite. One writer noted that by 1841 the otter and the beaver that had been abundant in California had been exterminated. The Russians had basically exterminated the otter, while the Columbians (trappers from the Columbia River) had almost made the beaver disappear.[17]

Before the 1840s, during the Mexican colonization of what is now California, the ultimate goal was to change the land and its people into a space that could produce actively for the Spanish empire—for New Spain and its imperial goals. The initial idea was that the "Indians" would learn the Spanish religion, language, and ways of dressing (covering the body). It was typical for Native American male contacts to be given a blanket and a loincloth. "When I was a boy, the way the Indians was treated was not good at all. They didn't pay us anything. They only gave us food, a loincloth, and a blanket which they replaced every year."[18]

In the early 1840s, around Monterey, more foreigners began to move into the area, bringing with them a new cluster of beliefs. Whereas the earlier merchant immigrants of the 1820s and 1830s had assimilated fairly readily into the dominant Mexican society, the newer arrivals believed that "the United States was destined, by providence, geography, and cultural and racial superiority, to extend its rule west to the Pacific."[19] This was Manifest Destiny—an idea promoting cultural superiority over nature.

FROM "NATURE" TO "CULTURE" AND BACK

The Uses of Native Fashion

The settlers coming from the eastern part of the United States and Europe had a certain perception of the West, not only as offering promise but also as requiring a taming of "nature"—of the wilderness and the "uncivilized" peoples the settlers associated with nature. In Alaska as well as elsewhere, the idea that native peoples were "nomadic" was used as a justification to take their lands. Inasmuch as native peoples symbolized the wilderness to European colonizers,[20] this perception extended to native peoples' very bodies. The fact was that Hawaiians and other natives of the Pacific Region did not cover the same parts of the body as did peoples of European (Christian) descent.

Based upon Christian beliefs about modesty, which go to the very foundations of ideas about Western clothing and fashion, the settlers and explorers of the Pacific Region assumed that the native peoples they found were primitive and closer to nature than to culture. (comments to this effect are often found in missionary newsletters sent back to their congregations). Ironically, some of the same female images that had been viewed as savage or wild and that needed to be tamed by the missionaries (e.g., covering women's breasts) became adapted to a tourist image that would sell about 100 years later in the form of the hula girl (now wearing a bra top). The Christian missionaries had isolated girls from their families and friends, dressed them in "proper" blue cotton dresses, and taught them how to wash and iron clothing. But the myth of the hula girl—a myth about her link to the goddess of nature and the "embodiment of passion"—was still compelling (and profitable) for the tourist industry that was rapidly developing from the 1920s onward.[21]

Rooted in the split between nature and culture that characterized how European settlers viewed the distinction between indigenous peoples and themselves was an assumption that somehow these indigenous peoples were closer to the land:

Men become like the land in which they live. This is not true of people such as ourselves. . . . We have made a life apart for ourselves in our houses and our cities. We have removed ourselves from nature. But it is true of savages living close to nature. Such savages must become like their land, or they will die. . . . The Indians were savages, close to nature. They had to become like their land. . . . The whites were a stronger and more advanced people. They could not be stopped from entering the Indian country and putting the country to better use.[22]

Here then, we have the greatest problem of the missionary: how to transform a savage race such as these into a society that is human, Christian, civil, and industrious. This can be accomplished only by denaturalizing them. It is easy to see what an arduous task this is, for it requires them to act against nature. But it is being done successfully by means of patience, and by an unrelenting effort to make them realize that they are men.[23]

One of the problems with the "disconnect" between nature and culture—so embedded in modern European thought—was that it undermined the potential to appreciate indigenous relationships with nature as cultural and aesthetic practices. For example, the Athabascan culture in what is now Alaska had used porcupine quills as decoration in clothes for centuries.[24] In the North Pacific, clothing made from animal skins were made in a process of production that was a sacred art. The artists tended to be women who processed and sewed the skins in a manner that respected the spirits of the animals from which they were derived. For example, Inuit (Eskimo) women had a number of well-documented taboos against sewing at the beginning of the hunting season ("to pierce the caribou hide with a needle would offend the spirit of the caribou waiting to be captured").[25] In the mythology of the North Pacific region, there was an intimate relationship between the spirits of humans and animals; they could transform from one into the other. In Athabascan indigenous culture, animals were regarded as beings that had permanently donned masks or skins. Humans showed their primary relationship with animals by wearing animal skins—a way of demonstrating the close, transforming bond between humans and animals. Additionally, the use of red ochre (thought to symbolize blood—a metaphor for life and a source of unity between humans and animals) decorated much Athabascan clothing, serving a protective as well as a decorative function. Red ochre was much like a visual "joint" that bound the seams and edges of clothing; it could also be found underneath porcupine quillwork or alongside tassels of hide, feathers, or later, beadwork.

A similar show of unity was demonstrated by the Chukchi and Koryak cultural practice of using alder bark to soften reindeer hide and to give it a reddish brown tone. The material also made the hides more moisture resistant. The resulting hides were sewn into dance coats. These were knee length and had a flared skirt, full sleeves, and a hood trimmed with wolverine or black dog fur. The chest was often decorated with white caribou fur arranged in geometric patterns, and the hem was embroidered. When whales were trapped and killed, Koryak women would wear these coats to welcome the whale to a new world and to symbolize through color a shared association with blood.

Inuit design motifs on fur clothing also revealed a relationship between humans and animals. The reindeer fur coats worn by women and men alike had a triangular-shaped gusset at the throat, which made a reference to the walrus, which was respected for its size and its tusks.[26] In the animistic religions of Inuit (Eskimo) and Aleut cultures, there was a belief in a central power (an earth spirit) that permeated all of nature.[27]

Inuits displaying reindeer-skin suits in contest, 1916. Courtesy of the Library of Congress.

The Relationship between Nature and Culture

Overall, there are several themes that pervade the history of the relationship between nature and culture(s) in the Pacific Region. First, there was an assumption on the part of European settlers that indigenous peoples who had lived in the region for centuries were part of its "natural" history, but they lacked culture. Second, the dominant European attitude was that people who were not white were "savages" who were not as advanced as peoples of European descent. This rationale was used not only to displace indigenous peoples from their lands but also to justify imposing European cultural practices—including ways of producing, consuming, and dressing—on indigenous peoples. Third, the history of the Pacific Region is one of a tension between preserving nature and having control over it. Before colonization by people of European descent, indigenous cultures tended to use their natural resources carefully, and it was not until the settlers themselves realized the limits of the environment that they, too, developed a philosophy of environmental preservation. This was especially true in the northern part of the region (from Northern California to Alaska)—an area that has been called "Ecotopia." This term comes from a 1975 novel by Ernest Callenbach, in which he describes Northern California, Oregon, and Washington seceding from the United States. The idea was: "We're here now, so let's seal off the borders and keep this environment the same—now that we've mastered it."[28]

As it turned out, the "disconnect" between nature and culture that had formed much of the rationale for European colonization had not offered a sustainable model for the future. The Pacific Northwest (the northern part of the Pacific Region), in particular, still experiences a tension between mastery over and protection of the environment. In part, this stems from an appropriation of the indigenous philosophy of unity with nature, in part from the compelling and majestic nature of the landscape (i.e., the ocean, the mountains, the plant life), and in part from an outdoor lifestyle—whether at work or at play. The philosophy of Ecotopia was to live simply and close to nature, in realization of the limits of natural resources.

To the Euro-American cultures of the Pacific Northwest, the close-to-nature philosophies of indigenous hunter-gatherer peoples could be used or appropriated into a discourse of "deep ecology." These philosophies helped to cure the nature-destroying problems associated with Western culture. At the same time, indigenous peoples themselves were "contained" (e.g., on reservations) or fixed in the past so as to be contrasted with Western ideas of progress and modernity.[29] An ecological philosophy was used as a way to redress the modern "disconnect" between nature and culture.

A "Natural" Way of Dressing

Some of this ecological philosophy plays out in a "natural" way of dressing—a look of studied indifference to style. Consider the following examples: In the 1990s, Phil Knight, CEO of the Nike Corporation based in Beaverton, Oregon—a CEO with an "unconventional management style" was described as wearing a wrinkled green business suit—"the wrinkles having become something of a trademark over time . . . and he clutched one stem of his ever-present wraparound sunglasses in his hand . . . with his longish, reddish-blond curls, close-cropped beard, and extravagantly designed eyewear—Knight looked for all the world, at the age of fifty-five, like some prosperous, if mellowed, rock-and-roll star."[30] Sixty years earlier, in Alaska, John Collier, appointed the Commissioner of Indian Affairs in Alaska in 1933, assumed an unconventional look of studied indifference. Collier, who was described as being infatuated with native cultures, would often wear a baggy green sweater, had long and unbrushed hair, and sometimes was known to carry a frog in his pocket.[31]

Another example of studied indifference, coupled with attention to the natural elements and to commercial culture, comes through in the advice in a travel book about how to dress while visiting Alaska:

> Bring plenty of T-shirts, short pants (temperatures in the interior can reach 90 degrees in the summer), casual slacks, sweats, socks, and a rain poncho, and you'll be comfortable most of the time. (However, locals advise not to wear cotton into the wilderness, even during the summer months. Cotton has no insulation value when wet and it does not dry quickly. Therefore, wearing it can result in hypothermia, which can kill.) Do not bring anything that needs ironing—or, if you do, wear it wrinkled. No one cares. . . . If you forget anything, Fairbanks, Juneau and Anchorage all have fully stocked outfitting stores.[32]

The ecological philosophy is very apparent in many Pacific Region clothing companies that specialize in outdoor apparel. In the philosophy of these companies, an adventurous, outdoor lifestyle can be integrated with environmentally sensitive production practices. And although there are environmental limits to production, an active and outdoor consumer lifestyle that has no limits is the ultimate in living (i.e., no mountain is too high to climb; no goal is too hard to be reached). One can get a sense of this by visiting the Web sites of outdoor companies such as The North Face, Patagonia, Royal Robbins, Eddie Bauer, and others. Patagonia advertises[33]: "Committed to the core in our commitment to the soul of the sport, enviro action, uncommon culture, innovative design." In 1999, Eddie Bauer [presented] American Forests with a check for $2.5 million, representing the 2.5 million trees planted nationally through Eddie Bauer's "Add a Dollar, Plant a Tree" retail program.[34]

But this ecological philosophy did not develop in a short period of time. The year 1876 marked 100 years after the founding of the United States, and by this time the Pacific Northwest had come to represent "a new frontier for exploration and a place of hope." However, by 1914, the limits of this help had become apparent to white settlers, who now realized that hope was balanced by hardship.[35] And about 200 years after the founding of the United States, clothing companies along the Pacific Coast of the United States, especially the northern part, were figuring out the importance of returning to a philosophy of hope—yet one blended with a philosophy of ecology. Increasingly haunting the industry, however, was the problematic philosophy of labor associated with global capitalism. There was a growing "disconnect" between the active, outdoor Pacific Region consumers and the offshore and immigrant garment workers who made their clothes.

NEGOTIATING WORK AND LEISURE

The Pacific Region's relationship with the outdoors, with nature and the environment, has deep roots in a larger negotiation between work and leisure. In fact, many of the casual (leisure) clothing companies in the region have historically responded to the needs of working people for functionality and comfort. From the native peoples of Alaska's whale hunting attire to Hawaiian plantation workers' clothing to the dress of the gold miners of California and loggers in much of the Pacific Northwest, there has been a theme of having clothes in which one can work outdoors comfortably. And inevitably these clothes have become popular with a larger mainstream audience for leisure as well as work. In many ways, the styles of working-class people (especially working-class men) have been appropriated as mainstream fashion.

The History of Blue Jeans

The story of Levi Strauss is a classic story in the move from work to leisure (and back). In 1847, San Francisco became a center of rapid population growth due to the gold rush. People came there from New England, the Pacific Northwest, China, and Mexico; from the south came free and runaway slaves; this great influx established San Francisco as the capital of California's nineteenth century.[36] Strauss was able to capitalize on this population growth. A tailor from Reno named Jacob Davis regularly purchased fabric from Strauss, a dry goods supplier in San Francisco, in order to supply the gold miners with sturdy pants that were then called "waist overalls." In 1870, Davis made some custom pants for a large woodcutter from some sturdy white, cotton fabric; his challenge had been to make the pants sturdy enough to withstand active wear. So he fastened the corners of the pockets and the base of the fly with rivets and then began to sell them to local teamsters; his business spread as the word got out about the new functionality. Davis wrote Strauss to tell him about the design and to seek his help in paying for a patent. He sent along two pairs of pants: One was in a white cotton duck, and one was in a blue denim. The latter (denim) is believed to have been derived from a twill fabric made in Nimes, France ("Serge de Nimes"). Initially, the twill fabric was made from a wool and silk mix, but it was translated into a different version in Manchester, New Hampshire. Strauss immediately recognized the potential for this unique garment and underwrote the patent fees. The patent was received on May 20, 1873, referred to by the Levi Strauss Company as the "birthday of blue jeans." In 1890 this style of pants was assigned the number 501, which it continues to bear today.

These distinctive pants became an international phenomenon: a blend of a good product with powerful marketing. Initially, Levi's marketed its pants (jeans) to workers in the mining and logging communities. But by the 1920s, jeans were being marketed to cowboys on the Hollywood silver screen. Cowboy stars such as William S. Hart and John Wayne wore them and popularized the idea of wearing jeans for leisure wear on dude ranches in California and Nevada. In the late 1930s, the denim industry was still catering largely to workers and cowboy-inspired consumers. Levi's was dominant in the West Coast jeans market, but the St. Louis–based Lee's brand was producing the most workwear clothes for the United States.

James Dean, 1955. Courtesy of Photofest.

The history of jeans (Levi's and other brands such as Lee's and Wrangler's) in the shift toward leisure (and "cool") wear must also be traced to Hollywood, when Marlon Brando appeared in *A Streetcar Named Desire* in 1951 and James Dean and Paul Newman appeared in subsequent films wearing jeans. By 1957, jeans had become "right for school" in San Francisco, and by 1966, they were becoming a symbol of hippie culture in the Haight Ashbury district of San Francisco. Bands such as the Jefferson Airplane, the Grateful Dead, and Santana all appeared in Levi's. The 1970s were to become the "golden age for denim," although competition from designer labels had quite an impact on Levi Strauss.[37] The company was to develop a new strategy by the 1990s: one that made khakis (Dockers) and even jeans a mainstay of professional men's wardrobes.

The Aloha Shirt and Hawaiian Influence on Dress

Understanding the concept of "business casual," however, requires going to another area within the Pacific Region: Hawai'i can be identified as "inventing" the idea of business casual with its use of the aloha shirt. The history of the aloha shirt is a complicated history of style that draws from diverse cultural influences. In the eighteenth century, shirts came to Hawai'i by way of sailors, whose loose and long shirts seem to have become translated into the "palaka"—a heavy cotton jacket in a white and dark-blue plaid; the idea of collars and buttons had been introduced by American businessmen. The palaka jacket was worn by immigrants coming into Hawai'i (often from Asia) to work in the fields and mills in order to protect them from the sharp sugar cane leaves or the spiny pineapple tops. By 1900, most plantation workers were wearing the palaka jacket, and within a few decades the style evolved into a short-sleeved shirt. It became lighter weight and was then worn for casual wear. The palaka was worn by teenagers and adults who were not doing physical labor and over time came to represent the plantation roots of ethnic identity in Hawai'i. By the early 1920s there were three small-scale factories producing palaka shirts, jackets, and work clothes.

Another form of casual shirt—Hawai'i's famous aloha shirt—developed soon thereafter in the tailoring shops, but soon these were produced in two of the factories. Garment companies sprang up to meet the demand, and by the 1940s, aloha shirts were becoming a symbol that employed thousands. The aloha shirt has multiethnic origins; the style lines came from sailors' shirts; that it is worn loose rather than tucked in comes from the influence of the Philippine's national shirt (*barong tagalong*) in Hawai'i; the early fabrics were generally kimono prints imported from Japan and brocades from China; the earliest shirts were crafted in Chinese and Japanese tailor shops. A Chinese tailor, Ellery Chun, trademarked the term "aloha shirt" in 1936, and aloha shirts were made of Asian fabrics with Asian prints until block printing began in the late 1930s. When importing ceased during World War II, block-printed Hawaiian designs became dominant in the 1940s and have dominated in aloha shirt design since then. In the 1944 film *Tahiti Nights*, aloha shirt fabric designs really made a splash nationally. At the same time, these designs were helping to develop a "local" Hawaiian look that blended elements from different cultures and ideas.

Aloha shirts brought in a new concept in men's shirting design; these were vividly patterned shirts—not solids or stripes. And it was to change what men could wear for leisure and, later, for work. By 1936, two companies, Kamehameha and Branfleet, were producing sportswear for tourists and for consumers in the U.S. mainland. In 1946, the Honolulu Chamber of Commerce launched a project promoting sport shirts (very plain versions of aloha shirts) that would be suitably comfortable for businessmen during the summer months. The next year, the chamber launched Aloha Week as a concept to attract tourists and to develop an esprit de corps locally. The idea was to wear aloha attire for the entire workweek, in part to benefit the fashion industry that produced muumuu dresses and aloha shirts, in part to offer some relief from the usual office wear. But the trend continued; Hawaiian themes in aloha wear had become a key trend by the 1950s. There was a fad for all things Hawaiian occurring in the United States by the late 1950s, when Hawai'i

In the 1961 film *Blue Hawaii*, Elvis was referred to as the "King of Aloha" and wore aloha shirts by Shaheen, a major aloha attire manufacturer in Hawai'i. Courtesy of Photofest.

joined the United States as the fiftieth state. Mainland companies such as Jantzen of Oregon sold "cabana sets" for men—a matching shirt with boxer-style shorts. And local businesses in Hawai'i encouraged more acceptance of the aloha shirt, if it was clean and tucked in, but only during Aloha Week.

In the 1960s, the Hawaiian Fashion Guild launched "Operation Liberation" and helped to make aloha attire suitable for Fridays and, eventually, an everyday possibility. Hawai'i's aloha shirt began America's movement toward business casual attire in 1962 when Hawai'i's government required men to wear it throughout the summer; later on, Aloha Friday was declared, and workers were (and still are) expected to dress in aloha attire every Friday. One could say that Aloha Fridays led to Casual Fridays on the U.S. mainland. Throughout the mid-twentieth century, tourists and soldiers brought the aloha shirt to the U.S. mainland, but more important, the aloha shirt migrated to California on the backs of surfers who brought the relaxed shirt and lifestyle to the mainland. This was the beginning of the business casual movement, as many of the young California surfers grew up to become Silicon Valley executives who shed three-piece suits for more relaxed attire at work and instituted Casual Fridays into the world of work. By the 1990s, the idea of Casual Fridays had spread to the West Coast of the United States, especially the Silicon Valley, where the computer industry promoted a casual and comfortable working situation (with which companies such as Levi Strauss were pleased to comply).

But the trend started in Hawai'i, and it had been used in part to help to establish a "local" identity—a panethnic identity that used aloha attire as a unifying theme. Today "identity apparel" drives the aloha attire industry in that most businesses in Hawai'i's tourist industry have uniform aloha attire with their corporate logo interwoven into the Hawaiian designs. Tori Richard is one of the key companies producing both identity apparel for Hawai'i and resort apparel for the rest of the world.[38]

The Business Casual Look

By the end of the twentieth century, the business casual look had transformed workplaces in a number of professional settings. Casual businesswear had become a flexible way to dress, and companies that focused on separates that could go into this look—moving from work to leisure and back—stood to profit. Accessible separates were the focus of San Francisco–based companies such as the Gap and Banana Republic. Banana Republic, which was part of the Gap company, competed with designer brands in the late 1990s by incorporating materials such as suede to give some of the separates a bit of punch. These items had a sense of luxury but still conveyed a casual silhouette and sold well, helping Banana Republic to become a $1 billion-a-year business by the late 1990s. According to *Wall Street Journal* reporter Teri Agins, "The end of fashion has led straight to Gap, which has mastered a modern way of marketing clothes. . . . To borrow a 1998 cover line from *Fortune* magazine: 'Gap Gets It.' Which means the shoppers get it, too."[39]

Something important occurred in the twentieth century to influence how work and leisure wear could be negotiated and transformed in the process. The idea was pretty different from a more traditional notion of what it meant to be professional. And it is evident that a number of images circulated in the tourist and film, as well as fashion, industries, to make this shift toward mixing and matching clothing separates an everyday reality for many, across the lines of work and leisure. The business suit was not dead, but it had some competition, and images helped to make this competition work.

SYSTEMS OF REPRESENTATION—CREATING NEW IMAGES AND IDENTITIES

Fashion, as a social process of identity and difference, becomes a key factor in representing local or regional identities. The Hawaiian aloha shirt is a profound example of this process; it represents a sense of being "Hawaiian" in the context of remarkable ethnic diversity: It is something—a symbol—that people have in common across ethnic differences. Ironically, it comes to mean being "local" in a state whose identity has been influenced by a blend of diverse ethnic influences, tourist imagery (what sells Hawai'i), and comfort and practicality for a tropical climate.

Similar examples and processes are part of the histories of the other states in the Pacific Region. Indeed, part of having any kind of local or regional identity is a process of creating new images and identities. Much of the Pacific Region had to figure out ways to sell images and identities to themselves, as well as to the rest of the United States and the world. Hollywood, for example, became a dream-making machine that was part of a larger effort to sell Los Angeles in the 1910s and the 1920s. And the Pacific Northwest—even though there has often been an attempt to seal its borders from the outside world—has paradoxically produced global companies such as Nike. So the idea of representing a sense of place involves a complex negotiation between local culture and globalization.

Hollywood Fashion Influence

Perhaps the process of creating new images and identities through style and fashion, of representing a sense of both the local and (hopefully) the global at the same time—is nowhere more evident than in Hollywood. Indeed, the major export of much of Southern California has historically been "image-creating ideas": a visual culture that offered an alternative to the print culture of older major cities such as New York.[40] One of the major ideas created in the early twentieth century was that of California as paradise—a kind of Eden that appealed to white midwesterners who were pleased to escape from labor or hardship to a landscape that seemingly produced abundant beauty (e.g., oranges, lemons, flowers) with ease.[41] And this was a largely homogeneous, white paradise, ethnically speaking. California, of course, was far more diverse ethnically than the images represented in the Hollywood film industry and elsewhere. Further, class relations complicated the development of California images. By the 1930s, California had become a place of contradiction; photographic images of poor Oklahomans migrating from the dust bowl during the Great Depression could be contrasted with the images of a fairy-tale Hollywood: a world of sophisticated glamour. Hollywood was all about being modern in a new, sensual way.[42]

By the mid-1920s, a number of Jewish immigrants from eastern Europe, by way of New York, had established some of the film studios in Hollywood that played a major role in representing a world of sophisticated glamour. Studio founders such as Samuel Goldwyn, Jesse Lasky, and Adolph Zukor had previously worked in the garment industry—an industry that also involved the use of image creating to foster new hopes and dreams. Once they came to California, they innovated images for Hollywood that sold very well to audiences in the United States and the world. The costume designers they and their film industry colleagues hired were a major factor in their ability to create a Hollywood look. For example, director Cecil B. DeMille hired Adrian to serve as head of the fashion department at Metro-Goldwyn-Mayer between the early 1930s and 1942. Adrian created gowns for Joan Crawford and other major female film stars.[43] Adrian had an enormous influence on international fashion trends during his time at MGM. In the 1920s, film clothing styles were the most glamorous images to which the average woman had access; this was before glossy fashion magazines such as *Vogue* and *Bazaar* were available:

> By the early twenties women for the most part had thrown away the corsets that had been restricting them for centuries, exposed the full length of their lower legs for the first time, and bobbed their hair. By the thirties they were wearing trousers and shorts for sport and informal occasions without being considered scandalous. The women of the United States and Europe were hungry for this change, and they turned to the movies to tell them of the latest styles.[44]

There is a great deal of controversy about whether *haute couture* (high fashion) in Paris was influenced by costume designs for Hollywood films. However, it is clear that the Parisian fashion designers—still arguably the arbiters of world fashion in the official sense—were exposed to Adrian when they went to the movies.[45] It seems that Paris was not the only international arbiter of fashion any more. The United States had its own fashion industry, and Hollywood certainly helped to launch a "golden age" that can be traced at least to the crash of the stock market. Many more women were going to the movies than they were studying high-fashion magazines to experience a different reality (to escape, so to speak . . .).[46]

It was during one of the bleakest periods in the history of the United States that Hollywood imagery began to resonate so deeply and importantly. By the mid-1930s, Hollywood fashions were creating "fictions for the eye" and cinematic illusions that perfectly matched film women's dresses to the scene. These gowns were made to be photographed rather than worn.[47] At the same time, a number of fashionable products were "placed" in film scenes in a way that created a new form of advertising, especially for middle- and upper-class consumers. In the late 1910s and 1920s, Cecil B. DeMille commented on the extent to which publicity and salespeople wanted modern clothes to be depicted, to create new desires. And in the coming decades, the Hollywood "outdoor" lifestyle—represented by casual separates such as bathing suits, pedal pushers, slacks, and jeans—revolutionized the way people dressed for leisure activities even in the smallest towns of the United States. Perhaps it is no accident that the number of clothing manufacturers increased dramatically between 1900 and the late 1930s. By this time, Los Angeles was becoming recognized as the international leader in the fields of sport clothes, street dress, and modern and outdoor furniture; and Los Angeles was probably second only to New York and Paris in high fashion.[48] The British costume historian

Christopher Breward argues that by the late 1930s Hollywood's "marketing and publicity prowess" had outdone Parisian models of fashion. Costume designers such as Adrian and Edith Head had created a new kind of femininity: one with "a source of power and purpose, achieved through a more structured approach to tailoring, padding and accessories."[49] This was a new model for fashion—one that offered glamour in an accessible way to wider audiences. Macy's department store became a leader in the Hollywood fashion field with its Cinema Fashion shops (there were 400 of these by 1937).[50]

A good example of the influence of Hollywood fashion on the general public is the impact of the 1951 film, *Place in the Sun*. In this film, Elizabeth Taylor starred in a role as a debutante who wore evening gowns. Costume designer Edith Head created two styles for her; one of these had a large white tulle skirt over pale green satin, and the bust was covered with white violets. Manufacturers copied this style, which quickly caught on with the consuming public: "Go to any prom this season and you'll see dozens of them," one fashion editor remarked.[51]

It is also no accident that the swimwear industry was launched in the Pacific Region in the 1920s. Three big firms emerged, all of whom evolved from the manufacture of knitwear: Jantzen emerged from the Portland Knitting Mills; Cole was West Coast Knitting Mills; and Catalina evolved from Bentz Knitting Mills. All of these were inspired to some extent by the glamour of Hollywood. For example, in 1952, Fred Cole hired Esther Williams (a swimming film star) to advertise his bathing suits. This suit hugged every curve of a woman's body (thanks, in part, to Lastex-and-nylon technology).[52]

The image of the hula girl grew up in the early part of the twentieth century, and this image also relied upon an exotic alternative to white images of glamour. By the early twentieth century, the image of the hula girl already seemed to be everywhere: on "tourist poster, key chains, apple boxes, and cigar containers."[53] The idea was that tourists and other visitors were to think about the hula girl as a sensual image that was alright to enjoy. In 1932, Latina actress Dolores del Rio performed a mating dance for the film *Birds of Paradise*, and she repeated this role in *Hawaiian Buckaroo* (1938). The idea was that the hula girl was a seductress, and it was okay to toy with her affections, but she was not the girl a man would eventually marry. Hers was a "forbidden sensuality"—the path for a white male to "a forbidden paradise. . . . She is a creation of the imagination, not of reality, a sexual interlude concocted to fit the needs of early to mid-twentieth century America."[54] Ironically, the very same image that missionaries had tried to destroy about 100 years ago now became an important advertising figure. Yet this new image, promoted by the Hawai'i Tourist Bureau as in 1930s brochures, can be compared to her counterpart in Hollywood films. She was more likely to look white than Hawaiian; she referred to "a mythological America: a land of WASPs, white bread, and old-fashioned values." This "girl-child" forged a connection between the hula girl and burlesque and vaudeville images of sexuality. This was an image designed to Americanize Hawai'i; there was no longer a need to fear the hula dancer; she had been tamed.[55]

It is ironic that the same sexuality that had been so problematic to the missionaries had now become appropriated by the tourist industry in order to sell Hawai'i. Accordingly, it is not too surprising that the hula girl remains as a central figure in the imagination of what it means to be Hawaiian or to experience Hawai'i. The

Aloha Elvis Style

There is an important connection between Hollywood and Hawai'i: Elvis. He first visited Hawai'i in 1957, and it became his second home. For the next three decades, he was to return to Hawai'i for vacations, concerts, and three films that further boosted tourism to the state. Popular aloha-wear maker Reyn Spooner marketed lines of Elvis Presley clothing, and some of these featured scenes from his album covers.[57] In the film *Blue Hawaii* (1961), Elvis was referred to as the "King of Aloha" and wore aloha shirts by Shaheen, a major aloha attire manufacturer in Hawai'i. Alfred Shaheen's goal was to produce textiles that authentically represented Hawai'i and Polynesia. The Hawaiian print Elvis wore on the cover of his *Blue Hawaii* sound track was Shaheen's Tiare Tapa print designed by Bob Sato.[58]

commercial image of the hula girl has become a stereotype of what it means to be Hawaiian, although her history is a much more complex blend of diverse Polynesian cultures and mainland desires for an exotic image.[56] This image, it seems, had the ability to "spice up" the white popular imagination.

Sexuality and Hollywood Fashion

As Hollywood has presented the "Pacific Region" to the outside world, there have been various images and stories. But a common thread can be identified. There is a common theme of an outdoor, active lifestyle: one that creates a sense of "coolness" by way of technologies and lifestyle choices. Hollywood is not the only venue available for creating images. Consumers in the region, savvy to certain ideas and ideals, use clothes to create not just looks, but entire identities.

TECHNICAL, ACTIVE "COOLNESS": OUTDOOR GEAR FOR ACTIVE LIVES

Bathing Suits

To a large extent, some of the dominant, glamorous images of Hollywood and Hawai'i have been feminine and fashion-attuned. This certainly applied to the development of the active swimwear industry in the Pacific Region. Jantzen, for example, was/is a company that has focused on the need for women to replace their old-fashioned, nineteenth-century "bathing costumes" with modern bathing suits. In 1910, Jantzen was known as the Portland Knitting Company; it began to manufacture suits that adjusted to the swimmer's body, using a riblike formation. The idea was to flatter the female body while also promoting beauty. In 1931, the company—now Jantzen (since 1918)—introduced the "Shouldaire," which allowed strap-free tanning. The company blended Lastex, a rubberized yarn, with the fabric to help to define the bustline and provide a better fit to the suit overall.

The difference was the extent to which it could sell to a mainstream audience. Jantzen recognized the necessity to cater to the needs of changing consumers. In the 1940s, the company added sweaters, foundations, and active sportswear to its basic swimwear line. After the attack on Pearl Harbor, the company shifted its focus to military items during World War II; these included sweaters, swim trunks, sleeping bags, gas mask carriers, and parachutes. About thirty years later, the company recognized the need to appeal to working women's desire for attractive beachwear for weekends and vacations. The company blended its commitment to new swimwear technologies with Hawaiian and other floral motifs; the idea was to be both functional and fashionable.[59]

Surfing Fashion

The idea of blending function and fashion goes back much further, however. The outdoor cultures associated with much of the Pacific Region compelled a number of innovations for work and/or leisure. For example, the Kodiaks in what is now California would wear shirts made from seal gut, and the flaps of the shirts were fastened to the rim of the canoe opening to protect against water in the canoe.[60] Surfing was another sport that developed a connection with the environment. It was a sport invented by the Austronesians (people of the Southern Islands), traced to around 2000 B.C.E. among seafarers in the Philippines and Indonesia; these were the first Polynesians to develop what was to become an elaborate sport in Hawai'i by at least 1200. In 1885, three Hawaiian princes attempted to introduce the sport to Santa Cruz, California. They fashioned boards from local redwood trees, but the sport did not really capture the imagination of local Californians at that time. It was not until the early 1900s, when there was a revival of the sport in Waikiki, that surfing started to catch on in the United States. Duke Kahanamoku—the Olympic swimming champion—did a lot to popularize the sport in the United States as well as Australia. Postcards featured him as a "human fish." The sport of surfing was in the United States in the 1930s, and by the 1960s and 1970s, surfing had become a commercial success, with clothes and other gear (i.e., surfboards) to go with the whole identity of being a surfer.

Surfing is a good example of the outdoor lifestyle that influenced fashion in Hawai'i and Southern California. But there is another outdoor and "cool" image in the Pacific Region: a rather earthy, funky "cool" image that is more focused on an active lifestyle on a regular basis. The company REI is a stellar example. Founded in 1938 by twenty-five mountain climbers from the Pacific Northwest, Recreational Equipment, Inc. (REI) is a consumer cooperative and has grown into a renowned supplier of specialty outdoor gear and clothing. Sales associates are sportsmen and women who have firsthand knowledge of the equipment and apparel needed for the sport. Today REI is the nation's largest consumer cooperative with more than 2 million members who enjoy special benefits. A portion of the company's profits are donated in support of the outdoors and outdoor recreation.[61]

Outdoor Cool

In gender terms, the cool image focused on an active lifestyle may be described as a distinction between "appearing" (in the sense of Hollywood images that are most compelling) and "doing" (in the sense of a number of industries that have emerged in the Pacific Region—especially in the Northwest—to express an active and outdoor lifestyle). While the former can quickly and easily be described as more "feminine" and the latter tend to be more "masculine," there are a number of ways this distinction can be complicated. This is just one of the many ways that fashionability—being timely, cool,—becomes gendered, and there are many reasons to contest the simplicity of this gender-based framing of "coolness," although at the same time there are some reasons to understand the basic, hegemonic need to establish and reestablish this distinction on an ongoing basis.

A number of apparel companies have emerged in the Pacific Region to convey and sell an athletic, outdoor lifestyle. On some level, these companies have attempted to communicate that they are making "authentic" products that happen to capitalize on the latest technologies to help consumers run faster, swim better, ski more comfortably and ably, and engage in a number of other outdoor sports with finesse and style. These "natural" or "authentic" products have often been framed primarily as masculine, although there are some notable exceptions. Overall, "outdoor gear" companies have portrayed a healthy, active lifestyle that is simultaneously glamorous. It is a new kind of cool—one that does not rely as much on fashion as it does on function.

By the 1980s, it had become fashionable to look athletic, a product of the fitness revolution in the late 1970s. By the late 1970s, there was a real interest in running—the ultimate independent sport. In addition to Nike, companies such as InSport (based in Portland, Oregon) were catering to this market. InSport produced running shorts out of garages at the same time that companies such as Nike and Adidas were marketing the product under their own labels but expanded in the late 1980s and 1990s into fitness, cycling, and triathlon apparel: clothes for the serious athlete. The company also became known for its use of highly technical and innovative fabrics.[62] Sporthill also emerged from a desire to produce athletic wear that was highly technical and functional. Its founder Jim Hill discovered that nylon running shorts and cotton sweats were not suitable for the Pacific Northwest's cold and rainy weather when he moved from Virginia to run track for the University of Oregon. (Visitors to Alaska are also warned about cotton not being well suited to the cold and damp climate.) He later started the company with a philosophy of merging European fit with the best fabrics from the United States.[63] Another action sportswear company, Columbia, established in 1937, grew from a small family-owned company in Portland to one of the world's largest outerwear brands. The company is known for its skiwear, as well as other active sportswear and rugged footwear; it was one of the first outerwear companies to make jackets from waterproof and breathable fabrics. Columbia also introduced a breakthrough technology in which the outer shell layer and liner combine for multiple wearing options,[64] a feature suitable to the Pacific Region's changing weather.

CONCLUSION

Pacific Region fashion cannot be described succinctly or easily, as myriad climates, peoples, and lifeways influence this large area. But there are some common threads: casual separates (from Pendleton blankets and shirts to Levi jeans to Alaskan parkas to aloha shirts), incredibly complex cultural histories, and attention to creating images of reality through style in the context of—or in spite of—natural environments. These images relate to everyday work and leisure, from the production of clothing and other goods to glamorous consumption that seems pretty far removed from this production, especially in a global economy. And these have not been the same kinds of images that were historically portrayed as fashionable in traditional fashion centers such as Paris or even New York in the nineteenth and twentieth centuries. Rather, these were pieces of fashion: fragments that could be mixed and matched in a variety of ways to construct identities that could be worn for manual labor, for active outdoor sports, or for the construction of identities that represented an array of ethnic, gender, sexual, and class identities.

The clothes produced and consumed in the Pacific Region have offered a way of thinking about fashion that is less prescriptive and more flexible. For example, women in Hawai'i began to wear aloha shirts when they were introduced for men, West Coast women adopted flannel plaid shirts, and people of all classes wear jeans to make all kinds of statements—including professional or dressy ones. The diversity of fashions in the Pacific Region can be linked to the fundamental need to differentiate while also seeking ways of expressing commonality. To the extent that this blend of identification and differentiation is flexible and global, it is able to capture a sense of what the Pacific Region is all about.

RESOURCE GUIDE

Printed Sources

Agins, Teri. *The End of Fashion: The Mass Marketing of the Clothing Business*. New York: William Morrow, 1999.

Arthur, Linda B. *Aloha Attire: Hawaiian Dress in the Twentieth Century*. Atgen, PA: Schiffer Publishing Ltd., 2000.

Barron, Stephanie, Sheri Bernstein and Ilene Susan Fort, eds. *Made in California: Art, Image, and Identity, 1900–2000*. Berkeley: University of California Press, 2000.

Beebe, Rose Marie, and Robert M. Senkewicz. *Lands of Promise and Despair: Chronicles of Early California, 1535–1846*. Santa Clara, CA: Santa Clara University, Berkeley, CA: Heyday Books, 2001.

Breward, Christopher. *The Culture of Fashion*. Manchester, UK: Manchester University Press, 1995.

Brown, DeSoto, and Linda Arthur, *The Art of the Aloha Shirt*. Waipahu, HI: Island Heritage Publishing, 2002.

Bullis, Douglas. *California Fashion Designers*. Layton, UT: Peregrine Smith Books, 1987.

Colburn, Bolton, Ben Finney, Tyler Stallings, C.R. Stecyk, Deanne Stillman, and Tom Wolfe. *Surf Culture: The Art History of Surfing*. Corte Madera, CA: Gingko Press, 2002.

del Mar, David Peterson. *Oregon's Promise: An Interpretive History*. Corvallis: Oregon State University Press, 2003.

Emberley, Julia V. *The Cultural Politics of Fur*. Ithaca, NY: Cornell University Press, 1997.

Fitzhugh, William W., and Valerie Chaussonnet, eds. *Anthropology of the North Pacific Rim*. Washington, DC: Smithsonian Institution Press, 1994.

Fregoso, Rosa Linda. *MeXicana Encounters: The Making of Social Identities on the Borderlands*. Berkeley: University of California Press, 2003.

Gaines, Jane, and Charlotte Herzog, eds. *Fabrications: Costume and the Female Body*. New York: Routledge, 1990.

Garreau, Joel. *The Nine Nations of North America*. Boston, MA: Houghton Mifflin, 1981.

Hall, Marian, Marjorie Carne, and Sylvia Sheppard. *California Fashion: From the Old West to New Hollywood*. New York: Harry Abrams, 2002.

Marsh, Graham, and Paul Trynka. *Denim: From Cowboys to Catwalks*. London, UK: Aurum Press, 2002.

Reilly, Maureen. *California Casual Fashions, 1930s–1970s*. Atglen, PA: Schiffer Publishing Ltd., 2001.

———. *California Couture*. Atglen, PA: Schiffer Publishing Ltd., 2000.

Robbins, William G. *The Great Northwest: The Search for Regional Identity*. Corvallis: Oregon State University Press, 2001.

Rosen, Ellen Israel. *Making Sweatshops: The Globalization of the U.S. Apparel Industry*. Berkeley: University of California Press, 2002.

Web Sites

Columbia Sportswear
February 24, 2004.
http://www.columbia.com/who/who_history.cfm

Eddie Bauer
March 3, 2004.
http://www.eddiebauer.com/about/company_info/history.asp

InSport
October 30, 2003.
http://www.insport.com/history.cfm

Jantzen
March 3, 2004.
http://www.jantzenswim.com/start.htm

The North Face
June 11, 2004.
http://www.thenorthface.com/

Pacific Trail
February 18, 2004.
http://www.pacifictrail.com/history.htm

Patagonia
June 11, 2004.
http://www.patagonia.com/

Pendleton
June 11, 2004.
http://www.pendleton.com/

Royal Robbins
June 11, 2004.
http://www.royalrobbins.com/

Sporthill
January 17, 2004.
http://sporthill.com/

Museums with Clothing Exhibitions

Alaska

Alaska Native Heritage Center
8800 Heritage Center Drive
Anchorage, AK 99506
http://www.alaskanative.net

Alaska State Museum
395 Whittier Street
Juneau, AK 99801-1718
http://www.museums.state.ak.us/asmhome.html

Anchorage Museum of History and Art
121 West 7th Avenue

Anchorage, AK 99519-6650
http://www.anchoragemuseum.org/

Sheldon Jackson Museum
104 College Drive
Sitka, AK 99835-7657
http://www.museums.state.ak.us/sjhome.html

University of Alaska Museum of the North
907 Yukon Drive
Fairbanks, AK 99775
http://www.uaf.edu/museum/main.html

California

Fullerton Museum Center
301 N. Pomona Avenue
Fullerton, CA 92832
http://ww.ci.fullerton.ca.us/museum/

J. Paul Getty Museum
The Getty Center
1200 Getty Center Drive
Los Angeles, CA 90049

Museum of the American West
4700 Western Heritage Way (in Griffith Park adjacent to L.A. Zoo)
Los Angeles, CA 90027
http://artscenecal.com/AutryMsm.html

The Oakland Museum of California
1000 Oak Street
Oakland, CA 94607
http://www.museumca.org/

San Jose Museum of Quilts and Textiles
110 Paseo de San Antonio
San Jose, CA 95112-3639
http://www.sjquiltmuseum.org/

Hawai'i

Bailey House Museum
2375 Main Street # A
Wailuku, HI 96793
http://www.mauimuseum.org/

Bernice Pauahi Bishop Museum
1525 Bernice Street
Honolulu, HI 96817
http://www.bishopmuseum.org/

East-West Center Gallery
1601 East-West Road at the corner of Dole Street
Honolulu, HI 96822
http://eastwestcenter.org/

Honolulu Academy of Arts
900 South Beretania Street
Honolulu, HI 96814-1495
http://www.honoluluacademy.org/

Maui Arts & Cultural Center
1 Cameron Way
Kahului, HI 96732
http://www.mauiarts.org/

Oregon

Corvallis Arts Center
Linn-Benton Arts Council
700 SW Madison Avenue
Corvallis, OR 97333
http://www.caclbca.org/

Grants Pass Museum of Art
229 SW "G" Street
Grants Pass, OR 97526
No Web site

Latimer Quilt and Textile Center
2105 Wilson River Loop Road
Tillamook, OR 97141
http://www.oregoncoast.com/latimertextile/

Portland Art Museum
1219 SW Park Avenue
Portland, OR 97205
http://www.portlandartmuseum.org/

University of Oregon Museum of Art
1223 University of Oregon
Eugene, OR 97403-1223
http://uoma.uoregon.edu/

Washington

Burke Museum of Natural History and Culture
University of Washington
17th Avenue NE and NE 45th Street
Seattle, WA 98195-3010
http://www.washington.edu/burkemuseum/

Frye Art Museum
704 Terry Avenue
Seattle, WA 98104
http://www.fryeart.org/

Northwest Museum of Arts and Culture
2316 West First Avenue
Spokane, WA 99204
http://www.northwestmuseum.org/northwestmuseum/

Seattle Art Museum
Downtown:
100 University Street
Seattle, WA 98101-2902

Seattle Asian Art Museum
1400 East Prospect Street
Seattle, WA 98112-3303
http://www.seattleartmuseum.org

Washington State History Museum
1911 Pacific Avenue
Tacoma, WA 98402
http://www.washingtonhistory.org/

FILM AND
THEATER

*Georges Van Den Abbeele,
John T. Caldwell, Jan
Goggans, and Jeff Purdue*

Understanding film as in any way regional (with the possible exception of locally oriented documentaries) flies in the face of traditional film history, which has taken special pride in the international reach of the cinema since its invention in 1895 by the Lumière brothers, who quickly proceeded to dispatch cameramen all around the globe to document local scenery and cityscapes. While the narrative of film history typically details stylistic variation as a function of *national* schools or movements, the shared viewing of the same images by audiences worldwide is understood to represent a departure from the language boundaries of literature and the site-specific limitations of the visual arts. Yet this internationalism of the new media should not obscure the regional basis of much filmmaking, *a fortiori*, in the Pacific Region of the United States, which has not only housed the acknowledged capital of the film industry in the Los Angeles suburb of Hollywood but whose landscapes from the Hawaiian islands to the rugged West Coast shoreline to the Mojave desert to the streets of Los Angeles and San Francisco have served as the acknowledged or unacknowledged backdrop for many of the images that have come to define the worldwide culture of modernity. The received filmic representations of the old American West, traditional New England, the cotton fields of the Old South, the deserts of North Africa and Arabia, even extraterrestrial worlds (as in the *Star Wars* series) are predominantly West Coast locations filmed (and in many cases built) to portray those other localities. David O. Selznick (1902–1965), for example, famously trucked in tons of crushed brick to the San Fernando Valley shooting location for *Gone With the Wind* (1939), mixing it into the soil to emulate the "red" earth of Georgia.

Eadweard Muybridge, c. 1910. Courtesy of the Library of Congress.

THE BEGINNINGS OF FILM IN HOLLYWOOD

Early History

Even before the advent of "Hollywood" as the industrial center of the U.S. movie industry, California can claim a key role in the very invention of the cinema. It was no one less than Leland Stanford (1824–1893), the transcontinental railroad baron turned California state governor, then horse fancier, and eventual founder of a university named after himself, who encouraged, subsidized, and massively publicized Eadweard Muybridge's (1830–1904) early experiments with motion photography in the early 1870s. Using multiple cameras timed to shoot individual snapshots of animals and people in motion, revealing a reality hitherto inaccessible to the human eye (such as, most famously, the flickering moment when a moving horse actually has all four hooves off the ground, "flying" ever so briefly), Muybridge also invented a corresponding projection device, the zoopraxiscope, by which he could display his photos as rapid, sequential movement upon a commonly viewed screen. This early prototype of the motion picture was first exhibited in Palo Alto to the Stanford family and friends in 1879.

The Exodus to California

The subsequent U.S. development of the cinema, though, in the 1890s and early 1900s was primarily an East Coast affair orchestrated by the likes of Thomas Edison (1847–1931) and George Eastman (1854–1932). But by the end of the first decade of the twentieth century, the further development of the film industry came up against two obstacles that triggered the sudden, grand, and definitive migration of filmmakers and studios from New York to Los Angeles in a kind of celluloid-driven gold rush that in its turn fueled the concomitant growth of the Los Angeles area into a world city. First, crippling patent disputes pitted Edison against those he accused of pirating his invention. The apparent resolution of these conflicts by the 1909 establishment of a consortium called the Motion Picture Patents Company (MPPC)—in essence a monopolistic front for Edison and eight other major producers—only aggravated the problem as distributors chafed under the requirements they show *only* MPPC films or be allowed none. By way of response, distributors decided instead to begin producing their own films, preferably as far away as possible from the East Coast patent barons (one of the less overtly acknowledged reasons for choosing Southern California was its quick proximity to the Mexican border, should legal or financial issues get too hot).

Perhaps the most important of these renegade producers was Carl Laemmle (1867–1939), whose Independent Motion Picture (IMP) Company moved to Hollywood in 1912, then reorganized itself as Universal Studios, opening its Universal City location in 1915 with unparalleled fanfare and publicity—including a myth that the Pacific Coast fleet upon the order of the secretary of the navy had sailed up the Los Angeles river (a technical impossibility) to deliver a gun salute in honor of the new studio home. Other independent producer/distributors soon followed suit and established studios in Hollywood all within the same time period. By the 1920s, the "majors," as they came to be called— Fox, Warner Brothers, Paramount, MGM, United Artists—would dominate world film production *and* distribution, while those who did not break free from the New York–based MPPC would go out of business and indeed out of modern memory.

A second force driving the development and choice of Hollywood as the hub of the cinema world arose from the

The zoopraxiscope—a couple waltzing, c. 1893. Courtesy of the Library of Congress.

ever-pressing need for more content and variety as movie watching dramatically grew in popularity with audiences both within and beyond the borders of the United States. Even MPPC loyalists, such as Biograph, Vitagraph, and Kalem, began sending film teams to Southern California to take full advantage of year-round sunshine and easy access to a stunning variety of scenic backdrops for location shooting. As early as 1909, D. W. Griffith, then working for Biograph, decided to "winter" in L.A. (when weather conditions made outdoor shooting virtually impossible back East) and subsequently decided to make that his permanent, year-round base of operations. Many of these early filmmakers were responding to publicity put out by the Los Angeles Chamber of Commerce claiming some 350 days of sunshine per year as well as works such as John McGroarty's *History of California*, which emphasized not only the "great variety of scenery—mountains, desert, sea, islands and rivers—" to be found close by but also "the vast variety of architecture in which every state and nation had here expressed itself."[1] Consequently, Southern California became a kind of massive set for almost any location and situation imaginable:

> Private homes were gratuitously used for elopements and domestic dramas. Banks were utilized on holidays, Saturday afternoons, and Sundays for hold-up scenes. Drug stores and other places of business were regularly robbed before the camera. Citizens were halted on the street to augment mob scenes. Streets were roped off for automobile accidents. . . .
> Robin Hood "robbed them good" in the woodland north of Hollywood mountain, and Custer's massacre occurred in the valley now occupied by

D. W. Griffith, c. 1925. Courtesy of the Library of Congress.

Silver Lake reservoir. Pirates had their treasure on Catalina Island, and the mushers with their dog trains mushed summer or winter in perpetual snow 11,000 feet up on San Jacinto mountain, while the Foreign Legion fought to the death in Death Valley.[2]

Moreover, the studios themselves were usually positioned on relatively copious tracts of land (unlike the cramped brownstones rented in New York) with offices, postproduction facilities, and interior sets (eventually sound stages) near the front with the "back lot" reserved for the construction of increasingly ambitious outdoor sets where once had stood groves of lemon and orange trees. Between these sumptuous studio sets and the panoply of closely accessible urban as well as natural decors, the Hollywood studios were able to work year-round and without the expense of remote location shooting, thus generating a film production rate unmatched anywhere else either in quantity, pictorial quality, or financial profitability, thereby acquiring a dominance over world film production that would last well through the mid-twentieth century. This formula of cost cutting through the use of local scenery may have reached its *nec plus ultra* (last word) when producer Henry Lehrman (1886–1946) of L-KO famously overruled a director's request to film some scenes up in Yosemite: "A rock is a rock—a tree is a tree—shoot it in Griffith Park!"[3]

The Draw of Regional Decor, Peopling, and Architecture

The "regional" decor of classic Hollywood cinema can be viewed in different ways. On the one hand, the California land- and seascapes opened up the stunning possibilities of the fledgling movie medium with the evocative exploration of vast new vistas of plains, mountains, and deserts. Longer films with such spectacular views definitively moved the film narrative out of Edison's black box and the nickelodeon onto wider screens and into the spacious movie palaces that remain as a great architectural tribute to the golden age of Hollywood in cities across the United States and around the world. On the other hand, a more ambiguous legacy lurks in the implicit equation of the California landscape with any or every region of the world. To the extent that these images are perceived not as regional but as generic, they contributed to the general cultural sense of rootlessness associated with the increasingly globalizing, flattening, and abstracting effects of modernity. In other words, they worked against the very sense of place and region studies such as those gathered in this volume strive to recover. And yet every cinematic image stamped with the imprimatur of "Hollywood"—and this means the virtual entirety of mid-twentieth-century American film production—at some level hearkens back to that Southern California location just as surely as the famous hilltop sign spelling out the letters of the town name of Hollywood (erected in 1923 and declared an official cultural historical monument in 1973), a sign that has itself become a cultural icon. Moreover, the age of classic Hollywood cinema and the industrialized "studio system" that brought it into being is coterminous with the great migratory movement that would make L.A. the second largest city in the country and California the most populous state in the union. The role of the landscape as it appears in Hollywood film surely contributed, whether explicitly or implicitly, to the lure of the West Coast as that last American dreamland where, like the protean screen actor, one could do anything or become anyone, just as the regional decor could itself morph into any given destination.

Such protean diversity is reflected, too, in the very peopling of Hollywood. Some of the century's best-known authors worked at one time or another as screenwriters (F. Scott Fitzgerald [1896–1940], William Faulkner [1897–1962], Raymond Chandler [1888–1959], among notable others). Moreover, many of the first filmmakers and eventual movie moguls were Jewish immigrants from eastern Europe who found opportunities in a disreputable new media. In the 1930s, a new generation of European émigrés, fleeing the rise of Nazism, reestablished their acting, directing, or screenwriting careers in Hollywood, which continues today to attract talent from around the globe. This "foreign" presence in Hollywood has at times served as fuel for attacks on the industry, from anti-Semitism in the 1930s through Joseph McCarthy's (1908–1957) charges of supporting communist sympathizers, up to more recent criticisms of failing to uphold American family values. Yet Hollywood has always protested by asserting its claim to be as American as anyone, from the production of World War II propaganda films, full cooperation with the House Un-American Activities Committee (HUAC) investigations, and the development of self-censorship procedures through production codes and movie ratings.

Well before larger studios such as Universal City, Disney, or Paramount caught on to the lucrative use of their own locations as tourist attractions and theme parks, California was already being architecturally transformed by the ambitions of set designers as well as of towns eager to promote themselves as niche shooting locations. The pioneering legacy of D. W. Griffith (1875–1948) cannot be underestimated here again, for the man who first came to Hollywood to profit from the year-round sunshine and location-rich topography of Southern California also left his own additional marks on the urban landscape of Los Angeles. Much of the gigantic Babylon set he built in 1915 for his epic *Intolerance*—easily the largest and tallest structure in L.A. at that time—stood near the corner of Sunset and Hollywood for years afterward. Today, a full-scale replica of the set's core, the Babylon Court, serves as a Mesopotamian-styled shopping mall in the Hollywood-Highland complex, which also houses theaters and the new official venue for the Academy Awards ceremony.

Other location-hungry filmmakers have teamed up with developers to get filming rights at large construction projects after their completion but before being opened for their intended use. For example, the underground chase scene in George Lucas' first feature film *THX 1138* (1970) was by special arrangement shot deep below San Francisco in the B.A.R.T. subway tunnels as yet unopened to the public. In other cases, certain nearby localities have highlighted their distinctive town architecture or natural topography for filmic use. North Coast towns, such as Mendocino or Bodega Bay, have successfully traded on their resemblance to New England (rugged shoreline, quaint marinas, Cape Cod–style homes, and classic-looking lighthouses) for a variety of horror and mystery films as well as historical dramas and romantic comedies set back East. Conversely, the sparse California chaparral has become the defining backdrop to the western genre, no matter whether the "action" is set in Texas, Wyoming, or the Dakotas, and communities sporting that look profited. The most wildly successful of these was the San Fernando Valley town of Chatsworth, home to the Iverson Movie Ranch, which served as the primary location not only for thousands of westerns featuring the likes of John Wayne, Gene Autry, Roy Rogers, the Lone Ranger, and Hopalong Cassidy but also a surprising variety of other terrains, including the "Africa" of the Tarzan movies. Ironically, rapid urban development in the early 1970s, spearheaded by the construction of the Simi Valley Freeway, hastened the end of this area as a filmic location and its conversion into a decidedly uncinematic sprawl of condominiums, shopping centers, and gated communities.

The cast of a Tarzan filming at the Iverson Movie Ranch in the San Fernando Valley, California, 1934. © MGM/The Kobol Collection.

While such niche location shooting still continues and West Coast localities often remain the unnamed stand-ins for places around the world, significant changes took place with the decline of the classic studio system in the 1940s, spurred by antitrust legislation (the 1948 *U.S. v. Paramount* case) that forced film production companies to divest their distributional control of theater chains as well as by the rise of television as a rival medium. Though less of an economic threat, the new film aesthetics of postwar Italian and later French cinema, which placed a high premium on location shooting, served as further encouragement to broaden the available decor of the Hollywood cinema. One response was found in the increasing use of "second-unit" film crews, which allowed a much more spectacular set of backgrounds to be used by dispatching cameramen to places further and further afield. The results of their filming could then be rear-projected in the studio while principal actors read their lines. The middle films of Alfred Hitchcock (1899–1980), from *Rebecca* (1940) and *Suspicion* (1941) up through *Vertigo* (1958) and *North by Northwest* (1959), are prime examples of this development (though Hitchcock's personal penchant for backgrounds featuring San Francisco and the Northern California coastline must be duly noted).

A second development is the increasing production of films shot in California not to represent faraway lands but as explicitly representative of California itself. Interestingly, this tendency, far from celebrating the fantasy myth of Hollywood, takes its strongest form by representing the gritty, urban underside of Los Angeles, most notably in the genre of film noir, as it develops from *Double Indemnity* (1944) through *LA Confidential* (1997), including such dark futuristic spinoffs as Ridley Scott's *Blade Runner* (1982) or the *Terminator* series (1984–2003). In many cases, a primary object of critical depiction has been the Hollywood film industry itself, such as Billy Wilder's *Sunset Boulevard* (1950), Robert Altman's *The Player* (1992), or David Lynch's *Mulholland Drive* (2001).

Perhaps no film epitomizes the California film as much, however, as Roman Polanski's 1974 *Chinatown*, which follows the narrative norms of classic film noir (the burned-out and cynical detective, the morally ambiguous femme fatale, a murder mystery that points to a wider and wider set of players, a slowly revealed social atmosphere of corruption that threatens to engulf the characters) while rejecting its cinematographic trademarks: black and white film, low-key lighting, chiaroscuro, and so on. Instead, *Chinatown* presents its 1930s L.A. unremittingly sun-drenched and brightly colored only to expose the devastating crime and perversity that lurks beneath that utopian exterior. The ultimate subject matter is, of course, the inglorious history of Los Angeles, developed by rich schemers who unscrupulously exploited land and water resources. (Indeed, the modern growth of Los Angeles, including the rise of Hollywood as the film industry's home, was significantly enabled by the building of the California aqueduct, which brought water to L.A. from the Owens Valley some 200 miles away. The aqueduct was completed in 1912, the same year the first studios set up shop in Hollywood.) The modern gleaming metropolis of L.A. and its artistic crown jewel Hollywood are shown to be founded upon urban scheming and manipulation so effective it has all but driven its misdeeds from public memory. The "L.A." film would thus be a way not only to reinsert the locality of place into the cinema but also to reintroduce the narrative of history into both an urban and a studio culture of timelessness and indeed placelessness.

Perhaps no film epitomizes the California film as much as Roman Polanski's 1974 *Chinatown*, starring Jack Nicholson and Faye Dunaway. Courtesy of Photofest.

Los Angeles is, of course, not the only California location overtly featured in film noir. John Ford's 1940 adaptation of John Steinbeck's (1902–1968) *The Grapes of Wrath* (1939), while filmed at a variety of locations along the road from Oklahoma to California, is most memorable for its scenes at the Weedpatch migrant camp (still in active use today) in the southern central Valley near Bakersfield. Here again, it is the obverse of the California dream that is highlighted in a film that is explicitly represented as taking place in California. Though more of a gangster movie than film noir per se, *High Sierra* (1941) serves as an important precursor while also launching the career of Humphrey Bogart and foregrounding the forbidding and wild mountain range that marks California's eastern border. In fact, to the extent the inhospitable Sierras visually enhance the contrast between the gangster protagonist played by Bogart and a postprison world in which he is in every way out of his element, the landscape starts to function as a kind of character, acting upon the protagonist and stoking his sense of alienation. Orson Welles similarly stages the southwest desert along the California-Mexico border in his 1958 *A Touch of Evil*.

And, further north, San Francisco, too, features prominently as a film noir locale for its combination of breathtaking beauty and a seedy underworld in such classics as *The Maltese Falcon* (1941), *The Lady from Shanghai* (1947), *Dark Passage* (1947), *Vertigo* (1958), *Jagged Edge* (1985), and *Basic Instinct* (1992). In a similar vein, Clint Eastwood's "Dirty Harry" series of movies deploys that tough cop character in noir-inspired plots at a variety of locations throughout the Bay Area, venturing as far as Santa Cruz and Big Sur. Finally, *The Birdman of Alcatraz* (1962) should be mentioned as spawning a kind of crime-based subgenre featuring the Bay Area's best-known prison.

Independent Filmmakers in California

Another consequence of the reorganization of the studio system in the 1940s was its encouragement of *independent filmmakers*, a term whose use covers several distinct categories. On the one hand, independent filmmaking refers to the practice of making individual motion pictures by special arrangements between financiers and film producers, often including use of studio facilities and individual contracting of directors, actors, and technical personnel. The profitability of such arrangements is, in turn, typically ensured by predictability of plot, name recognition, and high production values, that is, the working formula for a "blockbuster" capable of handsomely returning the enormous cost it takes to produce such films. Aesthetically, though, such films typically cannot be said to depart significantly from traditional Hollywood fare.

A secondary category of "independent" filmmakers refers to the rise of small low-budget companies such as AIP (American International Pictures), whose most noted director was Roger Corman, and which typically underwrote sensationalist or "exploitation" pictures targeted to specific audiences, such as teenagers. In keeping with the need to minimize expenses, location shooting was kept to a minimum, and as in early Hollywood, schlock horror and science fiction thrillers were filmed in the L.A. area but represented as taking place somewhere else. Other AIP-produced genres, however, often made the most of their California locations, such as "beach" movies of the 1960s, whose comedic plot typically featuring the likes of Frankie Avalon and Annette Funicello invariably took a backseat to the depiction of scantily clad teenage bodies frolicking on the sands of Malibu to the accompaniment of the surf sound popularized by Dick Dale, the Beach Boys, and others.

Another genre, the biker film, exploited the California-linked notoriety of the Hollister riot and, later, the Hells Angels motorcycle gang, starting with László Benedik's *The Wild One* (1953), featuring the young Marlon Brando (1924–2004) on up through Roger Corman's *Wild Angels* (1966) and Dennis Hopper's *Easy Rider* (1968), which portrayed the drive east out of California as an exodus from the utopian hippie culture of tolerance, drugs, and free love into a nightmare of intolerance, prostitution, and murderous violence (a *Grapes of Wrath* trajectory in reverse). Michelangelo Antonioni's *Zabriskie Point* (1970) likewise examines the contradictions at the heart of the 1960s counterculture in the shadows of yet another liminal California landmark. The most profound filmic contribution to the postwar culture of alienated youth remains, however, *Rebel without a Cause* (1955), directed by Nicholas Ray and starring James Dean in his most enduring role. Shot at various locations in midtown Los Angeles, Santa Monica, and Mendocino, the film's most memorable scene remains the climactic episode at the Griffith Observatory, perched high above L.A. on Mt. Hollywood itself.

The regional dimension of independent filmmaking is also evident in the oppor-

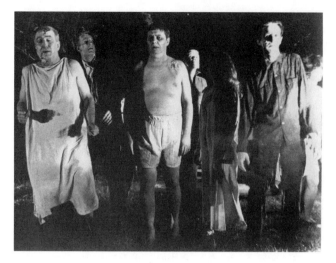

Zombies from George Romero's cult classic, *Night of the Living Dead*. Courtesy of Photofest.

tunities such companies gave younger directors as they emerged from the film schools of southern California. George Romero's *Night of the Living Dead*, produced in 1968 as a University of Southern California (USC) film project, quickly became a cult classic (even though initially rejected by none other than AIP itself). The so-called brat pack of film school graduates—Francis Ford Coppola (University of California at Los Angeles), George Lucas (USC), Steven Spielberg (California State University at Long Beach), and others—have successfully moved up the ranks of independent filmmaking companies to become their own producers of blockbusters with as much economic power and cultural sway as the old moguls who first came from modest origins to found the capital of the film industry in Hollywood.

Lucas' first major success, the 1973 *American Graffiti*, produced by Coppola, significantly revises and enhances the teenager movie while being the first major non-western picture since *High Sierra* to foreground a California location outside the two urban areas of L.A. and San Francisco Bay. A quasi-autobiographical evocation of Lucas' own youth in Modesto, the film portrays the reality of growing up in the small towns or rural settings of the Central Valley, far away from the glamour of Malibu and Hollywood, yet strangely mirroring their lure of reinvented possibilities. *American Graffiti* thus nimbly presents the California dream and its obverse, which turns out to be not the corrupting debacle staged by film noir but the quotidian drudgery of middle-class working existence after the exuberance of high school social life. Building upon the success of his later movies, Lucas himself went on to build his own version of the California dream, abandoning Hollywood to set up his own shop at his Skywalker Ranch in Northern California with his own production company, Lucasfilm, noted especially for its special effects unit (Industrial Light and Magic), its computer graphics division (later bought by Steve Jobs of Apple Computers and rechristened Pixar Animation Studios), and a patented sound system (THX). By dint of physical location and technical preoccupation, Lucas thus came to bridge the celluloid world of Hollywood with the digital revolution in Silicon Valley, adventurously linking the two prime technological loci of the West Coast into a potent aesthetic for the twenty-first century.

Since *American Graffiti*, the California location has at last become a context like any other, freely used or not to situate the locus of dramatic action, neither a stand-in for another place nor a myth to be mercilessly exposed. Whether romantic comedy (*L.A. Story* [1991], *Pretty Woman* [1990]), blockbuster action thriller (*Top Gun* [1986], *Breathless* [2003], *Speed* [1994]), science fiction (*Star Trek IV [1986]*, *Independence Day* [1996]), historical drama (*Seabiscuit* [2003]), or independent alternative (*Barton Fink* [1991], *Grand Canyon* [1991], *The Man Who Wasn't There* [2001]),

California has increasingly become simply one background among others, regardless of genre or film type. Moreover, the dramatic rise of ethnic filmmakers in the 1980s and 1990s has also enlarged the range of California locations depicted, such as the South Central L.A. seen in Melvin Van Peebles' *Sweet Sweetback Baad Asssss Song* (1971) or John Singleton's *Boyz N the Hood* (1991); the East L.A. of Luis Valdez's *Zoot Suit* (1982), Cheech Marín's *Born in East LA* (1987), or Ramón Menéndez's *Stand and Deliver* (1988); or the urban Chinese diaspora in Wayne Wang's films (*Eat a Bowl of Tea* [1989], *The Joy Luck Club* [1993]). Finally, John Caldwell's documentary project on "California Suburban Plantation Culture" brings the camera to those most hidden locations: the distressed hovels where undocumented immigrants live, in the gullies just below the multimillion-dollar mansions of San Diego's unsuspecting elite. Not content to document this polarized social landscape with the liberal good conscience of a supposedly impartial outsider, Caldwell boldly turns over the filming equipment to the local residents who tell their own stories and film the reality they live over and against a culture that would deny their very existence.

California's Continuing Dominance in the Film Industry

With location increasingly determined by the specificity of plot, California's place in film (majoritarian as it still is) also more and more resembles the role played by the other Pacific states in the much smaller number of films made either in or about them. The statistics developed by the Internet Movie Database[4] reveal the starkness of the contrast: While well over 12,000 films have been shot in California, one finds only 355 for Oregon, 421 for Washington, 296 for Hawai'i, and 109 for Alaska. As many movies have been filmed in the city of San Francisco alone (912) as in the four other states combined. Of course, these statistics do not exclude that a certain number of films shot in California may represent locations in the other states, but the preponderance of California, for better or for worse, remains indisputable in this domain.

OTHER PACIFIC LOCATIONS FOR FILM

Alaska in Film

While comparatively fewer films have been made in or about Alaska and Hawai'i, both states can be said to have a signature impact on the cinematic world through their own distinct image profiles as well as an indelible association with several recognizable subgenres. Both states sport breathtaking scenery that has served as a backdrop to represent not only themselves but other locations as well. Alaska, for example, has come to represent all things "northern," with much of the state's film industry providing locations or film clips for use in a variety of venues, including wildlife or sports documentaries, such as those produced by the successful Sprocketheads LLC in Anchorage. Not surprisingly, many of the most memorable films set in Alaska are those that follow in the tradition of Jack London's (1876–1916) novels *The Call of the Wild* (1903; no less than eight filmic adaptations from 1908 to 2000) and *White Fang* (1906; at least six cinematic renditions from 1925 to 1991), depicting the human encounter with wolves (*Never Cry Wolf*

[1983]) or the ubiquitous sled-dog race (*Balto* [1995]; *Snow Dogs* [2002]). A number of films further portray the difficulties of confronting the harsh wilderness within the historic period of the Klondike: *The Gold Rush* (1925); *The Trail of '98* (1928); and the John Wayne classic *North to Alaska* (1960). Of these, only *The Trail of '98* and the 1991 version of *White Fang* were actually shot on location in Alaska. The others were filmed in a wide variety of locations from the ever-available Iverson Ranch and the Owens Valley in California to Colorado to multiple sites in Canada (Alberta, British Columbia, Quebec) and places as far away as Finland, Norway, Spain, and Austria. Even the noted television series *Northern Exposure*, set in fictional Cicely, Alaska, was filmed in the Cascades of Washington state. The trend is continued by Christopher Nolan's recent *Insomnia* (2002), which is entirely set in Alaska, yet only a few segments, including the opening, were filmed near Hyder and Valdez, with most of the work going on in British Columbia.

On the other hand, some of the major motion pictures actually filmed in Alaska in fact represent alternative locations. *The Hunt for Red October* (1990) used Resurrection Bay near Seward for the Russian submarine base at Murmansk. John Carpenter's 1982 remake of *The Thing*, starring Kurt Russell, was filmed in Juneau but is set in Antarctica. And the Siberian scenes from *Lara Croft: Tomb Raider* (2001) were filmed in Glacier Bay National Park. A rare film that is both actually filmed in Alaska *and* purports to represent life as it is actually lived up North is John Sayles' remarkable *Limbo* (1999), which explores complex interpersonal relationships between characters in a small fishing town. Finally, a good number of locally focused documentaries explore the history of native peoples and reflect Alaska's ongoing attempt to preserve its traditional culture, most seriously by the private, nonprofit Alaska Moving Image Preservation Association, founded in 1991 and housing thousands of films and videos, including stock footage, dating as far back as the 1920s.

Hawai'i in Film

Long considered Hollywood's "tropical backlot," Hawai'i has also frequently provided the stage for any number of other locales, including islands in the South Pacific and the Caribbean, jungles in Southeast Asia, Africa, and Latin America, as well as beaches or volcanoes wherever they may be found. While exoticism and romance defined the subject matter of most early films made in Hawai'i from 1913's *Hawaiian Love* and culminating in the classic *South Pacific* (1958)—though persisting in such recent fare as *Joe versus the Volcano* (1989), *Don Juan deMarco* (1995), and *50 First Kisses* (2003)—the legacy of World War II made the islands *the* location postwar for just about any movie dealing with any event in the Pacific Theater of Operations: *Operation Pacific* (1951) with John Wayne, *From Here to Eternity* (1953), *The Caine Mutiny* (1954), *The Wackiest Ship in the Army* (1960), *None But the Brave* (1965), *In Harm's Way* (1965), *Midway* (1976), *Final Countdown* (1980), *Windtalkers* (2000), to mention only the most memorable. In particular, the traumatic bombing of Pearl Harbor has repeatedly served as the subject of cinematic realization, most ambitiously in *Tora! Tora! Tora!* (1970) and the 2000 blockbuster *Pearl Harbor* (directed by Michael Bay and starring Ben Affleck), which manages to combine both traditions of exotic romance and World War II action.

A few films have attended to earlier events in Hawaiian history, such as the partial realization of James Michener's eponymous epic in *Hawaii* (1966) and the sequel, *The Hawaiians* (1970). *Diamond Head* (1963) focuses on early plantation history, while several films have taken the charitable labors of Father Damien for their subject matter (especially *Molokai* in 1998).

In recent years, aided by a lucrative combination of tax incentives, a ready and experienced labor pool of film technicians, and the construction of the thoroughly modern and sprawling Hawaii Film Studio complex (built in 1994 and the only such facility in the nation to be owned and operated by a state government), the Hawaii Film Office has been quite successful in marketing the island to potential filmmakers across the full spectrum of genres and types—including science fiction movies from *Jurassic Park* (1993) and its sequels to *Waterworld* (1994); action flicks like *Under Siege* (1992) or *Charlie's Angels II* (2002); even animation, such as Disney's *Lilo and Stitch* or Hironobu Sakaguchi and Moto Sakakibara's computer-generated *Final Fantasy* (both released in 2001). Japanese as well as American filmmakers have been attracted to the islands, Kayo Hatta among others, whose moving historical drama *Picture Bride* was filmed on Oahu and the Big Island in 1995. But it is in the realm of television rather than film proper that Hawai'i has made its stake, with over forty-five television series filmed in the state since 1964. These run the gamut from the frivolous *Gilligan's Island* and *The Brady Bunch* through a long list of police dramas (*Hawaii Five-O*, *Magnum, P.I.*, *Jake and the Fatman*, and others) to more serious fare such as *War and Remembrance* and *China Beach*.

But even when such productions claim Hawai'i overtly as the plot location (and not just about any other island or tropical locales in the world), the islands tend to remain the beautiful background for a story that could just as well take place elsewhere rather than exploring the rich cultural significance the state has had for the many waves of people who have come to settle in the archipelago.

Not all filmmaking in Hawai'i, however, is about attracting film producers or marketing the island image, for the Hawaiian islands are also home to one of the nation's most dynamic and vibrant native film movements. One dimension of this movement involves the documentation and preservation of traditional Hawaiian culture through the use of archival materials and videotaped interviews. Cultural institutions such as the Bishop Museum and the Hawaiian Legacy Foundation have been instrumental in realizing such projects as renowned musician Eddy Kamae's remarkable seven-part series of documentaries on key traditions and personalities in Hawaiian folk culture and music. Another related dimension has been the activist use of film and video to promote the aims, aspirations, and rights of the native Hawaiian community. In 2000, the first feature film made entirely in the Hawaiian language was released: *Ka'ililauokekoa*, directed by Kala'iokona Ontai and winner of the Hawai'i Video and Film Maker Award at the 2000 Hawai'i International Film Festival (HIFF). Finally, an impressive array of interconnecting institutions, such as the HIFF, the Hawaiian Filmmakers Initiative ("building Hawaii's cinematic army . . . one filmmaker at a time"), the Maui Film Institute and Academy of Cinematic Arts (including a summer training program in digital arts and animation), and the Film Offices of the Hawaiian Islands together lend major support and encouragement to emerging independent and indigenous Hawaiian filmmakers to ensure the continuing productivity of a cinema fully engaged in exploring and understanding the rich culture and history of the archipelago and its most long-standing inhabitants.

The Pacific Northwest in Film

Relatively speaking, the Pacific Northwest has more often served as either the shooting location or filmic setting for a variety of well-known films, especially in the last two decades, though neither Oregon nor Washington can be said to have generated the same kinds of widely recognized trademark values as either (arctic) Alaska or (tropical) Hawai'i. Beyond the predictable mix of westerns, murder mysteries, horror, and action movies, the most memorable films set in the Pacific Northwest have typically situated characters at odds with the world in a "wilderness" setting that underscores their social isolation and physical vulnerability but also a certain freedom and willful assertion of independence. In this sense, the quintessential film is the 1971 filmic adaptation of Ken Kesey's epic *Sometimes a Great Notion*, set and shot entirely in Oregon. Directed by Paul Newman and starring Newman and Henry Fonda as father and son loggers whose independence of spirit pits them not only against the merciless wilderness, endless forests, and raging torrents that comprise the Central Oregon Cascades but also against the competing interests of neighbors and their own family members. This depiction of rugged endurance and irreverential individualism in the face of constant danger (whether from falling logs, social ostracism, or personal betrayal) not only powerfully captures a regional ethos but also offers a kind of eulogy to the Northwest's most fabled and risky occupation at the very moment of its incipient decline.

The Journey of Natty Gann (filmed in 1985 in British Columbia but set in depression-era Washington state) even explicitly correlates the devil-may-care attitude of the lonely logger with a suicidal and misanthropic desperation. This same film also explores the outlaw in the wilderness theme through its poignant narrative of a runaway girl overcoming social and natural adversities with the sole help of an equally outlawed and outcast wolf: Reminiscent of *The Call of the Wild* (one of whose strongest versions was filmed in 1935 in the Mt. Baker area and starring a young Clark Gable in the lead role), such narratives of children—with or without animal companion—finding solace from human interference in the wilderness appear frequently in films set in the Pacific Northwest: *Stand by Me* (1986) or even *Free Willy* (1993) come to mind as well as Disney's *Homeward Bound: The Incredible Journey* (1993), which features the wilderness odyssey of two domestic dogs and a cat to reconnect with their owners. *This Boy's Life* (1993), based upon the autobiography of writer Tobias Wolff, more somberly explores the attraction of delinquency for abused or neglected youth as do the better-known films of Gus Van Sant (a director with a particular attraction to filming in the Pacific Northwest): *Drugstore Cowboy* (1989), *My Own Private Idaho* (1991), *Even Cowgirls Get the Blues* (1993), and *Elephant* (2003).

The theme of social ostracism and alienation in a wilderness setting is cast in an ethnic frame with the powerful *Snow Falling on Cedars* (1999), about a Japanese American fisherman suspected of murder. Even darker versions of this same theme can be found in *The Parallax View* (1974), *Rambo: First Blood* (1982), and *The Vanishing* (1993). Finally, paranoia yields to the supernatural in *The Shining* (1980; the so-called Overlook Hotel in Colorado is actually filmed on the grounds of the Timberline Lodge, on the slopes of Mt. Hood, Oregon) and the 2002 blockbuster *The Ring*.

That independence of mind prefigured in such films (and mirrored in such other alternative cultural manifestations as grunge or the antiglobalization movement) finds its corollary less in any general depictions of the Pacific Northwest as a coherent region than in the vibrant "independent" film culture nurtured all along the urban corridor linking Portland, Olympia, Seattle, Bellingham, and Vancouver, constituting a kind of anti-Hollywood. This locally grown "Indie" film movement should not be confused with the poststudio system of "independent" filmmaking described earlier that gave rise to the "blockbuster" model of film production and its dependence on deep-pocketed financial investors. Both Oregon and Washington, like Hawai'i, have state film offices whose mix of tax incentives, organizational assistance, and aggressive advertising reveals their mission to be that of attracting out-of-state producers to invest in the local economy by shooting their big-budget projects on location, thus bringing in dollars, jobs, and the further opportunities enabled by the states' heightened profiles as "good" places to make movies.

The Indie film culture of the Pacific Northwest and its counterparts elsewhere represents an alternative to this model (without precluding of course the occasional crossover success of an Indie production that gets picked up by the larger distributors), one whose origins go back to the so-called art house cinemas of the 1970s and 1980s. Often an outgrowth of the local art scene in proximity with galleries, libraries, colleges, or community centers (many of which served—and in some cases still serve—as venues for film exhibition), art house cinemas screened a variety of non-Hollywood fare, especially foreign pictures, classic movies, shorts, documentaries, and experimental art films. The success of these alternative venues also provided opportunities for local filmmakers to screen their own movies (often explicitly made for local consumption) and in some cases to help provide financial or technical support for local film production. These filmmakers are true independents in the sense that their movies are funded by a variety of sources, including their own pockets, competitive grants, and community donations. Their aims are equally varied but generally have a lot less to do with making money than addressing issues of interest and import to them or their communities.

In the 1980s and 1990s, Indie filmmaking gained increasing visibility by the dramatic growth of film festivals as the venue of choice for alternative cinematic production. Films shown on the "festival circuit" offer an alternative to the increasingly restricted distribution networks of corporate-owned multiplexes, and they foster a more widely regional sense of community among both filmmakers and viewers. Finally, in contrast to the high production values and expensive special effects displayed by blockbuster film production, independent filmmakers have been in the forefront of creatively using and manipulating recent technological advances in film, video and digital art (camcorders, DVDs, cheap editing software for personal computers, etc.) whose low cost and ease of use are in the process of radically democratizing film production just as the Internet allows for a new, unfettered field of distribution.

These developments have the paradoxical result of rendering local, independent films both more possible on the regional level yet more global in their reach. Whereas the early invention of the Hollywood studio system created a global art form based on the regional topography of Southern California, today's digitally driven film revolution (generated by the high-tech industry based on the West Coast stretching from Palo Alto's Silicon Valley up to Seattle) holds the promise

An Emerging Local Film Culture

One example of an independent film community in the Pacific Northwest can be found in Bellingham, Washington, with its heart at the Pickford Cinema. The Pickford opened on 20 November, 1998. Supported by the Whatcom Film Association (WFA), which had been formed earlier in that same year, the Pickford shows primarily first-run films with the occasional re-release of classic films. The focus is entirely on American independent and foreign films, and documentaries are especially popular in Bellingham.

The Pickford's annual Projections Film Festival, open to local amateur filmmakers from Whatcom County (where Bellingham is situated) and the immediately surrounding counties, occurs in early November. Perhaps the most locally celebrated film to emerge from Projections so far has been *Creek Story*, by Dan Hammill and Suhki Sanghera. The film concerns Whatcom Creek, where, in June of 1999, a catastrophic pipeline explosion claimed three lives and caused an enormous amount of damage.

A former student of Hammill's, Michael Shepard, currently works at the Northwest Indian College in Bellingham as a Documentation Coordinator. Shepard and his students at NWIC recently made a video of the desecration of a Native American grave site at Semiahmoo Spit near Blaine, Washington, and this video was shown to a number of people, including United States Senators, to try to get an anti-desecration law passed through Congress. Shepard cites the developing film scene in Bellingham, which in his view really came together in 2002–2003, as a major source of support for his work. The developing network gives filmmakers a place to show work, to get critique, and to get instant film crews and equipment.

Other people who figure prominently in this burgeoning film community include James Gillies, who was involved in such early Bellingham-area films as Randy Allred's *Beat Angel* and Tom Ensign's *Immortality Machine*; and David Adams, who is the main force behind the Indie Film Group (IFG). The IFG invite prominent film industry professionals to talk to the group's members, and also conduct screenwriting workshops in this vibrant and resourceful film community of the Pacific Northwest.

for a truly global exchange of regionally produced visual expressions. That promise is rapidly being fulfilled in socially responsible and artistically exciting ways.

THEATER OF THE PACIFIC REGION

Theaters

If independent film houses and local films hold out an exciting new venue for directors, actors, and movie watchers, the small theater house stands at the beginning point of theatrical productions in the region. Most of the major cities in the Pacific Region built their first theaters in response to the Gold Rush. Built in 1849, The Eagle Theater in Old Sacramento is the oldest standing theater in California. Still in operation, an occasional show is still billed there. San Francisco had theaters by 1852, including the Jenny Lind Theatre, which it used as a city hall, and the American Theatre, at which in 1853 Lola Montez opened in *School for Scandal*, an English comedy, and where she would later perform her famous Spider Dance. Seattle, Washington's first theater was Squire's Opera House, built in 1879 by future governor and senator Watson Squire. In 1880, Rutherford B. Hayes (1822–1893), the first president to visit Seattle, held a reception there. Then, in 1900, John Cort built the Grand Opera House, "the finest theater in the city."[5] Cort eventually moved to New York, where, in 1912, he opened the Cort Theater on Broadway, which is still in operation. Fortymile, the first white town on the Yukon, in Alaska, had a theater by 1895 operated by Anna and George Snow, and a year later they built a log opera house in Circle City. After word of the massive Klondike gold strike first reached the outside world in July 1897, the Klondike became known throughout the world, and prospectors flocked to Alaska. When railroad and steamboat transportation became available from Skagway to Dawson in 1900, theater companies from Canada and the United States scheduled performances. Legitimate theater and dance hall entertainments were featured on many stages in Dawson.

Beyond the Gold Rush, vaudeville had the most impact on theaters in the Pacific Region. Increased social participation by women and a heightened sensibility to a need for a more "democratic" theater have long been acknowledged as playing a large role in the emergence and popularity of vaudeville, so it is no wonder that in the immigrant West, vaudeville became immensely popular. Indeed, Seattle's Palomar Theater continued playing vaudeville runs until the 1950s; its last show starred Sammy Davis, Jr. Although no specific date has ever been set as the official start of vaudeville, Tony Pastor, credited with being the father of American vaudeville, began presenting vaudeville shows in New York in the 1880s. It was advertised as family entertainment, a "clean" variety show that relied heavily on the minstrel show and featured songs, skits, and farcical entertainment.

Both the theaters and performers were on "circuits," and the Orpheum vaudeville circuit, the West Coast's most successful, began on June 30, 1887, when it opened its first theater in San Francisco. Under the leadership of Martin Beck, the Orpheum's performers were paid better than average salaries, and they stayed in first-class hotels on the road. The circuit was particularly known for its orchestras that played classical overtures prior to performances. After purchasing the Grand Opera House on Main Street in 1895, the Orpheum started permanent operations in Los Angeles. In 1903, the circuit moved its performances to a theater it purchased on Spring Street. Rather than purchase yet another theater in Los Angeles, in 1910 the Orpheum commissioned G. Albert Landsburgh, a prominent theater architect, to design a 2,000-seat house on Broadway. The new Orpheum, combined with the opening of Alexander Pantages' theater in 1910, anchored the theater district in Los Angeles on Broadway. Fifteen years later, Pantages opened his "New Pantages" Theater in San Francisco, with a plush, elegant interior evocative of pre-Reformation Spain. The gala opening night featured one of vaudeville's biggest shows ever, with a cast of over sixty. Ultimately, the Orpheum had a theater in every big city on the West Coast: Seattle, Portland, San Francisco, Oakland, Los Angeles, and San Diego. Some of the biggest names performed, including Ethel Waters and Bill "Bojangles" Robinson. Hawai'i, too, participated in the vaudeville run. The Hawaii Theatre, nicknamed the "Pride of the Pacific," opened its doors on September 6, 1922, in downtown Honolulu. The Hawaii Theatre operated as a showplace for vaudeville, plays, musicals, and silent films.

The most famous theater in the Pacific Region is, however, neither vaudevillian nor historic. Instead, it is an exquisite outdoor venue—the Oregon Shakespeare Festival—voted by *Time* magazine in 2003 as one of the five best regional theaters in the country. The site staged its first production, *Twelfth Night*, on July 2, 1935. Over the years the festival grew, as did the theater. Currently, there are four theaters on the grounds: the Elizabethan stage; the Angus Bowmer, which seats 600; the Black Swan, a venue seating 140; and the 350-seat New Theatre.

Theatrical Movements

While the theaters themselves have often been built and housed "imported" productions from the East Coast, and even Europe, the Pacific Region's most distinctive theatrical movements have come directly out of its ethnic and social concerns. In 1915, a theatrical group called "The Footlights" began in Honolulu, Hawai'i. Beginning as a somewhat straightforward group of actors and artists, their first production was *The Amazons* by Arthur Wing Pinero. The troupe regrouped in 1934 with a new name—the Honolulu Community Theatre (HCT)—and a new mission: "community service through the art of theater, involving the people of Hawaii as audience members, stage crew and performers."[6] During World War II, the HCT entertained thousands of troops throughout the Pacific. The Honolulu Community Theatre became the Diamond Head Theatre in 1990—"the Broadway of the Pacific" and the third oldest, continuously operating theater in the United States. In addition to the long-standing HCT, community and university theater troupes such as Ka' 'Uhane o na Honu Tribe and venues such as Gallerie Ha in Wailuku, which hosted a staged reading of *Kamau A'e*, a play written by O'ahu's Alani Apio, strive to bring indigenous works to the stage.

Perhaps the first aggressively political performers came out of the Haight Ashbury scene of the late 1960s. In May 1965, the director of the San Francisco Mime Troupe presented an essay titled "Guerilla Theater" that served as a sort of blueprint for radical theater groups working to change society. A few months later, the San Francisco Mime Troupe began its guerrilla tactics in earnest, as they performed, and were arrested for, a play without possessing a permit (the permit to perform had been revoked on grounds of obscenity). As the months followed, the Mime Troup frequently performed without the permits they were routinely denied, and both performers and directors were just as routinely hauled off to jail. The theatrical performances soon drew a number of intellectuals, writers, artists, and musicians, who eventually organized into the Artists Liberation Front.

An additional result of the San Francisco Mime Troupe is Luis Valdez, a renowned playwright who has had an extraordinary influence on Pacific regional theater. Valdez left the Troupe in 1965 to join César Chávez (1927–1993) in organizing farmworkers in Delano, California. While there, Valdez organized El Teatro Campesino (The Farmworkers Theater). Three years later, El Teatro Campesino began touring, and within a year, the company was awarded an Obie and Los Angeles Drama Critics Awards. Just as significantly, the theater movement began to grow. In 1968 Teatro Chicano was founded in Los Angeles by Gaudalupe Saavedra, and a year later, Teatro Mecha was founded at the University of California, Santa Barbara. In 1970 Ruben Sierra began Teatro de Piojo at the University of Washington. A 1974 graduate of the university, Sierra stayed on teaching drama and Chicano/Latino studies until 1979. He and his students also founded Teatro Quetzalcoatl at the University of Washington.

1970 also marked the year that El Teatro Campesino stopped performing exclusively on the road (whether on the backs of trucks or in theaters) and set up a permanent home in San Juan Bautista, a small rural town that allowed the group to focus on their work and develop their style. That style, now known as "teatro chicano," incorporates the "spiritual and presentational style of the Italian Renaissance commedia dell'arte with the humor, character types, folklore and popular culture of the Mexican theater,"[7] a theater with which vaudeville has much in common.

With a defined style and philosophy, El Teatro Campesino sought ways to venture into the commercial theater sector. Collaborating with Peter Brook, former artistic director of England's Shakespeare Academy, El Teatro Campesino produced *The Conference of the Birds*, which toured colleges and farm labor camps throughout California. Soon after, *La Carpa de los Rasquachis* (The Tent of the Underdogs) was produced, including an eight-country tour in Europe. The following year, the production was produced and aired on public television. In 1981, Valdez wrote and directed *Corridos: Tales of Passion and Revolution* for the El Teatro Campesino's workshop/playhouse. It was awarded eleven Bay Area Critics Awards and, six years later, adapted for television. In 1991, Valdez adapted and directed *La Pastorela*, a traditional shepherd's play, for PBS Great Performances series, starring Linda Ronstadt and Paul Rodríguez. Always striving to honor its ethnic roots and nurture its new visions, El Teatro Campesino remains the Pacific Region's best-known and most enduring teatro: "Like a serpent crawling out of its own skin," its official Web site states, "El Teatro Campesino continues to evolve and refine its aesthetic in order to realize its full artistic potential."[8]

At roughly the same time that teatro Chicano was beginning to solidly define itself, Asian American theater began to establish its own identity in the Pacific Region. In 1973, playwright Frank Chin founded the Asian American Theater Company (AATC). Beginning as a workshop sponsored by the American Conservatory Theater, by 1975 AATC had become its own professional theater company dedicated to the production of plays by Asian Pacific Islander American dramatists and the development and support of Asian Pacific Island American actors, designers, and technicians. In its thirty-year history, AATC has served as fertile ground for playwrights Chin, David Henry Hwang, and Philip Kan Gotanda as well as actors Margaret Cho and Dennis Dun, designer Lydia Tanji, and director Judi Nihei. Topically, AATC has secured its place in the racial discourse of postmodern identity politics; it still considers itself one of the only places in the country where Asian Pacific Islander American artists can enter into significant social and emotional dialogue with their own community. And within the structures of postcolonial discourse, AATC provides a rare opportunity for writers, actors, designers, and directors to control the depiction of Asian Pacific Islander Americans.

Additionally, AATC presents queer-positive plays and in 1997 received a Cable Car Award, which recognizes "outstanding achievement in the lesbian and gay community." AATC has also staged productions that explore interracial dating, disability issues, and masculine identities; in addition, the theater has sponsored spoken word and jazz collaborations, sketch comedy, erotic readings, teen work debuts, and "coffee house" open nights. Along with significant community involvement, AATC has also explored the politics of ethnicity, premiering in 1999 Philip Kan Gotanda's *Sisters Matsumoto*, a telling of the story of three sisters returning home from the internment camps of World War II. As it celebrates thirty years, AATC prepares to move into the future by focusing on both the historical traditions of Asian American theater and the avant-garde visions of new artists.

Playwrights/Directors

Frank Chin, born on February 25, 1940, in Berkeley, California, spent much of his childhood in Oakland's Chinatown. He attended the University of California at Berkeley and Santa Barbara and participated in the creative writing program at the University of Iowa. He writes novels, short stories, comic books, and essays as well as plays; he has worked in documentary television and as a Hollywood script consultant as well as directing and producing plays and taught college courses in Asian American literature. His central concerns are the emasculating effects of anti-Asian stereotypes, although he is nearly as famous for his unrelenting criticism of fellow Asian American writers such as Amy Tan and David Henry Hwang. His plays include *Gee, Pop!* (1974, unpublished); *Lullaby* (1976, unpublished); *America More or Less* (1976, unpublished); *American Peek-a-Boo Kabuki, World War II and Me* (1985, unpublished); *The Year of the Dragon* (1974); and *The Chickencoop Chinaman* (1981).

Philip Kan Gotanda (1951–), one of the nation's leading playwrights, has worked with the East West Players, the Asian American Theater Company, and a number of national institutions such as Boston's Huntington Theatre, the Manhattan Theatre Club, the Mark Taper Forum, and the New York Shakespeare Festival, among others, in the process creating one of the largest and most varied bodies of Asian Pacific American–themed work. His eclectic education includes a law degree from Hastings College of Law and time spent studying pottery in Japan with the late Hiroshi Seto. Currently, he lives in San Francisco and is an associate artist at the Seattle Repertory Theatre. Gotanda's work has long been familiar in American theater circles, but he has more recently begun receiving international acclaim beginning with his play *The Ballad of Yachiyo*, which opened at London's Gate Theatre in coproduction with the National Royal Theatre. Within the United States, Gotanda is presently developing works for San Jose Repertory (an adaptation of *Hedda Gabler*) and the American Conservatory Theatre (an adaptation of *Roshomon*).

David Henry Hwang, born in 1957 to immigrants in Los Angeles, is the son of a banker and a piano professor. He wrote his first play, *FOB (Fresh Off the Boat)* in 1978, the year before he graduated from Stanford University. *FOB* won an Obie Award for best new play of the season when Joseph Papp produced it off-Broadway in New York. After attending the Yale School of Drama, Hwang wrote *The Dance and the Railroad* and *Family Devotions*, both of which explored the problems immigrants face in trying to assimilate to a new culture. In 1988, *M. Butterfly*, which won a Tony Award for best play, established him as a major modern American playwright. His recent work *Golden Child* garnered three Tony Award nominations in 1998.

Cherie Moraga (1952–) is better known for her radical Chicana/lesbian poetry and essays as well as her theoretical work in the field of literary scholarship, but she is also the author of numerous award-winning plays, including *La extranjera* (The Foreigner; 1985); *Giving Up the Ghost: Teatro in 2 Acts* (1986); *Shadow of a Man* (1988), which won the Fund for New American Plays Award in 1991; *Heroes and Saints* (1989), which won the Pen West Award for Drama in 1992; and *Watsonville: Some Place Not Here*, which won a second Fund for New American Plays Award in 1995. Moraga has made a significant and lasting contribution to the growth of Chicano theater and to the development of Pacific regional theater in general. She has also received the National Endowment for the Arts (NEA) Theatre Playwriting Fellowship Award and is artist-in-residence in the Drama and Portuguese Departments at Stanford University in California.

Despite making a living for over twenty years in television, both as a writer (*St. Elsewhere* and *Homicide*) and a producer-writer (*Law and Order*), Eric Overmyer insists that he never forgets he is a playwright. Born in 1952, Overmyer grew up near, he says in an interview, "the shadow of Mt. Rainier."[9] After graduating from the local high school, Overmyer went to Reed College, in Portland, to study theater. Eventually, he moved east to pursue playwriting, and he won his first national recognition for *On the Verge, or The Geography of Learning* (1985). After that, he wrote a number of plays: *In a Pig's Valise* (1986); *In Perpetuity Throughout the Universe* (1988); *Hawker* (1989), *Kafka's Radio*, *Mi Vida Loca* (My Crazy Life), and *Don Quixote de La Jolla*, all 1990; and perhaps most famously, *Dark Rapture* (1992), which debuted in Seattle, near Overmyer's hometown. Not until 2004 did a second Overmyer play, commissioned by Seattle's ACT Theatre in 1990, finally get produced: *Alki* retells Henrik Ibsen's *Peer Gynt*, moving from Norway and Morocco to the Pacific Northwest and South America.

Octavio Solis writes mainly about the Southwest but makes his home in San Francisco, California. A playwright and director, his works *Man of the Flesh*, *Prospect*, *El Paso Blue*, *Santos & Santos*, *La Posada Mágica*, *El Otro*, *Dreamlandia*, and others have been staged at venues such as the Oregon Shakespeare Festival and El Teatro Campesino. *Burning Dreams*, cowritten with Julie Hébert and Gina Leishman, was produced by the San Diego Repertory, while his collaborative project with Erik Ehn, *Shiner*, was staged in Dallas, Texas. His most recent project, *The Seven Visions of Encarnación*, written for Shadowlight Theatre Company, is a shadow puppet work performed in San Francisco. Solis has received an NEA Playwriting Fellowship, two playwriting grants from The Kennedy Center, the Will Glickman Playwright Award, the 1998 McKnight Fellowship grant from the Playwrights Center in Minneapolis, and the 2000–2001 National Theatre Artists Residency Grant from Theater Communications Group (TCG). He is the recipient of a grant from the Pew Charitable Trust for a new project with the Oregon Shakespeare Festival.

Luis Valdez was born in 1940 in Delano, California, one of ten children of a mother and father who made their living as farmworkers. Like his parents, he worked in the fields until he was eighteen, when he went to San Jose State College, where he joined the theater and declared a major in English. There his first full-length play, *The Shrunken Head of Pancho Villa* (1964), was produced. After college he joined the famous San Francisco Mime Troupe, and in 1965, as a member of César Chávez's United Farm Workers Union, he founded El Teatro Campesino, for which he became artistic director and playwright. Although the teatro initially focused on productions highlighting the struggles and strengths of farmworkers, eventually Valdez began writing plays on a number of related subjects, such as the Vietnam War in *Dark Root of a Scream* (1967). He wrote several plays in a form he called *mito*, or myth. One of them, *Bernabé* (1970), introduced a figure who was a zoot suiter and focused on historical issues concerning Chicanos. Then, in 1978, Valdez produced *Zoot Suit*, which he also directed when it was turned into a film (1981). The next year he wrote *Bandido!* (1982), about a Mexican bandit named Tiburcio Vásquez, who was the last man publicly executed by the law in San Jose, California. *I Don't Have to Show You No Stinking Badges!* (1986), set in California during Ronald Reagan's presidency, concerns Buddy Villa and his wife Connie, who have spent their working lives as extras in television and film.

RESOURCE GUIDE

Printed Sources

Ashcroft, Lionel. *Movie Studios & Movie Theaters in Marin: A History since 1898*. San Rafael, CA: Marin County Historical Society, 1998.

Berelson, Bernard, and Howard F. Grant. "The Pioneer Theater in Washington." *Pacific Northwest Quarterly* 18 (1937): 115–136.

Booth, Michael R. "Gold Rush Theater: The Theatre Royal, Barkerville, British Columbia." *Pacific Northwest Quarterly* 51 (1960): 97–102.

———. "Theatrical Boom in the Kootenays." *The Beaver* (Autumn 1961): 42–46.

Caldwell, John. "California's Suburban Plantation Culture and Alternative Media." *Media, Culture, and Society* 25 (2003): 647–667.

———, ed. *Electronic Media and Technoculture*. New Brunswick, NJ: Rutgers University Press, 2000.

Carr, Steven Alan. *Hollywood and Anti-Semitism: A Cultural History up to World War II*. New York: Cambridge University Press, 2001.

Christensen, Jerome. "Hollywood's Corporate Art." *The Baffler* 13 (Winter 1999): 79–86.

Clarke, Charles G. *Early Film Making in Los Angeles*. Los Angeles, CA: Dawson's Book Shop, 1976.

Coutts, Robert. "Gold Rush Theatre and the Palace Grand." *The Beaver* (Spring 1982): 40–46.

DuPuis, Reshela. "Documenting Community: Activist Videography in Hawaii." Ph.D. dissertation, University of California, San Diego, 1997.

Engeman, Richard H. "The 'Seattle Spirit' Meets the Alaskan: A Story of Business, Boosterism and the Arts." *Pacific Northwest Quarterly* 81 (1990): 54–66.

Gabler, Neal. *An Empire of Their Own: How the Jews Invented Hollywood*. New York: Doubleday, 1988.

Giovacchini, Saverio. *Hollywood Modernism: Film and Politics in the Age of the New Deal*. Philadelphia, PA: Temple University Press, 2001.

Gomez-Pena, Guillermo. "The Virtual Barrio @ the Other Frontier." In *Electronic Media and Technoculture*, ed. John Caldwell. New Brunswick, NJ: Rutgers University Press, 2000.

Hamilton, Ian. *The Writers in Hollywood, 1915–1951*. New York: Harper & Row, 1990.

Hirschfelder, Arlene B. *American Indian Stereotypes in the World of Children: A Reader and Bibliography*. Lanham, MD: Scarecrow Press, 1999.

Hoffman, James. "Sydney Risk and the Everyman Theatre." *BC Studies* 76 (1987–1988): 33–57.

Hughes, Alan. "Charles Kean in Victoria: Touring Actors and Local Politics in 1864." *BC Studies* 74 (1987): 21–32.

Isto, Sarah A. *Cultures in the North: Aleut, Athabascan Indian, Eskimo, Haida Indian, Tlingi Indian, Tsimpshian Indian: Multi-Media Resource List*. Fairbanks: University of Alaska Press, 1975.

Keller, Betty C. "The Chastely Voluptuous Weblings." *The Beaver* 66.2 (1986): 13–18.

Levene, Bruce. *Mendocino & the Movies: Hollywood and Television Motion Pictures Filmed on the Mendocino Coast*. Mendocino, CA: Pacific Transcriptions, 1998.

MacDonald, Cheryl. "The Star from Hamilton: Julia Arthur." *The Beaver* 69.6 (1989–1990): 23–29.

Macdonald, Dwight. "Masscult and Midcult." In *Against the American Grain*. New York: Random House, 1962.

Mordden, Ethan. *The Hollywood Studios: House Style in the Golden Age of the Movies*. New York: Simon & Schuster, 1988.

O'Neill, P. B. "Regina's Golden Age of Theatre: Her Playhouses and Players." *Saskatchewan History* 28 (1975): 29–37.

Palmer, Edwin O. *The History of Hollywood.* Hollywood, CA: A. H. Cawston, 1937.

Puttnam, David. *The Undeclared War: The Struggle for Control of the World's Film Industry.* London: HarperCollins, 1997.

Rensin, David. *The Mailroom: Hollywood History from the Bottom Up.* New York: Ballantine Books, 2003.

Robinson, David. *From Peep Show to Palace: The Birth of American Film.* New York: Columbia University Press in association with the Library of Congress, 1996.

Shortt, Mary. "Curtain Time in Canada." *The Beaver* 70.4 (1990): 6–15.

———. "Victorian Temptations: Church and Stage Clash in Pioneer Canada." *The Beaver* 68.6 (1988–1989): 4–13.

Simmon, Scott. *The Invention of the Western Film: A Cultural History of the Genre's First Half Century.* New York: Cambridge University Press, 2003.

Todd, Robert B. "The Organization of Professional Theatre in Vancouver, 1886–1914." *BC Studies* 44 (1979–1980): 3–24.

Wallace, David. *Hollywoodland.* New York: St. Martin's Press, 2002.

Wright, Nancy Allison. "Glory Days of Vaudeville." *Columbia* 2.3 (1988): 3–9.

Zollo, Paul. *Hollywood Remembered: An Oral History of Its Golden Age.* New York: Cooper Square Press, 2002.

Web Sites

Alaska Film Program
July 21, 2004.
http://www.dced.state.ak.us/oed/film/production/productioncompanies.htm
A list of production companies and their credits.

Bedford/St. Martin's
July 21, 2004.
http://www.bedfordsmartins.com/litlinks/drama/
Playwrights' biographies.

Film Festival.Com
July 21, 2004.
http://www.filmfestivals.com/index.shtml
Headline news concerning festivals, new film, film.

Filmmaker Magazine
July 21, 2004.
http://www.filmmakermagazine.com/cgi-bin/fests.pl
An alphabetical guide to festivals.

Hawaiian Legacy Foundation
July 21, 2004.
http://www.hawaiianlegacy.com/
A foundation working to preserve Hawaiian cultural heritage through music, film, educational programs, and more.

Hawai'i Filmmakers Initiative
July 21, 2004.
http://www.hawaiifilmmakers.org/
Dedicated to nurturing Hawaiian independent filmmakers through a variety of mechanisms.

Hawai'i Film Office
July 21, 2004.
http://www.hawaiifilmoffice.com/

Hawai'i International Film Festival
July 21, 2004.
http://www.hiff.org/

Indie Film Group
July 21, 2004.
http://www.indiefilmgroup.com/
Provides networking opportunities to independent filmmakers.

The Internet Movie Database (IMDb)
July 21, 2004.
http://www.imdb.com/

MovieMaker
July 21, 2004.
http://www.moviemaker.com/festivals.html
Lists film festivals by state or territory and advertises festivals for their organizers.

Oregon Film and Video Office
July 21, 2004.
http://www.oregonfilm.org/

Right Angle Studios
July 21, 2004.
http://www.rightanglestudios.com/
One of the most unbiased Internet sites for listing of festivals, criticism, and resources for filmmakers and moviegoers.

Rodeo Film Company
July 21, 2004.
http://www.rodeofilmco.com/rfc/
The Web site for Portland independent filmmaker Matt McCormick.

Sacramento Bee Online: The Gold Rush
July 21, 2004.
http://www.calgoldrush.com/part2/02fun.html

Think-a-Tron Media Laboratories
July 21, 2004.
http://www.thinkatron.com/

University of Alaska Museum
July 21, 2004.
http://www.uaf.edu/museum/exhibits/tog/mania.html

Virtual Museum of the City of San Francisco
July 21, 2004.
http://sfmuseum.net/hist/chron3.html
Gold rush chronology.

Washington State Film Office
July 21, 2004.
http://www.oted.wa.gov/ed/filmoffice/

Whatcom Film and Video Group
July 21, 2004.
http://www.whatcomfilmandvideo.com/

Films

Alaska Patrol. Dir. Jack Bernhard. Burwood Pictures, Film Classics, Inc., 1949.
Kodiak: Red Snow, White Death. Dir. Robert Day. Kodiak Productions, 1974.
Treasures from American Film Archives: 50 Preserved Films. National Film Preservation Foundation. Curated Scott Simmon, 2000.

Film Festivals

AFI Los Angeles International Film Festival
2021 North Western Avenue
Los Angeles, CA 90027-1657
http://www.afi.com/AFIFEST/

Annual event in November that runs for ten days each year.

DancesWithFilms
1041 North Formosa Avenue
West Hollywood, CA 90046
http://www.danceswithfilms.com/

June.

Frameline28 San Francisco International Lesbian and Gay Film Festival
145 Ninth Street, Suite 300
San Francisco, CA 94103-2636
http://www.frameline.org/festival/

Mid-June.

Humboldt International Short Film Festival
Department of Theatre, Film and Dance
Humboldt State University
Arcata, CA 95521
http://www.humboldt.edu/~filmfest/

Early April.

IFP Los Angeles Film Festival
IFP/LA
8750 Wilshire Boulevard, 2nd Floor
Beverly Hills, CA 90211
http://www.lafilmfest.com/

June.

Mill Valley Film Festival
38 Miller Avenue, Suite 6
Mill Valley CA 94941
http://cafilm.org/

Mid-October.

Northwest Film and Video Festival
1219 SW Park Avenue

Portland, OR 97205
http://www.nwfilm.org/festivals/festivals.html
November.

Olympia Film Festival
416 Washington Street SE #208
Olympia, WA 98501
http://olympiafilmfestival.org/
November.
Sponsored by the Olympia Film Society.

Portland International Film Festival
1219 SW Park Avenue
Portland, OR 97205
http://www.nwfilm.org/festivals/festivals.html
February.
Features works from mainly outside the United States but also includes American features, documentaries, and shorts.

San Diego Film Festival
San Diego Film Foundation
7974 Mission Bonita Drive
San Diego, CA 92120
http://www.sdff.org/
September.

San Francisco Indie Fest
530 Divisadero Street #183
San Francisco, CA 94117
http://www.sfindie.com/index.php
Early to mid-February.

San Francisco International Asian American Film Festival
145 Ninth Street, Suite 350
San Francisco, CA 94103
http://www.naatanet.org/
Early March.
Sponsored by the National Asian American Association.

San Francisco International Film Festival
San Francisco Film Society
39 Mesa Street, Suite 110
The Presidio
San Francisco, CA 94129
http://www.sfiff.org/
April or May.
Presented by the San Francisco Film Society.

Seattle International Film Festival
Cinema Seattle
400 9th Avenue North
Seattle, WA 98109
http://www.seattlefilm.com/
May-June.

Slamdance Film Festival
5634 Melrose Avenue
Los Angeles, CA 90038
http://www.slamdance.com/

January.

Sonoma Valley Film Festival
P. O. Box 1613
Sonoma, CA 95476
http://www.cinemaepicuria.org/

March or April.
Sponsored by Cinema Epicuria.

Museums and/or Special Collections

Alaska Center for Documentary Film
907 Yukon Drive
Fairbanks, AK 99775
http://www.uaf.edu/museum/depts/docfilm/

Alaska Film Archives
Elmer E. Rasmuson Library
310 Tanana Drive
University of Alaska
Fairbanks, AK 99775-6800
http://www.uaf.edu/library/apr/filmarchives.html

Alaska Moving Image Preservation Association
1325 Primrose Street
Anchorage, AK 99508
http://www.amipa.org/

Grand Illusion
1403 NE 50th Street
Seattle, WA 98105
http://www.wigglyworld.org/grandillusion/

The best film education resource in Seattle.

Northwest Film Center
1139 SW 11th Avenue
Portland, OR 97205
http://www.nwfilm.org/

Affiliated with the Portland Art Museum, the Northwest Film Center shows a mixture of first-run and repertory films and features a comprehensive education program with classes and equipment rental. One focus of the education component includes film education for youth.

Northwest Film Forum
http://www.wigglyworld.org/index.shtml

The Northwest Film Forum is the center of independent film culture in Seattle. They run the only two not-for-profit independent film houses in Seattle, the Grand Illusion and the Little Theatre. In addition, they run Wiggly World Studios, an equipment rental and film education center that also screens local film.

Oregon Film and Video Office
One World Trade Center
121 SW Salmon, Suite 1205
Portland, OR 97204
http://www.oregonfilm.org/

Pacific Film Archives
Berkeley Art Museum
2625 Durant Avenue #2250
Berkeley, CA 94720-2250
http://www.bampfa.berkeley.edu/

FOLKLORE

Barre Toelken

FOLK GROUPS

In the archetypical West, certain recurrent ideas have functioned to define and express values shared by substantial numbers of people who have seen themselves as central to the West. In this often stereotypical world, the Japanese and Chinese remain as outsiders, the Indians as implacable foes (or occasionally as spiritual guides—as long as they are not interested in holding on to much land), the women as supporting players who sometimes rise to glory, the men (and male values) as central issues of reality. In many ways, thus, the West has functioned mythically as an idea that gives dramatic voice to attitudes that promote an "American" hegemony.

Folklore, because it springs from those whose voices resonate from within a region's cultures, can act as an antidote to mythologized notions of place. Most of the folk groups that have been prominent in the settlement of the West are multidimensional; that is, occupations that have their own lore and language have been developed or excelled in by members of certain ethnic or national groups that have as well their own insider lore. For example, much of the cowboy culture that has colored the life and attitudes (as well as fueled the stereotypes and myths) of the West was brought north from Mexico and developed into a highly articulate culture by Spanish-speaking ranchers. Much of the terminology still used in the cattle country comes directly from Spanish buckaroos (vaqueros). The preference for the word *buckaroo* by the cattle rangers over the word *cowboy* is still a locally distinctive feature in some areas within the region we call the West. In eastern Oregon, parts of Idaho, and much of Nevada, use of the word *cowboy* marks someone as an outsider. With such deep-seated usage of Hispanic terminology remaining so central to local conception of insider culture, one would expect to find other kinds of cultural expressions from the same background central to the ongoing value system, but they are rare, a fact that testifies to the malleability and selectivity of the folklore process. The buckaroos, working together with other knowledgeable buckaroos, developed a rich insider lingo for dealing with horses and cattle. At home, among their families—where other customs and ethnic values come into play—their folk expressions articulated those constellations. Obviously, ranchers of Hispanic background continue to live in a richly colonial Hispanic culture, even though in the intervening years, not all Hispanic people have remained ranchers. Significantly this strong central role in the development of ranching in the West is not often depicted so fully in the popular media, where the Mexican most often appears as a later interloper, a foreigner out of place in the Anglo system. Although historians estimate that as many as 30 percent of the working cowboys were Hispanic and black, and although their influence is easily seen in western occupational speech and slang, the popular images that appear in films and dime-novel format grow more directly out of later racist stereotypes. Such stereotypes were long politically and sociologically more important to the public than an acknowledgment of the cultural diversity suggested by folklore.

Nearly all folklore of the Pacific Region is similarly complicated for many of the same reasons. Not only is there sheepherder lore (both the lore of the sheepherders themselves and the ranchers who raised the sheep as well as the lore about sheepherders passed along by those—for example, cattle ranchers—who often saw the sheep ranchers as very odd people indeed, as outsiders to their own cultural views), but there is Basque sheepherder lore as well as Basque lore and lore about Basques by non-Basque people. Along the Northwest Coast there is the lore of the fishing people (the fishermen themselves, as well as their families at home); but there is also the lore of the Yugoslav fishermen as contrasted to that of the Scandinavian fishermen. Across the Pacific, many legends are told of shark men, with the islands Kauai, Maui, Hawai'i, and Oahu—as well as Samoa—all producing similar stories of shark men whose warnings to villagers or fishermen are a ruse that precedes the shark man's attack; yet each story differs in who is attacked, how the shark man hides his piscine identity, and how he is ultimately exposed. In California, clustered around Mt. Shasta, a volcano in the Cascade chain, native legends reflect the differing worldviews of the five tribes—Modoc, Wintu, Shasta, Achumawi, and Atsugewi—who lived there. As the area became populated by European immigrants and their descendants, tales of a lost race, called the Lemurians, living within the volcano began, although later pulp fiction versions cast the Lemurians as a "space faring" race. Another type of mythology comes from the most recent arrivals, New Age practitioners, and their claims of health and meditative transcendence.

For many places within the region, the distinction between native and immigrant cultures and their folklore is but one kind of split. Racial, social, and economic dichotomies also find their way into regional tales. One example is the region's prominent folklore of the lumber industry. Here, although loggers come from a variety of ethnic backgrounds, the important split seems to be between those who work in the woods and those who work in the mills. At least in the Pacific Northwest, the people make a distinction between *logger* and *lumberjack*, the latter being someone who stacks lumber in a mill; used by a logger, the term suggests a negative connotation. Since many of the eastern "lumberjacks" who left Michigan and Wisconsin to become "loggers" in the Northwest were Scandinavian, one might expect that national identification to have exercised a strong in-

Many of the eastern "lumberjacks" who left Michigan and Wisconsin to become "loggers" in the Northwest were Scandinavian and thus the stories about them became something like internal stereotypes of the logger image. Courtesy of the Library of Congress.

fluence on the lore of the occupation. And indeed it seems persistent today as a form of proud humor: Swedes (as most Scandinavians were called) were reputed to be hard and faithful workers who felt no pain, and thus the stories about them became something like internal stereotypes of the logger image. A Swede, in one story, tries to show his foreman how he cut his hand off in the buzzsaw by trying to work too fast: "Ooops, dammit, now dere goes da udder vun!" It is said that when a logger died on the job, his lower lip was pulled out to see if he had the distinguishing Swede characteristic: a hole the size of a quarter burned into the lip by snoose (moist, ground tobacco carried in the lip in preference to smoking). Young loggers trying to learn how to dip snoose were said to be "passing as Swedes." For the forest workers, ethnic differences showed up more precisely and distinctively at home or at weddings or church socials in which ethnic foods were served and national dances allowed for a retention of older community expressions.

One example of how folklore develops in response to ethnic immigration patterns comes with the waves of Chinese and Japanese immigrants. Initially imported in the 1860s mainly to work on the railroads and in the mines, both slowly developed their community stability in America largely because they originally did not bring their families with them. Much of their early folklore was men's lore, expressed, of course, in their own languages. Later, as wives and families joined the men, family lore (in the form of foods, customs, songs, and stories) grew apace, lore within the socially isolated immigrant communities and, in more economically advantaged Anglo communities, about them. A well-known phenomenon in folklore, often called *marginal* or *peripheral distribution*, accounts for the fact that people far from their original homes tend not so much to lose their traditions as to intensify them selectively by using them to adapt to the new situation while maintaining their own sense of normality. One example is in Japanese and Chinese immigrant communities, where customs found in the United States are actually older than the customs found today in the parent country. The Japanese lullaby "Naranda," sung to Japanese children born in America at the turn of the century, is still sung here but is virtually unknown in Japan. Innovation along ethnically "normal" lines is also found in new contexts: Thus, one finds several Chinese dishes that were "invented" in America, Japanese foods (such as sukiyaki) that have been altered by the addition of more meat (avoided once by Buddhists and rare anyway in Japan), or the exchange of one condiment or vegetable for another more readily available in the new situation.

Beyond that similarity, the differences in folklore between Japanese and Chinese folkore are deep, and they indicate how, in the Pacific Region, the two prominent immigrant groups differed in their arrival and settlement patterns. The Japanese eventually settled in rural areas and excelled in farming and developing previously marginal land; the Chinese, keeping large, extended family together, tended to settle in the urban areas and operated family-owned service businesses. Despite their differences, external perceptions of both nationalities made them in many ways the same, and a social folklore grew up to maintain that perception; thus, both Chinese and Japanese were classified together as the Yellow Peril, often coming under suspicion precisely because their own folklore was so different and because it was practiced in the privacy of their homes (a custom that Anglos saw as secretive and furtive). This outside stereotype came into political use during World War II when government "experts" testified that the very fact that the Japanese kept their culture alive secretly at home was a sure sign of their loyalty to the Japanese emperor, and the fact that no sabotage had ever been committed by a Japanese American showed just how well organized they were in their ultimate plan of waiting for the proper moment to strike. Such beliefs led to the internment without due process of 110,000 American citizens of Japanese ancestry in 1942. Equally remarkable is that the same stereotypes are today used to illustrate how successful Asians have been in America: They keep their families together, they mind their own business and keep their teenagers off the street, and they keep their ethnic heritage alive— all qualities highly valued in modern America. For the same reasons they were once a threat, Asians are now thought of as a model minority. Here is a striking example of the working of ethnic folklore and exoteric response in the American West. Of course, today, with the influx of Koreans since the 1950s and the Southeast Asians since the early 1970s, the picture becomes increasingly complex, and one sees and hears the beliefs once applied to the Japanese and Chinese being applied to the newer arrivals, most recently the Hmong.

Other groups that are valuable subjects in the study of Pacific Regional folklore are the many religious groups that have made themselves at home here, often in the expressed belief that somehow the West offered them a possibility for community independence that they could not find elsewhere. What *was* it they found, or thought they saw here? Consider their variety: the socialistic Puget Sound Utopian settlements; the extremely conservative Russian Old Believers near Woodburn, Oregon; the Buddhists and Shinto people in California; the Jews in every major city; the Catholics in the Southwest; the Protestants in the Northwest; the Amish in Oregon (once living near Amity, they suddenly picked up in the 1950s and moved to Florida). All of these groups have had an effect on the culture of this region, and all have undoubtedly been regionalized to one extent or another.

PRACTICAL THINGS OF TASTE AND BEAUTY

While not immediately thought of as folklore, material culture—cloth, wood, threads, plants, and other physical materials—transmits in concrete form concepts and designs and values parallel to the oral forms more often recognized as a folklore tradition. Cooking would of course be one of these expressions: local recipes (and names for them), local uses of wild vegetables and game, preferences for regional styles of food preparation and seasoning, favorite fuels or woods for smoking, customs about who does the cooking. Some western families restrict the raising and use of sourdough to men; in others, men cook meals prepared outdoors, while women take charge of those produced in the kitchen and control the language that is used there.

Like cooking, many material cultural expressions are clustered within domains traditionally associated with the female role and custom in a community. Quilting, for example, is largely but not exclusively a woman's form of expression. Most of the western quilters one hears about are women, but men show up with some frequency. Some take up quilting because there is no woman in the family passing on a mother's or a grandmother's tradition; in other cases, a man takes it up after retirement or after a difficult operation. Still others are drawn to it after helping their wives add the quilting (back and filling, together with whatever decorative stitches are used to bind them together) to a piecework top. The regular alternation of geometric patterns reflects the values of the agrarian society in which quilting became so central. Certain patterns are most likely to be given as gifts because they embody the thought or intent offered by the giver: for example, Double Wedding Ring, with its interwoven symbols of marriage, or Log

A woman in California works on a quilt given to her by her grandmother. Courtesy of Corbis.

Cabin, with its regular "log" walls and central spot (reminiscent of a hearth), are considered proper gifts for newlyweds, while erratic or humorous patterns like Drunkard's Path or Turkey Tracks, because of their characterizations of wandering away from the straight path, are considered dangerous for newly married couples. Do quilters believe that the quilt exercises a magical influence on those who sleep under it? No, but they obviously see the quilt as a statement, and they want the statement to be consistent with community value and practice. Folklore does not, however, need to be consciously planned in order to display intent and cultural resonance.

Other forms of western lore not limited to but traditionally associated with women would include other arts or crafts such as embroidery (extremely important for the Russian Old Believers), rug hooking or braiding (mainly a practical way of reusing older materials but subject to tremendous artistic variation), midwifery (almost exclusively a female tradition in the early West; old midwives will usually not even discuss it with a male researcher), and the performance of that great range of philosophical, medicinal, practical, and moral expressions that falls under the deceptively simple rubric of "housework." The housework itself is often done according to the traditions of routines long in the family: women report doing their washing and ironing on the same day their mothers did them, using certain procedures passed down in the family (like what order to wash clothes or dishes in), and even having the same attitudes toward color combinations that were thought normal by older female members of their families. Even as late as the 1930s, when government photographers like Dorothea Lange and Russell Lee moved up and down the Pacific states of Oregon, Washington, and California, documenting the migrant influx of "Okies" into the region, they tended to focus on the domestic practices of the women who struggled, despite their highly itinerate lives, to set homesteads and keep up the traditional homemaking practices, such as "Blue Monday"—clothes washing day—that inscribe the idea of permanent homes.

A different kind of material expression in folk design is the folk boat: the distinctively local boat built by local people for local conditions and use. Usually these are modifications of some earlier kind of boat known to the first boatbuilder who tried regionalizing the idea. Practically every western river, from Alaska's bustling Chena to the fly-fishing paradise of the Salmon and Rogue, has its own distinctive boat. They are practical, usually built of local materials, and although the users would probably be the first to say that their construction is more practical than aesthetic, there is often a very strong note of grace, balance, and symmetry that demonstrates an ongoing taste in good design as well as technical command of functional detail. The same can be said of the boatbuilding practices of the native tribes of Alaska and Hawai'i, whose boats and their history are often the subject of museum displays and scholarly study. The fact that local styles remain relatively stable over the years is a good sign that ends more complicated than technical necessity are being served. These are visible articulations of a shared sense of the good, proper, and beautiful.

The same can be said of traditional barns and outbuildings, fence styles and gates, mailbox supports, and ranch entryways. So ubiquitous in the West is the high, two-posted entry with crossbeam that even weekenders from the city living in prefab or mobile homes will erect one soon after obtaining a piece of property in ranch country. In earlier times, the high entryway no doubt helped people to find the gate opening in a long fence stretching for miles across the range. And of course it had to be built high enough that people could ride through without dismounting. But its practical functions are nearly always augmented by personal decoration of very specific sorts: A plank with the family or ranch name may hang in the middle; a saddle may ride in the cross-piece; wagon wheels, single and doubletrees, may dangle from overhangs; bison or cattle skulls, horse and oxen shoes, large models of the family's cattle brand, boots, hats, and the like, may be affixed over all. All of these are of course emblems of the ranch life, and the better they detail the accepted notions of the "real" ranch life of earlier times, the more they testify to the owner's tenure in the county. Fences, once the abomination of the cattlemen, have become in more recent years emblems of domain and familiar self-produced signs of ownership. There are preferred ways of stretching or repairing wire fence, locally developed methods of anchoring fence lines (such as "rock traps," bins of rock in eastern Oregon where land is too hard for post holes, explained to tourists as a means of catching rocks before they are blown out onto the road by high winds). Scraps of wire fencing are saved for use in repairing gates, machinery, and tackle. Oregon old-timer Reub Long once said, "If heaven hasn't any old rusty patched-up wire fences, I'll never feel at home there."[1]

Perhaps the most dramatic of material folklore in the region are totem poles. Generally carved of red cedar, with images of animals and people, they tell stories of times before humans lived on earth as well as tribal stories of marriage, deaths, births, heroic deeds, and supernatural transformations. The poles serve different functions—poles for the entrance of a house; "ridicule" poles to mock someone; mortuary poles, some of which contain a storage receptacle for the ashes of the deceased; and commemorative poles. They also act as family crests, and for Native tribes such as the Tlingit, Haida, Tsimshian, Nisga'a, Gitksan, and Kuakiutl, the poles record genealogical history. While it is not known how long totem poles have been part of culture, eighteenth-century expeditions to what are now Alaska and Vancouver Island record in words and drawings elaborate totem poles. Recently, after watching the practice nearly die out, Native artists have revitalized not only the carving art but the ceremonies—such as the elaborate potlatch (a lavish gift-giving ceremony) that go with the completion of a new totem pole.

FOLK SONGS IN THE PACIFIC REGION

Many of the songs sung traditionally in the West have survived not only the transcontinental journey but the transoceanic voyage as well—often with surprising fidelity to earlier versions. Of course, few folk songs have a single version that can reasonably be called the "correct" one, because constant variation in text and tune is the hallmark of the traditional process. Some older songs from England appear in western American versions in what first appears to be eroded condition. An old British broadside street ballad of some forty stanzas once became one of the most popular songs in the English language; it described in what we would today consider extremely melodramatic language the slow deaths of a wealthy husband and wife and the later deaths of their two children. What remains in western American tradition are a mere three verses, the ones that detail the death of

Singing cowboy songs at a camp in Odell, Oregon, 1941. Courtesy of the Library of Congress.

the lost children. The song now makes a somewhat different point: instead of moralizing about the duties of adults to their minor charges, the ballad now places full spotlight on the plight of the children, without rationale, background, or moral lesson. Why would singers do this, and why would the song have been so popularly sung in the West? It does not seem to be the result simply of poor memory. One way to approach such a question is to ask about how and when a song was actually sung and by whom. Researchers in the field of folklore have found that elderly people in the West remember hearing this song as a lullaby sung to them by their mothers, who probably shared with other mothers along the wagon trails, and later on the western homesteads, the fear that their children might wander off and die in the woods. Thus, because of the deep-seated fears the region produced in its inhabitants, one of the most popular songs ever to exist in England became also one of the most popular songs ever to be sung in the Pacific Region.

Two Babes in the Woods

Oh do you remember a long time ago
When two little babes, their names I don't know,
They wandered away one bright summer's day
And were lost in the woods, I heard people say.

And when it was night, so sad was their plight,
The moon had gone down and the stars gave no light.
They sobbed and they sighed and bitterly cried,
And those two little babes laid down and died.

And when they were dead, a robin so red
Brought strawberry leaves and over them spread.
And all the day long they sang their sweet song,
Those two little babes who were lost in the wood.[2]

Marital rites and courting traditions are another area in which the geography of culture makes its mark. Early and especially post–Civil War ballads may have detailed the lament of a father unable to find a suitable, or any, husband for his daughter. But in the Pacific West, the courting situation was entirely different. Western Oregonians were beginning to settle in small towns or in clusters of relatively nearby farmsteads. Their problem was not finding their daughter a husband, for the place was overrun with men. The bigger problem was keeping the house from filling up with mud:

I've reached the land of rain and mud,
Where flowers and trees so early bud;
Where it rains and rains both night and day
For in Oregon [pronounced O-ree-gun] it rains always.

Oh Oregon, wet Oregon
As through thy rain and mud I run;
I stand and look out all around
And watch the rain soak in the ground,
Look up and see the waters pour
And wish it wouldn't rain no more.

Oh Oregon girls, wet Oregon girls,
With laughing eyes and soggy curls;
They'll sing and dance both night and day
Til some webfooter comes their way:
They'll meet him at the kitchen door
Saying, "Wipe your feet or come no more."

MÜNCHAUSENS, LIARS, AND LOCAL CHARACTERS

Meaningful folk expressions coming from the Pacific Region are not found in a single genre of folklore, for there are always overlaps and interchanges with other forms, such as legend and local tall tale. In the latter, there is more than a humorously hyperbolic *text* in question, for most of the best texts available were narrated by people who themselves relished the role of the local "liar." Here is a genre in which the performer is a living part of the tradition and usually tells the stories as having happened to himself (even when the scholar can show without question that the story is several generations old). Often the storyteller is a local marginal "character," a retired farmer or an early settler who has been bypassed by younger and more aggressive folks who do not appreciate what the good old days were all about. The local "liar," then, is often not at the center of his community's current life in practical terms but is capable of projecting his community's values in a way that all insiders will recognize (because they know where reality leaves off and hyperbole begins, and they also know what it is that local taste considers worthy of hyperbolic treatment). In many ways, the western tall tale represents the inverse of myth (that is, the reverentially received and accepted story of the great, the powerful, the central): Instead of describing the exploits of heroes and founders, or even of cowboys who may stereotypically characterize values that many people *believe* to be central to their culture, the Münchausens, or tall tales, glorify mistakes, coincidences, and odd occurrences that *are* at the center of local values. They brag about local geographical or meteorological conditions that no one likes, they extol the use of outdated equipment, they savor the details of patently impossible events, and most of all, they love to do this in front of an audience made up in part of local folks who know the score and innocent outsiders who do not.

One such myth, extolling the virtues of California's "healthy climate," tells of a 200-year-old man who was simply unable to sicken and die in that state. Weary of life, he left California and died, but upon his corpse's reentry into the state for burial, he revived and rose out of his coffin. Folk exaggeration runs from these examples of narrative misinformation to lies that are acted out while the naive person watches (a mechanic pulls his head back from a battery as if shocked: "Did it get you?" he is asked by a concerned observer. "Nope, I was too fast for it.") to lies that come up casually in conversation after some peculiar action has taken place.

In stories about animals—the classic example being the fish that got away—folk exaggeration provides a narrative by which humans create their role in a region whose geography, climate, and geology combine into extreme patterns of the wild. Most stories about animal size and/or behavior generally reveal a myriad of cultural perspectives toward a specific region. In dry country, one hears that the cows have to keep one foot on their hay to keep it from being blown away, that a heavy logging chain hung from a post tells how hard the wind is blowing (when links begin snapping off the end and the chain is straight out, it is a "fair breeze"), that one time the wind blew the streetlight and headlight beams off the roads (but of course that was back when the lights were not as strong as they are now), or that the wind blew all the dirt from around a well or a prairie-dog hole, leaving the hole standing in the air. In the rainy areas on the Olympic Peninsula in Washington a farmer will tell you how his rain barrel overflowed during one storm; the water running over the lip of the barrel washed out the dirt under one side, and the barrel tipped over: "You know, it rained into the bunghole faster than the water could flow out the open end of that barrel, and before I knew it the water got all compacted in there, and it kept flowing out for a couple of months after the storm was over! Watered my stock on that one barrel the whole summer! I can show you the barrel itself if you don't believe me."

Reub Long, a loquacious central Oregon rancher, once said, "We measure humidity by the amount of sand in the air. When it rains, we keep our hired man in—we want all the water on the land."[3] The same rancher once told anyone who would listen that he had never seen rain until he was eighteen years old, and then he had run outside to see what the strange sound was of something hitting the tin roof of the ranch house. "You know, one of those big desert raindrops hit me on the back of the head and knocked me cold. They had to throw six buckets of sand in my face to bring me around!" Rapidly changing weather and resultant difficulties of raising livestock were not direct topics in Long's conversations but instead became articulated through folkloric humor and exaggeration. "The reason I've been able to produce some fast horses is that, where I graze them, they have to feed at thirty miles an hour to get enough to eat." One of his favorite stories, especially in front of strangers, was his account of how he tried to get rid of rats on a ranch he once bought. He had heard that if you caught one of them and painted it white, the others would think it was a ghost and leave the place. Long and a group of buckaroo friends finally caught one of the rats and, to keep it from escaping, took it out into the middle of the road. Then, while they kneeled on it, they argued over which was the best way to apply the paint: with the grain of the hair or against it—Did they want a shiny finish or a rough one? While all this was in progress, someone came down the road in a car and of course stopped at the sight of this strange crowd (one imagines that the stranger in the car in the story functions as the equivalent of the stranger listening to the story). "What in the world are you doing there, for God's sake?" "Why, we're whitewashing a rat," replied Long testily, whereupon the stranger turned around in haste and drove quickly out of sight.

Local exaggerations provide great insight into the living conditions of the region. Student Susan Mullin collected a tremendous range of tall tales, as recalled by Arthur Belknap from the first-person performances of his grandfather, Benjamin Franklin Finn (who claimed being the model for Mark Twain's [1835–1910] Huck Finn).[4] Among Belknap's performances of his grandfather's daily narratives was the well-known "Liar Too Busy To Lie."[5] Some Eugene newspapermen had come up the McKenzie River to interview him and collect some of his lies, but he was too busy to lie to them that day. "My best friend, Old Man Pepiot, died just last night, and I've been up all night working on his coffin. Now if you boys will just come back another time, why I'd be happy to tell you some lies." The newspapermen of course apologized profusely for their intrusion and went on down the road, where the first person they met was—naturally—Old Man Pepiot. Other yarns also found widely in the Münchausen tradition feature Granddad being caught in a tree or in a split stump (had to go all the way back to the house and get an ax to come chop himself loose), one that explained the great hunter bringing back only one wolf hide (he had been treed by a whole pack, and each time he shot one, the rest ate him up, so that finally, although he had shot twenty, he had only one pelt to show for it, but of course used the hide as proof of the whole story), a version of the Great Hunt (a hunter, with very few shots, kills an unbelievable amount of game and often falls in water only to emerge with his pants full of fish), which was narrated only when outsiders—hopefully game wardens—were present so that when they said, "Do you know who we are? State game wardens!" he could reply, "You know who I am? Huck Finn, the biggest damn liar on the McKenzie!"

Probably his best known story locally, outside the immediate circle of family and friends, concerns the naming of Finn Rock, a large monolith that stands beside the McKenzie River Highway. The local story (of course originally narrated by B. F. Finn himself) tells how Finn moved the rock to its present position by using a new buckskin harness that stretched as he drove his skittish team out across the roaring McKenzie. "That didn't bother Granddad none, though; he just hung the harness on a tree, and when the sun come out, why over come the rock!" said Arthur Belknap in one conversation. Later, when asked to repeat the story, he claimed that the stretching harness episode occurred when Granddad Finn brought a wagon load of groceries home through the Oregon rain. The wagon got mired in the muck along the way, while the wet buckskin harness continued to stretch. "That didn't bother Granddad none, though," said Belknap to Mullin. "He just hung the harness on the gatepost and when the sun came out, why along come the wagon." With just two versions of the same story from the same narrator, we begin to understand more clearly one of the standard maxims of folklore study: No single version can be said to be the "original" or the "correct" one, for the narrators themselves are accustomed to using them in various ways depending on the circumstances. The people who actually perform these "yarns" are engaged in expressing locally perceived truths using a very special kind of humorous hyperbole. It *is* unbelievably rainy on the Olympic Peninsula; the wind *does* blow furiously east of the Sierra Nevadas. It is the shared attitudes and emotions on those bothersome subjects that reach expression through the Münchausen, the yarn-spinner, and the local folk raconteur.

Still current in Reub Long's repertoire was the story of a frontier judge who was such a drunkard that one of the local businessmen, a prissy newcomer from the East, was moved to run against him in an election. On election day, as the citizens gathered to begin voting, the judge staggered out onto the porch in front of his office and said, "I really feel sorry for you people today. You haven't got much of a choice, because you've got to decide between a drunkard and a fool. There's only one thing that's worth remembering as you vote today, friends, and it's this: with a drunkard, you know that at least *sometimes* he's sober."[6]

LEGENDS AND OTHER TRUTHS

Unlike Münchausens, legends are stories, or idea clusters, passed along by people who actually believe either that they are true or that at least they are very likely to be true, usually because they have come from a culturally unimpeachable source. In some regards, legends are like rumors, and they pass through the same channels of the culture, propelled by our fascination with the almost unbelievable. Poodles are exploded in microwaves by old ladies ignorant of modern appliances, spiders are found in uncombed hairdos, escaped mental patients with hooks on arms accost people on lovers' lanes, countless innocent women from the country are embarrassed by urban chefs into paying for recipes for Red Velvet Cake, and so on.[7] Unlike rumors—which, after all, usually die out after a while—legends live on and propagate themselves astronomically. Clearly the story has some function in our society, or it would not persist. Among other things, it portrays an older woman as ignorant of a newer electronic way of life, both a sexist and an "ageist" stereotype that is found abundantly on other levels and in other kinds of expressions in our culture.

Photo shows what former rodeo rider Roger Patterson said is the American version of the Abominable Snowman, also known as Bigfoot or Sasquatch. He said pictures of the creature, estimated at 7½ feet tall, were taken northeast of Eureka, California. © Bettmann/Corbis.

One of these fascinating modern "urban" legends—already well discussed by Jan H. Brunvand—is an earlier, yet persistent legend of the West, that of Bigfoot, or Sasquatch. In this constellation of motifs and narratives, one central idea continues to emerge: alive in the mountains of the West is a kind of primate creature with shaggy hair and primitive build, one who is reminiscent of gorillas or larger apes but who apparently has some kind of social system like our own. The Bigfoots (the plural form is unclear, but there is a parallel to the plurals of *Webfoot* and *Tenderfoot*) try to keep to themselves, but they are troubled by our civilization and are often described as performing selected deeds of revenge (an empty oil barrel is found crushed by a logging crew, a Bigfoot steps out of the bushes and scratches the top of a government pickup truck, unsuspecting campers are scared off by a screaming Bigfoot, and so on). On occasion, they kidnap a human, taking the prisoner back to their "camp."

Both male and female humans are usually forced to accept Bigfoot sexual attentions and are seldom released afterward. Police and others who have gone in search of missing persons are said to have had mysterious accidents or to have disappeared themselves. The stories seem to cluster along certain mountain areas: the Siskiyous in Northern California, the Cascades in west central Oregon and Washington, and the coastal ranges of British Columbia, including Vancouver Island. Only Hawai'i has no formal Bigfoot encounters within the region, for while man-eaters appear in Hawaiian myth, the Northcoast Salish tribe's placement of Bigfoot on Whidby Island seems as far out into the Pacific Islands as it goes. Sightings are abundant in Alaska, where one Yukon village deserted as recently as 1992 because of a Bigfoot appearance. The Kenai Peninsula, near Homer, Alaska, shelters a rich lode of Bigfoot tradition. According to author Robert Pyle, English Bay residents tell of many encounters with "Nantiinaq," who can change from Bigfoot into any form. One explanation for the persistence of these stories that cannot be ruled out—especially since there are many eyewitness reports by very credible persons and since a number of anthropologists have busied themselves with the details of the issue—is that there is such a creature.

A Sasquatch crossing sign in Washington. Courtesy of Getty Images/PhotoDisc.

In folklore itself, however, what is more interesting is what function such a character plays in the Pacific Region, whether or not it expresses something important in the culture. Going as far back as *Beowulf*, there is a wealth of "wild man of the forest" stories in medieval woodcuts, in tapestries, and even in statuary. The wild men are depicted as covered with wavy, unruly hair, matted with twigs and bits of grass and leaves; the wild women are a bit less hairy and very voluptuous. They are shown as intruding on the affairs of civilized human beings by angrily rushing out of the woods to kidnap people. It may be that they represent, at least in some cases, a metaphorical statement about non-Christian or nonreligious people or even incarnations of the devil; in other cases, they may represent earlier gods of the field and wood who were put into shade (or out of business) by the advent of Christianity. But in all cases, they actually pictorialize a clash between the civilized and cultivated world and the uncivilized, uncultivated world. In other words, one of their functions seems to be to epitomize a condition of human existence against which civilization measures itself and without which it has little meaning. Indeed, the image is at least as old as the Gilgamesh epic.

In New England, especially in Maine, the legend of Yoho Cove (certainly not named by Jonathan Swift) tells how a local geographical area received its name when one of those Yohos came out of the woods and kidnapped a human girl who was out huckleberrying with her family. She was forced to mate with the Yoho and escaped some years later, the Yoho running after her, ripping their child in half and throwing one-half after her departing boat.[8] The same story is told in Kentucky, according to Leonard Roberts, where the creature is called Yeahoh.[9] All of the American stories stress the apelike qualities of the animal, in contrast to the distinctly human attributes of the European variety, and they all have much in common (viewed in retrospect) with the images that have made King Kong such a compelling character in the popular media. What is there in the American West that would nurture such stories as if they had local roots? Well, for one thing, the West, with all its reducing of the land (and people) to cultivated properties, also featured a number of distinctly uncivilized central episodes, among them the treatment of the Indians during the change of ownership. In addition, the frontier was a mixture of excitement and danger, a kind of tenuous boundary between the known and the unknown. There were indeed Boggarts and Boogers that would come and get you; at least the imagination seems to have created that scene. And the paranoid, almost fanatic way in which wolves, rattlesnakes, and Indians were ruthlessly attacked, when for the most part they kept trying to move out of the way, is a vivid indication that the Order brought about on the frontier was paid for with a large dose of mental disquietude. It is also worth saying that many of the common motifs of the Bigfoot stories are also common in racial/racist narratives, beliefs, and jokes: uncivilized and aggressive behavior, strong and offensive smell, apelike looks and movements, primitive culture, and a taste for white women, to name only a few. Yes, whether there really are Bigfoots or not, the populating of the Pacific Region nearly guarantees that they would appear here, for cultural "ghosts" seem to require animation and narrative performance.

Legends allow the scholar a chance at least to speculate about what sorts of emotions lie under the western surface nicely mythologized by historians but uncorked and set loose every now and then in oral narratives and by good writers. Not coincidentally, many of the local legends in the West have to do with monsters or mysterious animals who live under lakes (again, European antecedents come easily to mind, and they must surely have provided the cultural willingness to believe in the phenomenon), and what a strikingly appropriate image for further reflection and deeper scrutiny: the unfathomed lake with its hidden monster that comes into view every now and then and eats someone or bashes a boat to smithereens (or, more recently, swallows up a flight of air force jets without a belch). Carl Jung (1875–1961) would have been more than pleased to find this dream-stuff so widespread in oral tradition presented as living truth, for in psychological terms, that's precisely what it is. Mono Lake, California, Crater Lake, Oregon, Lake Chelan, Washington, and smaller lakes along the Oregon coast—there is hardly a lake in the Pacific Region that does not have its monster or at least a subterranean passage that links it to another lake that does. And—it is worth noting—many of these lakes have stories of similar contents by Indian backgrounds.

Native myths are often associated with the attempt to explain phenomenological events and perhaps in no place more than Hawai'i, where volcanoes form an ever present shadow on the lives of inhabitants. Thus, Hawai'i's most famous goddess, Pele, presided over volcanoes and had a tumultuous relationship with Kamapua¢a, the hog man and deity, who enjoyed special protection from the gods. As if that ongoing strife were not enough, Pele often had to confront the inappropriate actions of Hawai'i's kings. In one story, a king named Puna refuses to stop boasting about the beauty of his country, even though it is well known that Pele dislikes boasting. Insisting that he has nothing to fear from Pele, the king sings the following:

> My country is beautiful Puna,
> Land where all food plants are growing,
> Land where bananas hang heavy,
> Where potatoes burst from the earth,
> Where sugar-cane stalks are the sweetest.
> My country is sweet smelling Puna.
> To the seaman who comes near our coast
> The winds bear the fragrance of hala.
> Birds gather over our trees
> Drinking the nectar of blossoms.
> My country is beautiful Puna.[10]

Warned by a wise kahuna that his beautiful Puna has been laid to waste, the king, despite his brave front, returns. There he finds a pall of black smoke over all his land. Worse still, when winds lift the smoke, he sees all the fields and gardens have been buried beneath lava. The king learns in this hardest of ways that no one beneath Pele is safe from her power.

It is not only the stories associated with geographic formations that provide a folkloric insight to the Pacific Region. Names of towns and places are clues to earlier settlements and attitudes. The principal cities of Washington are named after Indians or Indian tribes, while the principal cities of Oregon are named after white settlers or the New England towns they came from. Even the brief legend told of Francis W. Pettigrove from Maine and A. L. Lovejoy from Massachusetts tossing a coin to decide if their city would be called Portland or Boston gives us a feel for the times: Who was making the decisions, and what was the range of alternatives they allowed themselves? Here is the establishment of a solid New England male Protestant stamp on Oregon, portrayed in a tableau scene of incredible economy of image. The various Murder Creeks, Bloody Washes, Bear-tooth Runs, and so on, throughout the West also have their legends to give flesh to the name, and in each area the legends do not necessarily agree: Murder Creek, Oregon, was named because of a murder that occurred there, but there are at least six different accounts of who was murdered and who was guilty (each one, of course, its narrator aware of the others, presents itself as the "real" one, passed on by a grandfather who knew the sheriff or who was a school friend of one of the culprits and heard a private confession). The genre has also been used to make fun of places one especially does not like or to praise places of special value. Walla Walla is supposedly the place they loved so well they named it twice; but one also hears that the name came about during a ritual bathing after the local tribe's annual bean festival: The chief, waist deep in water, broke wind, and the resulting sound, taken to be the chief's command, was ever after applied to the spot (needless to say, this is neither a real Indian legend nor a favorite anecdote of the Walla Walla Chamber of Commerce).

Just as place names, when explicated, reveal a polyglot of source material, so do certain place-based practices themselves. For much of the lower Pacific Region, water is a valuable commodity. Remember, John Wesley Powell's notation of the

100th meridian was a rainfall line; west of that line, average rainfall decreases, making agriculture a more and more difficult enterprise. Thus, the hunt for free groundwater was in the West as vigorous at times as the hunt for gold, and the means of the hunt are the stuff of lore. Witching for water is still a widespread phenomenon in the West, sometimes being performed by professional well-drillers, whose income, after all, depends on their success. Some western dowsers use two welding rods bent pistollike, one in each hand, and watch to see where they suddenly move together or cross. Some claim that by using a piece of metal spring or a stick they can witch water from a map (moving in their imaginations over the area depicted there), or while riding along in a car, and some believe they can locate uranium and other metals and even tell how deep they are. Other belief systems in the West include those of the fishermen along the coast, who still pass on and use a combination of the most ancient and modern beliefs imaginable. Many will not leave port on a Friday, one of the oldest of seafarers' beliefs; some place a golden or silver coin under the radar housing (a modern variation of insuring or buying wind by placing a coin under the mast); and almost all fishermen honor Lady Luck in one fashion or another, chiefly by not "pushing their luck" too far. If it is raining, someone will note that since salmon love fresh water, the fishing will be bound to get better; if the weather starts to clear, someone will just as cheerfully point out that since salmon like warm weather and a rising barometer, the fishing will start to pick up. Neither belief really indicates what fishermen think about, but both are based on a shared set of beliefs that encourage fishermen to speak only in positive terms about a change in the fishing: no matter what happens, the fishing will get better.

FAMILY FOLKLORE

Family folklore is found throughout the country, of course, but in the Pacific Region families are often also the contexts for occupational lore: One example is the family-operated ranch, where all family members participate in roundup, roping and tying, castration, and branding. One sees a ranch wife on horseback, roping an escaping calf; another wife, with cigarette dangling, sitting on a calf while it is branded and castrated, while her ten-year-old son comes dragging another calf by its neck and forelegs, taking time only to shift his snoose to the other cheek and spit. These would be rare sights in a western movie, but they are not rare in the daily reality of ranchers, especially today, when ranch hands are hard to find and salaries hard to pay. But such a matter is not only a part of reality; it becomes also a part of custom, jargon, gesture, anecdote, and legend. It may not fit the public image of "the cowboy," but it accurately expresses local community values about the occupation *and* family. Women, traditionally discouraged or prevented from coming aboard fishing vessels, are often found as integral units on family-owned and -operated fishing boats in the West Coast fishery. This in turn has led to the employment of single women on board otherwise male-operated boats. Skippers who will still assure the listener that one never allows a woman on board are discovered nonetheless to have employed women on their very own boats. One can conclude from such evidence that fishermen are lying, of course, but it is far more likely that their oral traditions are simply carrying a set of values that still exist on one level, even though they may have begun to disappear on another. Attitudes and customs about family relationships can thus affect traditional attitudes on other matters. Folk belief and custom seldom remain static in function, although the spirit of a region may persist for generations.

Family legends testify to the seriousness with which people take their own family myth, or sacred story (the term is not too forced here): Stories of how ancestors crossed the ocean or crossed the Plains, why they settled in a certain place, why they left their original homeland, and so on, are not simply homey attempts to capture a few facts of history but are usually delicately structured cameos of family, regional, religious, and cultural values. Succeeding generations who try to keep their hands clean delight in detailing how their grandparents had to learn to cook with buffalo chips, for it puts a slight reek of sainthood into their own plastic lives. Descendants of the Aurora Colony in Oregon recount how their founder, Dr. Wilhelm Keil, transported the body of his dead son Willie on the lead wagon westward in a casket lined with lead and filled with alcohol preceded by a German band; it is no wonder that his wagon train had no trouble with the Indians. But in any case, their sense of having come on a mission of religious peace and friendship—in contrast to many of their secular contemporaries—is a strong feature of their own subsequent evaluation of themselves, even though the Colony as such no longer exists.

A number of families in the Pacific West tell legends of close calls with the Indians or with large animals. An innocent child is followed all the way to the cabin door by a nice kitty whose footprints later identify it as a large and heavy cougar. A young boy living in the Cascade Mountains with no playmates keeps referring to his best friend Amos, who turns out not to be a fantasy friend but a giant rattler who threatens all who dare to come near the boy. A legend found in more than a dozen Northwest families was called "Goldilocks on the Oregon Trail" by Francis Haines, who spent a large part of his life tracing the story.[11] He found that most of the early families in Oregon had a version of the story in their oral traditions, while none of them was able to find any account of it in the otherwise detailed journals that had been kept on the way west. The story, in its broadest outlines, goes something like this:

On their way across the Plains, our family's wagon train was visited several times by the braves of Chief Joseph's [or Sitting Bull's or Geronimo's] band who were always trading for provisions, ammunition, or horses. The Chief kept coming back to the wagon train day after day, and it turned out that his attention had been drawn to the cute little blond four-year-old girl who was to become our grandmother. He kept offering the little girl's father more and more ponies for her, but the answer was still no. The father kept acting as though an eventual trade might be made, but finally, of course, he told the Chief that it had all been in fun, and that the girl was not for sale at any price. The Chief departed in great sorrow, and the family says to this day the "Grandma was almost sold to the Indians."

It does seem strange that in families where a journal record was kept of daily temperatures, miles covered, trees sighted in the horizon, rivers crossed, and so on, there would have been no mention of this rather striking event. Even so, we are not entitled to make the snap decision that it must never have happened. On the other hand, as with the exploding poodle story of more recent times, we would be foolish to overlook the fact that the story is told by more families than coincidence could suggest could have been approached by that busy chieftain. Moreover, the story has other familiar elements to it: A dark, powerful, aggressive male is believed to be infatuated with a small, prepubescent, white girl. Aside from its misunderstanding of Indian canons of beauty, its stereotypical presentation of the cliché of interracial sexual threat, so common in race-based stories, plus the common theme of a young female saved from doom by a male representative of the adult world (cf. policemen rescuing the stranded girlfriend from the backseat of the murdered boyfriend's car in countless lovers' lane legends), should suggest to us that at least the continued *telling* of the narrative does something more culturally complex than merely recalling an interesting incident in Grandma's early years, one that everyone now chuckles over. Why does one chuckle at it, indeed? And why does one assume that Grandma would not have liked life among the Indians, especially in the company of so illustrious a leader as Chief Joseph? Why, the family could have been *really* famous then. With this suggestion, one begins to hear the hum of pioneer ancestors spinning in their cerements, for that is not what they had in mind, one may well imagine. The story seems to function, among other things, as a hallmark of early arrival on the scene, for most of the later pioneers, though they had no easy time of this journey into rain and mud, did not get confronted by the Indians in such an intimate way. There is a heady quality to being first in line for the spoils that no amount of fact-finding will ever eradicate.

CONCLUSION

In the long movement of Manifest Destiny, the shores of the Pacific have held out the call of the Last West—even after Hawai'i became part of the United States. Because of that terminal position in the country's movement, many of the pioneer stereotypes that have underlain the sense of American identity are both larger than life and, somehow, slightly different by the time they reach the Pacific Region. The Pacific Regioner is an unabashed combination of outlaw and preacher, pioneer mother and dance-hall girl, buckaroo and oil baron, iconoclast and chauvinist. In this sense, each native, each settler, each pioneer mother and struggling logger—either in real life or in song and story—is a metaphor for some important aspect of the western cultural view, or it would not be passed on. Like all good poetry, folklore mediates, foregrounds, and makes palpable the most bothersome of these discrepancies in a way that not only entertains and edifies but somehow as well gives voice to the otherwise inarticulate features of the culture. Everything done and said by and in a culture is unavoidably a part of its larger language, has meaning in its larger picture. Thus, the aggregate of everyday expressions available in the living record of folklore provides the poetic grammar through which the emotional realities of all regions in America are articulated and understood.

RESOURCE GUIDE

Printed Sources

Armistead, Samuel. *Hispanic Balladry among the Sephardic Jews of the West Coast*. Berkeley: University of California Press, 1960.

Beckwith, Martha. *Hawaiian Mythology*. New Haven, CT: Yale University Press, 1940.

Botkin, B. A. *A Treasury of Western Folklore*. New York: Crown, 1955.

Bouchard, Randy, and Dorothy Kennedy, eds. *Indian Myths and Legends from the North Pacific Coast of America: A Translation of Franz Boas' 1895 Edition of* Indianisch Sagen von der Nord-Pacifischen Kuste Amerikas. Trans. Dietrick Bertz. Vancouver, British Columbia: Talon Books, 2002.

Bringhurst, Robert, ed. and trans. *Being in Being: The Collected Works of Skaay of the Qquuna Qiighawaay*. Lincoln: University of Nebraska Press, 2001.

Cameron, Anne. *Dzelarhons: Myths of the Northwest Coast*. Madeira Park, British Columbia: Harbour, 1986.

Craig, Robert D. *Dictionary of Polynesian Mythology*. Westport, CT: Greenwood Press, 1989.

Cunningham, Scott. *Hawaiian Magic and Spirituality*. St. Paul, MN: Llewellyn Publications, 2001.

Jones, Suzi. *Oregon Folklore*. Eugene: University of Oregon Press, 1977.

Judson, Katharine Berry. *Myths and Legends of the Pacific Northwest, Especially of Washington and Oregon*. Chicago: A. C. McClurg, 1910.

Kaeppler, Adrienne L., and H. Arlo Nimmo, eds. *Directions in Pacific Traditional Literature: Essays in Honor of Katharine Luomala*. Honolulu, HI: Bishop Museum Press, 1976.

Margolin, Malcolm, ed. *The Way We Lived: California Indian Stories, Songs, and Reminiscences*. Berkeley, CA: Heyday Books, 1993.

Morrill, Sibley. *The Kahunas: The Black and White Magicians of Hawaii*. Boston: Branden Press, 1969.

Napier, John. *Bigfoot: The Yeti and Sasquatch in Myth and Reality*. New York: E. P. Dutton, 1973.

Nimmo, H. Arlo. *The Pele Literature: An Annotated Bibliography of the English-Language Literature on Pele, Volcano Goddess of Hawaii*. Bishop Museum Bulletin in Anthropology. Honolulu, HI: Bishop Museum Press, 1992.

Pyle, Robert Michael. *Where Bigfoot Walks: Crossing the Dark Divide*. Boston, MA: Houghton Mifflin, 1995.

Shipley, William, ed. *The Maidu Indian Myths and Stories of Hanc'ibyjim*. Berkeley, CA: Heyday Books, 1991.

Taylor, C. J. *How We Saw the World: Nine Native Stories of the Way Things Began*. Montreal, Quebec: Tundra Books, 1993.

Webber, Willliam. *The Thunderbird "Tootooch" Legends: Folk Tales of the Indian Tribes of the Pacific Northwest Coast Indians*. Seattle, WA: Ace, 1936.

Westervelt, W. D. *Legends of Old Honolulu*. Boston, MA: Ellis Press, 1916.

Wyatt, Gary. *Mythic Beings: Spirit Art of the Northwest Coast*. Seattle: University of Washington Press, 1999.

Web Sites

Folklore of Mount Shasta
College of the Siskiyous Library. August 1, 2004.
http://www.siskiyous.edu/shasta/fol/index.htm

International Society for Contemporary Legend Research
August 1, 2004.
http://www.panam.edu/faculty/mglazer/isclr/isclr.htm

Films

In the Land of Totem Poles. Dir. Michel Viotte. La Sept Arte, Nester Productions, 1999.

Festivals and Events

Fall Folklore Festival
Spokane Folklore Society
P. O. Box 141
Spokane, WA 99210-0141
http://www.spokanefolklore.org/
Held annually in the late fall.
Features traditional and ethnic music as well as workshops.

Northwest Folklife Festival
305 Harrison Street
Seattle, WA 98109-4623
http://www.nwfolklife.org/P_F/festival.html
Held annually on Memorial Day weekend.
Located on the seventy-four-acre grounds of the Seattle Center in downtown Seattle.

Portland Old-time Music Festival
Norse Hall
NE Couch Street & 11th Avenue
Portland, OR 97232
http://www.bubbaguitar.com/festival/
Held annually in January.
A gathering of musicians honoring the traditional country/folk music and dance community in Portland.

Yakima Folklife Society Festival
Yakima Valley Folklife Association
2105 Tieton Drive
Yakima, WA 98902
http://folklife.yakimavalleymuseum.org/about.html
Held annually in July.
Various venues held at Franklin Park and the Yakima Valley Museum.

Organizations

American Folklife Center
Library of Congress
Thomas Jefferson Building, Room LJG49
101 Independence Avenue SE
Washington, DC 20540-4610
http://www.loc.gov/folklife/

American Folklore Society
Timothy Lloyd
AFS Executive Director
Mershon Center
Ohio State University
1501 Neil Avenue

Columbus, OH 43201-2602 USA
http://www.afsnet.org/

British Columbia Folklore Society
info@folklore.bc.ca
http://www.folklore.bc.ca/

California Folklore Society
Department of Folklore
University of California
Berkeley, CA 94720
http://ls.berkeley.edu/dept/folklore/index.html

National Council for the Traditional Arts
1320 Fenwick Lane, Suite 200
Silver Spring, MD 20910
http://www.ncta.net/

Smithsonian Center for Folklife and Cultural Heritage
Smithsonian Institution
750 9th Street, NW, Suite 4100
Washington, DC 20560-0953
http://www.folklife.si.edu/

Museums and Special Collections

Archive of Folk Culture
American Folklife Center
Library of Congress
Thomas Jefferson Building, Room LJG49
101 Independence Avenue SE
Washington, DC 20540-4610
http://www.loc.gov/folklife/

Material on the music of the American Indians of the Northwest Coast.

Mingei International Museum of Folk Art
1439 El Prado
Balboa Park
San Diego, CA 92101
http://www.mingei.org/

UCLA Folklore and Mythology Archives
http://www.humnet.ucla.edu/humnet/folklore/archives/

Online.

Western Folklife Center
501 Railroad Street
Elko, NV 89801
http://www.westernfolklife.org/site/

FOOD

Kimberly D. Nettles,
Melissa Salazar, and
Alice McLean

The Pacific Region includes five states with a dizzying array of climates, land types, animal and plant products, and peoples. Indeed, the very idea of a unifying Pacific regional food identity stretches the imagination, considering the physical distance and dramatic differences in foods, peoples, and climates between states such as Hawai'i and Alaska. The regional food culture cannot be adequately described by a few trademark foods or industries. What various parts of this region do have in common, however, is their fertility: from the nut orchards of California's Central Valley to the fishing banks of Alaska to the tropical plantations of Hawai'i, the lands (and waters) of the Pacific Region are so bountiful that they produce much of the food for the rest of the nation. Perhaps more than any other activities, food production, distribution, and consumption serve to define this region and to ground it.

The diversity of foods both produced and consumed in the Pacific Region is in large part due to its multicultural populace. As David Bell and Gill Valentine argue, regions are "products of both human and physical processes: a natural landscape and a peopled landscape."[1] The varied demographic of the region, which is home to the majority of the U.S. Asian and Hispanic ethnic populations, is a reflection of the region's long history as a landing ground for explorers, traders, and immigrants, many led by their desire for a new life of prosperity. Diverse groups such as Polynesians in Hawai'i, the Spanish *conquistadores* in California, and prospectors from all over the world during the Klondike and Californian gold rushes have all contributed their culturally distinct food habits, values, and agricultural practices, as well as redefined their own cuisines to fit their new home.

The wealth and variety of food industry in the Pacific Region combined with the multicultural fabric of the region make it a hub of agricultural and food innovation. The massive food production of the region means that what happens here affects food availability, food politics, and policies in the rest of the nation. Likewise, the gastronomy of the Pacific Region also has a cosmopolitan, groundbreaking spirit—a direct result of this bringing together of groups of people who have never before lived in the same vicinity. Pacific regional food culture is not merely the sum of its parts; rather, it is an amalgam of many cuisines that continuously develop and cross-pollinate, the weaving together of a wide variety of ingredients and cultural practices that lead in new directions.

THE ENVIRONMENT AND FOOD

The presence of the Pacific Ocean and the resultant long coastlines of Oregon, Washington, Alaska, California, and Hawai'i play a large role in defining the food and cuisine of this region. The ocean not only supports a large fishing industry but also provides a temperate shore climate. The ocean serves as a connecting force between the distant parts of the Pacific Region, as most of the major cities in the region have long histories as trading and shipping centers that have brought new foods—as well as food habits—into and out of the region. However, the vastness of the Pacific Ocean also means that the region includes landforms with dramatic contrasts in climate such as Alaska and Hawai'i, where there are more differences than similarities in foodstuffs.

Fishing, however, is one of the hallmarks of the Pacific food industry that ties the region together. The billion-dollar fishing industry accounts for more than 50 percent of the total U.S. domestic harvest. Alaska is also the number-one fishing state in the nation, catching a harvest valued at over $900 million in 2000. Seafood

Fishing for cod and halibut in Alaska, 1924. Courtesy of the Library of Congress.

is a staple found in most Pacific regional cuisines, beginning with native peoples, who later introduced their main food-stuff to subsequent settlers to the region. In addition, Native American populations in Alaska fished for sea mammals such as seal, walrus, sea lion, and whale, although the latter is the only one still commonly eaten. Fish such as salmon, halibut, tuna, herring, sardines, pollock, and squid, crustaceans such as shrimp and crab, and shellfish such as oysters, mussels, scallops, clams, and abalone are among the most well-known foods harvested from the Pacific Region. Several areas of the region also provide unique specialty seafoods that have become highly valued in food circles. Hawaiian waters are particularly abundant and well known for tuna, mahi-mahi, bonito, mackerel, marlin, scad, and pink and red snapper. The enormous Alaskan King crab is one of the most identifying Alaskan foods, thriving in the cold waters and reaching weights of twenty-five pounds, legs spanning six feet. Geoduck (pronounced gooey-duck) clams are another such specialty item. Typically found along the Oregon and Alaskan coasts, these clams have necks that stretch several feet; the clams can live up to 100 years. Asia remains the largest export market for Pacific regional seafood, where there is high demand for items such as squid (China) and herring roe used for sushi (Japan).

One fish, however, is perhaps the most important to the region's food identity: the Pacific salmon. The ocean is home to numerous varieties of salmon, the most common being the king, coho, sockeye, chum, and pink, all with different tastes and properties that have been utilized for maximum economic benefit. The roe of the sockeye is particularly prized in Japan; pink salmon, however, is less tasty as a fresh fish and is typi-

The enormous Alaskan King crab is one of the most identifying Alaskan foods. Courtesy of Corbis.

A woman holds a fresh Pacific salmon at a fish market in Washington. Courtesy of Getty Images/PhotoDisc.

Salmon canning in Oregon, 1915. Courtesy of the Library of Congress.

cally used for canning. Salmon was particularly important to the diets of Native Americans in the Pacific Northwest and Alaska, who settled along freshwater streams and rivers where salmon went in large numbers to spawn. They often used drying and smoking processes to preserve and extend their main food source, techniques that continue to be used in present Pacific cookery.

Farming, Overfishing, and Canning

Battles over fishing made up a large part of the region's food politics. Upon the arrival of settlers for the gold rush in the mid-1800s, the first "farmed" salmon fishery was established in the Sacramento, California, area, which was also the home of the first West Coast fish cannery. Farmed fisheries produced abundant and cheaper salmon supplies but reduced prices and encouraged larger-scale fishing operations in order to compete. The increases in fishing takes spurred on the canning and fish processing industry, and large canning operations were established in Monterey Bay, Oregon's Columbia River region, Hawai'i, and Alaska. Canning provided easy transportation and preservation of fish and seafood from the region not only to areas in the United States but also worldwide. All of these factors contributed to overfishing, which has dramatically reduced fish numbers over the past century. Wild salmon in the Pacific Northwest drastically declined in numbers due not only to overfishing but also to major destruction of habitat as large dams constructed along the Columbia River in the twentieth century eliminated many of the tributaries used by salmon for spawning runs. While salmon has shown a remarkable comeback in recent years, farmed salmon has decreased prices so dramatically that salmon fishing is no longer as economically viable as it once was.

Overfishing has not been limited to salmon. The California sardine has suffered a worse fate: In 1936–1937, 750,000 tons were harvested from California waters; twenty years later, the catch was a mere 17 tons. As a result, many sardine canning operations became "extinct," such as Cannery Row in Monterey, and sardine populations have never recovered. The Monterey Bay

Fishing Rights

As the populations of the Pacific Region have increased, wild fishing populations have declined due to overfishing and destruction of native fish habitats. In the twentieth century Native American tribes depended upon these fish not only for sustenance but also to preserve their cultural identity. Tribes in the Pacific Northwest began to pressure the federal government to uphold original fishing rights as agreed upon in treaties signed in the mid-nineteenth century, resulting in major court cases such as the *Boldt* decision in 1974 that upheld the Native rights to fish one-half of the commercial salmon harvest every year. The decision was expanded in the 1990s to include native peoples' right to shellfish stores. Declines in fishing stores have created tensions between native and nonnative fishermen, who must work together to protect the remaining fish and shellfish populations.

Aquarium now publishes a popular guide called "Seafood Watch" for the growing number of fish consumers, detailing which fish are currently overharvested or farmed using destructive environmental practices.

Wild Game, Livestock, and Dairy Industries

Mountain ranges and forests in the region are home to another characteristic Pacific food source: game. Native Americans in the region, as well as later settlers, sustained themselves on hunting game, traditions that influence Alaskan cuisine to this day. Caribou in the past was a traditional Alaskan game meat, but similar to the buffalo in the Plains states, destruction of habitat and sport hunting have reduced their numbers to less than 600,000. Currently, only residents are allowed to hunt caribou in order to help protect the species.

Monterey Bay Aquarium Seafood Watch

The Monterey Bay Aquarium in Monterey, California, runs a program called Seafood Watch: Choices for Healthy Oceans. It began in 1997 with an exhibit called "Fishing for Solutions," which showed how consumer demand for popular seafood was depleting fish stocks around the world and harming the health of the oceans. The exhibit was designed to help consumers become advocates for environmentally friendly seafood, by making better choices in restaurants and supermarkets to support sustainable fisheries and fish farms, by recommending which seafoods to buy or avoid. The program was so successful the Aquarium developed a pocket guide for consumers that can be downloaded for free off their Web site at http://www.mbayaq.org/cr/seafoodwatch.asp. The Web site is also an excellent resource for consumers to read about the health of specific fish and other sustainable fishing industry news. Currently Seafood Watch guides reflect what is sold in most West Coast markets, but development of similar guides for Hawai'i, the southern United States, the Northeast, Great Lake states, and the Midwest is under way.

Another interesting but mainly historically consumed Alaskan game food is reindeer. An American missionary introduced the species in the late 1800s, and by 1920 Alaska was exporting reindeer meat to the lower forty-eight states. However,

The spoils of a caribou hunt in Alaska, 1915. Courtesy of the Library of Congress.

failed pasturing efforts led to their wipeout in the region by the end of the twentieth century.

Domesticated cattle ranching is a huge industry in all parts of the region except Alaska—although there is a small industry of cattle farming there despite needing to feed cattle indoors for much of the year. Ranching in the majority of the mainland Pacific Region had its beginnings with Spanish settlers, then expanded dramatically with the surge of pioneers moving west, who found the plains and basins of California and Oregon particularly amenable to cattle. California now leads the Pacific Region in livestock and poultry farming, a $7 billion industry in 2001. Sheep and poultry farms are common throughout Oregon, particularly in the hills located in the southeastern part of the state and the prairies found in the Willamette Valley in the north. Hawai'i also has a long history of cattle ranching, beginning in 1793 with the introduction of the first cattle from

Artisanal Cheeses: A Women's Tradition

Project Truffle (http://www.projecttruffle.com/), an organization devoted to marketing artisanal cheeses made both in the United States and around the world, defines artisanal cheese making as a process that focuses on quality and "shows respect for the broader traditions of their environment, their locale, and their craft." Because artisanal cheeses are often handmade, their production is extremely small, often at a fraction of the rate of a larger cheese maker that uses industrial methods. In addition, these cheeses tend to be more expensive since most use only the highest-quality ingredients: the difference in price between a gallon of high-quality, organic, whole milk and a gallon of mass-produced, heavily processed milk can be as much as four to one.

Northern California and the Pacific Northwest are home to a number of artisanal cheese makers. Interestingly, the American artisanal cheese makers tend to be women, a tradition that goes back to early European cheese making where men tended the animals, while the women made the cheese. The environment of these areas of the United States is also reminiscent of Europe: The grazing areas are often next to vineyards, in a foggy, pastoral setting. One of the most successful of the artisanal movement is the Vella Cheese Company, based in Northern California. Begun by Tom Vella seventy years ago using methods he learned in France, his son Ig Vella now carries on the tradition of award-winning cheese making: Vella's signature is the Vella Dry Jack, a version of Monterey Jack, a California invention. Sally and Roger Jackson in Washington make a range of sheep, goat, and cow's milk cheeses and have such exacting standards they reportedly grow their own feed. Sonoma and Marin County are also home to a number of other artisanal cheese makers: Laura Chenel makes her signature Chevre goat's milk cheese, and is often credited with leading the boom in California cheese making in the late 1970s. Other famous cheese making women are Cindy Callahan at Bellwether Farms, who makes handmade goat's milk and cow's milk cheese, while upstarts at Cowgirl Creamery in Marin County, Sue Conley and Peggy Smith, make several soft cheeses with organic milk provided by a Straus Dairy (headed by Ellen Straus) just a few steps up the road. Jennifer Bice of Redwood Hill Farm tends her 400 goats herself, while three sisters from the Giacomini family run the family dairy and make Point Reyes Original Blue, one of the hottest-selling new cheeses in California. Finally, Mary Kheen makes the award-winning Humboldt Fog, a cheese named after the weather in her region of Northern California near the Oregon border.

California. King Kamehameha (1748/1761–1819) initially placed a taboo on slaughtering cattle, but their numbers increased so dramatically that by 1830 he removed the ban.

Pig, poultry, and lamb are all also raised in the region, but to a much lesser extent than cattle. The pig in Hawai'i is in fact a somewhat "wild" food source. Asian species introduced to the islands by the first Polynesians and later European species brought by explorer Captain James Cook (1728–1779) have both "gone wild" in the woods, multiplying so fast that they are now a major problem to farmers as they destroy crops. Although pork is a staple of the Hawaiian diet, wild pigs are not hunted in large enough numbers to control the population. Domesticated pig farming peaked during the gold rush years with exports to feed California but has declined ever since.

The most profitable animal-related agriculture in the Pacific Region, however, is dairy farming. California's number-one moneymaker is milk and dairy. It leads the nation in milk (both cow and goat) production, as well as butter and ice cream. California's cheese production is a close second to Wisconsin, but due to rapid growth, it is expected to take the number-one spot within a few years. The popular Monterey Jack cheese is a California invention, based on a type of soft cheese produced in the California missions more than 200 years ago. Oregon is also famous for its cheese and milk products, especially that produced in the Tillamook region. Cheese makers making specialty artisanal cheeses are continuing to crop up in small-scale operations across the region.

Crops

Although connected by the Pacific Ocean, the region stretches from the coldest climes of Alaska to the desert suns of Southern California and the tropical humidity of Hawai'i. As a result, vastly different crop industries are found throughout the region.

California has the largest amount of cultivated farmland of the region, while Hawai'i has the least, its volcanic and mountainous terrain leaving only 7 percent arable lands. The huge farming industry of California is its real gold: the state has the biggest agricultural production in the entire United States, earning more in *one year* from agriculture than the total earnings made from gold mining since 1848. California agriculture produces more than 350 types of crops and grows more than half of the nation's total fruits, nuts, and vegetables. California farms are responsible for nearly all of the nation's olive oil, almonds, artichokes, dates, figs, raisins/grapes, kiwis, nectarines, olives, peaches, persimmons, pistachios, plums, and walnuts. Production is so large that domestic markets are insufficient: In 2003 more than 14 percent of California's crops were exported all over the globe. Canada, the European Union, Mexico, Japan, China, and South Korea are the top recipients of California foods. The coastal Salinas Valley is nicknamed the "Salad Bowl of the Nation," with more than 75 percent of the state's total production of salad greens. In addition, its fertile soils and temperate weather are amenable to a variety of vegetable crops such as artichokes and garlic, spawning huge industries and two of the most famous food festivals in the Pacific Region, the Gilroy Garlic Festival and the Castroville Artichoke Festival, attended by hundreds of thousands of people every year.

The Pacific Region

Garlic Kisses vendor at the Gilroy Garlic Festival, 1993. © Catherine Karnow/Corbis.

Number Ones in Agriculture for California

California leads the nation in a number of crop and livestock commodities. It is particularly high in production of milk, with an average dairy size of 700 cows, compared to the national average of 100. The milk production per cow in California dairies is also 16 percent higher than the national average. The table below lists some of the crop and livestock number ones for California. Items in bold denote commodities of which California is the sole producer in the United States.

Almonds	Garlic	Pears: Bartlett
Apricots	Grapes: **raisins**,	Peas: Chinese
Artichokes	table, wine	Peppers: bell
Asparagus	Herbs	Persimmons
Avocados	Kale	Pigeon and squab
Beans: black-eyed,	**Kiwi**	**Pistachios**
lima, garbanzo	Lemons	Plums: fresh, **dried**
Broccoli	Lettuce: head, leaf,	Pomegranates
Cabbage	romaine	Rabbit
Carrots	Melons	Rice, sweet
Cauliflower	Milk: cow and goat	Spinach
Celery	**Nectarines**	Strawberries
Chicory	**Olives**	Tomatoes,
Currants	Onions	processing
Dates	Parsley	Greenhouse vegetables
Endive	Peaches: **Clingstone**	Oriental vegetables
Figs	and Freestone	**Walnuts**

242

California's agricultural core, however, is the Great Central Valley, which contains some 15 million acres of farmland, one-sixth of all the irrigated farmland in the United States. Tucked lengthwise between the coast and Sierra Nevada mountain ranges, the long and skinny valley extends nearly 500 miles, yet in most areas it is only about 45 miles across. Crucial to the valley's success as an agricultural region is its rich soil, mainly due to its alluvial geology—it drains two major rivers, the Sacramento in the northern part and the San Joaquin in the south. In addition, a deep channel from the San Francisco Bay Area to the Delta allows tankers and ocean vessels to access ports as far inland as Stockton and carry production from the valley all over the world. Adding to the amenable conditions is the temperate climate that provides crops an extremely long growing season: typically it is freeze-free for 225 to 300 days out of the year. The Native

The Flavr Savr Tomato

The Flavr Savr tomato was a variety of tomato engineered by Calgene, a Sacramento-area biotech company that researches ways to tinker with crops' genetic codes in order to improve pest resistance and flavor retention. In the early 1990s scientists there found a way to alter tomato genes to allow tomatoes to soften more slowly. Ripe tomatoes undergo this softening process rapidly, and this makes them difficult to transport without losses. To account for this, tomatoes were picked weeks ahead of ripening and "ripened" artifically using ethylene gas. With the new "hardness gene" the Flavr Savr tomato could be left on the vine longer and develop more flavor before picking. However, the Flavr Savr, renamed the "MacGregor," was not to be: Pushes for its introduction to consumer markets before it was ready, and noisy protests by antibiotech consumer groups (the latter of which resulted in big businesses like Campbell's Soup rejecting the tomatoes for use in their products) ultimately led to the tomato's demise. The tomato variety was last harvested in 1997, and Calgene lost millions as a result. In her book *First Fruit*, Belinda Martineau chronicles the discovery of the Flavr Savr and its impact on agriculture.[2]

Americans grew the first crops here, but larger-scale farming began with agrarian settlers in the region in the 1800s who established small vegetable farms that became well known for lettuces and asparagus and orchards of fruit, especially apples, plums, pears, grapes, apricots, strawberries, oranges, and avocados. In Southern California, orange and citrus groves thrived in the sunshine, and today California produces more than 160 varieties of citrus fruits and is particularly well known for navel and Valencia. In the early part of the twentieth century, nut farming became widespread in the northern Central Valley near Sacramento and Modesto, with almond, pecan, and walnut farms dotting the region. The valley also supports extensive grain farming, especially wheat and rice, the latter being introduced into the Sacramento area in the early 1900s.

The enormous agricultural output of the Central Valley is due to the past 100 years of agricultural innovation, particularly in the development of new crop varieties that began with agricultural scientist Luther Burbank (1849–1926) in the late 1800s. University agricultural researchers used Burbank's work to develop new disease-resistant fruits and vegetables (of particular fame is the Flavr Savr tomato). Large farm machinery helped to make farmwork more efficient. The Caterpillar tractor, invented by Benjamin Holt (1849–1920) in the Stockton area in the early 1900s, was the first to be designed with wide tracks rather than wheels, making farming possible on the moist, soft earth of the Valley Delta areas. The Caterpillar track method revolutionized not only tractors but also other earthmoving machinery and was even applied to tanks used in World War I. Finally, dramatic increases in agricultural production occurred in the early twentieth century with large irrigation water projects that diverted fresh water and pumped groundwater to transform previously arid valley lands into arable farmland. The huge influx of water, largely subsidized by the taxpayers, supported the growth of crops unsuited to the hot, dry conditions of the valley, and an inefficient "flooding" style of irrigation became heavily used.

Pesticides in Food

Increases in pesticides and herbicide development, as well as the invention of equipment to spray them, allowed farmers to plant larger fields of single crops and made larger farms possible. Between 1950 and 1970, the average size of farms in California more than doubled, from 260 to 560 acres. During this same time, the number of single-person-owned farms decreased by half, as large corporations entered the farming business. A cycle began where increases in food production drove down prices, which led to further support of technologies to improve yields yet again. Water policies also led to destructive environmental practices. The plentiful water to farmers supported their increased practice of utilizing a wasteful "flood-irrigate" technique, which over time has not only built up the salinity of the soil but has also concentrated agricultural chemicals and natural toxins in topsoil. Removal of this agricultural waste is now one of the most problematic and expensive issues for current farmers.

A critical outcry against these types of practices used by California farmers gained momentum in the 1960s and 1970s as environmentalists such as Rachel Carson (1907–1964), through books like her *Silent Spring* (1962), brought to the public's attention the harmful effects of pesticides and large-scale farming on the environment. Labor activists like César Chávez (1927–1993) and Dolores Huerta (b. 1930) additionally publicized the negative effects of these practices on the people who worked the land. The large farms of California (and historically the Hawaiian plantations) were made possible and profitable by an enormous pool of cheap labor from Japan, China, and the Philippines during the 1800s and early 1900s. Mexican labor has been particularly crucial in California, beginning en masse in 1918 and continuing through to World War II and the Bracero Program. During those years Mexican workers were brought into the country to alleviate labor shortages caused by the wars. Workers had few rights or wages for often backbreaking work that included significant exposure to the increasing use of pesticides and fungicides. These unfair working conditions spawned one of the most famous labor movements in history, the United Farm Workers (UFW) which blossomed in the 1960s and 1970s. Led by Chávez and Huerta, UFW's strength was its unity of farmworkers with students and politicians, as well as its use of peaceful strike methods such as hunger fasts. The most famous of their efforts was the Delano Grape Strike in 1965, during which 5,000 Filipino and Mexican farmworkers walked off the job, gaining them the first health and benefit plans for farmworkers in history. Subsequent strikes and campaigning by the UFW in the 1970s and 1980s led to the largest consumer boycott ever—more than 14 million Americans supported a boycott of California grapes and table wines. The combined effort led to the passing of the Agricultural Labor Relations Act in 1975, the first law to allow farmworkers the right to organize and bargain for better rights and working conditions. Today, however, conditions remain poor for agricultural workers, and the right to better working conditions is a continual struggle for the floods of Mexican, Central American, and Asian Indian migrant workers who work as seasonal labor in the Central Valley.

Farms of the Pacific Northwest also have made considerable contributions to agriculture. Agricultural output, however, is significantly less here than in California, since the varied lands—ranging from prairie grasslands and rugged mountain terrain to temperate, rainy coasts—make smaller farms and specialty products suited for a less sunny climate more profitable in this region. Although farmlands are smaller, there are bigger payoffs per acre for apples, pears, grapes, and berries grown in the Pacific Northwest than in California. The cold and rainy climates are ideal growing conditions for fruits, particularly apples and cherries. The Pacific Northwest is the number-one producer of both of these products in the United States and also produces 100 percent of the U.S. crops of specialty berries (loganberries, raspberries) and hazelnuts. The marionberry is a Pacific Northwest invention: a cross between the wild blackberry, loganberry, and the raspberry. The Pacific Northwest farms promote the "premium" quality of their berries and obtain high values in niche markets such as Japan and Canada. Therefore, substantial portions of these specialty foods are not consumed domestically but are exported. Other unique foods that have become trademarks of the Pacific Northwest region are the yellow and red mottled Rainier cherries and sweet onions from the Walla Walla area.

Rainier Cherries

The Rainier cherry is named after the highest point in the Pacific Northwest's Cascade Range, Mt. Rainier. Dr. Harold W. Fogle at the Washington State University Research Station in Prosser, Washington, created the Rainier cherry in 1952 by crossbreeding the sweet Bing and Van cherry varieties. The Rainier is a delicate, light-colored cherry and is expensive since it cannot be transported far from harvest, and is generally available only on the West Coast. Dark brown discolorations are an indicator of sweetness.

Incidentally, the Bing cherry also originated in the Pacific Northwest: one of the first cherry farms, Lewelling Farms, became known for its sweet cherries, with orchards coming into production during the 1870s and 1880s. The extremely sweet red Bing was named after a Chinese worker on the farm. Oregon and Washington are responsible for about 60 percent of the total U.S. sweet cherry crop.

Specialty Crops in Alaska and Hawai'i

Alaska and Hawai'i represent two extremes of climate within not only the Pacific Region but also the United States. Despite their extremes, they have something in common: both states have small amounts of arable farmland—due to three mountain ranges in Alaska and the small land mass of the Hawaiian islands, making both populations challenged to produce food for local consumption in order to keep their food import costs low.

Hawaii's land mass might be small, but agriculture there is a vastly profitable enterprise. As food authors Waverly Root and Richard De Rochemont posited in their historical account of American food, *Eating in America*, "Hawai'i is probably the only state that entered the Union primarily because of food."[3] Hawaii's arable farmland exists only near the coast, but it has been put to good use; conditions are ideal for valuable tropical crops such as pineapple, sugar cane, coffee, ginger, and taro, as well as fruits such as starfruit, guava, papaya, banana, and avocado. Hawai'i produces 100 percent of the domestic U.S. crop of macadamia nuts and pineapple, and it is the only state still growing coffee, famous for its Kona variety (originally from Guatemala). Most of these crops were introduced from other tropical regions, brought by Polynesian, Asian, and European explorers as well as immigrants from Asia. During the 1800s, plantations of sugar cane, pineapple, rice, and coffee boomed, bringing in immigrant labor as well as processing industries. The introduction of canning on Hawai'i made it possible to export food goods more cheaply. This advent reduced the impact of the quarantine imposed after 1910 on all fresh imports from and exports to the mainland due to fear of agricultural exposure to the Mediterranean fruit fly.

Sugar cane, or "King Cane" as it was called, and the pineapple industry were particularly instrumental to Hawai'i's agricultural economy. In the 1960s, during the industries' peak output, Hawai'i processed over 80 percent of the world's canned pineapple and exported over 1 million tons of sugar per year. However, in the last twenty years, rising costs and development of these industries in other countries have ended the twin grip of sugar and pineapple on Hawai'i. Although both sugar cane and pineapple are still grown, most large canneries and processing plants on the islands have closed. The closures, however, have opened up possibilities for a more diverse agriculture. Local farmers are taking the opportunity to experiment with growing industries such as organic crops and ethnic vegetables such as daikon and ginger for niche markets in Hawai'i and worldwide. In addition, the recent development of postharvest technologies such as irradiation has created hope of sending more fresh fruit and vegetable exports from Hawai'i to the mainland without fear of pest contamination.

In a vastly different climate than Hawai'i's, Alaska's agricultural production is affected by its weather and its geography. The largest growing valley is the Matanuska near Anchorage, which contains nearly one-half of the state's arable farmland. Due to its northern location, the growing season is extremely short. However, Alaska has longer-than-normal daylight hours in the summer months, and these conditions produce larger vegetables. Stories of seventy-pound cabbages and four-foot-high rhubarb abound. Alaskans also believe their vegetables taste better, a claim supported by these unique growing conditions: Although the extreme sunlight during the summer accelerates growth, the lower average temperature decreases the plants' respiration rates, and sugars and flavors are stored in the plant for a longer period. American immigrants to the region during the gold rush started a substantial wheat agriculture (using a hardy variety from Siberia), as well as oats, rye, and barley. Prohibitive transportation costs for fresh foods from the lower forty-eight states have increased interest in attempting to farm more foods for regional use.

Land-use policies in Alaska and Hawai'i have created tensions in both states. In Alaska, much of the land has been protected in federal wildlife preserves, preventing agriculture and ranching development and restricting big game hunting. Hawai'i's agricultural space is being threatened by the development of resorts for the tourist industry, and the urban population continually competes for agricultural water resources. The future of agriculture in both of these regions is dependent on its ability to coexist with population growth that threatens to pave over farmlands and with environmental preservation issues.

Wine, Beer, and Coffee

No discussion of Pacific regional foods would be complete without a discussion of wine and beer, two of the region's most famous food-related exports. The region is home to the "big 3"—that is, the states with the largest wine-making industries in the United States, namely, California, Washington, and Oregon. The region's wine production is supported by the large grape-growing industry. California alone produces more than 90 percent of the nation's table grapes and raisins as well as wine grapes. Although wines made in California's Napa and Sonoma Valley regions are the most well known, most California grapes are actually grown in the Central Valley. Fresno County alone produces more than 5 percent of the entire world output of grapes.

California leads the region and the nation in wine making and is responsible for three out of every four bottles produced in the United States Wines from California range in quality and quantity from the small vineyards in the Napa and Sonoma regions that are competitive with the French wine industry in quality to the lesser-quality table wines manufactured by larger companies based in the Central Valley.

Grape growing began in the Napa and Sonoma Valleys around 1770 with Franciscan missionaries, who were responsible for the majority of wine making in the state until the gold rush eighty years later. The population explosion due to the gold rush quickly expanded vineyard plantings around the San Francisco Bay Area, and the first traditional European grape cuttings of classic wine varieties *Vitis vinifera* were planted. Historians hypothesize the great demand for wine during this time was due in large part to the fact that gold rushers were mainly single and male. The wine industry grew steadily throughout the twentieth century, espe-

A vineyard in Sonoma Valley. Courtesy of Getty Images/PhotoDisc.

Viticulture Research at UC Davis

The Department of Viticulture and Enology at the University of California at Davis (UC Davis) has played a major role in developing viticulture methods that have made the California wine industry a world leader. The program began in 1880 at Berkeley and moved to Davis in 1935. Research focused on identifying ideal growing conditions and vineyard practices that would allow defect-free wines to be produced reliably year after year. More recent research has focused on how vineyard practices impact grape characteristics and wine character. Wine researchers hope to be able to someday produce wines "tailored" to individual tastes, with desired flavor and aroma profiles. The sensory evaluation of wine is one of UC Davis' specialties: In 1984, Dr. Ann Noble developed the wine "aroma wheel," which contains a standardized vocabulary to describe wines, used now throughout the wine industry.

cially in the past thirty years as more U.S. consumers have taken up wine drinking. The lack of viticulture (the science of grape growing) traditions, combined with scientific research begun at the University of California in the late 1800s, has cultivated an aggressive and innovative industry where engineering, science, and biology have created entirely new varieties and a wine culture unlike that of Europe. Wine making in the Pacific Region can be more influenced by people and method than place. The so-called cult wines made by California wine makers currently in fashion are collected by wealthy connoisseurs of wine and can fetch higher prices than even first-growth Bordeaux wines from France.

Washington and Oregon have substantial wine industries of their own. Their cooler climate is ideal for white grapes such as Riesling and Chardonnay, which are unsuited for the sunnier California weather. Both states focus on producing smaller yields of finer quality grapes and wines in order to compete with the sheer volume of California's wine industry. The Yakima Valley and Walla Walla Valleys are the most important wine-producing regions in Washington. Oregon trails Washington in wine production, but was vaulted to fame in 1979 when a Pinot Noir from Eyrie Vineyard placed a surprise second in a world wine competition. Oregon's largest wine region is in the Willamette Valley.

Beer is an additional important food product of the region. Washington and Oregon are the largest hop growers in the United States, and in 2001, Washington produced some 76 percent of the U.S. total production of hops. Like its wine industry, emphasis is placed on producing unusual "microbrewed" beers that have smaller output but yield higher prices. The region is therefore host to some of the most well-known microbreweries in the United States, such as Northern California's Anchor Steam and Sierra Nevada, Washington's Red Hook and Pyramid Breweries, and Oregon's Descutes and Bridgeport Brewing Companies. Alaska has lagged behind in beer brewing due to a territory law in the 1800s that banned alcoholic production. The Klondike gold rush in the early 1900s, however, established several breweries, but prohibition and transportation issues made it difficult for them to survive. Currently the leader in Alaskan beer is the Alaskan Brewing Company in Juneau, which produces several popular ales. Hawai'i's largest microbrewery, Kona Brewing Company, is enjoying success both on the islands and in Southern California, where it exports several of its most popular ales. The microbrewing industry there is small, however, and other operations have folded recently due to rising costs of exporting and production.

The Pacific Northwest is viewed as the hub of coffee drinking society in America. A coffee revolution occurred there beginning in the 1970s with the inception of coffee shops, modeled after Italian espresso bars, near major universities and in urban areas such as Seattle and Portland. Starbucks Coffee Company began in 1971 and operated out of a stall at Pikes Place Market until 1984 when founder Harold Schultz began expanding the chain. Starbucks now has close to 2,000 outlets worldwide, but many Pacific Northwest residents prefer independent coffee chains to Starbucks' commercial and sanitized atmosphere, and the coffee competition continues to thrive.

NATIVE AND ETHNIC CUISINES

The Pacific Region, which includes five states with diverse topographies and ecologies, might also be said to include at least four miniregions: The Northwest (Alaska, Oregon, Washington), The Tropical West (Hawai'i), The Coastal Desert (Southern California), and the Western Heartland (Northern California). However, the links between these seemingly disparate entities—particularly the Pacific Ocean as a trade route and source of foodstuffs, the abundance of rich agricultural lands, and the availability of natural resources for socioeconomic gain—have served to attract peoples from around the world and across the nation to settle and make the region home.

The Pacific Region has a population of over 46 million persons, with about 75 percent of them located in California—the second largest land mass and the most populated state in the United States. California and Hawai'i have the most racial-ethnic diversity, with significant numbers of people of Asian, Pacific Islander, or multiracial descent and less significant numbers of African Americans. While the numbers of indigenous peoples are low, there are significant pockets of Alaskan Natives and American Indians in Alaska and Polynesian natives in Hawai'i. The region also includes over 12 million people of Latino/Hispanic origin, more than 90 percent of whom live in California. The majority of the population in the region (over 75 percent) descended from early American settlers and past and recent immigrants from various European countries (e.g., Britain, France, Greece, Italy, Russia). In various ways, each of these groups has made and continues to make important contributions to the region's food cultures. Given the racial/ethnic and geographic diversity of the region, there is no one cuisine that defines it.

Native American—The Original Pacific Regional Cuisine

Contrary to *The Prudence Penny Regional Cook Book*'s claim that "when the far West was settled . . . there were practically no native food products,"[4] the precontact diet of natives in this region varied depending on their location. Indigenous peoples in the coastal and mountainous areas of California, Oregon, and Washington (e.g., Shoshone) had access to a particularly rich array of foodstuffs, allowing them to eat widely from a variety of food groups: seafood (abalone, clams, fish, mussels), fruits and berries (blackberries, blueberries, buffalo berries, groundcherries, cactus fruit), wild greens (cattail, clover, pokeweed, watercress) and vegetables (cacti, fiddleheads, mushrooms, Jerusalem artichokes), wild game and other meats (duck, grouse, turkey, buffalo, deer, rabbit), nuts (acorn meal, piñon nuts, pumpkin seeds), and natural sweeteners (honey, maple syrup). Fresh salmon was often roasted over an open fire or smoked for later consumption. Fish was also steamed in a pit. While animal protein was abundant, a large portion of the diet

Indian dancers at Potlatch, Chilkat, Alaska, 1895. Courtesy of the Library of Congress.

consisted of wild plants, indigenous fruits, and vegetables. Roots were roasted or baked, and fresh wild greens were eaten. In central California, an acorn-based diet was common.

The diet of indigenous peoples living in Alaska and northwest Washington (Inuits/ Eskimos, Aleuts, Tlingit, for example), on the other hand, was more limited in its variety. Fish and sea mammals (whales, seals, walrus) were the primary foodstuffs. Other game and meats (ducks, geese, mountain goats, polar bears) were available on occasion. Two dishes have frequently been associated with traditional Alaskan Native cuisine: *muktuk* and *kopalchen*. *Muktuk* is a frozen chunk of meat (either whale or walrus) with the fat and skin attached, while *kopalchen* is prepared by rolling the *muktuk* in herbs and fermenting it in a pit for a lengthy period of time. Mammal fat is highly prized; blubber is a key component in the preservation of meats, greens, and berries. While native groups in California, Oregon, and Washington cooked their foodstuffs, Alaskan Natives were more likely to consume their food raw due to unreliable fuel sources. Even though food sources were sometimes scarce, extravagant feasts called potlatches were typical among Arctic populations.

Traditional Native American cuisines reflect the diversity of the ethnic/tribal groups located throughout the region.

Potlatch in Alaska

Potlatches, or feasts, are important ceremonies that mark an event or stage of life among Alaskan and other Arctic Native American groups. The potlatch may be held for an individual person but usually includes the entire village. The host of the potlatch generally gives food and other gifts to guests, in a quantity intended to "overwhelm" the guest. These extensive quantities can sometimes be competitive between villages, with each village attempting to outdo the other with extravagance. Potlatches usually feature traditional foods, especially game such as moose, as well as salmon and plant foods such as berries. A salmon potlatch is commonly held after the first salmon catch in the spring.

The cooking/food preparation emphasized local ingredients and great care was paid to preserve foods for consumption during periods of scarcity. The indigenous peoples' knowledge of the land and its resources became an invaluable resource for white explorers and settlers from other parts of the Americas and Europe. Con-

Recipes for Typical Russian Dishes
Buckwheat Kasha
(from *Vegetarian Cooking for Everyone* by Deborah Madison)

1 c. kasha
1 egg
½ tsp. salt
pinch pepper
1½ c. boiling water
1 T. butter

In saucepan, combine kasha, egg, salt, and pepper; cook over medium-low heat, stirring, for 3 minutes or until dry and kernels separate. Stir in water and butter; cover and cook, without stirring, for 10–12 minutes or until water is absorbed. Fluff kasha with fork. Makes 1½ cups, or 2 servings.

Yukon Gold Potato Blini Recipe
(from *The French Laundry Cookbook* by Thomas Keller)

1 pound Yukon Gold potatoes
2 T. all-purpose flour
2 to 3 T. crème fraîche, at room temperature
2 large eggs
1 large egg yolk
Kosher salt and freshly ground white pepper

Place the potatoes in a saucepan with cold water to cover by at least 2 inches. Bring to a boil over high heat, reduce the heat, and simmer until the potatoes are thoroughly cooked and tender. Peel the warm potatoes and press them through a tamis. Immediately weigh out 9 ounces of pureed potatoes and place them in a medium metal bowl. Working quickly, whisk the flour into the warm potatoes, then whisk in 2 tablespoons crème fraîche. Add 1 egg, whisking until the batter is smooth, add the second egg, and then add the yolk. Hold the whisk with some of the batter over the bowl. The batter should fall in a thick stream but hold its shape when it hits the batter in the bowl. If it is too thick, add a little more or crème fraîche. Season to taste with salt and white pepper.

Heat an electric griddle to 350 degrees F. Note, if you do not have a griddle, heat a large nonstick skillet over medium-low heat. Spoon between 1 and 1½ teaspoons of batter onto the griddle or skillet for each pancake. Cook until the bottoms are browned, 1 to 2 minutes. Then flip them to cook the second side, about 1 minute. The blini should be evenly browned with a small ring of white around the edges. Transfer the blini to a small baking sheet and keep warm while you make the remaining blini, wiping the skillet with a paper towel between batches. Serve the blini as soon as possible. Makes about 3 dozen.

tact with the American and European settlers, however, did not bode well for the indigenous peoples. Like the plants and the animals on which they subsisted, many tribal/ethnic groups have disappeared. Others have been separated from their lands of origin and their traditional cultural practices. The forced movement of indigenous peoples to reservations and away from their traditional lands has had a profoundly negative impact on the health and diet of Native Americans today. However, the incursion of whites into the Pacific Region, also heralded the beginnings of a differently complex multicultural society which has drawn not just upon Europe, but also from Asia, the Pacific Islands, and Latin America.

White American and European Settlers

In the 1700s, 1800s, and early 1900s whites arrived in the region from various directions. Russian seal hunters established the first permanent settlement in Russian America (now Alaska) on Kodiak Island in the late 1700s. Although wheat was introduced and became a staple of the area, the hunters continued journeying southward in search of an environment to support food crops that would supply the Russian colony and the fur trade. After Russia sold Alaska to the United States in 1867, many established permanent settlements in Northern California. They brought with them a hearty food culture rich in the use of whole grains (particularly buckwheat), potatoes, cabbage, and fish.

The promise of land in the frontier West and the discovery of gold in California's Mother Lode (1848) and the Alaskan Klondike (in 1896) propelled hundreds of thousands of Americans from New England, the South, and the Plains states into the Pacific Region. Those on the Oregon Trail were more likely to be families seeking to homestead in the "new" frontier. These pioneers were primarily farmers of English, Dutch, German, and Scandinavian descent. They settled in Oregon and Washington, though some "turned left" and headed into California in search of gold. In both Oregon and Washington, the homesteaders became small farmers and adapted their ethnic cuisines to the local foodstuffs available. Traces of their ethnic origins remain in some of Oregon's food culture. In both states, fresh local seafood and game, newly cultivated fruits (apples, pears, cherries, and berries), nuts (particularly the hazelnut in Oregon), and vegetables (onions, asparagus, and corn) figure prominently in Northwestern cuisine.

Unlike the homesteaders, gold prospectors were usually single men. Immigrants from northern Italy, Portugal, and Britain (particularly the Cornish) made their way to California to search for gold. The miners subsisted on foods that were easily prepared and transported. While working the gold mines, their

Walla Walla and Maui Onions: Sweet Onions from the Pacific West

Walla Walla Sweet Onions originally came to America from Corsica at the beginning of the twentieth century. Approximately forty growers today cultivate the "onions with no bite" on about 1,200 acres. The town of Walla Walla additionally hosts a yearly Walla Walla Sweet Onion Festival (at Ft. Walla Walla in July) and Walla Walla Sweet Onion History Museum. A similar onion is also grown in Maui, Hawai'i. These have a yellowish color and flattened globe shape and are usually sold in West Coast markets from April to June. It is thought that the volcanic soil contributes to their sweetness. Ideas for cooking with these sweet onions can be found in the *Maui Onion Cookbook* by Barbara Santos.[5]

diets often consisted of breads either un-leavened or made with a sourdough cul-ture, beans with salt pork for seasoning, and coffee. It is thought that some min-ers, particularly in Alaska, hunted game to supplement their diet. In California, however, mining in and around the Central Valley and in "Gold Country" created a culture of hospitality due to the miner's reliance on boarding houses, hotels, and restaurants for meals and lodging. In fact, in the early days of the gold rush, Hawai'i was a center for sup-plying food for the gold miners—in particular, Irish potatoes grown in the mountainous regions of Hawai'i were sold to the forty-niners in California. Hawai'i also served as a site for recre-ation for California miners during the winter months. However, by the late 1850s San Francisco was already on the verge of becoming a cosmopolitan city. Other immigrant groups, especially Southern Italians, Greeks, and Japa-nese, fostered a rich restaurant culture in the San Francisco Bay area and in-troduced/created dishes like cioppino and fried calamari that we now associ-ate with the area. Even French chefs went to San Francisco to cook for those made newly rich by gold.

Foodways of the Asian Diaspora

Native Polynesians from the Mar-quesa Islands and Tahiti had already set-tled the islands that came to be known

"Sourdoughs" and Sourdough Bread

Sourdough bread gets its name from the sour taste im-parted by a lump of dough allowed to ferment and turn "sour." This method is used all over the world, as cooks save a bit of dough for the next day's starter, but the term *sourdough* seemed to stick in California and became well used as a way of making bread (as well as other bread prod-ucts such as biscuits and pancakes) during the gold rush era and even became the nickname for Alaskan miners themselves. San Francisco is now world renowned for making sourdough bread, but sourdough starter is possible to make anywhere there is wild yeast, which will impart its own special local flavor to the bread.

Sourdough Starter (from *Bon Appetit*, November 1993)

4 medium russet potatoes, peeled
4½ cups water
1 cup unbleached all-purpose flour
1½ teaspoons sugar
½ teaspoon salt

Combine potatoes and 4½ cups water in pot. Cover and boil until potatoes are tender, about 35 minutes. Drain cooking liquid into measuring cup. Transfer 1¼ cups liq-uid to large ceramic or glass bowl. Add flour, sugar, and salt to bowl; stir to combine. Cover bowl with cheesecloth and let stand at room temperature until starter begins to ferment and bubble, about 4 days. Transfer to covered plastic container; store in refrigerator. To freshen starter, every 2 weeks discard all but 1 cup. Mix 1 cup each flour and warm water into remaining mixture. Cover with plas-tic; let stand at room temperature overnight. Replace lid and return to refrigerator.

Use starter as part of "yeast" requirement in any bread recipe.

as Hawai'i by the time British explorer James Cook landed there in 1778. Ameri-can missionaries from New England were not far behind. Indigenous foodstuffs on the islands prior to the arrival of the Pacific Islanders were quite minimal. Hawai-ian culinary expert Rachel Laudan asserts that there was primarily fish, shellfish, birds, and ferns but no edible carbohydrates on the islands.[6] The Pacific Islanders who settled the area and are now referred to as Native Hawaiians brought with them over twenty-five edible plants and domesticated dogs and pigs for consump-tion. The most important plant products were taro, sweet potato, breadfruit, yams, sugar cane, and coconut. Poi—made by roasting taro and sometimes sweet potato

"Hangtown Fry"

Hangtown Fry consists of fried breaded oysters, eggs, and fried bacon, cooked together like an omelet or scramble. There is some controversy over its origins, although it is generally agreed that it originated in the Placerville area, a gold rush town in California nicknamed "Hangtown" after several criminals were hanged there in one day. Some say Hangtown Fry was a one-skillet meal for hungry miners who struck it rich and had plenty of gold to spend, since a meal featuring an expensive item such as oysters would have cost approximately $6.00, a fortune in those days. Others claim it was the last request of a man about to be hanged. Still others say it is simply a one-pot meal made up of the only foodstuffs left in the restaurant. However it came to be, ordering a Hangtown Fry became a mark of prosperity for gold-rich miners, and the recipe became known throughout the Northwest Territory, from California to Seattle, in the mid-1800s. Hangtown Fry is still the official dish of both the city of Placerville and the county of El Dorado, California.

in an earth oven or *imu*, pounding it with a stone on a wooden board, and mixing it with water to form a paste—is a staple of the diet. Fish was consumed raw, cooked, or dried/salted, and the diet was rounded out with seaweed and groundnuts of the candlenut tree. European settlers and explorers brought many foods now considered to be Hawaiian, particularly pineapple, mangos, and coffee. They also introduced domesticated cows, horses, and goats.

Two parallel cuisines developed: Hawaiian food associated with the Polynesians and *haole* food associated with the white settlers from New England. The introduction of large-scale sugar cane plantations in the late 1800s brought with it substantial numbers of laborers, primarily Chinese, Japanese, Koreans, Portuguese, Asian Indians, and Filipinos. Hawaiian cuisine, like much of the region's food culture, is a "salad bowl" rather than a "melting pot": the various ethnic groups who populate the islands contribute particular dishes to the culinary landscape, adapting their own cooking styles to the ingredients that could be found locally as well as bringing some of their indigenous foodstuffs with them. For instance, Portuguese sweetbread, known as "Hawaiian Bread," and *malasadas*— fried sweetbreads filled with sweetened and flavored creams, nuts, even poi—are commonly eaten by all Hawaiians. Chinese, Japanese, Korean, and Filipino immigrants brought with them *dim sum*, lotus root, ginger, *sashimi* (raw, thinly sliced fish), teriyaki-grilled meats and fish, *kimchi* (hot pickled cabbage relish), and *lumpia* (Filipino egg rolls). Each impacted the Hawaiian culinary landscape and signified the centrality of a pan-Asian cuisine throughout the Pacific Region.

In fact, the region is home to over 5 million persons of Asian descent. This is nearly half of the total number of Asians in the U.S. population. The majority of the Asians in the Pacific Region live in Hawai'i (about half a million) and California (over 4 million), but significant numbers are in Washington (over 300,000) and Oregon (over 100,000). The first significant immigration of Asians to the U.S. mainland were the Chinese who joined the gold rush to California in the early 1850s. This largely male population worked in the mines, but they also opened businesses (particularly restaurants, laundries, and import-export shops to provide goods

Cioppino

Cioppino is an Italian American invention, based perhaps on a fish stew called *ciupin*, a mariner's fish soup from Genoa. The Californian cioppino features fishes found in Pacific waters and generally includes tomatoes, green peppers, and herbs, although each restaurant and cook has their own "secret recipe" such as using jalapeño peppers or adding brown sugar to the tomatoes to remove the acidity.

and services for other Chinese immigrants) or were fishermen, farmers (working primarily in the cultivation of sugar beets), and railroad workers (laying the western half of the first transcontinental railroad). The import-export shops played a key role in making available Chinese foodstuffs (rice, noodles, bamboo shoots, dried shrimp, salted fish, dried bean curd) to the immigrant population. Chinese farmers and fishermen supplied them with fresh fruits, vegetables, and fish and other meats. Due to racial discrimination and exclusion laws, most Chinese immigrants lived in what became known as "Chinatowns" in San Francisco, Oakland, and later Los Angeles. Due to the poor living conditions in the China-

Hawaiian Luau

The luau is a traditional Hawaiian feast generally used to display hospitality. While feasting is a common occurrence in Polynesian society, the *luau* is a modern term that became widely used by European traders and sailors in the 1820s to describe the feasts put on by their hosts. The name *luau* refers to the luau leaves, the green tops from the taro plant that are usually served at the feast. Dishes served at a luau generally include a kalua pig, taro, poke, squid, shrimp, crab, and seaweed. Most of the food is served in large serving bowls, sometimes in a hollowed-out coconut, and is meant to be eaten with the hands. King Kamehameha, the ruler of the Hawaiian islands from 1758 to 1819, was known to hold luau-type celebrations for hundreds of people, lasting for weeks. Modern Hawaiians still hold luaus to celebrate important events in families and communities.

towns and the hostile environment outside them, the population of Chinese dwindled in the period between the mid-1800s and the mid-1900s. However, after the repeal of the Chinese exclusion laws in 1943, immigration of Chinese into the United States increased and was more likely to consist of families and couples. The Chinatowns remained the first point of contact for new immigrants into the United States until the latter part of the twentieth century.

Japanese migrated into the Pacific Region—again largely California and Hawai'i—in the late 1800s. They came to seek relief from the increasing taxation that fell primarily on Japanese farmers during the Meiji era. They were also enticed by the need for laborers in the United States, particularly after the Chinese Exclusion Act of 1882 served to interrupt the influx of Chinese-born laborers. Unlike the Chinese immigrants before them, however, Japanese immigrants maintained close ties with the Japanese government. Indeed, the Japanese government arranged the labor contracts for the Japanese immigrants into the region. They worked as fishermen and abalone divers, in the canneries of Monterey, on the railroads, and most important, became primary figures in agriculture. While the Chinese before them were largely unable to purchase land, the Japanese who began as farm laborers often became landowners. However, like the Chinese, the Japanese encountered intense anti-Asian sentiment that led to the passing of the Alien Land Law in 1913. The law, while not naming Japanese immigrants per se, prohibited the ownership of property in California to anyone not eligible for American citizenship. So because there were antinaturalization laws already on the books, Japanese and Chinese immigrants were heretofore barred from owning land in their own names. To circumvent this, some Japanese families registered the births of children born on United States soil and subsequently put land titles in their names. Throughout the early 1900s, Japanese farmers (as either owners or lessees) continued to dominate the region's agricultural industry—growing grapes, strawberries, tomatoes, onions, celery, and stonefruits. While primarily located in California, Japanese tenant farmers were also highly visible in Oregon and Washington. They also made significant contributions to the fishing, canning, and abalone diving industries. With the United States declaration of war on Japan after the bombing of Pearl Harbor in Hawai'i in 1941, Japanese immigrants and their American-born children living in the Pacific Region were removed from their homes and placed in "relocation camps." The camps were located throughout the Pacific Region (particularly in California) and parts of the West (Colorado, Idaho, Arizona). The rich food cultures of the Japanese were severely hampered in the living conditions at the camps. Those who survived internment to return to their homesteads within the region found them vandalized and dilapidated. However, many managed to pick up the pieces and continue to play a significant role in the region's agricultural and fishing industries.

In the postwar era, migration from Asia, Southeast Asia, and the Pacific Islands has created a vast panoply of Asian diasporic communities within the Pacific Region. Korean immigrants who in the early part of the twentieth century lived and worked primarily in Hawai'i have recently settled in Los Angeles, California, where there is an expansive Koreatown featuring Korean food shops (particularly barbecue) and other import-export businesses. There are also significant numbers of Koreans in Washington. Like the Koreans, early Filipino immigrants resided primarily in Hawai'i, but now over half the Filipino population in the United States lives in California, and smaller numbers can also be found in Washington. Cambodians, Thais, and other Southeast Asians have also found their way to California; the U.S. Hmong population resides largely in the rural communities of California's Central Valley. Three waves of Vietnamese migration in the 1970s have resulted in a substantial Vietnamese population in the region, perhaps a slight majority of all Vietnamese in the United States. Immigrants from Thailand make up a much smaller percentage of the Southeast Asian population; however, Thai cuisine is more widely known and consumed than either Vietnamese or Filipino cuisines in the mainland Pacific Region. It is perhaps the region's love of spice, first cultivated by the Hispanic/Latino cuisines, that has popularized what some characterize as the "hottest cuisine in the world," known for its lavish use of hot chili peppers and complex mixes of herbs and spices, like turmeric, cardamom, basil, cilantro, garlic, ginger, lemon grass, and tamarind.

A Return to Origins—Spanish/Latino Past and Present

The Spanish have a long history of settlement in parts of the Pacific Region. Spanish explorer Hernan Cortes subjugated the Aztecs (who had conquered the native Mayans) in the mid-sixteenth century, and Spain ruled Mexico until the early 1800s. After the Mexican-American War, Mexico ceded parts of what is now California to the United States. Consequently, the Spanish influence throughout California is pervasive. Of particular importance were the Spanish missions that were responsible for introducing many of the fruits and spices associated with Pacific Regional and California cuisines—for example, garlic, olives, grapes, tomatoes, figs, cinnamon, onions, and lemons. And the domestication of hogs added to the protein source formerly supplied primarily by cattle under the Mexican ranchero system. Corn, already a staple in the area, was supplemented by cultivated wheat. The missionaries also brought wine production to the region.

Once divided into two countries—California as part of the United States and

Mexico—the relationship between them has evolved primarily around the movement of Mexican laborers in and out of California. While those Mexicans who remained in the territories ceded to the United States became citizens and others who later migrated legally also became citizens, the use of Mexican *braceros* to work primarily in agriculture and on the railroads was rampant in the mid-1900s. The Bracero Program, where Mexican citizens were encouraged to become temporary workers in the United States, began as a way for the U.S. government to deal with its decision to forcibly "relocate" Japanese farmers to internment camps during World War II. The use of Mexican migrant labor increased in the post–World War II economy, particularly in the ever-expanding agricultural industry in the Pacific Region and specifically in California. Migrant farm laborers have occupied a status similar to that of Chinese immigrants before them—residing in culturally isolated rural and urban communities and maintaining a sojourner quality to their residence within the region. Given the nature of their lack of incorporation into the mainstream of the society, they had been more likely to have restaurants and other food shops that catered to their particular food preferences. But the influence of Mexican culture and cuisine on the Pacific Region has been felt in ways not easily documented. While many Mexican and Mexican Americans continue to work in the agricultural industry and many more are employed in the service industry, there has been a growth of middle- to upper-class Mexican Americans. Mexicans and Mexican Americans, working in food preparation in private homes and restaurants and using their ever-increasing visibility in the mainstream, have provided the environment in which an early fusion cuisine—Cal-Mex—originated.

At the same time, however, there has been an influx of new Latino immigrants from Central and South America and the Spanish-speaking Caribbean. More recent immigrants from Cuba, Colombia, Peru, Venezuela, Guatemala, El Salvador, and Nicaragua have made their way to the Pacific Region. Most significant are those immigrants from the Central American countries (Guatemala, El Salvador, Nicaragua) who have largely settled in the Pacific Region cities of Los Angeles and San Francisco. Like other immigrants, patterns of residence create pockets of particular ethnic groups within the larger metropolis. While the overall numbers of some of these individual groups in the Pacific Region may be small, taken in total the vast numbers of people of Mexican, Central and South American, and Caribbean descent have created, particularly in California, a culinary landscape similar to that of Hawai'i—such that in one day, one might partake of Mexican sweetbread for breakfast, a mid-morning snack of an El Salvadoran *pupusa* (a thick tortilla filled with pork, cheese, and/or black beans and deep fried), a lunch of small tacos with stewed *lengua* (cow tongue), chopped raw onions, cilantro and salsa fresca, accompanied by fresh radishes and cabbage and a tart *jamaica* beverage (sweetened punch made with hibiscus flowers), and a dinner of Cuban-inspired roasted chicken with lemon-marinated roasted onions and stewed black beans.

TWENTIETH-CENTURY CUISINES AND FOOD TRENDS

It is perhaps ironic that California was the birthplace of some of the most successful fast-food chains, since the region is most known for its use of fresh, local, and seasonal foodstuffs. In fact, the development of the late-twentieth-century American cuisine is due in large part to the innovations from chefs and food writ-

Fast Food in California

Southern California was the birthplace of one of the largest names in fast food: McDonald's. In San Bernardino the McDonalds brothers opened a single drive-in restaurant in the late 1930s: McDonalds Brothers Burger Bar Drive-In. Nearby, Carl Karcher in Anaheim ran a successful business "Carl's Drive-In Barbeque" that was later to become Carl's Jr. The rise of car culture and freeways made both businesses a raging success, particularly since the McDonalds brothers had perfected an assembly-line system of cooking and assembling many burgers at once that increased the speed of service; they called this the Speedee Service System. This new system meant labor was cheaper, which lowered prices. Ray Kroc took over the business and started the McDonald's system of franchising, dreaming of putting a McDonald's at every busy intersection. The success of McDonald's and Carl's Jr. inspired many other fast-food restaurants that had their beginnings in Southern California, especially Taco Bell and Jack in the Box, which are still around today. Interestingly, although California is arguably the birthplace of fast food, it is now one of the lowest fast-food-eating states.

ers from the Pacific Region. Formidable food personalities of the twentieth century such as James Beard (1903–1985), Julia Child (1912–2004), and M.F.K. Fisher (1908–1978) all spent considerable time on the West Coast and helped to popularize West Coast ingredients and styles of eating and cooking. Born and raised in Oregon, James Beard wrote extensively on the development of a modern West Coast cuisine and is credited with not only popularizing grilled foods (a Pacific Coast cooking style) but also bringing West Coast chefs like Alice Waters to the national scene in his nationally syndicated column. In 1980, he declared in his book *American Cookery* that

> today more and more people are forced to agree that we have developed one of the more interesting cuisines of the world. It stresses the products of the soils,

native traditions, and the gradual integration of many ethnic forms into what is now American cooking.[7]

In short, the new American cuisine was a way of cooking that focused on the food itself, using the best of local ingredients, crafted into a unique combination of native and ethnic flavors. It was a perfect description of the modern gastronomy that developed out of the Pacific Region during the latter half of the twentieth century and that has now taken hold in the rest of the nation.

Ethnic Flavors

One of the Pacific Region's most powerful contributors to the national palate was the ethnic restaurant. Walking down the street in many Pacific cities, and even in smaller towns, offers a diner any number of ethnic restaurant choices. In fact, "ethnic" dining is as common on the West Coast as eating American, and many supermarkets carry "the standards": frozen tamales, Chinese food, Indian, and in particularly upscale locations, freshly made sushi in their take-out section. School lunch fare features tacos, nachos, and even *teriyaki* bowls. *Taqueria*s and Chinese restaurants seem to be ubiquitous throughout the Pacific West, and Clement Street in San Francisco has in a stretch of just a few blocks Taiwanese "Hot-Pot," Thai, Indonesian, Persian, Vietnamese, Japanese, Chinese, Malaysian, and Burman restaurants. The states of Washington and California have the highest concentration of Thai restaurants in the nation, and there are an estimated 200 to 300 Thai restaurants in Los Angeles alone, the craze there beginning with the stylish Chan Dara, which opened in 1976. California has the most taco shops of any state, and Los Angeles has one of the largest numbers of barbeque restaurants outside the South, due to its relatively high African American population.

The popularity of ethnic dining on the West Coast—although dating back to Chinese American restaurants that cropped up during the San Francisco gold rush—is actually a relatively recent phenomenon. In the 1960s there were few ethnic restaurants on the West Coast, save for in Hawai'i, which since the 1800s had been home to a number of "East," "West," and "Local" restaurants in order to feed increasing numbers of immigrants. The U.S. Immigration Act of 1965 opened the Pacific West to a veritable flood of immigrants, who found opening restaurants (and employing U.S. citizens) as one way to facilitate obtaining green cards. Thai, sushi (including the invention of the California roll—a combination of crab and avocado), Indian take-out, North African and Middle Eastern, and later Vietnamese *pho* and Central American *pupuserias* appeared on the culinary landscape, as these pockets of immigrants gained a critical mass in West Coast cities like Seattle, San Francisco, and Los Angeles.

Fusion Cuisine

As ethnic restaurants began to flourish, the chefs with French training took notice of the popularity of these new styles and ingredients and began to incorporate them into the creation of altogether new dishes that combined, or "fused," ingredients and styles from more than one cuisine. The result was that the "fusion," craze began to sweep the West Coast in the 1980s and 1990s.

California Soul—African Americans in the Golden State

At just over 2.5 million, the African American population in the Pacific Region is only about 7.5 percent of the national black population; and nearly all of the blacks in the region live in California. While many scholars have documented the movement of African Americans from the South to the northern United States, fewer have focused on black movement west, and none has assessed the impact, if any, African Americans have had on the food cultures of the Pacific Region. While the numbers have remained quite low, there has been a steady migration of blacks to the West since the late 1700s, prior to the passage of the Thirteenth Amendment in 1865. In these early years black migration west consisted primarily of servants and slaves attached to white owners settling in the Plains states or gold prospectors in California, although there were a few free blacks prospecting during the gold rush. Up to the late 1800s, African Americans settled primarily in the Sierra Nevada Mountains, Sacramento, and San Francisco. After the completion of the Santa Fe Railroad and the subsequent land boom in Southern California, Los Angeles became an increasingly important destination for black migrants. Migration continued steadily, increasing in the postdepression years, and reaching a peak during and after World War II. Although African Americans had been primarily living in rural areas and employed in agriculture in the South, blacks who migrated into the Pacific Region lived in urban areas and were employed in the defense industry (largely aircraft and other manufacturing) and the domestic and civil service sectors. Restrictive housing practices generally kept them located within particular neighborhoods. One such area, along a stretch of Central Avenue in Los Angeles, became the center of African American food culture. Blacks who migrated to California brought with them a southern food culture that emphasized smoked meats (pork and beef), fried chicken, slow-cooked greens (mustards, turnips, collards) and peas/beans (black-eyed peas, cowpeas), and cornbreads (fried and baked). And, like other migrants, they opened restaurants and stores where they could make and eat the foods that sustained them in their places of origin. One typically African American food that has taken root in California is barbecue. However, as barbecue expert Lolis Eric Elie argues, there is nothing that can be labeled "California barbecue."[8] There are, instead, a number of barbecue joints throughout Los Angeles (and some in the San Francisco/Oakland area) whose menus reflect the southern roots of its founders: for example, Texan or Louisianan.

A variety of sushi, including California rolls (on the left).
Courtesy of Getty Images/PhotoDisc.

European-Asian Fusion

Roy Yamaguchi is often credited as one of the original Asian "fusion" chefs to inspire the West Coast movement. Yamaguchi was born and raised in Japan but spent summers cooking in Hawai'i and eventually studied at the Culinary Institute of America in New York. After moving to Los Angeles, he began cooking what he called "Euro-Asian" cuisine. Dishes like "Sea Urchin Rolled in Oysters Served with a Seaweed Cream Sauce" bespoke not only of his training in the preparation of fine cuisine but also of his ethnic background. Alan Wong is another Asian fusion chef who, with cookbooks such as *New Wave Luau*, (1999), has helped to bring attention to the fusion cuisine of Hawai'i. His cooking features Hawaiian dishes and ingredients with an upscale, French preparation. Of Japanese Chinese Hawaiian ancestry, Wong was raised in Hawai'i and trained at a local community college cooking program. He then spent several years with French chef Andre Soltner at Lutèce on the East Coast, where he learned traditional French cooking. He and Yamaguchi recently helped to found the New Hawaiian Regional Cuisine Group that includes other Hawaiian-French fusion chefs such as Sam Choy and Jean-Marie Gosselin.

The Asian-French fusion style began to be imitated on the mainland by none other than Los Angeles chef Wolfgang Puck, who opened an enormously popular Chinese-fusion restaurant in 1983, Chinois-on-Main, that brought the style to new heights with novel combinations of exotic ingredients. In the late 1980s Barbara Tropp carried on the tradition with her San Francisco Chinese-Californian restaurant China Moon Cafe, and in Los Angeles Nobu Matsuhisa dazzled critics with Japanese-French-Latin-style (after classic training in Japan and working in South America) at his restaurant Matsuhisa. Today the cuisine is alive and well, particularly in the Pacific Northwest. One of the largest Asian markets in the United States, the Uwajimaya market in Seattle, makes Asian ingredients easy to obtain for local chefs, and as a result, "Rabbit Satay" or "Wok-fried Lamb" are just a few of the Asian-inspired dishes to be found here. Tom Douglas, the chef/owner of popular restaurants like Palace Kitchen in Seattle, is one of the leaders in the Pacific Northwest fusion cuisine, combining his love for local fish and Asian ingredients to create dishes such as "Wok-Fried Crab with Ginger and Lemongrass." Chefs from the San Francisco region such as JoAnn Asher have even brought the Asian fusion style to the Alaskan dining scene. Her restaurant, Sacks Cafe in downtown Anchorage serves "regional food with an Asian and Mediterranean twist." In

The New Alaska Cookbook, Asher says, "People say it looks like what you'd find in San Francisco. . . . I say why can't we have this in Alaska?"[9]

Latin Fusion

The ongoing immigration of Mexicans and Central and South Americans into the West Coast created a parallel Latin "fusion" cuisine. Mexican food in California, or Cal-Mex as it has been called, is now ingrained into the Pacific cuisine beginning with the proliferation of burrito and taco stands along the West Coast, as well as restaurants such as El Cholo, a Los Angeles establishment since 1927. In addition, Mexican chefs and cooks make up the bulk of the workforce in most West Coast restaurants, and their influence has crept into nearly every corner of West Coast cuisine. Mexican food began to be taken seriously by upscale diners in the 1980s due to restaurants like José Rodríguez's La Serenata de Garibaldi and Mary Sue Milliken and Susan Feniger's Border Grill in Los Angeles. Milliken and Feniger showcased their culinary philosophy and cooking style on their cable television program *Too Hot Tamales*, which began airing in 1995.

A Return to the Soil: The Salad Generation, Hippies, and the Beginning of a "California Cuisine"

At the same time these fusion cuisines were brewing, another movement was afoot in California that had a profound effect on gastronomy. Counterculture groups in the 1960s that were rebelling against the "mainstream" began to apply their new lifestyle to their eating habits, particularly in their disdain for the consumption and promotion of increasingly processed and homogenized foods of the 1950s. The Diggers in San Francisco were one such group that put food at the center of the counterculture movement: They regularly hosted "Feeds," where they offered scavenged food to hippies living on San Francisco streets and handed out papers that declared people should "return to the land" as a way to "straighten our heads in a natural environment, to straighten our bodies with healthier foods."[10] They envisioned a new food nation, where stores would provide food free to the hungry and food co-ops, city gardens, and communal farms would support a more decentralized food system.

During this "return to nature" movement, many on the West Coast (and beyond) changed their diets, embracing health foods such as brown rice, New Age diets such as macrobiotics, and foods grown without pesticides, so-called organic foods. Books out of California, such as Francis Moore Lappé's *Diet for a Small Planet* (1971) and Edward Espe Brown's *Tassajara Cooking* (1970) from the Zen Buddhist Center, argued that food choices were political and promoted the ideals of the vegetarian lifestyle—as a way not only to better feed oneself but also to protest agricultural practices that were harming the environment. Throughout the 1960s and 1970s cooperatives, health food stores, and communes that grew their own food were popular in California, Oregon, and Washington. The magazine *Organic Gardening and Farming* called Los Angeles a "food shopper's paradise" because of its 300-plus health food stores and twenty-two organic restaurants. The Berkeley Food Co-op, one of the oldest and largest of the food cooperatives, boasted a membership of over 50,000 during the same period. The Berkeley Co-op even produced a "Cookbook" that did not contain a single food recipe: Instead, it contained "recipes" to becoming "an informed, active consumer." Although the Berkeley Co-op closed in 1986, many co-ops did survive, and today there are nineteen co-ops in California and Washington, ten in Oregon, and two in Hawai'i. The result of the movement of the 1970s was to produce a critical mass of people not only on the West Coast but nationwide who supported a decentralized way of farming and food distribution and who used their purchasing power to support "sustainable" sources. Organic foods, and farming, have continued to grow in popularity and are now the fastest growing food industry. Supermarkets nationwide have incorporated organic food sections and "local food" labeling into their produce sections.

These socially conscious ideals of "returning to the land" and of obtaining foods locally coincided perfectly with the goals of many high-end restauranteurs, who during this time were focused on trying to duplicate the type of eating they had experienced in France: dishes that featured the ingredients themselves, using simple preparations and foods in season. But since many French ingredients were not available in the Pacific Region, chefs began to find their own substitutes and make or grow their own *frisée* salad greens and foie gras and became leaders of the "local and fresh" movement.

Farmers' markets were one of the places that became critical for obtaining local produce. Chefs, as well as the public, supported a renaissance of farmers' markets that had faded away during the 1950s to 1970s. For instance, only two active farmers' markets were operating in the entire state of California by the end of the 1970s.

The famous Pikes Place Market in Seattle. Courtesy of Corbis.

A stone fruit glut, and the continued high prices charged for them at supermarkets, caused antihunger activists and the California Department of Food and Agriculture to push through legislation in 1979 that made it possible for farmers to sell to the public directly without packaging and labeling requirements. As a result, many farmers' markets were established in the 1980s and 1990s, the first in low-income areas of Southern California such as Gardena and Compton, then expanding to yuppie areas such as Santa Monica and Marin County. Today more than 350 farmers' markets exist in California alone, and there are several hundred throughout Oregon and Washington. The sunny climate of Hawai'i is particularly amenable to the open-air market, with more than 60 operating among the various islands, and even 11 currently operate in Alaska.

Alice Waters and her restaurant purveyor Sibella Kraus at Berkeley's Chez

Pikes Place Market

Pikes Place Market in Seattle is one of the most famous farmers' markets in the United States. Although today it is going strong, it has had a tumultuous history and has almost been destroyed several times over its 100-year history. The market began when consumers protested the markup of produce by middlemen, and housewives were happy to cut out the extra cost and buy directly from area farmers. The market was so successful that nearly 3,000 farmers were supplying the market in the early 1900s, many of them recent immigrants such as Germans, Italians, Chinese, Japanese, and Filipino farmers. Racist sentiment in Seattle came to a head during World War II when nearly two-thirds of the stalls sat empty as Japanese Americans were sent to internment camps. Proposals to develop the site into parking garages and office buildings almost razed the market several times, but in 1971 voters decided to make the site a seven-acre preservation zone, saving it from future destruction. Today there are millions of visitors per year to the market, and it remains one of the most popular tourist destinations in the Pacific Northwest.

Panisse in the 1970s and Michael McCarty of Bertranou's in Los Angeles were particularly instrumental in introducing to their well-heeled restaurant clientele the pleasures of foods just picked or harvested and the unique tastes and flavors of the region. Their purchasing power helped to support a resurgence of artisanal cheesemakers, breadmakers, fish "wranglers," and other food foragers, who in turn became famous for their association with the restaurant, such as the Acme Bread Company in Berkeley.

The new technique—using ingredients grown or produced in California and preparing them in the French style—ultimately produced something not exactly French but instead "Californian." Waters wrote in the introduction of her classic cookbook *The Chez Panisse Menu Cookbook*, first published in 1982:

> Chez Panisse began with our doing the very best we could do with French recipes and California ingredients, and has evolved into what I like to think of as a celebration of the very finest of our regional food products. . . . Our quest for the freshest and the best of the region has led us to Amador County for suckling pigs . . . to the Napa Valley for Zinfandel . . . to Sonoma County for locally made goat cheeses.[11]

The trend quietly gained momentum, and these ideas have now infiltrated current cuisine trends throughout the region: More often than not, fine restaurants consider *appellation*, or place of origin, to be a crucial part of the selling point of dishes. Chez Panisse became a launchpad for many chefs such as Paul Bertolli (Oliveto), Jeremiah Tower (Stars), and Mark Miller (Coyote Cafe), who have carried the "local and fresh" movement to other parts of the region and across the nation. The "local" ingredients movement is particularly evident in restaurants like Mustards in Napa Valley, Herbfarm in Washington, and Wildwood in Oregon, which feature ingredients found either in extensive backyard gardens or "just a few miles from the restaurant." In addition, Alaskan chefs like Kirsten Dixon (Riversong Lodge) and Jens Hansen (Jen's Restaurant and Bodega) as well as California transplants Jens Nannestad (Southside Bistro), Al Levinsohn (Aleyska Resort), and Kirk McLean (Fiddlehead) are at the forefront of the "regional" movement there. Their focus on finding the best local ingredients, as well as a higher demand for fresh produce, has jumpstarted the Alaskan agricultural industry.

THE FUTURE OF PACIFIC REGION FOOD CULTURE

Alice Waters is not the only household name from the Pacific Region; there are a host of chefs here who are arguably as famous as the movie stars they serve. These "celebrity" chefs, such as Sam Choy in Hawai'i, write cookbooks that sell copies on their name alone or, like Wolfgang Puck in Los Angeles and Caprial Spence in Portland, have popular television shows and continue to make a name for Pacific regional food and dining.

Although the Pacific Northwest, Alaska, and Hawai'i have made substantial contributions to dining movements, San Francisco as the port connecting these regions continues to be the anchor of the Pacific coast cuisine. It is home to some of the nation's finest restaurants, from the California French cuisine served at Fleur-de-Lys and Jardiniere in San Francisco to the irreverent dishes at Thomas Keller's French Laundry in nearby Yountville that defy labels. The organic and vegetarian roots of the area are still felt through vegan fine dining at Millennium in San Francisco and Roxanne's in Larkspur, which features one of the latest food trends, "raw food" that has not been cooked over 115 degrees. In addition, the Napa Valley is now home to a new West Coast Culinary Institute of America (CIA) in order to serve the many professional chefs in the region. Another addition to the region is COPIA, a unique museum funded by wine industry leaders Robert and Margrit Mondavi that celebrates American fine wine, food, and the arts.

M.F.K. Fisher

Mary Frances Kennedy Fisher (1908–1982), one of the most celebrated and widely published women in the culinary arts, wrote about appetite and hunger with such passionate skill that she inspired leading food authorities such as James Beard. Born and raised in Whittier, California, Fisher published her first book of gastronomic literature, *Serve It Forth*, in 1937. Three more books followed in quick succession: *Consider the Oyster* (1941), *How to Cook a Wolf* (1942), and *The Gastronomical Me* (1943). In these books, Fisher pioneered a form of gastronomic memoir, developed from the belief that how we gather, prepare, and eat food is inextricably linked to the quality of our lives.

While California first taught Fisher to taste the natural order of freshness, flavor, ripeness, then decay, several years living in France from age twenty taught her to prize the pleasures of eating dishes that capture the essence of this natural progression. During her years in Dijon, Fisher learned the importance of local products by watching the French prepare and eat regional dishes. Upon her return to the United States in 1932, Fisher brought back with her the French emphasis on regional ingredients prepared to taste of themselves. Fisher's philosophy has played a profound role in shaping the contemporary California table, influencing chefs and restaurateurs such as Deborah Madison, the founding chef of Greens restaurant in San Francisco, and Alice Waters, founder of Chez Panisse in Berkeley, whose efforts materialize the essence of Fisher's gastronomic philosophy—a devotion to the pleasures of gathering, preparing, and eating food fresh from the land and a deep respect for the wisdom these pleasures enhance.

Growing populations will generally mean shrinking farmlands; it is a simple, American equation. As more and more people move in or are born into a finite area, housing, roads, light industry—all drive up land values enough that farmers are faced with the painful prospect of making far more money selling their land than farming it. In the Pacific Region, growing population has also meant diversified demographics and a wide palette of food interests, cuisines, and cultures, creating both an increased need for locally grown foods to prepare and an increased interest in imported commodities. Even without the added tension created by global markets, the region's delicate, even intricate, balance between housing and tourist industries, environmental protection and extractive economies such as farming and fishing remain intense and sometimes volatile. A growing response has come in the form of food education. Starting with the trend of local Farmer's Markets, at which residents can see firsthand what foods actually grow within their landscape, and moving to concerted efforts at nutrition education that includes "edible gardens" and locally grown lunches, the Pacific Region is attempting to capitalize both economically and culturally on the rich diversity of foods it produces and supports. As immigration continues to change the cultural and social landscape of the region, food culture, and all it means, will become more complex and ultimately significant in new, perhaps as yet unimagined, ways.

RESOURCE GUIDE

Printed Sources

The Art Institutes. *American Regional Cuisine*. New York: John Wiley & Sons, 2002.

The Associated Press. "After Sustaining Alaska for Years, Salmon Fishing Industry Faces Crisis." *The Olympian*, March 19, 2002. http://www.theolympian.com/home/news/20020519/business/24064.shtml (accessed February 3, 2004).

Beard, J. *James Beard's American Cookery*. New York: Little, Brown, 1980.

Belasco, W.J. *Appetite for Change: How the Counterculture Took on the Food Industry*. Ithaca, NY: Cornell University Press, 1993.

Bell, D., and G. Valentine. *Consuming Geographies: We Are Where We Eat*. New York: Routledge, 1997.

Berholzheimer, R., ed. *The United States Regional Cook Book*. The Prudence Penny Binding. Chicago: Consolidated Book Publishers (for the *San Francisco Examiner*), 1955.

Black, H. *The Berkeley Co-op Food Book: Eat Better and Spend Less*. Palo Alto, CA: Bull Publishing, 1980.

Brennan, J. *Tradewinds and Coconuts: A Reminiscence & Recipes from the Pacific Islands*. Boston, MA: Tuttle Publishing, 2000.

Brenner, L. *American Appetite: The Coming of Age of a Cuisine*. New York: Avon Books, 1999.

Carson, R. *A Silent Spring*, 40th Anniversary Edition. 1962. New York: Houghton Mifflin, 2002.

Cass, B. "California." In *The Oxford Companion to Wine*, ed. J. Robinson. 2nd ed. New York: Oxford University Press, 1999. 124–130.

Chan, S. *Asian Americans: An Interpretive History*. Boston, MA: Twayne Publishers, 1991.

Davidson, A., ed. *The Oxford Companion to Food*. London: Oxford University Press, 1999.

de Graaf, L.B. *Negro Migration to Los Angeles, 1930 to 1950*. 1962. San Francisco, CA: R and E Research Associates, 1974.

Deutschman, A. *A Tale of Two Valleys: Wine Wealth and the Battle for the Good Life in Napa and Sonoma*. New York: Random House, 2003.

Deverell, W. "Privileging the Mission over the Mexican: The Rise of Regional Identity in Southern California." In *Many Wests: Place, Culture and Regional Identity*, ed. D. M. Wrobel and M. C. Steiner. Lawrence: University Press of Kansas, 1997. 235–258.

Dorenburg, A., and K. Page. *Becoming a Chef: With Recipes and Reflections from America's Leading Chefs*. New York: John Wiley & Sons, 1995.

Douglas, T. *Tom Douglas' Seattle Kitchen*. New York: HarperCollins, 2001.

Editors of American Heritage. *The American Heritage Cookbook and Illustrated History of American Eating and Drinking*. New York: American Heritage Publishing, 1964.

Elie L. E. "Smoke and Mirrors." *Gourmet: The Magazine of Good Living* (June 2002).

Ferrary, J., and L. Fiszer. *The California-American Cookbook: Innovations on American Regional Dishes*. New York: Simon and Schuster, 1985.

Findlay, J. M. "A Fishy Proposition: Regional Identity in the Pacific Northwest." In *Many Wests: Place, Culture and Regional Identity*, ed. D. M. Wrobel, and M. C. Steiner. Lawrence: University Press of Kansas, 1997. 37–70.

Frenkel, S. "A Pound of Kenya, Please or a Single Short Skinny Mocha." In *The Taste of an American Place: A Reader on Regional and Ethnic Foods*, ed. B. G. Shortridge and J. R. Shortridge. New York: Rowman and Littlefield, 1995. 57–63.

Grader, Z. "A Brief History of Fish Processing in California and Oregon." In *Microbehavior and Macroresults: Proceedings of the Tenth Biennial Conference of the International Institute of Fisheries*. 2000.

Hall, L. "Washington." In *The Oxford Companion to Wine*, ed. J. Robinson. 2nd ed. New York: Oxford University Press, 1999. 768–770.

Haslam, G. W. *The Other California: The Great Central Valley in Life and Letters*. Santa Barbara, CA: Capra Press, 1990.

Hess, J. L., and K. Hess. *The Taste of America*. New York: Grossman Publishers, 1977.

Ingle, S., S. Kramis, and B. Kafka. *Northwest Bounty: The Extraordinary Foods and Wonderful Cooking of the Pacific*. Northwest. Seattle, WA: Sasquatch Books, 1999.

Insight Guides. *The Pacific Northwest*. Maspeth, NY: APA Publications, 2002.

Johnson, S., G. Haslam, and R. Dawson. *The Great Central Valley: California's Heartland*. Berkeley: University of California Press, 1993.

Jones, E. *American Food: The Gastronomic Story*. New York: Overlook Press, 1990.

Kaplan, A. R., M. A. Hoover, and W. B. Moore. "Introduction: On Ethnic Foodways." In *The Taste of an American Place: A Reader on Regional and Ethnic Foods*, ed. B. G. Shortridge and J. R. Shortridge. New York: Rowman and Littlefield, 1986. 121–133.

Kelly, J. L. "Loco Moco: A Folk Dish in the Making." In *The Taste of an American Place: A Reader on Regional and Ethnic Foods*, ed. B. G. Shortridge and J. R. Shortridge. New York: Rowman and Littlefield, 1983. 39–43.

Kittler, P. G., and K. P. Sucher. *Cultural Foods: Traditions and Trends*. Belmont, CA: Wadsworth/Thomson Learning, 2000.

———. *Food and Culture*. 4th ed. Belmont, CA: Wadsworth/Thomson Learning, 2004.

Kroeber, A. L. "The Food Problem in California." In *The California Indian: A Sourcebook*, ed. R. F. Heizerand and M. A. Whipple. Berkeley: University of California Press, 1925. 297–300.

Lappé, F. M. *Diet for a Small Planet: High Protein Meatless Cooking*. New York: Ballantine Books, 1971.

Laudan, R. *The Food of Paradise: Exploring Hawai'i's Culinary Heritage*. Honolulu: University of Hawai'i Press, 1996.

———. "Hawaii." In *The Oxford Companion to Food*, ed. A. Davidson. London: Oxford University Press, 1999.

Levenstein, H. *Paradox of Plenty: A Social History of Eating in Modern America*. Berkeley: University of California Press, 2003.

Lyon, S. *The Japanese in the Monterey Bay Region: A Brief History*. Capitola, CA: Capitola Book Company, 1997.

Majka, L.C., and T.J. Majka. "Organizing U.S. Farm Workers: A Continuous Struggle." In *Hungry for Profit: The Agribusiness Threat to Farmers, Food, and the Environment*, ed. F. Magdoff, J.B. Foster, and F.H. Buttel. New York: Monthly Review Press, 2000. 161–174.

Martineau, B. *First Fruit: The Creation of the Flavr Savr Tomato and the Birth of Biotech Food*. New York: McGraw-Hill Companies, 2002.

Matthews, G. "Forging a Cosmopolitan Civic Culture: The Regional Identity of San Francisco and Northern California." In *Many Wests: Place, Culture and Regional Identity*, ed. D.M. Wrobel, and M.C. Steiner. Lawrence: University Press of Kansas, 2001. 211–234.

Mintz, S. "Eating American." In *Food in the USA: A Reader*, ed. C.M. Counihan. New York: Routledge, 2002. 23–33.

Morgan, J. "Starting with Sourdough." *Bon Appetit: The Food and Entertaining Magazine* (November: 1993).

Pillsbury, R. *No Foreign Food: The American Diet in Time and Place*. Boulder, CO: Westview Press, 1998.

Reisner, M. *Cadillac Desert: The American West and Its Disappearing Water*. New York: Penguin Books, 1987.

Robbins, J. *Diet for a New America: How Your Food Choices Affect Your Health, Happiness, and the Future of Life on Earth*. Tiburon, CA: H.J. Kramer, 1987.

Root, W., and R. De Rochemont. *Eating in America: A History*. New York: William Morrow, 1976.

Savage, M., and L. Hall. "Oregon." In *The Oxford Companion to Wine*, ed. J. Robinson. 2nd ed. New York: Oxford University Press, 1999. 500–503.

Schlosser, E. *Fast Food Nation: The Dark Side of the American Meal*. Boston: Houghton Mifflin, 2001.

Severson, K., and G. Denkler. *The New Alaska Cookbook: Recipes from the Last Frontier's Best Chefs*. Seattle, WA: Sasquatch Books, 2001.

Shaw Guides. *The Guide to Cooking Schools: 2003*. New York: Author, 2003.

Shindler, M. *El Cholo Cookbook: Recipes and Lore from California's Best-Loved Mexican Kitchen*. Los Angeles, CA: Angel City Press, 1998.

Takaki, R. *Strangers from a Different Shore: A History of Asian Americans*. New York: Little, Brown, 1998.

Tannahill, R. *Food in History*. New York: Three Rivers Press, 1988.

Tower, J. *California Dish: What I Saw (and Cooked) at the American Culinary Revolution*. New York: Free Press, 2003.

Vaught, D. *Cultivating California: Growers, Specialty Crops, and Labor, 1875–1920*. Baltimore: Johns Hopkins University Press, 1999.

Waters, A. *The Chez Panisse Menu Cookbook*. New York: Random House, 1982.

Wells, M.J. *Strawberry Fields: Politics, Class, and Work in California Agriculture*. Ithaca, NY: Cornell University Press, 1996.

Whitehead, J.S. "Noncontiguous Wests: Alaska and Hawai'i." In *Many Wests: Place, Culture and Regional Identity*, ed. D.M. Wrobel and M.C. Steiner. Lawrence: University Press of Kansas, 1997. 315–341.

Wong, A., and J. Harrison. *Alan Wong's New Wave Luau: Recipes from Honolulu's Award-Winning Chef*. Berkeley, CA: Ten Speed Press, 1999.

Zrally, K. *Windows on the World Complete Wine Course* (2003 ed.). New York: Sterling Publishing, 2002.

Films

The Fight in the Fields: César Chávez and the Farmworkers' Struggle. Prod. Tejada-Flores, R., and R. Telles. Paradigm Productions, 1997.

Web Sites

California Department of Food & Agriculture. "Agricultural Statistical Review." 2002. California Department of Food & Agriculture Resource Directory 2002. January 12, 2004.
http://www.cdfa.ca.gov/card/card_new02.htm

César E. Chávez Foundation. "An American Hero." January 15, 2004.
http://www.cesarechavezfoundation.org/Default.aspx?pi=33

County of Hawai'i. "Organic." February 10, 2004.
http://www.hawaii-county.com/bigislandag/organic.html

County of Hawai'i. "Post Harvest Treatment." February 10, 2004.
http://www.hawaii-county.com/bigislandag/phtintro.html

Hall, L. "History of the Oregon Wine Industry." 2001. January 22, 2004.
http://www.avalonwine.com/Oregon-Wine-history.htm

Hawai'i's Agricultural Gateway. "Some History of Hawai'i Agriculture." 1999. February 9, 2004.
http://www.hawaiiag.org/history.htm

Monterey Bay Aquarium. "Geoduck Clam: Panopea generosa." March 2, 2004.
http://www.mbayaq.org/efc/living_species/default.asp?hOri=1&inhab=137

National Oceanic and Atmospheric Administration. "Overview of the U.S. Fishing Industry." 1996. February 12, 2004.
http://www.st.nmfs.gov/st1/econ/oleo/oleo.html

Oregon Department of Agriculture. "History of Oregon Agriculture." January 10, 2004.
http://www.oda.state.or.us/information/aghistory.html

Oregon Department of Agriculture. "Oregon's Growing Regions." January 10, 2004.
http://www.oda.state.or.us/information/oregon_ag/growing_regions/

Viticulture and Enology University of California Davis. June 15, 2004.
http://wineserver.ucdavis.edu/

Washington Agricultural Statistics Service / USDA NASS. "Agriculture in Washington." *Washington 2003 Annual Bulletin.* January 11, 2004.
http://www.nass.usda.gov/wa/annual03/content3.htm

Washington Agricultural Statistics Service / USDA NASS. *Washington Agri-Facts.*
March 10, 2004.
March 20, 2004.
http://www.nass.usda.gov/wa/rlsetoc.htm

Wine Aroma Wheel
Ann C. Noble. June 15, 2004.
http://wineserver.ucdavis.edu/Acnoble/home.html

Cooking Schools

Alaska

University of Alaska at Anchorage
Community and Technical College
3211 Providence Drive, AHS169
Anchorage, AK 99508
907-786-6400
http://ctc.uaa.alaska.edu/pgms.html

California

California Culinary Academy: Le Cordon Bleu
625 Polk Street
San Francisco, CA 94102
800-BAY-CHEF
http://www.baychef.com

California School of Culinary Arts: Le Cordon Bleu
521 East Green Street
Pasadena, CA 91101
http://www.houseofedu.com/csca/index.jsp

Culinary Institute of America at Greystone
2555 Main Street
St. Helena, CA 94574
800-333-9242
http://www.ciachef.edu/

Hawai'i

Kapi'olani Community College
Food Service & Hospitality Education
4303 Diamond Head Road
Honolulu, HI 96816
808-734-9000
http://programs.kcc.hawaii.edu/fshe/index.htm/

Oregon

Western Culinary Institute
1316 W. 13th Avenue
Portland, OR 92701
800-666-0312
http://www.westernculinary.com/

Washington

Art Institute of Seattle
School of Culinary Arts
2323 Elliott Avenue
Seattle, WA 98121
206-448-0900
http://www.ais.edu/

Food and Wine Festivals

Alaska

Kodiak Crab Festival
Kodiak, AK
http://www.kodia.org/crabfest.html

Late May

California

American River Salmon Festival
Nimbus Hatchery
Rancho Cordova, CA
http://www.salmonfestival.net/

October

Castroville Artichoke Festival
Castroville, CA
http://www.artichoke-festival.org/

Mid-May

Gilroy Garlic Festival
Gilroy, CA
http://www.garlicfestival.com/

Late July

Napa Valley Mustard Festival
Napa Valley, CA
http://www.mustardfestival.org/

February through March

Pacific Rim Street Fest
Old Sacramento, CA
http://www.pacificrimstreetfest.org/

May

Stockton Asparagus Festival
Stockton, CA
http://www.asparagusfest.com/

Third week in April

Hawai'i

Kona Coffee Cultural Festival
Big Island, HI
http://www.konacoffeefest.com/
November

Taste of Honolulu
Honolulu, HI
http://www.taste808.com/
June

Oregon

Oregon Brewers Festival
Portland, OR
http://www.oregonbrewfest.com/
Late July

Salmon Festival
Oxbow Regional Park
Portland, OR
http://www.metro-region.org/parks/salmon.html
October

Washington

Issaquah Salmon Days Festival
Downtown Issaquah, WA
http://www.salmondays.org
October

Museums

COPIA: The American Center for Wine, Food and the Arts
500 1st Street
Napa, CA 94559
888-51-COPIA
http://www.copia.org/

A Sampling of Distinctive Pacific Restaurants

Alaska

The Homestead
Mile 8.2 East End Road
Homer, AK 99603
907-235-8723

Marx Bros. Cafe
627 West Third Avenue
Anchorage, AK 99603
907-278-2133

Sacks Cafe
328 G Street
Anchorage, AK 99501
907-274-4022

Within the Wild Lodges (Riversong, Winterlake, and Redoubt Bay)
2463 Cottonwood Street
Anchorage, AK 99508
907-274-2710

California

The Border Grill
1445 Fourth Street
Santa Monica, CA
310-451-1655

Campanile
624 South La Brea Avenue
Los Angeles, CA
323-938-1447

Chez Panisse
1517 Shattuck Avenue
Berkeley, CA 94709
510-548-5525

El Cholo Cafe
1121 South Western Avenue
Los Angeles, CA 90006
323-734-2773
(7 locations from Orange County to Santa Monica)

French Laundry
6640 Washington Street
Yountville, CA 94599
707-944-2380

Jardiniere
300 Grove Street
San Francisco, CA 94102
415-861-5555

Millennium
580 Geary Street
San Francisco, CA 94102
415-345-3900

Nobu Matsuhisa
129 North La Cienega Boulevard
Beverly Hills, CA
310-659-9639

Roscoe's Chicken 'n' Waffles
5006 West Pico Boulevard

Los Angeles, CA
323-934-4405

(5 locations from Long Beach to Pasadena)

Roxanne's Raw Restaurant
320 Magnolia Avenue
Larkspur, CA 94939
415-924-5004

Spago
176 North Canyon Drive
Beverly Hills, CA
310-385-0880

Woody's Bar-B-Que
3446 West Slauson Avenue
Los Angeles, CA
323-294-9443

Hawai'i

Alan Wong's Restaurant
1857 South King Street
Honolulu, HI
808-949-2526

Hawai'i Regional Cuisine Marketplace
Liberty House at Ala Moana, 4th Floor
Honolulu, HI
808-945-8888

L'Uraku
1341 Kapiolani Boulevard
Honolulu, HI
808-955-0552

Oregon

Caprial's Bistro
7015 SE Milwaukee Avenue
Portland, OR 97202
503-236-6457

Higgins Restaurant and Bar
1239 SW Broadway
Portland, OR 97205
503-222-9070

Wildwood
1221 NW 21st Avenue
Portland, OR 97209
503-248-9663

Washington

Herbfarm
14590 NE 145th Street
Woodinville, WA 98072
425-485-5300

Palace Kitchen
2030 Fifth Avenue
Seattle, WA 98121
206-448-2001

LANGUAGE

Kevin Donald, Ritsuko Kikusawa, Karen Gaul, and Gary Holton

"MAINLAND" LANGUAGES OF THE PACIFIC REGION

First Speakers

Within the Pacific Region, three states—California, Oregon, and Washington—form the eastern portion of the Pacific Rim and offer a fascinating history of early language contact as well as contemporary dialectical developments. Significantly, an extremely diverse array of languages and attending dialects was spoken by the numerous indigenous populations of the West Coast, and these were supplemented by various trade jargons. Well over 100 distinct cultural groups had been established before the coming of Europeans, although these groupings—primarily according to language families—often lump together dozens of independent tribes differing in custom, belief, and territory. Within such language-based groupings, linguistic differences between speakers can range widely, from slight accents in pronunciation to mutual incomprehensibility.

According to linguistic maps like those developed by Edward Sapir, language phyla specific to California, Oregon, and Washington include Salish, the Penutian Phylum, the Aztec-Tanoan Phylum, the Macro-Siouan Phylum, the Hokan Phylum, Wappo, and Yuki. Several language phyla of the coast states—including Salish, Beothuk, Timuca, Karankawa, Tarascan, Yuki, Wappo, and the Keres—fall into the category of "undetermined or isolated" phyla. Statistical comparisons of shared cognates have found no links between these "undetermined" and any of the other major phylum groups in North America. In Alaska, Eska-Aleaut and Na-Dene languages form the dominant families.

Many languages spoken for thousands of years are still used on a day-to-day basis within the region. Hokan languages of California and Mexico, Penutian languages of California and Oregon—both controversial groupings—and Salish languages of Washington State and British Columbia are the most prominent of the early languages still spoken in the region in some aspect. Some of the specific

Tracing the Geographical Origins of Culture and Language

By comparing language traits, or cognates, an anthropologist may determine the geographical origin of a culture and certain patterns to its migration. Through structural analysis—using knowledge of root words, affixes, and endings to decode words—anthropologists may also find that during migration a culture could have shared words and ideas with other cultures through language. The comparative method, or glottochronology, is another form of analysis used by linguists and anthropologists. Glottochronology is a linguistic method that measures the rate at which words are replaced in a particular vocabulary. After the rate is established, a relative date can be estimated as to the divergence for distinct but genetically related languages. Using the comparative method, modern linguists such as Edward Sapir (1884–1939; University of California at Berkeley) and anthropologists such as Alfred Kroeber (1876–1960; University of California at Berkeley) worked closely together to create language phyla (plural of *phylum*) for North America.

Sapir arranged North America into seven phyla: the Na-Dene, the American Arctic Paleo-Siberian, the Macro-Siouan, the Macro-Algonquian, the Aztec-Tanoan, the Hokan, and the Penutian.[1] Sapir noted that the areas of diversity could be generalized to be older because it would take longer for languages to split. Areas of uniformity could be generalized as younger because of the lack of diversity. Phyla also raised questions about age of a particular language, phylum relationships and migration.

languages spoken today consist of Makah (Algonquian-Wakashan Phylum, spoken regionally by people of the Pacific Northwest Coast and once the most widespread of Native American language phyla), Mohave (Hokan Phylum, spoken by people in California), Paiute (Aztec-Tanoan Phylum, spoken by people in California), and Navajo (Na-Dene Phylum; spoken by about 150,000 people, Navajo is the most widely used Native American language in the United States).

The Makah, Mohave, Paiute, and Navajo languages are all undergoing active tribal preservation projects. Most of the tribal language preservation projects are in conjunction with major efforts by university linguistic programs. The University of Washington's Linguistic Department, under the direction of Julia Herschensohn, the University of California at Berkeley's Linguistic Department, under the direction of Leanne L. Hinton, and the Northwest Indian Language Institute (NILI) on the University of Oregon campus are all forms of regional language revitalization projects for the specific languages listed above. Many of the revitalization projects, like the NILI, include training local speakers to teach their language to other reservation members and to use their first language whenever possible. However, the future looks dim for many indigenous languages. Of the 3,000 or so languages that are estimated to have been spoken in America at the time of European contact, at the beginning of the twenty-first century approximately 200 Native American languages are being spoken on a daily basis. About one-fifth of these languages are widely known, and a few tribal elders speak about 10 percent of these languages.

The First Settlers and Their Effect on Established Languages

The Spanish were the first Europeans to reach the southernmost portions of the region when Juan Rodríguez Cabrillo (?–1543) sailed into the San Diego Bay in 1542, claiming the land for Spain and establishing the first European settlement there. A Franciscan missionary, Junipero Serra (1713–1784), established the Mission San Diego de Alcala and dedicated the Presidio (the first Spanish fort in California) in 1769. Mexico had jurisdiction over San Diego until 1846 when it was captured by a U.S. naval force. A major colonial power, the Spanish intentionally

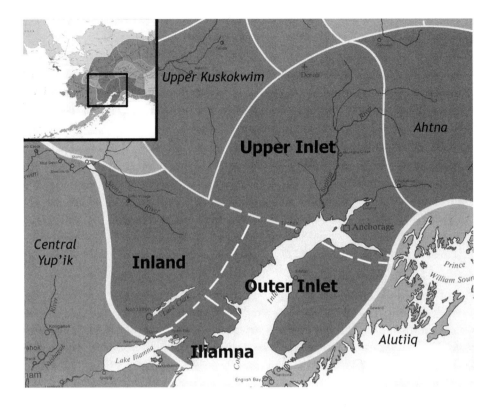

destroyed most all of the indigenous texts they encountered and trained indentured California Indians to speak Spanish at newly founded missions.

The northern reaches of the West Coast experienced their first European contact when, in the eighteenth century, Russian, and later British and French, fur trappers arrived. The largest of the fur companies was John Jacob Astor's (1763–1848) American Fur Company, which often came into conflict with the Canadian North West Company, notably in 1812–1813 at the Pacific Coast establishment of Astoria. The Spanish reached these northern areas in the 1770s, and Captain James Cook (1728–1779) spent some time on the Columbia River in 1778. The U.S.-funded expedition party of Meriwether Lewis (1774–1809), William Clark (1770–1838), York (Clark's black "manservant"), and Sacagawea (1786/1788–1812/1884) reached Fort Klatsop, in Astoria, in 1806. A variety of European languages could be found in the fur outposts, although English, Russian (particularly in Alaska), and French dominated.

While these pioneers made important inroads, the settlement of western lands can be directly associated with the Northwest Ordinance of 1787. The Ordinance guaranteed Indigenous Peoples their rights to continue to live their lives the way they had been living. But treaty violation after treaty violation made it clear that the words forming the ethical core of the Northwest Ordinance of 1787 were shallow and meaningless in the face of European colonialism, economic gain, and expansionism.

The overall effect on Indigenous Peoples and their languages was overwhelming. As traders paved the way for more sedentary settlers, the Indigenous Peoples found that their way of life was threatened and would be eventually eliminated.

Exploration, trade, and commerce within the region account for much of the earliest contact between indigenous and European speakers. Much of the nature and impact of European contact on indigenous languages can be generally characterized as having negative effects on the diversity of indigenous languages spoken at the time of contact. French, Spanish, and English are some of the languages most responsible for the displacement of indigenous languages in the region. For example, Mutsun, a dormant language spoken by Indigenous Peoples of California, was believed to have been lost in all the war, famine, and disease that swept the entire region as settlers flocked to the region in the nineteenth century. But Mutsun is beginning to be reexamined by linguist Natasha Warner, now a professor at the University of Arizona.[2]

When these indigenous and European speakers initially encountered each other, they had no formal means of language communication. Vocabulary and meaning were conveyed through a complex system of physical and verbal gestures, typically identified as pidgins and creoles. A *pidgin* is usually an auxiliary language that has come into existence through the attempts by the speakers of two different languages to communicate, resulting often in a simplified form of one of the languages with a reduced vocabulary and grammatical structure as well as considerable variation in pronunciation. *Creoles* are usually a pidgin that has become the native language of a speech community. On the Pacific mainland, one of the most noted pidgin languages to emerge was Chinook Jargon. A trade language probably existed prior to European contact that evolved into Chinook Jargon in the late 1700s. Chinook Jargon enjoyed widespread usage throughout the Pacific Northwest during the 1800s. During this time dictionaries were written for settlers to aid in communicating with the indigenous populations. Although Chinook Jargon does not enjoy the widespread use it once commanded, it appears that it will remain of linguistic interest. Some of the words still in use today from Chinook Jargon include the following:

> *Potlatch.* A ceremony where someone destroys or gives away his or her possessions to gain social status.
> *Cayuse.* A horse or pony.
> *Skookum.* Big/strong, powerful; today in English people use it to mean something firmly built.
> *High Muckimuck(s).* The chief, the boss; its modern usage and meaning refer, disparagingly, to upper management.

Chinook Jargon should never be confused with the Chinook language of the Indigenous People of the Pacific Northwest. The original Chinook language spoken by these people is now extinct.

Not surprisingly, considering U.S. settlement history, English is the dominant language of the region. However, global immigration into the region (see **Ethnicity** chapter) has made certain that there are few, if any, extant languages that are not being spoken within the region. Northward Mexican migration has ensured widespread use of Spanish. Russian, Polish, Chinese, and Hindi newspapers, for example, can easily be found in many urban newsstands, and Tagalog, Farsi, and Korean can be heard on local radio stations. This influx of languages means that more speakers in the region will become multilingual, proficient in one or more languages for day-to-day functioning and activity. Bilingualism, the ability of a speaker to articulate in two languages, is important to the region because of the necessity of the regional population to communicate across a diverse and broad range of individuals. An estimated 70 percent of speakers in the region are bilingual, primarily speaking Spanish and English. At least 69 percent of the coast states' population speak more than two languages. The trend for the future appears to be moving toward the fundamental requirement of linguistic diversity as a means to basic day-to-day functioning, despite attempts at standardizing English as an official language.

DIALECTS AND PRONUNCIATION

Subtle variations in dialect exist throughout the West, yet two significant dialects are relatively widespread in the Pacific Region: Spanglish and Ebonics. Every individual speaks his or her language in a different way, and this variation in speech is termed an *idiolect*. *Dialects* are groups of idiolects that share grammar, punctuation, and vocabulary. Spanglish and Ebonics represent two modes by which dialects established themselves in the region. Spanglish is an outgrowth of the Spanish/English bilingualism prevalent on the West Coast, a dialect formed where the two speech communities interface. Ebonics developed similarly—though through its own distinct process—among early African communities. The dialect has spread as a cultural tradition and was introduced to the Pacific as an increasing number of African Americans migrated westward during the twentieth century. Both examples demonstrate a certain stability in traditional use and yet are linguistically flexible enough to develop regional variations.

Spanglish: An Emerging Global and Regional Dialect

While contemplating the demise of many indigenous languages of the region, linguists can point to one dialect that is emerging globally and regionally: Spanglish, the linguistic result of speakers of Spanish incorporating English terminology into their speech patterns. Much of the responsibility for the global and regional emergence of Spanglish has to do with technology and forms of media communication (newspapers, television and music). In Latin America and Spain, it is not unusual to hear phrases like "superbien" (the equivalent in English being "excellent," or "awesome") or "colored" (taken from the English equivalent "caller ID"). Regionally speaking, Spanglish can be heard from the barrios of San Francisco and East Los Angeles to the migrant worker camps of Oregon and Washington to the suburbs of Seattle.

A precise or rigid definition of Spanglish, at this point in its linguistic evolution, does not exist. Some of the distinctive features of Spanglish are not completely systematic or the result of regularly occurring linguistic rules and patterns. However, there are some linguistically distinctive features that are evident, many of which hold true whenever one language absorbs part of another. Some of Spanglish's distinctive features include:

Code switching. Or the movement from one language to another. For example:
"Tengo que ir al bus stop para pick up mi hija."

Straight phonetic translation. A political meeting is sometimes called a "mitin," and a block for buildings is a "bloque."

Translation of an English expression into Spanish using English syntax. For example: "Te llamo para atrás" for "I'll call you back."

Adaptation of an English word into a Spanish form. The use of *reportear* for "to report" instead of *informar*, and *remover* for "to remove" instead of *sacar*.

Some words used in Spanglish have a different meaning in Spanish. For example: "Voy a vacumear la carpeta." In Spanish, *carpeta* means "folder," or "file."

The addition of "ear" to English words to form Spanglish verbs. For example: *butear*—to turn on or boot up one's computer.

Evidence of the linguistic creativity involved in the evolution of Spanglish (or any dialect) can also be witnessed in its immense regional variation. Spanglish spoken in the migrant worker camps of Oregon is different than the Spanglish spoken in East Los Angeles, which is different from the Spanglish in San Francisco. The main difference is that each geographical area has developed its own dialect terms—for example, "mucho muy groovy," "cholos" (guy gangsters), "cholas" (female gangsters), and "Hollywoodiano," a term used to define the Hollywood lifestyle.

Language is not always predictable, and Spanglish is going in its own direction. Sometimes there just is not a word in Spanish to convey the meaning of something, to capture the flow and meaning in one culture with the tongue of another, so Spanish speakers broadly borrow and use English words within their respective Spanish dialects. The result is Spanglish, which is one of the most talked about linguistic phenomena currently taking place. Despite the controversies surrounding the emergence of Spanglish, its contamination of "pure" Spanish, and an aging public's negative interpretation of its youthful speakers, there is no doubt that Spanglish is here to stay.

Ebonics: Regional English Dialect Import

Distinctive Features of Ebonics Pronunciation

Distinctive features of pronunciation in Ebonics include the substitution of the "d" sound for "th" (i.e., *dat* for *that*, *de* for *the*, and *wid* for *with*). A second distinctive feature of pronunciation in Ebonics is the omission of "g" at the end of some action verbs (*doin'* for *doing*, *goin'* for *going*, for example). A third distinctive feature is that Ebonics speakers can produce sentences by omitting *is* and *are* ("Kevin trippin'" and "De aw ight" for "They're all right) and changing the present tense of *am* (i.e., "ama" for "I'm going to" and "ahm talkin'" for "I'm talking"). Finally, there is the distinctive pronunciational quality of completed and habitual actions signified by the use of *done* and *be*, respectively (i.e., "De done gone" for "They have gone" and "Kevin be trippin'" for "Kevin is [always] mad").

In 1996 the Oakland, California, School Board proposed resolutions to consider drawing students' attention to the contrasts between African American Vernacular English (AAVE)—also known as Ebonics—and standard English primarily because of the school board's overwhelming African American student population. The school board's desire was to consider the nature and use of Ebonics (a combination of the terms *ebony* for "black" and *phonics* for "sound") in teaching its student population standard or academic English. There was an enormously negative public reaction to the school board's resolutions due largely to the misinterpretation of the intent of the resolutions. Regardless, Ebonics is

Valley Girls and Valspeak

One of the more dramatic contributions to pop cultural vernacular is tied to the sprawling San Fernando Valley on the outskirts of Los Angeles. When a new mall—the Sherman Oaks Galleria—opened in the Valley in 1980, local teenagers adopted it as an afternoon and weekend gathering place. Among the rituals and mores refined in this Southern California mall culture was a highly stylized pattern of speech. Alongside a notable "uptalk"—that is, ending a simple declaratory statement with a rising intonation—speakers also incorporated a variety of exaggerated slang interjections such as "fer sure," "grody to the max," "oh my god," or the classic "gag me with a spoon."

Among teens who gathered at the Galleria was fourteen-year-old Moon Unit Zappa, daughter of legendary musician and songwriter Frank Zappa. Moon took the kitschy, materialistic mall culture and wrote an anthem from the ostentatious teen speech mannerisms. "Valley Girls," which Moon recorded with her father, appeared on the Frank Zappa album *Ship Arriving Too Late to Save a Drowning Witch* (1982), bringing Valley Talk, or Valspeak, to radio stations across the country. Embraced and ridiculed in equal measure, Valspeak nevertheless entered the cultural mainstream. Widespread appeal among youth pop culture would even grow as movies like 1982's *Fast Times at Ridgemont High* (with Sean Penn as surf-slacker Jeff Spicoli) and 1983's *Valley Girls* (with Nicholas Cage and Deborah Foreman) set themselves around the Valley and featured characters with strong local accents.

Though Moon Zappa's song tied this "dialect" to the San Fernando Valley, such speech patterns had already become recognizable throughout Southern California before the record was released. Indeed, Valspeak derives from and shares elements with other local language patterns, including the jargon of California surf culture (e.g., "tubular," "bitchen"). "Pure" Valley Talk has become an iconic stereotype of the 1980s, a trying affectation of airheaded, teenage Valley Girls. Yet Valspeak still resonates with regional and national culture. Later movies, for example, 1995's *Clueless*, have reprised the accent as representative of upscale California youth culture. Valspeak idioms like "awesome" and "totally" have permeated American speech practices, as has the ubiquitous placeholder "like." On the Pacific Coast, the broader Southern California accent is still prevalent in the area, although the exaggerations of Valspeak have generally receded. At the same time, linguistic researchers at Stanford University have begun analyzing a so-called Northern California Vowel Shift. Reminiscent of Valspeak, the shifting vowel patterns are found among a variety of men and women of all age ranges. Fittingly, researchers are examining how this vowel shift practice has been successfully developed among teenage girls to negotiate their positions within social groups.

one of the most exploited forms of English dialects in use within the Pacific Region today. Writers, preachers, poets, comedians, actors, singers (especially rappers), and others have and are using Ebonics either in their artistic medium and/or in everyday speech, primarily for dramatic or realistic effect.

The distinctive features of Ebonics, grammar and pronunciation, are all systematic. Grammar and punctuation are governed and are the result of regularly occurring linguistic rules. Slang terms such as *da bomb* (an adjective used to emphasize one's approval of something), *chillin'* (a verb meaning one is relaxing), and *trippin'* (getting mad or miscommunication within the immediate speaking context) have been co-opted by the general population, particularly young adults. However, Ebonics words such as *ashy* (the whitish appearance of dry black skin), its meaning nearly unknown outside the African American community, are more interesting than slang terms because they have been used for many generations. Many of these terms have been used to make connections between languages spoken in distant locales of the black diaspora.

The distinctive features of grammar and pronunciation in Ebonics, historically speaking, have been connected to English dialects of Caribbean Creole as well as West African languages. The presence of these distinctive features in Ebonics could be due to the large number of Caribbean slaves who were imported to the thirteen colonies and whose descendants then migrated westward. A more current concern among linguists concerning Ebonics is its direction: Is it diverging or amalgamating into other vernacular varieties of American English? Regardless, Ebonics is one of the most intensely studied varieties of American English and promises to be so for quite some time.

PACIFIC AUSTRONESIAN LANGUAGES

On a map of the Pacific Ocean, nothing seems to exist but water. If it is a satellite map, the color blue seems to cover as much as one-third of the surface area of the earth. However, at closer look, there are a great number of small islands scattered there, with cultures and languages unique to each island. The islands of the Pacific Ocean were for the most part uninhabited (except for some islands in the Western Pacific) until ancient voyagers who spoke "Austronesian" languages spread across the Pacific. The Austronesians, especially those in the areas now referred to as Micronesia and Polynesia, sailed freely across the ocean, making monthlong voyages of up to 2,500 miles in large, double-hulled sailing canoes. This seafaring knowledge was passed on from generation to generation by word of mouth. Oral tradition not only recorded and conveyed practical knowledge but stood as a form of art and a part of rituals. Between islands that were close to one another, there were more frequent contacts between people; artifacts and cultural practices were exchanged, and the languages influenced each other.

When Europeans began to sail throughout the Pacific during "the great voyaging era" (1000 C.E.), interaction between these vastly different languages and cultures began. Austronesian people sometimes welcomed the visitors but oftentimes saw them as a threat. Eventually, the European visitors established their own settlements in the region and claimed ownership of the land, introducing the colonial era in 1652. This, by its very nature, brought about significant changes in the relationship between the Europeans and the indigenous Austronesian people. Conflict between the colonial countries introduced modern warfare into the Pacific, with new rulers bringing massive changes to the local cultures as well as the languages. Meanwhile, priests and missionaries started describing the languages and translating the Bible, in an attempt to convert people to Christianity from their traditional animistic beliefs. Writing systems were introduced, resulting in the standardization of the languages; those dialects that were written down acquired prestige over other regional dialects that were oral. Immigrants from various countries, in addition to those from the neighboring areas, started moving in. An almost continual flow of immigrants from European and Asian countries also affected the local population both culturally and linguistically. In some areas, a "mixed" language called pidgin developed.

At the end of World War II, areas that shared the same culture and language were politically divided; so today, language boundaries and political boundaries do not always match. For example, two of the U.S. territories in the Pacific—Guam and Northern Marianas—are today administratively separate, although inhabitants speak the same Austronesian language, called Chamorro. Likewise, Western Samoa, which is an independent nation, and American Samoa, although speaking the same language, belong to two politically distinct administrations. In such cases, the way people speak gradually changes, affected by the different administrative systems. When political boundaries remain long enough, two dialects of the same language will develop, and their boundaries will match the political boundaries.

The languages of these territories and the Hawaiian islands, constituting the State of Hawai'i, reflect the checkered history that each area experienced. Austronesian languages Chamorro, Samoan, and Hawaiian, along with a late intruder, Saipan Carolinian, are still spoken, showing different degrees of influence resulting from their contact with the European languages of their colonial masters. In addition, because each of the regions is under U.S. administration, English is either the only official language or is one of the official languages. An English-oriented administrative and educational system has been gradually changing the societies. Some people have become more aware of the need to preserve traditional ways and to foster the use of their indigenous languages and cultural practices, resulting in some areas in considerable disagreement. Each society, moreover, has a number of other languages spoken by minority groups, complicating the linguistic picture even further.

Austronesian Settlement and Pre-European Contacts

Austronesian Settlement

Today we find four societies that show quite different sociolinguistic situations. All of the "indigenous languages" of the region are Austronesian. The major Austronesian languages spoken in the U.S. Pacific Region today are Chamorro (Guam and Northern Marianas), Saipan Carolinian (Northern Marianas), Samoan (American Samoa), and Hawaiian (Hawai'i).

Of the four territories, the first to be inhabited was Guam and Northern Marianas. The ancestors of today's Chamorro-speaking population arrived as early as 4,000 years ago, from somewhere in the Northern Philippines.[3] The languages both in the Philippines and in Guam and Northern Marianas have changed considerably since the

Pete Koktalash, 1986. Courtesy of the National Archives.

separation, and therefore the similarities between the languages in the Philippines and Chamorro are not that obvious today. Two other Austronesian languages, Saipan Carolinian and Tanapag, are spoken in some parts of Northern Marianas. The other two territories in the Pacific, namely, Samoa and Hawai'i, were inhabited by people who belong to a different subgroup of the Austronesian family of languages. While Micronesian people split from the north of Papua New Guinea, another group moved further east, to eventually reach Fiji and to subsequently spread into all the island groups of Polynesia. The Samoan and Hawaiian people both descended from this group.

Pre-European Contacts and Linguistic Influence

All four languages are similar to one another to some extent, reflecting the fact that they have developed from the same ancestral language. Samoan and Hawaiian are particularly similar to each other. However, despite sharing many features, the languages exhibit such substantial differences from one another that they are mutually unintelligible. Most of the changes that distinguish the languages from one another developed long before they were influenced by the languages of the Europeans and other non-Austronesians who migrated into the Pacific.

Moreover, the languages continued to change after they spread throughout the Pacific. As is the case with all languages, there were both internal and external mechanisms that resulted in language change. The internal mechanisms include some "natural" changes that take place as a result of the characteristics each language has, such as structural pressures. There is no society in the world where older people do not complain about young people's language. This is the way current speakers of a language most typically observe the changes happening in their language. Probably, a long time ago, on the little islands in the Pacific, old people were complaining about the "wrong" use of the language by the younger members of the population. In fact, internal factors are typically the major reason that a single ancestral language develops into a number of different daughter languages.

External mechanisms refer to the changes brought about by contact with speakers of other languages. There is clear evidence for such contact between neighboring and nonneighboring Austronesian languages in the languages spoken today. Chamorro shows certain grammatical features that are commonly seen in Oceanic languages but that were originally not part of the Chamorro language. In Chamorro, in a phrase that expresses the idea of possession (e.g., "my fish," "your book," etc.), what is called a "classifier" has to be used. There are four classifiers in Chamorro—namely, *na'*, "edible things"; *ga'*, "non-human animals"; *iyo*, "inanimate objects"; and *gimen*, "drinkable things." A form is chosen from the four, according to the nature of the thing that is possessed and the relation between the person who possesses it and the thing that is possessed. There are no Philippine languages that exhibit such a system, while it is commonly observed in Oceanic languages spoken in Melanesia. One can therefore assume that Chamorro did not inherit this kind of possessive construction but acquired it as a result of contact with languages in Melanesia that have it.

When a language changes, regardless of whether it is a result of internal or external mechanisms, the change does not always spread throughout the entire community that speaks the language. Rather, changes are frequently restricted to certain geographical areas or social groups, resulting in "dialectal differences." Speakers from different areas can still understand and communicate with each other, but notice that the person with whom they are speaking has a different "accent" or uses words in a different way. All Austronesian languages are also dialectically diverse. As for Chamorro, Donald Topping notes:

> The dialects of the southern villages of Guam . . . differ from the dialect spoken in Yoña, Anaña, or Yigo. The dialect of Rota differs from the dialect of Saipan or Guam. Although these dialect differences have never been formally described, a native speaker of Chamorro has no difficulty in detecting a dialect that is different from his own. And in most cases he can identify the dialect being spoken.[4]

Likewise, in Hawaiian, it is well known that the dialect that is spoken on the island of Ni'ihao has some distinct characteristics that are different from the dialects of Hawaiian spoken on other islands.

In short, before the arrival of Europeans, each of the four territories had its own indigenous Austronesian language, and that language consisted of a number of more or less diverse dialects.

Arrival of Non-Austronesians in the Pacific and Their Influence

Once European people started visiting the Pacific in the fifteenth century, their languages began to affect the indigenous languages. To understand the linguistic situation after this period, it is convenient to classify the new languages into two kinds: those of the colonial power(s) and those of other immigrants. Both affected the local languages.

The languages of the colonial rulers typically involved the whole society, being used in many social contexts, such as administration and education. However, these languages did not replace the indigenous languages in personal contexts, although they were often considered to be "superior" to the local Austronesian language. On the other hand, the languages that were introduced by immigrants were typically spoken within the immigrant community, mostly for private communication purposes, and were not normally used in public contexts outside of this community.

The presence of the language of a ruling power along with multiple languages spoken by immigrants from different countries yielded a linguistic situation unique to each area. For example, in Guam during the twentieth century, the United States attempted to convert the local people to American cultural standards by restricting the use of the Chamorro language. Encouraging the use of English provided a "lingua franca," a common language used among people with different linguistic backgrounds. This resulted in the proliferation of English among the members of the society, and it is clear that today English is replacing the local languages, even in private contexts.

A completely different situation is found in Hawai'i. In early-twentieth-century Hawai'i, where there was also a large immigrant population from different countries, a new language, called Hawai'i Creole English (HCE), developed as a lingua franca. Hawai'i Creole English is based on English but exhibits various characteristics that are also observed in the immigrant languages spoken in the community.

Foreign Influences on Austronesian Languages

The influence of the earlier colonial powers on the local languages is most typically observed as lexical borrowings (loanwords) in their vocabulary. Under a colonial situation, the power relationship usually gives the language of the ruling group higher status than the local one, and it becomes prestigious to use words that are found in the language of the ruling power. In addition, it is commonly observed that the ruling power introduces new concepts and material items into their colonies. The local languages do not have names for such things, and the introduction of the foreign materials commonly results in the adoption of the foreign names of these items into the local language.

European occupation in the U.S. Pacific Region has left the influences of many languages. The languages of the former colonial powers include Spanish, Japanese (Guam and Northern Marianas), German (Northern Marianas), and English (all). Borrowings from the languages of the former rulers in Chamorro are spoken in Northern Marianas. Similar situations are readily observed in the other Austronesian languages.

In Northern Marianas, the Chamorro language (with its dialectal varieties) was spoken at the beginning of European occupation. The first ruler was Spain, an occupation that lasted for three and a half centuries (1556–1898). Spanish was used not only in administrative contexts but also at churches and schools, to the extent that some local "elites" spoke Spanish in public contexts. Names of things as well as verbs and other grammatical forms were borrowed because of the hundreds of years that Spanish influenced Chamorro. The long period of Spanish rule in Northern Marianas is reflected clearly in the Chamorro language.

At the end of the nineteenth century, German rule began in Northern Marianas. There are relatively few borrowings from German in the language, reflecting the fact that the occupation was rather short (1899–1914) and also that Germany did not set up an elaborate administrative system. Under the Japanese administration that followed (1914–1944), however, a sociolinguistic situation similar to that which developed during the Spanish occupation occurred. This time, mainly names of manufactured objects were borrowed, such as *denke'* ("flashlight"; Jpn. *denki*—"lamp, light") and *chirigame'* ("toilet paper"; Jpn. *chirigami*—"tissue paper"). Just as under the Spanish administration, many Chamorro speakers learned to speak Japanese, and had the Japanese occupation lasted longer, the linguistic influence would perhaps have been as great as Spanish had been on Chamorro spoken in Northern Marianas. Samoa and Hawai'i, unlike Guam and Northern Marianas, have been occupied for a relatively short period. In these areas the major occupying power has been the United States. As a result, there are numerous lexical borrowings from English found in both languages.

Development of the Writing Systems and the Loss of Oral Tradition

Most Austronesian languages had no writing systems before European contact. Traditional knowledge and other forms of culture, such as songs, poems, and family history, were all passed on from generation to generation by word of mouth. These oral traditions constituted a form of traditional art. There was always a person who knew the old stories.

Once contact with European people began, writing systems were introduced in all of the areas that constitute the U.S. Pacific Region today. The establishment of orthography systems was mainly associated with the missionaries, who considered translation of religious literature and literacy of the local populations to be essential steps in their program to convert the local people to Christianity. The translation of religious literature into the local languages required that the missionaries become fully fluent in the local languages. As a result, some missionaries wrote grammatical descriptions of the local languages, primarily as a tool to enable later missionaries to understand the structures of the languages and to help them acquire the languages efficiently. These grammatical descriptions are some of the earliest published records that we have of many of the languages in the Pacific.

For Chamorro, Spanish priests were the first ones to write down the language using their own alphabet in the late seventeenth century, and the very first grammatical description of Chamorro appeared in 1668. The early Spanish writing system underwent several changes as the territory was occupied by Germany and subsequently by the United States, resulting in several competing ways to write the language. The writing system that is commonly used today was adopted in 1971 and is the official Chamorro Orthography. For Samoan, missionaries first made an attempt to establish an orthography in the nineteenth century, a process initiated by the London Missionary Society. About the same time, attempts to establish an orthography system for Hawaiian were initiated by Protestant missionaries from New England.

The introduction of a writing system did not immediately influence the oral traditions of the local populations, but it is clear that it was a major factor in eventually causing their disappearance. The introduction of literacy and the development of school systems took children out of the home for much of the day and away from the influence of their parents and grandparents. Traditional methods of passing on knowledge were replaced by Western education, with the result that today much of traditional lore has now disappeared from the areas heavily influenced by the former colonial powers.

Immigrant Populations and Their Influence on Social Communication

Colonial rulers were not the only visitors to the Pacific. In each area, immigrants from other areas in the Pacific and elsewhere constituted part of the population. Unlike the languages of the colonial powers, the languages of immigrants typically remained minority languages, usually used only by a fixed group of people for communication within their own group. They were and still are spoken only within the group of those with the same or similar ethnic background for private communication; if they are used in public contexts, usually these are social activities within the community such as special cultural events. Although sometimes radio and television programs in the languages spoken by immigrants are available, the assumed audience is the particular ethnic group that speaks the language.

The immigrants' languages, then, do not in general affect the indigenous language to the extent that the language of the former colonial powers does.

However, the need for a lingua franca probably encourages rapid movement of the whole society toward greater English dominance. This is reflected in the fact that the use of English is more widespread in communities where there is a high percentage of immigrant population. In American Samoa, the Samoan population is the majority, in contrast to the situation in Hawai'i, where Hawaiians and other Pacific Islanders form the minority. Northern Marianas and Guam are somewhere in between, with nonindigenous people outnumbering the indigenous population. In American Samoa, where most of the population is Samoan, only 2.9 percent of the population speak English as their only language at home. Compare this with Hawai'i where there is no majority ethnic group population and 73.4 percent of the population claim to speak only English at home. In Guam and Northern Marianas, the numbers are between those of American Samoa and Hawai'i (38.3 percent and 10.8 percent, respectively). The population of those who use English only at home is extremely high in Guam, considering the relatively small Caucasian population and the large Chamorro and Asian population there.

The official annexation by the United States of Hawai'i, Samoa, and Guam took place at roughly the same time. This means that the length of exposure to English as the language of administration is about the same in these regions. The differences today in how widespread English is used among the local population, therefore, can be attributed at least partially to the distributions of people with different ethnic backgrounds in each society.

Emergence of Hawai'i Creole English (Pidgin)

On colonial plantations, such as those found in Hawai'i in the second half of the nineteenth century, speakers of two or more different languages had to maintain continuous close contact with one another. A simplified form of speech, referred to as a "pidgin," often developed to establish and maintain communication between the speakers of the different languages. A pidgin language typically develops when each speaker tries to establish communication by adopting lexical items of the other person's language. Example (1) shows a sentence uttered by a Japanese person trying to communicate with an English speaker. The speaker utilizes English words he knows, but he produces them following Japanese word order and with a Japanese affirmation ending *ne*.

(1) *Me, tomorrow, come, ne?* "I'll come [to see you] tomorrow, okay?"

Grammatical features are often simplified. For example, in the case of English, the plural marking *s* on nouns and the past tense marker *ed* on verbs typically are not used. Articles *the* and *a* and certain prepositions are also eliminated. Although some tendencies can be noted as to how speakers develop sentences such as these, there are no shared grammatical rules at this stage.

If this situation continues long enough, though, a group of people start sharing the same grammatical rules and the same set of vocabulary. In other words, the pidgin begins to become systematized, with regular patterns of usage developing. Typically this stage develops when children begin speaking only this language as their mother tongue. Some linguistic features may be attributable to the languages spoken in the community, but the language as a whole is not the same as any that had previously existed. Once this stage is reached, the language is recognized as a "creole" language, a new language that has developed from the contact situation.

In the U.S. Pacific Region, considering the fact that there have been continuous language contact situations among both genetically related (that is, belonging to the same language family) and nonrelated languages throughout the region, "pidginization" has probably not been at all an uncommon phenomenon in all the four areas.

Hawai'i is the only area in the U.S. Pacific Region where an entire creole language developed. The particular variety now spoken in Hawai'i is commonly referred to as "Pidgin" (with a capital "P") or more formally as "Hawai'i Creole English," commonly abbreviated as HCE. Hawai'i Creole English is an English-based creole language that integrates various features from other languages, such as Japanese, Chinese, Tagalog, Ilokano, Portuguese, and Hawaiian. There is no record as to exactly how this creole language developed, although there is evidence that it was preceded by a form of pidgin based on the Hawaiian language. Some scholars believe that it must have developed as a result of influence by speakers of Pacific pidgin, which was widely spoken in the eighteenth and nineteenth centuries between European and American sea traders, who came to the Pacific for sandalwood, spices, furs and whaling, and locally employed crews, which must have included some from Hawai'i. If such was the case, those who picked up the pidginized English on board their ships must have contributed to the communication on land once the plantations started in Hawai'i. Others believe that Hawai'i Creole English must have developed locally. Sugar cane plantations arose in 1835 in Hawai'i, and to supplement the local Hawaiian labor force, plantation laborers came from Japan, China, Puerto Rico, and Portugal. Immigrants also started coming from the Philippines in 1905. These people, speakers of different languages, were thrown together and needed an interlanguage, as well as a language to communicate with their overseers (typically Portuguese immigrants).

The Current Sociolinguistic Situation

What one finds today in the Pacific Region is a result of all the historical events that have been described in the previous sections. In each of the four U.S. regions in the Pacific, multilingualism is found in both social and individual contexts. There is English, a dominant Austronesian (indigenous) language, and some other languages spoken by immigrants. One commonly shared phenomenon observed throughout the four U.S. territories today is that English is rapidly becoming the main communication tool, gradually replacing the other languages. The Austronesian languages, with a much longer history than that of the United States as a nation, are being lost. Efforts are being made, however, to protect the indigenous languages.

U.S. Policy and English Dominancy

Once each territory was officially annexed to the United States, the U.S. government actively sought to make local people adapt to U.S. customs, including the use of the English language. For example, in Guam, the use of the Chamorro language was restricted. In American Samoa, although traditional rights were protected in the first half century or so, the sudden modernization policy of the U.S. government in the 1960s wiped out a large part of the traditional cultural heritage in each area. English did not merely remain a language that was used by the federal government in administrative contexts but became something that non-English speakers had to learn and use in place of their own language and culture.

Today, in each of the U.S. Pacific Regions, English is one of the official languages, and it is typically also used as the language of instruction in the schools. Its use is gradually changing the local languages as well as the linguistic attitudes of the indigenous populations, just as Spanish and Japanese did in the Mariana Islands in the past. The fact that English is now becoming the major international language of communication seems to be accelerating this phenomenon. For example, the 2000 U.S. Census shows that the percentages of the population that do *not* speak English *at all* at home are 0.7 percent in Guam, 14.6 percent in Northern Marianas, and 3 percent in American Samoa, suggesting that the use of English is now quite common even in private contexts.

Re-recognition of the "Indigenous" Languages and Revitalization Movement

As American modernization progressed, some individuals became alarmed over the loss of traditional heritages. Rerecognition of indigenous cultures and languages of the Pacific began in the late 1960s and 1970s, as in many other places in the world. Movements to prevent the complete loss of indigenous Austronesian languages exist today in all areas of the Pacific Region, although the nature and degree differ depending on the area. In Guam and Northern Marianas, some academic efforts are being made under the initiation of the University of Guam. Chamorro reading materials for children have been developed for use in the schools in addition to English reading materials. Grammatical descriptions and dictionaries have either been published already or are in progress, and more and more interest is seen in understanding how and why the Austronesians came into the areas where they now live. In American Samoa, after the extreme "modernization project" by the U.S. government was halted at the end of the 1960s, local people voted for a democratically elected leadership of their own and some degree of autonomy. Although their lost material heritage will never come back, fortunately the Samoan language is still somewhat intact among the local population.

Finally, in Hawai'i, a language revitalization program has been developed with highly gratifying results. Whereas fifty years ago the Hawaiian language was moribund, with very few native speakers left, now, as a result of the revitalization programs, there are growing numbers of native speakers in many communities throughout the Islands. Hawaiian, the first language to be spoken in Hawai'i was a "healthy," live language until 1898, when Hawai'i was annexed by the United States. The use of English in education was encouraged, and the Hawaiian language went into rapid decline as a result. Eventually there were relatively few native speakers left. Almost no one spoke Hawaiian at home any more, apart from on privately owned Ni'ihao island, where the local community is removed from modern political movements.

Revitalization of the Hawaiian language started around 1970, forming a part of what has been called the "Hawaiian Renaissance," initiated by those who were alarmed by the foreseen loss of a heritage that had been passed down for more than a thousand years. The Hawaiian language was declared to be an official language, in addition to English, in 1978. The number of speakers had dropped to around 2,000, whereas the total number of residents in Hawai'i was over 1 million. Active efforts have been made by Hawaiian language specialists at the University of Hawai'i (UH) and in the Department of Education to revitalize the language. In 1987 a school was established where Hawaiian is the language of communication with children in each of the grades. Because there were so few speakers left, those who were learning how to speak the language had to sometimes consult specialists at the university for Hawaiian expressions, thus yielding the term "UH dialect" to refer to the variety of Hawaiian that was being revitalized. In 1990, the U.S. government finally adopted a policy to recognize the right of Hawai'i to preserve, use, and support its indigenous language.

Today, the program continues, taking advantage of modern tools such as computers and the Internet.[5] The revitalization of Hawaiian has been meeting some success. It is reported that by 1993 the total number of speakers had already increased to 8,000. There are now several schools where most subjects are taught using the Hawaiian language, and Hawaiian language classes are popular at all levels of education. To date, Hawaiian is the only Native American language that is used officially by a state government.

The Future for Austronesian Languages

Among the islands belonging to the U.S. Pacific Region today, one sees four sociolinguistically unique areas. These have developed as a result of their diverse historical and linguistic backgrounds. The current linguistic situation in each of these areas has developed through the interaction of English with the indigenous Austronesian languages. In Guam, while Chamorro is still being spoken to some extent, the language is not being acquired by younger members of the community. The situation is similar in Northern Marianas, where not only Chamorro but also Saipan Carolinian is competing with English. Some effort is being made in each of these areas to foster the use of the indigenous languages, but funding for special programs is very limited, and the prospects for the survival of the indigenous languages is bleak. In Hawai'i, the indigenous language Hawaiian is actively being promoted, and the outlook for its survival appears brighter. Hawaiian Creole English, while still commonly heard, is also undergoing change, with more and more speakers adapting their form of speech toward the American Standard dialect of English. Finally, in American Samoa, the indigenous language is still commonly spoken, although English is gradually influencing the language; unless active steps are taken to promote the use of Samoan, one can expect that eventually English will also dominate the language at all levels of communication.

HANGING ON IN ALASKA: DENA'INA LANGUAGE REVITALIZATION IN SOUTH CENTRAL ALASKA

Dena'ina is one of the many endangered languages of Alaska. It belongs to the language family that is composed of some forty languages spread across Alaska, parts of Canada, and parts of the northwest coast of the United States.[6] Dena'ina speakers have historically lived in the areas wrapped around the region of Cook Inlet, but differences in pronunciation and vocabulary have developed into various dialects correlated with particular regions (the Upper Inlet, Outer Inlet, Inland, and Iliamna dialects.[7]

The fate of Dena'ina is not unique. All of Alaska's indigenous languages are severely endangered. They have been helped along the path to oblivion for many years by both official and unofficial policy. Beginning in the 1880s official U.S. educational policy forbade all use of Alaska Native languages in school.[8] The removal of children to residential school furthered the process of severing transmission of Native language from parent to child.

Today, children no longer grow up speaking Dena'ina, and there are few fully fluent speakers of Dena'ina remaining. Some elders learned Dena'ina as a first language, but most of them were taught English in grade schools at a very young age. In many cases, this meant that they were forbidden to speak their native language and were punished for doing so.

Some twenty years ago, anthropologist Linda Ellanna predicted that Dena'ina was moribund.[9] Such a prediction is fairly ominous. Whether Dena'ina can be revitalized into a widely and actively spoken language remains to be seen. A growing number of people in the south central Alaska area, however, are hoping to turn the tide.

Much of the initial work of language revitalization involves the bringing together of speakers and learners and a high level of commitment. When the learning process is reinforced and supported by textbooks, reading materials, media, and large speaker communities—as with many world languages—the task is hard enough. In the case of Dena'ina, there are few materials available, and the language is not spoken on a daily basis by a large community of speakers. Thus the learning process is all the more difficult. The Dena'ina language area spans a large territory, which includes both urban and remote bush areas. Connecting people across this vast and geographically diverse region is crucial to maintaining the Dena'ina language.

An important first step in the direction of Dena'ina language revitalization was taken in Kenai in May 2003 when the Kenaitze Indian Tribe hosted the first-ever Dena'ina Festival. This event drew speakers from across all the Dena'ina regions and dialect areas to discuss the prospects for language revitalization. More than 100 people attended. The festival was followed by a three-week Dena'ina language course held at Kenai Peninsula College and sponsored by the University of Alaska at Fairbanks. One of the important outcomes of the festival and the language course was the bonding between speakers and students. Speakers were encouraged by the presence of interested and dedicated students, many of whom had been long anxious to learn but lacked a teacher who shared their enthusiasm. Since then people have traveled periodically to additional language workshops to teach and learn from one another as part of a U.S. Department of Education Project.[10] Another three-week Dena'ina Language Institute was held in June 2004.

Meetings provide crucial contact between all those involved in language revitalization efforts. But the distance between villages makes travel more than a few times a year impractical. In order to maintain such contact, Dena'ina learners and teachers continue regular meetings by audio-conference. Those interested in learning Dena'ina can also subscribe to a Dena'ina "Word-of-the-Day" email list, or *Jan Gu Dena'ina Qena*. The Alaska Native Heritage Center in Anchorage is offering occasional classes in Dena'ina.

All of these grassroots initiatives are supported by and benefit from research, recordings, and technologies sponsored by a number of agencies and institutions. The National Park Service (NPS) has supported various research projects that include the recordings of oral narratives by Dena'ina elders and published reports.[11] Currently, an Ethnographic Overview and Assessment is being conducted for the Lake Clark National Park and Preserve and neighboring regions. Elements of that broader project include gathering new oral narratives from elders in remote Dena'ina communities, as well as creating an inventory and catalog of all existing recordings in Dena'ina. Also accounted for are recordings held in NPS archives as well as at the Alaska Native Language Center, at the Bureau of Indian Affairs, and in individual collections and elsewhere.[12] It is an important step in taking stock of the existing Dena'ina documentation and contributing to ways these recordings could be used in revitalization programs as well as related future research.

In the late 1990s, Project Jukebox compiled interviews of elders, photos, and maps into an interactive CD rom.[13] Viewers can listen to elders speak on various topics, describe contents in photos, and guide the viewer through trails on a map. The recordings in Project Jukebox also offer Dena'ina words for various places and objects. These tools contribute to both cultural and linguistic preservation. Additionally, James Kari, along with Jim Fall, has also tracked down hundreds of Dena'ina place names throughout the region, building maps and tying the names to stories, families, and their seasonal use patterns.[14]

Publications in Dena'ina plant lore, bird traditions, resource use, and village economy in some of the more interior inland areas have been produced by anthropologist Priscilla Russell, often in conjunction with James Kari.[15] Kari and Russell, along with anthropologist Alan Boraas, worked with Peter Kalifornsky, a Dena'ina elder and recorder of Dena'ina culture and history, to produce a collection of writings called *A Dena'ina Legacy: K'tl'egh'i Sukdu*.[16]

Complementing these efforts is a new project at the University of Alaska at Fairbanks that will create digital access to Dena'ina materials housed at the Alaska Native Language Center (ANLC). The ANLC maintains a comprehensive collection of nearly everything written in or about the Dena'ina language. This collection includes some of the first written materials, such as William Anderson's (1784) Dena'ina wordlist, collected on Cook's (1778) expedition; field notes from linguists who have worked with the language over the past fifty years; and more recent curriculum materials. In addition, the collection includes more than 200 audio recordings of stories, songs, and linguistic material. The Dena'ina Archiving, Training and Access (DATA) project will help to make all of these materials discoverable and accessible.

When a language disappears, an entire way of viewing and thinking about the world goes with it. Poetry, puns, lullabies, and endearments are gone forever. The collective history, culture, and values of the Dena'ina people are embedded in the sounds, words, and grammatical structures of the Dena'ina language. English may function equally well as a system of communication, but it lacks the long-standing connection with the Dena'ina people.

Dena'ina language revitalization remains an achievable goal. Revitalization can take many forms, but in all cases it requires a strong commitment from within the community. And community effort like that among contemporary Dena'ina in south central Alaska may just be what it takes to bring back into flourishing use an almost forgotten language. Institutions such as the National Park Service, the Alaska Native Language Center, and others can support this effort by providing access to research, documentation, and recordings of Dena'ina language. Communities can come to see archives as their own language reservoir, holding resources that can help to build and develop language and culture in creative and dynamic ways that will be sustainable in a rapidly changing world.

LANGUAGE IN THE PACIFIC REGION

The Pacific Region of the United States exhibits perhaps the largest and most diverse group of languages in the country today. From Spanish and Asian languages to the Austronesian languages of the Pacific Islands to the American Indian languages of the Northwest and Alaska, and hundreds of other dialects, the region boasts a true polyglot population.

RESOURCE GUIDE

Printed Sources

Bickerton, Derek. *Roots of Language*. Ann Arbor, MI: Karoma, 1981.
Biggs, Bruce. "Direct and Indirect Inheritance in Rotuman." *Lingua* 14 (1965): 383–445.
Blust, Robert A. "The Proto-Austronesian Pronouns and Austronesian Subgrouping: A Preliminary Report." *Working Papers in Linguistics, University of Hawai'i* 9.2 (1977): 1–15.
———. "Subgrouping, Circularity and Extinction: Some Issues in Austronesian Comparative Linguistics." In *Selected Papers from the Eighth International Conference on Austronesian Linguistics*, ed. Elizabeth Zeitoun and Paul Jen Kuei Li. Taipei: Academia Sinica, 1999. 31–94.
Carr, Elizabeth B. *Da kine Talk: From Pidgin to Standard English in Hawaii*. Honolulu: University of Hawai'i Press, 1972.
Elbert, Samuel. *Spoken Hawaiian*. Honolulu: University of Hawai'i Press, 1970.
Elbert, Samuel H., and Mary Kawena Pukui. *Hawaiian Grammar*. Honolulu: University of Hawai'i Press, 1979.
Grimes, Barbara F., ed. *Ethnologue: Languages of the World*. 13th ed. Dallas, TX: Summer Institute of Linguistics, 1996.
Hunkin, Galumalemana Afeleti L. *Gagna Samoa: A Samoan Language Coursebook*. Auckland: Polynesian Press, 1992.
Jackson, Frederick H. "The Internal and External Relationships of the Trukic languages of Micronesia." Ph.D. dissertation, University of Hawai'i, 1983.
Jackson, Frederick H., and Jeffrey C. Marck. *Carolinian-English Dictionary*. PALI Language Texts Micronesia. Honolulu: University of Hawai'i Press, 1991.

Kalifornsky, Peter. *A Dena'ina Legacy: K'tl'egh'i Sukdu. The Collected Writings of Peter Kalifornsky*. Fairbanks: Alaska Native Language Center, University of Alaska, 1991.

Kari, James. "*A Classification of Tanaina Dialects*." Anthropological Papers of the University of Alaska 12.2 (1975): 19–53.

Kari, James, and Priscilla Russell Kari. *Dena'ina Elnena, Tanaina Country*. Fairbanks: Alaska Native Language Center, 1982.

Krauss, Michael E., and Victor K. Golla. "Northern Athabaskan Languages." In *Handbook of North American Indians*. Vol. 6: *Subarctic* ed. J. Helm. Washington, DC: Smithsonian Institution Press, 1981.

Lynch, John. *Pacific Languages: An Introduction*. Honolulu: University of Hawai'i Press, 1998.

Lynch, John, Malcolm Ross, and Terry Crowley. *The Oceanic Languages*. London: Curzon Press, 2002.

Marck, Jeff. *Topics in Polynesian Language and Culture History*. Canberra: Pacific Linguistics, 2000.

Mosel, Ulrike, and Even Hovdhaugen. *Samoan Reference Grammar*. Oslo: Scandinavian University Press, 1992.

Murray, Thomas E. "American English Loanwords in Samoan." *American Speech* 66.1 (1991): 109–112.

Odo, Carol. "Orthography Outline for Hawaiian English Project." Unpublished manuscript, Social Sciences and Linguistics Institute, University of Hawai'i, Honolulu, 1973.

Reid, Lawrence A. "The Demise of Proto-Philippines." In *Papers from the Third International Conference on Austronesian Linguistics*. Vol. 2: *Tracking the Travellers*, ed. Lois Carrington, Amran Halim, and Stephen Wurm. Canberra: Pacific Linguistics, 1982. 201–216.

———. "Morphosyntactic Evidence for the Position of Chamorro in the Austronesian Language Family." In *Collected Papers on Southeast Asian and Pacific Languages*, ed. Robert S. Bauer. Canberra: Pacific Linguistics, 2002. 63–94.

Reinecke, John E. *Language and Dialect in Hawaii: A Sociolinguistic History to 1935*. Ed. Stanley M. Tsuzaki. Honolulu: University of Hawai'i Press, 1969.

Robinson, Andrew. *Lost Languages*. New York: McGraw-Hill, 2002.

Ross, Malcolm D. "Is Yapese Oceanic?" In *Reconstruction, Classification, Description: Festschrift in Honor of Isidore Dyen*, ed. Bernd Nothofer. Hamburg: Abera, 1996. 121–166.

Schütz, Albert J. *All about Hawaiian*. Honolulu: University of Hawai'i Press, 1995.

Silva, Kalena, ed. *Ka Ho 'oilina: The Legacy. Puke Pai 'Olelo Hawai'i: A Journal of Hawaiian Language Sources*. Hilo: Kamehameha School Press and University of Hawai'i. 2003.

Tanaka, Sachiko. "Hawai eigo (Hawai'i English)." In *The Sanseido Encyclopaedia of Linguistics*. Vol. 3: *Languages of the World, Part Three*, ed. Takashi Kamei, Rokuro Kono, and Eiichi Chino. Tokyo: Sanseido, 1992. 344–349.

Topping, Donald. *Chamorro Reference Grammar*. PALI Language Texts: Micronesia. Honolulu: University of Hawai'i Press, 1973.

———. "Loan Blends: A Tool for Linguists." *Language Learning* 13 (1963): 281–287.

Warschauer, M., and K. Donaghy. "Leokï: A Powerful Voice of Hawaiian Language Revitalization." *Computer Assisted Language Learning* 10.4 (1997): 349–362.

Wurm, S. A., and Shirô Hattori, eds. *Language Atlas of the Pacific Area, Part 1: New Guinea Area, Oceania, Australia*. Canberra: Pacific Linguistics, 1975.

Web Sites

Alaska Native Knowledge Network
Sponsored by Alaska Federation of Natives, University of Alaska, National Science Foundation, and Alaska Department of Education.

July 13, 2004.

http://www.ankn.uaf.edu/

A resource for compiling and exchanging information concerning Alaska Natives.

Alaskool
July 13, 2004.
http://www.alaskool.org/language/languageindex.htm

Online materials about Alaska's native history, education, languages, and culture.

The California Foreign Language Project
July 13, 2004.
http://www.stanford.edu/group/CFLP/

Established in 1989 by mandate of the California legislature to challenge language professionals to improve and expand language programs in California as well as to promote student access and equity within educational institutions.

City College of San Francisco Language Center
July 13, 2004.
http://www.ccsf.edu/Departments/Language_Lab/splinks.htm

Online links to Spanish-language learning resources.

The Hispanic Reading Room
Library of Congress
July 13, 2004.
http://www.loc.gov/rr/hispanic/

Contains catalogs and finding aids, collections, databases, and so on.

Inforain
July 13, 2004.
http://www.inforain.org/maparchive/native_lang.htm

A map of Northwest Coast indigenous languages.

Language Links
College of Letters & Science, University of Wisconsin
July 13, 2004.
http://polyglot.lss.wisc.edu/lss/lang/langlink.html

MIT Indigenous Languages Initiative
July 13, 2004.
http://web.mit.edu/linguistics/www/mitili/Links.html

A master's-level program at Massachusetts Institute of Technology, sponsored by the Department of Linguistics and Philosophy, with the aim of helping speakers of threatened languages to use their linguistic expertise to help their communities preserve their native languages.

The Native American Language Center
Sponsored by the Department of Native American Studies at the University of California at Davis and the Humanities, Arts, and Cultural Studies Division of the College of Letters and Science.
July 13, 2004.
http://cougar.ucdavis.edu/nas/NALC/home.html

Promotes linguistic research on American Indian languages and intergenerational transfer of language knowledge in Native American communities.

Native American Language Resources
July 13, 2004.
http://www.plumsite.com/palace/native.htm

Alphabetical listing of languages, with links.

Pacific Resources for Education and Language (PREL)
July 12, 2004.
http://www.prel.org/reading/

PREL, an independent, nonprofit organization, provides a range of products and services in the areas of reading and language development for multilanguage and multicultural communities.

Project Jukebox
University of Alaska Fairbank's Oral History Program. 1988.
July 12, 2004.
http://uaf-db.uaf.edu/Jukebox/PJWeb/pjhome.htm

Project Jukebox is an interactive, multimedia computer system designed to access Alaskan oral histories and their associated photographs, maps, and text.

University of California Linguistic Minority Research Institute
Established in 1984.
July 13, 2004.
http://www.lmri.ucsb.edu/

Provides information to anyone interested in issues of language, education, and public policy, especially as they relate to linguistic minorities.

WWW.Virtual Library—American Indians
July 13, 2004.
http://www.hanksville.org/NAresources/

Index of Native American resources on the Internet.

Yamada Language Center
University of Oregon.
July 13, 2004.
http://babel.uoregon.edu/

Yamada Language Guides provide information on over 140 languages, news groups, fonts, and language-related mailing lists.

Research Centers

Advocates for Indigenous California Language Survival
Alliance for California Traditional Arts
Fresno Arts Council
1245 Van Ness
Fresno, CA 93721
559-237-9813
info@actaonline.org
http://www.actaonline.org/TADP/2001_grants/AICLS.htm

Alaska Native Language Center
University of Alaska Fairbanks
Box 757680

Fairbanks, AK 99775
907-474-7874
fyanlp@uaf.edu
http://www.uaf.edu/anlc/

Jonathan Napela Center for Hawaiian Language and Cultural Studies
Brigham Young University–Hawai'i, #1970
55-220 Kulanui Street
Laie, HI 96762
http://www.lds.org/ldsfoundation/accelwork/priority/1,7476,536-1-1-142,00.html

Native California Network
1670 Bloomfield Road
Sebastopol, CA 95472
707-578-0307
No Web address

LITERATURE

Jack Hicks, Michael Kowalewski, and Chris J. Sindt

Traditional histories of regional literatures are constructed from the first churning waves of stolid explorers' logs, natural inventories of discovery and contact to the crown and church, private citizen diaries and daybooks, rough-hewn traders' journals and scouts' accounts, and Christian sermons and moral exhorta to stray not into the forest, lest we become sinners in the hand of an angry god or—worse—go native. But the Pacific Region has far deeper roots, in the oral literatures of indigenous peoples from Mexico to the Arctic Circle, arcing across the Pacific Ocean and south to Hawai'i and the archipelago groups beyond. A few thousand years later, the region was more fantasized than sketched faithfully to the page from live models. García Rodriguez Ordoñez de Montalvo dreamed California into being in *The Adventures of Esplandian* (c. 1510), a romance of a fantastical island "very close to the side of the Terrestrial Paradise," a fierce kingdom paved with gold and peopled with Amazons, ruled over by the warrior Queen Calafia, who used men briefly as breed stock, thereafter feeding them to her herd of prized griffins.

Most broadly, when we speak of the American Pacific Region, we mean the American side of the Pacific Rim, and the root narrative of the Pacific Rim itself has been situated by geologists as the "ring of fire," the necklace (or noose) of earthquakes and volcanoes that encircles the Pacific Ocean. Characteristically, the geologic concept has been quickly appropriated and exercised as literary metaphor by contemporary American Pacific writers, notably novelist and nonfiction writer James D. Houston, in his novel *Continental Drift* (1987) and the more recent collection *The Ring of Fire: A Pacific Basin Journey* (1997). More than 100 years earlier, Mark Twain (1835–1910) took the first writer's stab at imaging what the Pacific Rim (with California at the heart) could become in the mock-heroic tones of *Letters from Hawaii* (1866). Beset by money troubles for much of his life, in "Letter 23," his Pacific ruminations take a financial cast:

With the Pacific Railroad creeping slowly but surely toward her over mountain and desert and preparing to link her with the East, and with the China mail steamers about to throw open to her the vast trade of our opulent coast line stretching from the Amoor river to the equator, what State in the Union has so splendid a future before her as California? Not one, perhaps. She should awake and be ready to join her home prosperity to these tides of commerce that are so soon to sweep toward her from the east and the west. To America it has been vouchsafed to materialize the vision, and realize the dream of centuries, of the enthusiasts of the old world. We have found the true Northwest Passage . . . the enchanted land whose mere drippings, in the ages that are gone, enriched and aggrandized ancient Venice, first, then Portugal, Holland, and in our own time, England—and each in succession they longed and sought for the fountain head of this vast Oriental wealth, and sought in vain. The path was hidden to them, but we have found it over the waves of the Pacific, and American enterprise will penetrate to the heart and center of its hoarded treasures, its imperial affluence. The gateway of this path is the Golden Gate of San Francisco. . . . She is about to be appointed to preside over almost the exclusive trade of 450,000,000 people— the almost exclusive trade of the most opulent land on earth.[1]

By the 1920s, geological theories of the formation and continuity of the Pacific Rim and American Pacific were roughly in place, and over the next fifty years, vulcanologists and plate tectonicists refined the cohesive scientific narrative that informs our matrix sense of the region today. But it remained for Robinson Jeffers (1887–1962), the first great poet of the American Pacific, to extrapolate from the early science to imagine the deep continuity of the region. In poems such as "Continent's End" (1924), he stood on his Carmel headland and addressed the Pacific Ocean and the primordial "tides of fire" that gave it birth and saw in "the boundaries of granite and spray" a vision that would "yoke the Aleutian seal-rocks with the lava and coral sowings that flower the south." In such visionary poems, he imagined the beginning face of a continuous American Pacific (with finally tragic ends for Jeffers) with the sorts of complex biological, demographic, and cultural features that characterize the region as it defines itself in our time.

In truth, the American Pacific as metaregion is still emerging, much as a volcanic island is first shaped by submarine lava flow and hardens only as it emerges and becomes visible. Unlike regions such as the Deep South or New England, both defined by a geographic and historical continuity, homogenous demography, and enduring sociopolitical traditions, the American Pacific Region is spatially immense and geologically complex, paved by colonialism, layered by immigrations (and the mixed messages of welcome and exclusion newcomers found), and fractured by tensions between the forces of assimilation and those of cultural preservation. It is defined more by sudden economic booms and busts and political change and characterized by ongoing conflicts over the uses of natural resources (gold, lumber, oil, water, open land); and the sciences—more than literary history, critical theory, history, sociology, or anthropology—offer disciplines, information, and approaches that can best inform the humanist's task of getting a handle on the American Pacific Region. For example, the emerging science of ecology and the study of bioregion have offered especially valuable windows into grasping how the literature of *place*—first, wild and natural and, more recently, urban and built—emerges both topically and aesthetically from the natural and constructed Pacific landscape, whether situated in postmodern Los Angeles, the Cascades, or the Hana rainforest in Maui.

To contextualize and inform a discussion of the region and its literary manifestations, five stages of the development of the American Pacific may be considered. They are:

1. The earliest indigenous literatures of the "First Nations"—the oral, preliterate, polyphonous body of creation myths, legends, cautionary tales, prayers, chants, visions, invocations, and accounts of the coming of the new people that existed prior to (and only shortly after) the initial Mexican, American, and European contact. Fragments of this corpus have been preserved by tribal practice and transferred to us by linguists, archaeologists, and anthropologists as they worked to prevent the extinction of first peoples, their languages, and folkways.

2. The collected narratives (journals, accounts to the crown, diaries, letters) of discovery, exploration, and conquering by the first waves of Spanish, Russian, and other European, Mexican, and American explorers and conquerors.

3. The bipolar stage in which (a) a body of populist forms of literary entertainment emerges—doggerel verse, declaimed ballads, folksy anecdotes, whimsical memories, tall tales, and nostalgic sketches that were featured in weekly newspapers and dramatized at community gatherings and barroom and gambling den diversions in the mid-nineteenth century—and (b) an emerging tide of writing with greater literary aspirations. But just as many frontier towns of the Pacific West erected opera houses to demonstrate their newfound civility, so, too, were many of the first serious literary ventures—especially poetry—imitative of romanticized East Coast and European literature, the more abstract and loftier, the better.

Luis Valdez (center), author of *Zoot Suit*, poses in front of the Broadway theater where his play is running. He is flanked by a costumed actor from the production and his brother Daniel, who wrote the music and appears in the show. © Stephanie Maze/Corbis.

4. The literature that emerged in the mid-nineteenth century and began to incorporate the themes that live to the present in the American Pacific, rooting them in specific western landscapes, regions and bioregions, cultures, and shared and unique histories and attitudes, beginning the first experiments with forms styles that might be uniquely expressive of Pacific Western experience. The inherent danger here was of willful provincialism, limited local color, and self-parody, particularly—as early figures such as Mark Twain, Bret Harte (1836–1902), and Joaquin Miller (c. 1839–1902) were aware—to feed the insatiable East Coast appetite for colorful accounts of the romantic and barbarous New West.

5. The multigeneric (encompassing drama, lyric poetry, short and long fiction, biography, and narrative history) and transgeneric (ritual theater and pageants, fantasy and science fiction, the long poem, and the

many hybrids of creative nonfiction) mature literature, one both self-conscious and self-critical of its origins (as in the works of Josiah Royce [1855–1916]) and capable of treating founding history and myths in a self-reflexive, critical, and often comic manner. Simultaneously and perhaps paradoxically, such a mature and coherent national or large regional literature ranges beyond its boundaries to engage larger human and universal sympathies and readerships. James Joyce (1882–1941) was rooted first in Dublin, William Faulkner (1897–1962) in Mississippi, John Steinbeck (1902–1968) in California's Great Central Valley, and Gary Snyder (1930–) in the foothills of the Sierra Nevada. A key attribute of such a mature regional literature is its ability to circle back on its origins, to revive, reimagine, remake the past into a viable contemporary literary instrument. Consider Sherman Alexie's (1966–) reservation fiction and film, Garrett Hongo's (1951–) *Volcano*, a memoir of Hawai'i, Brenda Hillman's (1951–) poetic collection *Cascadia*, informed as it is by plate tectonics, and Luis Valdez's (1940–) *Zoot Suit*, a dramatic exploration of El Pachuco as a powerful cultural presence, the spirit of Aztlan alive in contemporary Los Angeles.

These five stages are not strictly chronologically sequential or separated—they should be envisioned as bright beads on one string—and a mature regional literature may manifest three, four, or five tendencies simultaneously. The Pacific Region encompasses a great sweep of cultures and ecosystems. Their sheer size and diversity poses daunting challenges to anyone trying to understand the cultural metabolism of this region. How can we comprehend the polyethnic flows of language, culture, and technology that began in the early sixteenth century, when Spanish explorers first ventured north from Acapulco in search of the legendary Strait of Anián, or Northwest Passage, from the Pacific to the Atlantic? The challenge of trying to fully "fathom" this region has proven irresistible to writers, who have produced a truly remarkable profusion of fictional and nonfictional works that include everything from novels, plays, and short stories to letters, diaries, autobiographies, expeditionary reports, travel accounts, and scores of personal narratives.

NATIVE AMERICANS AND LITERATURE

This outpouring of printed material documenting and dramatizing life in the Pacific Region was, of course, predated by age-old oral traditions that celebrated and embodied the deep history, spirituality, and ecological know-how of the first inhabitants of these areas. The first maritime explorations and settlements in the Pacific Region were undertaken for several thousand years by native peoples ranging from the Aleutian archipelago to the Baja Peninsula. North Pacific coastal peoples (including Eskimo, Aleut, Tlingit, Haida, Nootka, Pomo, Miwok, and Chumash) utilized rich marine environments for fishing and sea mammal hunting. Around 3,500 years ago, Polynesians began to leave Tahiti and venture north to Hawaii, part of the long-distance canoe voyaging that the scholar Max Quanchi has called "the most remarkable achievement in exploration history."[2] The familiarity of all these native peoples with the Pacific Ocean infused everything from boat design to ceremonial regalia. Likewise, the earliest land-based explorations of the West Coast were undertaken, for centuries, by tribes from the Bering Strait to Baja California. They managed diverse plant communities, established complex trade networks, and possessed a detailed knowledge of their local terrain. These cultures were sustained by complex oral cultures and traditional songs, chants and dances (such as the *hula* in Hawaii). Malcolm Margolin, who publishes the journal *News from Native California*, reminds us that California, for instance, had the densest pre-Columbian population anywhere north of Mexico, reflected in the more than 100 Indian languages, "seventy percent of them as mutually unintelligible as English and Chinese," spoken in California when the first European explorers arrived.[3]

While literary scholarship long ignored this oral tradition, since the 1970s, native language preservation movements and publications such as *News from Native California* have brought to the greater public an awareness of many of the beautiful and poetic origin myths from tribes like the Maidu, the Chumash, the Paiute, and the Wintun. Along with myths that explain how the world was created, Native tribal literature often sought to explain and inscribe what in the modern world constitutes a legal system. Thus, there are also stories of how love, marriage, and family should work, just as there are prayers and chants for the order of the world, both within the tribe's structure and without—songs about the "dream time" from the Ohlone or the Yokuts Rattlesnake Ceremony Song, to name a few. Finally, just as so much pre-modern and modern literature seeks to explain the "meaning of life," native chants, stories, songs, and prayers addressed the complex issue of old age, death, and the afterlife. Many are collected in *The Literature of California, Volume I* (UC Press, 2000), *The Way We Lived: California Indian Stories, Songs, and Reminiscences* (Heyday Press, 1991), *Indian Legends of the Pacific Northwest* (University of California Press, 1953, reissued 2003), *Tales from the Dena: Indian Stories from the Tanana, Koyukuk, and Yukon Rivers* (University of Washington Press, 1995), and *Hawaiian Folk Tales: A Collection of Native Legends* and *More Hawaiian Folk Tales: A Collection of Native Legends and Traditions*, both by Thomas G. Thrum (Ams Press, 1987 and University Press of the Pacific, 2001). Additionally, contemporary writers have worked successfully to inscribe novels and stories with the native legends of Pacific Region tribes, producing intelligent and sensitive works such as Darryl Babe Wilson's *The Morning the Sun Went Down*, Nancy Lord's *Man Who Swam with Beavers* (Coffee House Press, 2001) and the title story of Leslie Marmon Silko's *Storyteller*.

A SURVEY OF NONFICTION ACCOUNTS OF THE FAR WEST

This extraordinary palimpsest of indigenous life, spirit, language, and culture, however, remained undocumented in *writing* until the incursions of European merchants and military explorers. Thus our knowledge of the precontact lives of native peoples in the Pacific Region is heavily dependent upon the writings of nonnative missionaries, soldiers, miners, and anthropologists (the majority of whom, sadly, were ill-informed about or even actively hostile towards native cultures).

Particularly in nonfictional accounts of the Far West, a close attention to the particularities of topography, botany, weather, and animal life has been a continuing preoccupation. It was present in the accounts of early diarists like Father Juan Crespí (?–1782), who kept a unique mile-by-mile diary of Gaspar de Portolá's "Sacred Expedition" in 1769 northward from San Diego on a route later designated El Camino Reál (the King's Highway). Crespí recorded details about wildlife, earthquakes and encounters with Native Americans. While accounts such as his and those of fellow missionary/explorers Pedro Fages and Junipero Serro lacked the overt religious typology of accounts such as those by Puritans William Bradford, they still "looked" at the Pacific Region with an eye dominated by the Catholic missionary vision. Similarly, ten years later, in 1779, captain Cook's expedition sailed into *Karakakooa* (Kealakekua) bay on the island of Owhyhee (Hawai'i). Initially treated with great respect by the island's natives, he was eventually killed when he tried to take a Hawaiian chief hostage to force the return of a boat. When his crew returned to England, they circulated text and drawings of the exotic island culture that reflected more about the attitudes of a conservative Christian Europe than the indigenous Islanders and their life.

More secular accounts of the region were often just as biased, for they fulfilled the writer's need to dramatize his own actions and, perhaps, his perception of what might most impress posterity. John Charles Fremont reported on Oregon and North California, as did Lansford Hastings. Lewis and Clark's arrival at the mouth of Oregon's Columbia River in 1812 is but part of their collected journals, the subject of a recent PBS documentary. The journal entries of the Meriwether Lewis (1774–1809) and William Clark (1770–1838) Expedition provide a detailed record of natural phenomena, rich with immediacy and hardship. On November 18, 1805, at the aptly named Cape Disappointment, Clark writes about a foray to the ocean:

> made a fire and dined on 4 brant and 48 Plever which was killed by Labiech on the coast as we came on. Rubin Fields Killed a Buzzard of the large Kind [a California condor] near the whale we Saw measured from the tips of the wings across 9½ feet. . . . Some rain in the after part of the night. Men appear much Satisfied with their trip beholding with estonishment the high waves dashing against the rocks & this emence Ocian.[4]

The perceptive, often meditative journal of fur trapper Jedediah Smith (1799–1831) in the 1820s or the records of the dauntless Scottish botanist David Douglas (1799–1834) (after whom the Douglas fir is named), who explored the Pacific Northwest and the Hawaiian Islands in the 1820s and 1830s, offer similarly engaging accounts of frontier ecosystems and fledgling settlements. Clarence King's (1842–1901) *Mountaineering in the Sierra Nevada* (1872) won international fame for California's Geological Survey (founded in 1860) and, along with Mark Twain's *Roughing It* (1872), created a vogue for self-dramatizing western emigrant writing that mixed lyrical description with tall-tale humor. Indeed, the need to extol one's own abilities stretched beyond the explorer's realm. Photographers such as Eadweard Muybridge and Carleton Watkins were nearly as admired for their physical prowess as their camera work, and recently, Nathanial Lewis argued in *Unsettling the Literary West: Authenticity and Authorship* that nearly all western writing grapples to some degree with the author's need to establish his—or her—own mystique as a westerner.

Along those lines, women's pioneer diaries told the story of the landscape as it first confronted the eyes and hearts of adventurous women charged with "taming" this vast region. Sarah Eleanor Royce, who crossed the Sierra Nevada range and eventually settled in California; Diane Lucina Spicer Block, who lived, among other places, in Oregon and California; Esther Roloefson Johnson, who came across the Oregon Trail and helped found the Cumberland Presbyterian Church in Oregon; Elizabeth Wisdom Rhoads Hamrick, who brought three children across the Oregon Trail during the height of the Gold Rush, to eventually settle in California's gold country to raise eight more children—the numerous diaries of west-bound women offer yet another perspective on the region.

Poet-naturalist John Muir (1838–1914) wrote several books, notably *The Mountains of California* (1894), about his ramblings and sojourns in the Sierra Nevada mountains or, as he called them, the "Range of Light," which created a new rhetoric of the alpine sublime and advocated wilderness preservation. Muir personified a distinctively West Coast notion—vaguely bohemian—that the "good life" was linked to hiking, camping, mountaineering, and outdoor recreation. This notion of the Far West as a splendid scenic wonderland, full of outdoor adventure and genial good health, appears in works from James Mason Hutchings' (c. 1824–1902) *Scenes of Wonder and Curiosity in California* (1860) to Albert S. Evans' (1831–1872) *À La California* (1873), J.

John Muir, 1909. Courtesy of the Library of Congress.

Smeaton Chase's California trail books (1910), Charles Nordhoff's promotional narratives (1872, 1874), Francis Fuller Victor's *Atlantis Arisen* (1891), and new aesthetic appreciations of the deserts by Mary Austin (1868–1934), John C. Van Dyke (1856–1932), and George Wharton James (1858–1923). Magazines like *Land of Sunshine* (founded 1894; *Out West* after 1902), *Touring Topics* (founded 1925; *Westways* after 1934), and *Sunset* (founded 1898) promoted cultural tourism, recreation, and a new outdoor, often suburban "lifestyle" on the West Coast.

A number of contemporary works have also focused upon the nuances of particular places in the Pacific Region: works like David Rains Wallace's meditations on myth and evolution in *The Klamath Knot* (1983); Barry Lopez's (1945–   ) *Arctic Dreams* (1986); the essays in David James Duncan's *My Story as Told by Water* (2001); Richard Nelson's exploration of subsistence living on the southeast coast of Alaska, *The Island Within* (1989); Gary Snyder's (1930–   ) essays on wildness, freedom, etiquette, and place in *The Practice of the Wild* (1990), *Totem Salmon* (1999) by Freeman House; and Dan Duane's account of a surfer's year on the central California coast in *Caught Inside* (1996).

Because its population and wealth have eclipsed that of the other states in the Pacific Region, California has been the epicenter of many of the cultural contradictions that have come to characterize the region as a whole. Despite a popular image of laid-back informality and good living, the state has also insistently been identified with transience and unchecked growth. California has been the stage for an intensified version of a scenario enacted throughout American history: the collision between restless mobility and "place." Variations of this historical tension orbit throughout California history in battles over wilderness preservation and restrictive immigration laws, water engineering projects and residential zoning restrictions, offshore oil drilling and lettuce boycotts, lumber sales, and the character of urban police departments.

CALIFORNIA'S MAGNETISM

Yet no matter how disorienting, the vertigo inspired by expanding growth in the state has often been seen as stimulating, as Bayard Taylor (1825–1878) revealed as early as 1850 in his travel narrative *El Dorado*. The San Francisco of the late 1840s, Taylor notes, increased daily "by from fifteen to thirty houses." "The change which had been wrought in all parts of town during the last six weeks," he says, "seemed little short of magic." "The very air" in San Francisco "is pregnant with the magnetism of bold, spirited, unwearied action, and he who but ventures into the outer circle of the whirlpool is spinning, ere he has time for thought, in its dizzy vortex."[5] It was the gold rush that established the boomtown swagger and cosmopolitan "magnetism" of the Golden State and that catapulted it permanently into the national imagination as a radiant emblem of possibility and life in the fast lane. As Kevin Starr, the state's preeminent historian, asserts, the gold rush forever linked the state with a charge of hope: "As a hope in defiance of facts, as a longing which could ennoble and encourage but which could also turn and devour itself, the symbolic value of California endured."[6]

In pursuit of hope and happiness, the blessing or the curse of California, depending upon one's perspective, is the state's openness to new ideas (whether community colleges, tax revolts, no-smoking initiatives, or political recalls) and its willingness to take a chance (in architecture, new cuisine, or the psychedelic counterculture).

The Enduring Lure of California

The lasting power of the California dream legacy has been affirmed by even so wry a commentator as the novelist Stanley Elkin (1930–1995). Encountering "all the PR of a tanned and chosen people" on a visit in 1990, Elkin still felt the indisputable allure of the state. "It strikes me," he said, "that California is a choice one makes, a blow one strikes for hope."

Oh, St. Louis, where I'm from, is a choice, too, but not in the way California is. Unless a job's waiting, or he has other, very specific, reasons, no one ever wakes up one day and says, I must move to Missouri. No one chooses to find happiness in Maryland. And California, whether it delivers or not, is *about* happiness, as America, whether it delivers or not, is about freedom.[7]

The Perennial Death of the California Dream

What is often forgotten, however, is that Bad News about California is nothing new; it has an intricate, sometimes predictable history. *Time* and other mainstream eastern publications steadily churned out special issues on the death of the California Dream long before the L.A. riots in 1992 and the Loma Prieta and Northridge earthquakes in 1989 and 1994, respectively. The late 1960s and early 1970s—when talk was of Charles Manson, Patty Hearst, the Watts riots, and the mass suicides of Jim Jones' People's Temple rather than of O.J. Simpson or Kobe Bryant—saw headlines

like "Shades of the Sunbelt Shift: California Dream in a Body Bag" and book titles such as *Anti-California: Report from Our First Parafascist State* (1971) by Kenneth Lamott. In fact, a fascination with watching hope turn and devour itself in
California has been a long-standing preoccupation. Mike Davis' cultural histories
City of Quartz (1990) and *The Ecology of Fear* (1998), works of historiography that
often read like novels, are part of a noir tradition that has its inception in the beginnings of Anglo settlement. Few know the names of the pioneers who successfully made it over the Sierras in the 1840s, but everyone knows of the Donner
Party (partly because George Stewart's riveting narrative of the disaster, *Ordeal by
Hunger* [1936], still keeps spellbound readers up all night).

California Writers

For every California booster gleaming with optimism about the state, there has
been a countervailing naysayer, from Henry David Thoreau (1817–1862), who
considered the gold rush exodus a sign of moral bankruptcy ("Going to California," Thoreau fumed in his journal, "It is only three thousand miles nearer to
hell"),[8] to Nathanael West (1903–1940), who so memorably chronicled the bored,
emotionally vacant automatons who "came to California to die" in *The Day of the
Locust* (1939). Because there has historically been an aura of expectation and glamorous possibility about the state, because the dream of a better life away from cold
weather or the past or political persecution has fueled the expectations of the millions who arrive in California, failure or disappointment there is usually magni-
fied: made to seem more dramatic and more damning. It can also, especially in the
popular eastern media, be edged with a complicated mix of envy, resentment, and
self-righteousness.

California writers are generally more willing to explore rather than simply exploit
the animating contradictions of the state, but a negative, sometimes pessimistic
cast of mind is still highly polished in the California literary grain. As many critics have noted, California writers (from Bret Harte [1836–1902] to Ambrose Bierce
[1842–1914] and Raymond Chandler [1888–1959], from James Cain [1892–1977]
to Sam Shepard [1943–], Carolyn See, Joan Didion [1934–], and Walter
Mosley [1952–]) repeatedly explore the dark ironies that lurk behind the California of postcards. The most engaging artistic works about California and the
larger Pacific Region, however, are those that suggest that ironic juxtaposition too
must be used carefully, lest it become too predictable a response. The best works
intimate that the complexity and contradictions of California have a way of out-
stripping or undermining our best attempts to understand them. Works like T. Cor-
aghessan Boyle's novel *The Tortilla Curtain* (1995) or Anna Deavere Smith's
Twilight—Los Angeles, 1992 (1994) raise barbed questions about how one makes
sense of a region in which gleaming space shuttles land in the desert while migrants
sleep in cardboard refrigerator boxes in the hills outside San Diego. What kind of
stories will best register the texture of life in cities where fifty different languages
are spoken in a single political district? How does one dare to be optimistic—but
also, how does one dare to settle for only cynicism—in thinking about the historical complexities and injustices of the Pacific Region?

John Steinbeck, 1966. Courtesy of the Library of Congress.

John Steinbeck

Many earlier literary works about this region demonstrate that such questions are not new—only more publicized. John Steinbeck's novel *The Grapes of Wrath* (1939) juxtaposes hope and bigotry, resiliency and brute force in the struggles of migrant Okies. Like Frank Norris (1870–1902) before him, in *The Octopus* (1901), Steinbeck saw, in the large-scale agribusiness of the Far West (a corporate operation analogous to commercial overfishing in Hawai'i and oil drilling and industrial logging in Alaska), an ideal betrayed and a dream deferred. Steinbeck predicted dire consequences for a system of absentee landowners, flows of national and global capital, and a dehumanizing industrial technology that destroyed surpluses of oranges, potatoes, and livestock just in order to keep prices artificially high:

There is a sorrow here that weeping cannot symbolize. There is a failure here that topples all our success. The fertile earth, the straight tree rows, the sturdy trunks, and the ripe fruit. And children dying of pellagra must die because a profit cannot be taken from an orange. . . . The people come with nets to fish for potatoes in the river, and the guards hold them back; they come in rattling cars to get the dumped oranges, but the kerosene is sprayed. And they listen . . . to the screaming pigs being killed in a ditch and covered with quicklime . . . and in the eyes of the people there is the failure; and in the eyes of the hungry there is a growing wrath. In the souls of the people the grapes of wrath are filling and growing heavy, growing heavy for the vintage.[9]

Rose of Sharon undergoes a hard labor and gives birth to a stillborn child, and unlike the movie version of the novel, the end of the book is extremely bleak, with the Joad family living in a boxcar, watching the floodwaters rise and the orchards fill with mud. The Joads are homeless, broke, and down on their luck. The scene would seem to endorse the bitter sentiment of the crippled black character, Crooks, in *Of Mice and Men* (1937): "Nobody never gets to heaven," Crooks declares, "and nobody gets no land. It's just in their head. They're all the time talkin' about it, but it's jus' in their head."[10]

Yet even in the face of such stark realities, and the angry social realism designed to indict them, there is always room for something more in Steinbeck's fiction. If the point of his work was simply to demonstrate that all dreams are illusions, that human nature is innately cruel, and that we can reliably count on the worst in people, he would be too smug and too limited an author. Rose of Sharon's now famous act of suckling a starving man at the end of *The Grapes of Wrath* is a case in point here. The old man is frightened and humiliated, and he does not wish to accept the young woman's help.

> Rose of Sharon loosened one side of the blanket and bared her breast. "You got to," she said. She squirmed closer and pulled his head close. "There!" she said. Her hand moved behind his head and supported it. Her fingers moved gently in his hair. She looked up and across the barn, and her lips came together and smiled mysteriously.[11]

This image was controversial at the time, and Steinbeck was asked to change the ending. He refused. The ending was no more significant than other parts of the novel, he told his publisher, but it was still important. "If there is a symbol," he wrote, "it is a survival symbol not a love symbol, it must be an accident, it must be a stranger, and it must be quick."[12] Rose of Sharon's wonderful, mysterious smile holds in it all the elusive strength and resilience and—despite all they have faced—the tenderness of the Joads and those like them. "Their blood is strong," Steinbeck wrote of the migrant workers he encountered in the Central Valley.[13] And he considered their strength of character and their will to survive one of the noblest things he had encountered in America.

WRITING ABOUT OREGON, WASHINGTON, ALASKA, AND HAWAI'I

Other authors in the Pacific Region have memorably used history to create the future by recovering the past. This might, at first, seem odd, as the insistent demographic pressures of growth and development in much of the region have extinguished a sense of the past. Many residents of Portland, Tacoma, Honolulu, and Sacramento have watched in astonishment at an accelerated rate of growth that, particularly since World War II, has obliterated familiar landmarks and outstripped residents' capacity to orient themselves to new surroundings. In response, some authors in the Pacific Region have looked to the past with a revisionist historical imagination, attempting to give voice to characters and populations that had been previously silenced or ignored.

Other important historical works set in the Pacific Northwest include David Guterson's bestselling novel about race relations in post–World War II Puget Sound, *Snow Falling on Cedars* (1994); Shannon Applegate's history of her Oregon pioneer family, *Skookum* (1988); James D. Houston's powerful retelling of the ordeal of the Donner Party, *Snow Mountain Passage* (2001); Annie Dillard's novel about frontier Washington, *The Living* (1992); Murray Morgan's history of Seattle, *Skid Road* (1951); and the philosophical explorations of Washington writer Charles Johnson.

The West Coast's vaunted hospitality (at least in urban areas and college towns) to the offbeat and the eccentric has provided a cultural atmosphere since the late 1950s that has been receptive to street theater, Be In's, Happenings, Gay Pride parades, and a vast array of countercultural experiments. The impulse, in literary works, can be seen in everything from the comic raunchiness of Ishmael Reed's fiction or the mischievous metaphors of Tom Robbins' novels such as *Another Roadside Attraction* (1971) and *Still Life with Woodpecker* (1980) to the wacky narratives of Jim Dodge's *Fup* (1983), Gerald Vizenor's *The Trickster of Liberty* (1988), and the earlier "merry pranksterism" of Richard Brautigan and Ken Kesey. It can be felt in the generic blurring of literary fiction and fantasy in novels by Portland author Ursula LeGuin, such as *Always Coming Home* (1985) and *Searoad: Chronicles of Klatsand* (1991). LeGuin, a pioneer in feminist and science fiction, was born in California but moved to Portland, Oregon, where she wrote, and garnered numerous awards for, books such as *The Left Hand of Darkness, Always Coming Home* (considered by many to be the only bioregional novel), and *The Lathe of Heaven*. Brautigan, born in Tacoma, Washington, is considered by many to be the supreme representative of the countercultural movement, a writer whose antiestablishment prose went hand in hand with his often law-breaking lifestyle. Tom Robbins, a transplant to Seattle, Washington, began as a writer at the Seattle *Post-Intelligencer* before embarking on a career as novelist whose outrageous characters and their practices embody the independence and nonconformist attitudes of the Pacific Region. Ken Kesey's *Sometimes A Great Notion* is a powerful and adamantly regional tale of an Oregon logging clan embroiled in the bitter strike that has harnessed a small lumber town along the Oregon coast. The Stamper men—Henry, the fierce patriarch, Hank, a son entangled in trying to be his father, and Leland, the outcast intellectual son—and the woman in the middle, Hank's wife Viv, play out a modern day Greek tragedy in the quickly disappearing first growth forests of Oregon's wilderness.

Of course, any attempt to characterize a region (particularly a region as complicated and far-flung as the Pacific Region) in terms of a given aesthetic can be only suggestive, not prescriptive. For instance, any overemphasis of styles of postmodern urban eclecticism and self-subversion is likely to overlook an equally powerful tradition of dryland realism in the Pacific Region, which has focused on rural areas in the interior of Oregon, Washington, Alaska, and California and the tough, working-class laborers who make their living there. In the 1970s and 1980s, Yakima, Washington native Raymond Carver, whose most famous short story, *Cathedral*, is one of American literature's most frequently anthologized works, created a new brand of spare, unblinking fiction (dubbed "minimalism" by the critics) that focused on the bankruptcy, alcoholism, and infidelities of characters in the Pacific Northwest trapped in economic hardship, failing marriages, and self-doubt.

Carver joined fellow Pacific Region resident William Kittredge to create a body of work that used the spartan landscape of east or urban Oregon and Washington as a parallel to the bleak landscape of existential despair and unending personal isolation. *Hole in the Sky* (1993), Kittredge's harrowing account of his own psychological breakdown and the breakdown of the Western myth, fittingly includes a drunken episode with Raymond Carver at the historic Benson Hotel in Oregon.

If the literature of the Pacific Northwest and Alaska often seeks to create an aesthetic of Paradise, or its counterpoint, Pacific literature must more frequently work to engage in some sort of dialogue with prevailing notions of Paradise. The extent to which Hawaii and the Pacific Islands are a Paradise, and, more important, whose Paradise—one that belongs to the discourse of pre European contact or that which has been created by the tourist trade—all are themes that drive the literature of the Pacific Islands. *The Girl in the Moon* (1996), for example, by Sia Figiel, presents collected stories about Samoan girls to make the point that Paradise is not all that it seems. Figiel's *Where We Once Belonged* (2000), an exploration of gender, class and sexuality in the lives of Samoan women, uses a variety of narrative techniques, including the informal "talk story," the traditional Samoan storytelling form of su'ifefiloi, and more elegiac poetic reflections on the landscape of Samoa, to look at the difficulties of growing up female in an objectionably patriarchal, yet physically desirable, culture. In addition, novels like Kiana Davenport's *Song of the Exile* (2000) explore the aftermath of the attack on Pearl Harbor on Hawaiian culture while *Blu's Hanging* (1997), by Lois-Anne Yamanaka, uses the cultural crossroads of the Hawaiian island of Molokai to examine the lives of three children trying to hold themselves together after the death of their mother.

THE ESSENCE OF A PLACE?

The critic Pierre Sansot suggests that instead of asking, "What is the essence of a place?" one should substitute the question, "What can one dream about it?"[14] Rainsford Chan, a fourth-generation Chinese American in Shawn Wong's novel *Homebase* (1979), offers one way of answering that question when it applies to the Pacific Region. Rainsford remembers his father taking him to Yosemite as a boy to show him "the stump of a once giant redwood tree." He "showed me its rings of growth. Like a blind man, he made me run my fingers over each year grain to feel the year of my great-grandfather's birth, my grandfather's birth, his own birth, and my birth." "Out of all this I will see dreams," Rainsford says, "[I will] see myself fixed in place on the land, [and] hear stories my father taught me."[15]

The Pacific littoral has for eastern Americans inspired an exceptionally strong projection of desire and freedom that Wallace Stegner once lovingly termed "the geography of hope," but it is now being increasingly enriched and complicated as other cultural "directions" come into view. The sustaining metaphor of the westward migration of easterners heading for the setting sun retains its historical potency. In Steinbeck's story "The Leader of the People" (1945), a Salinas Valley rancher who "led a wagon train clear across the plains to the coast" tells his impressionable young grandson: "There's no place to go. There's the ocean to stop you. There's a line of old men along the shore hating the ocean because it stopped them."[16] The title of the first important West Coast literary anthology, Joseph Henry Jackson's *Continent's End: A Collection of California Writing* (1944), seemed to evoke that same sense of limits and reaching the verge of westward yearning. Yet the Robinson Jeffers' (1887–1962) poem that provides the title actually provides a slightly different sense of imaginative location. His speaker stands on a sea cliff, at the thundering "boundaries of granite and spray." He faces the vast Pacific expanse and feels "the immense breadth of the continent" behind him. Yet in his address to the ocean, the speaker provides an image not of limits but of cross-

Wallace Stegner, 1937. Courtesy of the Library of Congress.

directional contact, because "the long migrations" have met across the Pacific, which "yokes the Aleutian seal-rocks with the lava and coral/ sowings that flower the south." The Pacific links "the life that sought the sunrise faces ours that/ has followed the evening star."[17] The word "ours" here suggests a connection with the westering population. But Jeffers' poem presents a valuable way of visualizing the West Coast as a four-way intersection rather than a cultural stop sign. The historical and cultural complexity of the West cannot be fully imagined until one acknowledges the mobile flows of people, viruses, plant and animal species, ideas, and art forms moving back and forth from multiple centers along multiple strands: a spider web whose filaments are a net of airlines, bloodlines, and story lines.[18]

CULTURAL FUSION WRITERS

Luis Valdez, for his part, proposes the idea of "cultural fusion," a force that reverses the destructive potential of *fission*: "instead of splitting the cultural atom, we are going to integrate it even more. . . . Instead of coming into a place and blowing it apart, why not fuse?" Valdez knows this will not be an easy process in "this maddening reality of ours."

> I address myself to ancient fears, fears of miscegenation. "What will happen to our kids if they end up looking and being like *them*?" It is a fearful thing that touches every community, but nevertheless it is inevitable. Fusion. It is not just a question of dealing with the newly arrived Vietnamese; it is a question of one day *being* Vietnamese. It is not a question that whoever does not speak Spanish learn Spanish; you are already more Spanish than you realize. You have been living here for a long time, and there's more in those tacos than you realize. We know herbs and plants. We absorb, and then we become and we evolve.[19]

Pacific Region authors—particularly authors of color—have been hard at work in the last several decades exploring the ironies, challenges, and rich rewards of such cultural fusion. The trans-Pacific consciousness at work in Maxine Hong Kingston's *Tripmaster Monkey* (1988) and *The Fifth Book of Peace* (2003); Sherman Alexie's collection of short stories, *The Lone Ranger and Tonto Fistfight in Heaven* (1993); Jess Mowry's fiction about African American teenagers in Oakland; poet Garrett Hongo's memoir of Hawai'i, *Volcano* (1995); Richard Rodriguez's remarkable reflections on ethnicity, eroticism, and history in *Brown* (2002); Louis Owens' metaphysical mystery novels, set in Washington and California, about mixed-blood Indian characters; works by Native Hawaiians such as John Dominis Holt's novel *Waimea Summer* (1976); the Englishman Jonathan Raban's wry commentary on metropolitan Seattle in *Hunting Mister Heartbreak* (1990) or his sea voyage from Puget Sound to Alaska in *Passage to Juneau* (1999); Haunani-Kay Trask's impassioned essays in *From a Native Daughter* (1993); George Hu'Eu Sanford Kanahele's *Ku Kanaka: Stand Tall* (1993); and the work of Native Alaskan writers like those featured in the anthology *Raven Tells Stories* (1991)—all these works, and many others, demonstrate the ways in which Pacific Region authors continue to send their verbal imaginations into the vortex of contemporary life and return with remarkable stories to share. Those

Sherman Alexie, 1995. Rex Rystedt/MPI/ Getty Images.

tales are not for the easily disoriented or the faint of heart, but they can help provide, as William Kittredge says, "a fresh dream of who we are" so we can do good work together.[20]

THE POETRY OF THE PACIFIC REGION

Facing west from California's shores,
Inquiring, tireless, seeking what is yet unfound,
I, a child, very old, over waves, towards the house of maternity, the land of migrations, look afar,
Look off the shores of my western sea, the circle almost circled.
—Walt Whitman, "Facing West from California's Shores"[21]

Walt Whitman's "Facing West from California's Shores" set the tone for a century and a half of poetry that comes to terms with life along the Pacific Rim. The poem reveals a romantic image of the western poet, an image adopted and practiced by countless figures who came to, or came of age in, the western states: the seeker, the childlike visionary, and the immigrant all rolled into one. The stance that Whitman identified is unique to poetry from the Pacific states. This stance almost always points westward—not toward the east and its European culture and publishing power but toward the sea, the Pacific islands, and the Asian continent beyond.

Though much of the poetry of the region was written far inland—in the valleys, deserts, interior mountains, and volcanic highlands of Alaska, California, Hawai'i, Oregon, and Washington—the poetry of the West often returns to Whitman's "shore," the coastal tide line: shifting, marginal, a place of great fragility, and a place of constant change. Robinson Jeffers (1887–1962) captured this spirit well in his "Continent's End," which describes the poet "gazing at the boundaries of granite and spray" while he feels behind him "the immense breadth of the continent" and before him "the mass and double stretch of water."[22] Yvor Winters (1900–1968) is struck by the "chaos of commingling power" as "the whole Pacific hovers, hour by hour."[23] In the work of these poets, the tide line begins to serve as a metaphor for the unstable space so many westerners thrive in. It is betwixt and between, embodying flux, and rife with the possibility of change. Even a poet such as Michael Palmer (1943–), who stresses the unpredictable nature of language and meaning, reveals his western spirit in a poetics of the tide line: "Once I fell in the Ocean/ when I didn't know I fell in the ocean."[24]

The early poetry of the Pacific states (notwithstanding the chants and songs of the Native American tribal cultures) comes out of exploration, immigration, and settlement, which ranged from the 1840s in California to the 1890s in Alaska. The poetry from this experience is characterized by the hardships of daily life and the persistent and creative spirit—often guided by religious devotion—that immigrants needed to survive.

The poetry of the region came of age—with some notable exceptions—along with the developing urban centers and universities of the region, particularly in the San Francisco Bay area and Seattle. But no single state or city can claim dominance in the region, and rich vibrant poetry has sprung from Los Angeles, Honolulu, and Fairbanks, from the Olympic Peninsula, the island of Maui, and the great Central Valley of California. Across the vast region, there have been striking conflicts and unusual alliances, often transcending regional identity: A poet from San Francisco's North Beach might have more in common with a poet from Seattle than he does with a poet from across the Bay at the University of California. Still, the poetry of the Pacific states has forged a cumulative identity fitting the vastness and wildness of the region.

Writing Conferences and Festivals in the Pacific States

Mendocino Coast Writers Conference
Fort Bragg, CA
Directors: Suzanne Byerley and Ginny Rorby
Established: 1989

Napa Valley Writers Conference
St. Helena, CA
Director: John Leggett
Established: 1980

Squaw Valley Community of Writers
Squaw Valley, CA
Director: Oakley Hall
Established: 1969

Whidbey Island Writers' Conference
Langley, WA
Director: Celeste Mergens
Established: 1997

Writers Studio at UCLA Extension
Los Angeles, CA
Director: Linda Venus
Established: 2001

MAJOR THEMES AND POETS

Immigration

The poetry of the Pacific states has very often been the poetry of an immigrant culture—fresh, innovative, and emerging from the margins. Following nearly 200 years of exploration and conquest by missionaries and explorers from England, Spain, and Russia, the California gold rush in 1848 led to a massive overland immigration and the growth of urban centers. From 1864 to 1872 the population of San Francisco tripled in size, and it was in this city that writers such as Bret Harte (1836–1902), Samuel Clemens (1835–1910), Ina Coolbrith (1841–1928), and Charles Warren Stoddard (1843–1909)—all recent immigrants—created the West's first literary community. Harte, Stoddard, and Coolbrith, known as the "Golden Gate Trinity," edited the *Overland Monthly* (1868–1871), which sought to elevate the literary tastes of the rugged gold-mining readership.

Like Harte, Coolbrith was an active poet, editor, and literary mentor. She discovered and nurtured the precocious talent of Jack London (1876–1916) while working at the Oakland Public Library, and her Sunday afternoon salons—held in her North Beach apartment—were legendary. She is also credited with choosing a name—and an identity—for one of the most memorable western poets of the nineteenth century, Joaquin Miller (1837–1913). In such poems as "By the Pacific-Ocean," "Dead in the Sierras," and "Columbus," Miller's poetry reveals a larger-than-life mythic figure, a traveling western bard who encounters wild nature, easily transforms his persona time and time again, and provides commentary on the greatness of the land and the age.

While poets like Miller, Harte, Coolbrith, and Stoddard immigrated to the West via overland routes, others came by sea from the Asian continent. Throughout the nineteenth and twentieth centuries, immigrants from China, India, Japan, Korea, the Philippines, and Vietnam arrived in the ports of San Francisco, Los Angeles, and Seattle, largely to work in various jobs associated with the gold rush and the building of the railroads. An estimated 20,000 Chinese laborers passed through the Port of San Francisco in 1852, the same year the California state legislature passed a Foreign Miners Tax. The Chinese Exclusion Act of 1882 forced newly arrived immigrants to be detained, sometimes for months.

One of the most striking examples of immigrant writing in the West is the collection of poetry retrieved from the former immigration station at Angel Island off the coast of San Francisco, now collected in the book *Island: Poetry and History of Chinese Immigrants on Angel Island.*[25] Angel Island was both a holding station for Chinese immigrants and a prison for deportees awaiting transportation to China. The

Joaquin Miller, 1906. Courtesy of the Library of Congress.

poems were found carved into the walls in Chinese characters beneath layers of paint in the dilapidated remains of the immigration station. The poetry expresses frustration and explores the ironies between myth and reality. As Karen Polster notes, "These poems refer to Angel Island as a world in between worlds, and outside the tangible universe. No longer in China, and unable to enter the American mainland, the poets highlight the displacement, anxieties, and alienation that is so often at the heart of the assimilation process."[26]

> I told myself that going by this way would be easy.
> Who was to know that I would be imprisoned at Devil's Pass?
> How was anyone to know that my dwelling place would be a prison?
>
> A flickering lamp keeps this body company.
> I am like pear blossoms which have already fallen.
> Pity the bare branches during the late spring.

The unsigned poems of Angel Island capture the experience of immigrants trapped literally on the margin between their homeland and the new world—a land of supposed opportunity and freedom.

Japanese immigrants, too, settled permanently in Hawai'i and locations along the Pacific Coast, primarily between 1890 and 1910. With their works, *The American Diary of a Japanese Girl* (1902), *Poems* (1890), and *Naked Ghosts* (1898), immigrants such as Yone Noguchi and Sadakichi Hartmann (1867–1944) quickly entered the American literary establishment, combining rich Japanese literary traditions with the English language and European literary conventions. No discussion of the Japanese American experience can fail to mention the devastating consequences of the 1942–1945 imprisonment by the War Relocation Authority of Japanese Americans residing in the western United States. On February 19, 1942, President Franklin Delano Roosevelt (1882–1945) signed Executive Order 9066, which removed all Japanese and Americans of Japanese ancestry from western coastal regions and placed them in guarded camps (euphemistically called "Assembly Centers" and "Relocation Centers") in the interior western United States. These camps were typically located on county fairgrounds and racetracks, and detainees were issued nothing but cots, army blankets, and straw-filled mattresses. The detainment of Japanese Americans during World War II coincided with the heyday of haiku clubs—such as the Valley Ginsha Haiku Kai in Fresno, California—where participants voted on the best haiku. This tradition carried over into the relocation centers and produced some of the richest poetry of the twentieth century. This poetry is collected in *May Sky: There Is Always Tomorrow*.[27]

The great complexity of the contemporary period of Asian American poetry is due in large part to the pluralism achieved by years of immigration to the Pacific states. Second-, third-, and fourth-generation immigrants have found a continued integration into mainstream culture and with that a continued set of difficulties. Many contemporary poets, such as Lawson Inada (1938–), Garrett Hongo (1951–), and Cathy Song (1955–), take these issues head-on, exploring the relationship between cultural, family, and personal history. Song was born in Honolulu, Hawai'i, to a Chinese American mother and a Korean American father. Her paternal grandmother had come to Hawai'i as a "picture bride" from Korea, and the exploration of this heritage became the subject of her first book, *Picture Bride* (1983), which was chosen by another western poet, Richard Hugo (1923–1982), for the Yale Series of Younger Poets in 1983. Song's spare, imagistic poetry moves back and forth between past and present, examining family history and reconciling it with her own place as a woman and mother living in contemporary Hawai'i.

The past several decades have also shown the emergence of Latino/a and Chicano/a poets in the Pacific states. In the 1960s, as a result of evolving self-consciousness of cultural heritage after the civil rights movement, various kinds of Chicano protest literature emerged. Poets such as Lorna Dee Cervantes (1954–), Juan Felipe Herrera (1948–), and Gary Soto (1952–) continue that tradition to the present day. Soto's work describes the violence of life in the city, the exhausting and demeaning reality of migrant labor and rural life, with a particular interest in children's themes. Herrera's poems bridge the gap between performance poetry and the written word and consider such themes as illegal immigration, migrant farmwork, and the L.A. riots. Cervantes' work explores cultural and gender identity through an exploration of family and the linguistic riches of bilingualism, often combining Spanish and English to create rich new word sounds, rhythms, and poetic forms.

Poetry of Place

The poetry of the Pacific Region is uniquely interested in landscapes, nature, and place. Early poets of the region marveled at the awesome beauty of the natural world, and poets such as Robinson Jeffers, Hildegarde Flanner (1899–1987), Kenneth Rexroth (1905–1982), Theodore Roethke (1908–1963), John Haines (1924–) Gary Snyder (1930–), Richard Hugo, David Wagoner (1926–), Michael McClure (1932–), Robert Hass (1941–), and Brenda Hillman (1951–) have continued to explore the landscape and ecology of specific regions, the spiritual power of nature, and the political fight to preserve the natural world for future generations.

Poetry of the nineteenth century wrestled with a relationship to place that was undeniable largely because the West itself was wild, uncultivated, and uncivilized. The poetry of Joaquin Miller, Bret Harte, Ina Coolbrith, and George Sterling attempts to capture that large, wild spirit, and the poetry of Edwin Markham captures the plight of the working farmer. But none of these poets were able to transcend the strictures of the high romantic poetic style, characterized by archaic diction, rhymed iambic pentameter, and classical themes. It was not until the early twentieth century that poets began to align a sense of place with the modernist impulses to "make it new," and no poet did more to bring the western landscape into modern literary history than Robinson Jeffers.

After immigrating with his family to Los Angeles, Jeffers studied literature and medicine and eventually earned a master's degree in forestry from the University of Washington. In 1913 he moved with his wife Una to Carmel, already a noted artist colony and occasional home to Stoddard, Sterling, and Mary Austin (1868–1934). In 1916, Jeffers produced his first commercial publication, *Cali-*

Robinson Jeffers, c. 1935. Courtesy of the Library of Congress.

fornians, and with his second publication, *Tamar and Other Poems* (1924), he found his voice, a voice intimately linked with the landscapes and narratives of his local region.

Jeffers is often viewed as an environmentalist writer because of the rich, natural imagery in his work and in part because of his evolving position on the human encroachment into the natural world, a position he labeled "inhumanism." Jeffers advises in "Carmel Point" that "we must uncenter our minds from ourselves;/we must unhumanize our views a little, and become confident/As the rock and ocean that we are made from."[28] Jeffers was often characterized as misanthropic, but he insisted that his beliefs were not against human beings but in favor of a more integrated relationship between people and the divinity of the natural world. His poetry, which employs long breathless lines influenced by Walt Whitman and the King James Bible, is particularly suited for the wide expanse of land and sea he encountered on a daily basis.

Jeffers' great innovations changed the literary character of the West forever and particularly influenced a number of poets associated with a movement known as the San Francisco Renaissance. While the innovations of the San Francisco Renaissance went far beyond an exploration of place, three poets in particular—Kenneth Rexroth, William Everson (1912–1994), and Gary Snyder—expanded on Jeffers' lessons and thrived in the aesthetic and political landscape of the 1940s, 1950s, and 1960s. Rexroth moved to San Francisco in 1927 with his wife Andrée Schafer, studying mysticism, participating in the Communist Party's John Reed Clubs, and publishing poems and essays in *New Masses*, *Partisan Review*, *New Republic*, and *Art Front*. Espousing pacifism and objecting to war measures, he helped a number of Japanese Americans evade internment. His later work was dominated by Eastern philosophy and Asian poetry, and his last major project was a series of poems presented as translations of a fictional Japanese poet named Marichiko.

Rexroth's poetry is often plain-spoken and imagistic, owing to his interest in Jeffers as well as the other Modernist masters Ezra Pound (1885–1972) and William Carlos Williams (1883–1963). But his interest in the natural world—seen in his repeated descriptions of woods, lakes, and animals—sets his poetry apart from many of his contemporaries. His knowledge of the natural world is often scientific—he names rare plants and animals and understands larger geologic or astronomical systems. But also like Jeffers, Rexroth's education in the classics sets him apart from most nature lyricists. He often reveals in the midst of a nature poem a deeper interest in the moral fabric of the universe.

A key member of Rexroth's circle, Everson was born on a farm near Sacramento. He attended Fresno State College in the 1930s, but after discovering Jeffers, he dropped out of college in order to devote his life to poetry. He was a conscientious objector during the war, and owing to this, he was relocated to a series of work camps in the Pacific Northwest. It was during these years that he wrote his first mature poetry, collected in *The Residual Years* (1948). After the war, Everson settled into the San Francisco Bay Area, and soon he was a major figure in the San Francisco Renaissance. In the 1950s he joined the Dominican Order and took the name of Brother Antoninus, a title and association he renounced in 1969. He also established himself as an important scholar of the literature of the West with the publication of *Archetype West: The Pacific Coast as a Literary Region* (1976).[29]

Everson's initial reputation was as a poet of the Central Valley—a poet of farming and work, stressing the existential dignity of the natural world. After his conversion to Catholicism, he replaced, as Lee Bartlett puts it, "his early concerns with man's relationship to nature with man's relationship to God."[30] Still, the conversion only deepened and broadened Everson's connection to the natural world. In his classic poem "Canticle to the Waterbirds," Everson critiques the human impulse to deny the natural world. But unlike Jeffers, he allows for a divinity (expressed in nature) that returns to humans the same willful disregard that they show toward nature. The waterbirds are portrayed as having access to the will of God, while the humans are existentially bound by their own ignorance. While Rexroth's poetry added a layer of political engagement and scientific rigor to Jeffers' project, Everson complicates the poetry of the natural world through a deep exploration of the spiritual power of nature.

Another member of Rexroth's circle of influence, Gary Snyder was born in San Francisco but grew up in Oregon and Washington. Along with poets Lew Welch (1926–1971) and Philip Whalen (1923–2002), he attended Reed College. Throughout the 1950s, Snyder worked as a logger, a trail-crew member, and a seaman on a Pacific tanker. During this time, he was a major participant in the San Francisco Renaissance and Beat Movement. In the 1960s, he lived in Japan, writing and studying Buddhism. Later, he returned to the West Coast, settling in the foothills of the Sierra Nevada mountains and eventually teaching at the University of California, Davis.

With books such as *Riprap* (1959), *Turtle Island* (1974), *Axe Handles* (1983), *No Nature* (1992), and *Mountains and Rivers without End* (1996), Snyder established himself as the nation's preeminent poet of nature and environmental activism. His interest in Zen Buddhism and mythopoetics—including the great literatures of indigenous peoples in the West—has helped define the nature and parameters of West Coast poetics, and his interest in bioregionalism has helped shape the modern conception of place. His poetry blends all of these things: America's deep geologic and human history, the wild surprises of the natural world, the discipline of Zen Buddhism, and the knowledge of the language and culture of China and Japan. Snyder's poetry is often joyous, musical, and playful, but it also contains a spirited environmental ethic. It combines a scientific knowledge of ecology—the way man-zanita reproduces, for instance—and also professes an ethic of land management modeled on indigenous peoples and the latest discoveries in the fields of geology, biology, and ecology.

While Rexroth served as the mentor to the generation of poets surrounding the San Francisco Renaissance and Beat Generation, Theodore Roethke (1908–1963) served as the master teacher and host to many poets who developed in the Pacific Northwest. Roethke was already a distinguished American poet and the author of *The Open House* (1940) and *The Lost Son* (1948), when he moved to Seattle to begin teaching at the University of Washington. In Seattle, he found talented protégés in Richard Hugo, David Wagoner, Carolyn Kizer (1925–), and James Wright (1927–1980), along with many others.

Roethke's first years in Seattle were a time of great national celebrity: His two collections of poems, *The Waking* (1953) and *Words for the Wind* (1958), won just about every major American prize, including the Pulitzer and the National Book Award. While living and teaching in Seattle, he composed the sixty-one new poems that were to be published posthumously in *The Far Field* (1964). *The Far Field* opens with Roethke's "North American Sequence," which might be read as a tribute to life in his adopted home. In this sequence of four long poems, Roethke reveals a facility with describing the landscape of the Pacific Northwest. Often in these poems the natural world takes on the symbolism of the primitive, standing in for childhood associations and landscapes. Roethke's pioneering explorations of na-ture, regional settings, depth psychology, and personal confessionalism—coupled with his stylistic innovations in open form poetics and his mastery of traditional, fixed forms—have secured his reputation as one of the most distinguished and widely read American poets of the twentieth century.

Another poet of the Pacific Northwest, William Stafford (1914–1993) was born in Hutchinson, Kansas, and received his doctorate at the University of Iowa. He lived the great majority of his life in Oregon, prolifically producing poems largely set in the natural world around his home. He taught at Lewis and Clark College in Portland and served as Oregon's Poet Laureate from 1975 to 1993. Stafford is known for recording ordinary life and the intellectual pursuits of daily life. His poetic idiom, too, strives to be ordinary, readable, lucid, and conversational. Ac-cording to Robert Bly, "He believes that whenever you set a detail down in lan-guage, it becomes the end of a thread . . . and every detail—the sound of the lawn mower, the memory of your father's hands, a crack you once heard in lake ice, the jogger hurtling herself past your window—will lead you to amazing riches."[31] Stafford's subject is often the awesome beauty of nature and the power it has over us. A classic Stafford poem "Traveling through the Dark" describes a speaker who finds a dead doe "swollen in the belly" with a stillborn fawn on the side of the road. Kneeling with his hand on the doe's belly, Stafford's speaker can "hear the wilderness listen" before he rolls her off the road, over a cliff and into the river below.[32]

Like Stafford, Robert Hass (1941–) chronicles the rich possibilities found in daily life. He grew up in the Marin County suburb of San Rafael, and as a teen-ager, he was impressed by the burgeoning San Francisco Bay Area poetry scene of the 1950s. After receiving his Ph.D. from Stanford University, where he studied briefly with Yvor Winters, Hass was awarded the Yale Younger Poet's Prize for his book *Field Guide* (1973). From 1994 to 1996, he served as the nation's Poet Laureate, the first time a poet from the Pacific states has held that post. An accomplished translator, Hass served as the chief English translator of the Nobel Prize–winning Polish poet Czeslaw Milosz. Like Rexroth and Snyder, Hass has translated from Eastern languages, publishing the *Essential Haiku: Versions of Basho, Buson, and Issa* in 1994. In his essay "Some Notes on the San Francisco Bay Area as a Culture Region: A Memoir," Hass recognizes Rexroth as "the first one to teach me that there could be an active connection between poetry and my own world."[33] Hass has spent his career exploring his place—the detail of the San Francisco Bay and coastline, the Sierra Nevada, and the more allusive human culture of suburban California. Hass' poetry might be viewed as part of the distinctive tradition of Pacific poets that includes Jeffers, Rexroth, and Snyder. It relishes in detailed description, often of the natural world, but it is also deeply meditative, considering modern philosophy and human psychology in clean, clear-headed language. Along with Rexroth and Snyder, Hass' interest in history and politics informs his vision of our place on earth.

Poetry of the New

The poetry of the Pacific Region is characterized by a series of writers willing to invent and reinvent themselves—not in order to mask experience but in order to create new mythologies out of the place and the experience of encountering it. Western poets try again and again to create hybrid mythologies, taking liberally from Native American traditions, their own cultural traditions, the traditions of the Pacific Rim religions—such as Buddhism and Hinduism—and the traditions of Islam adopted by poets associated with the Black Arts Movement.

As a result, western poets have created a new poetics that fits the diversity of the place and its people. We find in this poetry a spirit of openness that includes the sacred and profane, a spirit that can be found in the work of William Everson, Gary Snyder, Robert Duncan (1919–1988), and Brenda Hillman. The poetry of the Pacific states is dominated by experimentation with lifestyle, image, and aesthetics. The word *Bohemian* has been used to apply to a wide range of western artists, from Robert Service (1874–1958) to George Sterling (1869–1926) to poets associated with the Beat Movement. The word generally characterizes the traveling or "lost" poet who records the experience of isolation and ceaseless encounter. It is this bohemian spirit that led to experimentations with style and language often associated with the San Francisco Renaissance and the Beat Movement. The story of these literary movements begins with Kenneth Rexroth's Friday-evening salon where Bay area poets would meet to discuss theories of politics and poetry. In attendance were many young Bay area avant-garde poets, such as Robert Duncan, William Everson, Richard Eberhart (1904–), Philip Lamantia (1927–), and later, Allen Ginsberg (1926–1997), Lawrence Ferlinghetti (1919–), Gary Snyder, and Jack Spicer (1925–1965).

Probably the most prominent member of Rexroth's circle, Duncan was born in Oakland, California, and raised by devout Theosophists. He grew up in a social world that included séances and meetings of the Hermetic Brotherhood. Duncan attended the University of California in 1936 and began writing poems on social issues and class conflict. His circle of friends included Mary Fabilli (1914–) and

Pauline Kael (1919–2001). In 1938 he quit Berkeley, attended the experimental Black Mountain College in North Carolina, and lived in a commune in Woodstock, New York. After being dishonorably discharged from the army during the war after he confessed his homosexuality, Duncan returned to San Francisco in 1945.

In 1947, he published his first book of poetry, *Heavenly City, Earthly City*, and before long, Duncan was at the center of the San Francisco Renaissance. In the 1960s he published three influential collections, *The Opening of the Field* (1960), *Roots and Branches* (1964), and *Bending the Bow* (1968), which contain his most memorable and influential works. His work is representative of the poetry of the West from the mid-century. It moves freely from frank explorations of sexuality to complex religious symbolism to innovations with the use of language and the poetic line. Duncan is typically western in a variety of ways: His interest in and use of the occult exhibits a willingness to experiment with the freedom of religious practice; his sincere interest in the wildness of both nature and mind provide a transition to postmodern thought and the Language movement of the 1980s; and his difficult but important stand on homosexuality predicted the social transformations of the 1960s and 1970s often associated with San Francisco.

At some point in the mid-1950s, the movement known as the San Francisco Renaissance evolved or combined with the larger American phenomenon known as the Beat Movement. Poets such as Rexroth, Everson, Snyder, Duncan, Spicer, Fabilli, and Lamantia are often associated with both movements, but Lawrence Ferlinghetti might be considered the greatest bridge between the two. Ferlinghetti moved to San Francisco after serving in the war and receiving a Ph.D. from the University of Paris. After working as a teacher and art critic, writing, and attending Rexroth's discussion groups, he met Peter Martin, editor of *City Lights* magazine. Ferlinghetti and Martin launched City Lights Books, the country's first all-paperback bookstore in San Francisco's North Beach. Soon the bookstore became the hub of San Francisco's literary and political scene, the home of poetry readings, anarchist demonstrations, and the Pocket Poet Series. Though the Series would publish all of the great Beat writers and many influential translations of avant-garde European poetry, its most famous publication is by far Allen Ginsberg's *Howl*.

Ferlinghetti decided to publish *Howl* after hearing the title poem at the historic Six Gallery reading on October 7, 1955, a reading that featured Gary Snyder, Philip Whalen, Michael McClure, and Philip Lamantia, along with Ginsberg. *Howl and Other Poems* was released in 1957, and on March 25 of that year, 500 copies were seized for charges of obscenity. The subsequent trial became a national story that put Ginsberg, Ferlinghetti, City Lights Books, and the Beat Generation on the map for good. In June, Ferlinghetti and Shigeyoshi Muroa (City Lights' then manager and future co-owner) were arrested on obscenity charges by the San Francisco Police Department. The summer-long court case ended with a not-guilty verdict, and the case molded the writing of Ginsberg and his contemporaries into a definable movement.

The Beat Movement, centered in the bohemian artist communities of San Francisco's North Beach, Los Angeles' Venice West, and New York City's Greenwich Village, expressed a weary ("beat") alienation from conventional society. It is associated culturally with a "hip" vocabulary, jazz music, and casual dress. Beats advocated a personal spirituality ("beatitude") through states of consciousness sometimes associated with drugs, music, sex, or the disciplines of Zen Buddhism. Beat poets rebelled against academic writing and wrote poems that celebrated and mirrored speech and street talk. They stressed also the oral traditions of poetry and rediscovered the art of the public poetry reading, sometimes reading to the accompaniment of jazz. Though the aesthetics of poets like Ginsberg, Snyder, Jack Kerouac (1922–1969), McClure, Bob Kaufman (1925–1986), Joanne Kyger (1934–), and Diane DiPrima (1934–) are quite varied, Beats are often associated with various "free verse" techniques designed to convey the immediacy of experience.

Third World Poets

In the 1970s many writers then known as "Third World" found a home in *Yardbird*, edited by Ishmael Reed (1938–), and writers associated with the women's movement, such as Adrienne Rich (1929–), Diane Wakoski (1937–), and Sandra M. Gilbert (1936–) gained national reputations. Poets associated with the San Francisco Renaissance, such as Robert Duncan, Diane DiPrima, Michael McClure, and

Allen Ginsberg, Timothy Leary, and Ralph Metzner (left to right) standing in front of a ten-foot plaster Buddha, preparing for a "psychedelic celebration" at the Village Theater, New York City. Courtesy of the Library of Congress.

Gary Snyder, continued to publish through the 1960s, 1970s, 1980s, and 1990s, and their work defined the West Coast as the place for cutting-edge experimentation.

This experimentation took another leap forward with the Language Poetry movement. The beginnings of the movement might be traced to 1975 when Ron Silliman (1946–) edited a collection of nine "Language-centered" poets in the journal *Alcheringa*, among them western writers Clark Coolidge (1939–), Barrett Watten (1948–), Larry Eigner (1927–1996), and Silliman himself. This publication, along with numerous subsequent manifestos and journals, defined the Language movement as an ideological critique of the "naturalness" of poetic language, expressed in one of the movement's earliest and most characteristic mottos, by Robert Grenier: "I HATE SPEECH."[34] Language poets typically call into

Literary Journals That Publish Poetry in the Pacific States

Alaska Quarterly Review
University of Alaska
Anchorage, AK
Established: 1980

Bamboo Ridge
Honolulu, HI
Established: 1984

Crab Creek Review
Varshon Island, WA
Established: 1983

580 Split
Mills College
Oakland, CA
Established: 1999

Haight Ashbury Literary Journal
San Francisco, CA
Editors: Alice Rogoff, Indigo Hotchkiss
Established: 1980

Lynx Eye
Los Osos, CA
Editor: Pam McCully
Established: 1994

Manoa
University of Hawaii
Honolulu, HI
Editor: Frank Stewart
Established: 1989

Northwest Review
University of Oregon
Eugene, OR
Established: 1957

The Seattle Review
University of Washington
Seattle, WA
Established: 1978

Tameme
Los Altos, CA
Editor: C. M. Mayo
Established: 1996

The ThreePenny Review
San Francisco, CA
Editor: Wendy Lesser
Established: 1980

Tin House
Portland, OR
Editor: Win McCormack
Established: 1999

Transfer
San Francisco State University
San Francisco, CA
Established: 1956

26
Saint Mary's College of California
Moraga, CA
Editors: Avery Burns, Rusty Morrison, Joseph Noble, Elizabeth Robinson, and Brian Strang
Established: 2001

Zyzzyva
San Francisco, CA
Editor: Howard Junker
Established: 1985

question the ability of language to represent the world and in particular the poetic self. Instead, they pay special attention to the materiality of language—its sounds, shapes, and structures, and its inherent political implications.

The influence of radical experimentation has touched many western poets, poets often grouped with the Language movement, such as David Bromige (1931–), Lyn Hejinian (1941–), Michael Palmer (1943–), Rae Armantrout (1947–), and Carla Harryman (1952–), and it has deeply influenced poets of more eclectic aesthetic influences, such as Leslie Scalapino (1947–), Heather McHugh (1948–), Marth Ronk (1940–), Donald Revell (1954–), Gillian Conoley (1955–), Amy Gerstler (1956–), Harryette Mullen, and Brenda Hillman, whose book *Cascadia* (2001) forges together influences as diverse as Gary Snyder, Robert Duncan, Language poetry, and the more mainstream confessional poem. *Cascadia* seeks to capture the geology and history of the West in a set of complex lyric experiments, exploring the architecture and art of California missions, the history of the gold rush and hydraulic mining, and dioxin-tainted sunsets. As Walt Whitman does in "Facing West from California's Shores," Hillman asks us to continually imagine the West Coast's rapturous instability: "A left margin watches the sea floor approach/It takes 30 million years//It is the first lover."[35]

In many ways, the literature of the Pacific Region encompasses, draws upon, and influences a large number of cultural characteristics. The languages of its fictions and narratives are colored by the many native and immigrant tongues that make up its linguistic shape; the rhythms of its text and poetry are influenced by the musical patterns of First Nations peoples, European, South American and Asian immigrants; the stories of exploration, perseverance, defeat, and renewal are told poly-vocally and polytonally, with each culture and each generation confronting the myth of the Last West in a variety of ways, but all of them dreaming into a new shape the region that is, ultimately, their home.

RESOURCE GUIDE

Printed Sources

Anthologies

Applegate, Shannon, and Terence O'Donnell, eds. *Talking on Paper: An Anthology of Oregon Letters and Diaries*. Corvallis: Oregon State University Press, 1994.

Beckham, Stephen Down, ed. *Many Faces: An Anthology of Oregon Autobiography*. Corvallis: Oregon State University Press, 1993.

Beebe, Rose Marie, and Robert M. Senkewicz, eds. *Lands of Promise and Despair: Chronicles of Early California, 1535–1846*. Berkeley, CA: Heyday Books, 2001.

Bruchac, Joseph, ed. *Raven Tells Stories: An Anthology of Alaskan Native Writing*. Greenfield Center, NY: Greenfield Review Press, 1991.

Chan, Jeffery Paul, et al., eds. *The Big AIIIEEEEE!: An Anthology of Chinese American and Japanese American Literature*. New York: Meridian, 1991.

Chock, Eric, ed. *Talk Story: An Anthology of Hawaii's Local Writers*. Honolulu, HI: Petronium Press and Talk Story, 1978.

Chock, Eric, and Darrell H.Y. Lum, eds. *The Best of Bamboo Ridge: The Hawaii Writers' Quarterly*. Honolulu, HI: Bamboo Ridge Press, 1986.

Dodds, Gordon B., ed. *Varieties of Hope: An Anthology of Oregon Prose*. Corvallis: Oregon State University Press, 1993.

Hedin, Robert, and Gary Holthaus, eds. *Alaska: Reflections on Land and Spirit*. Tucson: University of Arizona Press, 1989.

Hiura, Arnold, Stephen Sumida, and Martha Webb, eds. *Talk Story: Big Island Anthology*. Honolulu, HI: Bamboo Ridge Press and Talk Story, 1979.

Houston, James D., ed. *West Coast Fiction: Modern Writing from California, Oregon and Washington*. New York: Bantam Books, 1979.

Jackson, Joseph Henry, ed. *Continent's End: A Collection of California Writing*. New York: McGraw-Hill, 1944.

Kowalewski, Michael, ed. *Gold Rush: A Literary Exploration*. Berkeley, CA: Heyday Books, 1997.

Lerner, Andrea, ed. *Dancing on the Edge of the World: An Anthology of Contemporary Northwest Native American Writing*. Tucson: University of Arizona Press, 1990.

Love, Glen, ed. *The World Begins Here: An Anthology of Oregon Short Fiction*. Corvallis: Oregon State University Press, 1993.

Mergler, Wayne, ed. *The Last New Land: Stories of Alaska Past and Present*. Anchorage: Alaska Northwest Books, 1996.

Monaghan, Patricia, ed. *Hunger and Dreams: The Alaskan Women's Anthology*. Fairbanks, AK: Fireweed Press, 1983.

Murray, John A., ed. *A Republic of Rivers: Three Centuries of Nature Writing from Alaska and the Yukon*. New York: Oxford University Press, 1990.

Rich, Ives, ed. *From Timberline to Tidepool: Contemporary Fiction from the Northwest*. Seattle, WA: Owl Creek Press, 1986.

Sarris, Greg, ed. *The Sound of Rattles and Clappers: A Collection of New California Indian Writers*. Tucson: University of Arizona Press, 1994.

Stewart, Frank, ed. *Passages to the Dream Shore: Short Stories of Contemporary Hawaii*. Honolulu: University of Hawaii Press, 1987.

———, ed. *A World between Waves*. Washington, DC: Island Press, 1992.

Ulin, David L., ed. *Writing Los Angeles: A Literary Anthology*. New York: Library of America, 2002.

Further Reading

Bartlett, Lee. *The Sun Is But a Morning Star: Studies in West Coast Poetry and Poetics*. Albuquerque: University of New Mexico Press, 1989.

Bingham, Edwin R., and Glen A. Love, eds. *Northwest Perspectives: Essays on the Culture of the Pacific Northwest*. Seattle: University of Washington Press, 1978.

Cristoforo, Violet Kazue de. *May Sky: There Is Always Tomorrow: An Anthology of Japanese-American Concentration Camp Kaiko Haiku*. Los Angeles: Sun and Moon Press, 1997.

Davidson, Michael. *The San Francisco Renaissance: Poetics and Community at Mid-century*. Cambridge: Cambridge University Press, 1989.

Dawson, Robert, and Gray Brechin. *Farewell, Promised Land: Waking from the California Dream*. Berkeley: University of California Press, 1999.

Didion, Joan. *Where I Was From*. New York: Alfred A. Knopf, 2003.

———. *The White Album*. New York: Simon and Schuster, 1979.

Dunne, John Gregory. *Quintana and Friends*. New York: Pocket Books, 1988.

Everson, William. Archetype West: *The Pacific Coast as a Literary Region*. Berkeley, CA: Oyez Press, 1976.

Fine, David. *Imagining Los Angeles: A City in Fiction*. Albuquerque: University of New Mexico Press, 2000.

Fine, David, and Paul Skenazy, eds. *San Francisco in Fiction: Essays in a Regional Literature*. Albuquerque: University of New Mexico Press, 1995.

Gutiérrez, Ramon, and Richard J. Orsi, eds. *Contested Eden: California before the Gold Rush*. Berkeley: California Historical Society and University of California Press, 1998.

Harstad, Cheryl A., and James R. Harstad. Island Fire: An Anthology from Hawai'i. Honolulu: University of Hawaii Press, 2002.

Haslam, Gerald. *The Other California: The Great Central Valley in Life and Letters*. Reno: University of Nevada Press, 1994.

Henderson, George L. *California and the Fictions of Capital*. New York: Oxford University Press, 1999.

Hicks, Jack, James D. Houston, Maxine Hong Kingston, and Al Young, eds. *The Literature of California: Writings from the Golden State*. Berkeley: University of California Press, 2000.

Houston, James D. *Californians: Searching for the Golden State*. Santa Cruz, CA: Otter B Books, 1982.

Kollin, Susan. *Nature's State: Imagining Alaska as the Last Frontier*. Chapel Hill: University of North Carolina Press, 2001.

Kowalewski, Michael, ed. *Reading the West: New Essays on the Literature of the American West*. New York: Cambridge University Press, 1996.

Lai, Him Mark, Genny Lim, and Judy Young, eds. *Island: Poetry and History of Chinese Immigrants on Angel Island, 1910–1940*. Seattle: University of Washington Press, 1980.

McWilliams, Carey. *California: The Great Exception*. New York: Current Books, 1949.

———. *Southern California: An Island on the Land*. Salt Lake City, UT: Peregrine Smith, 1973.

Murphet, Julian. *Literature and Race in Los Angeles*. New York: Cambridge University Press, 2001.

O'Connell, Nicholas. *At the Field's End: Interviews with 22 Pacific Northwest Writers*. Seattle: University of Washington Press, 1998.

Schwartz, Stephen. *From West to East: California and the Making of the American Mind*. New York: Free Press, 1998.

Skelton, Robin. *Five Poets of the Pacific Northwest: Kenneth O. Hansen, Richard Hugo, Carolyn Kizer, William Stafford, and David Wagoner*. Seattle: University of Washington Press, 1964.

Snyder, Gary. *A Place in Space: Ethics, Aesthetics, and Watersheds*. Washington, DC: Counterpoint, 1995.

Stanton, Joseph. *A Hawai'i Anthology: A Collection of Works by Recipients of the Hawai'i Award for Literature, 1974–1996*. Honolulu: University of Hawaii Press, 1997.

Starr, Kevin and Richard J. Orsi. *Rooted in Barbarous Soil: People, Culture, and Community in Gold Rush California*. Berkeley: California Historical Society and University of California Press, 2000.

Stegner, Wallace. *The American West as Living Space*. Ann Arbor: University of Michigan Press, 1987.

Stewart, Frank, and John Unterecker. *Poetry Hawaii: A Contemporary Anthology*. Honolulu: University of Hawaii Press, 1979.

Sumida, Stephen H. *And the View from the Shore: Literary Traditions of Hawai'i*. Seattle: University of Washington Press, 1991.

Walker, Franklin. *San Francisco's Literary Frontier*. New York: Alfred A. Knopf, 1939.

Wallace, David Rains, and Morley Baer. *The Wilder Shore*. San Francisco: Sierra Club Books, 1984.

Wendt, Ingrid, and Primus St. John. *From Here We Speak: An Anthology of Oregon Poetry*. Corvallis: Oregon State University Press, 1993.

Western Literature Association, eds. *Updating the Literary West*. Fort Worth: Texas Christian University Press, 1997.

Wilson, Edmund. *The Boys in the Back Room: Notes on California Novelists*. San Francisco: Colt Press, 1941.

Wyatt, David. *Five Fires: Race, Catastrophe, and the Shaping of California*. New York: Oxford University Press, 1997.

Libraries and Archives

Alaska State Library and Historical Collections
P. O. Box 110571
Juneau, AK 99811-0571
907-465-1300
http://www.library.state.ak.us/

The Bancroft Library
University of California, Berkeley
Berkeley, CA 94720-6000
http://bancroft.berkeley.edu/

California State Library
Stanley Mosk Library and Courts Building
914 Capitol Mall
Sacramento, CA 95814-4869
http://www.library.ca.gov/

Hawai'i State Library
Hawai'i Center for the Book
478 South King Street
Honolulu, HI 96813-2901
http://www.hcc.hawaii.edu/hspls/hsl/hslov.html

The Huntington Library, Art Collections, and Botanical Gardens
1151 Oxford Road
San Marino, CA 91108
626-405-2100
http://www.huntington.org/

Oregon State Library
250 Winter Street NE
Salem, OR 97301-3950
503-378-4243
http://www.osl.state.or.us/home/

Sutro Library (Bay Area Branch of California State Library)
480 Winston Drive
San Francisco, CA 94132
415-731-4477
http://www.library.ca.gov/

Washington State Library
Point Plaza East
6880 Capitol Boulevard
Olympia, WA 98504
http://www.secstate.wa.gov/library/

Important Bookstores and Publishers

City Lights Bookstore
261 Columbus Avenue at Broadway (North Beach)
San Francisco, CA 94133
415-362-8193
http://www.citylights.com/

Heyday Books
2054 University Avenue, Suite 400
Berkeley, CA 94704
510-549-3564
http://www.heydaybooks.com/public/home.html

Oregon State University Press
101 Waldo Hall
Corvallis, OR 97331-6407
541-737-3166
http://oregonstate.edu/dept/press/

Powell's City of Books (Burnside)
1005 W Burnside
Portland, OR 97209
http://www.powells.com/home.html

Powell's has numerous satellite stores throughout the Portland area.

University of California Press
2120 Berkeley Way
Berkeley, CA 94704-1012
510-642-4247
http://www.ucpress.edu/

University of Washington Press
1326 Fifth Avenue, Suite 555
Seattle, WA 98101-2604
https://www.washington.edu/uwpress/index.html

Festivals

The *Los Angeles Times* Festival of Books
http://www.latimes.com/extras/festivalofbooks/

A two-day celebration of the written word and one of the country's premier literary events. The festival is free to the public and held each year on the last weekend of April on the UCLA campus.

California Book Awards
http://www.commonwealthclub.org/bookawards/

Established in 1931 by The Commonwealth Club of California, a nonprofit, nonpartisan public affairs forum established in 1903. From the beginning the book awards have sought to recognize exceptional literary works by California's writers, poets, and publishers.

Organizations

Alaska Center for the Book
Loussac Library
3600 Denali Street
Anchorage, AK 99503-6093
907-345-2363
akctrbk@akcenter.com
http://www.alaskacenterforthebook.org/

California Center for the Book
Department of Information Studies
University of California, Los Angeles
207 GSE&IS Building
300 Young Drive N Box 951520
Los Angeles, CA 90095-1520
310-206-9361
cfb@ucla.edu
http://www.calbook.org/

Hawai'i Center for the Book
478 South King Street
Honolulu, HI 96813-2901
http://www.hcc.hawaii.edu/hspls/hsl/hslov.html

John Muir Center
University of the Pacific
3601 Pacific Avenue
Stockton, CA 95211

209-946-2527
http://ets.uop.edu/muir/about.htm

The National Steinbeck Center
One Main Street
Salinas, CA 93901
831-796-3833
http://www.steinbeck.org/MainFrame.html

El Teatro Campesino
705 Fourth Street
San Juan Bautista, CA 95045
831-623-2444
http://www.elteatrocampesino.com

Oregon Center for the Book
Oregon State Library Building
250 Winter Street NE
Salem, OR 97301-0640
503-378-2112, ext. 239
http://www.osl.state.or.us/home/libdev/CFTBoverview.html

Robinson Jeffers Tor House Foundation
26304 Ocean View Avenue
Carmel, CA 93923
831-624-1813
http://www.torhouse.org/

The Washington Center for the Book at the Seattle Public Library
800 Pike Street
Seattle, WA 98101
http://www.spl.org/default.asp?pageID=about_leaders_washingtoncenter

Western Literature Association
Utah State University
http://www.usu.edu/westlit/

The WLA publishes *Western American Literature*, a leading journal of western American literature, and holds an annual conference every October.

MUSIC

Pauline Tuttle, Valerie Samson, Sydney Hutchinson, Rob Kirkpatrick, and Jan Goggans

Perhaps because its borders are so broad, and languages so varied, the Pacific Region turned to music as a means of communication that both defined and crossed its many cultures. The region has a long and rich musical history. First Nations, Asian American, Mexican American—cultures have created musical forms that have evolved over many years. And despite the many homogenizing efforts of global music industries and programming playlists, even in contemporary forms, the varied cultures of this region find diverse expression.

FIRST NATIONS MUSIC IN THE PACIFIC REGION

As is true for almost any rigidly bounded geographic area defined and demarcated by political boundaries rather than cultural markers or paths of transmission and interaction, the Pacific Region of the United States cannot be adequately understood in isolation from the northern and western relationships that have shaped and given meaning to First Nations lifeways for countless generations. Such relationships do not follow imposed political boundaries such as state lines or artificially created borders that have been delineated through the machinery of colonization and subsequent nation building but, rather, are delineated by topographical, linguistic, and shared cultural traits, as well as familial lineages that cross all borders. This is particularly true when we look at the performing arts that lie at the core of First Nations community life—music, dance, carving, storytelling, the ceremonial cycle, and others.

From the nineteenth-century Prophet Dance to the contemporary rez rap circuit, the song paths of First Nations Peoples in the Pacific Region have served as fluid vehicles for the transmission of songs, stories, dances, and their embedded teachings since the beginning of remembered time. Along these paths, it is said, pockets of stillness have served as sites of gathering, visioning, dreaming, catching, and reawakening songs that have lain dormant in the land for generations.

The reawakening of such songs is said to be triggered, at times of ceremonial interaction between singer and site, through the power of the Thunder Beings, perhaps the most potent Native American heraldic figures in the Americas.

The Thunderbird in Native American Music and Dance

From Alaska to California the Thunderbird, a powerful spirit in the form of a bird, serves as a catalyst for change, for transformation and renewal. Coast Salish author and cultural mentor William White (Xelimuxw) explains that this power, brought into the contingent world through the prerogatives of the Thunder singers and dancers, has the capacity to change the very fabric of both individual and community life.[1] This transformative power of the Thunderbird is not surprising, for it is said that they are so large and so strong that they can readily swoop down and grasp a whale in their talons, carrying it back to their mountain homes to eat. According to mythology, a simple wink of a Thunderbird's eyes is enough to cause lightning bolts to shoot down from the sky; and the air rushing through its massive wings as the Thunderbird takes flight will cause the thunders to roll across the sky. The resultant winds and rains serve as cleansing forces, preparing the way for change, for clarity of vision, for the return of the calm and stillness required when new songs come into being and old songs are reawakened. For these reasons, Thunder songs serve as an appropriate starting point for an overview of the music of the vast Pacific Region.

Tribal Territories and Influences

In the Pacific Region of the United States, which includes the states of Alaska, Washington, Oregon, California, and Hawai'i, the First Peoples are members of over 400 federally recognized tribes, and numerous unrecognized tribes, living in the culture areas of the Northwest Coast, Plateau, Great Basin, Sub-Arctic, Arctic, Southwest, California, and Hawai'i.

Here, the fabric of music changes in accordance with seasonal ceremonial and festival cycles, with the life cycles of both individual and community, and with the larger cycles of lived experience in relation to other villages and nations. Regardless of regional and cultural differentiation in musical style and form, in language, or in geographic setting, the rights to sing the Thunder songs, to wear the crests, to dance the dances, to don the regalia, and to tell the stories in which the experiences of Thunderbird are embedded, as with any other heraldic figure, are hereditary prerogatives handed down from one generation to the next, originating from those who were first given the songs by these powerful beings and in some cases from those who received them in vision quests or dreams at sites where Thunderbird is known to have visited.

Thunder Songs

Thunder songs throughout the Pacific Region are often accented by the sounds of the Thunder Beings, which are created through rapid and loud drum tremolos and conjoined with the rapid flapping of the wing of an eagle, the shrill cry of whistles made from cedar, river cane, or whatever particular natural materials are

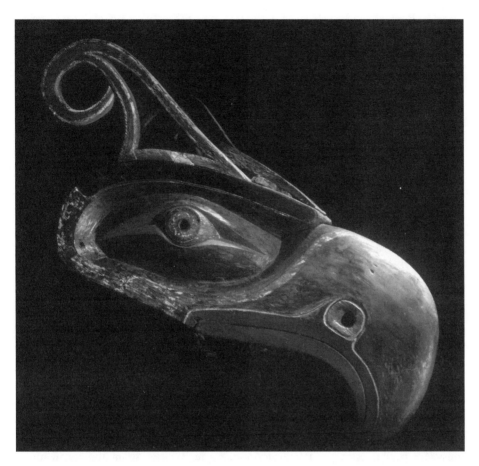

Kwakwaka 'wakw Thunderbird Hamat'sa Headdress (Kwanxwaml) from the Northwest.
© Werner Forman/Art Resource, NY.

present in the diverse topographies of this region, and the crackling sound of clappers or two sticks being sharply struck together. These sounds, and the imagery linked to the Thunders, are given form through the movements and regalia of dancers, the masks of carvers, the stories that tell of ancestral relationships and rights to perform such powerful songs, to wear and display the crests of such auspicious figures. These songs, and many others, originate from sacred sites of musical interaction dotting the coastal landscapes from northern Alaska to Southern California, and well beyond, sites where Thunderbird rests, feeds, creates, rescues, and winters.

As one of many examples found in the Pacific Region, Frederico de Laguna reiterates a story told to him in 1949 by a Tlingit singer, Frank Italio, who explained the significance of the Thunderbird screen in his house in Yakutat, ten years prior to Alaska becoming a state. In this story, a young Cʌnkuedi boy of about four years, a boy named GòxȺk, had been left behind at Síťȿayi (Glacier Point) by his family while stopping for a rest on a canoe journey down the Alesk river. By the time they realized he was missing, it was nightfall. Knowing that he would not survive the four days it would take them to travel back upriver against the current, the family held a potlatch for the boy, and mourning songs were composed in his honor. Perhaps it was the power of these songs that protected GòχÁk, for this boy was rescued by Xèt_ (Thunderbird). Xèt_ raised him in his mountain cave as his own child, training him to be strong with keen vision, and when GòχÁk was grown, he even grew feathers and quills like Xèt_. He missed his family so much, though, that Thunderbird brought him back home. Here, he became the leader of the CAnkuedi, teaching them all that he had learned from Xèt_ and recreating the house of the Thunderbird in his Yakutat home in honor of his experiences. From then on the CAnkuedi were the people of the Thunderbird, an ancestral story that continues to this day to be reiterated at memorial potlatches through songs, regalia, story, artistry, and dance by the CAnkuedi and Kagwantan in Alaska.[2]

The Historical Record of Native American Music

While there are more than 400 distinct First Nations in the Pacific Region, not including the indigenous peoples of Hawai'i, and the songs of each are distinct, the vast majority share certain musical characteristics such as song cycles and a predominance of vocal music accompanied by drums of various forms. The earliest record of Indigenous music on the Northwest Coast of the Pacific Region known to date was provided by Fray Juan Crespi, the chaplain on Captain Juan Pérez's *Samtiago*, which sailed from Monterey California to Trinity Bay on the Alaskan Pan Handle in 1774.

On Dall Island, in 1774, Pérez and his crew were welcomed by 200 people who came out to meet them in 21 canoes, playing drums and rattles, singing and dancing, and likely tossing feathers around on the water as a welcoming gesture, much as they had witnessed at Langara but on a smaller scale.[3] While Crespi's record of musical interactions offers a valuable contribution to the historical record of early musical experiences in the Pacific Region, we learn little about the actual music that was heard. For this, we must turn to the journals from Captain James Cook's expedition, which document the music they heard on their arrival in Nootka Sound in 1778, followed three years later by the musical observations made by Bodega y Quadra's botanist José Mariano Moziño. While the perceptions of Cook and his crew range from describing the music as "the most warlike and awful they had ever heard" to that of songs "composed of a variety of strange placed notes, all in unison and well in tune,"[4] Moziño's detailed descriptions tell of harmonious voices singing in unison at the octave and accompanied by "a noise which the singers make on some boards with the first solid object they find," and wooden rattles that sound similar to Aztec gourd rattles."[5] Cook collected rattles, which he describes as being carved in the form of a bird. He also describes, regalia, a "cape" "with deer hooves hanging from it, which rattled with every motion he [the singer] made" and both Cook and Moziño describe a lead singer who begins the song and is followed by others, with shouts interjected from time to time.[6]

Native American Music from the Contiguous States of the Pacific Region

Early transcriptions discussed, have not surfaced in the literature documenting the early history of interaction between the First Peoples of the Washington and

Oregon areas and their early Russian, European, and British trading partners. This is not so for California, though. The lands occupying what is now the state of California were first visited by Juan Rodríguez Cabrillo in 1542 and revisited by Sebastian Vizcaino in 1602; by 1769 the first of twenty-one missions were established, almost a century before the 1843 establishment of the First Mission school in Alaska (established by the Russian-Greek Orthodox Church). These mission schools, set up to break familial and cultural ties and further the acculturation process by ensuring that Indian children were educated according to European Christian standards and doctrine, prohibited the use of indigenous languages, artistic practices, dance, and lifestyle, thus having an immediate and devastating impact on the music and lifeways of California's First Peoples. Between the years 1815, when Fray Felipe Arroyo do la Cuesta (1780–1840) published the first of several manuscripts with transcriptions of songs he had heard while working with the Mutsun Indians at San Juan Bautista, and 1907, when Alfred Kroeber published *Indian Myths of South Central California*, the myths in which hundreds, if not thousands, of songs were traditionally embedded had already shrunk to "nothing but fragments."[7]

Not unlike the many mission schools throughout the Pacific Region, San Juan Bautista was a California mission, boasting 1,200 enrolled Indian students, 8,000 cattle, 9,000 sheep, 270 horses, 500 mares and colts, and an orchard by 1831.[8] Here, the performance of music was often limited to the singing of English hymns, many of which have since been translated into local indigenous languages, and an array of musical ensembles that included Indian brass bands and, in British Columbia's Capilano, an accordion band. Today the Yakima in Washington even have a Trinidadian steel band. In later years, Kroeber wrote that the California Indians were "among the least characteristic of the Indians of North America," because of the absence of pottery, agriculture, war, totemism, artistic realism, intensity, and complex ceremonial activities; more importantly, he found that "dancing and singing played no less crucial a role among the California Indians than elsewhere."[9] Throughout the Pacific Region, dancing and singing were always linked to one aspect or another of procuring, preparation, and consumption, or avoidance, of food.

Songs related to primary subsistence are extremely important throughout the Pacific Region, from food-gathering songs to whaling songs to hunting songs to the songs of the First Salmon Ceremony. Songs are sung prior to the onset of the food expedition, as a means of finding the food, before and after the first catch (be it salmon, berries, deer, etc.), before the food is prepared to eat, before the food is eaten, during the meal, and of course, afterward. Jeanette Timentwa, a Lake Indian from Colville, describes the seasonal dinners she hosts each year, from her "New Year" root feast in April to the dinner for salmon and service berries in June to "Indian Thanksgiving" in October to the many feasts held during the winter dance season. Always, the earth is thanked through the sprinkling of tobacco and a prayer of gratitude, and a plate is set for the ancestors who play a crucial role in the ongoing survival of the culture.[10]

While there are songs for each season, many individuals acquire their own "spirit power song" at different points in their lives, which can be drawn on and utilized for many purposes, depending on what is required at any given time. These songs provide strength throughout the entire life span of the individual and sometimes come through dreams, sometimes through visions, sometimes through cleansing baths in the cold mountain streams, and sometimes through processes of initiation during the winter ceremonials, a two- to three-month process that is undergone by sixty to seventy dancers a year in twenty longhouses (smokehouses, bighouses), with the support of about 1,000 family members in each longhouse, in southern Vancouver Island alone.

Songs that are not specifically spirit power songs also come to different people in different ways. Sometimes they are "caught"—that is, it is said that they reside in the memory of the landscape, or in the collective spirit memory of the people, lying dormant, waiting to be awakened and caught by a singer who will make them his or her own. Other times they are received during a vision quest or simply during prayer or even everyday activities like a walk on the beach or in the woods. There are songs that come in dreams, songs that come through ceremony, and sometimes songs that are consciously composed for a specific purpose, such as the honoring of an individual, the inauguration of an important community institution or building, or the onset of a historic gathering. And then there are hereditary songs that are handed down from one generation to the next, with the rights for use given to others through marriage or as restitution for damage done.

Songs are used for healing purposes, for gaming, for the validation of familial and heraldic status, for opening meetings and enabling political processes to be rooted in spirit, for celebrating life-cycle markers such as receiving a name, puberty, marriage, even divorce and reconciliation, and for passing into the world beyond. Basically, songs are an integral part of all aspects of life and are used in both work and play, just as was found in the earliest documented sources of the music of the Pacific Region that appeared a full century before Thomas Edison's (1847–1931) 1877 invention of the phonograph had reached the commercial market. This recording tool, originally designed to ease the work of stenographers, dramatically changed the face of musical transmission and research in the Pacific Region; it allowed ardent collectors to amass large recording collections for purposes of preservation and future analysis, such as those of Willard Rhodes (housed at the UCLA Ethnomusicology Archives); Frances Densmore (housed at the American Folklife Centre); Melville Jacobs (housed at the University of Washington); Edward Curtis, who coordinated the production of approximately 10,000 wax cylinder recordings, only 279 of which have survived (housed at the Indiana Archives of Traditional Music); and those of Frederico de Laguna in Alaska; among many others.

Preserving Native American Music Today

Today, the practice of recording songs and gatherings for cultural preservation, family and village record keeping, and entertainment purposes has permeated the entire region. One such example is found in the work of the Storyscape project, initiated in 1998 by Melissa Nelson and Philip M. Klasky, who were asked to preserve the collection of Mojave Creation Songs that had been recorded by the late amateur ethnographer Guy Tyler in 1972. From this work, other projects grew, beginning with a much fuller documentation of the Mojave Creation Song Cycle that was inspired by the sung testimony of Wally Antone, a Quechan Bird Song singer, at a federal environmental hearing in Needles protesting a proposed nuclear waste dump on Mojave ancestral lands in Ward Valley, California. Antone, with his singers and dancers, sang the Bird Songs into the court record as a sacred oral map of their traditional territory, identifying the valley as a landmark site for the collection of mesquite seeds. On hearing of the work of Klasky and Nelson, they subsequently requested their assistance in preserving their Creation Song Cycle, comprising hundreds of songs.[11]

Other projects Nelson and Klasky have worked on include the "restorying" of the traditional territories of the Kashaya Pomo through the sung mapping of sites of sacred, experiential, ecological, and historical importance to the identity of the Kashaya, and the 142-song cycle of Nuwuvi Salt Songs telling the entire history of the world through the eyes of the Southern Paiute. These songs tell of the houses, experiences, sacred sites, and diverse peoples encountered on their thousand-mile journey from Bill Williams River to California. The collections recorded by Klasky and Nelson are housed at the University of California at Berkeley Language Center, with copies distributed to the diverse bands and singers involved and additional copies being housed at the Storyscape archives in San Francisco. Key to the success of efforts such as these is the close collaboration of local First Nations singers, elders, and communities with ethnomusicologists and academic institutions and meaningful reciprocity with the goal of First Nations empowerment rather than subjugation. Too often, in the past, vast recording collections such as those of Willard Rhodes, Edward Curtis, Franz Boas, Melville Jacobs, Frances Densmore, and many others have remained virtually inaccessible to community members. For those undertaking research on the music of the First Nations in the Pacific Region today, this applied approach plays a crucial role in the building of ruptured bridges and the elimination of historical prejudices that have obfuscated our mutual efforts, in varying degrees, to move forward, to redress past injustices, and in so doing, to deepen the understanding of the importance of the role song, music, and ceremony play in the sustainability of indigenous community-based lifeways that are key to the preservation of identity and diversity.

Part of Klasky and Nelson's mandate, like many ethnomusicologists and oral historians working in the Pacific Region today, is to provide training that will allow First Nations community members to professionally record and document their own culture for archival preservation and ongoing community use.

Native American Musical Instruments

Today, there are no First Nations groups who do not use drums of some form in one aspect or another of their current musical practices. Traditionally, though, rather than using skin drums, many groups, such as the Maidu of California, the Coast Salish of Washington and Oregon, the Kwakwakewakw of Vancouver Island, the Yakutat of Alaska, and many others, used drums made from hollowed logs that were played by several drummers at the same time. Unlike other areas, where the logs were struck with handheld sticks, the Maidu struck these drums (*ki'le*) with their feet. For the Maidu, the log drum was placed over a shallow trench dug into the ground that served as a resonator. The drum was played by two or three men standing on top of the log and dancing, stamping their feet to keep the beat of the music. At other times they would use long drum sticks, or stamping tubes, of about four feet long to stamp the log.[12] Stamping tubes were also used in Alaska, and this type of percussion instrument has also been used to keep time by stamping a talking stick on the hard ground by Makah singers at Neah Bay.

Also commonly used in the Pacific States were plank drums, particularly at *slahal* (bone/stick) games. Frances Densmore reports that long planks resting on blocks were struck with sticks by several men, and in Neah Bay they were arranged "as three sides of a square."[13] Among the Maidu, a handheld short plank was struck to keep rhythm. Also found in some California areas are basket drums. Further north, the Makah made bentwood box drums in the shape of a square, and the Inuit in Alaska hung open-ended rectangular ceremonial box drums (*kaylukuk*) from either a tripod or the ceiling, which today are used by many contemporary dance groups in concert performances. Along the coastal areas, other vessels used as drums included the rhythmic striking of paddles against canoes, commonly reported in the documentation of early explorers and traders and heard today in the Canoe Festivals and Tribal Journeys as the Canoe Nations arrive and are welcomed in the various coastal bays on their annual canoe journeys. Entire longhouses have been known to be transformed into drums, with the striking of paddles and long poles on the rooftops, giving perhaps the most palpable expression of the teaching that the drumbeat is the heartbeat of the Nation, for in the womb of the longhouse, which serves as a ceremonial center for ritual rebirth, the entire community and their guests become an integral part of the resonating chamber of the drum.

The one type of drum that can be found in all areas of the Pacific Region today is the large skin drum that rests on a stand and is played by several singers who sit in a circle around the drum and strike the drum simultaneously with long drum sticks. These drums provide the accompaniment for a variety of dance competitions, from traditional to warrior to fancy to jingle dress and more, at annual powwows held throughout the Pacific states, the continent, and abroad. Likewise, the powwow drum provides the beat for the dancers who come from all corners to enter the annual World Champion Hoop Dance competition at the Heard Museum in Phoenix, Arizona. Regardless of the type of drum, as with the crafting of most musical instruments in the Pacific Region, the process of preparing the materials to be used and constructing drums was accompanied by ritual prayer and song, with large feasts often being held on the occasion of the first use of the finished instrument. Such honorings are crucial aspects of the process, as the materials are derived from living organic parts of creation imbued with powers that are transferred to the drum through song and ceremony. Likewise, in all areas there are specific unique symbologies linked to the materials and sounds of the drum and the drum stick, just as there are for the various rattles and whistles used.

Throughout the Pacific Region, the function of the drum is much more than that of marking time. The drum is considered to be the heartbeat of the nation; it is the vehicle by which the sung prayers are carried to the hearts of the people and to the spirit world; conversely, the drum beat is the vehicle, coupled with voice and sometimes the rattle, by which the ancestors in the spirit world are called to become active participants in a gathering. In some areas of the Pacific Region the drum primarily reinforces the vocal line as the regular underlying pulse, while in other areas the beat of the drum serves as the foundation for the movement of the dancers, with the vocal line serving as a counterrhythm of sorts. Deeper meanings are embedded in various types of drum beats, such as strong accented beats like the "honor beat" in songs heard on the powwow circuit. These beats place added emphasis on the text and communicate to the audience the respect held for the individual who is being honored in the song. As a prelude to the song proper, rapid tremolos on the drum sometimes accompany spoken prayer, sometimes with the first verse of a song being quietly sung behind the prayer or even by itself, announcing to the audience and to the ancestors that something important is about to happen, preparing the way for the coming out of the dancers or of an important song.

Since the 1960s contemporary First Nations musicians in the Pacific Region have become increasingly involved in indigenous expressions of identity in popular music circuits from Intertribal Powwows to the rap circuit to Native American flute circles to jazz, rock, gospel, and even opera. In California, a strong united American Indian voice was first heard in the driving rhythms of the powwow songs sung during the watershed nineteen-month occupation of Alcatraz island that began on November 20, 1969, marking the beginning of a proliferation of coastal powwows, the onset of a vital Native voice in the folk music scene and the popular music industry, and serving as a springboard for the intense activism of the American Indian Movement throughout the 1970s and into the 1980s. Here, the gathering of thousands of First Nations people from all over North and South America, including many who identified with their cause, served as a celebration of newfound pride in cultural identity, a vehicle for political autonomy and self-governance efforts, and a call for long-overdue respect. Today, hundreds of powwows are held throughout North America on an annual basis, with the "powwow trail" that straddles the Pacific states and British Columbia drawing singers and dancers from across the country and abroad.

Other important musical instruments in the Pacific Region include rattles and whistles, although many do not think of whistles as musical instruments but rather as spirit voices. Nevertheless, whistles and aerophonic calling devices of various types are sometimes used in public performance as a means of calling on the spirit of the animal who inspired a given song, such as the loon, the eagle, or even the Thunderbird. Often the sound production is veiled or hidden and indicates the presence of particular spirit beings. Generally the use of these instruments is limited to the songs and dances of the winter ceremonials held in traditional big houses, an annual cycle of spirit dance and initiation activity that signifies renewal and provides the participants with the strength and spiritual foundation required as they move through two worlds in their daily lives. In the Southwest, whistles were traditionally made of crane wing-bones or sometimes swan or blue heron. The Maidu are known to have used many different sizes of these whistles, variously pitched depending on the length of the bone, at the same time, with five or six men blowing them alternatively in order to create a melody.[14] In the northern coastal areas whistles were often made from wood, with elaborate carvings of heraldic figures with rich ancestral lineages.

Also found in the literature are discussions of duct flutes whose sound production is dependent on exterior blocks made of leather, cloth, a carved wooden block, or even just the finger of the flute player and include end-blown open-ended flutes played with a split-breath embouchure similar to that of the Persian *ney* (*nai*, *nei*, or *nay*), such as the Hopi and Yuman end-blown flutes Richard Payne documents.[15] Payne asserts that the historic duct flute, perhaps most highly developed in the Plains areas, originated with the Northern Utes and its knowledge traveled south to the Taos community, which further dispersed it to the other Southwestern tribes. It also traveled to the Plains tribes of Oklahoma, spreading then to other Plains tribes, northward and eastern.[16]

Whether or not this is so, for there are as many flute origin stories and ideas as there are flute players, the flute that has captured the hearts and marketing venues of First Nations contemporary musicians and their audiences is that played by flutists such as Mary Youngblood, an Aleut/Seminole woman born in Alaska and living in California. Inspired by the music of R. Carlos Nakai, Youngblood was the first woman to release a full-length CD of solo flute music, winning Native American Music Awards (NAMA) "Flutist of the Year" in 1999, "Best Female Artist" and "Best New Age Recording" in 2000, and the Association for Independent Music (AFIM) Indie award in the North American Native Music category in 2000.

While it is important to keep in mind that recent musical developments such as flute circles, drum circles, Native hip-hop among the youth, and even powwows are greeted with varying degrees of acceptance, or strident objection, by local First Nations community members, just as the American Indian protest music of the 1970s and 1980s was, they remain a vibrant part of the musical life of many American Indian musicians in the Pacific Region. Equally vibrant are the traditional genres of song that have in many areas retained their form, style, and musical traits, while finding new avenues and venues of expression that celebrate cultural identity, such as the annual Makah Days in Washington, Seattle's annual Folklife Festival, California's Strawberry Festivals, Round Valley's revived Ghost Dances, Shaker Church and Native American Church services, and the Neah Bay Annual Council Fire. Perhaps most vibrant of all are the ceremonial activities that show less evidence of the decimation caused by the nineteenth-century prohibition of traditional practices, such as potlatches, First Salmon ceremonies, and winter ceremonials. Throughout the history of this region, the ongoing change and transformation represented in the songs, dances, and stories of the Thunder Beings have supported, engendered, and nurtured the transitions and journeys of First Nations singers, dancers, and communities for generations; and, it is said by the old ones, this will continue to be so as future generations traverse and forge new songpaths linking the First Peoples of the Pacific Region to their indigenous sister communities around the world.

MUSIC AND DANCE OF MEXICAN AMERICANS IN THE PACIFIC STATES

The Mexican American population of the Pacific states can be divided into two main groups defined by their different histories and origins. *Chicanos* are American-born of Mexican descent, many of whom have lived in the region since well before western statehood. This is true particularly of California, which was part of Mexico until the Mexican-American War concluded in 1848. *Mexicanos* are people born in Mexico who now live in the United States, and they range from naturalized citizens to permanent and temporary residents to migrant workers. Mexicanos typically maintain strong ties to the regional cultures of their Mexican states of origin. Although a number of different terms have been used historically for these two groups, these two have been chosen for the sake of clarity.

Geography, politics, and history have all affected which group predominates in a given area. California has a larger and more deeply rooted Chicano population than other states. At the same time, its proximity to Mexico means that it also receives more immigrants than other areas and that this immigration has occurred constantly and consistently. In Oregon and Washington, Mexican American communities were not established until the twentieth century, when growth presented immigrants with new economic opportunities. Some Chicanos have lived in the Northwest for two or three generations, and new immigrants continue to arrive. Alaska and Hawai'i did not have established Mexican communities until just the last two decades because of their geographic distance from Mexico. At present, the Mexican American communities of those states are formed almost entirely of immigrant Mexicanos.

The differing heritage and history of these groups have also determined different musical preferences. In areas like Oregon and Washington that have received substantial numbers of Texas Mexicans, *tejano* music has naturally been strong. Communities of recent immigrants in all the Pacific states tend to choose popular Mexican styles like *ranchera* ("ranch" songs), *banda* (brass band), *norteña* (border accordion music), or *grupera* (romantic ballads played by keyboard-heavy groups). The more cosmopolitan Chicanos of large Pacific cities have eclectic musical tastes that vary substantially from individual to individual, including everything from pan-Latino music like salsa, merengue, and *rock en español* (Spanish-language rock) to American jazz, rock, or hip-hop to Mexican mariachi, *banda*, *grupera*, or *norteña* music. In Los Angeles, both Mexicanos and Chicanos have contributed to the development of unique styles of music and dance by innovating within traditional styles like *corridos* and *banda* as well as popular ones like rock and hip-hop.

Mexican American Music in California

California's colonization began with the missions established by Fray Junípero Serra in the late eighteenth century. Some of the earliest recorded musical activity dates to this period, when the Franciscan monks at Los Angeles' San Gabriel Mission taught local Indians to play and sing religious music. After Mexican independence in 1821, the area was secularized, and the Mexican government gave land grants to encourage immigration to the frontier state; the population grew to about 7,300 in 1845. Contemporary historical records show that music making was then a popular pastime, with string ensembles playing Spanish dances, waltzes, and quadrilles for formal, upper-class *bailes* (balls) and popular *fandangos*. California's population was concentrated in coastal cities such as Los Angeles, San Diego, Santa Barbara, and Monterey.

At the conclusion of the Mexican-American War in 1848, General Antonio López de Santa Anna (1794–1876) ceded California and the other southwestern states to the United States, and those residents who chose to stay were made American citizens. The ensuing gold rush brought an estimated 25,000 Mexicans and 100,000 Anglos to the state. The Anglos quickly came to dominate the state demographically, economically, and politically; discrimination against the Californios (Californians of Mexican descent) resulted in their increasing awareness of a unique ethnic identity. They began to identify themselves as *La Raza* ("The [Mexican] Race") and to establish barrios, Mexican American enclaves in the cities. Euro-American music was introduced to the area through traveling military bands and minstrel groups, while Californios maintained some established musical practices, such as the performance of *pastorelas*, nativity plays, and *posadas*, Christmastime gatherings enacting Mary and Joseph's search for an inn, where traditional Christmas songs were sung. Dances continued to be popular activities, including *bailes de cascarones*, at which egg shells filled with perfume, ashes, or confetti were broken over suitors' heads. In addition, Los Angeles' newly constructed concert halls hosted touring classical performers from Mexico, South America, and Europe.

The twentieth century dawned on a dramatically different California: The previously dominant Californios now accounted for only 1 to 2 percent of the state's 1.5 million residents. However, the imbalance would not last. Federal reclamation programs brought water to arid regions, facilitating the growth of urban centers, agriculture, and industry. By 1929, approximately 100,000 Mexicans had immigrated to California, mainly as a result of upheavals caused by the Mexican Revolution in 1910. In Los Angeles, they settled on the East Side, establishing a barrio with its own newspapers and radio stations that is still an important cultural center for Mexican Americans today. A nascent recording industry released recordings of local guitar trios and mariachis playing *canciones* (songs, usually romantic), boleros, and *huapangos* (a type of *son* native to the Huastecan region between the Sierra Madre and the Gulf of Mexico). The 1930 census lists 368,013 Mexican immigrants and first-generation Mexican Americans in California.

The 1930s were a difficult time for Mexican Americans—besides suffering the economic effects of the Great Depression, many thousands were uprooted and "repatriated" either voluntarily, to avoid racism and harassment, or by force. One response to these hardships was made musically: *Corridos*, narrative ballads of northern Mexico, became an important way to discuss current affairs like the Work Projects Administration and interethnic tensions. A number of important musical groups arose in Los Angeles during the 1930s, including Los Madrugadores, a trio who performed their *corridos* and *canciones* regularly on local radio, and Las Hermanas Padilla, a pair of singing sisters who became popular recording artists in both Mexico and the United States.

Things changed during the 1940s as a result of the high demand for labor created by World War II. A 1942 agreement known as the Bracero Program allowed approximately 220,000 Mexican men to enter the United States legally as agricultural workers before its expiration in 1947; in the next two years, an additional 142,000 undocumented laborers were given legal status. Most *braceros* went to California or Texas, with Washington, Idaho, and Oregon the next most visited destinations. In a pattern that would become familiar, the influx of newcomers resulted in both intra- and interethnic tension. For example, in 1943 the Los Angeles "Zoot Suit Riots" erupted between white sailors and young Mexican American pachucos, members of a bilingual subculture identified by their baggy "zoot" suits. Also, though public facilities like swimming pools remained segregated in Southern California until the 1950s, in 1945 Orange County Mexican American parents challenged school segregation policies and won. Tensions between Mexicanos and Chicanos also increased: Some Californios felt the new immigrants were taking away their jobs and driving down wages.

Even while the percentage of Mexican American families with Mexican-born members was dropping, new immigration increased the local community's cultural ties to Mexico. Mexican musical films were shown regularly in Los Angeles theaters, and popular Mexican singers like Tito Guizar appeared in live concerts. Cultural organizations formed during this period include La Casa del Mexicano (1945), a community center, and the Mexican American Movement, a youth group that organized cultural festivals. The Mexican Consulate contributed to musical interchange and growth, hiring performers like Las Hermanas Padilla to entertain at *bracero* camps. Performances by the orchestras of Xavier Cugat (1900–1990) and Carlos Molina introduced cosmopolitan Mexican Americans in Los Angeles to the latest Latin dance craze, the rumba.

Los Angeles continued to produce talented performers, including Las Hermanitas Mendoza, bolero singers who dressed in traditional Mexican attire, and classical artists like tenor Ruben Reyes and organist Juan Aguilar. Other local musicians recorded "jump blues," a style considered a link between swing and rock and roll, aimed at the pachuco subculture. Songs like Lalo Guerrero's "Chuco Suave" and Don Tosti's "Pachuco Boogie" mixed American and Latino idioms just like the pachuco *caló* dialect fused Spanish and English words. A number of local recording labels focusing on Mexican music emerged in the 1940s and 1950s, attracting many talented Mexicans and Mexican Americans to the city.

In the early 1950s undocumented immigration rose dramatically, encouraged by American employers who benefited from the cheap labor supply. The new arrivals faced harsh discrimination and, after 1954, a massive campaign by the U.S. government to "secure" the border, known as Operation Wetback. The cultural divide between agricultural workers from Mexico and urban Mexican Americans increased. In Los Angeles, Afro-Cuban styles were favored, and East L.A. began to emerge as a musical destination as new clubs opened up in the area, many featuring the Cuban-style music like mambo that was popular at the time. Chicano rockers began to emerge in the same area, heavily influenced by local black artists like saxophonist Chuck Higgins. L.A.'s Chuck Rio composed the 1958 hit "Tequila," and Ritchie Valens (born Valenzuela; 1941–1959) became famous around the same time for "La Bamba."

In the 1960s, immigration accelerated still further. Though the Bracero Program ended in 1964, new legislation in 1965 created a quota system that allowed for greater numbers of legal immigrants from Latin America. At the same time, entry requirements became stricter and illegal immigration rose as well. An increasing political and cultural awareness paralleling the African American civil rights movement defined this period and was known as the Chicano Movement. Chicano students in Los Angeles and across Southern California were particularly active, organizing strikes and political groups intended to advance equality and to unify the Mexicano and Chicano communities.

Mexican American artists, writers, and musicians were at their most creative and prolific during this period, and the movement's emphasis on *mestizo* heritage meant that many looked to Mexican traditions for inspiration. *Folklórico* groups that performed dances from many regions of Mexico sprung up at universities throughout the Southwest, as did mariachi music ensembles. Interest in border music like *tejano* and *norteño* also grew. A few performers like vocalist Vicki Carr, born in El Paso but raised in the San Gabriel

Carlos Santana performing at Shoreline Amphitheater in Mountain View, California on October 5, 2002. © Tim Mosenfelder/ Getty Images.

Valley, and Carlos Santana (1947–), who started his career in San Francisco but was born in Jalisco, Mexico, made inroads into mainstream popular culture. East L.A. bands like Thee Midniters, Tierra, and El Chicano developed a unique style of Chicano rock by combining rhythm and blues (R&B), rock, salsa, Mexican and other musical influences.

Some of the most important political and artistic activities of the time took place in California's central San Joaquin Valley. There César Chávez (1927–1993), a migrant farmworker born in Arizona and raised in San José, organized the National Farm Workers Union (now United Farm Workers of America) in 1962. In 1966, Chávez orchestrated the five-year grape workers strike (*huelga*) in Delano that brought the country's attention to the plight of the mostly Mexican and Filipino laborers. Numerous *corridos* have been composed about the leader, now a folk hero who has attained mythic status. In order to further Chávez's goals, Luis Miguel Váldez and Agustín Lara formed, in 1965, El Teatro Campesino (Peasant Theater), a traveling theater group that spread news and educated *braceros* while entertaining them with a combination of skits, adaptations of Mexican myth, and songs. Their performances included dramatizations of *corridos* and performances of Mexican folk songs like "De Colores" (Of Colors). The group later evolved into El Teatro Campesino Cultural, which moved to Fresno and then San Juan Bautista. Váldez continues to work with the Teatro, while Lara works in the Fresno area with composer Patricia Wells Solórzano, with whom he founded the musical group Alma in 1979 to continue the Teatro's aims.

A 1986 bill granted amnesty to 2.7 million undocumented immigrants, 70 percent of them Mexicans, while large-scale immigration from Central and South America and the Caribbean further increased diversity in the U.S. Latino population. At the same time, economic recessions increased fear among many Americans and anti-immigrant sentiment grew, often resulting in highly discriminatory legislation; California Mexicans were the hardest hit after the passage of Proposition 187 in 1994, which denied basic benefits and rights to undocumented workers and their families. California Latinos fought back both politically and culturally. Politically, their efforts ended the effects of Prop 187 in 1999. Culturally, they retaliated with increased interest in traditional and semitraditional Mexican art forms. Throughout the 1990s Mexican and Mexican-derived music and dance grew in popularity among youth, and none was more popular than *banda*, brass band music originally from the state of Sinaloa. The first Sinaloan-style banda in the United States was founded in Los Angeles in the mid-1970s, but the style did not become popular until an updated version was imported from Guadalajara in the early 1990s. Whereas the original instrumental *bandas* featured upwards of twenty musicians, the new *tecnobandas* replaced many instruments with electric guitar, keyboards, and drum sets and added vocalists. The genre gained national attention when *banda*-format radio station KLAX became Los Angeles' top station in any language in 1992.

These *tecnobandas* introduced a new dance called *quebradita* ("little break," sometimes also termed *caballito*, or "little horse"). Though the rhythm—actually a speeded-up *cumbia*—was likely developed in Mexico, the dance seems to have originated in the Los Angeles area. Its distinctive movements are a combination of *folklórico*, hip-hop, salsa, swing, and country line dancing, though it is most easily recognized by the deep backbends that gave the dance its name, dangerous flips, and flashy western clothing style. In the early 1990s hundreds of competitive *quebradita* clubs formed across Southern California and in other cities with large Mexican American populations. Though some disapproved of the *quebradita*'s sensual movements, most viewed the clubs as a positive alternative to gang activity. Many young *quebradita* dancers saw their participation in the dance as an affirmation of their pride in Mexican culture, and the dance's popularity cut across lines of class and national origin.

Corridos, narrative ballads, were another traditional Mexican style Los Angeles musicians resuscitated in a new form. Called *narcocorridos*, these timely songs dealt with the drug trade. Though *norteño* group Los Tigres del Norte had recorded such songs in the 1970s, they did not develop into a distinct subgenre until the late 1980s, when Sinaloan immigrant Rosalino "Chalino" Sánchez recorded them in Los Angeles. Chalino's raspy voice, macho image, and country origins earned him many devoted fans and, after his violent death in 1992, numerous emulators. His recordings are still selling strong a decade later, and other L.A. artists have taken this tough genre a step further. Most prominent among recent *narcocorridistas* are the Rivera family. Father Pedro runs the label Cintas Acuario on which Chalino's recordings were released; son Lupillo and daughter Jenni, who grew up listening to as much rap and R&B as Mexican music, bring an urban edge to their *corridos* that has drawn comparisons to gangsta rap.

At present, Mexican Americans in California are making every type of music imaginable and giving each their own unique twist. In the realm of the traditional, mariachi groups abound, and both student and professional groups can be found in all parts of the state. Mariachi masses have been a part of Southern California Catholic worship since 1968. Women's groups, still a novelty in the primarily masculine genre, are active in Los Angeles and Fresno. The popularity of traditional music among Mexican American youth is evidenced by the hundreds of juvenile folklórico dance groups and mariachi ensembles throughout the state—over twenty youth mariachi groups exist in the San Joaquin Valley area alone. Among the professionals, Arizonan Linda Ronstadt's popular 1988 mariachi recording "Canciones de mi Padre" (Songs of My Father) featured three of L.A.'s best-known groups: Los Camperos de Nati Cano dates to 1961 and is known as an originator of the popular "show" format that blends dance, theater, and music; leader Natividad Cano received a National Heritage Fellowship in the United States and a Sylvestre Vargas Award in Mexico for artistic excellence. Los Galleros de Pedro Rey was formed in 1970 by a former member of Mariachi Vargas de Tecalitlán, Mexico's premier group. José Hernández, the son of Galleros founder Pedro Hernández, organized Mariachi Sol de Mexico in 1986; the group has since become known for its "classical" performances with orchestras. Among the many other traditional genres practiced in California are the Sinaloan *banda* music played by several Los Angeles and Bay Area groups and the religious *danzas* maintained by immigrants from Apatazingán, Michoacán, in Redwood City.

In the area of popular music, many small, local, keyboard-driven groups, sometimes known as *grupos tropicales*, play Mexican *cumbia* music or *grupera* ballads. Others focus on accordion-driven *norteño* music, and indeed, many Mexican groups including top *norteño* band Los Tigres del Norte now make their home in California. Narcocorridos remain strong, as do Sinaloan *tecnobandas*. Eastside Chicanos like Los Lobos continue the tradition of Chicano rock even as they investigate more traditional Mexican music like *tejano/norteño* or *huapango*. Other artists like *conguero* Poncho Sánchez enliven the Latin jazz scene. Many Mexican Americans also enjoy dancing to salsa and merengue; in fact, they have contributed to the development of a distinctive L.A. salsa dance style. As in the past, young Los Angeles Mexicano and Chicano musicians are showing themselves to be particularly adept in fusing diverse musical styles. One innovative group is Ozomatli, whose members have Mexican, African, and even Japanese roots; their songs combine rap, salsa, *cumbia*, merengue, funk, *norteño*, and Indian musical influences.

Although Los Angeles, as the home to the largest Mexican-origin community in the United States (nearly 3 million strong), continues to be an important center for musical production, Chicano and Mexicano cultural organizations are active in many other cities across the state. In the Bay Area, San Jose has one of the older Mexican communities. There, Los Lupeños and the Aztlán Academy have been teaching *ballet folklórico* and other Mexican traditions to area youth since the 1960s, while the Mexican Heritage Plaza hosts an annual mariachi festival. Meanwhile, recent immigrants living in the newer communities of Oakland and Richmond have been active on the *banda sinaloense* scene. In San Pablo, Los Cenzontles Mexican Arts Center has since 1989 been home to a unique musical group led by Eugene Rodríguez. The group aims to preserve and disseminate a variety of traditional Mexican rural genres from *son abajeño* to *banda* through collaborations with Mexican artists. In Fresno, almost half of the population has Mexican ancestry, and the city has produced many well-known Mexican American authors, poets, and scholars, including Teatro Campesino founder Agustín Lira. Annual mariachi festivals in Fresno, San Diego, and other cities attract both internationally famous artists and local groups.

Mexican American Music into the Northwest

The Mexican community of the Pacific Northwest is not as old as California's, but it goes back for several generations. Mexican *vaqueros* (cowboys) and *arrieros* (mule train drivers) had worked in the area in the nineteenth century but did not stay; the earliest settlers were most likely longshoremen of Mexican descent who lived and worked in Seattle, Washington, in the 1910s and 1920s. Today's flourishing northwestern Mexicano/Chicano community was established by migrant workers who arrived from Mexico through the Bracero Program in the 1940s; many others came up from Texas to fill the rising need for agricultural laborers. The first Mexican American–owned businesses in the Northwest opened in the early 1950s; these included a tortilla factory in Ontario, Oregon, and a restaurant in Seattle, Washington. Beginning in the 1980s, some farmworkers became landowners as they bought out their former employers.

As in California, Mexican immigration to the Northwest increased throughout the twentieth century, with the greatest growth occurring at the end of the century. In 1930 the census found only 562 Mexicans in Washington and 1,568 in Oregon (though second-generation Mexican Americans were not counted), and outmigration further depleted the population during the Great Depression. However, things picked up after World War II, and by 1990 Washington was home to 155,864 and Oregon 85,632 persons of Mexican origin. Those numbers more than doubled again in the following decade, with 2003 estimates placing nearly 350,000

Mexicans or Mexican Americans resident in Washington and 230,000 in Oregon. If the migrant population were included, these totals would be still larger.

In Washington, following World War II a large number of Texas Mexicans settled in the Yakima Valley region, where most worked as farm laborers. Some were also musicians who played for social functions like *quinceañeras* (fifteen-year-old girls' coming-out parties), weddings, baptisms, and dances. Their *conjunto tejano* music became central to the community, symbolic of their ethnicity and their connections to the borderlands. This dance music can be in polka or waltz time and is centered on the button accordion and *bajo sexto* (twelve-string guitar), often accompanied by electric bass and drum set. Though thousands of Mexican immigrants also arrived as a result of the Bracero Program, Chicanos dominated the community's cultural life.

In the 1950s, popular *tejano* artists like Tony de la Rosa began to travel to Washington towns like Toppenish and Sunnyside on tour, expanding local musicians' repertoires and reinforcing their connection to the *conjunto* style. Local theaters showed Mexican films, bringing the music of popular Mexican singers and actors like Jorge Negrete and Pedro Infante to the Northwest. Then as now, Washingtonians with *tejano* roots like Los Astros del Norte, Conjunto Rangel, and Los Guzmanes performed *rancheras*, *corridos*, and romantic *canciones*. Spanish-language radio broadcasts also began at this time on Sunnyside's KREW. A few musicians who immigrated to the Yakima Valley during the 1950s became teachers and mentors. Santiago Almeida, a *bajo sexto* player who recorded with Narciso Martínez (a founder of the *conjunto tejano* style), was still playing and teaching in Sunnyside into the 1990s, as was traditional violinist Trinidad Márquez, a native of Michoacán who moved to Toppenish and was recently given a National Heritage Award. As in California, the Chicano Movement of the 1960s reinforced the centrality of such Mexican and Mexican American musical styles to the local communities, ensuring their survival.

The newly arrived Mexicanos also introduced new musical styles to the Yakima Valley. One of the most popular genres among new immigrants is *norteño*, another accordion-based music similar to *tejano*, though the former is faster-paced and focused on the *corrido* form, while the latter is closer to country western two-step and concentrates on romantic song. In addition, because the immigrants have come from a number of different Mexican states, several traditional regional ensemble styles have made their way to the Yakima Valley. Among these are the traditional *sones* and *huapangos* (regional songs) for *conjunto arpa grande* (large harp ensemble) as played by Yakima group Los Campesinos de Michoacán and the mariachi styles of Mariachi Guanajuato, a Sunnyside group made up of members from the states of Guanajuato, Jalisco, and Sinaloa.

Today, Yakima County is home to over 78,000 Mexicans. Marion, Salem, King, and Washington Counties also have significant populations. New communities are blossoming on the Olympic Peninsula and in the Skagit valley. The population's vitality is evident through its commitment to traditional music: Five schools now host mariachi programs; among them, Mariachi Huenachi of Wenatchee High School was given a Governor's Heritage Award in 2000 and has won two national competitions. *Tejano* ensemble Grupo Sueño is composed entirely of young Mexican Americans in the Yakima Valley area who have learned traditional musical styles through an afterschool program initiated by accordionist Cruz

Rangel. Seattle, which historically has had only a very small Mexican American population, is home to several mariachis and *folklórico* dance groups that include the University of Washington's thirty-year-old Bailadores de Bronce and the community-based Mexican American Association of Baile Folklórico. Mexican American musicians in the city also participate in salsa and other popular music groups, and Seattle now boasts its own Sinaloan brass band, Banda Vagos. The many recent Central American immigrants in the Puget Sound area also listen to Mexican musical styles and will likely make their own contributions to the region's musical life.

Oregon's Mexican American community, centered in the Snake River Valley, is smaller than but similar to that of Washington State. Here, too, Texas and Mexican *braceros* moved into the area after World War II, establishing one early community in the town of Independence. Today, the largest communities are found in Marion County (47,000), Multnomah County (41,000), and Washington County (30,000), with the largest urban group in Portland (30,000), but smaller populations can be found throughout the state. *Folklórico* dance groups, often the first cultural organizations to be formed in any Mexican American community, are active in Portland, Independence, and Woodburn as well as in Clackamas, Hood River, and Lincoln Counties. Several mariachi groups have formed in Salem and Portland. Portland is also home to notable musicians such as Candelario Zamudio, a *requinto* (five-string guitarlike instrument used by some mariachis) player originally from Guadalajara, and singer/guitarist Estella Lerma, who moved to Portland from Laredo, Texas, as a child.

One distinguishing characteristic of Oregon's Mexican Americans is their commitment to indigenous Mexican art forms. Many Purépecha speakers from Michoacán live in Corvalis, where musician Hugo Nava makes clay flutes and sings in Nahuatl, Purépecha, and Spanish. Several towns boast indigenous dance groups: In Cornelius, Cuernavaca native Rocío Espinoza Cotero teaches pre-Hispanic dance; in Milwaukie, Rigoberto Hernández leads Aztec dance group Flor y Canto; and in Independence, Salomón and Mercedes Falcón perform religious dances of the Huichol Indians each year on December 12, the feast day of the Virgin of Guadalupe. In addition, Mexican Oregonians in Portland have engaged in creative interchange with other Latino groups. Some are collaborating with local South Americans to create fusion groups like Mexican/Andean Grupo Condor; others have joined up with Guatemalan marimba ensembles or Salvadoran musicians like *vihuela* and *jarana* player Jesus Rivas.

New Frontiers: Mexican American Music in Alaska and Hawai'i

Since the 1980s, Mexican immigrants have been moving in increasing numbers to the furthest reaches of the United States in search of new frontiers of economic opportunity. Alaska's Mexican community grew from about 9,000 in 1990 to a current official figure near 13,000. Likewise, Hawai'i's Mexican population rose to over 17,000 in 2000 from the 14,000 of a decade earlier; upper estimates that include undocumented immigrants run as high as 40,000. Higher wages and living standards along with less competition for jobs were the attraction for central and southern Mexican immigrants to these nontraditional settlement areas. In Hawai'i, the Mexican community is centered in Kona on the Big Island, where most work in the coffee industry, and on the islands of Maui and Oahu. In Alaska, many Mexicans work in the fishing industry.

Even though the growth of the Mexican American community in Hawai'i is a recent development, Mexicans do have a historical presence on the islands. In 1832, California *vaqueros* (Mexican cowboys) were brought in by King Kamehameha III (1813–1854) to teach the Hawaiians about raising the cattle Captain John Vancouver had established on Hawaii Island in the late eighteenth century. The *vaqueros* brought guitars with them, and their musical practices influenced the other islanders to such a degree that a new style of Hawaiian slack-key guitar was developed. The Hawaiian cowboys as well as their music came to be called *paniolo*, a Hawaiian pronunciation of the word *español*. However, these early Mexicans did not establish a lasting community, so Hawai'i's current Mexican population maintains no connection to such musical practices. Cultural activities of the new Mexican community include the establishment of *ballet folklórico* "Los Amigos" in 1993 in Waianae, Oahu island.

In Alaska, Mexicans have worked as seasonal laborers since the early twentieth century, filling spring openings at businesses such as canneries. Today, the largest Mexican American community in Alaska is in Anchorage. It numbers from 5,000 to 7,000 and is centered on the Mountain View neighborhood. In 2002, four Mexican American mothers in Anchorage formed what appears to be the first Mexican cultural organization in Alaska. The activities of Xochiquetzal-Tiqun, which takes its name from the Aztec goddess of the arts and a native Alaskan word for "wolf," include a children's *folklórico* dance group. Cinco de Mayo is now celebrated in Anchorage as well, and Mexico's patron saint, the Virgin of Guadalupe, is given her due through the traditional singing of "Las Mañanitas" (often called "The Birthday Song") on December 12 at the Our Lady of Guadalupe Parish. Spanish-language radio programming can be heard in locations as disparate as Anchorage, Fairbanks, Juneau, and Kodiak.

THE ASIAN INFLUENCE ON MUSIC IN THE PACIFIC REGION

The Asian influence on the arts in the Pacific Region is complex, especially in music. This influence is not limited to the musical arts that immigrants bring with them and practice when they settle in America. It includes many elements from the immigrant cultures, including the other arts, religion, technology, and philosophy. In addition, continuing widespread contact between America and Asia has been transforming the musical cultures of each. By many of the same processes that African and European cultures have shaped American culture, Asian cultures also shape our culture.

History of Asian Immigrant Music in the Pacific Region

From the very earliest days of the settling of the American West, Asian immigrants have brought with them their own music and continued to practice it. In California, immigrants from Asia arrived contemporaneously with immigrants from Europe and the eastern parts of the United States. The first public western opera performance in San Francisco (1851) preceded the first Chinese opera performance (1852) by only one year.

The San Francisco Bay Area has the largest population of ethnic Chinese outside of Asia. One-third of all foreign-born in the United States are in California. Honolulu, Hawaii, and Seattle, Washington, are also extraordinarily multiethnic cities. Honolulu has the highest percentage of ethnic Asians of any city in the United States. Alaska has its own unique mix of ethnic groups, but with fewer Asians than the other Pacific states. The musical culture of the Pacific Region is strongly shaped by the cultures of the many different ethnic groups that live there.

Perhaps the most defining characteristic of the music of the Pacific Region is that it has developed in an environment both rich in many traditions and rich in active links with the rest of the world. Regional boundaries have been porous. Musicians, teachers, scholars, and audiences all continue to move freely from one area to another. National boundaries of the Pacific states with Canada and Mexico continue to be open. Many individual musicians and arts organizations keep in touch with each other across these borders.

In addition, direct contact with the people and organizations of Asian countries continues, and cultural exchange is an important component of this contact. As a result, the musical culture of the Pacific Region has not developed in isolation. The importance of this cannot be overestimated. Ongoing contact maintains the complex and ever-changing web of relationships that have made the Pacific Region what it is culturally. Instead of diminishing regional identity, it defines it.

The development of twentieth-century recording technology made a major impact on the cultivation of Asian music in the Pacific Region. Immigrants both imported and made their own 78 rpm records when equipment became available. Local radio stations in ethnic communities also made recordings. The invention of the tape recorder in 1948 and the many technological advancements since then have further expanded the ability of individuals and organizations to record. Recordings facilitate the maintenance and dissemination of musical culture.

By the 1960s long-playing records brought "world music" to the general population, and by the early 1970s, half of all Western composers in the San Francisco Bay Area had studied Asian music enough for it to influence their own music. Among these composers were Richard Felciano (b. 1930), Gerhard Samuel (b. 1924), Ingram Marshall (b. 1942), Douglas Leedy (b. 1938), Loren Rush (b. 1935), Lou Harrison (1917–2003), and Dane Rudhyar (1895–1985). Concepts of timbre, time, texture, structure, instrumentation, and notation all expanded as a result of contact with Asian cultures.

Asian Musicians and Composers

Composers of the Pacific Region have been both very original and influential as a result of contact with Asian cultures. Early twentieth-century composer Henry Cowell (1897–1965) learned Chinese music in San Francisco and studied other Asian music in the 1930s. He became famous for his experimentation with timbre, microtones, tone clusters, and form. After studying the Chinese text the *I Ching*, Los Angeles–born composer John Cage (1912–1999) applied chance techniques to music composition. His experiments sparked a major movement in mid-century

American composition. Cage's influence on other composers and artists was so great that he became known as the father of the avant-garde.

Many Asian performers visited or immigrated independently. Leo Lew (c. 1900–c. 1990, China) stayed long enough to teach Chinese music to pianist/composer Betty Siu Jun Wong (b. 1938, San Francisco). Wong then formed Chinese and new music ensembles and taught at the Community Music Center in San Francisco.

Asian American musicians in other parts of the United States have influenced musical developments in the Pacific Region. Chinese American composer Wen-Chung Chou (b. 1923) in New York taught James Tenney (b. 1934), who then taught a generation of musicians at the California Institute of the Arts. Korean American composer Earl Kim (1920–1998) in Massachusetts taught Chinese American composer Melissa Hui (b. 1966), who currently teaches at Stanford University in California.

Asian Americans have participated in many western music organizations. One example is the Del Sol String Quartet (f. 1992, Banff, Canada), with two Asian American members, which has had residencies in California and in San Francisco performed a premier of a work by Japanese composer Toshio Hosokawa (b. 1955).

Henry Cowell, 1964. Courtesy of the Library of Congress.

Many Asian or Asian American conductors have conducted symphonies in the Pacific states. These include Seiji Ozawa (b. 1935) in San Francisco, Kent Nagano (b. 1951) in Berkeley, and Jung-Ho Pak (b. 1962) in San Diego. Chinese Canadian Samuel Wong (b. 1962) has conducted the Honolulu Symphony since 1996.

Visiting Asian musicians and music ensembles have repeatedly irrigated the musical culture of the Pacific Region. Among those who have come are the most accomplished performers and composers from many different cultures. A list of Chinese musicians who came to San Francisco to perform in the 1990s would include numerous Cantonese and other Chinese opera troupes not only from China but also from Singapore and Taiwan. The Chorus of the Central Philharmonic Society, the National Ensemble of Chinese Music, and the Shanghai National Music Orchestra all performed in California. In 1998 the Chinese new music group Huaxia Ensemble also gave concerts.

The Balinese gamelan Burat Wangi (f. 1972) came to the California Institute of the Arts in 2004. This ensemble performs new styles as well as traditional Balinese court music.

Indonesian gamelan music has flourished in the United States. One-third of all gamelan ensembles in North America are in the Pacific Region, and about half of these—about twenty—are associated with educational institutions. In academia, gamelan music has been combined with other kinds of music and instruments, including the organ, Indian percussion, and electronic music synthesizers.

Taiko drumming has become extremely popular, and many groups have been established in the Pacific Region. Many outdoor public events in this region's cities would be incomplete without Taiko drumming.

Audiences in the Pacific states have been able to experience performances of traditional music from Israel, Iran, India, Mongolia, Korea, Vietnam, and many other Asian countries. Performers from Asia traveling to other parts of the United States often pass through the Pacific Region, which serves as a gateway to America. Many immigrants temporarily reside in this region before moving on to other regions.

The development of electronic music in California during the 1960s was both a result of and a catalyst for continuing contact with Asian music. The San Francisco Tape Music Center (f. 1961) helped familiarize Western audiences with drones, repetition, phrase lengths, and structural concepts not common in Western music.

In 1975, composer John Chowning (b. 1934) invented frequency modulation synthesis in Palo Alto, California, opening the way for the development of digital music synthesizers. New electronic instruments designed in Japan, such as those by Roland, could simulate non-Western instruments as well as Western instruments. As a result, the sounds of the shamisen and other Asian instruments became readily available to musicians in the West.

A young woman performs with the Japanese traditional drum team, Northwest Namukai Taiko, at the International District Festival in Seattle, 1990. © Bohemian Nomad Picturemakers/Corbis.

Circumstances in the Pacific Region—extraordinary opportunities for musicians to experience the music of other cultures, and the continual movement of people into and out of the region—have affected the development of music around the globe. Many immigrant musicians did not have opportunities to experience the music of other cultures in their own countries. In America they have been able to build on their earlier training and undergo dramatic transformation in their new environment. In addition, continuing contact with their Asian homelands helps spread their knowledge to those still at home while also providing new stimulation for growth. This ongoing contact and exchange has given rise to terms such as "transnationalism" and "interculturalism."

Many music conservatories in China, Korea, Japan, and in other Asian countries train musicians almost exclusively in Western music. When these Western musicians—composers and performers—

arrive in the United States and come into contact with different cultures, they often develop an interest in the traditional music of their homelands. Their attempts to learn, integrate, and imagine traditional culture stimulates the development of new hybrid forms.

The Younger Generation of Immigrant and Asian American Musicians

The younger generation of immigrant Asian instrumentalists, such as those from China, often hear older styles of performance in America than the styles they were trained to play in their homelands. This contact with the past, as preserved in the New World, expands their understanding of their cultural history and eventually enriches the culture of the mother country as well.

Other American-born descendants of Asian immigrants have developed similar interests in their cultural heritage after studying Western music. Nurtured in the experimental environment of Mills College in Oakland, California, composer and koto performer Mia Masaoka (b. 1958) has created unique works reflecting her heritage, education, time, and place. The well-known pianist Jon Jang (b. 1954) and other members of the Asian American Orchestra learned to play jazz first and later added ethnic musical characteristics to their work. Some scholars identify the resulting music as a new genre: Asian American jazz. The work of bassist/bamboo mouth organist/composer Mark Izu (b. 1954) has been seminal in the development of this new music.

Collaborations between musicians and other performers from different cultures have become so common that audiences can now hear single compositions combining music from several continents. For example, "Dream of the Desert" (2003) by Betty Siu Jun Wong and performed by the Phoenix Spring Ensemble (f. 1975, San Francisco, CA) includes a Japanese shakuhachi, an Australian digeridoo, an American Indian cedar flute, a Chinese xiao, both Turkish and Iranian ney, and an Arabian qanun, all combined with guitar, saxophones, and assorted other instruments. "The Hear and Now" (2004) by Jon Raskin (b. 1954) performed at the Other Minds International Music Festival in San Francisco featured the Rova Saxophone Quartet (f. 1977, Oakland, CA) along with Korean kayagum, Japanese koto, Burmese pat waing, Indian table tarang, and Chinese instruments.

Collaborations sometimes feature dancers, such as the 1999 "Common Ground" performance in San Francisco of the Lily Cai Chinese Dance Company (f. 1988, Shanghai) and the Dimensions Dance Theatre (f. 1972, Oakland, CA), specializing in African and African-derived dance forms.

Through their activities, a number of music clubs have served vital roles in the community. These roles include (1) maintaining ethnic identity through food, language, music, and ritual, (2) maintaining strong community social bonds through collaboration, cooperation, and sharing, (3) helping newcomers adapt to their new country, and (4) constructing a positive identity of Chinatown to outsiders.

During times of hardship, music clubs have helped raise funds and feed those in need. The Cantonese Opera Club Hoy Fung, in San Francisco, sent funds for famine relief to China in 1961. During World War II, this club provided daily meals to members. It also organized a basketball team for recreation.

Music has been a vehicle for political expression in Asian American communities in the Pacific Region throughout the twentieth century. The connection between music and politics is complicated and often so subtle it escapes notice, but it has not diminished over time. Public performances of Cantonese opera in San Francisco are always occasions for political speeches. Asian American jazz musicians frequently choose historical events of racial injustice as topics for their performances. California's reputation as a place of political foment has been built on the actions of its many ethnic groups, and the arts have contributed to this in very important ways.

WEST COAST POP AND ROCK

West Coast Jazz

In the eyes of many music critics, West Coast jazz is a brief and perhaps even errant moment in musical history, a period following World War II during which California produced an identifiable sound that has been alternately esteemed and demeaned. As Ted Gioia recounts in his seminal study *West Coast Jazz*, musicians Art Pepper and Chet Baker, who enjoyed critical and popular success during the 1950s and 1960s, found themselves out of favor by the 1970s, even, in Baker's case, reduced to pumping gas for a living.[17] Beginning as what one critic terms a "mutation" of the popular bebop jazz sound of the East Coast, West Coast jazz found its way into existence in Los Angeles, in places such as the short-lived Cotton Club, of the 1950s, in Hollywood, and Billy Berg's club on Vine Street or Central Avenue's Club Alabam and the Downbeat. In a highly racialized city (African Americans needed a permit to be in Glendale after 6 P.M.), black jazz nightclubs were marked by racial tolerance and an atmosphere that welcomed and embraced all creeds and colors, as long as they loved jazz.

American jazz saxophonist Dexter Gordon sits with his instrument, smoking in a dark nightclub during a performance, New York City, 1948. Herman Leonard/Getty Images.

Robert Gordon's *Jazz West Coast* pinpoints the beginning of the West Coast sound in December 1945, the date of Dizzy Gillespie's (1917–1993) appearance at Billy Berg's club.[18] Charlie Parker (1920–1955) showed up for a set, and despite a host of problems with both musicians (Parker's erratic behavior a result of his heroine addiction) and audience, the combination of a one-month stand and records Gillespie and Parker cut while in California solidified a West Coast scene. After their recording session, Gillespie headed back to the East Coast, and Parker stayed on, landing a job in Los Angeles' Little Tokyo, his presence attracting a host of musicians who would soon create the sound of West Coast jazz: Gerry Mulligan, Stan Getz, Charlie Ventura, Gene Krupa, and Dexter Gordon, among others.

Parker's problems continued, however, and he eventually returned to the East Coast, claiming California's reputation as "square," to use the terminology of the day, and that perception was cast in stone in the minds of urban and urbane New Yorkers. But if Parker had failed to light a jazz fire in Hollywood, Central Avenue was still hot, with the incomparable Dexter Gordon and the extraordinary Art Pepper playing with frequency. Working through and with the established bebop sound that a first-rate combo, the Howard McGhee Sextet, had brought out west, Pepper and Gordon crafted what became the archetypal West Coast jazz sound: fluid, lyrically precise, smooth, even-keeled, with an emotional detachment that could only be called "cool."

For many, West Coast jazz's rejection of the spontaneous, sometimes frenetic jams of bebop made it not cool but bland. What was for some a relaxed, easily digestible composition was for others predictable. Therein began a short-lived rivalry, with proponents of the up-and-coming hard bop sound coming out of the East referring to West Coast as "filleted bebop"—a sound served up too easily to its listeners. Yet a number of musicians, all of whom were showcased by West Coast jazz's emphasis on instrumental soloists, broke ground. Trumpeter Miles Davis (1926–1991), hardly a Pacific coaster, began the trend when he "cooled" his sound down in his nonet recordings (1949–1950), producing an understated sound and style that emphasized arrangements by West Coasters such as Gerry Mulligan (1927–1996). Capitol records later issued the recordings on a 12 inch LP they rightly called *Birth of the Cool* (1957). Davis' nonet, a nine-piece group, also set the tone for cool jazz's orchestral timbres.

Instrumental Soloists

More than anything, perhaps, it is the emphasis on precise, nonspontaneous instrumental solos that characterizes the West Coast jazz sound. Of all the musicians, Dave Brubeck (b. 1920) is the most famous. Brubeck's trademark polytonal, polyrhythmic style was born and bred in California. He studied in Stockton, at the University of the Pacific, which currently houses the Brubeck Collection. While Brubeck formed both an octet and a trio at one point, it was the Dave Brubeck Quartet that thrust him and his smooth sound into international prominence. "Take Five," a song in 5/4 time on his album *Time Out* (1959), helped the album become the first jazz album to go gold. The song was at the top of jazz charts and is still a favorite with music fans of all ages.

Brubeck's success opened a number of doors and spurred controversy as well, since many of the musicians who walked through those doors were white. West Coast jazz is still sometimes referred to as "white jazz," for its stable of talent included a host of white jazz musicians: Chet Baker (1929–1988), a photogenic singer and trumpeter whose career failed because of drug addiction; Cal Tjader (1925–1986), often re-

Portrait of Dave Brubeck, with sheet music as backdrop, 1954. Courtesy of the Library of Congress.

ferred to as "the greatest Anglo musician in Latin music"; Gerry Mulligan (1927–1996); and Vince Guaraldi (1928–1976), whose 1963 hit "Cast Your Fate to the Wind," a smooth, jazzy piano instrumental, is still overshadowed by Guaraldi's most famous work: the sound track to the Charlie Brown animated television specials (first released in 1965).

Whether the result of public taste changes or a lack of innovation among its practitioners, West Coast jazz was indeed a scene that was all but over by the 1960s. Some of the scene's more experimental artists, such as Charles Mingus (b. 1922), Ornette Coleman (b. 1930), and Dexter Gordon (1923–1990), moved to the East Coast and went on to have varied and highly respected careers.

Surf Rock and the California Sound

Long a haven of West Coast surfers, the state of California was the cradle of an early form of 1960s rock and roll known as *surf music*, or *surf rock*. Dick Dale (b. 1926) was a Southern California guitarist known for a high-speed, reverberating staccato style. His signature sound, which would prove to be the foundation for surf music, actually blended eastern European and Middle Eastern melodies with contemporary rock and roll riffs. Dale and his band the Del-Tones scored a regional hit with the 1961 single "Let's Go Trippin'," often credited as the first surf rock song. After a number of regional hits, Dale and the Del-Tones released two full-length albums, *Surfer's Choice* (1962) and *King of the Surf Guitar* (1963), which brought his music to a national audience. Dale played up-tempo instrumentals, as did other California surf bands such as the Chantays ("Pipeline," 1963) from Santa Ana and The Surfaris ("Wipe Out," 1963) from Glendora. A Tacoma, Washington, band, The Ventures also spread the gospel of surf music with hits such as "Walk-Don't Run" (1960) and the "Theme from *Hawaii Five-O*" (1969).

After the original guitar-based surf bands, subsequent surf music placed more emphasis on vocal harmonies than on guitar instrumentalism. Undeniably the kings of this "second wave" of surf music, The Beach Boys were the most successful group to come from the California shores at the time. The Beach Boys, formed in the Los Angeles suburb of Hawthorne by brothers Carl, Dennis, and Brian Wilson, along with cousin Mike Love and friend Al Jardine, sang simplistic, upbeat pop/rock songs distinguished by irresistible vocal harmonies, such as "Fun Fun Fun," "Little Deuce Coupe," "Surfin' USA" and "Surfin' Safari." The band reached its creative apex with its 1966 album *Pet Sounds*. This album, displaying Brian Wilson's growing skills as a music producer, yielded innovative vocal and instrumental layerings, as heard in such hits as "Wouldn't It Be Nice" and "God Only Knows"; in fact, many critics have pointed to *Pet Sounds* as an inspiration for The Beatles' landmark *Sgt. Pepper's Lonely Hearts Club Band*, released one year later. While *Pet Sounds* also represented a subtle move toward more introspective lyrics, the group still stayed true to their surf rock roots, as shown in their hit "Good Vibrations," recorded shortly after the *Pet Sounds* sessions.

Jan Berry and Dean Torrence, who recorded as Jan and Dean, rivaled The Beach Boys as leaders of the surf music craze during the early 1960s. Their hit singles "Surf City" (1963) and "Little Old Lady from Pasadena" and "Dead Man's Curve" (both from 1964) were just as catchy as the early Beach Boys hits. Groups such as The Beach Boys and Jan and Dean mixed descriptions of surfing, hot rod

Hawaiian Slack Key Music

For many, Hawaiian slack key guitar, *ki ho'alu*, is both the least known and greatest of guitar traditions. *Ki ho'alu*, meaning "loosen the key," relies on slacked tunings that present a variety of open tunings, generally based on a major tonality. The tunings are combined with techniques such as the hammer-on, a sharp pluck of the fret that produces a secondary, higher tone, and the pull-off, in which the guitarist pulls off the string to produce a secondary lower note. The techniques mimic certain sounds rooted in ancient Hawaiian chants and songs.

Because the history of the Hawaiian Islands contains so much immigration, and because music is such a mobile art form, many theories exist as to how slack key began in the Islands. Some believe that European sailors, arriving around the beginning of the nineteenth century, introduced Hawaiians to the gut string guitar, and the Portuguese, who arrived in the 1860s with steel string guitars, shifted Hawaiians to the steel string sound, which remains the most popular guitar sound today. Others believe that Mexican and Spanish *vaqueros* hired by King Kamehameha III around 1832 to help with Hawaiian cattle brought their guitars and played them around campfires during cattle drives.

However the form developed, it clearly received an important boost during the reign of King David Kalakaua (1836–1891), the ruler responsible for the great Hawaiian cultural resurgence of the 1880s and 1890s. He supported the preservation of ancient music while also promoting newer sounds such as the guitar and ukulele. Kalakaua and his siblings composed a host of superb songs, still well known today, and generated a national pride that remained long after Hawaii lost its monarchical system and became part of the United States.

Currently, Hawaiian slack key may be experiencing its highest level of popularity yet. Keola Beamer's first solo album was recorded in 1972, and he has since recorded and produced more than a dozen albums. He has appeared on *Sesame Street*, has won many Hoku Awards (the Hawaiian equivalent of the Grammies), and toured the United States as one of the "Masters of the Slack Key Guitar." Ozzie Kotani is a respected teacher, arranger, composer, and accompanist as well as a solo performer. He has played *ki ho'alu* for over twenty years on the Mainland, in Spain and Japan, as well as all around the Hawaiian Islands. He recorded his landmark first album *Classical Slack* in 1988. Most recently, Israel Kamakawiwo'ole brought a combination of traditional Hawaiian and contemporary Hawaiian, including open ukulele tuning, to a short but lasting career. His 1993 CD *Facing Future* is still one of the bestselling Hawaiian music recordings, due to the inclusion of the medley "Over the Rainbow/What a Wonderful World." His death in 1997 has done nothing to diminish his immense popularity in Hawai'i and elsewhere.

culture, and youthful innocence to transform a local lifestyle into American mythology.

The Mamas & The Papas, with members John Phillips, Michelle Phillips, Cass Elliot, and Denny Doherty, were another California group that found success by offering harmony-rich pop tunes. Between 1966 and 1968, the Mamas & the Papas had big hits with the folk-inspired pop hits "Monday, Monday," "Go Where You Wanna Go," "I Saw Her Again," and "California Dreamin'."

The Psychedelic Sound

Cities such as Los Angeles and, especially, San Francisco became centers of 1960s American counterculture. The Jefferson Airplane, a band rooted in folk and blues, formed during the so-called San Francisco Bay folk boom of 1965. After releasing *Jefferson Airplane Takes Off* (1965), the group recruited Grace Slick, the singer in a local San Francisco group The Great Society. The Jefferson Airplane became a leading band in late 1960s psychedelic rock, and the band participated in the "Human Be-In" celebration that took place in January 1967 in Golden Gate Park. Their album *Surrealistic Pillow* (1967) contributed to the unofficial sound track of the Summer of Love with hit songs "Somebody to Love" and "White Rabbit." The band experimented with psychedelic drugs lyrics for inspiration, and "White Rabbit," inspired by the Lewis Carroll novel *Alice in Wonderland*, was also seen to contain drug-trip imagery. Jefferson Airplane became intrinsically linked with hippie counterculture. In 1969, the Airplane released their most political album to date, *Volunteers*, and performed the titled track at the Woodstock Arts and Music Festival in August 1969.

Woodstock may not have happened if not for the success of The Monterey International Pop Festival, held at the Monterey (California) County Fairgrounds from June 1967. Over 200,000 people attended the three-day festival, which featured such diverse acts as soul singer Otis Redding, Indian sitar master Ravi Shankar, and pscyhedelic blues band Big Brother and the Holding Company (featuring Janis Joplin [1943–1970]). The festival marked the first American performance of British rock group The Who and also an emerging guitarist named Jimi Hendrix (1942–1970), who hailed from Seattle. Hendrix, backed by his band The Experience, provided the most memorable moments of Monterey Pop when he sacrificially lit his guitar on fire at the end of "Wild Thing."

Monterey is seen by many people to have touched off the Summer of Love in 1967, but San Francisco is generally seen as the home of this cultural phenomenon. That spring and summer, thousands of youths migrated to the city's Haight-Ashbury district to celebrate the hippie movement. John Phillips of The Mamas and the Papas wrote the song "San Francisco" (released by Scott McKenzie in May 1967), telling the incoming youths to wear flowers in their hair and to prepare for the city's "love-in."

The combination of hippie counterculture and the vibrant music scene produced some of the leading bands of psychedelic rock, which featured comparatively free-form song structures often influenced by Eastern music. In addition to the Jefferson Airplane there was Vanilla Fudge and also Tommy James and the Shondells. But the one band who would have the most lasting legacy was the Grateful Dead.

The Grateful Dead (or The Dead, as they are often called) was formed in the mid-1960s by Jerry Garcia, Ron "Pigpen" McKernan, and Bob Weir. (Bill Kreutzmann, Phil Lesh, and Mickey Hart soon joined, and the band has gone through numerous lineup changes over the years.) The Dead was perhaps the most important band in the Haight-Ashbury musical scene of the late 1960s. Musically, the group drew on the eclectic influences of its many members, combining blues, jazz, country, folk, and psychedelic rock. They released their first album, *The Grateful Dead*, in 1967; a number of their albums, especially two releases from 1970, *American Beauty* and *Workingman's Dead*, have gone down as classics.

The Dead have become most known, though, for their live performances—and the phenomenon surrounding these performances. The band toured almost regularly from 1965 until the year 1995, when Jerry Garcia died. The band's performances were marked by extended jams in which members improvised individually while seeking to blend their different directions into cohesive songs. Over the years, fans of the band's live performances (often called Deadheads) grew into a dedicated following with an unrivaled fanaticism. The Dead was an especially "fan-friendly" band; they not only allowed fans to tape their shows but encouraged it, and the trading of fan-recorded concerts has become an established practice among Deadheads. The use of mind-altering drugs such as marijuana, mushrooms, and LSD has also been a long-standing tradition among many Deadhead concertgoers.

In 1966, a Mexican-born guitarist named Carlos Santana formed a San Francisco group that would become known as Santana. The band played a unique blend of jazz, fusion, rock, and Latin influences, as popularized on albums such as *Santana* (1969), *Abraxas* (1970), and *Santana III* (1971), which featured hits such as "Evil Ways," "Black Magic Woman," and "Oye Como Va." In June 1968, the band played its debut live performance at San Francisco's famous Fillmore West venue. The band's performance of "Soul Sacrifice" was a highlight of the 1969 Woodstock festival.

Another musically eclectic group that highlighted Woodstock was Sly & the Family Stone. Sly Stone (b. Sylvester Stewart in 1944) worked as a record producer in San Francisco with such bands

Historic Festivals

Monterey International Pop Festival
June 16–18, 1967
Monterey, CA
Twenty-five hours of music in two and a half days that brought over 50,000 people together. Bay Area musicians like the Grateful Dead and Jefferson Airplane performed with the first major U.S. appearance of the Who, Jimi Hendrix, and Janis Joplin, all of whom would later be major attractions at Woodstock.

Altamont
1969
Altamont Speedway, Altamont, CA
The culmination of the Rolling Stones' tour of America, Altamont was a free concert near San Francisco with Santana, the ever-present Grateful Dead, Jefferson Airplane, Crosby Stills Nash and Young, and the Flying Burrito Brothers. The concert proved to be one of the largest rock disasters ever, when a fan was murdered at the concert and crowd control was nonexistent.

California Jam
April 6, 1974
Ontario, CA
A festival concert held at the Ontario Motor Speedway. It attracted over 200,000 fans and was one of the last of the original wave of rock festivals as well as one of the most well-executed and financially successful, and it presaged the era of media consolidation and the corporatization of the rock music industry.

The U.S. Festivals
1982–1983
Glen Helen Regional Park, San Bernardino Desert
A "huge party" Steve Wozniak (cofounder of Apple Computers) threw in the remote Southern California desert in September 1982, then again the following year. The "us" in this case was the as-yet-unnamed cultural phenomenon now called "the creative class."

as the Beau Brummels and also Grace Slick's pre-Airplane band, The Great Society. By 1967, Sly was the front man of Sly & the Family Stone, a rock group that mixed soul, funk, rock, pop, and even early hip-hop. After scoring a hit with the title track to *Dance to the Music* (1968), the band broke through with the 1969 album *Stand!* The band's landmark album *There's a Riot Going On* (1971) inspired further generations of musicians and activists as Stone, an African American, expressed militant Black Power sentiments embraced by the civil rights struggle within counterculture America.

While bands with California roots contributed to the August 1969 Woodstock festival, a crowning achievement in the free love/flower power movement, California was also the setting for the ill-fated Altamont Speedway concert. That festival was headlined by such groups as the Grateful Dead, Jefferson Airplane, and—most notoriously—the Rolling Stones. Conceived as a free concert, Altamont became a disaster when crowds became too large for speedway capacity. Tragically, during the Rolling Stones' performance, a fan named Meredith Hunter was killed by members of the Hells Angels motorcycle gang, who were acting as security during the Stones' set. Debate has since raged regarding whether the Stones had hired the Hells Angels to work the concert; regardless, the incident has been cited (superficially) as the end of the Woodstock era.

Arising from Los Angeles during the days of Summer of Love and Woodstock, The Doors seemed to fly in the face of West Coast "flower power." Electric keyboardist Ray Manzarek, guitarist Robby Krieger, drummer John Densmore, and singer/lyricist Jim Morrison played a unique form of psychedelic blues, sans bass guitar. Musically the band mixed in such diverse elements as lounge jazz, Tin Pan Alley, even Kurt Weill. But on their six studio albums—*The Doors* (1967), *Strange Days* (1967), *Waiting for the Sun* (1968), *The Soft Parade* (1969), *Morrison Hotel* (1970), and the heavily-bluesy *L.A. Woman* (1971)—Morrison's poetic, psychedelic, sometimes shamanistic lyrics took center stage. His charismatic and unpredictable stage performances became a notorious element of the band's live performances, until he died in Paris in 1971.

Country Rock and the Singer-Songwriter

The Byrds combined elements of rock and folk guitar, later adding a twangy electric-guitar style of early surf rock (albeit at slower tempos) to create a pioneer sound known as country rock. The group was formed in the early 1960s by Roger McGuinn, Gene Clark, David Crosby, Chris Hillman and Michael Clarke. Between 1965 and 1967, the group scored hits with "Mr. Tambourine Man," "Turn! Turn! Turn!" and "Eight Miles High," all of which were distinguished by McGuinn's melodic voice. But the group's most influential album, *Sweetheart of the Rodeo* (1968), was a step back into pure country; the album inspired a generation of country rock and alternative country artists.

The Flying Burrito Brothers, formed in Los Angeles in 1969, were also instrumental in the beginnings of the country rock genre. The All Music Guide Web site says the Brothers' debut album *The Gilded Palace of Sin* "virtually invented the blueprint for country-rock."[19] Gram Parsons, one of the founding members of the band, went on to forge a respectable career as a singer-songwriter. Another country rock Los Angeles band, Poco, made their debut performance at the Troubadour in Los Angeles in November 1968 and then performed at the famous Fillmore West in December on the same bill with The Steve Miller Band and Sly & the Family Stone. Poco was one of the most enduring bands in West Coast country rock, reaching a breakthrough with *Crazy Eyes* in 1973 and then its commercial peak in 1978 with *Legend*. Interestingly, two former members of Poco, Randy Misener and Timothy B. Schmidt, would go on to play for another Los Angeles band, The Eagles.

If The Byrds pioneered the Southern California country rock sound, then The Eagles brought the sound into the 1970s. The band was formed in 1971 when John Boylan, who was then managing singer Linda Ronstadt, helped guitarist/keyboardist Glen Frey, guitarist/mandolinist/banjo player Bernie Leadon, and bassist Randy Meisner get together. Frey then recruited drummer Don Henley. Not one of the musicians hailed from California, but the band set up headquarters in Los Angeles and began to tour as opening act for Linda Ronstadt.

Unlike The Byrds, who successfully recorded a number of cover songs, The Eagles emphasized the singer/songwriter ethos. Their first album, *The Eagles* (1972), presented a "pure, innocent" style of country-tinged pop and rock; their second, *Desperado* (1973), focused on outlaw mythology of the Old West, highlighted by the balladic title track. The Eagles' next two albums, *On the Border* (1974) and *One of These Nights* (1975) featured more lushly produced songs, and the band's sound moved toward the 1970s guitar-driven rock and roll featured on album-oriented radio. Their 1976 album *Hotel California* would go down as a classic. Songs such as the title track "New Kid in Town" and "Life in the Fast Lane" presented images of the rich-and-famous lifestyle in 1970s California. The band's 1978 album *The Long Run* yielded their last number-one single, "Heartache Tonight."

While emerging in the late 1970s as a straightforward rock band, The Eagles generally played a "softer" type of rock that shied away from the excesses of volume and experimentation that marked much of 1970s classic rock. Jackson Browne was another leading figure in the soft rock sound that came from many West Coast singer-songwriters in the 1970s. Browne moved to Los Angeles at an early age and sang folk music in local venues before joining The Nitty Gritty Dirt Band in 1966. Browne penned songs for such artists as The Byrds, The Eagles, Linda Ronstadt, and Tom Rush. In 1971, Browne signed as a solo artist and scored a big hit with the song "Doctor My Eyes" the following year. He broke through with the successful albums *The Pretender* (1977) and *Running on Empty* (1978).

Hard Rock, Hair Metal, and Speed Metal

While California produced many country rock and soft rock stylists during the 1970s, it was also home to many hard rock bands in the 1970s and 1980s. The band Van Halen began performing on the Los Angeles club circuit during the mid-1970s. Their 1978 self-titled album (with "Running with the Devil," "Ain't Talkin' 'Bout Love," and a cover of The Kink's "You Really Got Me") was one of the more successful debut recordings in rock history. The group's most distinctive elements were Eddie Van Halen's "lickety-splity" guitar technique, which hearkened back to Dick Dale's surf stylings, and David Lee Roth's flamboyant vocals. Roth, in particular, was particularly video-friendly, as he milked the showman aspect of rock and roll, striking sexual poses that were part burlesque and part Hollywood, in tight leather pants and long, teased hair.

Los Angeles played a key role in the formation of the "hair metal" subgenre. Just a year before, another L.A. band, Mötley Crüe, had a nationwide hit with the album *Shout at the Devil*. The group played up-tempo heavy metal that reveled

California Hardcore

The L.A. hardcore punk/metal scene had thrived since the late 1970s. Black Flag, widely considered the archetypal L.A. hardcore band, combined hard-driving music with social and political commentary, in a way predicting the harder edges of the grunge scene that would emerge in the Northwest years later. The band was founded in 1977 by Greg Ginn and Chuck Dukowski, who would also form the indie label SST, which released such bands as Hüsker Dü, the Minutemen, Meat Puppets, Sonic Youth, Soundgarden, Dinosaur Jr., and the Screaming Trees. Farther up the coast, San Francisco's Dead Kennedy's developed a cult following with a similarly avant-garde mix of political dissent and hard-edged punk.

While such bands were somewhat ahead of their offerings of hard-edged hybrid punk, the Red Hot Chili Peppers perhaps set the mold. Heavily influenced by the hardcore movement but also by eclectic sources such as funk artist George Clinton and bluesman Robert Johnson, this California band emerged as a leader of the West Coast underground scene with such recordings as *The Uplift Mofo Party Plan* (1987) and *The Abbey Road EP* (1988) before achieving phenomenal success with 1991's *Blood Sugar Sex Magik*.

lyrically in sex, alcohol, and drugs. Fellow Los Angeles bands Faster Pussycat, Great White, L.A. Guns, Poison, and Ratt sold a blend of heavy metal machismo and androgynous fashion, including long-sprayed hair and even makeup.

Guns n' Roses emerged from the Los Angeles heavy metal club scene in the late 1980s and released a self-produced extended play (EP) record, *Live ?!*@ Like a Suicide*, in 1985. Although originally demonstrating hair metal tendencies, the group's *Appetite for Destruction* (1987) offered even darker views with songs on topics ranging from heroin addiction to sadomasochism. But underneath these darker trappings, Guns n' Roses songs possessed surprising pop sensibilities, as evidenced in the voice of Axl Rose and the lyrical melodies of lead guitarist Slash. Songs such as "Welcome to the Jungle," "Sweet Child o' Mine," and "Paradise City" became staples on MTV.

Rivaling Guns n' Roses for hard rock supremacy during the late 1980s and early 1990s was Metallica. The band formed in Los Angeles in 1981 and played the club scene with a high-energy form of heavy metal characterized by speed, volume, and virtuosity. Their 1983 debut, *Kill 'Em All*, is now seen as the beginning of trash metal or speed metal. With *Ride the Lightning* (1984) and *Master of Puppets* (1986), Metallica developed a cult following. They reached new heights with the 1989 release *. . . And Justice for All*. By then, the genre of speed metal was an established phenomenon also practiced by bands such as Megadeth, which was formed by Dave Mustaine, a member of Metallica during the band's early days. Ironically, the band who practically invented speed metal reinvented its trademark sound on *Metallica* (1991). With this album, the band shunned technical virtuosity for more deliberately paced songs and reached a wider audience. In 1999, the band released the album *S&M*, a live album from its performance with the San Francisco Orchestra.

From Garage Rock to Grunge—The Northwest Music Scene

Since the 1960s, the Pacific Northwest had been home to a strong independent rock music scene. In 1961, a Seattle band named The Wailers (who played behind vocalist Rockin' Robin Roberts) turned a little-known R&B tune called "Louie Louie" into a local hit. Two Portland bands, Paul Revere and the Raiders and (more famously) The Kingsmen, would later release versions of the song nationally. The Wailers played a "stomping, hard-nosed R&B/rock fusion" that inspired other regional bands, such as the Sonics from Tacoma, Washington.

While the garage bands scene thrived throughout Washington and Portland, Seattle became the leader in regional rock. In the 1970s, Seattle had a strong punk rock and hardcore scene, led by such bands as The Mentors and Solger. In 1980, a Seattle-based "fanzine" newsletter called *Subterranean Pop* began covering the underground American music scene and distributed cassette compilations of locally produced music. By 1986, *Subterranean Pop* had morphed into Sub Pop, a record company that specialized in local bands, beginning with a sampler titled *Sub Pop 100*. In the fall of 1987, Sub Pop released the debut recording of Soundgarden. Sub Pop would also release a three-EP boxed set, *Sub Pop 200* (1988), which captured the work of Seattle musical acts at the time. In 1989, Sub Pop released *Bleach*, the debut release from Nirvana, a band that had formed in Aberdeen in 1987 before moving to Seattle. Both Soundgarden and Nirvana would become synonymous with grunge rock and the Seattle sound.

The term *grunge rock* was applied to bands, many of whom arose from the Northwest independent scene in the late 1980s, whose music combined elements of punk, hard rock, and heavy metal, featuring angry vocals and a murky and often distorted guitar sound. Also sometimes called the "Seattle Sound," grunge music was distinctive and readily recognizable as an emerging musical phenomenon, although area musicians resisted the attempts of the rest of America—especially corporate America—to label them as parts of the latest rock music "scene." Still, a number of grunge rock acts shared similarities not only musically but also lyrically, as their songs presented angst-ridden stories or sentiments straight out of late-twentieth-century youth culture dealing with issues of alienation, addiction, and isolation. The first recording by a grunge band to gain national attention was Alice in Chains' *Facelift*, released in April 1991. But really it was the release of Nirvana's *Nevermind* in September that popularized the genre. With the release of the album's first single, the raucous yet catchy, "Smells Like Teen Spirit," as well as subsequent hits from the album, Nirvana gained an unprecedented level of fame for a band from the Seattle scene. The release of Soundgarden's *Badmotorfinger* and Pearl Jam's debut *Ten* further spread the grunge sound to the rest of the country. The Cameron Crowe film *Singles* (1992), set in Seattle and featuring a sound track of songs almost entirely from Seattle-area rock acts, seemed to cement the transformation of the Seattle sound from a local scene to a nationwide trend—though it also gave ammo to critics who claimed that this was just the latest example of regional culture to be co-opted by corporate America.

As Northwest grunge rock grew in

Members of rock group Nirvana (left to right) Krist Novoselic, Dave Grohl, and Kurt Cobain. Courtesy of Photofest.

notoriety, regional bands featuring entirely female lineups also came to the forefront. Bands such as Bikini Kill and Sleater-Kinney (both from Olympia), as well as Hole—whose lead singer Courtney Love married Kurt Cobain of Nirvana in 1992—and L7, a band signed by Sub Pop in 1987, found increasingly receptive audiences among both female and male listeners. The purposefully in-your-face style of these pioneer bands, which combined hard rock and hardcore music (arenas that had been largely limited to men) with female empowerment, feminist sensibilities, and overt sexuality, became known as "riot grrrl" bands. The term *riot grrrl* may have been inspired by a comment made by Bratmobile singer Alison Wolfe during the International Pop Underground in Olympia in August 1991.

Overall, though, the "second wave" of grunge music that went nationwide in the early 1990s was perhaps more melodic and less heavy than its late 1980s precursor, but its aggressive sounds and lyrics ushered in a revolution in American music that effectively put an end to the popularity of the hair metal craze of the late 1980s. Rock radio stations routinely played grunge rock, and MTV placed videos from grunge acts into its regular rotation. The grunge scene became so predominant that it seeped into other areas of American culture, especially fashion. The distinctly unglamorous style evidenced by many grunge bands—which generally consisted of flannel shirts (an element stemming more from practical concerns of the American Northwest climate than from self-conscious trends), ripped jeans, and long, unkempt hair—became popular throughout the nation in the early 1990s. These elements became associated with American "slacker" culture and Generation X. The band Nirvana, and especially Kurt Cobain, symbolized (in mainstream media, at least) an apathetic, disillusioned, late-twentieth-century lost generation.

This symbolism became all too obvious when Cobain committed suicide in April 1994, which in retrospect has been seen as a harbinger of the fall of grunge music. The original grunge bands began to evolve and experiment with new styles as mid- to late 1990s rock bands in general leaned more toward a "power-pop" direction. As the decade progressed, bands such as Seattle's Candlebox offered a sound that was hard-driving though less harsh and more melodic. When the remaining members of Nirvana disbanded, drummer Dave Grohl became front man of the newly formed Foo Fighters, which combined hard rock and commercial pop and went on to become a staple of MTV, album-oriented radio, and "hit" radio stations alike.

West Coast Hip-Hop

Just as West Coast jazz reacted to and, in the eyes of some, improved upon its East Coast progenitor, the West Coast hip-hop sound came after East Coast rap had become a staple of some East Coast clubs. Beginning with breakdancing in the 1970s, the Afro-influenced hip-hop and house music had been thriving in urban areas such as Chicago, Philadelphia, New York, and Detroit, but as late as the 1980s, Los Angeles had produced only a few hip-hop or rap artists—Ice-T and Captain Rapp, whose "Gigolo Rapp" is considered the first West Coast hip-hop recording. Meanwhile, with successful releases by hardcore rappers such as Run DMC, Kurtis Blow, LL Cool J, and Public Enemy, East Coast rap had developed a sound all its own.

Despite the East Coast's dominance, it was a West Coast group, N.W.A., that made the first album to successfully break into the mainstream. "Straight Outta

Compton" (1988), which names a relentlessly poverty-stricken African American neighborhood in Los Angeles, featured subject matter including drugs, violence, and sex. Its grim sound and message helped popularize what became known as gangsta rap (said to have begun with Ice-T's "6N' Da Morning") and earned N.W.A. a strongly worded letter of discontent from the Federal Bureau of Investigation. Notoriety aside, however, N.W.A.'s most lasting impact was in placing the West Coast on the hip-hop map.

After N.W.A. broke up, one of its members, Dr. Dre, released *The Chronic* (1992), which took West Coast rap in a new direction by melding funky beats with slowly drawled lyrics. This sound was popularized by a whole roster of West Coast artists signed to Death Row Records, most notably Snoop Doggy Dogg (Doggystyle). The sound, which was aimed at pop markets, dominated mainstream hip-hop for several years, and during that time, the West Coast eclipsed the East Coast in popularity and sales. The long-standing rivalry between the coasts was given ample fuel by rap and hip-hop's tendency to "MC battles" and sometimes criminal attitudes. While many felt the rivalry was more in the minds of media than the artists themselves, one real battle existed between the West Coast's Tupac Shakur and the East Coast's Notorious B.I.G. In 1996, Shakur was murdered in a crime that remains unsolved to this day. A few months later, Notorious B.I.G. was murdered as well. Copious theories exist, including a wealth of conspiracy theories, but general opinion holds that both murders were somehow related to the East Coast–West Coast rivalry.

As rap's direction began to change once again, dominance shifted back to the East Coast. However, alternative rap and hip-hop sounds have lately begun to flourish across the country, and alternative Los Angeles artists Black Eyed Peas found their way onto the scene with *Behind the Front* (1998), a critically acclaimed album by a group once rejected for its unusually peaceful lyrics. *Bridging the Gap* (2000) and *Elephunk* (2003) promise to keep West Coast rap alive.

RESOURCE GUIDE

Printed Sources

Azerrad, Michael. *Come as You Are: The Story of Nirvana*. St. Hillsboro, OR: Main Street Books, 1993.

Beresford, William. "Letter XXXVIII." In *A Voyage Round the World; but more Particularly to the North-West Coast of America: Performed in 1785, 1786, 1787, and 1788, in The King George and Queen Charlotte, Captains Portlock and Dixon*, with introduction and two appendices by Captain George Dixon. London: Geo. Goulding, 1789.

Bush, James. *Encyclopedia of Northwest Music*. Seattle, WA: Sasquatch Books, 1999.

Caitlin, Amy. "Music of the Hmong: Singing Voices to Talking Reeds." *The Hmong in the West: Observations and Reports*, ed. Bruce T. Downing and Douglas P. Olney. Minneapolis: Center for Urban and Regional Affairs, University of Minnesota, 1982.

Castro, Rafaela G. *Dictionary of Chicano Folklore*. Santa Barbara, CA: ABC-CLIO, 2000.

Curtis, Edward S. *The North American Indian, Being a Series of Volumes Picturing and Describing the Indians of the United Sates and Alaska*. Ed. Frederick Webb Hodge. 20 vols. 1907–1930. New York: Johnson Reprint Corporation, 1970.

de Laguna, Frederica. *Under Mount Saint Elias: The History and Culture of the Yakutat Tlingit*. 3 vols. Washington, DC: Smithsonian Institution Press, 1972.

Densmore, Frances. "Maidu Musical Instruments." *American Anthropologist* 40 (1939): 113–118.

———. *Nootka and Quileute Music.* Smithsonian Institution. Bureau of American Ethnology, Bulletin 124. 1939. New York: DaCapo Press, 1971.

Eels, Myron. "Indian Music." *American Antiquarian* 1 (1879): 249–253. (24 transcriptions of Clallam, Twana, and two unspecified songs)

Gaines, Steve. *Heroes & Villains: The True Story of the Beach Boys.* New York: New American Library, 1986.

Gioia, Ted. *West Coast Jazz.* New York: Oxford University Press, 1992.

Gleason, Ralph J. *The Jefferson Airplane and the San Francisco Sound.* New York: Ballantine, 1969.

Gordon, Robert. *Jazz West Coast: The Los Angeles Jazz Scene of the 1950s.* New York: Quartet Books, 1986.

Griswold del Castillo, Richard. *North to Aztlán: A History of Mexican Americans in the United States.* New York: Twayne Publishers, 1996.

Gunter, Erna. *Indian Life on the Northwest Coast of North America, as Seen by the Early Explorers and Fur Traders during the Last Decades of the Eighteenth Century.* Chicago: University of Chicago Press, 1972.

Halpern, Ida. "On the Interpretation of "Meaningless Nonsensical Syllables" in the Music of the Pacific Northwest Indians." *Ethnomusicology* 20.2 (1976): 253–271.

Harrison, Lou. "Asian Music and the United States." Paper presented at the Conference of the Asian Composers League, Manila, Philippines, 1975.

Haslam, Gerald. *Workin' Man Blues: Country Music in California.* Berkeley: University of California Press, 1999.

Hitchcock, H. Wiley, and Stanley Sadie, eds. "Asian American Music." In *The New Grove Dictionary of American Music.* London: Macmillan, 1986. 1:79–85.

Hoskyns, Barney. *Waiting for the Sun.* New York: Griffin Trade Paperback, 1999.

Keeling, Richard. *Cry for Luck: Sacred Song and Speech among the Yurok, Hupa, and Karok Indians of Northwestern California.* Berkeley: University of California Press, 1992.

Kimberlin, Cynthia Tse, and Akin Euba, eds. "Introduction." In *Intercultural Music.* Point Richmond, CA: Music Research Institute, 1995. 1:2–5.

Koranda, Lorraine D. "Music of the Alaskan Eskimo." In *Musics of Many Cultures: An Introduction,* ed. Elizabeth May. Berkeley: University of California Press, 1981. 332–362.

Kroeber, Alfred. *Indian Myths of South Central California.* Berkeley: University of California Press, 1907.

Lowie, R. H. "The Emergence Hole and the Foot Drum." *American Anthropologist* 40 (1938): 174.

Loza, Steve. *Barrio Rhythm: Mexican American Music in Los Angeles.* Urbana: University of Illinois Press, 1993.

———, ed. *Musical Aesthetics and Multiculturalism in Los Angeles.* Selected Reports in Ethnomusicology. Vol. 10. Los Angeles: University of California, 1994.

Martínez, Oscar J. *Mexican-Origin People in the United States: A Topical History.* Tucson: University of Arizona Press, 2001.

Miller, Leta E., and Fred Lieberman. *Lou Harrison: Composing a World.* New York: Oxford University Press, 1998.

McNally, Dennis. *A Long Strange Trip: The Inside History of the Grateful Dead.* New York: American Library, 2002.

Moziño, José Mariano. 1791. *Noticias de Nutka.* Trans. I. H. Wilson. Seattle: University of Washington Press, 1970.

Nelson, Melissa, and Philip Klasky. "The Power of Song in the Protection of Native Lands." *Orion Magazine.* (August 2001). http://www.oriononline.org/pages/oa/01-4oa/01-4oa_Storyscape.html (accessed June 20, 2004).

Parnas, Sam. *A History of Filipino Rondalla Music and Musicians in Southern California*. Los Angeles: University of California, 1999.

Payne, Richard. "Indian Flutes of the Southwest." *Journal of the American Musical Instrument Society* 15 (1989): 5–31.

Peña, Manuel. *The Texas-Mexican Conjunto: History of a Working-Class Music*. Austin: University of Texas Press, 1985.

Riddle, Ronald. *Flying Dragons, Flowing Streams*. Westport, CT: Greenwood Press, 1983.

Sadie, Stanley, and John Tyrrell, eds. *The New Grove Dictionary of Music and Musicians*. 2nd ed. Oxford: Oxford University Press, 2001.

Samson, Valerie. "Chinese Music in the San Francisco Bay Area." *Association for Chinese Music Research* 12 (1999): 47–101.

Selvin, Joel. *Summer of Love: The Inside Story of LSD, Rock & Roll, Free Love and High Times in the Wild West*. New York: Cooper Square Press, 1999.

Simonett, Helena. *Banda: Mexican Musical Life across Borders*. Middletown, CT: Wesleyan University Press, 2001.

Smith, Barbara. "Chinese Music in Hawaii." *Asian Music* 6.1–2 (1975): 225–230.

Smith, Dick. *Condor Journal*. Santa Barbara, CA: Capra Press and Museum of Natural History, 1978.

Timentwa, Jeanette, and Rebecca Chamberlain. "Native Songs and Seasonal Feed-Gathering Traditions." (Jeanette Timentwa Interview and Transcription by Rebecca Chamberlain). In *Spirit of the First People: Native American Music Traditions of Washington State*, ed. Willie Smyth and Esmé Ryan. Seattle: University of Washington Press, 1999. 50–61.

Titon, Jeff, and Bob Carlin, eds. *American Musical Traditions*. Vol. 5. New York: Schirmer, 2002.

Tuttle, Pauline. "The Hoop of Many Hoops: The Integration of Lakota Ancestral Knowledge and Bahá'í Teachings in the Performative Practices of Kevin Locke." Ph.D. dissertation, University of Washington, Seattle, 2001.

Wald, Elijah. *Narcocorrido: A Journey into the Music of Drugs, Guns, and Guerillas*. New York: HarperCollins Publishers, 2001.

Washington State Arts Commission (WASAC), with Cathy Ragland and Erasmo Gamboa. *Gritos del alma: Chicano/Mexicano Music Traditions of the Yakima Valley*. Olympia: WASAC, 1993.

White, William/Xelimuxw, and Philip Cook. "Thunderbirds, Thunder-beings, Thunder-voices: The Application of Traditional Knowledge and Children's Rights in Support of Aboriginal Childrens' Education." *American Review of Canadian Studies* (Spring–Summer 2001): 331–347.

Bibliographies and Discographies

Gray, Judith A. "California Indian Catalog." In *The Federal Cylinder Project*. Vol. 5: *California Indian Catalog, Middle and South American Catalog, Southwestern* Catalog. Washington, DC: American Folklife Center, Library of Congress, 1990. 1–328.

———. "Creating and Disseminating Ethnographic Recordings: Washington State Materials in Washington, D.C." In *Spirit of the First People: Native American Music Traditions of Washington State*, ed. Willie Smyth and Esmé Ryan. Seattle: University of Washington Press, 1999. 169–180.

———, ed. "Northwest Coast/Arctic Indian Catalog." In *The Federal Cylinder Project*. Vol. 3: *Great Basin/Plateau Indian Catalog, and Northwest Coast/Arctic Catalog*. Washington, DC: American Folklife Center, Library of Congress, 1988. 79–288.

Keeling, Richard. *A Guide to Early Field Recordings (1900–1949) at the Lowie Museum of Anthropology*. Berkeley: University of California Press, 1991.

———. 2001. "Voices from Siberia: Ethnomusicology of the Jesup Expedition." In *Gateways: Exploring the Legacy of the Jesup North Pacific Expedition, 1897–1902*. Washington, DC: Arctic Studies Center, National Museum of Natural History, Smithsonian Institution, 2001. 279–296.

Seeger, Anthony, and Louise S. Spear. *Early Recordings: A Catalogue of Cylinder Collections at the Indiana Archives of Traditional Music*. Bloomington: Indiana University Press, 1987.

Sercombe, Laurel. "Ten Early Ethnographers in the Northwest: Recordings from Washington State." In *Spirit of the First People: Native American Music Traditions of Washington State*, ed. Willie Smyth and Esmé Ryan. Seattle: University of Washington Press, 1999. 148–168.

Web Sites, Organizations, Museums

Alaska

Alaska Flute Circle
Contact Person: Deborah Peterson
9641 Arlene Street
Anchorage, AK 99502

No Web site

Juneau Arts & Humanities Council
206 North Franklin Street
Juneau, AK 99801
http://www.juneauartscouncil.org/

California

Ali Akbar College of Music
215 West End Avenue
San Rafael, CA 94901
http://www.aacm.org/aacm/

Teaches classical music of north India.

Cantonese Opera Association Silicon Valley
3003 Bunker Hill, Suite 206
Santa Clara, CA 95054

Center for World Music
Dr. Robert E. Brown, President
4417 Shade Road
La Mesa, CA 91941
http://centerforworldmusic.org/

Centro Cultural de la Raza
2125 Park Boulevard
San Diego, CA 92101
http://www.centroraza.com/

Nonprofit organization that organizes exhibits, classes, and cultural events and sponsors the Ballet Folklórico en Aztlán.

Latino Arts Network
Marie Acosta, Director

867 Treat Avenue
San Francisco, CA 94110
http://www.latinoarts.net/

Sponsors events such as touring exhibits and musical performances.

Northern California Flute Circle
Contact Person: Mike Oitzman
135 Brenton Court, #B
Mountain View, CA 94043
http://www.naflute.com

Southern California Flute Circle
Contact Person: Guillermo Martinez
28691 Modjeska Canyon Road
Modjeska, CA 92626

No Web site

Hawai'i

Hawaiian Music Hall of Fame and Museum
P. O. Box 1619
Kailua, HI 96734
http://www.hawaiimusicmuseum.org/main/cover.html

Hawai'i State Foundation on Culture and the Arts
250 South Hotel Street, 2nd Floor
Honolulu, HI 96813
http://www.state.hi.us/sfca/

Oregon

Bellas Artes
425 SE 6th Avenue
Portland, OR 97214
http://www.milagro.org/BellasArtes-Pages/bellasartes.html

A division of the Miracle Theatre Group whose performances reflect the rich diversity of the Hispanic/Latino experience. Its productions include theatrical performances, dance, music, and literary readings.

Cascadia Flute Circle
Contact Person: Ellen Saunders
P. O. Box 5035
Manning, OR 97125
http://www.cascadiaflutecircle.org

Oregon Historical Society
Oregon Folklife Program
1200 SW Park Avenue
Portland, OR 97205
http://ohs.org/education/folklife/index.cfm

Conducts research on the arts of immigrant communities in Oregon and maintains a database of traditional artists, including musicians.

Washington

Experience Music Project (located on the Seattle Center Campus)
325 5th Avenue North
Seattle, WA 98109
http://www.emplive.com/index.asp

Explores and celebrates musical diversity. Galleries include exhibits on Jimi Hendrix, The Beatles, Nirvana, and more.

Folk Arts Program
Washington State Arts Commission
234 8th Avenue SE
P. O. Box 42675
Olympia, WA 98504-2675
http://www.arts.wa.gov/

Washington Flute Circle
Contact Person: Melinda Codling
Issaquah, WA 98027

No Web site

Videos/Films

American Cowboys. Wildbill Productions, 1998.
The Decline of Western Civilization. Dir. Penelope Spheeris. 100 min. Spheeris Films, 1981.
Hmong Musicians in America, 1978–1996. Prod. Amy Catlin. Apsara Media for Intercultural Education, 1997.
In the Light of Reverence. Prod. Christopher McLeod. Sacred Land Film Project of Earth Island Institute, 2001.
Monterey Pop. Dir. James Desmond, Richard Leacock, Al Maysles, D.A. Pennebaker, Nicholas Proferes, and Barry Feinstein. 98 min. Pennebaker Hegedus Films, 1968.
Na Paniolo o Hawaii. Dir. Edgy Lee. Filmworks, Ltd., 2001.
Pasajero: A Journey of Time and Memory. Prod. Los Cenzontles. Forthcoming.
Sacred Land Preservation.
Songs on the Wind: The Arlecho Creek Story. Prod. and dir. Richard Newman, 2002.

Recordings

Beach Boys. "Good Vibrations." *Smiley Smile.* Capitol Records, 1967.
Beach Boys. *Pet Sounds.* Capitol Records, 1966.
Corridos y Tragedias de la Frontera. Arhoolie, n.d.
The Doors. *The Doors.* Elektra, 1967.
Gritos de Alma [tape]. Washington State Arts Commission and Jack Straw Productions, 1993.
Los Angelinos. *The Eastside Renaissance.* Zyanya; distributed by Rhino, 1983.
Los Cenzontles. *Cancionero* (romantic ballads). Mockingbird Records, 2000.
Los Cenzontles. *Media Vida* (*son jarocho, pirecua, ranchera*). Mockingbird Records, 2002.
Love. *Forever Changes.* Elektra, 1967.
Nirvana. *Nevermind.* Geffen Records, 1991.
Norte y sur: Un solo pueblo. Northwest Folklife, 1998.
Songs of the Hawaiian Cowboy—Na Mele o Paniolo. Warner Brothers, 1997.
Tosti, Don, Lalo Guerrero, and others. *Pachuco Boogie.* Arhoolie, 2002.

Festivals/Events
Alaska

Fairbanks Summer Folk Fest
Pioneer Park
Fairbanks, AK 99707
http://www.mosquitonet.com/~gcn/faifolkfest/

Held in June

Sitka Summer Music Festival
Harrigan Centennial Hall
Sitka, AK 99835
http://www.sitkamusicfestival.org/

Held in June
Held since 1972, the festival features chamber music.

California

Coachella Valley Music and Arts Festival
Empire Polo Field
81-800 Avenue 51
Indio, CA 92201
http://www.coachella.com./main.html

Held annually in early May
Massive two-day alternative music festival.

Noise Pop Brand Music Festival
Various locations
San Francisco, CA
http://www.noisepop.com/festival/

Held in February
A microfestival that began in 1993; features the best national and local bands in the modern musical world.

Strawberry Music Festival
Camp Mather
Yosemite, CA
http://www.strawberrymusic.com

Held two times each year, over the Memorial and Labor Day weekends
Labor Day and Memorial Day weekend folk festival that features a wide range of musical acts representing many different musical genres including Americana, bluegrass, swing, rock, blues, and gospel.

UCLA Powwow
UCLA Campus
Los Angeles, CA 90095
http://www.studentgroups.ucla.edu/americanindian/powwowpage.htm

Held in May

¡Viva el Mariachi! Festival
Fresno Convention Center

Fresno, CA 93721
http://www.radiobilingue.org/
Held annually in February or March, sponsored by Radio Bilingüe

Yomen: Maidu Spring Ceremony
The Maidu Interpretive Center & Historic Site
1960 Johnson Ranch Drive
Roseville, CA 95661
http://www.roseville.ca.us/index.asp?page=379
Held in April

Hawai'i

Big Island Hawaiian Music Festival
Afook-Chinen Civic Auditorium
Hilo, HI 96720
http://www.ehcc.org/slack_key.htm
Held in July
Sponsored by the East Hawai'i Cultural Center. Features ukelele, steel guitar, and slack key guitar.

Hawai'i Music Awards
Music Foundation of Hawai'i
1019 University Avenue, Suite 4
Honolulu, HI 96826
http://www.hawaiimusicawards.com/
Held annually in April
Includes awards for local artists in both Latin and Paniolo categories.

Oregon

Cinco de Mayo Festival
Portland Waterfront Park
Portland, OR 97204
http://www.cincodemayo.org/
Held annually for several days around May 5
Hosted by the Portland Guadalajara Sister Cities Association

Fiesta Mexicana
Woodburn, OR
http://www.ohs.org/exhibitions/celebrate_fiesta.htm
Held first weekend of August
The festival includes a parade and mariachi mass.

Oregon Jamboree
P. O. Box 430
Sweet Home, OR 97386
http://www.oregonjamboree.com/
Held annually in late July
Features country music in the foothills of the Cascade Mountains.

Washington

Bumbershoot Seattle Arts Festival
Seattle Center
305 Harrison Street
Seattle, WA 98109
http://www.bumbershoot.org/

Held on Labor Day weekend
One of America's largest urban arts and music festivals.

Mariachi Northwest
Part of Washington State Apple Blossom Festival
P. O. Box 2836
Wenatchee, WA 98807
http://www.appleblossom.org/

Last weekend in April and first weekend of May

Northwest Folklife Festival
Seattle Center
305 Harrison Street
Seattle, WA 98109
http://www.nwfolklife.org/

Held annually over Memorial Day weekend
Features ethnic and folk music.

Sites of Important Pacific Region Collections of Music of the First Peoples

Archive of Folk Culture
American Folklife Center
Library of Congress
Thomas Jefferson Bldg., Room LJG49
101 Independence Avenue SE
Washington, DC 20540-4610
http://www.loc.gov/folklife/archive.html

Archives of Traditional Music
University of Indiana
Morrison Hall 117 and 120
Bloomington, IN 47405-2501
http://www.indiana.edu/~libarchm/

Burke Museum
University of Washington Archives
17th Avenue NE and NE 45th Street
Seattle, WA 98195
http://www.washington.edu/burkemuseum/

UCLA Ethnomusicology Archive
1630 Schoenberg Music Building
Box 951657
Los Angeles, CA 90095-1657
http://www.ethnomusic.ucla.edu/Archive/

University of Washington Ethnomusicology Archives
Music Building
University of Washington
Seattle, WA 98195
http://depts.washington.edu/ethmusic/archives.html

RELIGION

Jeremy Bonner, Vivian Deno, and Aaron DiFranco

The Pacific Rim states have a religious culture that is peculiarly individualistic. Originally settled by Spanish Catholics who left a firm imprint on much of California, the region was subject to a sizable influx of immigrants from Asia during the nineteenth and early twentieth centuries, which helped diffuse knowledge of Buddhism, Shintoism, and Hinduism to a nation that had hitherto viewed such practices as merely primitive superstition. The 1906 Azusa Street revival in Los Angeles also served to make the West Coast a region peculiarly hospitable to Pentecostal sects, most notably the Assemblies of God. These two religious traditions have helped shape the Far West's religious identity, yet the region is also internally divided. Southern California—the most culturally conservative section—is heavily Catholic, like much of the neighboring Southwest, but also includes enclaves of Southern Baptists whose increasing strength has added to the political conservatism of the Los Angeles suburbs. Northern California, Oregon, Washington, and Alaska are much more secular in outlook, with many people avoiding ties to any religious body. Hawai'i is in a peculiar position, so far from the mainland United States. With its large Asian population, its ties to China and Japan inevitably shape its religious outlook, though it has also been a springboard for Mormon missionaries headed for Asia. Taken as a whole, the Far West is probably the least religious section of the United States, especially in the Pacific Northwest, whose affluent white-collar population generally favors a completely secular society. Nevertheless, religious phenomena can be found throughout the region, ranging from communal experiments to New Age and homosexual "denominations." The Theosophical Society and the Church of Scientology are also headquartered in California, adding to the area's religious diversity.

THE PACIFIC RIM BEFORE 1850

Early Native American Faiths

Considerable diversity characterized the religious practices of the pre-Columbian inhabitants of the Pacific Rim—the Hokan, Penutian, and Shoshone tribes of California and the range of Indian communities stretching north from the Puget Sound. In arid Southern California, much spiritual authority was vested in the keeper of the ceremonial enclave where tribal rituals were performed. Such rituals included the *tolache* ceremony, which served to initiate boys into manhood. The ceremony commenced with the consumption of a jimsonweed infusion intended to aid visualization of a personal, totemic guardian animal. Over the course of the next month the boys received instruction in ceremonial dancing and concluded this period of preparation by jumping over a pattern of stones superimposed over the representation of a human figure in a pit. The Southern California tribes also observed girls' puberty rites in which adolescent girls spent three days and nights in a stone-lined pit covered with grass and sand and refrained from consuming meat or salt for the next month. Most elaborate of all was the annual six-day rite of mourning for those who had died the previous year. After four days of singing and dancing, an eagle was killed and its feathers used to decorate images commemorating the deceased. On the final day of the rite, a boy of the tribe performed a dance wearing a shirt decorated with eagle feathers.

Tribes of central California—such as the Pomo—had rites similar to those of their southern neighbors but also laid special importance on what was known as the *Kuksu* cult, whose practitioners performed a series of god-impersonating dances that varied with the seasons. In Northern California and along the Northwest Coast, World Renewal cults—intended to re-form the earth through ritual recitations and activities—were more common. Among the California Hupa these took the form of Jumping Dances and Deerskin Dances, composed of a set of ritual maneuvers intended to wipe out any evil caused by members of the tribe in the course of the past year. Such dances were often performed in the course of first fruits ceremonies (such as observance of the first salmon or early acorns) but were intended to foster human health and improvement of the conditions of the earth. In the Pacific Northwest, World Renewal cults were very elaborate and often accompanied by a belief in the immortality of certain economically important species like salmon, deer, and elk. Tribes like the Salish also practiced Spirit Singing, in which individuals demonstrated the powers of their guardian spirit through song and dance, often while wearing elaborate costumes and masks.

Alaskan and Hawaiian

In Alaska's far north regions, survival depended on learning the behaviors of those flora and fauna able to live in that stark environment. The continual struggle against the elements did not provide much time for a formal, organized religion; rather, Native Alaskans developed a life philosophy integrating knowledge from the spirit world around them. In many Yupik and Inupiat villages, animals, plants and even landforms were believed to each possess its own spirit with whom people could communicate and learn how to exist. Specific knowledge was often gained with the assistance of a shaman-figure, who helped humans and animals speak with one another. An extremely delicate balance of life was maintained only by observing the lifeways of the ecological community. Proper respect was always demonstrated toward animals in ritual practices and in the smallest habits of daily life so that their spirits would be reincarnated and continue to provide for the community.

A polytheistic religious system marks Native Hawaiian practices. Along with eight primary gods and goddesses (akua), Hawaiians also have individual, family, and regional deities to whom they make offerings. As with many other native religions of the region, shamanistic impulses directed attention to local deities and spirits (aumakua). However, religious practice was also highly structured in Hawaiian society. Priests and other attendants (sorcerers, necromancers, medicine men) belonged to the second-highest social class. Priests lived in the *heiau* (temples) and were responsible for performing ceremonial chants, directing sacrifices, and maintaining certain oral traditions. Hawaiian religious practices went underground

Hupa Indian, half-length, standing, facing left, in ceremonial deerskin costume. Courtesy of the Library of Congress.

after the arrival of Christian missionaries in 1820, but they reemerged in the latter twentieth century variously influenced by Asian and European customs.

The Arrival of Christianity

The arrival of Christianity in the Far West came with Spanish settlement of present-day California in the late eighteenth century. Although the Spanish had laid claim to Alta California—the Spanish colonial holdings roughly comprising the present U.S. state—in 1542, it was not until 1769 that the Franciscan Order was charged with establishing a chain of missions from San Diego to San Francisco Bay to secure the loyalty of the region's Indian residents and counter French and British claims to the region. Under Father Junipero Serra, Mission San Carlos Borromeo was established in Monterey Bay in 1771, the first of twenty-one such missions. The Franciscan missions succeeded in completely reorganizing the social order of California, baptizing nearly 54,000 Indians and exercising complete control over the local economy. Despite teaching the Indians many new skills, the friars did not achieve their objectives without a cost. Indian labor was not voluntary, the "neophytes" were barred from leaving the mission, and many died as a result of poor sanitation and the harsh social discipline. Further north, Spanish hegemony was challenged by the arrival of English and American traders in the Puget Sound region. At the same time, the Russians, who had begun to colonize Alaska in 1799 and erected the Church of St. Michael the Archangel at Sitka in 1808, established Fort Ross (near San Francisco) in 1812—the first Eastern Orthodox community in North America.

With Mexican independence in 1821, the new government launched a concerted drive against church control, though with less success in California than in Texas or New Mexico. Many local officials feared that dissolution of the mission system would prove to be an economic disaster for the region, and only in 1833 was sec-

Illustration from a 1913 publication showing Junipero Serra holding a crucifix in one hand and a stone in the other preaching to a crowd of Natives. Courtesy of the Library of Congress.

ularization finally achieved. Even then, it was still necessary to be a practicing Catholic in order to own land or hold citizenship. While transferring much land to the Californio elite, secularization also destroyed the institutional Catholic Church in California, since few Mexican priests wished to serve the impoverished northern parishes. In 1846, there were only five priests in the whole of California.[1] In the Pacific Northwest, meanwhile, a slow but steady stream of American immigrants and missionaries—including the famous missionary couple Marcus (1802–1847) and Narcissa Whitman (1808–1847)—headed for Oregon's Willamette Valley during the late 1830s and early 1840s. Their presence, loudly proclaimed by the various national Protestant missionary societies, helped increase popular sympathy for annexation of the Oregon Territory in 1846 and led to the establishment by the Catholic Church of a metropolitan see at Oregon City in the same year—the first American Catholic diocese on the West Coast. The outbreak of war between the United States and Mexico in May 1846 resulted in a relatively swift invasion and occupation of California. Given the virtual absence of a Mexican Catholic hierarchy, an American bishop for California became a necessity, and in June 1850, the Dominican Joseph Alemany was consecrated bishop of the new American diocese of Monterey. While California Catholics would continue to wrestle with the issue of Mexican Catholics in their midst, future leadership of the Church in the Far West would be under American, not Mexican, auspices.

POST–GOLD RUSH RELIGIOUS SPHERES

The prospect of rich, arable lands in the Far West and the discovery of gold near Sacramento in 1848 brought a steady stream of immigrants to the Far West between 1840 and 1860 and in the years following the Civil War. These included a short-lived Mormon colony at San Bernadino, California, from 1851 to 1857, which Brigham Young (1801–1877) hoped would give his state of Deseret access to the Pacific Ocean. Unlike the situation on the trans-Appalachian frontier a generation before, however, many migrants had only weak ties to organized religion. This was particularly true among Protestants, many of whom were well supplied by their denominations with church buildings and ministers but failed to maintain a connection with the church of their birth. Although many colleges in California were begun as Protestant institutions, most had abandoned their denominational affiliation by 1900. Protestant pastors continued to enjoy a high profile in the Pacific states, but not generally because of the size of their congregation. During the late nineteenth century, however, they increasingly became involved in morality crusades, as evidenced in the career of Presbyterian Mark Matthews who fought bootleggers and political corruption in Seattle. The Far West tended to nurture, in an extreme form, the individualism and spirit of theological inquiry that has so often characterized American Protestantism. It is perhaps no accident that when Katherine Tingley sought to move the American Section of the Theosophical Society[2] out of New York in 1900, she selected Point Loma, California, as her destination, which soon became the home of Theosophical University and a popular place of retreat for educators, musicians, and artists.

Although few Catholic migrants abandoned their faith during the nineteenth century, the Church in the Far West continued to experience the disadvantages of frontier life. It was only with the support of the Catholic Extension Society and the generous financial backing of lay Catholics that many rural communities in Oregon and Washington were able to erect churches of their own, and until the 1880s, the principal function of a parish was to raise money (St. Brigitta's Church in Portland held twenty-three dances in one year for this purpose). With the passage of time, some other parish organizations did emerge, including the Altar and Holy Name societies, for women and men, respectively, and later the Young Men's and Young Ladies' Institutes concerned with the spiritual and intellectual development of young Catholics, the latter ministries unknown outside the Far West. The Church faced fewer problems from recalcitrant ethnic parishes than it did in the East, largely because there were fewer Catholic migrants from eastern and southern Europe, but the issue of reaching the Mexican minority continued to haunt the bishops. Moreover, the Church also undertook an extensive program of educational development, both at the school and college levels, which ultimately produced the universities of San Diego, Santa Clara, San Francisco, Portland, Seattle, and Gonzaga.

RELIGIOUS INDIVIDUALISM AND THE PENTECOSTAL EXPERIENCE

There was perhaps no more suitable place for the Azusa Street Revival than Los Angeles, with its vast array of religious groups. The impact of the 1906 revival swept across the Pacific West, and Florence Crawford carried the movement to Portland, where she set up the Apostolic Faith Mission of Portland, Oregon. While Pentecostals were generally less concerned with denominational distinctions than other religious groups, western Pentecostals showed a peculiar reluctance to become part of a large organization. Seattle's first Pentecostal congregation—Bethel Temple—chose not to affiliate with the emerging Assemblies of God in 1914, while Aimee Semple McPherson's International Church of the Foursquare Gospel prided itself on its Angelus Temple and KFSG Radio. A similarly independent approach characterized Charles Lochbaum's Apostolic Faith (Hawai'i), which won 4,000 converts between 1923 and 1927. Some effort was also made to accommodate the non-English-speaking portion of the Pentecostal movement, through such bodies as the Filipino Assemblies of the First Born, constituted in Delano, California, in 1933, on the Assemblies of God model but with preaching and teaching in the members' native tongue.

The Role of the Roman Catholic Church in the Pacific

While Pentecostalism was making inroads in the spiritual life of the West Coast, Catholicism was consolidating itself as the dominant religious tradition of the region. More and more communities began to place their faith in parish missions, which imitated the revivalist techniques of American evangelicalism to help recover lukewarm and fallen-away Catholics. Homilies on death and salvation delivered by members of the religious orders were accompanied by frequent opportunities to make a sacramental Confession and receive the Eucharist. The early 1920s also witnessed an increased readiness on the part of lay Catholics to receive the Eucharist (at St. Ignatius Church, Portland, Oregon, the number of Communions rose from 330 in 1919 to 14,400 in 1923) and to engage in nonliturgical devotions, such as novenas, which emphasized personal spirituality over corporate worship.

Despite this privatization of religious practice, Catholics remained the subject of considerable suspicion among Protestants and the irreligious. The rise of the Ku Klux Klan in the West during the 1920s owed much to anti-Catholic sentiment, embodied in the Oregon legislature's 1923 decision to require all children to attend public school, but in 1925 the U.S. Supreme Court ruled in *Pierce v. Society of Sisters* that the Oregon statute was unconstitutional. In the wake of the Great Depression (1929–1941), the Catholic Church enjoyed a new opportunity to demonstrate its social concern through the relief work of the St. Vincent de Paul society and other Catholic charities. Bishops like Robert Armstrong of Sacramento and John Cantwell of Los Angeles also worked to integrate their Mexican coreligionists into the life of the Church (a concern enshrined in the 1936 decision to raise Los Angeles to the status of an archdiocese, making California the only state with two archbishops).

The early twentieth century was also a time when religious organizations for Chinese and Japanese immigrants acquired a markedly higher profile, beginning with Hawaii's Jodo Buddhist mission, launched by Okabe Gekumo in 1896 (the mission boasted fifteen temples and 1,800 members by 1997). Buddhism arrived in the Pacific Region during the mid-nineteenth century as maritime traders, laborers, immigrants and other "sojourners" from Japan and China brought local religious practices to Hawai'i and California. Developing practice in these pioneering emigrant communities—which also nurtured Daoist, Shinto, Confucianist, and other Asian spiritual beliefs—remained in the hands of individual practitioners until they developed enough specific gravity to draw teachers to them at the turn of the twentieth century. The Kuan Yin Temple in Honolulu—the oldest Chinese temple in America—was erected during the early twentieth century. Also active in Hawai'i was the Soto mission, which began in 1915—the oldest Zen Buddhist group in the United

Amida Buddha Statue at the Jodo Mission. © Robert Holmes/Corbis.

Goodwin J. Knight smiling and in suit and tie, 1954. © Bettmann/Corbis.

States—which ministered largely to Japanese Americans and was among the most resistant to assimilation. By contrast, the Honpa Hongwanji mission headquartered in San Francisco—which taught Pureland Shin Buddhism—was a significant factor in Japanese American assimilation, ultimately becoming the Buddhist Churches in America. Two Rinzai Zen Centers—in Los Angeles and San Francisco—were founded in the 1920s by the missionary Nyogen Senzaki (1876–1958).

Buddhism may be the dominant Asian tradition in the Pacific, yet several other significant religions also established themselves on the coast during the early twentieth century. Sikhs from the Punjab province of northern India settled in California's Central Valley, and the first *gurdwara*, or Sikh temple, in America was completed in 1912 in Stockton, California. Hindu adherents entering the United States through San Francisco built there the first Hindu temple in the Western world in 1905. Japanese missionaries for the Tenrikyo tradition of Shinto were active in Portland, Seattle, and Los Angeles during the 1920s. Immigrants from India and other South and Southeast Asian countries also carried Islam to the Pacific during this era, where they established organizations like the Islamic Center of Southern California, now one of the largest Muslim entities in the United States.

One religious group that experienced rapid growth from 1920 to 1950 was the Church of Jesus Christ of Latter-day Saints, which increased from under 4,000 members in California in 1920 to 100,000 in 1950, with significant growth in and around Los Angeles. As well as establishing many church auxiliaries, the California Mormons took part in the church-wide Welfare Plan, implemented during the 1930s to take care of needy Mormons, and won from other Christian groups the right to participate in interdenominational services and activities (such as campus ministries). In 1953, Goodwin Knight (a Mormon) succeeded Earl Warren as governor of California, and the Los Angeles Temple was consecrated. After 1950, California—and other states in the Far West—would become a magnet for Mormon families living further east (the Mormon population of California had grown to 300,000 by 1965).

RELIGIOUS LIFE SINCE 1950

Since 1950, the Pacific region has witnessed both consolidation of formal religious institutions as well as a slackening of dogmatic strictures. While Catholic and charismatic Christian movements still maintain strong presences, a liberal spiritualism has enabled a variety of faiths to develop in the region. This is supplemented by ongoing immigration that has diversified established religions. Vietnamese and Tibetan arrivals, for example, have contributed to the growing Buddhist population; new Russian and European groups have helped vitalize Orthodox communities. Recent immigrants from Jordan, Iran, and Palestine have not only expanded the region's Muslim population but also brought Syriac and Chaldean practices.

The Roman Catholic Church

During the late 1960s, Catholics in the Far West found themselves obliged to grapple with a new set of structures imposed by the reforms of the Second Vatican Council (1962–1965). Liturgical changes shifted the focus from the individualized rosary and novena devotions of the 1950s to an emphasis on corporate worship embodied in Scripture and the Eucharist. Well-educated parishes like St. Julie's Church, San Jose, California, developed a wide range of forms of the Mass to serve different age groups. Parish councils were also created during this period and assumed responsibility for many aspects of parish life, especially in places like St. Francis de Sales Church, Oakland, California; and even in more traditional settings, pastors found it necessary to obtain the support of the laity for major projects. A new emphasis on social justice programs also became evident during the 1960s. Other lay-led spiritual groups like Cursillo and Marriage Encounter enjoyed an increasingly prominent profile and helped further ecumenical dialogue with local Protestant churches. Finally, in the region that had nurtured the seminal Pentecostal event of the twentieth century, Charismatic Renewal—a nationwide Catholic Pentecostal phenomenon—developed a hold through the Southern California Renewal Conference, supported by parishes like Blessed Sacrament Church in Orange County, California.

Protestant Churches in the Region

While Catholics grappled with reform, Southern California Protestants continued to experience a conservative revival that had begun with the founding of Fuller Theological Seminary in Los Angeles in 1947—a vital instrument in the mainstreaming of American fundamentalism—and the 1952 decision of the Southern Baptist Convention to expand its mission work outside the American South. The Far West increasingly became a target for conservative evangelicals, and branches of groups like Campus Crusade for Christ appeared on many western campuses. In 1965, Chuck Smith launched a ministry to the hippie community of Costa Mesa, California, which ultimately became the mother church of a group of Calvary Chapel churches in California and elsewhere. Repudiating denominationalism, Smith stressed *agape*, verse-by-verse expository Bible teaching and outreach ministry. The movement grew apace and was soon followed by a number of California nondenominational megachurches, including Grace Community Church in Riverside, the West Angeles Church of God (a black Pentecostal body), and Robert Schuller's Crystal Cathedral in Garden Grove. In 1986, a group of congregations formerly affiliated with Calvary Chapel broke away to form the Association of Vineyard Churches, based in Anaheim, which laid a greater stress on the Gifts of the Spirit than did the mother church. The megachurch phenomenon has persisted in the Pacific West. Twenty-four of the nation's largest churches in 1990 (including seven of the largest twenty) were in California, with another four in Washington and three in Oregon. Such churches have learned how to serve suburban populations, to adjust rapidly to changing circumstances, and to provide a range of specialized ministries. The conservative trend also included smaller Pentecostal groups like Donald Barrett's Community Chapel and Bible Training Center in Seattle and the Music Square Church in Alma, Alaska.

The rise of independent churches in the Far West during the 1960s and 1970s was not confined to conservative fundamentalist circles. Communal experiments like The Family, which began in Huntingdon Beach, California, in 1968, or San Francisco's Kerista Commune, begun three years later, testified not only to the disaffection of the young from conventional religion but also their more relaxed attitudes toward sex and marriage. A feeling that the major denominations had failed adequately to address the needs of homosexuals led Troy Perry to found Metropolitan Community Church in Los Angeles in 1968, which ultimately spawned the nation's first gay "denomination"—the Universal Fellowship of Metropolitan Community Churches. Minority religion also took on a new prominence with the rise of powerful black churches including Los Angeles' First African Methodist Episcopal (AME) Church (which helped foster the career of future mayor Tom Bradley) and the Crenshaw Christian Center, Allen Temple Baptist Church in Oakland, Mount Zion Baptist Church in Seattle, and San Francisco's Glide Memorial Methodist Church, the home of the West's most well-known black clergyman, Cecil Williams.

Buddhism

Buddhism, too, emerged as a more mainstream religious avocation, in large measure due to Alan Watts, who helped found the American Academy of Asian Studies in San Francisco during the 1950s. Spearheading the spiritual renaissance was the Sino-American Buddhist Association, launched in 1959 and directed by Tipitaka Master Hsuan Hua. Emphasizing the formation of monastic communities, the Association opened its first monastery near San Francisco in 1970, with additional foundations in Los Angeles (1976) and Seattle (1984). Now based in Talmage, California, and known as the Dharma Realm Buddhist Association, it operates the first Buddhist university to be established in the Western Hemisphere and is a major publisher of Buddhist literature.

Both Rinzai and Soto Zen missionaries established themselves on the coast with regularity after World War II, encouraged by the United States' increasing familiarity with Asian affairs and the Beat Movement's popularizing of Zen in the 1950s and 1960s. Taizen Maezumi Roshi (1930–1995) opened the Zen Center of Los Angeles in 1956, while Nyogen Senzaki's student, Robert Aiken (b. 1916) founded the Diamond Sangha in Honolulu in 1959. The influential Soto Zen priest Shunryu Suzuki (1904–1971) arrived in San Francisco in 1959 and established the San Francisco Zen Center two years later. A variety of literary introductions to Zen Buddhism also appeared in the West at this time. These included works by the popular, if "square," Watts (1915–1973) to the catalyzing guidance of Dr. D. T. Suzuki (1870–1966), a powerful and prolific early proponent. *Zen Mind, Beginner's Mind* (1970), by Shunryu Suzuki Roshi, became a particular favorite for those challenged by Buddhism's investigations of Emptiness and Enlightenment. These works led many counter-culture adherents to centers like Suzuki Roshi's San Francisco Zen Center.

Post-1960 Buddhist organizations included specialized ethnic associations for immigrants from Thailand and Vietnam and groups more open to general participation such as the Tiep Hien Order in Berkeley, California, founded by Thich Nhat Han, who advocated the engagement of Buddhism with contemporary social issues, and the True Buddha School of Redmond, Washington, founded by Sheng-Yen Lu, which draws from Tibetan Buddhism to teach that culture's older, mystic tantric traditions. In 1987, an ecumenical Buddhist initiative resulted in the

Alan Watts (right) watching a group of people performing Taoist experiments, 1960.
Truman Moore/Time Life Pictures/Getty Images.

formation of the American Buddhist Congress in Los Angeles to bring together
Buddhists of all persuasions in common endeavors, to promote understanding of
the different traditions, and to educate the American public in the practice of Buddhism. Succeeding waves of emigrants from numerous Asian countries have continued to transfer not only the teachings of the three primary Buddhist
traditions—Mahayana, Vajrayana, and Theravada—to the region, but also a variety of socially and historically inscribed practices. As in the rest of the country,
Buddhism in the Pacific Region frequently concentrates around major urban
areas—Honolulu, Los Angeles, San Francisco, Seattle. However, the long history
of transnational contact has seen Buddhist practice permeate the culture, impacting events as diverse as the Hollywood vogue for the Dalai Lama's Tibetan teachings, the 1996 political fundraising "scandal" at the Taiwanese-established Hsi Lai
Temple, as well as the rising popularity of online Cyber-Sangha's.

Pacific Buddhism

One of American Buddhism's most widely respected figures during the last half-
century is the Pulitzer Prize–winning poet, preeminent environmental thinker, and
regional activist Gary Snyder (b. 1930). As a graduate student in East Asian Languages at the University of California–Berkeley in 1952, Snyder came in contact with
the San Francisco Bay Area's well-established "Pure Land" and other schools of Mahayana Buddhism and participated in a literary and cultural explosion conspicuously
anchored in Buddhist spiritualism. With Allen Ginsberg (1926–1997), Jack Kerouac
(1922–1969), Joanne Kyger (b. 1934), Philip Whalen (1923–2002), Kenneth Rexroth

Beat poet Gary Snyder at a protest march, 1965. © *The Observer*/Getty Images.

(1905–1982) and other writers and Beat artists of mid-century San Francisco, Snyder nurtured Buddhism's spread into the mainstream-American popular imagination. His fictionalization as Japhy Ryder in Kerouac's novel *The Dharma Bums* (1958) solidly fixed Snyder as an exemplar for this cultural turn. With little formal training available in the United States, Snyder chose to travel to Japan in 1956 to study Rinzai Zen. Based in Kyoto for the next decade, Snyder would also travel through Asia, encountering various Buddhist sects and their local spiritual customs, before he finally returned to the West Coast to continue his practice.

Though critics occasionally grumble that Beat Generation writers could misappropriate Buddhist concepts in their unorthodox and "hedonistic" poetry, the creative energy the Beats generated ushered Buddhism into the imagination of the American public. Charles Prebish, a leading scholar of American Buddhism, has claimed that "Beat Zen" was one of the most significant developments in Buddhism since it came to U.S. shores, and its legacy is still apparent.

Both formal and creative roots had fomented, as increasing numbers of Chinese, Japanese, Korean, and South Asian immigrants began filtering across the Pacific to Hawai'i, California, and Washington. These late-nineteenth and early-twentieth century pioneer experiences made the developing culture of the Pacific Region familiar with and receptive to Buddhist thought. Immigrant communities soon established formal temples that nurtured Buddhist thought in the region. Such historical influences also led to a growing acceptance of Asian religious practices in the region, as Snyder elucidates:

> What the West Coast Buddhists have that maybe the rest of the country doesn't have so much—this goes back to that question of "what is the legacy of the Beats"—it also has a significant population of people who know a lot about Buddhism, and thought about it in some cases for many years, and read a lot, have been in and out of Buddhist places, but who won't call themselves Buddhists. And who live in all kinds of situations and have a happy kind of irreverence in regard to Buddhism, like say Jim Dodge up in Arcata . . . it's exactly that kind of irreverence that I think something the West Coast has because it has been comfortable with Buddhism longer. It can afford to poke fun at it.
>
> Then there are a lot of people who think of themselves Daoists, informally speaking. I know a lot of people who say, "Oh, that Buddhism stuff is too serious; I'm a Daoist." And then you know the joke is, "What Buddhists do is meditate; what Daoists do is take naps." (laughs) A lot of people say Daoists like to drink too, so they drink and then they take naps. They're very relaxed and good-natured. The Daoists are also very serious practicers, with some distinctive differences from Buddhists. We all get along, and that goes for Confucianists too.

When Jack Kerouac and Allen Ginsberg and I all got together at Rexroth's place and it was the first time that Kerouac had met me or met Rexroth or met Whalen—Whalen was there too—Jack was spouting Buddhist stuff all the time. He had really discovered it in a big way, so finally Kenneth says to him—this was 1955—he said (does Rexroth imitation) "Ah, slow down Jack, everybody's a Buddhist here in San Francisco" (laughs). That was in 1955.

It had taken hold here in the sense that everyone was aware of the basic thinking and had read some books and was certainly cheered up by it, was sort of pleased by it. Not that there was much in the way of formal Buddhist activity. There was Alan Watts teaching, and there were the Japanese community temples. It was in the air, and even then—like with Rexroth—Buddhist thought was to some degree linked to philosophical anarchism and pacifism a la Gandhi, and resistance to both the capitalist and the Soviet communist model. It suggested a third path.[3]

Among European American converts to Buddhism, sects that promote meditation—including Zen and its Chinese precursor Ch'an, as well as some Tibetan and Theravada sects—are by far the most favored. Zen enlarged its appeal to non-Asians in the late 1950s as Soto and Rinzai Zen schools were established throughout the Pacific Region. The influx of teachers like Taizen Maezumi Roshi and Shunryu Suzuki Roshi to the region provided a path for those adherents who were looking for more formal training.

Since the Zen expansion of the 1950s and 1960s, a vibrant atmosphere of Buddhist practice has developed along the Pacific, an atmosphere churned by the continued East–West flows of people and ideas. The Dharma Realm Buddhist Association, established by adherents of Ch'an, has affiliates from Seattle to Los Angeles; forest-oriented practices from the Theravada tradition can be found in Oregon and Northern California; and large numbers of non-Asian Americans are still drawn to the nontheistic and individualistic aspects of Zen spiritualism. As Snyder points out, the style of American Buddhism must still contend with these cultural and historical trends:

There's a great deal of variety on the West Coast. I do think that we can say that they all share a few features though that are—quote—"new." One is that women are very much involved from one end to the other. From Vancouver, British Columbia, to San Diego. Actually, from Fairbanks, Alaska, to San Diego because there are some Buddhist groups in Fairbanks and in Juneau and in Anchorage and in Sitka—I've visited almost all of them at one time or another. Women have been drawn to Buddhism, and women have transformed it by their presence. Jan Bays of the Zen Community of Oregon is a teaching Roshi. She was a disciple of Maezumi Roshi of Los Angeles and became his Dharma heir. So women's engagement and equality in Buddhism is a new thing. And the concern for social justice and ecological justice—or environmental issues, if you like—are pretty much up and down the whole Coast. Where you can see that all happening is in the periodical *Turning Wheel*, the magazine of engaged Buddhism [published by the Buddhist Peace Fellowship] which comes out of Berkeley.[4]

The Buddhist Peace Fellowship, an inter-sectarian organization focusing on social causes, is just one model of how Buddhist groups in the West interact. Throughout its history, Buddhism has acknowledged and fostered multiple tradition of practice: Ch'an practice, for example, often emphasizes an eclectic assortment of teachings from other Mahayana sects. Buddhism's core principles, the Buddhadharma, has enabled contact and shared teaching between differing communities as diverse practices spread within the Pacific context. Cross-cultural exchanges between Asian, Asian American, and European American Buddhist communities in the Pacific Region are ongoing, and this interaction that bodes well for the sharing of ideas beyond conventional Buddhist communities.

Since his resettling in California in 1969, Snyder himself has advocated a particular blend of ecological consciousness and social activism grounded in Buddhist practice, along with traditional Zen meditation. His books, whether the poetry of *Turtle Island* (1974) and *Mountains and Rivers Without End* (1996) or the prose of *The Practice of the Wild* (1990), have promoted alternative, ethically minded ways of conceiving one's relationship with the world. Though dedicated to Zen practice, Snyder is a student of all traditions and visits local sanghas, or Buddhist communities, throughout the Pacific Rim. Besides his writings and talks, Snyder's contributions to an "American Buddhism" include his helping found a meditation retreat, the Ring-of-Bone Zendo, in the Sierra Nevada Mountains. In 1998, he received the Buddhism Transmission Award from the Bukkyo Dendo Kyokai Foundation of Japan for his career-long integration of Zen practice and environmental concern.

Unconventional Religious Experiences

In addition to conventional religion, the Far West continues to foster a variety of religious experiences. From the United Church of Religious Science in Los Angeles to Roy Masters' Foundation of Human Understanding (which enjoyed an extensive California radio following in the 1960s and 1970s but is now based in Oregon), the mail-order Universal Life Church in Modesto, California, and L. Ron Hubbard's Church of Scientology, many options exist for the curious.

Religious Science was founded by Ernest Holmes, who was heavily influenced by Ralph Waldo Emerson (1803–1882), Mary Baker Eddy (1821–1910), and others, key figures in the development of the New Thought tradition, from which Religious Science draws many of its key tenets. His *Science of Mind*, written in 1926, describes belief based more on science than mysticism and stressing an intellectual approach to spiritual matters and striving toward oneness with God and all things.

Roy Masters, originally a diamond cutter in Great Britain, became fascinated with hypnosis as a young man. Believing that people are already hypnotized in negative ways that create stressful living, his interest in the power of suggestion and study of the way the mind influences behavior led him to develop a program based on a meditative technique called *psychocatalysis* to "unhypnotize" people. While his Foundation, originally called the Institute of Hypnosis and begun in 1961, is legally considered a church, opponents identify cultlike qualities.

Begun by Reverend Kirby James Hensley (1911–1999), the Universal Life Church opened its doors in 1959 to everyone. Its main tenet is that everyone is part of the Universal life, and religious freedom is stressed. For a donation, the church, upon application, will ordain anyone as a minister, and ordination is for life. Since Hensley's death in 1999, his wife Lida has been the president of the church board.

L. Ron Hubbard's (1911–1986) Church of Scientology is known worldwide. It is a many-tiered organization whose multiple layers allow membership at various levels. Membership has been variously estimated, as high as 8 million. The first church was formed in Los Angeles in 1954 in response to public interest in Hubbard's *Dianetics: The Modern Science of Mental Health* (1950), which outlines his religious philosophy and is considered a sacred text. With elements of science, Freudian psychoanalytical theory, and Eastern philosophies, Hubbard's philosophy asserts that human beings are

Scientology Goes Hollywood

Among the Church of Scientology's members are well-known personalities, including some of Hollywood's most famous actors, who are actively recruited at Scientology's Celebrity Centers, created specifically to attract and nurture artists and actors. The centers offer career and spiritual guidance in luxurious surroundings. Recognizing that artists and actors exert enormous influence in society, impacting cultural values and social trends, L. Ron Hubbard began recruiting celebrities as early as 1955, when he initiated "Project Celebrity." According to critics, famous faces help to recruit members, increase Scientology's acceptance in mainstream America, and deflect some of the criticism Scientology has received over the years concerning, for example, its business practices. Among Scientology's most famous adherents are Tom Cruise, John Travolta, Kirstie Alley, Anne Archer, and Priscilla Presley.

spiritual beings capable of solving their own problems and reaching high states of awareness. Survival is the primary urge that drives all other activities. Hubbard introduced *Dianetics* as a mind-tool to improve the quality of survival—conquering the reactive mind, which is unconscious, and empowering the analytical mind, which analyzes and resolves problems. The goal of Scientology's Religious Technology Center is to ensure that Dianetics and Scientology doctrine are taught according to Hubbard's dictates. Since 1987, David Miscavige has headed the organization.

Despite the presence of mainstream and more unconventional religions such as Scientology, the ultimate truth is that many residents of the West Coast are extremely secularly minded. In four states, the level of participation in religious organizations falls below 40.0 percent, while in California it is 46.1 percent, helping to lift the regional figure to 42.8 percent.[5]

A Survey of Religious Bodies in the Pacific Region

Which bodies help provide the basis for California's more vibrant religious life? Almost two-thirds of the state's churchgoers are Roman Catholics (64.6 percent), and another 6.4 percent are Jews. Conservative Protestants account for much of the remainder, with 3.4 percent for the Church of Jesus Christ of Latter-day Saints, 3.0 percent for the Southern Baptist Convention, and 2.0 percent for the Assemblies of God. The fringe states of Hawai'i and Alaska present a study in contrasts. In Hawai'i, Catholics account for only 54.9 percent, and the Latter-day Saints are their closest rivals, with 9.7 percent. Liberal Protestantism claims 5.2 percent for the United Church of Christ, while Pentecostals are represented by the Assemblies of God (5.0 percent) and the International Church of the Foursquare Gospel (3.4 percent), and the Southern Baptist Convention has 4.8 percent. Alaska is only 25.3 percent Catholic and 8.8 percent Mormon, while having a significant number of members of the Southern Baptist Convention (10.7 percent) and the Orthodox Church in America (9.3 percent). Other groups include the Assemblies of God (5.4 percent), the Evangelical Lutheran Church in America (ELCA) (5.3 percent), and the Episcopal Church (3.1 percent). The state also boasts a large number of independent noncharismatic churches (3.5 percent).

In the secular Pacific Northwest, the influence of Catholicism declines to 36.9 percent in Washington and 32.5 percent in Oregon. The Latter-day Saints, by contrast, sustain levels comparable with Hawai'i, achieving 9.2 percent in Washington and 9.7 percent in Oregon. Oregon has a more diverse range of denominations, with a strong Pentecostal presence, including the Assemblies of God (4.6 percent) and the International Church of the Foursquare Gospel (4.2 percent). Other conservative groups include the Christian Churches & Churches of Christ (3.6 percent), the Conservative Baptists (3.4 percent), and the Southern Baptist Convention (3.0 percent). Liberal Protestantism is represented by the Evangelical Lutheran Church in America (4.4 percent), the Presbyterians (3.2 percent), and the United Methodists (3.2 percent), while Jews account for 3.0 percent of religious believers. In Washington, the range of groups is somewhat smaller. The ELCA is the third largest group, with 6.6 percent, followed by the Assemblies of

Table 1. Religious Adhesion in the Pacific Rim, 2000

Denomination	Number	Percentage of total adherents
Roman Catholic	11,438,854	59.3%
Jewish congregations	1,079,650	5.6%
Church of Jesus Christ of Latter-day Saints	873,664	4.5%
Southern Baptist Convention	609,721	3.2%
Assemblies of God	498,963	2.6%
Evangelical Lutheran Church in America	359,791	1.9%
United Methodist	352,993	1.8%
Presbyterian Church in the United States of America	346,281	1.8%
Muslim	282,529	1.5%
Seventh Day Adventists	271,363	1.4%
Episcopal Church in the United States of America	252,632	1.3%
Independent Charismatic	248,630	1.3%
American Baptists, U.S.A.	218,416	1.1%
International Church of the Foursquare Gospel	209,743	1.1%
Lutheran Church– Missouri Synod	199,286	1.0%
Independent Noncharismatic	197,775	1.0%
Other	1,841,834	9.6%
TOTAL	19,282,125	100.0%

Source: Dale E. Jones, Sherri Doty, Clifford Grammich, James E. Horsch, Richard Houseal, Mac Lynn, John P. Marcum, Kenneth M. Sanchagrin, and Richard H. Taylor, *Religious Congregations and Membership in the United States 2000: An Enumeration by Region, State and County Based on Data Reported for 149 Religious Bodies* (Nashville, TN: Glenmary Research Center, 2002).

God, with 5.4 percent. The Southern Baptist Convention accounts for 3.2 percent, while liberal Protestant groups include the United Methodists (3.9 percent) and the Presbyterians (3.8 percent).

Americans in the Pacific Rim states have probably been exposed to a greater variety of religious practices than any other section of the United States. While most of America experienced migration as an east-to-west process, the Far West also experienced—and continues to experience—substantial migration from both Asia and Central America. When this was combined with

The Gift of Tongues

Pentecostals, influenced by nineteenth-century Wesleyan and Keswick holiness and sanctification movements, sought the gift of tongues or the Baptism in the Holy Spirit as experienced by the first group of Apostles, in the first century of the Common Era. They generally take their cue from Acts 2:4: "All of them were filled with the Holy Spirit and began to speak in other languages, as the spirit gave them ability." Pentecostals characterize their experience as the third and final blessing of Christianity, with conversion being the first and sanctification, the eradication of inward sin, the second. Theologically, the first is accepted by all Christians and the second and third by a more limited group.

the habitual weakness of traditional American Protestant institutions in the region through the twentieth century, many non-Catholics adopted a stance of benevolent (or sometimes malevolent) neutrality toward institutional religion. The strength of spiritual individualism among believers has also contributed to the presence of a great array of religious institutions and programs that repudiate denominational affiliation, some of these extremely conservative and some remarkably liberal. The success of Pentecostalism in the region could be attributed, in some measure, to its emphasis on the *individual*'s personal connection with God through the action of the Holy Spirit. The Catholic Church, meanwhile, has been forced to grapple with the individualist critiques of its hierarchical structure and governance and with the need to accommodate the increasingly large proportion of its membership that is Spanish-speaking and newly arrived in America. More and more residents of the Pacific Rim states, however, no longer practice any form of religious observance, preferring to uphold the values of secular humanism. For non-Hispanics, in particular, it seems unlikely that religious commitment will ever attain the levels evident in the rest of the nation.

PACIFIC COAST PENTECOSTALISM

Historical Background

In April 1906 the *Los Angeles Times* reported a "weird babble of tongues" coming from a church in the city's African American Central District. By the close of the year, dailies from across the country—Atlanta, Spokane, New York, Chicago, and all points in between—reported similar phenomena. The source of this "weird babble of tongues" was the Azusa Street Revival (1906–1909) located at the Los Angeles Apostolic Faith Mission (Los Angeles AFM [1906–1922]). Led by William J. Seymour (1870–1922), the son of former slaves, the AFM or Azusa Street Mission was home to a largely working-class, mixed-race congregation of Mexican washwomen, Swedish housewives, day laborers of many nationalities, and African American maids, cooks, and janitors. The Mission became the focal point of the faith over the next several years as it developed in the region and around the nation. Moreover, the congregation's eclectic working-class background attracted considerable media interest as the Revival became known for its mixed-race worship and religious enthusiasm. Sensational headlines greeted morning and evening readers, inviting them to read the latest accounts of the "Holy Rollers," as they labeled the religious phenomenon. What these papers, along with the nation's sizable religious press, were witnessing and helping to midwife through their reports was modern Pentecostalism, which in less than a century would grow into 300 million adherents worldwide, with nearly 6 million in the United States and 1.1 million in the Pacific West.

Pentecostal Beliefs and Culture

Pentecostalism quickly spread across the Pacific West. Its growth was facilitated by a preexisting network of Holiness associations that connected the region through tent revivals, healing services, and itinerant evangelists. Early West Coast converts Carrie Judd Montgomery (1858–1946), publisher of the *Leaves of Healing*, Dr. John G. Lake (1870–1935), and William F. Manley, among many others, reflected the Holiness background of the early faith and served to connect the new faith to a well-established body of believers and churches in the region. As a result, many of the first converts to Pentecostalism encountered the faith in older Holiness Association churches. A shared emphasis upon divine healing attracted many Holiness believers to the new faith. Early Pentecostalism reflected its Holiness roots with its intense emphasis upon personal conduct and divine healing. For instance, the early faithful frowned upon tobacco and alcohol use, modern entertainments, and short hair for women, and they insisted on modest dress for both sexes and a strict observation of Sunday as a day of rest and restraint. More important, early Pentecostals rejected modern therapeutic culture that emphasized science and medicine for healing. Instead, they relied on divine or faith healing through the laying on of hands and prayer for the sick. Faith healing became a prominent feature of early Pentecostalism and a key point of attraction for early converts in the region. Moreover, letters exchanged between friends and families in Los Angeles, Portland, Tacoma, Spokane, and elsewhere aided in the propagation of the faith, as did evangelists sent from Azusa Street and other Los Angeles area churches, tabernacles, and missions. In Oregon and Washington some of the first Pentecostal churches were direct descendants of the original Azusa Street Meeting either through the development of new churches or through conversion of already established churches to the Pentecostal message. Sent out from Los Angeles, white Pentecostal Florence Crawford (1870–1936) helped to establish a number of missions in the region, including her Portland, Oregon, Apostolic Faith Mission (Portland AFM).

Alaska and Hawai'i both received the Pentecostal message through the missionary efforts of mainland Anglos. In the opening decades of the twentieth century, Hawai'i was a recent acquisition of American imperialism, and Alaska was still a predominantly male outpost in the cold wilderness; both were U.S. territories. The Portland AFM sent missionaries to Native Alaskan communities as well as to American Indian tribes in Washington in the 1910s. Charles and Florence Personeus, under the direction of the Assemblies of God (AOG), were the first to pioneer Pentecostal churches in Alaska in 1917. Together the two would serve the region for nearly forty years. Pentecostal work in Hawai'i has focused almost exclusively on the native Hawaiian population and imported Chinese, Japanese, Portuguese, and Filipino labor. Pentecostal missions first appeared on the larger islands of Hilo, Maui, and Kauai in the 1910s. Missionary efforts to Hawai'i and Alaska were stalled during World War II but regained momentum as both gained statehood in 1959. Today the AOG numbers 21,000; the International Church of the Foursquare Gospel (ICFG) has 15,000 members, with another 3,000 believers affiliated with independent charismatic ministries on the islands. Alaska, in contrast, has a smaller Pentecostal population, with nearly 12,000 in the AOG, less than 400 in the ICFG, and another 2,400 in independent churches.

Perhaps no one on the West Coast—indeed, in the nation—did more to attract adherents to the new faith than Aimee Semple McPherson. Known simply as "Sister Aimee," McPherson was the first true star or celebrity of the faith and has been credited with drawing tens of thousands to the faith in the 1920s alone. Hers was an exuberant, personal message of faith retold through a common language of daily experience and plain-folks metaphors. Services at her Angelus Temple were as well known for their theatricality as they were for their spiritual enthusiasm. Her religious pageants featured the usual bands and singing but also featured biblical reenactments, live animals, and a cast of costumed hundreds. In one rather famous instance, she rode down the aisles of Angelus Temple on a borrowed policeman's motorcycle to emphasize the need for congregants to stop speeding through life. Ultimately her spiritual entertainment bridged the divide between the burgeoning entertainment industry of Southern California and the animus

Aimee Semple McPherson

Aimee Semple McPherson (1890–1944), born in Ontario, Canada, was the daughter of a Canadian Salvation Army lass. She was widowed young when her husband, evangelist Robert Semple, died shortly after the two arrived in China in 1910. She turned her attentions to evangelical work and headed west in 1918. While she was known around the world for her ministry and a frequent traveler of the nation's tent revival sawdust trail, her home was in Los Angeles. On New Year's Day 1922 she opened her Angelus Temple, a spectacle of modern acoustics and the first church to be built by national donations. In 1924 she built the first religious radio station, KFSG—Kall Foursquare Gospel. The next year she founded L.I.F.E. Bible College and, two years later, her own denomination, the International Church of the Foursquare Gospel. At the pinnacle of her success in the 1920s the *New York Times*, *The New Yorker*, and *The Nation* all published detailed accounts of her ministry and life, including her attack on corrupt Los Angeles politics and her mysterious disappearance from the warm waters of the Pacific in 1926. Her disappearance and subsequent reappearance several months later occasioned hysteria locally and drew worldwide media coverage. McPherson claimed to have been abducted and held in the Arizona desert. Her detractors claimed that she had run off with her married radio engineer to Carmel, California. The subsequent fraud trial did little to clear up the controversy. She continued to minister and draw crowds to Angelus Temple until her death in 1944.

Aimee Semple McPherson at an evangelist meeting in London. Courtesy of the Library of Congress.

Midwestern migrants held toward popular culture and popular amusements in the 1920s.

The steady stream of immigrants to the Golden State turned to a flood as the dust bowl and the Great Depression loosed tens of thousands from the soils of Oklahoma, Kansas, Arkansas, and Texas and sent many more chasing a better life in the fields of California. The sheer volume of immigrants into the state, some 200,000 by 1935 and almost 500,000 by 1940, altered the social landscape of the state, including Pentecostalism. While the faith had always attracted the socially dislocated, these impoverished arrivals strapped already poor congregations. It was during this period that the haunting images of impoverished, uprooted whites first came to embody the Pentecostal faith during the Great Depression and after. Though depression-era images linger, regional believers as early as the 1950s sought to project a more polished and professional image.

The postwar push toward the American middle class by Pentecostals can be seen in the emergence of the Full Gospel Business Men's Fellowship International (FGBMFI). Founded in Los Angeles in 1951, the FGBMFI initially set out to evangelize Southern California's growing class of average business people. Meeting over breakfast at Clifton's Cafeteria in downtown Los Angeles, the FGBMFI sought to reach local businessmen through a carefully crafted image of restrained faith and professional polish. The first meeting in 1951 drew 200 local businessmen. Organized by Armenian immigrant, dairy farmer, and real estate developer Demos Shakarian (1913–1993), the FGBMFI quickly became both a local and national Pentecostal phenomenon as it helped to organize some of the largest revival and healing crusades of the postwar era. In particular, the FGBMFI provided crucial financial support and organizing power for young evangelists, including Pentecostal Oral Roberts (b. 1918) and Pentecostal-friendly Billy Graham (b. 1918), among others. The organization has been widely credited with moving the faith from the nation's tents and storefront churches and into its hotels and convention sites and into the lives of the professional and entrepreneurial classes. By 1972 the membership of the FGBMFI stood at 300,000, with 700 chapters in the United States and another 200,000 members around the world. In the 1980s and 1990s an estimated 600,000 to 700,000 businessmen across the world met regularly to share their faith over breakfast. Since Shakarian's death in 1993, his son Richard Shakarian has served as president of the organization.

Charismatic Religions

During the 1980s and 1990s nondenominational charismatic churches in the Pacific West experienced tremendous growth. Nondenominational charismatic churches have offered a casual, contemporary worship service and Bible studies geared toward an eclectic group of believers turned off by traditional religion. Services tend to focus on an enthusiastic, personal relationship with God, as they have avoided discussions of theology. Modern music styles, most notably rock, tend to accompany the services. Many meet in rented buildings or lease commercial space as a way to remain flexible as their churches grow or contract in size. These "new paradigm churches," as Donald Miller argues, reflect dissatisfaction with formal religion and represent an effort to embrace and utilize lay leadership to lead worship services and to lead Bible classes.[6] The two largest new paradigm umbrella affiliations are the Calvary Chapel Fellowship Churches, founded in 1965 by Chuck Smith in Corona, California, and Vineyard USA, founded by Jon Wimber (1934–1997) in 1982 after leaving the Calvary Chapel Fellowships. Although many of these new paradigm churches have sought to maintain small intimate congregations, others have given rise to spectacular megachurches, some with congregations of over 15,000. While Southern California leads the region and nation in the number of megachurches, both Oregon and Washington are home to a number of megachurches, including the Beaverton, Oregon, Foursquare Church with 6,000 members and the 2,500-member Spokane, Washington, Calvary Chapel.

Charismatic Movements

The term *charismatic movement* first appeared in the 1950s in response to Pentecostal phenomena that occurred in non-Pentecostal settings, particularly the Roman Catholic Church, Lutheran, Mennonite, and Presbyterian churches. *Charismatic* is also understood to describe a vibrant style of worship that borrows heavily from traditional Pentecostal services but does not necessarily profess an explicit Pentecostal theology. Thus all Pentecostals would consider themselves charismatics, but not all charismatics would label themselves and their faith Pentecostal. Currently, independent charismatics and members of Vineyard USA account for nearly a million believers, with approximately 285,000 believers in the Pacific West.[7]

Pentecostal Organizations

The Pacific West proved resistant to sustained denominational organization until the 1920s. In the first years, Pentecostals operated independent of church denominations. Many had been forced out of their churches for their less-than-orthodox spiritual beliefs and practices, especially glossolalia, or speaking in tongues. Not wanting to replicate the very institutional forms that had rejected them, the first generation of believers proved to be reluctant church members and even more reluctant institution builders. In general they adhered to a loose definition of church polity, eschewing most formalities, including ministerial education and formal applications for membership. The earliest institutions sprang from the Azusa Street Revival.

Along the Pacific Coast the Los Angeles AFM and its Portland counterpart planted new congregations in San Francisco, Port Angelus, Washington, and Tacoma, Washington, with a host of smaller branches throughout Oregon and Washington as well as scattered outposts in California through the early 1930s. Organized in 1908, the Portland AFM traced its origins to the hallowed grounds of the Azusa Street Revival. Led by Florence Crawford, an original participant at the Los Angeles Mission, the Portland Mission initially considered itself an offshoot of the Southern California revival. The Mission attracted members through Crawford's stern yet charismatic pulpit and radio sermons and through the Mission's extensive newspaper ministry. Over the years her ministry refused to soften its position on divorce and remarriage as she rejected remarriage if a divorced partner still lived. In 1919 a group of disgruntled AFM members started the Bible Standard Mission in Eugene, Oregon, under the direction of Crawford's close associate Fred Hornshuh (1884–1982). The group merged with the Open Bible Evangelistic Association in 1935, changing its name to its current Open Bible Standard Churches. The two organizations today claim around 40,000 members, each with the majority living in Oregon and Washington.

Pentecostal organizations from other parts of the nation, notably the Assemblies of God (founded in 1914), began to develop a following in the Pacific West during the 1920s. In 1919 the AOG organized the Southern California District Council (SCDC) and the Pacific Northwest District Council (PNDC), which included western Montana, Idaho, Oregon, Washington, and the territory of Alaska. Both district councils invited local well-established Pentecostal congregations and well-respected individuals to join with them in their organizing endeavors. While some refused, citing fears of potential institutional coercion or spiritual laxity, others were attracted to the benefits offered by the organization—the authority to bury the dead, to marry believers, and to obtain train discounts. The PNDC grew quickly throughout the 1930s as the region's population increased and as missionary efforts to Alaska and to local Native Americans expanded in this period. Yet it was in Southern California that Pentecostal organizations grew by leaps and bounds.

Organization dramatically altered the Pentecostal landscape of Southern California. Although the AOG initially accepted interracial fellowship, a hallmark of worship in Southern California, the denomination abandoned the practice as it organized. They reasoned that it would alienate Midwestern newcomers and argued that African American organizations should be the home of African American believers. Consequently, as the Azusa Street Mission declined in attendance and the SCDC retreated from interracial worship, African American and Latino believers found themselves increasingly isolated from white believers. African Americans were urged to join with the local Church of God in Christ (COGIC) and refused membership when they applied for credentials with the SCDC.

Headquartered in Memphis, Tennessee, the Church of God in Christ converted to Pentecostalism in 1907 after its charismatic leader, African American Charles H. Mason (1865–1961), experienced the Spirit Baptism at the Azusa Street Mission. As the only incorporated and thus federally recognized Pentecostal church, in the first years of the faith, white and black believers alike sought the credentialing authority of the COGIC. The COGIC incorporated in California in 1914. Led by African American Eddie Driver (1869–1929), the COGIC ministered to blacks and whites until the mid-1920s, when race lines were strictly observed for the first time in Pentecostal churches in the city. Efforts to organize chapters elsewhere in the Pacific West have met with little success. Currently there are no branches of COGIC in Washington and only one in Portland, Oregon.

Latino Pentecostals

For Latino believers in the Pacific West, the years after Azusa Street were mostly spent in independent Spanish-language missions and under the tutelage of Anglo home missionaries. Spanish-speaking congregations sprang up on Los Angeles' eastside in Montebello, El Monte, Pico Rivera, and Belvedere and in the factories in the fields of the San Joaquin and Imperial Valleys as well as Orange, Riverside, San Bernardino counties and wherever else men and women followed the harvest. Pentecostal growth in the region coincided with a dramatic increase in the Mexican population from 9,000 in 1900 to nearly 89,000 in 1920. Recognizing the tremendous missionary field in the region, the AOG under the direction of white Texan Henry Cleophas Ball (1896–1989) established the Latin American Bible Institute in 1926 in San Diego to train mostly white missionaries for service to the region's Spanish-speaking population. Other white Pentecostals, notably Alice Luce (1873–1955) and Florence Murcutt (?–1935), migrated to the region to proselytize to what Luce called "the floating population" of agricultural workers through the 1920s. Yet from the start of the Azusa Street Mission, Mexicans and Mexican Americans in the region sought to develop their own Spanish-language churches and assemblies, independent of whites and in conjunction with them.

California-born Mexican American Arthur C. Valdez (1896–1988) served for many years as one of the faith's most outspoken and well-recognized Latino converts. Converted at the Azusa Street Mission as a boy, Valdez served as a prime example of the racial diversity of the early faith. Other less well known converts worked to establish institutions that reflected their religious and cultural sensibilities. Antonio Nava (1892–1999) was one of a few Spanish-speaking converts in the region who evangelized Mexicans and Mexican Americans in the fields of Brawley, Calexico, and other towns in California's Imperial Valley. In 1930 Nava, along with Francisco Llorente, incorporated the Apostolic Assembly of the Faith in Jesus Christ in California. By the 1960s in Los Angeles the Apostolic Assembly numbered twelve churches and 1,000 members, the AOG had eighteen churches and 1,000-plus members, and there were another seventeen Spanish-language independent Pentecostal churches. Currently Spanish-speaking congregations are both pioneering new churches and resuscitating older Pentecostal venues. Los Angeles' Bethel Temple, the former denominational headquarters of the Southern California District Council of the AOG, is now a Spanish-language church with a membership of 1,500 and a vision of social justice that has led to a revitalization of the local eastside neighborhood. Latino Pentecostals number more than 900,000 in the United States, with approximately a third residing in Southern California.

The denominations founded by two of the most important early Pentecostal women, Crawford's Portland AFM and McPherson's International Church of the Foursquare Gospel, have weathered the deaths of their founders. After Crawford's death in 1936, her son Raymond Robert Crawford (1890–1965) took over the AFM. Crawford proved to be a charismatic and more amenable figure than his mother during his leadership. In a similar vein, after McPherson's death in 1946, the ICFG was led by her son Rolf McPherson (b. 1913) until his retirement in 1997. Where his mother had looked warily on ties with other Pentecostal organizations, McPherson allied the ICFG with larger umbrella organizations including the National Association of Evangelicals and the Pentecostal Fellowship of North America as well as the FGBMFI. Membership in the Portland AFM and allied branches mostly in the Pacific West stands at around 4,000, with another 50,000 worldwide. In contrast, the ICFG has 347,000 members around the nation, with 210,000 in the Pacific West.

Pentecostals and the Media

Early Pentecostals embraced American print culture—publishing an impressive number of newspapers and journals as well as religious tracts. Typically, Pentecostal papers consisted of revival notices, requests for prayers, sermons, and extended biblical exegesis or analysis. The Los Angeles AFM established a thriving newspaper ministry with nearly 50,000 papers printed per issue in 1909. Starting in 1908 the Portland AFM launched an impressive newspaper ministry that included newspapers, tracts, and newsletters in several languages, among them English, French, German, Polish, and Swedish. Other regional publications, notably *The Bridal Call* (Los Angeles) and *The Golden Grain* (Seattle), also boasted a thriving readership through the 1920s, yet the numbers of well-established Pentecostal papers remained small in the Pacific West. Although there were only a few sustained publishing endeavors on the West Coast, the region figured heavily in national coverage.

In Los Angeles, the Azusa Street Mission garnered considerable local and national interest. The mixed-race membership, the practices of speaking in tongues and laying on hands of the spiritually and physically sick, and the ministry of women elicited local interest. The *Pasadena Star* reported on the mixed-race meetings and the defiance of female adherents. In particular, they lamented that young, white working women were being lured away from all sensible activities—eating and working—by the carnivalesque atmosphere of the Azusa Street Mission and other local Pentecostal churches. In Oregon, Florence Crawford's "association with negroes" became the grounds on which a Portland court questioned her fitness as a mother in 1908. In other locales in the Pacific West, news of mixed-race meetings as well as women's spiritual leadership drew the ire of local nonbelievers and magistrates alike. Moreover, these headlines contributed to salacious caricatures of the early faith as a hotbed of "free-loveism," which covered everything from wife swapping to premarital sex. Yet the media also served the interests of the early faithful as it helped to spread their message and to keep the emerging Pentecostal nation informed of their activities.

For the highly mobile population of Pentecostals, radio through the 1950s proved a touchstone for faith and community. In the 1920s Crawford of the Portland AFM and her more famous Pentecostal sister, Aimee Semple McPherson, embraced radio as a tool of evangelization. McPherson's KFSG (Kall Foursquare Gospel) started broadcasting in 1924 and reached a national audience soon thereafter; in the process, she pioneered religious radio broadcasting. Other evangelists in the region sponsored weekly shows but were unable to sustain as wide a following. Radio was nowhere near as popular or as powerful a medium for Pentecostals as was television.

Starting in the 1950s, Pentecostals took to the airwaves to spread their message of faith and healing, and in the process, they helped to start a new phenomenon: televangelism. It was not until the 1970s, however, that the Pacific West experienced homegrown televangelism. Founded in 1972 in Santa Ana, California, the Trinity Broadcast Network, or TBN, was launched by Paul (b. 1934) and Jan Crouch, along with James "Jim" Bakker (b. 1940) and Tammy Faye Bakker Messner (b. 1942). The Bakkers were experienced television personalities. The two had starred in children's radio and television shows in the 1960s.

TBN quickly became the leading network for charismatic Christianity. It offered talk and Christian variety along with programming aimed at children. Currently, the station broadcasts over 5,000 stations worldwide and from thirty-three satellites. The network has developed innovative Christian programming geared toward an MTV generation of Pentecostal and charismatic youths interested in music videos, extreme sports, and urban culture. One of the station's highest-ranking programs is *Harvest*, hosted by Greg Laurie (b. 1953), pastor of Riverside, California's

Former Pentecostal Minister Troy Perry who now has his own homosexual Metropolitan Community Church. Grey Villet/Time Life Pictures/Getty Images.

Harvest Christian Fellowship. The show draws on the phenomenal success of Laurie's Harvest Crusades. Melding youth culture and Christian rock music with an evangelical message of a deeply personal relationship with God, the Harvest Crusades have witnessed to approximately 2 million in the Pacific West and another million in the United States since 1990. The Harvest Crusades and other contemporary youth-oriented programming and events reflect ongoing changes in Pentecostal culture in the region as the movement has increasingly moved away from formal denominational structures to independent, nondenominational churches.

RESOURCE GUIDE

Printed Sources

Afonsky, Gregory. *A History of the Orthodox Church in Alaska.* Kodiak, AK: St. Herman's Theological Seminary, 1977.

Alexander, Kay. *California Catholicism.* Santa Barbara, CA: Fithian Press, 1993.

Anderson, Robert M. *Vision of the Disinherited: The Making of American Pentecostalism.* New York: Oxford University Press, 1979.

Bartleman, Frank. *Azusa Street: The Roots of Modern-Day Pentecost.* Plainfield, NJ: Bridge Publishing, 1980.

Blumhoffer, Edith. *Aimee Semple McPherson: Everybody's Sister.* Grand Rapids, MI: Wm. B. Eerdmans, 1993.

Bradley, Martin B., Norman M. Green, Jr., Dale E. Jones, Mac Lynn, and Lou McNeil. *Churches and Church Membership in the United States 1990: An Enumeration by Region, State and County Based on Data Reported for 133 Church Groupings.* Atlanta, GA: Glenmary Research Center, 1992.

Brandt, Patricia, and Lillian A. Pereyra. *Adapting in Eden: Oregon's Catholic Minority, 1836–1986.* Pullman: Washington State University Press, 2002.

Burns, Jeffrey M. "Building the Best: A History of Catholic Parish Life in the Pacific States." In *The American Catholic Parish: A History from 1850 to the Present*, ed. Jay P. Dolan. Mahwah, NJ: Paulist Press, 1987. 2: 10–135.

Collins, John J. *Native American Religions: A Geographical Survey.* Lewiston, NY: Edwin Mellen Press, 1991.

Deno, Vivian. "God, Authority, and the Home: Gender, Domesticity, and U.S. Pentecostals, 1906–1926."

Fields, Rick. *How the Swans Came to the Lake: A Narrative History of Buddhism in America.* 3rd ed. Boston, MA: Shambhala, 1993.

Holland, Clifton L. *The Religious Dimension in Hispanic Los Angeles: A Protestant Case Study.* South Pasadena, CA: William Carey Library, 1974.

Jones, Dale E., Sherri Doty, Clifford Grammich, James E. Horsch, Richard Houseal, Mac Lynn, John P. Marcum, Kenneth M. Sanchagrin and Richard H. Taylor. *Religious Congregations and Membership in the United States 2000: an Enumeration by Region, State and County Based on Data Reported for 149 Religious Bodies.* Nashville, TN: Glenmary Research Center, 2002.

Mardsen, George. *Understanding Fundamentalism and Evangelicalism.* Grand Rapids, MI: William B. Eerdmans, 1991.

McPherson, Aimee Semple. *This Is That.* 1923. Los Angeles: Foursquare Publications, 1996.

Melton, J. Gordon. *Encyclopedia of American Religions.* 6th ed. Detroit, MI: Gale Research, 1999.

Prebish, Charles. *American Buddhism.* North Scituate, MA: Duxbury Press, 1979.

Strain, Charles. "The Pacific Buddha's Wild Practice: Gary Snyder's Environmental Ethic." In *American Buddhism: Methods and Findings in Recent Scholarship*, ed. Duncan Ryuken Williams and Christopher S. Queen. Richmond, England: Curzon Press, 1999.

Suiter, John. *Poets on the Peaks: Gary Snyder, Philip Whalen and Jack Kerouac in the North Cascades.* Washington, DC: Counterpoint, 2002.

Suzuki, Shunryu. *Zen Mind, Begginer's Mind.* Ed. Trudy Dixon. New York: John Weatherhill, 1970.

Szasz, Ferenc M. *Religion in the Modern American West.* Tucson: University of Arizona Press, 2000.

Tonkinson, Carole, ed. *Big Sky Mind: Buddhism and the Beat Generation.* New York: Riverhead Books, 1995.

Vaughan, John N. *Megachurches and American Life: How Churches Grow.* Grand Rapids, MI: Baker Books, 1993.

White, Richard. *"It's Your Misfortune and None of My Own": A New History of the American West.* Norman: University of Oklahoma Press, 1991.

Web Sites

Assemblies of God (U.S.A.)
June 28, 2004.
http://www.ag.org/top/

Buddhist Church of America
June 28, 2004.
http://www.buddhistchurchesofamerica.com/

Church of Jesus Christ of Latter-day Saints
June 28, 2004.
http://www.lds.org/

Fuller Theological Seminary
June 28, 2004.
http://www.fuller.edu/

Evangelical nondenominational institution of higher learning.

Roman Catholic Archdiocese of Los Angeles
June 28, 2004.
http://www.la-archdiocese.org/english

Events

Harvest Crusade
Edison International Field
Anaheim, CA
http://www.harvest.org/

Held annually in either July or August
The annual Harvest Crusade attracts local and national media coverage of its eclectic blend of Christian youth culture, including motorcross sports and skateboarding exhibitions along with a contemporary Christian music festival called "Harvest Jam."

Portland Apostolic Faith Camp Meeting
52nd Avenue and Duke Street
Portland, OR 97206
campmeeting@apostolicfaith.org
http://www.apostolicfaith.org/aboutus/camp.asp

Held annually in July
An annual event since 1908, the camp meeting draws visitors from across the country and from around the world to attend its youth services, gospel music, and Bible lessons.

Organizations

Angelus Temple
1100 Glendale Boulevard
Los Angeles, CA 90026
213-484-1100
http://www.angelustemple.org/

Buddhist Peace Fellowship
P. O. Box 3470
Berkeley, CA 94703
http://www.bpf.org/html/home.html

Flower Pentecostal Heritage Center
1445 North Boonville Avenue
Springfield, MO 65802
http://www.agheritage.org/

Fuller Theological Seminary
David du Plessis Archive
135 North Oakland Avenue
Pasadena, CA 91182
http://www.fuller.edu/archive/

Hartford Institute for Religion Research
Hartford Seminary
77 Sherman Street
Hartford, CT 06105
http://hirr.hartsem.edu/

International Church of the Foursquare Gospel
Executive Offices
1910 West Sunset Boulevard, Suite 300
Los Angeles, CA 90026
http://www.foursquare.org/index.cfm

Junipero Serra Museum
2727 Presidio Drive
Presidio Park
San Diego, CA 92103
619-297-3258
http://www.sandiegohistory.org/mainpages/locate4.htm

Kuan Yin Temple
170 North Vineyard Boulevard
Honolulu, HI 96817
808-533-6361
No web site

Buddhist temple.

Laie Hawaii Temple
55-600 Naniloa Loop
Laie, HI 96762
808-293-2427
No web site

Mormon.

Misión San Francisco de Asis (Mission Dolores)
3321 16th Street
San Francisco, CA 94114
415-621-8203
http://www.graphicmode.com/missiondolores/

The Old Church
1422 SW 11th Avenue
Portland, OR 97201
503-222-2031
http://www.oldchurch.org/

Old St. Mary's Catholic Cathedral
660 California Street
San Francisco, CA 94108
415-288-3800
http://www.sfarchdiocese.org/parishes/oldstmary.htm

San Francisco Zen Center
300 Page Street
San Francisco, CA 94102
415-863-3136
http://www.sfzc.com/

St. Michaels' Cathedral
Downtown Sitka
Sitka, AK 99835
907-747-8120
No Web site

Russian Orthodox church.

Vanguard University
Lewis Wilson Institute for Pentecostal Studies
55 Fair Drive
Costa Mesa, CA 92626
http://www.vanguard.edu/wilsoninstitute/

Supports study of Pentecostal and Charismatic movements.

SPORTS AND RECREATION

Mont Christopher Hubbard, Andrea Ross, and Patrick Moser

Diverse in culture, diverse in landforms, diverse in sports—the equation seems logical. Sports frequently are invented in response to place, and for many of the Pacific Region's most popular and long-lived sports, it is true that the culture of recreation has grown out of regional topography. Sports such as hiking, fly-fishing, hunting, sled dog racing, and surfing are intrinsically related to the survival activities of the region's indigenous peoples. Indeed, attitudes toward the land itself have played a major role in the development of sports culture, particularly wilderness sports. As land ethics have changed from conquering to conserving, many wilderness activities have become more aligned with both the practices and beliefs of native cultures, incorporating within their practice a respect for the land and its future. At the same time, some of the region's most competitive sports look at the mountains, rivers, and ocean as a challenge against which competitors can match their skills. Finally, for all the emphasis on recreation in response to place, many of the region's most popular sports are East Coast imports, sports that can be played nearly anywhere at any time, as long as there is room to shape a baseball diamond or build a basketball court.

PRO AND COLLEGIATE SPORTS

The origins of team rivalries vary. Baseball's Dodgers and Giants, once bitter rivals in New York, now equally at odds on the West Coast in Los Angeles and San Francisco, respectively, illustrate how team rivalries can be transplanted along with the team. Most often, however, rivalries are based on geographic proximity, like the long-standing competition between Stanford University and the University of California at Berkeley, situated across the San Francisco Bay from each other.

The most basic of rivalries is that of the West Coast versus the East Coast. One explanation for that rivalry is simply that on each coast sporting experiences are different. Eastern teams have 100-year histories, some of which are bitter, like the Boston Red Sox or Chicago Cubs, and their fans tend to be more tightly wound. Western pro teams are still relatively young, their histories more forgiving. This is not to say that western fans are not passionate about their teams. They can be outright rabid (see the "Black Hole" fan section of the Oakland Raiders), but they do not yet have annals of adversaries that years of competition have created. Another difference results from the width of the country and the time zone differences that broadcasting demands have complicated. Sunday football begins at noon for easterners, but in the West a fan must get up at 9 A.M. to watch the televised game. (Fans in Hawai'i and Alaska must get up even earlier!) With night games, the disadvantage turns to the East. A typical 7:05 P.M. first pitch or tip off in Los Angeles equates to 10:05 P.M. in New York. A normal three-hour game lasts until past 1 A.M. in the morning for easterners.

Broadcasting issues are just one of the results of professional sports' full scale economic thrust. In 1993, professional sports was a $55 billion a year industry. This includes admissions, retail, and television contracts. Even amateur sports are big business now. In 1997–1998 the NCAA alone hauled in $267 million in revenues. Football and basketball coaches at top schools command million dollar salaries, and athletic programs are under constant financial pressure to succeed. Money rules the sports world, including the way it dictates the geography of franchises, with teams leaving cities with waning attendance for greener pastures. The onset of professional sports in the Pacific Region owes much to that geographic/financial dicta, for most sports came to the West for the same reasons that drew explorers, pioneers, and entrepreneurs—the lure of money. In the late 1950s, when baseball's Brooklyn Dodgers and New York Giants relocated to L.A. and San Francisco, the reasons were financial. Officials in both western cities promised greater attendance in newer stadiums than the teams had in New York, and despite heartbreaking pleas from loyal fans, the franchises quickly moved. Giants owner Horace Stoneham's oft-cited response to the disappointed New Yorkers was, "I feel bad about the kids, but I haven't seen many of their fathers lately."

Collectively, these leagues are sometimes called the Big Four. It is no oversight that the states of Alaska and Hawai'i are barely represented in a discussion of professional and collegiate sports in the Pacific Region. The two states have never been home to a major professional franchise. The population of the entire state of Alaska is under 700,000. The largest city, Anchorage, is about 350,000 people. In comparison, the smallest cities with professional teams have around 500,000 people. The addition of metropolitan and outlying areas usually pushes this number up near the million mark, far more than the number of people in the entire state of Alaska. The islands of Hawai'i are more populated, with over 1 million residents.

The distance between Hawai'i and the mainland is an obstacle. Until jet travel in the 1960s, the trip was long and expensive. In 1961 baseball's AAA Pacific Coast League did expand to Honolulu, and a team played in Hawai'i for twenty-seven years. Visiting teams would play extended series, and Honolulu was expected to pay half of the travel expenses to defray costs. Sagging attendance and dilapidated facilities forced the franchise to relocate after 1987. Those twenty-seven years were as close as Hawai'i has come to a major league team. Alaska, meanwhile, has been home to a few minor league hockey teams, currently the Alaska Aces (in Anchorage). In the collegiate world, the University of Hawai'i Rainbow Warriors compete in the Division I Western Athletic Conference, while four other Hawai'i schools (three private institutions—Chaminade, Brigham Young–Hawaii, Hawaii Pacific—and one public—University of Hawai'i at Hilo) are members of the Division II Pacific West Conference. Two Alaskan universities compete in the Great Northwest Athletic Conference, also in Division II—University of Alaska at Anchorage and University of Alaska at Fairbanks.

Baseball

The game of baseball was brought to the Pacific Coast during the California gold rush. In 1859 the Eagles club of San Francisco was formed, competing against various pickup teams. Another San Francisco club, the Pacifics, was organized in 1862, and the two played frequently. When the first enclosed ballpark opened in San Francisco on November 26, 1868, the Eagles beat the Oakland Wide Awakes 37–23. By 1869, there were at least ten baseball clubs just in the city of San Francisco. That year, the Pacific railroad was completed, linking the previously isolated West to the East. Almost immediately, the Pacific got its first taste of "real" baseball when the mighty Cincinnati Red Stockings, the first professional baseball team, headed west to play exhibitions against three San Francisco teams, the Eagles, the Pacifics, and the Atlantics. Fans in the city were optimistic that their clubs could beat the visitors and show the East that the West could play ball. They were mistaken, as in five games the Red Stockings outscored the home favorites 289–22. Still, the visit only helped to further the popularity of the sport, and by the end of the decade, baseball was the most popular pastime in the region, truly becoming the "national sport" all over the nation.

In the following years, baseball spread around the state. A few teams would form a league, play for a year or two, and then disband, only to form a new league with different teams the following year. The quality of play increased, as more teams from the East barnstormed through the West, especially during the winter months when weather was not right for baseball back East. Additionally, more western players left to play in the professional leagues on the East Coast. To counter these losses, minor league teams around the country formed the National Association of Professional Baseball Leagues (NAPBL) in 1901, regulating the operating procedures and preventing major league teams from harvesting their talent. At that time, both the California League (with teams in San Francisco, Oakland, Sacramento, and Los Angeles) and the Pacific Northwest League (PNL—Portland, Seattle, Tacoma, Spokane, Butte, and Helena) were members of the National Association. However, in 1903, the California League left the NAPBL and expanded to Portland and Seattle, competing outside of organized baseball as the Pacific Coast League (PCL). Protesting that its territorial rights had been infringed upon, the Pacific Northwest League retaliated by placing franchises in San Francisco and Los Angeles (and changed its name to the Pacific National League). That season the two leagues competed for fans, often scheduling games on the same day in the same city, in ballparks only blocks from each other. The fans chose the PCL. Four of the eight PNL teams (San Francisco, Los Angeles, Tacoma, and Helena) disbanded during the season, and the Portland club moved to Salt Lake City. What remained was a successful Pacific

Coast League. Impressed by the success of the league, Organized Baseball wooed the PCL and convinced league officials to join the National Association. By 1904 the PCL was a legitimate Class A league.

The Pacific Coast League would remain successful and competitive. The fair weather allowed longer schedules: sometimes as many as 225 games a year, compared to the 154-game seasons in the major leagues, with seasons running from March into late November. At the time, major leaguers were paid meager wages, and since the PCL compensated its players for the extended schedule, it was possible to earn more money playing out West. With the added bonus of better weather and travel conditions, many players chose to stay with the Pacific Coast League. As a result, the quality of play rose to match the best of the Class A leagues.

For the next half century, the PCL survived many events that might have crippled a weaker league. In 1917 as the United States entered World War I, financial difficulties arose—dropping attendance, wartime travel restrictions, and drafted players hit the league hard. But it survived, and the postwar 1919 season arrived with renewed fan interest. In fact, the PCL expanded to eight teams, and each made money that season. The 1920s brought even more fans, with the end of the dead-ball era and the explosion of offense that followed. The decade saw impressive offensive performances; three players hit over .300, and new home run, runs, and runs batted in (RBI) records were set. In 1925, Salt Lake City's Tony Lazzeri (1903–1946) was the first player in the country to hit 60 home runs, albeit in an extended 200-game season. He also batted .355 with 202 runs and 222 RBIs. Two years later, Lazzeri was the starting second baseman for the New York Yankees when Babe Ruth hit 60 home runs himself. The exciting new brand of offense-oriented baseball brought record crowds to the ballparks. This momentum carried over into the 1930s and the Great Depression. While many teams around the country folded and some leagues ended play, the Pacific Coast League remained strong. Admission prices were lowered and expenses cut. In addition, the league began to play night games, catering to the fans who worked during the day. Attendance jumped at every ballpark that installed lights. Another factor that kept the PCL successful was the high level of play. Future Hall

17,500 fans assembled for the opening of Ewing Field, San Francisco's New Baseball Park, on May 16, 1914. Courtesy of the Library of Congress.

of Famers that played in the Coast League during the 1930s included Ted Williams (1918–2002) and Joe DiMaggio (1914–1999). As an eighteen-year-old rookie in 1933, DiMaggio hit safely in 61 consecutive games (eight years later as a Yankee he would set the major league record with a 56-game hitting streak).

The Pacific Coast League weathered the depression and would survive a slump during World War II as well. However, it could not withstand the imminent threat of major league baseball. PCL officials wanted to elevate their league to major league status and threatened to leave organized baseball. Compromises were hammered out, and for six years in the 1950s, the PCL was granted a new "Open" classification, in which the league would not be subject to the major league draft. Some league leaders were hopeful that

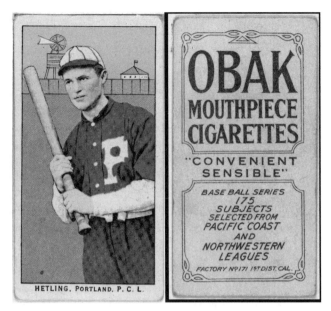

A baseball card for Gus Hetling promoting the Pacific Coast League. These cards were distributed in cigarette packets. Courtesy of the Library of Congress.

they were one step closer to major league status, but it was not to be. In 1957 the Brooklyn Dodgers and the New York Giants were both granted permission by major league baseball to move west and did so the following year to Los Angeles and San Francisco, respectively. The two cities embraced big league ball, but the PCL was irreparably damaged. Los Angeles and San Francisco had been cornerstones of the league since its start. The two franchises (Angels and Seals) moved to Spokane and Phoenix. PCL lost its "Open" classification, returning to AAA, and reduced its schedule to a standard length of 154 games. With clubs

now tightly affiliated with major league teams, players were called up and sent down frequently, and there was no continuity among rosters. Attendance sagged, franchises once again began relocating, and the league fluctuated wildly. For a time the Pacific Coast League had teams as far east as Arkansas and Indianapolis. A team also appeared in Hawai'i, lasting twenty-seven seasons. Today the PCL contains sixteen teams, with only four of them on the West Coast (Sacramento, Fresno, Portland, and Tacoma).

Meanwhile, major league baseball expanded to more West Coast cities. In 1961 Los Angeles gained a second team with the expansion California Angels (named after the former Los Angeles Angels of the PCL). In 1968 the Athletics, one of the oldest American League franchises, moved to Oakland from Kansas City. The next year San Diego and Seattle both received expansion teams, the Padres and Pilots, respectively. Although the Pilots left Seattle for Milwaukee after just one season, major league baseball returned to Seattle in 1977 with the expansion Mariners.

Los Angeles and Oakland had great success in their first three decades out West. The Dodgers won five World Series titles before 1989, and the A's won four, including three in a row in 1972–1974. The only other West Coast team to do so was the Anaheim Angels, who defeated the Giants four games to three in 2002.

Pac-10 College Sports

While baseball got its start on the professional diamond, the sports of basketball and football were popularized at the collegiate level. Football was born on the East Coast at Ivy League schools, where students adapted soccer and rugby into a new game. By the 1890s, football found its way to the West Coast. The University of California at Berkeley (Cal) and Stanford University, two of the few institutions of higher learning out West, played the first college football game on the West Coast in March 1892. The coaches were imported from the East Coast. It was a major event, with a noisy parade preceding the game and $30,000 in proceeds. (Perhaps everyone was too excited—the game was delayed because no one remembered to bring a football.) Through the end of the century, Cal and Stanford played mostly each other, as well as games against semi-pro teams and prep schools. This new sport was popular among the students, but not so with the presidents of the schools, who thought that the violent spectacles sent the wrong message to the students, overshadowing their academics. In 1906, the two universities pulled their football programs and ordered a move to rugby, with other colleges and high schools on the West Coast soon following their lead. Easterners ridiculed this practice. Finally, in 1915 Cal changed its rules and played a football game against the University of Washington. With new rules in place across the country, the game was much safer than before, and by the end of the decade, every school on the West Coast had returned to playing football.

There was a question as to whether the newer programs in the West could compete with the established ones in the East. In 1901, the director of the Pasadena Tournament of Roses proposed a game on New Year's Day to match the best eastern team with the best team. That year, the first Rose Bowl was held, and Michigan trounced Stanford 49-0. During the West Coast's rugby phase, there were no games, but the Rose Bowl returned in 1916. This time the West was victorious, with Washington Agricultural College (later Washington State) defeating Brown. The Rose Bowl would soon become a premier event in college football. The Rose Bowl Stadium, constructed in 1922 in Pasadena, is one of only three stadiums in the country (L.A. Coliseum, Michigan Stadium) with a capacity of over 100,000. It has hosted every Rose Bowl since 1923, except in 1942, following the attack on Pearl Harbor, when Duke University in North Carolina hosted the game (all large gatherings on the West Coast had been canceled). In 1947, the format was changed to pair up the champion of the Pacific Coast Con-

The 1989 World Series

The 1989 World Series was a highly anticipated event, as the Oakland A's and the San Francisco Giants were meeting in the postseason for the first time. It was dubbed "The Bay Bridge Series," after the span connecting the two cities. In fact, the series was anticlimactic, as the powerhouse A's swept the underdog Giants. The series, however, remains memorable not for what happened on the field but what occurred off it. To be more precise, it is what occurred *under* the field that left an indelible mark on baseball history. On October 17, as the teams were being introduced for Game 3 in Candlestick Park, an enormous earthquake struck the Bay Area. Measuring 6.9 on the Richter scale, the quake killed sixty-seven people and caused billions of dollars in property damage. (Fortunately, the ballpark withstood it, and no one there was injured.) The World Series was delayed ten days as the Bay Area tried to recover from the devastating disaster.

ference (PCC; now Pac-10) with that of the Big 10 Conference. That remained the format until 1999 when the Rose Bowl joined with the Sugar, Orange, and Fiesta Bowls in the Bowl Championship Series, with a national championship game pitting the number-one and number-two teams in the country and rotating among the four bowls. The other three pick from the best remaining teams.

Following the West's first Rose Bowl win in 1916, the notion of a vastly superior eastern football was quickly put to rest. The following year Oregon defeated Penn State in the Rose Bowl, and the easterners realized that western football was a force. Coaches imported from the East were building strong programs. Andy Smith came to Cal from Purdue in 1916—five seasons later Cal would be named national champion for the first of three consecutive seasons, running up a 27-1-0 record from 1920 to 1922. Glenn Scobey "Pop" Warner, already a legend in coaching, left Pitt for Stanford in 1924. In Warner's first season in Palo Alto, the Cardinals were undefeated (with a tie against Cal), and during his nine-year tenure, Stanford went 71-17-8, with three Rose Bowl appearances. Perhaps the most influential transplant was Howard Jones, hired at the University of Southern California (USC) in 1925 following eight successful years at Iowa. Jones would coach at Southern California for sixteen seasons, winning three national championships, five Rose Bowls, and seven Pacific Coast Conference titles.

Following a successful period in the 1920s and 1930s, the PCC began to slide in quality. Between 1943 and 1959, PCC teams lost sixteen of seventeen Rose Bowls. After the 1959 season, in the wake of a rules violation scandal involving the University of California at Los Angeles (UCLA) and Washington, the PCC disbanded. Five of the schools (Washington, Cal, Stanford, USC, and UCLA) formed the Amateur Athletic Western Union. Washington State joined a few years later, followed shortly by Oregon and Oregon State. This was the beginning of a renaissance for the newly named Pac-8, led by the USC Trojans. USC won national titles five times between 1962 and 1978 and played in the Rose Bowl seven times in nine years. Also in 1962 Terry Baker of Oregon State University became the first West Coast player to win the Heisman Trophy, awarded to the top player in college football. Including Baker, seven of the twenty Heisman winners between 1962 and 1981 played in the Pac-8. Four of them—Mike Garrett, 1965; O.J. Simpson, 1968; Charles White, 1979; and Marcus Allen, 1981—were USC Trojans.

In 1978 the Pac-8 expanded with the inclusion of Arizona and Arizona State and became the Pac-10. Since its heyday in the 1970s, the Pac-10 has had one national champion (Washington, 1991) and one Heisman Trophy winner (Carson Palmer, USC, 2002). Its national prominence may have faded slightly, but the heart of Pac-10 football has always been the strong intraconference rivalries. There are five sets of geographic, ready-made rivals, battling annually for bragging rights. Most years the rivalry game is the biggest game of the season. In Washington the two universities compete for the Apple Cup. Oregon's annual game is dubbed "the Civil War." USC and UCLA play for the Victory Bell, a bell originally owned by UCLA and stolen by USC pranksters in 1941. But the most storied rivalry is undoubtedly Cal versus Stanford. The "Big Game," as it is called, dates back to 1892 but became an annual event starting in 1919. On November 22, 1924, the largest crowd yet to attend a college football game watched Cal and Stanford play to a 20-20 tie; 76,000 fans crowded into Cal's Memorial Stadium, with another 24,000 on "Tightwad" Hill, which overlooked the stadium. In 1982 the Big Game ended with one of the most memorable and unique plays in college football history. After a field goal, Stanford led 20-19 with only four seconds left on the clock. Their kickoff was returned to around midfield, where it appeared that the Cal player was tackled to end the game. The Stanford band stormed the field in celebration. However, the Cal player had lateraled the ball to a teammate, and the play was continuing. Cal players lateraled four more times, avoiding Stanford tacklers and band members on their way to the end zone, scoring the game-winning touchdown and flattening a Stanford trombone player in the process. "The Play" immediately became a piece of Pac-10 and college football legend.

Pro Football

The first American Football League (AFL), founded in 1926, lasted just one season but long enough to give the West Coast its first pro football team in the Los Angeles Wildcats. When the AFL returned in 1936, L.A. received a franchise, the Wildcats. Los Angeles won the AFL championship in 1937. The league quickly folded again, and when it returned for another brief, two-year life in 1940–1941, it did not include any western franchises. A decade after their last team, Los Angeles became the new home of a National Football League (NFL) franchise when the Rams moved from Cleveland in 1946. The same year, another fledgling league, the All-America Football Conference (AAFC), was born and placed a franchise in San Francisco, calling it the 49ers in honor of the first year of the gold rush in California.

In 1950 the AAFC merged into the NFL. The AFL reemerged in 1960 with eight teams, including the Oakland Raiders and the Los Angeles Chargers. After one season the Chargers moved to San Diego, where they were AFL champions in 1963. In 1966 the champions of the NFL and the AFL began playing in the "Super Bowl" to determine one champion. The first Super Bowl was held on January 15, 1967, in the L.A. Coliseum, in front of almost 62,000 people. Since that time, the Super Bowl has become one of the largest and most anticipated sporting events in the United States, with millions of dollars in ticket sales and advertising revenues. The West Coast has hosted it ten times (five times in Pasadena; twice at the L.A. Coliseum; twice in San Diego; and once in Palo Alto, California). Every year it is one of the most anticipated and watched programs on television. In 1985, the year it was held at Stanford (in Palo Alto), the Super Bowl was the most watched live telecast in history (at the time).

In 1970 the AFL and NFL officially merged, leaving four West Coast teams: the San Francisco 49ers, the Oakland Raiders, the Los Angeles Rams, and the San Diego Chargers. The 49ers and the Chargers have stayed where they are since. In 1982, the Raiders moved from Oakland to Los Angeles, where they

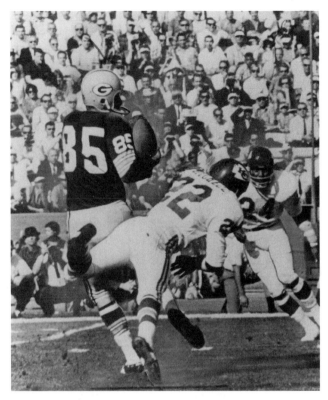

Green Bay Packers play Kansas City Chiefs in the first Super Bowl on January 15, 1967, in the L.A. Coliseum in front of almost 62,000 people. Courtesy of the Library of Congress.

spent thirteen seasons before moving back to Oakland in 1995. The Rams also left Los Angeles in 1995, relocating to St. Louis and leaving L.A. without a pro football team for the first time in fifty years. The fourth team on the West Coast is the Seattle Seahawks—they joined the NFL in 1976.

Arguably, the Oakland Raiders have been the most successful of the four. In the thirty-year period from 1963 through 1992, the Raiders had the highest winning percentage of any NFL team (.661)—in fact, of *any* major sports team—and won three Super Bowls, in 1976, 1980, and 1983. However, in recent years the most successful of the West Coast teams has been the San Francisco 49ers. In the 1980s and early 1990s, they dominated the NFL, winning four Super Bowls and changing the face of the game. Until then, offenses in the league were oriented around the running game, and teams ran the ball far more than they threw it. The 49ers head coach Bill Walsh (1931–) began using a system that emphasized short quick passes. The attack became known as the "West Coast offense," and it was hugely successful: The 49ers won Super Bowls in 1982, 1985, 1989, and 1990 under Walsh and star quarterback Joe Montana (1956–). In 1995, the 49ers became the first NFL team to win the Super Bowl five times. Today, about half of the teams in the NFL run some variant of the West Coast offense.

Although California and Washington remain the only Pacific states with NFL teams, pro football does make its way to Hawai'i once a year. Since 1971 Honolulu has hosted the Pro Bowl, the NFL all-star game held one week after the Super Bowl. In May 2004, NFL team owners agreed to keep the Pro Bowl in Hawai'i at least through 2009.

Pro Basketball

A few years after Los Angeles and San Francisco welcomed major league baseball teams, basketball teams relocated to the West, with the Minneapolis Lakers moving to L.A. in 1960 and the Philadelphia Warriors moving to San Francisco two years later. With the Warriors came star center Wilt "the Stilt" Chamberlain (1936–1999). In only his fourth season, Chamberlain had already become a dominant force in the game. In the 1962–1963 season, the first on the West Coast for the Warriors, Chamberlain averaged 44.8 points and 24.3 rebounds per game, both marks leading the league. In just their second season out west, the Warriors advanced to the finals, where they lost to the Boston Celtics, in a matchup between dominant centers: Chamberlain was pitted against Celtics star Bill Russell (1934–   ). (Russell had his own previous West Coast glory—at the University of San Francisco in 1954–1956—Russell led the Dons to fifty-five consecutive wins and two straight national titles.) However, after the Warriors traded Chamberlain back to the Philadelphia 76ers (formerly the Syracuse Nationals) in the middle of the 1964–1965 season, San Francisco finished in last place. They quickly rebounded and in just two seasons played again for the championship. And whom did they face? Wilt Chamberlain and the 76ers, who defeated the Warriors in six games. Following that year, the Warriors began to falter. The franchise had attendance problems and was losing money. In 1971 they moved across the Bay to Oakland, calling themselves the "Golden State" Warriors. Except for a surprise championship run in 1975, the team has not returned to the finals and has endured many losing seasons as of late.

While the Warriors experienced their decline, the Los Angeles Lakers were on the rise. Throughout the 1960s the Lakers were quite successful behind future Hall of Famers Elgin Baylor (1935–   ) and Jerry West (1938–   ) but could never win a championship, losing *six* times in the finals to the Boston Celtics. In 1968, after the fifth such loss, the Lakers upgraded at the center position by acquiring the only player who could match up with the Celtics' Bill Russell—Wilt Chamberlain returned to the West Coast in a trade with the 76ers. Although the Lakers lost again to the Celtics that year, Chamberlain would soon help turn them into champions. In the 1971–1972 season, the Lakers won sixty-nine games and lost only thirteen, the best record ever at the time. At one point in the season they won thirty-three straight games, still an American professional sports record. They stormed through the playoffs, losing just three games, and defeating the New York Knicks to win their first championship on the West Coast. Chamberlain was named the Most Valuable Player (MVP) of the series. The following season the Lakers again reached the finals but were defeated by the Knicks. At the end of the season, at age thirty-seven, Chamberlain retired, as did West a year later. In 1975, the Lakers would miss the postseason for the first time in seventeen years.

Again, however, they would acquire a dominant center, this time in the form of Kareem Abdul-Jabbar (1947–   ) from the Milwaukee Bucks. Abdul-Jabbar was the league MVP his first two years as a Laker, but the team could not reach the finals. However, in 1979 they drafted a guard out of Michigan State University (MSU) named Earvin "Magic" Johnson (1959–). Johnson was coming off a national championship during which he was thrust into the national spotlight, along with Larry Bird (1956–) of Indiana State University, whose team lost to MSU in the National Collegiate Athletic Association (NCAA) finals. Johnson's impact on the Lakers was immediate. In the 1979–1980 season, the team went 60-22, leading the Pacific Division. Abdul-Jabbar turned in one of his best seasons and won the MVP award, his third as a Laker. While Abdul-Jabbar carried the team during the season, Johnson was the hero in the playoffs. Having breezed into the finals, the Lakers met the 76ers, splitting the first four games. L.A. won game 5 but lost Abdul-Jabbar, who sprained his ankle. In game 6, twenty-year-old rookie guard Johnson started at center in Abdul-Jabbar's place. In one of the greatest performances in National Basketball Association (NBA) playoff history, Johnson scored 42 points, grabbed fifteen rebounds, and passed for seven assists, leading the Lakers to a 123-107 victory and the championship. He was named MVP of the finals.

Over the next eight years, the Lakers appeared in the finals six times, winning four more championships. Their squad, led by Johnson, was nicknamed "Showtime" because of their exciting style of play. The popularity of the Lakers helped boost the NBA to new heights.

Abdul-Jabbar retired after the 1989 season, in which the Lakers lost in the finals to the Detroit Pistons. Johnson shocked the basketball world two years later when, before the 1991–1992 season, he announced that he had contracted HIV (human immunodeficiency virus) and would retire at age thirty-two. He returned to coach the Lakers for half of the 1993–1994 season. Then, midway through the 1995–1996 season, he came out of retirement and rejoined the team. L.A. made the playoffs but fell to the Houston Rockets. The Showtime Era finally ended, as Johnson retired for the second and final time following the playoffs.

The current incarnation of the Los Angeles Lakers began that offseason when they acquired yet another dominating center, Shaquille O'Neal. They also drafted eighteen-year-old Kobe Bryant out of high school. Bryant soon blossomed into a superstar with O'Neal, and in 2000, the Lakers returned to the

Kareem Abdul-Jabbar reaches over backwards to score, 1967. Courtesy of the Library of Congress.

UCLA Men's Basketball Dynasty

Dynasties are a part of sports. Strong teams will arise and dominate for a time. How long a team must do so to be called a "dynasty" is debatable, but none can argue that one began at UCLA in 1964. In March the Bruins' men's basketball team completed a perfect season (30-0), capped off by their first NCAA championship. It would not be their last. The following twelve seasons brought a remarkable ten championships to UCLA. How did UCLA remain so dominant for such a long period? All the credit goes to Coach John Wooden (1910–   ). Considered one of the greatest coaches of any era, the Wizard of Westwood (named after the neighborhood surrounding UCLA) preached his Pyramid of Success, based on conditioning, fundamental skills, and teamwork. (Wooden taught as much off the court as on and took great pride in molding not just good basketball players but good citizens.) Under his tutelage, UCLA set NCAA records likely never to be broken, including seven championships in a row, eighty-eight consecutive victories, and thirty-eight straight NCAA tournament wins. He also coached and developed future NBA Hall of Famers such as Gail Goodrich, Lew Alcindor (later known as Kareem Abdul-Jabbar), and Bill Walton.

top, with the first of three straight championships. They continue to reside among the elite teams in the league.

While Los Angeles has enjoyed the majority of the NBA success, other West Coast teams have tasted victory. In 1977, the Portland Trailblazers, with former UCLA Bruin Bill Walton, became the third West Coast team to win a championship, doing so in their seventh season of existence. Two years later, the Seattle Supersonics (who joined the league in 1967) were champions, following a runner-up finish the previous year. Although each franchise has only one championship, they have both been relatively successful, with numerous winning seasons and playoff appearances.

The other West Coast teams have not been as fortunate. San Diego first had a team in the late 1960s with the Rockets, but they moved to Houston in 1971 after four mediocre seasons. In 1978 basketball returned with the relocated Boston Braves. Changing their name to the Clippers, the team struggled for six years, both with wins and attendance, before moving north to Los Angeles. The move did little to increase success. They endured twelve straight losing seasons before finally breaking .500 and making the playoffs in 1991–1992. They have not had a winning season since, although they did make the playoffs in 1993 and 1997.

The Sacramento Kings, too, have a sorry history. Relocating from Kansas City before the 1985–1986 season, they proceeded to run off thirteen consecutive losing campaigns to begin their Sacramento era. However, while the L.A. Clippers battled with poor attendance, the Sacramento fans doggedly supported their team. They were finally rewarded in 1999 with a winning season and playoff appearance. Since then, the Kings have made the playoffs each year and sported the league's best record in 2001–2002 (61-21), setting the franchise record for wins in the process.

There is also a women's basketball league, the Women's National Basketball Association (WNBA), which started play in the summer of 1997. The WNBA is owned and supported by the NBA. Currently there are thirteen franchises, including teams in Seattle (Storm), Sacramento (Monarchs), and Los Angeles (Sparks). The Sparks were champions of the league in 2001 and 2002. Although it is certainly too early to say, the WNBA seems primed to succeed, especially with the support of the NBA.

Pro Hockey

Of the four professional sports, hockey has the smallest following in the United States. This is not surprising. Hockey, of course, is a cold weather sport and took hold first in Canada in the latter part of the nineteenth century. The first professional league was wholly composed of Canadian teams. Only in the eighth year of the National Hockey League (NHL) (1925–1926) did the first franchise appear in the United States (Boston Bruins). Until 1967 the NHL was still a small league and had no teams west of the Mississippi River. Just as it was the last of the four major leagues to put down roots in the United States, so was the NHL the last to move west, doing so finally in its 1967 expansion. The league doubled in size, adding six new teams, including two on the West Coast—the Los Angeles Kings and the California (Oakland) Seals. Another team, the Los Angeles Sharks, arrived in 1972 courtesy of the fledgling World Hockey League (WHL), but after only two seasons, the Sharks left L.A. for warmer waters (Michigan). San Diego received a WHL franchise, the Mariners, in 1974, but it, too, had a short life when the WHL itself folded in 1979. Meanwhile, the California Seals had moved to Cleveland in 1976, leaving the West Coast with the L.A. Kings as their only professional hockey franchise. It would remain so for fifteen years, until the NHL introduced expansion teams in San Jose (Sharks) and Anaheim (Mighty Ducks) in 1991 and 1992, respectively. None of the NHL teams on the West Coast have ever won the Stanley Cup, though Anaheim and Los Angeles have advanced to the finals. Still, for a time California attracted the attention of the hockey world. In 1988, in a blockbuster trade, L.A. acquired Wayne Gretsky (1961–   ) from the Edmonton Oilers. Gretsky, whose nickname was simply "The Great One," was considered by many to be the greatest hockey player ever. He played for the Kings for most of eight seasons, during which time he broke Gordie Howe's (1928–   ) records for most career goals and most career points. By the time he retired after the 1999 season, Gretsky held or shared sixty-one NHL scoring records, some by absurd margins—his number of career assists (1,962) is more than 800 higher than second most (Paul Coffey—1,102).

The NHL on the West Coast may only date back to 1967, but hockey itself has a deeper history here. In fact, unlike the other sports, some of hockey's first professional franchises in the United States were west of the Rocky Mountains. Founded in 1911 by two former National Hockey Association players, the Pacific Coast Hockey Association (PCHA) began with three Canadian teams but added a team in Portland in 1915 and followed in successive years with teams in Seattle and Spokane. These were the first professional hockey teams on the West Coast. (A small semiprofessional league sprang up in California in 1928 with teams in Oakland, San Francisco, Los Angeles, and Hollywood, but it died after five seasons.) At the time, there were two hockey leagues, the PCHA and the National Hockey Association (NHA) (which would eventually become the NHL). Beginning in 1914, the champions of each league played each other for the championship and the Stanley Cup. In 1916, the Portland Rosebuds became the first American team to compete for the Stanley Cup but fell to the Montreal Canadiens. However, the following year the Seattle Metropolitans defeated Montreal and brought the Cup to the United States for the first time (a decade before the New York Rangers became the first American NHL team to win it). However, by the mid-1920s, the

Portland, Seattle, and Spokane teams had folded, and the remaining Canadian teams in the PCHA merged with the Western Canadian Hockey League. Professional hockey would not return to the West Coast for over forty years.

Today, although it has no NHL teams, the Pacific Northwest is home to five franchises that play in the Western Hockey League, an arm of the Canadian Hockey League, which is a professional league that mainly serves as a minor league for the NHL. The teams in the Northwest are the Portland Winterhawks, the Seattle Thunderbirds, the Spokane Chiefs, the Everett Silvertips, and the Tri-City Americans. In addition, there are four teams in California (Bakersfield, Fresno, Long Beach, and San Diego) and one team in Alaska (Anchorage) that are members of the East Coast Hockey League (ECHL), a minor development league in cooperation with the NHL. As of yet, there are no pro hockey teams in Hawai'i.

Not all professional sports in the Pacific Region carry the weight of coastal rivalry and generational associations with schools or cities. While surfing is clearly the quintessential regional sport, its "playing field" spanning all states and islands within the region, a number of other sports have developed in response to the unique climatological and geographical qualities of the region.

WILDERNESS RECREATION IN THE PACIFIC REGION

Early California mountaineer and conservationist John Muir (1838–1914) begins his classic book *The Mountains of California*, published in 1894: "Go where you may within the bounds of California, mountains are ever in sight, charming and glorifying every landscape."[1] From his statement one might extrapolate that the volcanic chain stretching from California to Alaska has a deep, if sometimes subtle, impact on those who live in the Pacific Western states; everywhere one looks, there are mountains—and hence mountaineers, rock climbers, backpackers, hikers, and river rafters. Yet despite its seeming plethora of wild lands, Robert Hass, former U.S. Poet Laureate and wilderness enthusiast, believes that "California is the most engineered landscape in the country; everyone who grew up in California has an elegy inside themselves about how this landscape looked when they were growing up."[2] Perhaps because of the prevailing "engineered" landscape, people take to the mountains in an attempt to regain a sense of the wild, and as a result, wilderness recreation is epidemic in the western states. As use of public lands becomes heavier, recreation areas become more crowded, and the landscape grows more impacted by humans. Some environmentalists argue that especially in densely populated California, the wilderness is being loved to death. Nonetheless, individuals continue to head outdoors for many reasons: to test their strength against the elements, to search for a feeling of wholeness in their lives, to clear their minds, and like the proverbial bear who went over the mountain, simply to see what they can see. Since mountains dominate the visual experience of all those who live in the Pacific states, they loom large in the collective unconscious. Even those who do not participate in outdoor recreation have an experience unique to the western states—as a constant backdrop, mountains are built into the psyche; they are burned onto the cerebral cortex.

Furthermore, the idea of the individual against the elements is iconic in the Pacific Region, as westerners are known as pioneers and adventurers, those willing to leave behind "civilization" to explore the wilds, both physical and psychological. Thus, the ways they test themselves in the wild become metaphors for how they survive quotidian challenges.

One outgrowth of this cultural connection to mountains is the long history of wilderness experience being paired with literary endeavors. Adventures beg to be written down, and written transcripts of adventures not only formalize them but enable others to live the experience vicariously and give the author a forum to brag. They also create a cultural bond; they help individuals define who they are in relation to the environment. Many western adventurers, both novice and accomplished, such as John Muir, Clarence King, Margaret Murie (1902–2003), Gary Snyder (1930–), Jack London (1876–1916), and Jack Kerouac (1922–1969), have immortalized their wilderness experiences in writing.

John Muir, full-length portrait, facing right, seated on rock with lake and trees in background, 1902. Courtesy of the Library of Congress.

Clarence King (1842–1901), one of the early California mountaineers, was a geology student at Yale in 1862 when he heard that Josiah Dwight Whitney and William Brewer of the California Geological Survey had summitted Mount Shasta in order to determine the mountain's height. Soon after, King set out on horseback for California to volunteer as an assistant with the California Geological Survey, climbing and measuring summits in the Sierra Nevada with Whitney and Brewer. Although he was not the first person to summit the mountain, he named the highest mountain in the continental United States Mount Whitney (14,494 feet), after the survey's director. King himself became the first director of the U.S. Geological Survey (USGS) in 1880. In 1872 he published his major work *Mountaineering in the Sierra Nevada*, which Pulitzer Prize–winning author Wallace Stegner later called "the most delightful book of its decade."[3] King's book is a blend of geology, scenery, action, and ideas, with much emphasis on harrowing details of his expeditions, many of which are thought to be literary embellishments.

John Muir's writing, on the other hand, is known for its understated treatment of the travails of his wilderness travel and laudatory, odelike descriptions of the landscapes he traveled during his extensive exploration of the mountains of the Pacific West. Muir was known to travel with very little gear; sometimes a blanket with bread rolled up in it was all that he carried for multiday expeditions. Muir was born in Scotland, then immigrated with his family to Wisconsin in 1849. He studied geology and botany at the University of Wisconsin, Madison, for two years; then in September 1867 he set out on a 1,000-mile walk from Indiana to Florida, after which he traveled to California, arriving in San Francisco in 1868. He walked for six weeks across the state of California to the Sierra Nevada mountains to take a job as a part-time sheepherder. While living in the remote mountains, he developed a deep, spiritual engagement with them and consequently dubbed them "The Range of Light." After California, Muir traveled to Alaska and wrote about its wonders in *Travels in Alaska* (1915). He published several other books about his travels, beginning in 1894 with *The Mountains of the Sierra Nevada*, which fostered in its readers an interest in the environment and its conservation. Muir became politically active on behalf of wild lands and thus was instrumental in the designation of Yosemite, Sequoia, Mount Rainier, the Petrified Forest, and Grand Canyon as national parks. He cofounded the Sierra Club in 1892 and served as its president until his death in 1914. Many of California's backcountry treasures are named in his honor, including the John Muir Wilderness, John Muir Trail, and Muir Woods National Park Monument.

While many of the first mountaineers in the Pacific Region were men, such as King and Muir, women also participated in the nascent days of mountain sports. When one thinks of mountaineering in the late nineteenth and early twentieth centuries, images of men come to mind—on skis, snowshoes, on belay, and on foot, making first ascents, exploring, and mapping uncharted territory. Yet in July 1894, 193 people summited Oregon's Mount Hood during the Mazamas Mountain Club's inaugural climb, and 38 of those people were women. An interest in fitness in the late 1800s and the advent of the bicycle as a popular sport in the 1890s aided popular acceptance of women's participation in sports and mountaineering. Similarly, beginning in the late 1960s, women began moving even more freely outdoors due to the second wave of the feminist movement, an increased emphasis on physical well-being, and innovations in gear that lightened the physical load.

There is no single reason women take to the backcountry, but as Ann Zwinger, author and natural historian, asserts, "I don't like being cold, wet, tired and hungry, but the irony is that being so evokes qualities of endurance I didn't know I had. It concentrates my powers of observation and intensifies the experience. It rearranges my relationship to the world and generates a different approach to thinking and to writing."[4] Many adventure travel companies offer women-only excursions. Many women prefer the noncompetitive, nonthreatening milieu of an all-women's expedition. They find their skills, such as campcraft, navigation, or paddling technique, improve more rapidly than on mixed-gender expeditions, as they are able to learn without competing with men who may have had more exposure to wilderness travel and may have more confidence and experience.

One early female backcountry traveler was Margaret "Mardy" Murie. Murie was born in Seattle, Washington, but moved with her family at the age of nine to Fairbanks, Alaska, where in 1924 she became the first female graduate of the University of Alaska. Soon after she married Olaus Murie, a wildlife biologist, and they honeymooned by dog sled in the Alaskan backcountry. She spent much time alone and with her children in the wilds of Alaska's Brooks Range while her husband was out tracking the herds of caribou that he studied; her book *Two in the Far North* (1962) is a reflection on her adventures in Alaska with her husband. She also published *Island Between* (1977) and *Wapiti Wilderness* (1987). Murie was a fierce defender of wild lands, and in 1960, along with her husband, she was instrumental in establishing the Alaska National Wildlife Refuge, a 20-million-acre preserve.

Mountaineering

Mountaineering is the sport of mountain climbing over difficult terrain, requiring the use of safety equipment such as ropes, ice axes, and crampons. Mountaineering in the Pacific states developed as people wanted to explore progressively steeper and more remote areas of the backcountry. While historically mountaineers were interested in "conquering" mountains, there is also a more philosophical aspect to the sport, as many feel that mountaineering is an act of conquering the self. Others feel that to successfully climb a mountain, the mountain itself must be a member of their team, an entity to be consulted in all expeditionary decisions. One such mountain is Mount McKinley, or Denali Peak, in Alaska. At 20,320 feet, Denali Peak is the highest in North America, a massif of 10,000 square miles of rock and ice. The first verified summit of the mountain was made in the spring of 1912 by a group of local mountaineers. Upon summitting, they found evidence on a lower peak of the mountain of a prior party of Alaskans known as the "Sourdoughs," whose claims to the summit of the North Peak of Denali in 1910 had, until then, been disputed. Decades later, in 1965, female mountaineer Arlene Blum applied to join an Alaskan expedition but was turned down due to the prevailing belief of the time that women had neither the emotional stability nor the physical strength to climb high mountains. Yet five years later, Blum proved her doubters wrong and led the first all-women's expedition up Mount McKinley.

Rock Climbing

The sport of rock climbing is an outgrowth of mountaineering, employing similar techniques but focusing solely on the ascent of steep rock surfaces that cannot be climbed safely without taking measures to protect the climber in the event of a fall. There are several categories of climbing, including soloing, free climbing, and aid climbing: To solo is to climb without protection of rope or anchors. Free climbing is climbing using only holds provided by the rock. Free climbers use ropes and anchor for protection but not to assist the climber in ascending the rock, as opposed to aid climbing, in which the climber uses the anchors and ropes themselves to ascend.

Modern rock climbing arrived in the Sierra Nevada in force in the early 1930s: Climber Robert Underhill joined a group of Sierra Club climbers in the High Sierra after mountaineering and rock climbing in the Tetons. In 1931, he and four others undertook and completed the ascent of the longest, steepest face of Mount Whitney. Independently of the Mount Whitney climb, Dick Leonard, a law student in the San Francisco Bay area, began practicing climb-

"The Last Great Race on Earth"

Known as "The Last Great Race on Earth," the Iditarod is a trail dog sled race held annually in Alaska. Over 1,000 miles long, the race begins in Anchorage and ends in Nome, drawing mushers from all over the world. The Iditarod commemorates a historic sled run in 1925 to save the town of Nome from a diphtheria epidemic. Twenty dog teams raced serum from Nenana to Nome, a distance of 674 miles, in just under twenty-eight hours. In 1967 the first Iditarod race was organized by Dorothy Page and Joe Redington, Sr., to preserve sled dog culture; in 1973 the race was expanded to its present course—the Iditarod Trail, a mail and supply route used during the gold rush days. The race begins on the first Saturday in March; entrants typically begin to arrive in Nome ten and a half days later and continue to arrive for another week and a half. The race draws people from all walks of life, each with his or her own reason for combatting the elements. Anywhere from fifty-five to seventy-five mushers compete each year for more than half a million dollars in prize money. Men and women, as well as amateurs and professionals, compete against each other and all are supported by an army of volunteers.

ing and safety techniques with some friends at Indian Rock, a steep formation in the Berkeley Hills. This group came to be known as the Cragmont climbers. As their skills and confidence grew, some of them, including Leonard, Jules Eichorn, and Bestor Robinson, decided to try their hand at rock climbing in the Sierra Nevada, with their sights set on Yosemite Valley's Cathedral Spires. In 1934 they made a first ascent of Higher Spire, and modern rock climbing in Yosemite was born. Another of this group was mountaineer and climber David Brower (1912–2000), who also pioneered some of the first rock climbs in Yosemite Valley in the early 1930s. Brower went on to become a conservation leader; he was the executive director of the Sierra Club from 1952 to 1969 and formed Friends of the Earth and the League of Conservation Voters in 1969 and Earth Island Institute in 1982. He is also the subject of environmental writer John McPhee's book *Encounters with the Archdruid* (1990).

The sport of rock climbing in Yosemite Valley grew in popularity until a veritable microculture developed and took hold in the now-famous campground known as Camp 4. Camp 4 became a city of climbers, with its own rules and ethics, who lived there for extended periods while climbing various routes throughout the valley.

Rock climbing also became popular in Oregon, Washington, and more recently, Hawai'i. For decades, climbers have scaled the crags of Oregon's Hood River Valley, Willamette Valley, and the Three Sisters Mountains. One stellar Oregon climbing spot is Smith Rock State Park in central Oregon, an impressive formation of volcanic tuff. Modern rock climbing in Hawai'i developed later than on the mainland, and most of the climbing spots known to the general public occur on the island of Oahu. These routes were first discovered by climbers and developed as climbing areas beginning in the 1980s, some as recently as 2001. The climbing community in Hawai'i has had a difficult time gaining access rights to climbing areas on the islands, so they admonish all would-be climbers to "malama ka aina"—respect, honor, and preserve the land.

Despite its popularity, for decades climbing remained a male-centric sport with a very macho reputation. However, in the late 1960s, a gradual shift began to take place. Beverly Johnson (1947–1994) was one of the first women climbers to enter this male culture, and climber Tom Carter calls her "the first woman to command the respect of men in a male-dominated kingdom."[5] Gradually, more women entered the climbing world and found themselves able to climb as well as—or in some cases, better than—male climbers: A fit woman's higher ratio of muscle to body weight can enable her to climb more difficult routes than a fit, yet heavier, man.

The 1980s were a boom period in women's climbing: In August 1987, *Climbing* magazine came out with its first women's issue. Lynn Hill emerged as a preeminent climber. Her first free ascent of The Nose, a difficult, sustained route on El Capitan in Yosemite, and her subsequent one-day free climb of it "secured her place in the elite of climbing."[6] Since then, climbing magazines have portrayed Hill climbing some of the hardest rock routes but have also included pictures of her in an evening gown and even in a wedding veil. In climber Nancy Kerrebrock's words, "[T]he message is clear: we are ready to accept as a standard of attractiveness and femininity a woman who can outcrank most of the men on the planet."[7]

Skiing

Unlike climbing, the allure of skiing is to descend, rather than to ascend. Skiing in the West grew up independently of the rest of the country. In California it was first popular in the mining camps of the gold rush. During the 1850s and 1860s, miners who worked in the high country used skis for transportation. Additionally, "doctors made rounds on skis when all else failed, . . . marriages and funerals required ski travel, and ladies did shopping and visiting on skis."[8] Perhaps the first ski lift in the country was composed of the ore buckets at the Johnsonville Mine, whose owners allowed members of the public to ride in the buckets on Sundays during the 1880s. On days when the snow was too deep to do mining work, the miners planned ski "race meetings," which offered large purses for the winners and side betting for anyone who wished to wager.

By 1911 the Lake Tahoe area was already known as a resort for city people, and clubs formed in the 1920s with emphasis on cross-country, or Nordic, ski trips and ski jumping for men. Modern downhill, or Alpine, skiing began to take hold in 1945 after World War II; long heavy skis gave way to shorter, lighter, more maneuverable versions, and the first Alpine resorts such as Sugar Bowl were built. A galvanizing moment in western ski history was the advent of the 1960 Winter Olympics, held at the then-little-known Squaw Valley ski resort near Lake Tahoe. It was the first Winter Olympics in the United States since 1932, and until shortly before the opening ceremonies there was very little snow on-site. Fortunately, the weather changed at the last minute, and a blizzard descended on the area, dropping much-needed snow just in time for the games to begin.

Unlike the ski resorts in California, Washington and Oregon ski resorts rarely experience a lack of snow. The terrain in Washington offers diversity and challenge for any level of skier, and skiing opportunities and resorts are found from Mount Baker, in the north, to Olympic National Park in the west, to Mount Rainier and Mount Saint Helens in the south. Oregon boasts its share of ski areas, such as the spectacular Mount Hood, featuring some of the driest snow in the Northwest, and Mount Bachelor, located southwest of the city of Bend in central Oregon.

Today, Alpine skiing remains a triumphantly popular sport, while Nordic skiing and Telemarking, an older technique of free-heel downhill skiing, have enjoyed a renaissance over the past several decades. Snowboarding, a snow sport that employs the balance and maneuvering techniques of surfing with the use of a wide, short platform, has become extremely popular throughout the West since the early 1980s. To commemorate ski culture, the Western Skisport Museum at Donner Pass, near Lake Tahoe, portrays the history of ski recreation in California.

Backpacking, Car Camping, and Day Hiking

While not everyone in the Pacific Region is a mountaineer or rock climber, many have been on some kind of camping trip, hike, or backpacking excursion. Since the 1960s and the advent of highways, the popularity of outdoor leisure activities for the average citizen has been on the rise. The Pacific West is rich in public lands, and hiking with friends or family to a waterfall, creek, or other natural attraction is a common pastime on weekends and holidays. State and national parks and other public entities manage and maintain campsites for those who wish to spend time outdoors without carrying all their supplies with them in a pack. These organizations also often sponsor guided hikes and discovery walks that focus on local flora and fauna or other items of interest regarding local natural history.

Additionally, vast networks of backcountry trails have been developed on public lands for those seeking a somewhat more rugged experience. Backpackers carry with them everything they need for a multiday trip, including tents, sleeping gear, clothing, and food, and set out on the trails to explore the forests, deserts, and mountain ranges of the Pacific West. The longest and most famous backpacking trail in the region is the Pacific Crest Trail, which extends from the Mexican border to the Canadian border through California, Oregon, and Washington and covers 2,650 miles. In recent years, about 300 people attempt to "through-hike," or hike the entire length of the trail, per year, and approximately 60 percent of those through-hikers complete the trip, which takes five to six months of hiking approximately 20 miles per day.[9] The Pacific Crest Trail can be accessed at many points by road and can thus be enjoyed also by those wishing to walk it for a day hike or shorter backpacking trip.

Water-related Sports

Fly-fishing

Fly-fishing has become increasingly popular over the last couple of decades and currently enjoys much popularity throughout the West. To fly-fish, the weight of the line is used to carry the nearly weightless fly to the fish. This technique requires practice, and some fly-fishing aficionados liken the technique to a kind of meditation, due to its focused, contemplative nature. Fly-fishing is popular throughout the rivers of the West but is especially popular in Alaska, where all kinds of fishing are prevalent, and fish are abundant. Alaska fly-fishers even have a mentorship program, providing casting lessons, information of fish biology, angling ethics, and fishing safety to local youths. This program originated because many Alaskan fly-fishers expressed interest in passing on the affection they have for Alaska and the ethics every good fisher applies.

Furthermore, fly-fishing has become very popular among women, and many women's fly-fishing companies have cropped up, offering safe and supportive environments in which women can improve their fly-fishing skills. There is even an International Women Fly Fishers Organization, which promotes such programs as urban in-school aquatics projects in Alaska; the Steelhead Restoration Project in California; and Casting for Recovery (CFR), a nonprofit organization that teaches breast cancer survivors to fly-fish, with the aims of reducing swelling and restoring mobility compromised by surgery.

Kayaking, Rafting, and Canoeing

Bounded by the Pacific Ocean, and veined through by countless rivers and streams, Hawai'i, Alaska, Washington, Oregon, and California are prime locations for boating. Sea kayaking is especially popular as it does not require much technical skill yet allows travel to otherwise inaccessible places of extraordinary beauty.

The sea kayaker has a front-row seat for viewing marine life such as sea otters, porpoises, dolphins, seals, sea lions, and whales. One favorite sea kayaking destination is Washington's San Juan Islands, where orcas are often sighted.

While sea kayakers take to the relatively calm waters of marine bays and sounds, river rafters and river kayakers tend to seek the fast-moving whitewater of rivers and creeks. Such whitewater is found in abundance in the rivers of Alaska including the Wind River and the Stikine River, among many others. Washington boasts many rivers to boat, such as the Nooksack, Skagit, Green, Wetatchee, and Snykomish. Oregon, too, has much whitewater, including runs on the Deschutes, Klamath, Umpqua, and Rogue. And California, though desertlike throughout much of the state, offers boating on the American, Stanislaus, Tuolumne, and Merced rivers.

In addition to this myriad of wilderness sports, a number of professional and semiprofessional sports have taken advantage of the region's temperate weather. Thus, tennis, a European sport that arrived in the Pacific via the east coast and, particularly, Florida, has long been popular as a high school and college sport. Most recently, however, with the emergence of the Arthur Ashe Safe Passage Foundation Tennis Program, established in 1990 to reach at-risk youth, and the international fame of Compton, California natives Serena and Venus Williams, more tennis players from the region are seeking professional status. Similarly, golfers have long flocked to world famous courses in Hawai'i and California, as well as lesser known but highly popular courses in Oregon and Washington. Monterey, California's Del Monte Gold Course opened in the 1890s and held the Pacific Coast Open in 1901. Pebble Beach, also in Monterey, with three courses of varying—including the challenging Spyglass Hill course—all with views of the ocean if not actually on the ocean, is one of the most famous golf courses in the world. Across the Pacific, the Mauna Kea Golf Course, on the Big Island was designed by Robert Trent Jones, Sr., who also designed Spyglass Hill and a host of other world class courses. Robert Trent Jones, Jr. designed the Wailea Golf Club, on Maui, home of the Wendy's Champions Skins Game and the Poipu Bay course on Kauai. Additionally, once solely leisure sports such as volleyball and skateboarding have professionalized in the region. The first beach volleyball tournament took place in 1948; less than forty years later, in Los Angeles, California, the Association of Volleyball Professionals was formed in 1983. Likewise, skateboarding, once a way for California surfers to "surf" the streets has, in the form of thrilling skateboarder Tony Hawk, found many devotees.

Of course, mainland surfing began as a means for the region's most all-encompassing sport, surfing, to survive when the surf was not "up," so to speak. In the long and fascinating cultural history of surfing, many of the region's most interesting aspects come to light.

SURFING

Surfing, one of the fastest-growing sports in the world, is also one of the oldest. Riding waves prone on wooden boards—what today is termed *body* or *boogie boarding*—probably dates back thousands of years. According to anthropologists Ben Finney and James Houston, many islands in the broad sweep of Oceania

Beaches with Muscles

America's love affair with fitness began in Southern California in the 1930s at a place called Muscle Beach. Santa Monica, California's Muscle Beach attracted individuals such as Jack LaLanne, Steve "Hercules" Reeves, Vic Tanny, Joe Gold, Charles Atlas, and Harold Zinkin, the first Mr. California. Huge crowds flocked to see their glistening hard bodies. The original attractions, however, were not bodybuilders but acrobats who entertained the crowds with feats of strength and agility, gymnasts, wrestlers, and weightlifters. Human towers and muscle men bench-pressing bathing beauties dazzled onlookers. In the 1950s Muscle Beach relocated to Venice Beach, California, there originally called "The Pen," and emphasis switched from acrobatics to bodybuilding. Arnold Schwarzenegger worked on his world-class physique there. Venice Beach holds a variety of annual competitions, including the Mr. and Ms. Muscle Beach bodybuilding contest; The Battle of Muscle Beach, a weightlifting contest; and the Annual Bench Press Championships.

shared this activity.[10] Yet only in Tahiti and Hawai'i did islanders refine this recreation to the point of standing on their boards; surfing most likely originated in Tahiti and arrived in the Hawaiian Islands by the twelfth century during the second wave of migration from Polynesia (the first immigrants are thought to have arrived from the Marquesas Islands around the fifth century). Geography and culture combined over the next 600 years to integrate surfing into Hawaiian religious beliefs, social relations, recreational activities, and oral ancestral histories.

Following the arrival of Captain James Cook (1728–1779) and other explorers in the eighteenth and nineteenth centuries, surfing entered a period of decline as Western customs, religions, and diseases swept through the Pacific Islands. Surfing soon became associated with immorality and idleness by influential Protestant missionaries. Royalty and urban natives, many of them educated by the missionaries, eagerly rejected traditional customs in an effort to show their dedication to Western ways.

The annexation of Hawai'i by the United States in 1898, and its subsequent interest as a tourist destination, helped foster a surfing revival early in the twentieth century: The sport grew steadily as native Hawaiians exported surfing first to California, then to the eastern United States, Australia, and New Zealand. After World War II, new technologies in surfboard design and a growing youth culture in Southern California combined to transform the pastime of a modest number of Island enthusiasts into an international fad. Surfing has since become a global sport enjoyed by millions and a reminder of how an ancient Pacific tradition continues to influence how the modern world interacts with nature.

Where Do Pacific Swells Come From?

Winter storms in the Aleutian Islands off Alaska send waves sweeping down the American coastlines and into the Southern Hemisphere, where they break, thousands of miles away, against the rock, reef, and sand of Asia and Oceania. In the summertime this flow reverses: Antarctic storms push swells into the Northern Hemisphere, where they roll against and connect the countless beaches of the Pacific Rim. As these seasonal storms touch all lands of the Pacific, so riding their surface energy on surfboards has become a shared recreation among the many cultures and peoples of this vast region.

Early Surfing Described by Europeans and White Americans

Their Strange Diversion

Explorers had witnessed Tahitians riding waves as early as 1769 on Cook's first voyage to the South Pacific (1768–1771). Generally speaking, recreational activities like surfing took a hard hit during the years when the missionaries were most influential in Hawai'i, from the time of their arrival in 1820 until the departure of their most prominent leader, Hiram Bingham (1789–1869), in 1839. Along with their Bibles and school supplies, the missionary families brought an austere view of life that held little room for the many pastimes that had become integral to Island life. Although some missionaries, like the explorers, expressed admiration for native surfing skill, their opinion nevertheless placed the sport among those evils that degraded moral values.

Early Hawaiian Surfboards

Early Hawaiian surfboards ranged from three-foot *paipo* or bodyboards to the grand *olo* boards, which could exceed seventeen feet; in between these was the *alaia*, a thinner board with a square tail measuring from six to thirteen feet. The larger boards had rounded decks, bottoms, and noses and no fins for turning. Shaped from native koa, breadfruit, and wiliwili trees, the heaviest weighed more than 150 pounds.

Surfing survived despite the arrival of Western explorers, their diseases, and their religions. William Ellis (1794–1872), one of the most tolerant and experienced missionaries in the region (he had spent six years in Tahiti before arriving in Hawai'i in 1822), commented that the decline of native traditions in Tahiti was "on no account, matter of regret." He added: "When we consider the debasing tendency of many, and the inutility of others, we shall rather rejoice that much of the time of the adults is passed in more rational and beneficial pursuits." Later, during a visit to the island of Hawai'i, Ellis passed an unusually quiet Sunday: "No athletic sports were seen on the beach; no noise of playful children, shouting as they gambol'd in the surf." He concluded, "It could not but be viewed as the dawn of a bright sabbatic day for the dark shores of Hawaii." Oddly enough, Ellis' lengthy description of surfing in his *Narrative of a Tour through Hawaii* (1825) became a foundational text for travelers seeking to witness, even try for themselves, this exciting native sport. Ellis' vivid tableau ends with these stirring words: "[B]ut to see fifty or one hundred persons riding on an immense billow, half immersed in spray and foam, for a distance of several hundred yards together, is one of the most novel and interesting sports a foreigner can witness in the islands."[11]

Surfing Revival: 1898–1945

Surfing and Hawaiian Tourism

By 1898 Hawai'i had become a territory of the United States, and more Americans turned their interest to the Islands. Promoters soon targeted surfing as a tourist draw and founded the sport's first official organization in 1908, the Hawaiian Outrigger Canoe Club at Waikiki. As Hawaiian political and social structures had Westernized during the nineteenth century, so too its recreations: Popular accounts of surfing stressed individual achievement over communal participation and a heroic, man-conquers-nature ethos that remains part of the sport's image today.

Jack London (1876–1916) sailed to Hawai'i from San Francisco in 1907, publishing that same year "Riding the South Seas Surf" in *Woman's Home Companion*. The same story reappeared in *The Cruise of the Snark* (1911) under a catchier title, "The Sport of Hawaiian Kings: Surfing at Waikiki." London's fame and writing skills were marshaled by promoter Alexander Hume Ford (1868–1945) to spotlight surfing as a unique Hawaiian sport. In London's adventure-story prose, surfing not only gained national attention but was recast into a decidedly Western mold that emphasized the individual overcoming nature. In the following excerpt from London's story, a local Hawaiian surfer is transformed into a Western-style hero:

> He is a Mercury—a brown Mercury. His heels are winged, and in them is the swiftness of the sea. In truth, from out of the sea he has leaped upon the back of the sea, and he is riding the sea that roars and bellows and cannot shake him from his back. . . . He is a Kanaka—and more, he is a man, a member of the kingly species that has mastered matter and the brutes and lorded it over creation.[12]

London lived in a time when many Americans rejected repressive Protestant values (like those of the missionaries) and embraced what President Theodore Roosevelt (1858–1919) championed as "the cult of the strenuous life," which included an enthusiasm for sports. People firmly believed that science led to progress, and an understanding of nature's laws led to mastery of nature itself. Thus London includes in his experience of surfing a detailed account of the physics of wave motion as a preliminary to conquering the "bull-mouthed breaker."

Both London and Alexander Hume Ford set out to debunk the popular myth that only natives could succeed at the sport. This tradition had gained much credence from, among others, Mark Twain, who recorded his experience of surfing in *Roughing It* (1872). "I tried surf-bathing once, subsequently," Twain wrote, "but made a failure of it. I got the board placed right, and at the right moment, too; but missed the connection myself. . . . None but natives ever master the art of surf-bathing thoroughly."[13] If surfing was to draw tourists to Hawai'i, it had to be portrayed as a relatively easy sport to enjoy. So London writes: "Go strip off your clothes that are a nuisance in this mellow clime. Get in and wrestle with the sea; wing your heels with the skill and power that reside in you, hit the sea's breakers, master them, and ride upon their backs as a king should."[14] Ford echoes him two years later in an article for *Collier's Outdoor America*, insisting that surfing is "not such a difficult feat after all, in the small surf where the waves are not more than two or three feet high at most."[15]

The combination of Ford's salesmanship and London's prose had an enormous impact on the popularity of surfing. By 1915, when Jack and Charmian London returned to the Islands, Charmian records that the Outrigger Club sported "twelve hundred members, with hundreds more on the waiting list."[16] Surfing had also been the sport of Hawaiian queens, commoners, and children, but London, picking up where Charles Warren Stoddard had left off, glorified the sport as regal, male, and heroic—as an individual fighting to overcome nature. Standing on the surfboard—rather than lying prone or kneeling—rising above the wave like "a brown Mercury," clearly symbolized this domination.

Long since severed from religious rites, its role in Polynesian myth largely unknown or ignored, its communal practice alive yet waning along with the native population, surfing became a cause célèbre that suddenly needed to be "saved" to enhance the economic growth of the Islands. While one might question how much the sport actually needed saving, there is little doubt that without the energetic marketing of Alexander Hume Ford, few Westerners outside the Islands would have experienced that "most supreme pleasure" that Captain Cook's mariners witnessed on the face of a Tahitian "while he was driven on, so fast and smoothly, by the sea."[17]

Duke Kahanamoku (1890–1968) emerged during this time as the sport's first ambassador and the father of modern surfing. The twenty-one-year-old native Hawaiian appeared on the cover of Ford's *The Mid-Pacific Magazine* in 1911. He was also given credit for the lead article "Riding the Surfboard," though Ford penned the piece himself, drawing partly from his earlier article in *Collier's*. Ford had chosen well. Surfing received a permanent boost the following year when Kahanamoku won the Olympic gold medal in the 100-meter freestyle in Stockholm, Sweden. Invitations followed for Kahanamoku to perform swimming and surfing exhibitions in New Jersey (1912), Australia (1914), and New Zealand (1915).

Back in Hawai'i, Kahanamoku and a group of locals had already organized their own surfing club, Hui Nalu, many of whose members also formed the first band of Waikiki's famous beach boys. These young Hawaiians found daily work at the new beachfront hotels giving surfing lessons, tandem surfing with hotel guests, playing impromptu music sessions, and leading paddling trips in outrigger canoes. They emanated the "aloha spirit" for which the Islands and its people became world renowned. The Waikiki beach

Duke Kahanamoku, head-and-shoulders portrait, wearing print shirt, 1955. Courtesy of the Library of Congress.

boys also became famous for performing agile tricks on surfboards, catching the attention of tourists like London and local residents who became increasingly interested in surfing and other native traditions. As early as 1898, Jean A. Owen notes in *The Story of Hawaii* that "the island-born foreigners emulate the natives in their surf-board riding, canoeing and fishing by torchlight."[18] Kahanamoku continued to spread surfing in the following decades and to win Olympic medals. Passing through Michigan in 1920 on his way home from winning gold in Antwerp, Belgium (again in the 100-meter freestyle), he met a young man from Wisconsin named Tom Blake whom he inspired to move to the Islands and make his own contributions to the history of surfing.

Hawaiian Surf Culture in California

Tom Blake (1902–1994) visited Hawai'i for the first time in 1924 and proved to be somewhat of a renaissance man for surfing. Intensely interested in the sport's history, including surfboard design, Blake began shaping replicas of the early Hawaiian *olo* and *alaia* boards housed in the Bishop Museum in Honolulu. Trying to reduce the great weight of these boards, some of which exceeded 150 pounds, Blake designed a hollow board in 1929 for both paddling and surfboard competitions, events in which he excelled. Blake is also credited with introducing the first surfboard fin in 1935, allowing riders to turn their boards more easily; his lighter, more maneuverable boards opened the sport to more enthusiasts at more surf spots. He went on to give the sport national exposure by publishing his surf photography in *National Geographic* and writing how-to articles in *Popular Science* and *Popular Mechanics* for surfboard construction and riding technique. His most enduring publication, *Hawaiian Surfboard* (1935), includes chapters on Hawaiian legends and an early history of the sport. In addition to these accomplishments, Blake had a profound impact on exporting Hawaiian surf culture to the burgeoning surf community in Southern California.

California surf culture gained momentum after the inaugural Pacific Coast Surf Riding Championship in 1928 held at Corona del Mar, an event in which Blake placed first with a prototype of his hollow board. The cross-pollination of ideas and rituals in surfing had been happening since at least 1885 when three Hawaiian princes attending boarding school surfed an impromptu session near Santa Cruz in Northern California. More Island influence arrived in 1907 when part-Hawaiian George Freeth performed several exhibitions in Southern California. (Freeth had surfed with London at Waikiki earlier that year and served as the model for the "brown Mercury" in London's account.) Duke Kahanamoku's visit to Southern California in 1912 marks another key moment of Hawaiian influence; however, following the pattern set by early and modern Hawaiian culture, surfing appears to have generated the most interest in California as a result of formal competition. Subsequent Surf Riding Championships were held at San Onofre, a remote beach north of San Diego that epicentered California's Hawaiian-based surf culture in the 1930s and 1940s. With gently rolling waves and a temperate climate, even a grass shack left behind by a Hollywood movie company, San Onofre became the Waikiki of the West Coast. Local surfers formed clubs, sported palm frond hats, and strummed ukuleles in an attempt to re-create an idealized version of Hawaiian beach life. In the process of imitating their Island cousins, these "coast *haoles*" were well on their way to establishing their own brand of surf culture.

Postwar California Surf Culture: 1945–2004

War Technology and Surfboard Design

A younger generation of surfers came into prominence after World War II, infusing the sport with Southern California culture and marking an important shift in both the practice and image of surfing. Whereas early Hawaiian accounts had emphasized the communal aspects of the sport, a tradition that lasted until London's glorification of surfing as uniquely royal and male, the new picture emerging after World War II relegates surfing to the domain of youth. In practice, surfing included as wide a demographic as it ever had in California; certainly the communal traditions among Hawaiians remained strong. However, the trend that emerges after the war—and this solidifies in the late 1950s and early 1960s—is dominated by Southern Californian youth culture: cars, clothing, language, and attitude. Malibu became their home, its higher-performance waves their testing ground for a new generation of surfboards shaped from lightweight balsa and wrapped in an innovative by-product of the region's military industry: fiberglass.

Bob Simmons (1919–1954), a machinist and mathematician for Douglas Aircraft, is credited with being the first to apply war technologies to surfboard production. Working with hydrodynamic designs wrapped in fiberglass, Simmons created lighter, higher-performance surfboards. Simmons, along with fellow surfers Joe Quigg, Matt Kivlin, and Dale Velzy, soon matched the new fiberglass material with balsa, producing user-friendly surfboards that weighed less than thirty pounds. By 1957, another new war technology—polyurethane foam—had replaced balsa as the principal board material, ensuring an easily shapeable, limitless supply of lightweight boards.

By the end of the 1950s, most of the elements that sparked surfing's launch into mainstream culture were in place: a large youth population in Southern California relatively well off thanks to postwar prosperity, a fast-growing car culture that allowed easy access to surf spots along the coast, an established film industry close at hand, and a small but growing number of surf shops ready to provide the latest surfboard designs.

Surfer Counterculture

"In 1968," Drew Kampion writes in *Stoked! A History of Surf Culture*, "surfing experiences the greatest cultural and conceptual shift in its history as virtually the entire sport threw away its 9- and 10-foot boards and took up shortboards."[19] What has become known as "the shortboard revolution" coincided with the counterculture of the late 1960s; their combined effect was not only to change *how* people surfed on waves in terms of equipment but also to make them rethink *why* they surfed waves in the first place.

Much of the background for this conceptual shift lies in the years leading up to the shortboard revolution. Influenced by the counterculture, most younger surfers no longer identified with a sport that spent most of the 1960s becoming more organized, more competitive, more commercial, and more mainstream. The most high-profile surfers of the postwar generation were focused either on conquering big waves on the north shore of Oahu or noseriding at smaller mainland breaks like Malibu. For a younger generation of surfers, now maneuvering vertically on waves because of new fin and board designs, redefining the sport meant opening up new spaces on the wave: flowing with the ocean, not trying to conquer it; riding *inside* the wave rather than standing outside and posing on the nose.

The prime movers for this change came from distant quarters: Australia. Shaper Bob McTavish and competitive surfer Nat Young had teamed up to win the 1966 World Surfing Championship in San Diego, California, heralding a new era that would ironically question the usefulness of contests. As Vietnam took its toll on American society, especially in the minds of young people, psychedelic drugs replaced surfing's postwar drinking culture; brotherhood

Surfing in the Pacific Northwest

As surfing hit mainstream in the 1960s, crowd-weary waveriders began to flee California and journey north to explore the rugged coastlines of Oregon, Washington, and Alaska. Year-round cold water, remote surf spots, and hazardous ocean conditions (including great white sharks) still keep crowds to a minimum throughout the region. With hard-core enclaves in Seaside, Oregon, and Westport, Washington, the Pacific Northwest recalls the grassroots surf culture of California's pre-*Gidget* era. The small town of Yakutat is the best-known surf destination in Alaska, having been pioneered in the late 1970s and subsequently gracing the cover of *Surfer* magazine in January 1993.

and "soul surfing" displaced individualism and competition. Grassroots shapers proliferated in place of established surf manufacturers, and for the first time since early Hawaiian culture, spirituality entered the sport as the counterculture embraced Eastern religions. Opening one's mind in the late 1960s translated to experimentation with shorter boards and new designs. By the end of the decade, top California surfers like Corky Carroll and David Nuuhiwa could ride six-foot boards that weighed less than ten pounds.

The Rise of Professionalism

By 1970 surfing had been established along the coastlines of the world's major continents. Films like Bruce Brown's *The Endless Summer*, distributed nationwide in 1966, inspired surfers to travel abroad in search of the perfect waves that Robert August and Mike Hynson had found at Cape St. Francis in South Africa. Surf films and magazines in the 1970s increasingly presented colorful images of exotic waves in Central America, Europe, Australia, West Africa, and the Pacific Islands. Surfing, born and nurtured in the Pacific, had successfully migrated to the oceans of the world. As high-quality surf spots proliferated, a young group of surfers, principally Australian and South African, began to dream of an international professional surfing tour.

The International Professional Surfers (IPS) completed its inaugural year in 1976 with fourteen events in five countries. Founded by former world amateur champion Fred Hemmings of Hawai'i, the IPS, with a few bumps over the years, continues today as the Association of Surfing Professionals (ASP). The men's World Contest Tour (WCT) now holds a dozen events in nine countries with a total purse of $3 million; the women's WCT maintains five events in as many countries with a total purse of $310,000. In addition to the WCT, the ASP holds the World Qualifying Series (WQS), an international network of contests linked to the WCT; the World Longboard Tour; the Junior World Championship; and the Masters World Championship.

As in the past, the rise of competition has spurred design innovations. Australian Mark Richards, winner of four world championships from 1979 to 1982, introduced a twin-fin design in 1977 that revolutionized the mobility of boards on waves. Simon Anderson, another Australian, introduced his tri-fin or "thruster" model in 1981. The board combined the strengths of both single- and twin-fin designs and has since become the standard for surfers around the world. Since 1992, when Florida surfer Kelly Slater won the first of six world titles on Al Merrick–designed, ultrathin surfboards, "New School" surfing has taken the sport into its latest high-performance phase of radical maneuvering, including aerials. With a rising number of national and international surf contests in the 1980s and 1990s, a small group of surfers had realized their vision of taking this Pacific sport and making a living out of a lifestyle.

Surfing Today

First among the trends that promise to have a continuing impact on surfing is the sport's broad demographic. At no period since Captain Cook landed in the Islands has a more diverse population ridden waves: old and young, male and female, all levels of society across the world taking to the ocean on every imaginable kind of water craft, from boogie boards and longboards to boards with sails and kites attached. Women in particular have entered the sport in the greatest numbers over the past decade, moving from less than 5 percent of the surf population in the early 1990s to between 10 and 15 percent in 2003.

Nostalgia is the second trend, evident not only in annual surf auctions where surfboards from the 1950s have sold for nearly $20,000 but also in the growing corpus of magazines, books, and videos dedicated to preserving surfing's past. *The Surfer's Journal*, founded by Steve and Debbee Pezman in 1992, is the spiritual leader of the movement. The nostalgia movement gains momentum from the growing realization that surfing, as Steve Pezman says, has "got a history." Older surfers recognize that this history, and surfing in general, has played an important part in how they have come to define themselves: Preserving the past is a way of validating that identity.

Surf writing received much cultural cachet in 1992 when William Finnegan published "Playing Doc's Games" in *The New Yorker*, a two-part article describing surf life in San Francisco. Thomas Farber's *On Water* (1994) and Daniel Duane's *Caught Inside: A Surfer's Year on the California Coast* (1996) have continued to plumb surfing's depths while evoking themes similar to Finnegan's: sounding the ultimate value of a pursuit considered "nonproductive" by society and yet whose mastery requires an enormous investment of time and energy. As native Hawaiians discovered in the nineteenth century, surfing does not integrate well into the Protestant work ethic; twenty-first-century surf writers, on the far side of the Industrial Revolution, are making a case reminiscent of Pacific Island lore where surfing reconnects us to the spiritual and salutary rhythms of nature.

RESOURCE GUIDE

Printed Resources

Allen, E. John B. *From Skisport to Skiing: One Hundred Years of an American Sport, 1840–1940.* Amherst: University of Massachusetts Press, 1993.

Ball, Doc. *Early California Surfriders.* 1946. Reprint of *California Surfriders.* Ventura, CA: Pacific Publishing, 1995.

Blake, Tom. *Hawaiian Surfriders:1935.* 1935. Redondo Beach, CA: Mountain & Sea, 1983.

Colburn, Bolton, et al., eds. *Surf Culture: The Art History of Surfing.* Corte Madera, CA: Laguna Art Museum/Gingko Press, 2002.

da Silva, Rachel. *Leading Out: Women Climbers Reaching for the Top.* Seattle, WA: Seal Press, 1992.

Duane, Daniel. *Caught Inside: A Surfer's Year on the California Coast.* New York: North Point Press, 1996.

Farber, Thomas. *On Water.* Hopewell, NJ: Ecco Press, 1994.

Finney, Ben, and James D. Houston. *Surfing: A History of the Ancient Hawaiian Sport.* Rev. ed. San Francisco, CA: Pomegranate Artbooks, 1996.

Fox Rogers, Susan, ed. *Solo: On Her Own Adventure.* Seattle, WA: Seal Press, 1996.

Gabbard, Andrea. *Girl in the Curl: A Century of Women in Surfing.* Seattle, WA: Seal Press, 2000.

Jenish, D'Arcy. *The Stanley Cup.* Toronto, Ontario: McClelland & Stewart, 1992.

Jones, Chris. *Climbing in North America*. Berkeley: University of California Press, 1976.

Kampion, Drew. *Stoked! A History of Surf Culture*. Rev. ed. Layton, UT: Gibbs Smith, 2003.

———, ed. *The Stormrider Guide North America*. Cornwall, UK: Low Pressure Publications, 2002.

King, Clarence. *Mountaineering in the Sierra Nevada*. New York: W. W. Norton, 1935.

Klatell, David A., and Norman Marcus. *Sports for Sale*. New York: Oxford University Press, 1988.

LaBastille, Ann. *Women and Wilderness*. San Francisco, CA: Sierra Club Books, 1980.

LaBlanc, Michael L., ed. *Professional Sports Team Histories: Basketball*. Detroit, MI: Gale Research, 1994.

Leifer, Eric M. *Making the Majors: The Transformation of Team Sports in America*. Cambridge, MA: Harvard University Press, 1995.

Messina, Lynn M., ed. *Sports in America*. New York: H. W. Wilson, 2001.

Moore, Terris. *Mt. McKinley: The Pioneer Climbs*. Seattle, WA: The Mountaineers, 1981.

Moss, Al. *Pac-10 Football*. New York: Crescent Books, 1987.

Mrozek, Donald J., ed. *Sports and Recreation in the West*. Manhattan, KS: Journal of the West, 1978.

Muir, John. *All the World Over: Notes from Alaska*. San Francisco: Sierra Club Books, 1996.

———. *The Mountains of California*. New York: Century, 1894.

Noverr, Douglas A., and Lawrence E. Ziewacz. *The Games They Played: Sports in American History, 1865–1980*. Chicago: Nelson-Hall, 1983.

O'Neal, Bill. *The Pacific Coast League: 1903–1988*. Austin, TX: Eakin Press, 1990.

Rojstaczer, Stuart. *Gone for Good*. New York: Oxford University Press, 1999.

Shebl, James M. *King, of the Mountains*. Stockton, CA: University of the Pacific Press, 1974.

Warshaw, Matt. *The Encyclopedia of Surfing*. San Diego, CA: Harcourt, 2003.

———. *Maverick's: The Story of Big Wave Surfing*. San Francisco, CA: Chronicle Books, 2000.

———. *SurfRiders: In Search of the Perfect Wave*. New York: HarperCollins Publishers, 1997.

Watterson, John Sayle. *College Football*. Baltimore, MD: Johns Hopkins University Press, 2000.

Weiss, Ann E. *Money Games*. New York: Houghton Mifflin, 1993.

Wellner, Alison. *Americans at Play: Demographics of Outdoor Recreational & Travel*. Ithaca, NY: New Strategist Publications, 1997.

Williams, Dennis C. *God's Wilds: John Muir's Vision of Nature*. College Station: Texas A & M University Press, 2002.

Wittingham, Richard. *The Rites of Autumn: The Story of College Football*. New York: Free Press, 2001.

Zimbalist, Andrew. *Baseball and Billions*. New York: Basic Books, 1992.

Web Sites

Alaska Fly Fishers
January 30, 2004.
http://www.akflyfishers.com/faq.html

Aubrecht, Michael. "The 1989 World Series." *Baseball Almanac*. 2000.
July 4, 2004.
http://www.baseball-almanac.com/ws/yr1989ws.shtml

Clarence King Timeline
Mount Shasta Companion. October 30, 2003.
http://www.siskiyous.edu/shasta/env/king/time.htm

Current View of Mt. McKinley from Talkeetna Waterfront
November 12, 2003.
http://www.alaskaairtours.com/webcam.html

Flyfishing in Alaska
January 30, 2004.
http://www.sf.adfg.state.ak.us/statewide/flyfish/home.cfm

Fuller, Mike. "The Seattle Pilots Baseball Team." 2003.
July 4, 2004.
http://www.brandx.net/pilots/

International Women Flyfishers Organization
January 30, 2004.
http://intlwomen.flyfishers.org

The John Muir Exhibit
Sierra Club. August 22, 2003.
http://www.sierraclub.org/john_muir_exhibit/

Litterer, David. "An Overview of American Soccer History."
The American Soccer History Archives. February 24, 2004.
http://www.sover.net/~spectrum/overview.html

Outdoors Directory
January 30, 2004.
http://www.outdoorsdirectory.com/fishing/htm

Real-time audio interviews with fisheries biologists.

Pacific Crest Trail Photo Gallery
Pacific Crest Trail Association. June 10, 2003.
http://www.pcta.org/about_trail/photo.asp

Rockclimbing.com
January 30, 2004.
http://www.rockclimbing.com/routes/listState.php?CountryStateID=52

Rock climbing in Oregon.

Rock Climbing Hawaii.com
January 30, 2004.
http://www.rockclimbinghawaii.com/

See You Outside
January 30, 2004.
http://www.seeyououtside.com/climbing.htm

Rock climbing in Oregon and the Pacific Northwest.

Ski Travel in Washington
January 30, 2004.
http://www.travel-in-wa.com/outdoor/ski.html

Snake Gabrielson's Surfing Library
July 4, 2004.
http://www.blackmagic.com/ses/surf/papers/home.html

Resources for surfing-related papers and historical studies.

SurfArt.com
July 4, 2004.
http://surfart.com/surf_history/site2.html
General site for surf history, especially the Hawaiian roots of surfing.

Surfer Resources
July 4, 2004.
http://www.sdsc.edu/surf/surfer_resources.html
General site for links and information on everything from surf art to wetsuits.

Surfline
July 4, 2004.
http://www.surfline.com/home/index.cfm
Surf forecasting, Web cams, and an A–Z encyclopedia section.

Ultimate Directory of Kayaking Links
January 30, 2004.
http://home.adelphia.net/~kwinter/kayakmain.html

Westfly.com
January 30, 2004.
http://www.westfly.com/
Online magazine and information source for fly-fishing in the West.

Women's Fly Fishing
January 30, 2004.
http://www.womensflyfishing.net/

Videos/Films

Condition Black. New Street Productions, Ltd., Tremendous! Entertainment, Inc., and Thirteen/WNET. New York, 2002.
The Endless Summer. Bruce Brown Films, 1990.
Five Summer Stories. MacGillivray Freeman Films, 1994.
The Golden Breed. Dale Davis Productions, 1968.
The September Sessions. Jack Johnson, c. 1999.
The Surfers' Journal: 50 Years of Surfing on Film. Opper Sports Productions, 1996.
Surfing for Life. David L. Brown Productions, 1999.
Surfing the 50's. Bud Browne, 1994.

Recordings

Cowabunga! The Surf Box. Rhino Records, 1996.

Organizations and Museums

Association of Surfing Professionals
P. O. Box 1095
Coolangatta, QLD
4225 Australia
61-7-5599 1550
asp@aspworldtour.com
http://www.aspworldtour.com

Groundswell Society
233 Ashland Avenue, Suite F
Santa Monica, CA 90405
info@groundswellsociety.org
http://www.groundswellsociety.org/

Knik Museum
Mile 13.9 Knik Road
Wasilla, AK 99654
http://home.gci.net/~wasillaknikhistory/KnikMuseum.html

Houses the Sled Dog Mushers Hall of Fame and includes Iditarod Sled Dog Race early history.

Surfrider Foundation
P. O. Box 6010
San Clemente, CA 92674-6010
1-800-743-SURF and 949-492-8170
http://www.surfrider.org/

Surfrider Oahu Chapter
Contact Person: Doug Rodman
66-077 Wana Place
Waialua, HI 96791
808-637-4151
http://www.surfriderhawaii.org/

Surfrider Wild Coast Chapter
Contact Person:Kris Balliet
425 G. Street, Suite 400
Anchorage, AK 99501
907-258-9922
orca@acsalaska.net
http://www.surfrider.org/wildcoast/

Western Ski Sport Museum
P. O. Box 829
Soda Springs, CA 95728
http://www.auburnskiclub.org/ski_museum/index.html

Exhibition of western North American ski history.

Westport Surfrider Chapter
Contact Person: Kevin Ranker
P. O. Box 3354
Friday Harbor, WA 98250
360-378-1091
kranker@surfrider.org
http://www.surfrider.org/westport/

TIMELINE

c. 80 million B.C.E.	Sierra Nevada batholith begins its rise on the earth's surface.
c. 70 million B.C.E.	Hot spot in Pacific Ocean begins formation of Hawaiian Island chain; Alaska's Brooks Range also begins to build.
c. 40 million B.C.E.	Cascade Mountain Range begins to form.
50,000–10,000 B.C.E.	Beringia land mass connecting Asia and North America left exposed during Ice Age.
c. 13,000 B.C.E.	Earliest known human migration wave crosses Beringia into North America.
c. 11,000 B.C.E.	Ice Age glaciers retreat from Columbia Plateau.
c. 10,000 B.C.E.	Dating of historic petroglyphs near Steam Wells in the Mojave desert; Clovis culture present along Pacific Coast.
c. 8000–5000 B.C.E.	Second major human migration from Siberia into Alaska brings Na-Dene speakers and, later, Eska-aleut speakers.
c. 300 C.E.	Polynesians, most likely coming from the Marqueses Islands, establish permanent settlement on Hawaiian chain.
c. 500	First temple, or *heiau*, erected on Hawaii's Big Island.
c. 1200	Polynesians from Tahiti conquer the original Hawaiian population and establish the kapu system.
1542	Juan Rodríguez Cabrillo, a Portuguese captain sailing for Spain, leads the first European exploration of the California coastline, meeting various California tribes.
1543	After Cabrillo's accidental death, Bartolomé Ferrelo continues the expedition as far north as Oregon before returning to Acapulco.

1579	English pirate Francis Drake sails along the Northwest coast; he lands near the Point Reyes peninsula and encounters California coast Miwok tribes.
1602	Sebastián Vizcaíno, seeking a port for Spain's Manilla-Acapulco trade route, names Monterey Bay and makes contact with Ohlone Indians.
1729	Vitus Bering, a Dane sailing for Russia, discovers the Diomede Islands; the pair of islands mark the present-day border between the United States and Russia.
1732	Russia's Ivan Fedorov, navigator on Bering's first voyage, charts the northwest coast of Alaska; Bering would land on the state's southern coast in 1741.
1769	New Spain's "Sacred Expedition," commanded by Captain Gaspar de Portolá and including Franciscan missionaries led by Father Junipero Serra, founds the first of California's missions, San Diego de Alcala.
1774	Spain's Juan Pérez explores the Pacific Northwest coast, sighting Washington's Olympic Mountains; the following year Bruno de Hezeta claims the region for Spain when he lands on the Washington shore.
1775	Kumeyaay Indians destroy the Spanish mission of San Diego; the mission was rebuilt but attacked again by the Quechan in 1781.
1776	San Francisco, the northernmost of the original nine missions, established by Junipero Serra's "Sacred Expedition."
1778	Captain James Cook's third Pacific voyage takes him to Hawai'i as well as into Cook Inlet, Alaska.
1784	Russia founds first permanent outpost in Alaska on Kodiak Island.
1786	France's Comte de La Perouse sails to the Queen Charlotte Islands.
1788	U.S. Captain Robert Gray sails the Oregon coast, discovering the mouth of the Columbia River.
1789	Chinese shipbuilders land in Hawai'i.
1792	British Captain George Vancouver penetrates Puget Sound.
1793	Spanish pueblo of Los Angeles founded.
1799	Russian American Company, directed by Aleksandr Baranov, given fur monopoly rights in Alaska.
1802	Tlingit under Katilan drive the Russians off Sitka Island; Russia regains island in 1805.

1804	Construction of the town of New Archangel, on Baranof Island, begins; later the capital of Russia's Alaskan holdings, it would be renamed Sitka under U.S. authority.
1805	Meriwether Lewis and William Clark lead their Corps of Discovery mission down the Columbia River to the Pacific Ocean.
1810	Kamehameha I consolidates political power over entire Hawaiian Island chain and establishes the Kingdom of Hawai'i.
	Spokane House fur trade outpost established by North West Company.
1811	Chinook Indians meet members of the Pacific Fur Company building Fort Astoria at the mouth of the Columbia River.
1812	Russians establish Fort Ross north of San Francisco.
1821	Mexico gains independence from Spain; California missions begin transformation to rancho system.
1824	Chumash Indians raid Santa Barbara and Santa Ynez, the last of the Mission Indian revolts.
1825	Fort Vancouver established by Hudson's Bay Company.
1833	Secularization of the Alta California missions.
1841	Bidwell-Bartleson party, the first emigrant wagon train to cross the Oregon Trail, leaves for California; half the party would head north into the Oregon Territory.
1844	George Washington Bush, an African American pioneer, settles north of the Columbia River, one of the first Americans to do so.
1846	Negotiations between President James Polk and the British government establish the 49th parallel as the northern border of Oregon Country, founding the present-day border between Washington State and Canada.
	Mexican-American War begins; in the first action of the Bear Flag Rebellion, U.S. settlers seize the town of Sonoma and declare the Republic of California.
1847	British traders establish Fort Yukon.
	Measles-ravaged Cayuse Indians under Tiloukaikt attack the Protestant mission at Waiilatpu, killing Dr. Marcus Whitman and fourteen others and prompting the Cayuse War.
1848	Treaty of Guadalupe-Hidalgo ends the Mexican-American War and cedes California to U.S. authority.

	Gold discovered at Sutter's Mill on American River, prompting the California Gold Rush.
	King Kamehameha III enacts the Great Mahele, redistributing Hawaiian lands and leading to their loss from native control.
	Oregon Country formally recognized as Oregon Territory by the U.S. government.
1850	California becomes thirty-first state.
1851	Chinese in San Francisco form the Sam Yup and Sze Yup Associations.
1852	Gold discovery in eastern Washington; the flood of miners into the state exacerbates conditions, leading to the Yakima War.
1853	Washington Territory crafted from the northern part of the Oregon Territory; the eastern boundary of Oregon was established along the Snake River and south to the Nevada border.
	Foreign Miners Tax crafted against Chinese immigrants during the gold rush.
1859	Oregon becomes thirty-third state.
1862	Homestead Act signed into law.
1867	U.S. Secretary of State William Seward negotiates purchase of Alaska from Russia.
1868	First Japanese immigrants arrive as contract laborers in Hawai'i.
1869	Central Pacific Line of the transcontinental railroad links Los Angeles with the East.
1872–1873	Modoc War, one of the costliest of the Western Indian Wars, flares along the Oregon-California border.
1873	Patent for denim work pants received by the Levi Strauss Company on May 20.
1876	Reciprocity Treaty allows Hawaiian sugar duty-free entry into the United States.
1878	Starvation and forced relocation of Northwest Tribes prompts the Bannock-Paiute War.
1882	Chinese Exclusion Act effected a nationwide ban on Chinese immigration.
1883	Northern Pacific Line of the transcontinental railroad links Portland and Tacoma with the East.
	Sarah Winnemucca publishes *Life among the Paiutes: Their Wrongs and Claims*.
1889	Washington becomes forty-second state.

1892	Mountaineer and conservationist John Muir cofounds the Sierra Club; he would publish *The Mountains of the Sierra Nevada* in 1894.
1893	American sugar cane plantation owners collude with the U.S. Consul in Hawai'i and overthrow the government of Queen Lilioukalani.
1894	Irwin Convention negotiates the arrival of 29,000 Japanese contract laborers to work in Hawai'i's sugar plantations.
1896	Gold discovered in Alaska's Yukon region.
1898	Hawai'i annexed by the United States; it would be officially designated a territory in 1900.
	Jodo Shinshu Buddhist priests land in San Francisco, precipitating the founding of the Buddhist Churches of America.
1899–1902	Philippine-American War confirms the Philippines (a spoil of the 1898 Spanish-American War) as a U.S. territory; Filipinos, as U.S. nationals, soon begin arriving on the West Coast.
1905	The first Hindu temple in the Western world built in San Francisco.
1906	The San Francisco earthquake and the ensuing fires devastate the city.
	Azusa Street Revival in Los Angeles spreads Pentacostalism in the West.
1907	The Gentleman's Agreement limits Japanese immigration to the United States; a loophole in this agreement, however, allows for the entry of Japanese wives.
1909	Bishop family factory in Pendleton begins producing Native American–inspired wool blankets.
1910	Angel Island immigration station opened.
1911	Ishi, the last surviving member of the California Yahi tribe, walks out of the wilderness and turns himself over to authorities in the town of Oroville.
1912	The first *gurdwara*, or Sikh temple, in America is completed in Stockton, California.
1915	San Francisco's Panama Pacific International Exhibition unveils modernist art on the West Coast.
1916	Boeing Airplane Company founded outside of Seattle.
1919	Centralia labor strikes in Washington erupt in violence.
1924	Federal Immigration Act completely bars the entry of Japanese into the United States.

1928	Inaugural Pacific Coast Surf Riding Championship at Corona del Mar affixes surf culture on the mainland coast.
1929	U.S. stock market crash and dust bowl poverty help initiate massive westward migration into California.
1936	Filipino and Mexican agricultural workers found the Field Workers Union.
1940	Angel Island Immigration Station closed.
1941	Pearl Harbor bombed by Japan on December 7.
1942	Franklin Delano Roosevelt signs Executive Order 9066 on February 19, incarcerating the Pacific Region's Japanese population in internment camps.
	Federal Bracero Program brings Mexican contract workers into West Coast states.
1943	Hanford Works built in Richland, Washington, to produce plutonium for first atomic bombs.
	Zoot Suit Riots break out in Los Angeles after U.S. Navy sailors brawl with Mexican American locals; sailors and white citizens cruise the streets, beating Mexican Americans, African Americans, and Filipino Americans.
1944	A bomb explosion at California's Richmond Naval Station kills 300 African American workers.
1955	Six poets at the Sixth Gallery reading launches the Beat Movement in San Francisco.
1958	Alaskan oil reserves discovered.
1959	Alaska becomes forty-ninth state.
	Hawai'i becomes fiftieth state.
1960	Winter Olympics held in Squaw Valley, California.
1962	United Farm Workers labor union organized by César Chávez and Dolores Huerta.
1965	Federal Immigration Act removes previous quota system and increases immigration opportunities for Asians.
	Watts Riot rages for six days among parts of Los Angeles' African American and Mexican American communities, the largest race riot in U.S. history.
1966	Black Panther Party organizes in Oakland; a second chapter would be founded in Seattle in 1969.
1969	In the first major display of modern, pantribal Native American activism, First Peoples under the leadership of Richard Oakes occupy Alcatraz Island in San Francisco Bay in November and hold the island for eighteen months.
1971	Alaska Native Claims Settlement Act passed by U.S.

	Congress resolves many land disputes with Alaskan Native villages.
1972	San Francisco City Supervisor Harvey Milk, one of the first openly gay elected officials in the country, is murdered in San Francisco.
1975	Fall of Saigon initiates wave of Southeast Asian refugees to the West Coast.
1980	Mount St. Helens erupts in southwest Washington.
1992	Race riots grip Los Angeles after four white officers of the Los Angeles Police Department are acquitted of using excessive force after they beat Rodney King, an African American, during his arrest.
1997	On October 27 physician-assisted suicide became a legal medical option for terminally ill Oregonians with passage of the Oregon Death with Dignity Act.
2003	Recalled California governor Gray Davis is defeated by actor Arnold Schwarzenegger, who becomes the state's thirty-eighth governor.
2004	Bush administration pushes Congress to open Alaska's Arctic National Wildlife Refuge to oil drilling. Environmentalists, including the Wilderness Society, file lawsuits in federal court to block the action, and public dissent encourages the Senate to reject the play.

NOTES

Architecture

1. Carlos Arnaldo Schwantes, *The Pacific Northwest: An Interpretive History*, rev. ed. (Lincoln: University of Nebraska Press, 1996).

2. Alison K. Hoagland, *Buildings of Alaska* (New York: Oxford University Press, 1993), 25.

3. From Charles Nordhoff, *California for Health, Pleasure, and Residence: A Book for Travellers* and Settlers, rev. ed. (New York: Harper & Brothers, 1882), 10.

4. Carleton Monroe Winslow, Clarence S. Stein, and Bertram Grosvenor Goodhue, *The Architecture and the Gardens of the San Diego Exposition* (San Francisco, CA: Paul Elder and Company, 1916), 6–7.

5. [Gustav Stickley], "Plans of the Craftsman for Next Year," *The Craftsman* 15 (October 1908): 115.

6. Irving Gill, "The Home of the Future: The New Architecture of the West," *The Craftsman* 30 (May 1916): 141–142.

7. James Cook, *A Voyage to the Pacific Ocean* (1784), 2:200.

8. For a discussion of Cook and Lono, See Gananath Obeyesekere, *The Apotheosis of Captain Cook*, (Princeton, NJ: Princeton University Press, 1992).

9. Cook, *A Voyage to the Pacific Ocean*, 2:211.

10. Robert Jay, *The Architecture of Charles W. Dickey: Hawaii and California* (Honolulu: University of Hawaii Press, 1992), 14.

Art

1. A petroglyph is a prehistoric rock carving.

2. A pictograph is a prehistoric rock painting.

3. Robert Tyler Davis, *Native Arts of the Pacific Northwest* (Palo Alto, CA: Stanford University Press, 1954), 5–6.

4. The stone adz is a tool used for carving wood or stone and is often attached to a hardwood handle and decorated with relief sculpture and/or paint. It is still in use today, though contemporary adzes often have a steel blade, as opposed to the ancient stone and bone blades.

Notes

5. The big boom days were essentially over by 1854, though newly engineered methods, such as hydraulic mining, were still being employed to extract gold from harder-to-reach sources.

6. The Oakland Art Museum in California contains the largest and most diverse collection of gold rush art in the world.

7. "The Domes of Yosemite," A letter from Samuel Clemens [Mark Twain] published in *The Alta California Newspaper*, June 2, 1867 at http://www.yosemitenews.net/yosemite_domes.html.

8. The Munich School was prominent in the 1870s, when Germany rose to the forefront as the hotbed of artistic innovation. The Munich School style was characterized by thick, painterly brushwork and a deliberately unfinished quality to paintings except for certain details, such as hands and faces in portraits.

9. The Barbizon School was a group of artists working in France in the region of Barbizon. They rejected the theory of the Academic tradition and developed new and bold methods to represent the landscape.

10. The second generation of the Hudson River School was a group of landscape painters working largely in the Hudson River Valley; they also spread out across the American West. These artists recorded intimate scenes of nature rather than the panoramic vistas of the first generation of the Hudson River School.

11. Charles Wilkes. *Narrative of the United States Exploring Expedition* (Boston: Gregg Press, 1970).

12. When artists work *en plein air*, that is to say that they work outdoors, on location.

13. In woodcut printmaking, the artist incises grooves into a block of wood with a flat surface and spreads ink or paint onto the surface. The resulting print is made by pressing the inked or painted side onto paper or other materials, leaving a register of those areas that have not been cut away.

14. In monotype printmaking, the artist spreads paint or ink onto a flat surface, then presses paper against that surface. It is called "monotype" because each print is unique.

15. In etching, a more complicated type of printmaking, the artist scratches the surface of a metal plate that has been treated with acid-resistant coating, using a needle or stylus. The plate is then submerged in acid, which eats grooves into the metal in all the places that have been scratched through. The acid-resistant medium is then removed, and the plate is treated by pressing ink into the grooves. To make prints, the plate is covered with paper and run through a press.

16. Fauvism was a movement in French painting from 1898 to 1906 that is immediately recognizable for its bright, primary colors, spontaneity, and flat forms. As one of the original avant-garde movements, it was very influential in the development of Abstract art. Henri Matisse (1869–1954) is probably the most well-known Fauvist.

17. Pointillism denotes a movement developed by the French painter Georges Seurat (1859–1891) that flourished between 1886 and 1906, characterized by the separation of color into points, or dots, that collectively create the illusion of a unified image.

18. Automatism denotes the process by which an artist works purely on instinct, with no negotiation between the subconscious and the conscious mind.

19. Administered by the Alaska State Council on the Arts, the Silver Hand Program protects the work of Alaska Native artists while guaranteeing the public that items bearing the Silver Hand identification seal were handcrafted in Alaska by an Alaska Eskimo, Aleut, or Indian craftsperson or artist and made wholly or in significant part of natural materials.

20. The 1972 Marine Mammal Protection Act exempted Indians, Aleut, and Eskimos (who dwell on the coast of the North Pacific Ocean) from the moratorium on taking provided that taking, was conducted for the sake of subsistence or for the purpose of creating and selling authentic Native articles of handicraft and clothing.

21. The Native American Graves Protection and Repatriation Act is a federal law passed

in 1990. NAGPRA provides a process for museums and federal agencies to return certain Native American cultural items—human remains, funerary objects, sacred objects, and objects of cultural patrimony—to lineal descendants, culturally affiliated Indian tribes, and Native Hawaiian organizations.

22. William W. Fitzhugh and Aaron Cromwell, *Crossroads of the Continents: Cultures of Siberia and Alaska* (Washington, DC: Smithsonian Institution, 1988), 162–163.

23. Kate Duncan, *Northern Athapaskan Art: A Beadwork Tradition* (Seattle: University of Washington Press, 1988), 56.

24. Cheryl Samuel, *The Chilkat Dancing Blanket* (Seattle, WA: Pacific Search Press, 1982), 14.

25. Frances Paul, *Spruce Root Basketry of the Northern Tlingit* (Sitka, AK: Sheldon Jackson Museum, 1981), 38.

26. Dinah Larsen, ed., *Setting It Free. An Exhibition of Modern Alaskan Eskimo Carving* (Fairbanks: University of Alaska Museum, 1982), 11.

27. Molly Lee, *Baleen Basketry of the North Alaskan Eskimo* (Barrow, AK: North Slope Planning Department, 1983; Seattle: University of Washington Press, 2000), 13. Citations are to the University of Washington Press edition.

28. Suzi Jones, ed., *Eskimo Dolls* (1982; Anchorage: Alaska State Council on the Arts, 1999), 40. Citations are to the 1999 edition.

29. See Rita Pitka Blumenstein, Earth Dyes (Nuunam Qaralirkai) (Fairbanks: Institute of Alaska Native Arts, 1984).

During the summer of 2000, the Alaska Native Heritage Center in Anchorage, Alaska, sponsored a traditional Native boatbuilding project wherein eight masters and their apprentices assembled eight traditional Alaska Native boats many of which hadn't been seen in over seventy-five years.

30. Ann Fienup-Riordan, *The Living Tradition of Yup'ik Masks: Agayuliyararput: Our Way of Making Prayer* (Seattle: University of Washington Press, 1996), 23.

31. Lydia T. Black, *Glory Remembered: Wooden Head Gear of Alaska Sea Hunters* (Juneau: Friends of the Alaska State Museum, 1991), 30.

32. See Jan Steinbright, *Qayaqs and Canoes: Native Ways of Knowing* (Anchorage: Alaska Native Heritage Center, 2001). (See also accompanying video, same title.)

33. Anfesia Shapsnikoff and Raymond C. Hudson, "Aleut Basketry," in *Anthropological Papers of the University of Alaska* 16 (1974), 41–69.

34. Ibid. 58.

35. In 1992 Teri Rofkar, Marie Laws, and Irene Jimmy, assisted by various other weavers, wove the *Tides People* Raven's Tail robe in Sitka for the Southeast Alaska Indian Cultural Center. The design depicts the last 100 years, from subsistence to cash economy: tree stumps representing clear-cut logging and dollar signs representing cash.

36. See http://www.imagesnorth.com/pages/Bevins.html (accessed June 6, 2004).

37. Jan Steinbright, ed., *Alaskameut '86: An Exhibit of Contemporary Alaska Native Masks* (Fairbanks: Institute of Alaska Native Arts, 1986), 14–15.

Ecology and Environment

1. Forbes Annual Survey, 2002.
2. *Newsweek*, April 2001.
3. Environmental Defense Fund.

Fashion

1. William F. Fitzhugh, "Crossroads of Continents: Review and Prospect," in *Anthropology of the North Pacific Rim*, ed. William W. Fitzhugh and Valerie Chaussonnet (Washington, DC: Smithsonian Institution Press, 1994), 37–38.

2. Sebastian Vizcaíno, qtd. in Rose Marie Beebe and Robert M. Senkewicz, *Lands of Promise and Despair: Chronicles of Early California, 1535–1846* (Santa Clara, CA: Santa Clara University; Berkeley, CA: Heyday Books, 2001), 38.

3. Michael Dear, "Peopling California," in *Made in California: Art, Image, and Identity, 1900–2000,* ed. Stephanie Barron Sheri Bernstein, and Ilene Susan Fort (Berkeley: University of California Press, 2000), 49.

4. Vicente de Santa María, qtd. in Beebe and Senkewicz, *Lands of Promise and Despair,* 182–183, 185.

5. Juan Bandini, qtd. in ibid., 382.

6. Aeko Sereno, "Images of the Hula Dancer and 'Hula Girl': 1778–1960" (Ph.D. diss., University of Hawai'i, 1990), vi, 6.

7. DeSoto Brown and Linda Arthur, *The Art of the Aloha Shirt* (Waipahu, HI: Island Heritage Publishing, 2002), 10.

8. Valerie Chaussonnet and Bernadette Driscoll, "The Bleeding Coat: The Art of North Pacific Ritual Clothing," in *Anthropology of the North Pacific Rim,* ed. William W. Fitzhugh and Valerie Chaussonnet (Washington, DC: Smithsonian Institution Press, 1994), 114.

9. http://www.pendleton-usa.com/ (accessed June 11, 2004).

10. Ibid.

11. Beebe and Senkewicz, *Land of Promise and Despair,* 293–294, 314.

12. Ibid., 413.

13. Ibid., 337.

14. Ibid., 357.

15. Ibid., 350.

16. Ibid., 434.

17. Ibid., 425–426.

18. Beebe and Senkewicz, *Lands of Promise and Despair,* 470.

19. Ibid., 464.

20. Ramona Ellen Skinner, *Alaska Native Policy in the Twentieth Century* (New York: Garland Publishing, 1997), 13–14.

21. Sereno, "Images of the Hula Dancer," 32, 33, 127.

22. Philip H. Parrish, *Historic Oregon* (New York: Macmillan, 1943), 10, 25.

23. Fermin Francisco de Lasuen, qtd. in Beebe and Senkewicz, *Lands of Promise and Despair,* 274.

24. Galina I. Dzeniskevich "American-Asian Ties as Reflected in Athapaskan Material Culture," in *Anthropology of the North Pacific Rim,* ed. William W. Fitzhugh and Valerie Chaussonnet (Washington, DC: Smithsonian Institution Press, 1994), 56.

25. Chaussonnet and Driscoll, "The Bleeding Coat," 109.

26. Ibid., 109–115.

27. Roza G. Liapunova, "Eskimo Masks from Kodiak Island," in *Anthropology of the North Pacific Rim,* ed. William W. Fitzhugh and Valerie Chaussonnet (Washington, DC: Smithsonian Institution Press, 1994), 177.

28. Joel Garreau, *The Nine Nations of North America* (Boston: Houghton Mifflin, 1981), 250.

29. Julia V. Emberley, *The Cultural Politics of Fur* (Ithaca, NY: Cornell University Press, 1997), 39.

30. Donald Katz, 5.

31. Skinner, *Alaska Native Policy in the Twentieth Century,* 31.

32. Jan Halliday, *Native Peoples of Alaska: A Traveler's Guide to Land, Art, and Culture* (Seattle, WA: Sasquatch Books, 1998), xiii–xiv.

33. http://www.patagonia.com/ (accessed June 11, 2004).

34. http://www.eddiebauer.com/ (accessed June 11, 2004).

35. Norman Clark, "Notes for a Tricentennial Historian," in *Northwest Perspectives: Essays on the Culture of the Pacific Northwest*, ed. Edwin R. Bingham and Glen A. Love (Seattle: University of Washington Press, 1979), 48, 57.

36. Dear, 1979 "Peopling California," 51, 52.

37. Graham Marsh and Paul Trynka, *Denim: From Cowboys to Catwalks* (London: Aurum Press, 2000).

38. Brown and Arthur, *The Art of the Aloha Shirt*.

39. Teri Agins, *The End of Fashion: The Mass Marketing of the Clothing Business* (New York: William Morrow, 1999), 194.

40. Garreau, *The Nine Nations of North America*, 219.

41. Sheri Bernstein, "Contested Eden, 1920–1940," in *Made in California: Art, Image, and Identity, 1900–2000*, ed. Stephanie Barron, Sheri Bernstein, and Ilene Susan Fort (Berkeley: University of California Press, 2000), 130.

42. Ibid., 105.

43. Ibid., 130–132.

44. From the Los Angeles County Museum of Art, "Adrian Retrospective" [August 17, 1995], qtd. in Maureen Reilly, *California Couture* (Atglen, PA: Schiffer Publishing Ltd., 2000), 21.

45. Ibid., 21.

46. Ibid., 22.

47. Jane Gaines, "Introduction: Fabricating the Female Body," in *Fabrications: Costume and the Female Body*, ed. Jane Gaines and Charlotte Herzog (New York: Routledge, 1990), 19–20.

48. Charles Eckert, "The Carole Lombard in Macy's Window," in *Fabrications: Costume and the Female Body*, ed. Jane Gaines and Charlotte Herzog (New York: Routledge, 1990), 100–121.

49. Christopher Breward, *The Culture of Fashion* (Manchester, UK: Manchester University Press, 1995), 187.

50. Ibid., 188.

51. David Chierchetti, *Edith Head: The Life and Times of Hollywood's Celebrated Costume Designer* (New York: Perennial/HarperCollins, 2003), 116–118.

52. Maureen Reilly, *California Casual Fashions, 1930s–1970s* (Atglen, PA: Schiffer Publishing Ltd., 2001), 56–57.

53. Aeko Sereno, 154.

54. Ibid, 189.

55. Ibid, 197–198, 204.

56. Ibid, 211–212, 245.

57. Jerry Hopkins, *Elvis in Hawai'i* (Honolulu, HI: The Bess Press, 2002), vii.

58. Dale Hope and Gregory Tozian, *The Aloha Shirt: Spirit of the Islands* (Hillsboro, OR: Beyond Words Publishing, 2000).

59. http://www.jantzen.com/ (accessed June 11, 2004).

60. Beebe and Senkewicz, *Lands of Promise and Despair*, 320–321.

61. http://www.rei.com/ (accessed June 11, 2004).

62. http://www.insport.com/ (accessed June 11, 2004).

63. Ibid.

64. http://www.columbia.com/ (accessed June 11, 2004).

Film and Theater

1. Recollection of David Horsley, president of the Nestor Film Company, in Edwin O. Palmer, *History of Hollywood* (Hollywood, CA: Arthur H. Cawston, 1937).

2. Ibid., 195–196.

3. Charles G. Clarke, *Early Film Making in Los Angeles* (Los Angeles, CA: Dawson's Book Shop, 1976), 30.

4. Internet Movie Base, http://www.imb.com/ (accessed July 19, 2004).

5. See http://seattletimes.nwsource.com/news/local/seattle_history/articles/story8.html.

6. Diamond Head Theatre, http://www.diamondheadtheatre.com/about/history.htm (accessed July 21, 2004).

7. El Teatro Campesino, http://www.elteatrocampesino.com/campesin/history/history.html (accessed July 21, 2004).

8. Ibid.

9. See http://seattletimes.nwsource.com/html/artsentertainment/2001_1951208_alki09.html.

Folklore

1. Reub Long's hyperboles are found throughout *The Oregon Desert* (Caldwell, ID: Caxton, 1969), which he edited and wrote with E.R. Jackman. Tall tales and other exaggerations that were his personal trademarks are still in healthy oral tradition in central Oregon. Gilgamesh—taken from stone tablets found in Assyria 669–633, the Gilgamesh legend is one of the oldest known "stories." Hundreds of versions, probably beginning around 2600–2500 B.C., were written about the Mesopotamian hero Gilgamesh, estimated to have lived around 2700 B.C. The legend itself and the long story of how it evolved and was discovered are in the realm of knowledge of many high school students and certainly college students since the Gilgamesh tablets are so seminal in the study of the written word.

2. Collected from Herbert Arnston, Pullman, Washington, in December 1958; text and tune are found throughout the West with only minor variations. The original broadside may have appeared as early as 1597, according to Hyder E. Rollins, in *The Pepys Ballads* (Cambridge, MA: Harvard University Press, 1930), 3, 57. The ballad became so popular that it inspired parodies of itself, some of which may be found in John Ashton, *Modern Street Ballads* (London: Chatto and Windus, 1888), 124–127.

3. Long.

4. Susan Mullin, "Oregon's Huckleberry Finn: A Münchausen Enters Tradition," *Northwest Folklore* 2 (1967): 19–27.

5. Recurrent single elements of folklore, called *motifs*, are cataloged for convenience in comparison and analysis in Stith Thompson, *Motif-Index of Folk-Literature: A Classification of Narrative Elements in Folktales, Ballads, Myths, Fables, Mediaeval Romances, Exembla, Fabliaux, Jest-books, and Local Legends* (Bloomington: University of Indiana Press, 1955–1958). Within category X, Humor, Thompson especially designated the numbers X900 to X1899 for the classification of Lies and Exaggerations in traditional narratives. In another work designed to categorize entire narrative clusters (*groups* of motifs in recurrent use, recognizable plots), Thompson and Antti Aarne provide Tale-Type numbers for a similar range of materials: *The Types of the Folktale*, Folklore Fellows Communication 184 (Helsinki: Suomalainen Tiedeakatemia, 1961). The section called "Tales of Lying" uses Type numbers 1875 to 1968 and includes such well-known "lies" as 1882A, Man Caught in Tree Goes Home to Get Axe; 1889F, Frozen Words Thaw; 1889L, The Split Dog; 1889M, Snakebite Causes Object to Swell; 1913, The Side-Hill Beast (short legs on one side); 1917, The Stretching and Shrinking Harness; 1920B, I Have Not Time to Lie; 1960M, Large Mosquitoes Fly off with Kettle. Motif and Type numbers have not been given for the texts quoted in this chapter, for their appearance here is relatively unsystematic; standard practice in folklore analysis, however, would require a survey of all texts of a given item and an account of their traditional provenance through reference to these basic research tools.

6. Long.

7. See Jan H. Brunvand, *The Vanishing Hitchhiker: American Urban Legends and their Meanings* (New York: Norton, 1981); and Brunvand, *The Choking Doberman and Other "New" Urban Legends* (New York: Norton, 1984).

8. The Yoho Cove story can be found in Richard Dorson's *American Folklore*, (Chicago: University of Chicago Press, 1959), 130–131.

9. Leonard Roberts, *South from Hell-fer-Sartin: Kentucky Mountain Folk Tales* (Berea, KY: Council of Southern Mountains, 1964), 192, with the title "Origin of Man."

10. Eye of Hawai'i, "Hawaiian Legends," http://www.eyeofhawaii.com/Legends/legends. htm (accessed July 30, 2004).

11. Francis Haines, "Goldilocks on the Oregon Trail," *Idaho Yesterdays* 9 (1966): 26–30.

Food

The authors would like to thank Scott Singer for his generous assistance in the preparation of this chapter.

1. D. Bell and G. Valentine, *Consuming Geographies: We Are Where We Eat* (New York: Routledge, 1997), 18.

2. Belinda Martineau, *First Fruit: The Creation of the Flavr Savr Tomato and the Birth of Biotech Food* (New York: McGraw-Hill, 2002).

3. W. Root and R. De Rochemont, *Eating in America: A History* (New York: William Morrow, 1976), 267.

4. *The Prudence Penny Regional Cookbook* (Chicago: Consolidated Book Publishers, 1955), 619.

5. Barbara Santos, *Maui Onion Cookbook* (Berkeley, CA: Celestial Arts, 1996).

6. R. Laudan, *The Food of Paradise: Exploring Hawai'i's Culinary Heritage* (Honolulu: University of Hawai'i Press, 1996).

7. James Beard's *American Cookery*, cited in L. Brenner, *American Appetite: The Coming of Age of a Cuisine* (New York: Avon Books, 1999), 195.

8. L. E. Elie, "Smoke and Mirrors," *Gourmet* (June 2002).

9. Quoted in K. Severson, with G. Denkler. *The New Alaska Cookbook: Recipes from the Last Frontier's Best Chefs* (Seattle, WA: Sasquatch Books, 2001), xv.

10. W. J. Belasco, *Appetite for Change: How the Counterculture Took on the Food Industry* (Ithaca, NY: Cornell University Press, 1993), 18.

11. A. Waters, *The Chez Panisse Menu Cookbook* (New York: Random House, 1982), x.

Language

1. Edward Sapir, various works.

2. To learn more about extinct languages within the region, see Andrew Robinson's *Lost Languages* (New York: McGraw-Hill, 2002).

3. Lawrence A. Reid, "Morphosyntactic Evidence for the Position of Chamorro in the Austronesian Language Family," in *Collected Papers on Southeast Asian and Pacific Languages*, ed. Robert S. Bauer (Canberra: Pacific Linguistics, 2002), 63–94.

4. Donald Topping, *Chamorro Reference Grammar*, PALI Language Texts: Micronesia (Honolulu: University of Hawai'i Press, 1973), 9.

5. For example, see M. Warschauer and K. Donaghy, "Leokï: A Powerful Voice of Hawaiian Language Revitalization," *Computed Assisted Language Learning* 10.4 (1997): 349–362.

6. Michael E. Krauss and Victor K. Golla, "Northern Athabaskan Languages," *Handbook of North American Indians*, vol. 6: *Subarctic*, ed. J. Helm (Washington, DC: Smithsonian Institution Press, 1981), 67–86.

7. James Kari, "A Classification of Tanaina Dialects," *Anthropological Papers of the Uni-*

versity of Alaska 12.2 (1975) 49–53; also James Kari and Priscilla Russell Kari, *Dena'ina Elnena, Tanaina Country* (Fairbanks: Alaska Native Language Center, 1982), 11–12.

8. Thomas Alton, "Federal Policy and Alaska Native Languages since 1867" (Ph.D. diss., University of Alaska, Fairbanks 1998).

9. Linda J. Ellanna, Lake Clark Sociocultural Study: Phase I, US National Park Service, Lake Clark National Park and Preserve, 1986: 3–5; see also Michael E. Krauss, "Alaska Native Languages: Past, Present and Future" (Alaska Native Language Center Research Papers, Number 4).

10. *Genaga Career Ladder Program*, U.S. Department of Education grant T195E980090 to University of Alaska, Fairbanks, in partnership with the Interior Athabascan Tribal College (principal investigator Patrick Marlow).

11. Linda Ellanna and Andrew Balluta, *Nuvendaltin Quht'ana; The People of Nondalton* (Washington, DC: Smithsonian Institution Press, 1992).

12. This inventory work is being conducted by James Kari, a linguist specializing in Dena'ina and professor emeritus at the University of Alaska, Fairbanks.

13. The Lake Clark Project Jukebox was a collaboration between Lake Clark National Park and the Alaska Native Language Center at the University of Alaska, Fairbanks.

14. James Kari and James A. Fall, *Shem Pete's Alaska: The Territory of the Upper Cook Inlet Dena'ina* (Fairbanks: University of Alaska Press, 2003).

15. See Priscilla Russell Kari's "Land Use and Economy of *Lime Village*," Technical Paper Number 80 (Alaska Department of Fish and Game, Division of Subsistence, 1983); Kari, "Wild Resource Use and Economy of Stony River Village," Technical Paper 108 (Alaska Department of Fish and Game, Division of Subsistence, 1985); Kari, *Tanaina Plantlore, Dena'ina K'et'una: An Ethnobotony of the Dena'ina Indians of Southcentral Alaska* (Anchorage: National Park Service, Alaska Region 1987); Priscilla Russell, *Bird Traditions of the Lime Village Area Dena'ina: Upper Stony River Ethno-Ornithology* (Fairbanks: Alaska Native Knowledge Network, 2003).

16. Peter Kalifornsky, *A Dena'ina Legacy: K'tl'egh'i Sukdu. The Collected Writings of Peter Kalifornsky* (Fairbanks: Alaska Native Language Center, University of Alaska, 1991).

Literature

1. Mark Twain, *Letters from Hawai'i*, ed. A. Grove Day (New York: Appleton-Century, 1966), 273.

2. Max Quanchi, "Pacific Ocean Islands," *Literature of Travel and Exploration: An Encyclopedia*, ed. Jennifer Speake, Vol. 2 (London: Fitzroy Dearborn, 2003), 905.

3. Malcolm Margolin, "Introduction," *The Way We Lived: California Indian Stories, Songs, and Reminiscences* (Berkeley: Heyday Books, 1993), 2.

4. *The Journals of Lewis and Clark*, Penguin edition, ed. Frank Bergon, 2003.

5. Bayard Taylor, *Eldorado; or, Adventures in the Path of Empire: Comprising a Voyage to California, via Panama; life in San Francisco and Monterey; Pictures of the Gold Region, and Experiences of Mexican Travel. With Illustrations by the Author* (New York: George P. Putnam, 1850).

6. Kevin Starr, *Americans and the California Dream* (New York: Oxford University Press, 1973), 68.

7. Stanley Elkin, "An American in California," in *Pieces of Soap* (New York: Simon & Schuster, 1992), 104, 135.

8. Henry David Thoreau, *Gold Rush: A Literary Exploration*, ed. Michael Kowalewski (Berkeley: Heyday Books, 1997), 297.

9. John Steinbeck, *The Grapes of Wrath* (New York: Penguin, 1986), 449.

10. Steinbeck, *Of Mice and Men* (New York: Penguin, 1994), 72.

11. Steinbeck, *The Grapes of Wrath*, p. 581.

12. John Steinbeck, Letter to Pascal Covici, January 16, 1939, qtd. in Jackson Benson, *John Steinbeck, Writer* (New York: Penguin, 1984), 390–391.

13. John Steinbeck, *The Harvest Gypsies* (1936; Berkeley, CA: Heyday Books, 1988), 22.

14. Pierre Sansot, qtd. in Gerald Kennedy, "Place, Self, and Writing," *Southern Review* 26 (1990): 496–516.

15. Shawn Wong, *Homebase* (New York: Plume, 1991).

16. Steinbeck, "The Leader of the People," from *The Red Pony* (New York: Viking Press, 1945), 112, 130.

17. Robinson Jeffers, "Continent's End," from *Continent's End: A Collection of California Writing* by Joseph Henry Jackson, (1944).

18. See James D. Houston, *In the Ring of Fire: A Pacific Basin Journey* (San Francisco: Mercury House (1997).

19. Luis Valdez, "Envisioning California," *California History* (Winter 1989–1990): 170–171.

20. William Kittredge, "Doing Good Work Together," in *The True Subject: Writers on Life and Craft*, ed. Kurt Brown (St. Paul, MN: Graywolf Press, 1993), 58.

21. Walt Whitman, *Leaves of Grass and Selected Prose* (New York: Modern Library, 1950), 92.

22. Robinson Jeffers, *The Selected Poetry of Robinson Jeffers* (Stanford, CA: Stanford University Press, 2001), 24.

23. Yvor Winters, *The Selected Poems of Yvor Winters* (Athens: Ohio University Press, 1999), 41.

24. Michael Palmer, *The Lion Bridge* (New York: New Directions, 1998), 137.

25. M. H. Lai et al, *Island: Poetry and History of Chinese Immigrants on Angel Island, 1910–1940* (Seattle: University of Washington Press, 1980).

26. Karen L. Polster, "Major Themes and Influences of the Poems at Angel Island" [online]. An Online Journal and Multimedia Companion to *Modern American Poetry* (Oxford: Oxford University Press, 2000), http:www.english.uiuc.edu/maps/poets/a_f/angel/polster.htm (accessed November 1, 2003).

27. Violet Kazue de Cristoforo, *May Sky: There Is Always Tomorrow: An Anthology of Japanese American Concentration Camp Kaio Haiku* (Los Angeles: Sun and Moon Press, 1997).

28. Jeffers, *The Selected Poetry of Robinson Jeffers*, 676.

29. William Everson, *Archetype West: The Pacific Coast as Literary Region* (Berkeley, CA: Oyez, 1976).

30. Lee Bartlett, *The Sun Is But a Morning Star: Studies in West Coast Poetry and Poetics* (Albuquerque: University of New Mexico Press, 1989), 25.

31. Robert By, "Introduction: William Stafford and the Golden Thread," in *The Darkness Around Us Is Deep*, by William Stafford (New York: HarperPerennial, 1993), vii.

32. Stafford, *The Darkness Around Us Is Deep*, 36.

33. Robert Hass, *Twentieth Century Pleasures* (New York: Ecco Press, 1984), 223.

34. Robert Grenier, *This* 1 (1971): "I Hate Speech."

35. Brenda Hillman, *Cascadia* (Middletown, CT: Wesleyan University Press, 2001), 3.

Music

1. William White/Xelimuxw and Philip Cook, "Thunderbirds, Thunder-beings, Thunder-voices: The Application of Traditional Knowledge and Children's Rights in Support of Aboriginal Children's Education," *American Review of Canadian Studies* (Spring–Summer): 331–347.

2. Federica de Laguna, *Under Mount Saint Elias: The History and Culture of the Yakutat Tlinglit*, 3 vols. (Washington, DC: Smithsonian Institution Press, 1972), 249–251, 804.

3. Gunther 1972:6–13.

4. Op cit.

5. Moziño 1791, in translation by Wilson 1970.

6. Cited in Gunther 1972: x.

7. Alfred Kroeber, *Indian Myths of South Central California* (Berkeley: University of California Press, 1907), 319. Note that the only exception Kroeber found to this pattern was that of the creation stories, which had remained intact.

8. Ibid.

9. Kroeber, *Indian Myths of South Central California*, 319.

10. Jeanette Timentwa and Rebecca Chamberlain, "Native Songs and Seasonal Feed-Gathering Traditions" (Jeanette Timentwa Interview and Transcription by Rebecca Chamberlain), in *Spirit of the First People: Native American Music Traditions of Washington State*, ed. Willie Smyth and Esmé Ryan (Seattle: University of Washington Press, 1999).

11. Melissa Nelson and Philip Klasky, "The Power of Song in the Protection of Native Lands," *Orion Magazine* (August 2001), http://www.oriononline.org/pages/0a/o1-4oa/01-4oa_Storyscape.html (accessed June 20, 2004).

12. R. H. Lowie, "The Emergence Hole and the Foot Drum," *American Anthropologist* 40 (1938): 174.

13. Frances Densmore, "Maidu Musical Instruments," *American Anthropologist* 40 (1939): 117.

14. Ibid.

15. In order to produce a pitch on the open-ended end-blown *ney*, the air column is split by a combination of the placement of the tongue and the mouth—the tongue must be curled up vertically, while the mouth must be placed in such a way that the canine teeth can serve as a node to split a very focused air stream between the back edge of the open-ended mouthpiece and the teeth. This is a very difficult embouchure to master. Richard Payne describes the use of this technique among Hopi and Yuman flute players in "Indian Flutes of the Southwest," *Journal of the American Instrument Society* 15 (1989): 5–31.

16. For much more in-depth discussion of the history of the American Indian flute, see Pauline Tuttle, "The Hoop of Many Hoops: The Integration of Lakota Ancestral Knowledge and Bahá'í Teachings in the Performance Practices of Kevin Locke" (Ph.D. diss., University of Washington, Seattle, 2001), 463–504.

17. Ted Gioia, *West Coast Jazz* (New York: Oxford University Press, 1992).

18. Robert Gordon, *Jazz West Coast: The Los Angeles Jazz Scene of the 1950s* (New York: Quartet Books, 1986).

19. All Music Guide Web site, "Flying Burrito Brothers," http://www.allmusic.com/cg/amg.dll (accessed June 22, 2004).

Religion

1. Richard White, *"It's Your Misfortune and None of My Own": A New History of the American West* (Norman: University of Oklahoma Press, 1991), 41.

2. The Theosophical Society was founded by Helena Blavatsky in 1875 to collect and diffuse knowledge of the laws governing the universe in the fields of philosophy, religion and science. In 1895, the American Section separated from its parent body and Katherine Tingley became its leader.

3. Snyder, Gary. Interview by Aaron K. DiFranco. Tape Recording. Davis, CA, June 4, 2003.

4. Ibid.

5. Unless otherwise stated, all percentages are derived from Dale E. Jones, Sherri Doty, Clifford Grammich, James E. Horsch, Richard Houseal, Mac Lynn, John P. Marcum, Kenneth M. Sanchagrin, and Richard H. Taylor, *Religious Congregations and Membership in the United States 2000: An Enumeration by Region, State and County Based on Data Reported for*

149 Religious Bodies (Nashville, TN: Glenmary Research Center, 2002). These figures do not include any estimate of the predominantly black denominations. In 1990, there were reported to be approximately 655,680 Black Baptists or 4.2 percent of the religious population.

6. Donald Miller, *Reinventing American Protestantism: Christianity in the New Millennium* (Berkeley: University of California Press, 1999).

7. The *New International Dictionary of Pentecostal and Charismatic Movements*, 3rd ed., s.v. "Charismatic Movement"; and Dale E. Jones, ed., *Religious Congregations and Membership in the United States: 2000* (Nashville, TN: Glenmary Research Center, 2000), 13–14.

Sports and Recreation

1. John, Muir, *The Mountains of California* (New York: Century, 1894).

2. "Writing Nature in the 21st Century: Panel Discussion with John McPhee, Gary Snyder, and Robert Hass," University of California, Davis, http://prhc.ucdavis.edu/ (accessed November 12, 2003).

3. James M. Shebl, *King, of the Mountains* (Stockton, CA: University of the Pacific Press, 1974), 53.

4. Susan Zwinger and Ann Zwinger, eds., *Women in Wilderness: Writings and Photographs* (San Diego, CA: Harcourt Brace, 1995), 10.

5. Gabriela Zim, *The View from the Edge: Life and Landscapes of Beverly Johnson* (La Crescenta, CA: Mountain N'Air Books, 1996), 54.

6. Kathleen Gasperini, "Going to Extremes with Lynn Hill and Nancy Feagin." MountainZone.com, 1998, http://classic.mountainzone.com/climbing/hill/ (accessed July 5, 2004).

7. Rachel da Silva, *Leading Out: Women Climbers Reaching for the Top* (Seattle, WA: Seal Press, 1996), 339.

8. John B. Allen, *From Skisport to Skiing: One Hundred Years of an American Sport, 1840–1940* (Amherst: University of Massachusetts Press, 1993), 15.

9. Pacific Crest Trail Association http://www.pcta.org (accessed July 5, 2004).

10. Ben Finney and James D. Houston, *Surfing: A History of the Ancient Hawaiian Sport*, rev. ed. (San Francisco, CA: Pomegranate Artbooks, 1996).

11. William Ellis, *Narrative of a Tour through Hawaii* (Honolulu: *Hawaiian Gazette*, 1917).

12. Jack London, "The Sport of Hawaiian Kings: Surfing at Waikiki," in *The Cruise of the Snark* (1911).

13. Mark Twain, *Roughing It* (1872).

14. London, Ibid.

15. Alexander Hume Ford, *Collier's Outdoor America* article.

16. Papers of Charmian London.

17. Ford, Ibid.

18. Jean A. Owen, *The Story of Hawaii* (1898).

19. Drew Kampion, *Stoked! A History of Surf Culture*, rev. ed. (Layton, UT: Gibbs Smith, 2003).

BIBLIOGRAPHY

Adix, William F., and Jerry Davis. *The Story of the Pacific Region*. Association for Clinical Pastoral Education, 2000.

Blank, Paul W., and Fred Spier. *Defining the Pacific: Opportunities and Constraints*. Burlington, VT: Variorum, 2002.

Glavine, Terry, and Carl Safina. *The Last Great Sea: A Voyage through the Human Natural History of the North Pacific Ocean*. Vancouver, BC: Greystone, 2000.

Iwamura, Jan Naomi. *Revealing the Sacred in Asian and Pacific America*. New York: Routledge University Press, 2003.

Lower, J. Arthur. *Ocean of Destiny: A Concise History of the North Pacific, 1500–1978*. Vancouver: University of British Columbia Press, 1978.

Maidment, Richard, and Colin MacKerras, eds. *Culture and Society in the Asia-Pacific*. New York: Routledge University Press, 1998.

Miller, Sally. *Studies in the Economic History of the Pacific Rim* (Routledge Studies in the Growth Economies of Asia 10). New York: Routledge, 1998.

Needham, Joseph, and Lu Gwei-Djen. *Trans-Pacific Echoes and Resonances: Listening Once Again*. Philadelphia, PA: World Scientific, 1985.

Tam, Kwok-kan, Wimal Dissanayake, and Terry Siu-han Yip, eds. *Sights of Contestation: Localism, Globalism and Cultural Production in Asia and the Pacific*. Hong Kong: Chinese University Press, 2002.

Thorne, Alan, and Robert Raymond. *Man on the Rim: The Peopling of the Pacific*. North Ryde, NSW, Australia: Angus & Robertson, 1989.

Wilson, Rob. *Reimagining the American Pacific: From South Pacific to Bamboo Ridge and Beyond*. Durham, NC: Duke University Press, 2000.

Wilson, Rob, and Arif Dirlik. *Asia/Pacific as a Space of Cultural Production*. Durham, NC: Duke University Press, 1995.

Wilson, Rob, and Wimal Dissanayake, eds. *Global/Local: Cultural Production and the Transnational Imaginary*. Durham, NC: Duke University Press, 1996.

INDEX

Illustrations are noted in italics.

ABOUT THE EDITORS AND CONTRIBUTORS

JAN GOGGANS received her Master's Degree in English from California State University, Sacramento in 1987. In 2002, she was awarded a Ph.D. in English from the University of California, Davis. Her dissertation, *The Shape of Community in the Visual West: Land, Water and Women in the Work of Dorothea Lange and Paul Taylor*, looks at the developing body of work by photographer Dorothea Lange and her husband, labor economist Paul Taylor. In 2001/2002, Dr. Goggans held an American Association of University Women Educational Foundation dissertation fellowship. Her Ph.D. dissertation was awarded a Kevin Starr postdoctoral fellowship award in California Studies for 2002/2003. She is finishing a book about the work Lange and Taylor did between 1934 and 1939.

She has published interviews with Isabel Allende, Carolyn See, and Pam Houston in *Writing on the Edge*. In addition, her essays for *Traditions in Transition*, a photo and word exhibit, appear online at the University of California, Riverside/California Museum of Photography. In 1999, she published *Living with the Land*, essays and interviews with farmers and growers in the Putah and Cache Creek watersheds. She published a similar pamphlet in 2003, featuring residents of the Sacramento River Delta, called *The Land of Give and Take*. Her critical essay, "Social (Re) Visioning in the Fields of *My Antonia*" was published in *Cather Studies, V. 5*. Currently, she is assistant to the Director of the Pacific Regional Humanities Center at University of California, Davis.

AARON DiFRANCO serves as program officer for the Pacific Regional Humanities Center at the University of California (UC) at Davis. He is completing his Ph.D. research in the UC Davis English Department and has published several pieces on American nature poets.

LINDA B. ARTHUR is a professor of apparel merchandising, design, and textiles at Washington State University. She is the author of *Aloha Attire: Hawaiian*

Dress in the Twentieth Century (2000), *The Art of the Aloha Shirt* (with David Brown, 2002), and *At the Cutting Edge: Contemporary Hawaiian Quilting* (2003).

JEREMY BONNER holds a Ph.D. in American history from the Catholic University of America in Washington, D.C., and is currently an independent scholar in Baltimore, Maryland. He has published on political and religious history in such journals as the *Journal of Mormon History* and *Anglican and Episcopal History*. He is currently working on a biography of Victor J. Reed, Catholic bishop of Oklahoma City and Tulsa, 1958–1971.

JOHN T. CALDWELL is a professor of film, television, and digital media at the University of California at Los Angeles and is the author of the book *Televisuality: Style, Crisis and Authority in American Television* (1995).

M. KATHRYN DAVIS is a lecturer in geography and women's studies at San Jose State University. She is the author of *Sardine Oil on Troubled Waters: An Environmental History of California's Sardine Industry, 1905–1955* (forthcoming).

VIVIAN DENO is an assistant professor at Butler University and is currently at work on a social and cultural history of working-class Pentecostalism in the United States.

KEVIN DONALD received his Ph.D. in anthropology from the University of Oregon. Donald's interests in linguistics are exemplified by his writing on topics such as creativity in language, hermeneutics, and the polysemic nature of language. He is currently an instructor in the Africana Studies Program, College of Humanities, at the University of Arizona where he teaches classes on African American religion and African traditional religions.

KAREN GAUL is a cultural anthropologist with the Lake Clark and Katmai National Parks. She is currently working on an ethnographic overview and assessment for Lake Clark National Park.

JACK HICKS teaches at the University of California at Davis, where he specializes in California literature, nature/wilderness literature, and contemporary American writing and digital culture. He is coeditor (with James D. Houston, Maxine Hong Kingston, and Al Young) of *The Literature of California* (*Volume I*, 2000; *Volume II*, 2005), a two-volume anthology of California literature from Native American origins to the present. He has also coedited (with Dana Gioia and Chryss Yost) *California Poetry* (2003), the most comprehensive collection of the poetry of the state.

GARY HOLTEN is assistant professor of linguistics at the Alaska Native Language Center, University of Alaska at Fairbanks. He has authored or coauthored several publications on the Athabascan languages of Alaska, including *Tanacross Phrases and Conversations* (2003).

SYDNEY HUTCHINSON is a doctoral candidate in ethnomusicology at New York University. She also holds an M.A. in ethnomusicology from Indiana University's Folklore Institute with a thesis on Mexican American *quebradita* dancing. Originally from Tucson, Arizona, she has worked for three years as a public sector ethnomusicologist in and around New York City.

MONT CHRISTOPHER HUBBARD is a musician and resides in Portland, Oregon.

SUSAN B. KAISER is professor and chair of textiles and clothing, and professor of women and gender studies at the University of California at Davis. She is the author of *The Social Psychology of Clothing: Symbolic Appearances in Context* (2nd ed. rev. 1997). Her current work focuses on the intersections among gender, ethnicity, sexuality, and age in relation to style and fashion theory.

RITSUKO KIKUSAWA is an associate professor at the Research Institute for Languages and Cultures of Asia and Africa, Tokyo University of Foreign Studies, specializing in linguistics, language change, and prehistory of Austronesian societies. Her recent publications include "Proto Central Pacific Ergativity: Its Reconstruction and Development in the Fijian, Rotuman and Polynesian Languages" (2002) and "Did Proto-Oceanians Cultivate *Cyrtosperma taro?*" (2003).

ROB KIRKPATRICK is senior acquisitions editor at Greenwood Publishing in Westport, Connecticut. He holds a Ph.D. in English from Binghamton University. He is currently completing his first full-length book, a biography of World War II–era baseball player Cecil Travis.

MICHAEL KOWALEWSKI is professor of English and director of American Studies at Carleton College. He is the editor of *Reading the West: New Essays on the Literature of the American West* (1996) and *Gold Rush: A Literary Exploration* (1997).

SPENCER LEINEWEBER is a professor of architecture at the University of Hawai'i at Manoa and director of the Heritage Center.

ALICE McLEAN is a scholar of women's food writing. She received her Ph.D. in English from the University of California at Davis.

PATRICK MOSER is associate professor of French at Drury University. He is currently compiling an anthology on the history and culture of surfing.

KIMBERLY D. NETTLES holds a Ph.D. in sociology from the University of California at Los Angeles. She is currently an assistant professor in the Women & Gender Studies Program at the University of California at Davis. Her research interests include gender, race, food production/consumption, and ethnic food cultures.

JULIE NICOLETTA is an associate professor of art and architectural history at the University of Washington at Tacoma. She is the author of *The Architecture of the Shakers* (1995) and *Buildings of Nevada* (2000). She is currently writing a book on architecture and globalization at the New York World's Fair of 1964–1965.

MERRY OVNICK, author of *Los Angeles: The End of the Rainbow* (1994), is an assistant professor of history at California State University at Northridge.

JEFF PURDUE is an assistant professor in the Libraries at Western Washington University in Bellingham, Washington. He is the coeditor of the online journal *Habits of Waste: A Quarterly Review of Pop Culture*.

LINDA NOVEROSKE RENTNER is a graduate student of art history at the University of California at Davis. Her work involves contemporary application of the Kantian sublime, using the monument of Stonehenge as a case study.

ANDREA ROSS is a lecturer in the English Department at the University of California at Davis, the writer-in-residence at the Cache Creek Nature Preserve, and a poet-teacher for California Poets in the Schools. She is also the cofounder of a wilderness adventure travel company.

MELISSA SALAZAR is a Ph.D. candidate in the School of Education at the University of California (UC) at Davis. She has a master's degree in food science and technology from UC Davis and a bachelor's degree in chemistry from UC Berkeley. She studies the sociology of eating, particularly in children and adolescents.

VALERIE SAMSON, Ph.D., is a musician and independent researcher in San Francisco, California. Her article "Chinese Music in the San Francisco Bay Area," was published in ACMR (Association for Chinese Music Research) *Reports*, vol. 12, 1999.

CHRIS J. SINDT is an assistant professor of English and director of the M.F.A. Program in Creative Writing at Saint Mary's College of California. He is the author of *The Land of Give and Take* (2002), and his work has appeared in *Hayden's Ferry Review*, *Poetry Flash*, *Swerve*, and *26: A Journal of Poetry and Poetics*.

JANET L. STEINBRIGHT is an assistant professor of Alaska Native art history and assistant director of the Native Studies Program at Sheldon Jackson College in Sitka, Alaska. She is the author of *Qayaqs and Canoes: Native Ways of Knowing* (2001) and *My Own Trail: Life History of Athabascan Elder, Howard Luke* (1998) and many other articles and catalogs focusing on Alaska Native art. She has been working with Alaska Native cultural programs for over twenty years.

KELLA DE CASTRO SVETICH is a doctoral candidate in English at the University of California at Davis, where she also works as a teaching assistant in the Asian American Studies Program. She is currently completing her dissertation, titled "Flesh and Blood: Trauma and Abjection in Contemporary Filipino American Fiction."

BARRE TOELKEN is a professor emeritus of folklore and Native American literature (in English) at Utah State University. He is the author of *The Anguish of Snails* (2003) and a number of books on folklore and Native American culture and religion.

PAULINE TUTTLE received her Ph.D. in ethnomusicology from the University of Washington. She currently teaches field school in ethnology, ethnohistory, and ethnomusicology for the Anthropology Department and music of the Northwest Coast and of the Pacific Rim in the School of Music at the University of Victoria on Vancouver Island. Her publications include "Traditional Music of Vancouver Island: Calling on the I'iich'abak'takud (the Ancestors)" (2003) and "Beyond Feathers and Beads: Interlocking Narratives in the Music and Dance of Tokeya Inajin (Kevin Locke)" (2001).

GEORGES VAN DEN ABBEELE is Director of both the Davis Humanities Institute and the newly established Pacific Regional Humanities Center at the University of California at Davis, where he is also Professor of French and Humanities. He is the author of *Travel as Metaphor* and coeditor of *French Civilization and its Discontents: Nationalism, Colonialism, Race* (2003). He is currently working on theories of national identity with particular attention to the case of Belgium.

The Greenwood Encyclopedia of American Regional Cultures

The Great Plains Region, *edited by Amanda Rees*

The Mid-Atlantic Region, *edited by Robert P. Marzec*

The Midwest, *edited by Joseph W. Slade and Judith Yaross Lee*

New England, *edited by Michael Sletcher*

The Pacific Region, *edited by Jan Goggans with Aaron DiFranco*

The Rocky Mountain Region, *edited by Rick Newby*

The South, *edited by Rebecca Mark and Rob Vaughan*

The Southwest, *edited by Mark Busby*